The **STEELERS** Encyclopedia

The photo collage on the title page spans the first 80 years of franchise history. *Left to right:* Byron "Whizzer" White (1938), the Steelers' first bonus baby and U.S. Supreme Court Justice; Joe Greene (1969–1981), the very foundation of the Steelers' success, in his famed "One for the Thumb" pose; Mike Webster (1974–1988) was a rock in the offensive middle and, after his career, contributed to the NFL in ways he couldn't have imagined; founder Art "The Chief" Rooney Sr. and his cigar affected Pittsburgh, the Steelers, the NFL and so many along the way; Steel Curtain member L. C. "Hollywood Bags" Greenwood (1969–1991); Dermontti Dawson (1988–2000), who followed Webster in the offensive middle; Big Ben Roethlisberger (2004–) helped to lift the Steelers back to the Super Bowl stage, reaching three over a five-year span.

A photo gallery of Steelers players and coaches through the years appears at the beginning of each chapter. Featured are, *left to right:* the colorful Bobby Layne (1958–1962) helped to make winners of the loveable losers. . . for a few years; their first star and third coach, Johnny "Blood" McNally; fiery Greg Lloyd (1988–1997) only looks like he's trying to remove Warren Moon's head; Larry Brown (1971–1984) started out a tight end, but wound up an anchor of an offensive tackle; Terry Bradshaw (1970–1983) early on received his strongest support in the locker room from Joe Greene (1969–1981); a pair of Notre Damers powered Pittsburgh's ground game in five different decades, Rocky Bleier (1968, 1970–1980) and Jerome Bettis (1996–2005); Franco Harris (1972–1983) hit the ground running as an Army-inspiring rookie and brought the Steelers playoff fortune every year of his career with the team, starting with that Immaculate Reception; Chuck Noll (1969–1991) did smile, but mostly the NFL's gods smiled on him; the dynamite duo of Lynn Swann (1974–1982) and John Stallworth (1974–1987) pushed one another; the teeth were merely part of the superficial, on-field persona of Jack Lambert (1974–1984); Troy Polamalu (2003–) spectacularly continues the standard of debilitating defense.

The STEELERS
Encyclopedia

CHUCK FINDER

TEMPLE UNIVERSITY PRESS
Philadelphia

Temple University Press
Philadelphia, PA 19122
www.temple.edu/tempress

This book is not sanctioned by the NFL or its teams.

Library of Congress Cataloging-in-Publication Data

Finder, Chuck, 1962–
    The Steelers encyclopedia / Chuck Finder.
         p.   cm.
    ISBN 978-1-4399-0832-7 (cloth : alk. paper)
1.   Pittsburgh Steelers (Football team)—Encyclopedias.   I. Title.
    GV959.P57F56 2012
    796.332'640974886—dc23

                             2012011396

♾ The paper used in this publication meets the requirements of the American
National Standard for Information Sciences—Permanence of Paper for Printed
Library Materials, ANSI Z39.48-1992

Printed in the United States of America

2   4   6   8   9   7   5   3   1

Contents

Acknowledgments

Since this project started, we've lost a few threads from the Steelers' fabric. All-Pro center Bill Walsh and Super Bowl XXX offensive coordinator Ron Erhardt—two gentlemen who graciously shared memories for this book—along with inaugural 1,000-yard rusher John Henry Johnson all passed away.

Since this project started, I lost my mother, Sorky, who along with my father, Sandy, introduced me to football via a steady diet of hot chocolate, hot dogs, and cold days at Pitt Stadium. I saw my career arc change and the nest go empty . . . except for a third dog to go with the two snakes.

It is a lesson of which we are constantly reminded: Times change. Life moves on.

This book attempts to trace the roots of an iconic franchise through its people and their tales. It would never have been possible without the contributions of more than 100 people.

First and foremost the thanks start with my own family. My wife, Cindi, and youngest son, Brendan, endured too much time without me—including a quiet Thanksgiving where my other son, David, escorted his mother to the movies. The wonderful photographers who so grandly lent their artistry are a close second. The magical memories of 90-some folks who lived them and the exquisite black-and-white photographs by Vincent J. Musi, George Gojkovich, Mike Fabus, Bill Amatucci, John Beale, and Bob Pavuchak are the beauty of this book.

Beyond Fabus, the Steelers' Tony Quatrini, Lynne Molyneaux, Burt Lauten, Nathan LoCascio, Emily Scerba, and former intern Ryan Scarpino, among others, also deserve considerable thanks for their geniality and help—especially Lynne. Her former boss, Joe Gordon, not only was a hospitable interviewee but a resource. The same goes for Art Rooney Jr., author of *Ruanaidh*. His brothers Pat Sr. and Tim Sr. also were extremely giving of their time.

My gratitude for photographic and interviewing assistance goes to the Carnegie Library; the Pro Football Hall of Fame; the universities of Pittsburgh, Duquesne, and Robert Morris athletics; the Green Bay Packers; and the New York Jets.

And a special thanks to the many other voices that helped to narrate this Steelers history:

- Pre-modern players Jack Butler, Chuck Cherundolo (to this book what Buck O'Neil was to Ken Burns), Dale Dodrill, Dick Hoak, Frank Varrichione, Walsh, the wife of Ralph Wenzel, and Al Wistert of the Steagles.

- Modern players John Banaszak, Charlie Batch, Tom Beasley, Steve Bono, Bubby Brister, Larry Brown, Rodney Carter, Ryan Clark, Dermontti Dawson, Tony Dungy, Gary Dunn, James Farrior, Larry Foote, Frenchy Fuqua, Joe Greene, Kevin Greene, Jack Ham, Casey Hampton, Santonio Holmes, Tunch Ilkin, John Jackson, Jon Kolb, Heath Miller, Troy Polamalu, Gabe Rivera (who months after our interview returned to public focus by getting inducted into the College Football Hall of Fame), Ben Roethlisberger, Andy Russell, Aaron Smith, John Stallworth, Max Starks, Jim Sweeney, Mike Wagner, Hines Ward, Gerald Williams, Craig Wolfley, and LaMarr Woodley.

- Coaches Bruce Arians, Dom Capers, Cherundolo, Bill Cowher, Dungy, Erhart, Russ Grimm, Dick Hoak, Dick LeBeau, George Perles, Dan Radakovich, Lou Riecke, and Joe Walton.

- Front-office, scouting, and sideline types Ralph Berlin, Kevin Colbert, Joe Gordon, Ed Kiely, Bill Nunn, Tim V. Rooney, Art Rooney II . . . plus the Steelerettes and Ingots.

- Media members Bill Hillgrove, Roy McHugh, and Carl Hughes; photographer Jim Klingensmith (who also passed away during this project); Marian Jane Drum, the wife of legendary sports writer Bob Drum; plus friends of Myron—Frank Haller and Dan Torisky.

- Super fans Al Vento of Franco's Italian Army, Bob Bubanic of Gerela's Gorillas, and Jimmy Pol the Steelers Polka guy, along with the mechanic who dresses like Jesus, the mother of NASA Col. Mike Fincke, and Carnegie Mellon University's Dr. Michael Tarr, plus globe-trotting, Towel-carrying photographers Gordon Dedmon of England, Donald Durdan of Pawleys Island, S.C., and Mark Davis of Summerville, S.C.

- Outsiders Ernie Accorsi, the general manager of several foes, Ralph Cindrich, who played against them and dealt with them as an agent, and performance-enhancing drugs expert Chuck Yesalis.

Finally, thanks to the Temple team of Micah Kleit, Alex Holzman, Amanda Steele, and the Urban Archives folks, Temple's marketing team of Gary Kramer, Ann-Marie Anderson, and Saul Markowitz Communications, plus editors/designers Peter K. Reinhart, Nancy Lombardi, Peggy Gordon, and more at P. M. Gordon Associates.

One last note: The fifth member of the Steel Curtain, backup Steve Furness, was a family friend (and tennis-court victim) since I was a teenager. I had an assist in naming one of his sons and spoke at his funeral, in front of a room filled with Canton honorees. His firstborn, Zack, is a man of letters who wrote a Temple book years ago. When Temple wanted to do *The Steelers Encyclopedia*, they asked Zack about it. He referred them to me. Ergo, this book never would've reached your eyes were it not for divine Steelers intervention.

—*Chuck Finder*

The *STEELERS* Encyclopedia

1

Beginnings (1933–1947)

IN THE OH-SO-HUMBLE BEGINNING, they were Pirates. They were transients and ruffians and gridiron soldiers of fortune in a three-river town that cleaved to other games as recreation. They were displaced citizenry with no firm day of the week on which to play because the Pennsylvania Blue Laws still hadn't been repealed by the time the team first set sail in late 1933.

True, there existed a National Hockey League entry by that same name in Pittsburgh eight years earlier. But this new bunch adopted the moniker and hues of the fabulously successful baseball team that occupied the same Forbes Field. In a region waging a tempestuous love affair with amateur football, these professional Pirates could hardly get to first base.

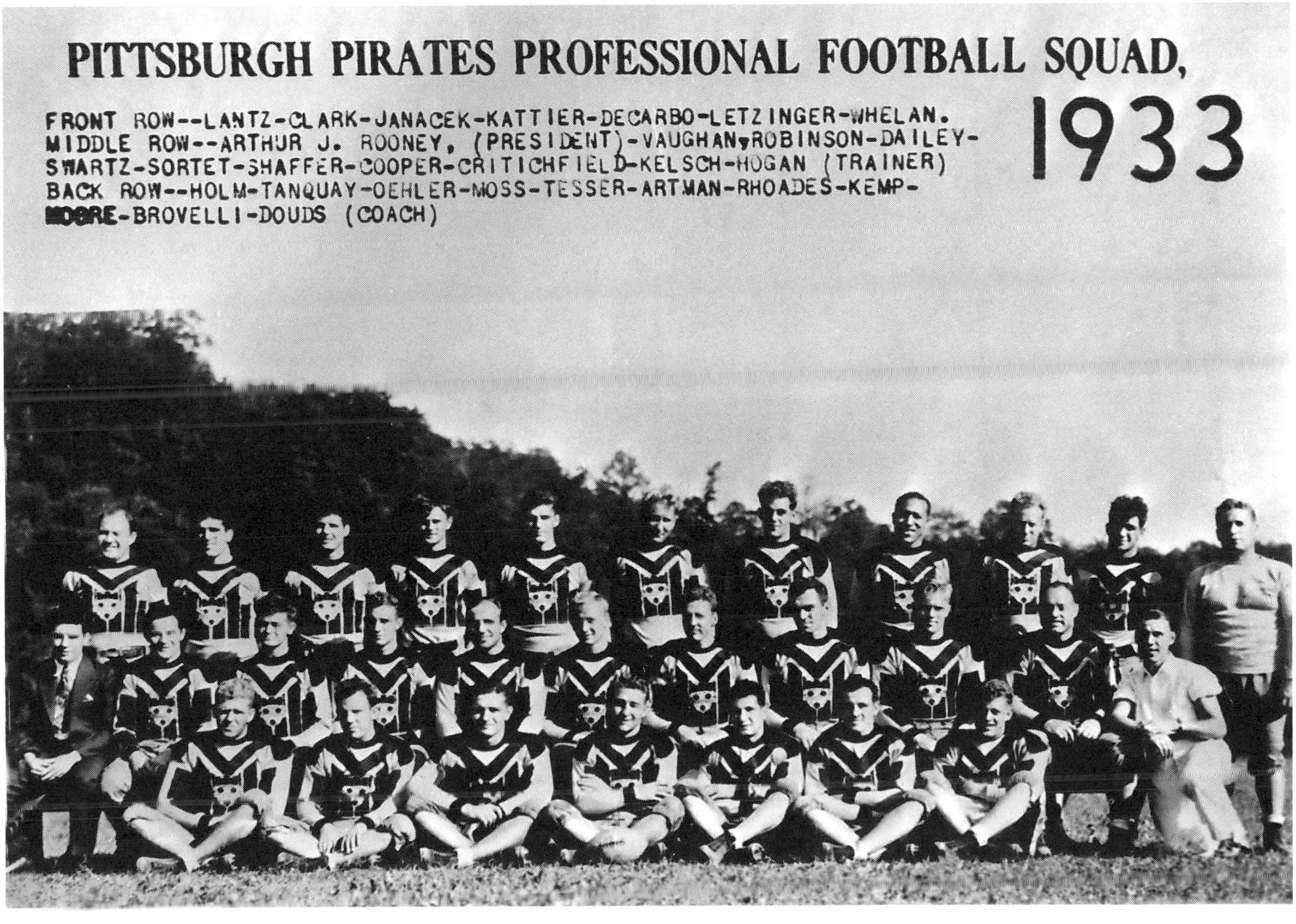

PITTSBURGH PIRATES PROFESSIONAL FOOTBALL SQUAD, 1933

FRONT ROW--LANTZ-CLARK-JANACEK-KATTIER-DECARBO-LETZINGER-WHELAN.
MIDDLE ROW--ARTHUR J. ROONEY, (PRESIDENT)-VAUGHAN-ROBINSON-DAILEY-SWARTZ-SORTET-SHAFFER-COOPER-CRITICHFIELD-KELSCH-HOGAN (TRAINER)
BACK ROW--HOLM-TANQUAY-OEHLER-MOSS-TESSER-ARTMAN-RHOADES-KEMP-MOORE-BROVELLI-DOUDS (COACH)

1933 team photo: Notice that Art Rooney is second row, far left. Coach Jap Douds is last row, far right. The third player in, from Douds' right shoulder, is Ray Kemp—the first African American player in franchise history and one of few in the NFL until Marion Motley and Company in 1946. (Courtesy of the Pittsburgh Steelers)

College football ruled. From the farms of immigrants, from the coal patches and steel mills that attracted waves of Irish, Germans, and Eastern Europeans, around the thriving neighborhoods of Polish Hill and Swissvale arose a thump of shoulder pads and leather helmets. Carnegie Tech, Pitt, Washington and Jefferson—these were local colleges that skirmished on fall Saturdays for the right to play in the Rose Bowl. Each did earn an invitation to that prestigious game: the granddaddy of them all.

Crowds flocked to their fields, their games, their embrace.

These professional Pirates?

Not so much.

They were swashbucklingly bad.

Stayed that way for decades, too.

Art Rooney Jr., son of the founder, about the early going: "I mean, how many winning seasons did we have in 30 years? We were always apologizing." Between 1933 and 1945 they had just one winning season. The majority of those years, they won three games or fewer.

Pat Rooney Sr., one of Art Rooney Sr.'s twin sons: "Pro football started playing on Sundays because colleges had Saturday wrapped up. You couldn't play football on Sundays because of the Blue Laws. That's why the Eagles and Steelers came around in the same time.

"The colleges didn't want anything to do with the pros. They wanted to separate it. The pros were the bastard child. Carnegie Tech and Pitt—we were sort of a nonfactor in all that stuff. I can remember when the baseball Pirates were first [in Pittsburgh, colleges second]. We were really the third sport . . . until we moved into Three Rivers Stadium."

A generation before he was known as the Chief or the Old Man, or even Sr., Art Rooney had coal-black hair and a pocketful of either cash or tickets from the racetrack—or both. He long had operated semipro football and baseball teams around Western Pennsylvania, barnstorming with both as player, coach, and owner. He was still a few years from launching the boxing gym and promotion business with pal Bernard McGinley.

It was 1933, and the political bent in Rooney—also a few years prior to his election campaign for an Allegheny County row office—caused him to take a flyer on this young professional football league. After all, Pittsburgh was found to be the birthplace of professional football, in a style a gambling man could appreciate: William "Pudge" Heffelfinger accepted $500 to play one contest for the Allegheny Athletic Association on November 12, 1892, and the rival Pittsburgh Athletic Club demanded the game be declared an exhibition so a ringer couldn't disrupt betting. On his own, Rooney had already spent years fielding a successful team of sandlotters, the Hope Harveys.

So he worked to petition for entry into what was called the National Professional Football League. At the same time, he worked to convince Pennsylvania's lawmakers to repeal the Blue Laws, allowing Sunday football, baseball, even motion pictures.

A railroad ticket cost $1 to Youngstown, New Castle, and Ellwood City. Stewing chickens ran you 59 cents apiece. A nice Hollywood frock for ladies set you back $16.75 at Joseph Horne Company. Hitler was the chancellor in Germany. Honus Wagner turned 59. The baseball Pirates opened spring training in Paso Robles, California. And the league meeting came to Pittsburgh for what the papers called a "confab," with representatives of teams from Portsmouth, Ohio; Brooklyn; Boston; New York; Staten Island; Chicago (Bears and Cards); and Green Bay, Wisconsin.

In the February 25, 1933, *Pittsburgh Post-Gazette* columnist Harvey J. "Chilly" Doyle opined:

> Pittsburgh fans will welcome the professional football officials who will meet here today and tomorrow. While this has never been in modern times a professional football center, the strides the big league game is making in other cities offer hope that Pittsburgh may be ready to support such an enterprise.
>
> Art Rooney, the former athlete, is interested in bringing the professional game here.
>
> There was a time in Pittsburgh, shortly after the boys came home from the Spanish-American War, that professional football flourished here to such an extent that the college game would not attempt to compete with it. College games were played on Friday and the professionals held sway on Saturdays.
>
> Some of the boys played both on college teams and professional teams at the time.
>
> Anything that will help widen Pittsburgh's clean amusement side deserves encouragement.

On July 8, 1933, the Pirates were approved for a franchise in the 10-team loop. The entry fee: $2,500. Rooney had that in track winnings, though his big day at the races came later in that Depression decade.

Art Jr.: "He could not get into professional baseball because he was a gambler. The NFL had bookmakers and bootleggers and him. Dad said he paid $2,500 for a franchise, and they [told him] that they would have given it to him for nothing. He always said a lot of the guys who played sandlot with him could play in the National Football League.

"He ended up changing the league."

Awaiting the November 7, 1933, blue-law referendum, the new franchise opened on a Wednesday night—September 20—under the lights at Forbes Field. (On any given Wednesday? Nah.) Player-coach Jap Douds from W&J told the *Post-Gazette*: "We have boys just out of college who are strong and fast and are imbued with confidence and desire to win."

The Pirates conjured one first down.

They scored just two points, on a safety.

They charitably donated the first score in franchise history, $400-a-game Angelo Brovelli tossing an interception that New York's Ken Strong returned for a touchdown.

The *Post-Gazette*'s Jack Sell wrote the next day's story, as he would for decades covering what he called "the Rooneymen:"

> The New York Giants proved real Gridiron Goliaths last night at Forbes Field when they ruined the debut of Pittsburgh's golden jerseyed Pirates in the National Professional League by running and passing their way to a brilliant 23-2 victory before a surprising crowd of about 25,000 local well-wishers.
>
> The local entry made a gallant effort to match the skill of the invaders, but showed conclusively the lack of players with experience in the paid-to-play class, especially in the late periods of the battle when the cool, clever victors piled up their big margin.

Pittsburgh should've gotten used to it.

That was professional football under Art Rooney for almost another 40 years.

Doyle opined in his post-debut commentary: "Unless this early sign is completely wrong, the professional game has come here to stay and will improve as time goes on. . . . It will never, however, I believe equal the college game as a spectacle or as a thriller. Fans will like [a] little less of the expert and a little more of the college spirit."

Rooney gave it the old professional try. He brought in a washed-up player named Johnny "Blood" McNally, one of the most colorful and reckless athletes in American sports history—his best scrambling came after curfew or just as the team's train departed the station. Then Rooney, who had claimed losses of $10,000 in the 1934 season with Blood playing for him, made him player–coach in 1937. It would figure that Blood would go AWOL for a game and go winless in nine consecutive games, including the first three of the 1939 season.

Creating a hoo-ha over the first bonus baby in pro-football history, the fellow more often known as penurious became a pariah in his own league for giving Colorado halfback Byron "Whizzer" White the sum of $15,800 to skip Oxford and a Rhodes scholarship to play in Pittsburgh. Pirates, indeed. Even

Whizzer White kicks long before he takes a seat on the most important bench in America—the Supreme Court. (Courtesy of the Pittsburgh Steelers)

Johnny "Blood" McNally even as the coach was a selling point—this was a promotional device showing the 1938 Pittsburgh Pirates home schedule. A sign of the times: three of the games listed there were played on different days of the week, sometimes months apart. (Courtesy of the Pittsburgh Steelers)

Rooney's partner/accountant from the start, Milt Jaffe, quit him over that transaction.

White led the league in rushing with 567 yards, and more than three-quarters of a century later the franchise awaits another rookie to top that category. From the sound of it, yards weren't easy for him that 2-9 season, either.

Jim Klingensmith, the late Pittsburgh Post-Gazette *photographer:* "I used to go over to Art's office all the time and smoke a cigar. He told me a story one day. The first game at Forbes Field, the linemen were making $4,000 a year and [White] was making almost $20,000. They called his number and he hit the line—he didn't go any place, couldn't make any yardage. The second time, he hit the line, and couldn't go anyplace. The next time they called his number to carry the ball, Art said, [White] asked the linemen, 'Could you please open a hole big enough for me to get through?' They said, 'We're making $4,000, you're making [$15,800]. Make your own hole.'"

White made good, anyway. He left for Oxford after that season, as both sides initially agreed, and landed Rooney

$5,000 of his investment back in a swap with Detroit. Much later in life, White became a U.S. Supreme Court Justice, but that still didn't help Rooney.

When Walt Kiesling directed the club to its first victory of 1939—in the 11th and final game of the season—a scant 9,663 were in Forbes Field to witness it. Fewer still likely admitted as much in later years. Kiesling was a character himself. Enshrined in the Pro Football Hall of Fame for his lineman career, he became a pal of Rooney's betting on the horses, a constant companion, and his go-to coach. Rooney hired him thrice to coach his club, each time as an interim or clean-up man. Discounting the shared 5-4-1 season with Greasy Neale and the 1943 Philadelphia Eagles—and also discounting the shared 0-10 season as the 1944 Card-Pitts—Kiesling had one winning season in the seven he coached solo over three separate terms.

In other words, Kiesling was a three-time loser, 30-55-5 all told.

And then Rooney sold out.

He handed over the Pittsburgh Steelers—newly renamed after a fan contest—to a millionaire playboy/heir, 28-year-old Alexis Thompson. So Rooney told the public prints after the 1938 season, Thompson had offered for years to buy the club for $50,000 and move it to Boston. They finally consummated the $160,000 deal in December 1940, the day after the Chicago Bears won the league championship by 73-0 behind the fancy passing of quarterback Sid Luckman . . . whom they drafted with a first-round pick they received in trade from Rooney and his woebegone Pirates. But that's for later in this book.

Problems began to arise with the deal. The league refused to allow Thompson to move the renamed Pittsburgh Iron Men to Boston. Rooney in the meantime purchased half of the Philadelphia Eagles from his pal and their owner-coach, Bert Bell. It was a complex transaction that involved 18 players changing addresses. As it turned out, they swapped franchises with Thompson four months after the original sale, and Rooney was back in Pittsburgh business with the Steelers. In a weird quirk, the swap caused the franchises to operate under each other's original charter: Pittsburgh under Philadelphia's, Philadelphia under Pittsburgh's. But it's only paperwork.

In 1941, the Pittsburgh Steelers went through one victory and three coaches—Bell followed by Buff Donelli, the Duquesne University coach who tried to work the two teams at once, followed by Kiesling yet again.

Chuck Cherundolo, center 1941–1942 and 1945–1948: "They were a bottom-class team [in perception around the league]. I really don't know why. Holy hell, I was satisfied.

"[Those Steelers] were just ordinary football. Actually, they didn't get good until. . . . I don't remember when they got good."

Roy McHugh, longtime sportswriter, columnist, and editor at the Pittsburgh Press: "They were regarded more or less as a sad, lost team. The Card-Pitts. The Steagles."

A funny thing happened on the way to those wild World War II years.

The Steelers won. Once.

Kiesling directed them to a 7-4 season in 1942. Yes, that fall of '42, they lost the opener to Philadelphia, which won only one other game that season, and lost the next game at Washington, which lost only one game that season. Then Big Kies' Steelers won seven of their final nine games, but didn't make the postseason—their record still was only fourth-best in the 10-team league.

The reason the Steelers got so good? It was all "Bullet" Bill Dudley, the rookie from Virginia, at age 23. He passed for 438 yards and two touchdowns, he rushed for a league-leading 696 yards and five more touchdowns, he punted, he intercepted three passes (Cherundolo had one), he topped the league in punt returns, and he topped the league in kickoff returns, where he scored yet another touchdown. That triple crown of league-leading categories has never been duplicated.

Cherundolo: "We had a helluva year that year."

After that, their 1940s went haywire.

THE '43 STEAGLES

Players such as Bill Dudley and Chuck Cherundolo were among the hundreds league-wide pressed into military service. Rationing came to the NFL as well as the rest of America: rosters were cut from 33 to 28, and travel was reduced by one-third to assist with the war effort. Players worked defense jobs in the off-season, too. So two seasons after their 1940–1941 sale and swap, the ownership parties—Alexis Thompson was an army corporal by then—were reunited for the Steelers-Eagles spawn. They came to be called the Steagles, courtesy of *Press* sports editor Chet Smith.

In their two Pittsburgh home games that strange season, they wore Philadelphia green and white—the only hiatus of the black and gold in franchise history.

They somehow emerged a winner, at 5-4-1. But in inimitable Pittsburgh fashion, they managed to finagle their way into the NFL record book: Most Fumbles, Game—10 on October 9, 1943, versus the Giants. (They also set a Steelers defensive standard that not even the Stunt 4-3 of the 1970s could touch: Fewest Yards Rushing Allowed, Game—minus 33 . . . one week earlier versus Brooklyn.)

Al Wistert, Eagles tackle–guard–defensive tackle 1943–1951: "I remember I was real surprised when I got to Philadelphia and found out that we were combined with Pittsburgh. The manager of the team [Harry Thayer] who signed me to a contract out in California, he never said anything about this. So it was a complete surprise to me. It ended up fine; it all came out all right. But I was really surprised to find out we were combined with the Steelers.

"Guys got along pretty well." Even when aligning alongside youngsters unfit or untapped for military service. Even when aligning alongside old-timers or fellows against whom you would compete for the next several years. "Yeah, that was strange . . . but not too bad. We could manage that.

"Greasy Neale was our coach and Kiesling—Walter Kiesling. They both coached the team. We players got along better than the coaches did. Greasy Neale . . . , he was a very dominant personality. He had to run the show wherever he was, you know. And the other guy wasn't used to that. So that's the way it worked."

It worked, period. Neale handled the offense, Kiesling the defense. Despite going a collective 2-1-1 against them, the players who formed this Pitt-Phila conglomerate—as it was officially listed—finished one game behind playoff-bound Washington and the New York Giants in the Eastern Division. These were the hatchlings of the 1947 NFL championship finalist Philadelphia Eagles. On the way to that title match, the Eagles had to beat a club brand-new to the postseason: the Pittsburgh Steelers. But, again, that's getting ahead of the story.

It was something of a watershed year for the NFL, with the introduction of helmets and unlimited substitution that prompted two platoon football, but more pointedly it was a watershed for the Pittsburgh franchise. For one thing, 1943 brought its first box-office success. Moreover, their headquarters moved up . . . an entire floor, to the second from the first. Their previous office, facing the parking lot at the Fort Pitt Hotel, had a window that most everyone used as a backdoor, hoisting it and climbing through it to get into the hotel faster instead of walking all the way around the block.

Cherundolo: "Matter of fact, I did that myself. For anyone on the first floor of that hotel, you did."

Carl Hughes, the Steelers beat reporter for the Pittsburgh Press *and later Kennywood Park's longtime president:* "The [Rooney–Barney McGinley] boxing carried the football club in those days, because they made money on boxing. And Art's winnings. I'm sure Barney put in a lot of money, too. [But boxing] was the big thing then. It was second only to Major League Baseball. Pro football was nothing. I remember when Bert Bell came to town. He would have the hotel put a cot in the office that the boxing club and the football club shared." Bell could outshout boxing matchmaker Jack Mintz on another phone, forcing Mintz under the desk to carry on conversations. The boxing club staged fights at Duquesne Gardens, Forbes Field, wherever, so Mintz was making a lot of matches. "There were only three employees then. Joe Carr was the ticket manager. Fran Fogarty was the business manager. And Jake Mintz." When your amalgamated football team is playing four games in Philadelphia's Shibe Park and only two in Forbes Field, how many employees would you need?

Say this for the Steagles of 1943: They were better than the 1944 wartime hodgepodge, the Car-Pitts.

Wistert: "Oh, yeah. Muuuuuch better."

THE '44 CAR-PITTS

Any alliance between what were for decades considered—rightly or wrongly—the most miserly men of the NFL, Charles Bidwill and Art Rooney, wasn't a good idea.

Wartime forced spasms. This one hurt.

In 1943, a year earlier, the Chicago Cardinals went 0-10 and lost on average by 24-10.

In 1944, they merged with the Steelers that remained from the Steagles, and somehow the team got even worse: 0-10 and lost on average by 33-11.

Their nickname was supposed to be Card-Pitts, probably because Cardlers, Steelinals, or Card-Steels just didn't roll off the tongue. Given their horrendous nature, it naturally morphed into Car-Pitts, as in: everybody walked across them.

Carl Hughes, the Steelers beat reporter for the Pittsburgh Press *and later Kennywood Park's longtime president:* "How bad? The Car-Pitts? They didn't win a game. I don't remember any close games. The players changed all the time. It depended if they got back from the service. They'd practice a couple of days; then they'd play.

"You couldn't give away tickets.

"I do remember a story about [Bidwill as] the owner. . . . He and his wife, the story goes, went to Comiskey Park to see a game—it wasn't a Steelers game. It was raining all day, and nobody came to see it. [Employees] came up to him and said, 'Mr. Bidwill, can we postpone it?' He said, 'My wife and I are here. Go ahead and play.'

"In those days, every day before the game, we stopped at a racetrack out of town. It was routine. Art, of course, was a big bettor. And everybody got used to it. The players went, too. Art was a great host. If you went, he'd buy you lunch or something."

Johnny Grigas was a running back for the Car-Pitts, and a successful one despite the circumstances. Entering the '44 season finale, he was in second place close behind the Giants' Bill Paschal in the race for the NFL rushing title. Apparently, Grigas wanted none of it.

Hughes: "He didn't show up for the final game at Forbes Field. The game was so one-sided, on one of the last plays they gave the ball to the Bears center, Bulldog Turner—he's in the Hall of Fame. And he ran [48 yards] for a touchdown, very easily. Big guy. So that's what precipitated an argument at the club [later]. . . .

"Afterwards, I went to [Grigas'] roommate, Don Currivan. 'He left me a note. I didn't even see him. I was at the hockey game last night, and he left me a note.'" In the note, Grigas wrote to Currivan that he was going back to the "stud farm." Hughes remembers that phrase running in the next edition of the *Press*, but an editor upon reading it yanked the phrase as too racy. "Art Rooney after [that] home game had all the writers from the visiting team together and took them down to a club on the South Side that had a house of ill repute upstairs. I remember [the Cardinals'] Motsy Handler was co–head coach with Walt Kiesling. Monk Anderson was one of the Bears' coaches. He and Handler got into a big argument. I remember Anderson yelling, 'You were a fumbler when you played.' Rooney tried to get between them, and then they put them in separate rooms. The Bears and the Cardinals, of course, hated each other [from sharing Chicago]."

Ed Kiely, publicity director and longtime aide-de-camp: "All I can remember is: 'When are you gonna win?' They used to call Rooney cheap and everything. You've got to get the players. Coaches are good, but the players are better."

JOCK TIME

Carl Hughes: "In '45, Jim Leonard was the Steelers coach, and they'd lost fourteen straight games [dating to the end of '43], as I recall. Probably still a Steeler record." It was, anyway, until 1969–1970 and 16 losses in a row under some guy named Charles Henry Noll. "They were playing the New York Giants. And ended their 14-game losing streak at the Polo Grounds. So, anyway, on the train back, the club car was sold out—Art bought drinks for everybody."

Perhaps it was less a toast to Leonard, who won two of his final seven games as coach, and more for the man who would replace him.

Go back to 1938, when Pitt deemphasized football—at the expense of a legendary coach. Dr. John Bain Sutherland, better known as Jock, immediately left the university where Pop Warner transformed a Scottish immigrant and wrestler into a football star and future coach. Art Rooney wanted to hire him right about the time of Sutherland's first footfall off campus. Sutherland preferred to converse with Rooney in private, at the Fort Pitt Hotel. When the story got out, he sat

The famed Jock Sutherland agrees to patrol the professional sidelines in Pittsburgh after having negotiations years earlier with Art Rooney about leaving the Pitt Panthers' sideline to coach the then-Pirates. (Courtesy of University of Pittsburgh athletics)

out the 1939 season and instead took the coaching position with the Brooklyn Dodgers' NFL club for a reported $18,000. Two years later, he went into the navy.

Rooney reached out to Sutherland again in October 1945, but he declined to talk in detail because Leonard was still on the Steelers job.

Hughes, about sharing a seat with Rooney on a train trip to the Cleveland Rams–Washington Redskins NFL championship game in Cleveland, December 16, 1945: "He asked, 'Atom [Hughes' nickname], what do you think of Bert Bell as commissioner?' Bert was his partner, and I liked him very much. I said, 'Bert would be terrific, but you already have a commissioner, Elmer Layden.' He was trying to give me a story: The next day, Bell was named commissioner.

"That same trip, we met Jock Sutherland in his naval uniform. Was handsome as hell in that uniform. And they signed him up to coach."

Art Rooney Jr.: "He brought Jock in. That was a brilliant move. He was a penny-pinching Scotsman. Fit right in with the Chief."

Sutherland told friends, "I'm back home." Amid postwar treaties and a mine explosion, it was front-page news in the *Pittsburgh Press*. He was named vice president and awarded a percentage of the gate. That worked out rather well for him: Forbes Field sold out for the 1946 and 1947 Steelers seasons, primarily due to his celebrity and his strength as a domineering teacher and coach. It probably didn't hurt that Sutherland personally wrote every single season-ticket holder a letter, either.

Sutherland moved the team offices to the Union Trust Building, kept the team in the single wing, and changed the face of the franchise.

Tim Rooney Sr., third-born son of Art Rooney and a camp ball boy at Alliance College in Cambridge Springs, Pennsylvania, at the time:

Jock Sutherland was our coach. He was a very, very strong disciplinarian. He used to work the players unbelievably. Scrimmage and scrimmage and scrimmage. What happens then, which is hard to believe when you think of football today and football then, we had to have somebody on the floors in the dormitories staying up at night to make sure no one snuck out and quit. They'd have sneak-outs so they could just disappear. They were fodder just for practice.

I remember one day, I was walking from my dorm to the dressing room—the dressing room in those days wasn't a dressing room as such; it was a gymnasium at the school. The lockers and hangars were put up around the basketball floor. I was with Jock Sutherland, and he had his arm on my head: "Are we going to scrimmage today?" I ask. He says, "We'd like to scrimmage, but we don't have enough players."

. . . Money was very short. You went on trains or on buses. It was tough sledding with the players and everything. Just making it. Just making sure you didn't go bust. Even as young kids, we were very cognizant of the fact that it took a lot of money to run a football team.

The players in those days were wonderful, wonderful people. Wages were hard to believe. You were talking about thousands of dollars, small thousands of dollars. These guys were making less than $5,000. Funny thing is, a lot of times you had a pretty good player, but when they'd get married they had to quit. It was hard enough taking care of themselves, you know.

Joe Walton, longtime NFL player and coach, whose father, Tiger, worked as line coach under Sutherland: "Dad always said he was a very stern guy, ran a very tight ship. Pretty stubborn, too."

Chuck Cherundolo, center 1941–1942 and 1945–1948: "Never said a word. When he spoke to you, you stood up and listened. 'Do it this way.' And, you know, that was the way you were going to do it. That's what made him a good coach."

Roy McHugh, longtime sportswriter, columnist, and editor at the Pittsburgh Press: "He got rid of [league MVP Bullet Bill] Dudley after '46 [and a 5-5-1 record]. They didn't get along. With Sutherland, everything had to be done by the book, his way. The single wing, which of course was becoming obsolete since 1941, the 73-0 [Bears–Redskins 1940 NFL championship rout]. Everybody went to the T formation after that. Except Sutherland, who learned the single wing from Pop Warner." Dudley, a future Hall of Famer, was a quintuple threat—defensive back, passer, rusher, field goals, and returns.

Quarterback Charley Seabright; halfback Tony Compagno; quarterback Bob Cifers, whom the Steelers received from Detroit in the Bullet Bill Dudley trade; and halfback Paul White, circa 1947. They helped to make the finest—and first playoff—Steelers team in the franchise's first 40 years of existence, at 8-4. Then coach Jock Sutherland died unexpectedly the next April. The franchise made the playoffs only once more over the next 24 seasons. (Carnegie Library Archives)

"Sutherland told him: 'You're a great player, but I don't have to have great players to win.' And they had a better record in '47 without Dudley than they had before."

Al Wistert, Steagles/Eagles tackle–guard–defensive tackle 1943–1951: "I'm surprised by that. Because Bill Dudley was the kind of a guy, I'd want guys like him on my team any day. But that's the way it goes, I guess."

Further toiling to improve the franchise, Sutherland hired the first scout in Steelers' history and reputedly only the second in the entire NFL. Pat Livingston didn't merely serve as a scout, though. McHugh talked about the taciturn coach once dispatching Livingston to fetch his suit at a dry cleaner. An argument ensued over the 25 cents in change from the dollar he gave Livingston. It became the sticking point between the two, and next thing anyone knew Livingston was a sportswriter at the *Press*.

McHugh: "Of course, nobody knew [Sutherland] had the brain tumor."

Sutherland's Starless Steelers, as they were nicknamed, went 8-4 in 1947. After losing two of their opening three games, they reeled off seven victories in their final nine regular-season games—including a 35-24 triumph over Philadelphia constructed on three fourth-quarter touchdowns. End Val Jansante and rookie guard Red Moore were the only Steelers to share a first team All-Pro stage with the Eagles' Wistert and Detroit's Dudley, among others.

The franchise record to date for victories resulted in the franchise's first playoff game in its decade-and-a-half history. Coaches from around the "National League" convened in Pittsburgh for the annual draft that Friday night at the Fort

Tailback Johnny Clement, aka "Johnny Zero" (for the number he wore), scores a touchdown at Forbes Field, circa 1946–1948. (Carnegie Library Archives)

Pitt Hotel. Les Biederman wrote in the game-day *Pittsburgh Press*: "A 15-year dream, nursed and coddled with heartaches and plenty of red ink, becomes a reality today for owner Art Rooney and his Cinderella Steelers. . . . The Steelers are sentimental choices because of Rooney's plight down through the years." Before 35,729 at Forbes Field at the end of an exciting pro-football week in Pittsburgh, the Steelers were blanked by Philadelphia, 21-0, en route to the Eagles' NFL-championship-game loss to the Chicago Cardinals. Interesting how those former mergers all fared in 1947.

For the Pittsburgh franchise, the suddenly brightening fortunes turned bleak . . . again.

Scouting through the South the next spring, driving from Washington, DC, to Durham, North Carolina, to New Orleans, Sutherland endured some sort of episode and went missing for days before he was discovered dazed in a field in Bandana, Kentucky. The Steelers hadn't heard from him between March 28 and the April 8 date he was found wandering that field with his briefcase. He spent two days in a Cairo, Illinois, hospital. "Nervous exhaustion," doctors originally diagnosed him. He had complained of headaches for two weeks before he left on the scouting mission, but an examination at a Pittsburgh hospital found nothing worrisome.

Sutherland was flown back to Pittsburgh, helped off the plane by protégé Johnny Michelosen, and nestled into the Steelers station wagon driven by publicity director Ed Kiely. Twenty-eight hours later, he was in the operating room for two surgeries on a malignant brain tumor. He died the next day, April 11, 1948. The banner headline across the top of the next day's *Post-Gazette*: "Jock Sutherland is dead at 59."

Steelers part-owner Barney McGinley compared it to the sad football day Knute Rockne passed. Chicago Bears coach George Halas called Sutherland undoubtedly the best coach in the NFL. The *Press* editorialized: "Pittsburgh has lost its most celebrated citizen. . . . He was universally admired, uncommonly esteemed and genuinely mourned."

Ernie Accorsi, general manager for Cleveland, Baltimore, and the New York Giants: "The Chief always told me, 'We would've won if he hadn't died.' That's the only would-have-been he ever said."

2

The Owners

F ROM BIRTHRIGHT TO BIG BUSINESS, from $2,500 investment to billion-dollar worth, the little football franchise that could has grown and changed. What started out as Rooney family hobby has morphed into much more in barely a quarter century's time. When the leadership was handed down from father to son a second time, the Rooneys retained the Steelers—but in order to do so they were required to add ownership outside the family circle for the first time. This transaction was on a much different scale than the concern of meeting the Monday payroll.

Such are the spasms and issues in guiding the Pittsburgh Steelers from one generation to the next to the next.

ART ROONEY SR.
Founder–President: 1933–1975

Colleges: Indiana University of Pennsylvania (formerly Indiana Normal), Georgetown, Duquesne, and Washington and Jefferson • **Birthplace:** Coultersville, Pennsylvania • **Born:** January 27, 1901 • **Died:** August 25, 1988

He had the horses, all right. He had them in Maryland, New York, New Jersey, Pennsylvania, Vermont, Quebec, Kentucky. He had them at the $100 window and higher. He had them before electronic tote boards, when pals such as Tim Mara legally made book from their pockets for thousands. He had a head for figures, a gut for playing the horses, a spine for long shots, and a driver so he could bone up by studying the *Daily Racing Form* or the papers. He had a multitrack mind, which explains how the family made quite a good living off the old man's wondrous wagering and, much later, a handful of raceways around the East Coast along with the rambling Shamrock Farms in Maryland. Pittsburgh's first family of sports made its living, paid its bills until about 1990, on the backs of the ponies.

That's the irony between Art Rooney Sr.'s avocation and his vocation.

In professional football, he never had the horses for the first 40 years.

He could pick a winner on any oval. He couldn't build a winner on any rectangle.

Art Rooney Jr.: "If horses could run there, he would win."

Tim Rooney Sr.: "My father was one of the best bettors who ever lived."

The man, the office, the usual pose—stogie in mouth or hand. Art Rooney Sr. sits at his desk in January 1980 after his team's fourth Super Bowl triumph. (George Gojkovich)

Pat Rooney Sr.: "Everybody talks about the football side, but the horse racing part was every bit as important. He talked about how making the payroll on Monday was bigger than winning on Sunday. And that depended on how he did Saturday."

For the longest time, the father whom even his own children addressed as the Chief (after Superman's editor Perry White) would leave on Mondays for a week of horses. The adventure might include a stop at their 350-acre Shamrock Farms in Woodbine, Maryland, then routinely follow a course of tracks; Laurel or Havre de Grace in Maryland, Liberty Bell in Philadelphia, then New Jersey or New York next. Come Saturday night, they would return to Pittsburgh, or meet up with the Steelers, for an NFL Sunday.

Every morning, the Chief attended Mass, no matter how close to a track or fairground post time.

Pat Sr.: "Hey, that was *his job*. And it was a tough-ass job, too, boy. There's nothing tougher than going to the track as your business." He knows from experience. Pat Sr. runs the

Rooneys' Palm Beach Kennel Club in Florida, where he has come across roughly a dozen professional gamblers over the years. "A lot of our success wasn't getting into tracks, it was getting out of them at the right time. [Regulations, tax-percentages, the art of business accounting,] my dad understood that stuff better than anybody I ever saw."

Joe Gordon, publicity director and vice president, 1969–1998: "That first year, '69, our offices were in the Roosevelt Hotel. There were two real big desks facing each other. . . . I had an opportunity firsthand to be exposed [to the Chief's savvy]. The most perceptive person I've ever known. And the greatest man I've ever known."

Roy McHugh, longtime sportswriter, columnist, and editor at the Pittsburgh Press *and a gent of 93:* "He was the most beloved sports personage I've ever known. I think I only heard a couple of guys in my whole life who didn't like him. Two. I can think of two. I won't tell you who. Everybody loved him. He was humble. Down to earth. Maybe that's what made him so good; he didn't make any affect. He could be real."

This gambling man was genuine Pittsburgh, Irish Catholic, humble, charitable, unlucky at football, and lucky at horses.

Arthur Joseph Rooney, the eldest of nine, was born southeast of Pittsburgh and moved to Beaver County before the family settled on the North Side before he was two—and never left. The family lived atop the saloon operated by his father, Daniel, on the grounds from which Three Rivers Stadium sprouted. Family, friends, and folks simply described as fellow North Side toughies lived nearby in row houses that existed until PNC Park was constructed. He nearly drowned at age 11 canoeing through a flood in what normally was the outfield at Exposition Park, professional baseball's Pittsburgh home before Forbes Field, Three Rivers Stadium, and PNC Park. He went to school at St. Peter's parochial. Those are firmly planted roots.

Art Jr.: "The North Side. His dad was a saloon owner. There were a lot of horseplayers around the saloon there. My dad was always like the runner; I don't know if he was running bets, but they didn't have pari-mutuels. For politicians, taking messages to other politicians. He was a really sharp guy at a young age. His dad would go to [horse tracks] in Cleveland and those places, and my dad would go with him, and he had that knack. So he grew up in that environment, horses, running winnings from saloon to saloon."

Pat Sr.: "I don't ever remember hearing a story about hard times for the Rooneys. And I always heard they fed a lot of folks around that neighborhood [in times of need]. That's where all the Irish lived . . . , and they all worked in the steel mills." Art Sr. later admitted to working just a half day in his entire life, walking out of that steel mill midway through his first shift and never even returning for his paycheck. All nine of Daniel and Margaret Rooney's children growing up around the Depression went to college, "and in those days that was unheard of. My dad went to four or five colleges. I don't think he ever graduated.

"I always heard he never gambled on anything else. He was only a horse player. The only card game I remember him playing was pinochle. That's how he got into the gambling business, just hanging around it [from the North Side saloons to regional racetracks]. He was raised . . . in an environment of wise guys, and those guys would do anything to make a nickel."

Art Jr.: "And he was a great athlete, a tough guy. He could take care of himself."

McHugh: "Looked tough. There was no big smile and all that stuff. That came later."

He boxed, barnstormed, and played football and baseball, sometimes finding ways to mix together all four. He won an AAU welterweight boxing title and beat two members of the U.S. team for the 1920 Olympics in Antwerp, Belgium, including gold medalist Sammy Mosberg. Such was his boxing reputation and moxie, he eventually went into business with partner Barney McGinley by opening a gym and staging cards. Billy Conn fought under the Rooney/McGinley banner for a time, and in 1951 they brought the Ezzard Charles–Jersey Joe Walcott heavyweight championship to Forbes Field.

Baseball seemed to be his first love as a sport. He played on teams that barnstormed the region against Negro League teams. Later, he bankrolled what became the Homestead Grays under Negro League Baseball Hall of Famer Cumberland Posey. He patrolled center field and managed a Wheeling minor league team along with his brother, Dan. A dead arm cut short his baseball career, by all accounts. The team's nickname: the Stogies.

Art Jr.: "All he talked about was playing . . . baseball with his brother, who became a priest. He loved baseball more than he loved minor league football."

By 1925, his baseball career over, he began to concentrate on horse racing—though football remained a factor.

See, back in his college days—or, more accurately, colleges days—young Art was quite the footballer. He received a recruiting letter from Notre Dame University's famed Knute Rockne, who supposedly twice offered him a football scholarship. He graduated from Indiana Normal School, now Indiana University of Pennsylvania, in two years' time and, from there, played baseball at Georgetown, plus football at Duquesne and Washington and Jefferson. These were the days long before the NCAA and its unwieldy rules manual. He became a devout believer in crisscrossing the demarcation between college and semipro, if not college and college.

McHugh: "In the morning, he played for both Indiana Normal [now IUP] and, in the afternoon, for Duquesne."

Art Jr.: "All the guys who played at Pitt, Carnegie Tech, W&J . . . would take the train out to Canton and Akron and play there [the next day]. He always said a lot of the guys who played sandlot with him could play in the National Football League."

Rooney founded and funded a couple of sandlot, or semi-pro, football teams, such as the Hope Harveys. And how did he fund them well enough to pay his players and afford their transportation? The track.

So if he could do that with sandlotters, perhaps he could make a go of it in the business that the newspapers labeled "the National Professional League," because the common "National League" could get confused with major league baseball—the far more popular game. After all, his bookmaker buddy Tim Mara had owned the New York Football Giants since 1925, and it cost him only $500 to start a franchise.

Becoming well connected politically through North Side Republicans, dipping his toe into the rising waters of change, Rooney figured the time was ripe for a repeal of the Blue Laws so pro football could play on Sundays. In 1933, he ponied up $2,500 to launch professional football in the Commonwealth of Pennsylvania: he in Pittsburgh, and his pal Bert Bell in Philadelphia. (One side benefit: Theater owners, giddy at having a new weekend day of business, granted Rooney free movie passes for life.) The franchise's inaugural game, September 20, 1933, arrived on a Wednesday night. They opened with a safety, then lost to Mara's Giants, 23-2. There was much work to do.

Ray Kemp, in that inaugural 1933 season the first African American to play for the franchise then nicknamed the Pirates, years later told the *Pittsburgh Post-Gazette*: "Often, when the Pirates were playing, he was at the races."

Art Jr.: "He told me once he won more money betting on Seabiscuit than Seabiscuit won on races." The horse's earnings from 1933 to 1939: $437,730.

Tim Sr.: "The most famous story of my father betting on horses was what he did in Saratoga. In fact, it was the week I was born, 1937. Every day they wrote stories in the New York papers how well my father was doing on the races in Saratoga. My father got his bankroll at Empire City. Tim Mara was a legalized bookmaker—you had bookmakers before the totes business. That's who I'm named after. What he said to Tim Mara when he left [Empire City for upstate New York]—and I was born while he was in Saratoga— . . . 'I'm never going to let you forget this day. Not because of the money I won off you, but I'm naming my son after you.' Of course my daughter married Chris Mara, who's the second oldest boy in the Mara family. Their daughter is [actress] Rooney Mara. I like Patricia [her birth name] better."

Those three August days at the races all reputedly started at a Harrisburg plumber's union banquet with two friends and a notion. At Empire City, a $20 bet earned $700 from Mara. Rooney kept on going until he concluded the sizzling Saturday with $21,000. The Saratoga meet opened Monday, and the betting party arrived despite what the Chief later described as a radiator problem that required four stops. First bet: $2,000 on an 8-1 shot named Quel Jeu, or What Game. It was the first of five long shots. It was the first of five big winners.

He made, by most accounting, maybe $250,000, maybe $380,000, maybe more. Whatever size was the actual pile of money, Rooney sent for a Brink's truck. He sent money to his brother Dan, by then known as Father Silas and a missionary in China. Upon returning to the North Side, he told his wife, Kathleen: We'll never have to worry about money again.

Oh, he worried just the same. He kept right on betting, taking to tracks with him various Pirates/Steelers players and a fellow horse player named Walt Kiesling, whom he hired not once, not twice, but three times as his head football coach. Usually, one of the Chief's sons or North Side friends drove him from track to track, occasionally two in one day.

Pat Sr.: "He drove . . . like [race-car pioneer] Barney Oldfield." He drove the tires off the car." By acclamation, the father rode in the passenger seat and someone else drove. "So the Chief was always reading the paper or the *Daily Racing Form*. He was reading the *Daily Racing Form* constantly in the car."

Tim Sr.: "The one thing he was consistent on, if anything ever happened to him and he died—and he used to always make these speeches at dinner—'sell all those horses of mine and *immediately* sell that football team of mine.'"

Pat Sr.: "It was definitely survival mode. It wasn't trying to win the championship. It was trying to keep it going. And a big, big part of that was the racetrack."

Consider his 1940s:

In December 1940, he sold the newly christened Steelers to Alexis Thompson and bought half of the Philadelphia Eagles from his friend Bert Bell.

Four months later, they swapped franchises—he got Pittsburgh back.

In August 1941, they opened camp in Hershey with co-owner Bell as coach. That arrangement lasted just shy of eight weeks, until Bell went 0-2 and quit. They hired Duquesne University coach Buff Donelli, who coached *both* teams, until the Steelers went 0-5 and Donelli went on a plane to California for a Duquesne game. Then Rooney named, for the second of three go-rounds, Kiesling as head coach. "What's next?" the *Pittsburgh Post-Gazette* asked.

Next came the 1943 Steagles, the 1944 Car-Pitts (perhaps the worst team in NFL history), and Rooney's proclamation about their attire and identity: "I told [a sportswriter]: 'The only thing different is the uniform. It's the Same Old Steelers.' The papers have never let me forget it."

The Chief later offered this synopsis of his first two decades as Pirates-Steelers owner: "When the Blue Laws were repealed in 1933 and I applied for an NFL franchise . . . , it was just a hop, skip and a jump from semipro ball. I never gave it any time. Only the guys like [Chicago's George] Halas, [Green Bay's Curly] Lambeau, and [Washington's George Preston] Marshall tried to win. But when I started trying to win in the '40s, everyone else did, too, and it became difficult. My worst break came when Jock Sutherland died after we tied for the division title [in 1947]."

Gordon: "He had a soft spot for Kiesling, obviously," hiring him in 1939, 1941, and 1954. "But he hired Jock Sutherland. If Jock Sutherland hadn't died, Pittsburgh could have had championship teams."

Tim Sr.:

After football games, we'd come home to dinner—we surely wouldn't go out to dinner after a football game. We'd all have opinions about why we lost and what went wrong, just like the fans do. So you're sitting there, you'd like to say what you think. But you never would open your mouth. Once [the Chief] made his statements, and he didn't always do it because he was generally mad after, but you waited for him to open the door. Then everybody would open up and argue what was the worst call, or the worst call by an official. They were interesting times.

One of the best stories I ever heard about my father: Bob Drum, who wrote for the *Press* and used to sit with my father at the games, my father told him the story. The day before he called Kies in. "You're going to start [quarterback Jack] Scarbath on Sunday." Kies got out of the chair. My father said, "Kies, sit down, you're forgetting I'm the boss. You're starting Scarbath." And those were the days where our first play was [a Fran Rogel dive play], all 30,000 people in the stands would all start singing "Hey, diddle diddle, Rogel up the middle" before the first play. Of course, he'd gain a yard and get tackled. And that's how we started every game.

So my father tells Drum he was starting Scarbath. And he told Kies that the first play he has to throw a pass. So [Scarbath] throws the ball, and it's, like, 85 yards for a touchdown. And we're offsides. They bring it back, and the next play they run Rogel up the middle.

And Drum said, "They went offsides on purpose."

That was the only time I ever heard of my father interfering with plays and the players.

Montage used in 1947 game program portraying center and later assistant coach Chuck Cherundolo, middle left, and others. (Carnegie Library Archives)

Hey diddle diddle, it's Fran Rogel . . . not going up the middle. Notice the Phillies scoreboard at Shibe Park. Rogel (1950–1957) was such a workhorse in the unimaginative Steelers offense that he averaged only 3.6 yards per carry. Star offensive tackle Frank Varrichione, voted to the Steelers' all-time team, is No. 74 in the background. (Temple Urban Archives)

Dan "Bad Rad" Radakovich, assistant coach 1971 and 1974–1977, illustrating that the Chief held onto that lesson for a generation and more: "He didn't interfere, probably to a fault. All that trouble he had through the years, it was probably because he didn't interfere. [Buddy Parker] trading his team away and all that [spit]."

McHugh: "When I was the [*Press*] sports editor, I got letters, 'You on Rooney's payroll?' They wanted to run Rooney out of town. They wanted somebody else to be in charge of the Steelers. Even '69, Noll's first year, when they won one game." One media note: Rooney was publicity savvy, which explained why he kept Ed Kiely and Joe Gordon on staff for three to four decades apiece. The Steelers invited media to join them on the road, free of charge, to secure coverage. They set up a hospitality room with plenty of alcohol after practices. They allowed coaches on the road to buy drinks for journalists and bill the club.

Pat Sr.: "We won, when, '46–'47? Then we went to the playoffs [next], when, '63? I think the Chief knew we couldn't win until we got a stadium. From the racing business and all that, the Chief knew numbers so well. Besides, you couldn't go to a football game like this . . . ," craning his neck to the left, mimicking Forbes Field's made-for-baseball seating.

To the old man, one side benefit to constructing Three Rivers Stadium: 81 games of baseball, right outside of his office door.

Often, baseball came through his office door.

Kiely: "When we were at Three Rivers, there wasn't a [major league] team that came in where somebody didn't say, 'Can I meet Art?'" Managers in particular relished his company, often squatting for long talks in the dugout.

V. Tim Rooney, nephew and Steelers pro personnel scout, about a former San Diego Padres base coach: "He told me, 'He would call me over and talk; I knew who he was. He knew

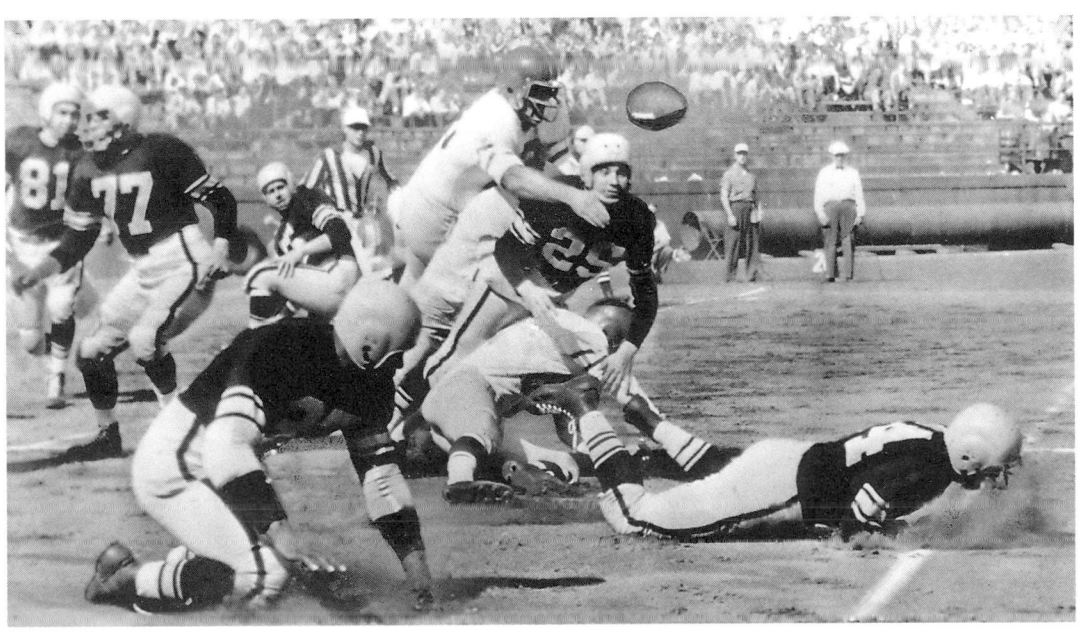

Ray Mathews, with Steelers teammates falling around him, watches the ball float away from his grasp in 1952. (Temple Urban Archives)

more baseball than half the people I ever knew in baseball. It was unbelievable the amount of baseball he knew.'

"I remember [Pirates third baseman Richie] Hebner coming through the Steelers offices to get a cigar. Four o'clock, he would walk through in his uniform, [the Chief] and Bradshaw would be in there."

Art Jr. recalled his dad giving the Pirates' call-ups $50 or $100 in welcome-to-town cash. There also were almost daily visits to the manager's office, when the Pirates were home, and kibbutzing with Roberto Clemente, Manny Sanguillen, and the fellows.

Ralph Berlin, trainer 1968–1992: "I think basically he really loved the Pirates. I was always surprised that he didn't buy them, truthfully. He never missed a baseball game. Never."

Gordon, who got nighttime calls from his boss, with no notice or pleasantries, just a sudden burst of pure baseball apoplexy: "'How could that guy throw the ball home?'

"When CBS sold the Yankees to [George] Steinbrenner's guys, I think CBS approached Tim Rooney Sr. I think [the Rooneys] considered it. How seriously, I don't know. When Carl Barger's [public-private] group bought them [in the mid-1980s], there were rumors the Rooneys were interested in buying the Pirates."

Art Jr.: "We did a bit of research in it [when the Galbreath family sold to Barger and the consortium]. Then the O'Malley family with the LA Dodgers called us [later looking to sell shares amid estate issues]. All I could think was how happy the Chief would have been. We thought, 'If you were going to own a team, who would you rather own, the Los Angeles Dodgers or the Pittsburgh Pirates?'"

Imagine if the Chief owned a baseball club? He already had a problem with chewing tobacco and, of course, cigars.

Most of the time, the cigars remained unlit. He just kept one in his lips, the way some people sport toothpicks and others chew gum. It was his public habit; chew was his private vice . . . and he was none too pleased when he found out Art Jr. had the same affliction.

Kiely: "Chew? He told me it was the worst thing to ever happen to him."

Berlin: "The Chief got me smoking cigars. When I came here, I was smoking Hav-A-Tampas; they were five for 45 cents. They were all paper filler. The Chief came to me and said Frank Sinatra would send him three boxes of cigars a month, and he had three, four, or five for me. Mr. Rooney gave me quite an education on cigars. There was a place in Jenkins Arcade called Bloom Cigars [across the street from their Roosevelt Hotel offices]. He would send me over. I would get four, five boxes of cigars for him, and he would always give me one. Then he died and left me with this expensive habit."

McHugh: "The joke was, he spent more on cigars than the education of his five sons."

Steve Bono, quarterback 1987–1988: "Earnest [Jackson, a 1986–1988 running back] would literally go in there and smoke cigars with him and put his feet up on the desk. I remember going in there once with Earnest and thinking, 'Oh my God, Earnest, what are you doing?'"

Ernie Accorsi, general manager of Baltimore, Cleveland, and the Giants: "The Chief and I had a special relationship for all things [pertaining to] cigars. And you could smoke them anywhere in those days. But he'd give me a cigar anytime he saw me at league meetings. The last meeting he attended, he didn't look good. I had a suspicion. So that last cigar he gave

me, I took it home and put it in a case—never smoked it. If I touch it, it's going to disintegrate. But I have a little note in there, 'Chief's last cigar.'"

Sharing a good stogie was but a speck of Rooney's charity, an eyehole peep into his open personality.

Stories, if not legends, abound about his generosity. A priest in New York, with whom he shared a cab, wound up with the $10,000 his parish needed for a new roof. *Sports Illustrated* wrote that the boss loaned his suite before the 1979 New England opener to a wedding party about to get betrothed in a crowded, standard hotel room. Beggars off the street in Stadium Circle at Three Rivers Stadium. . . .

Gordon: "Those panhandlers and deadbeats" who used to hang around the Chief.

But also the mayor, Joe Barr, would stop by the Steelers offices. Same for Governor David Lawrence and the Chief's protégé, longtime Pittsburgh-area politician Tom Foerster. (Rooney, by the way, ran on the Republican ticket in 1939 for register of wills. After a campaign speech the *Pittsburgh Post-Gazette* labeled "frank," in which Rooney admitted he didn't know where to find the office itself, he lost by 8,375 votes. He never made it out of the 1943 primary, either.)

Kiely: "I traveled all over with him. It really was an education, I tell you. Because he knew so many people." Once, the Chief ran into an acquaintance who just happened to be a member of President Franklin Delano Roosevelt's cabinet. Another time in Chicago, Mayor Richard Daley's office rang their hotel room to ask for an audience.

Larry Brown, tight end–offensive tackle 1971–1984: "I don't ever remember talking football with him. What I do remember is going up to the Hill to get my haircut. There always were a bunch of old guys there, doing that barbershop thing. Guys would talk about him coming up to the Hill, talking to them, interacting with them. That was just who he was. And that was a huge asset for the club. I think that legacy and respect are probably what even sustains the club now."

Tunch Ilkin, tackle–guard–center 1980–1992: "I was in for a physical before the [1980] draft—Nate Johnson, Ted Walton, and me—and we all wound up getting picked. We're in the lobby. We met with Chuck. We're waiting for the physicals. The Chief walks in, and he's dressed casually. He's got on a cardigan that's misbuttoned. He's got a golf shirt buttoned to the top. He's got the cigar. And he's dumping a large ashtray into a small one. And Nate Johnson says, 'So are you the janitor?' The Chief just laughed it off: 'I do a little of everything around here.' Just a picture of humility. If anybody could have been rolled up in himself, it was the Chief. And here was a guy [who acted like] he was a working man."

Berlin: "Greatest man I ever knew. He treated everyone the same. If he walked in here right now and he didn't know you, he'd walk over and say, 'Hi, I'm Art Rooney. Who are you?' I really feel like he was the father I never had."

As a rumpled elderly man, it made him all the more cute, cuddly, silly. When he took the elevator to the locker room with time still on the clock, you just had to laugh that the founder missed the watershed moment in his troubled franchise's history: the Immaculate Reception (see Sidebar in Chapter 8, pp. 158–162). "I didn't see the miracle."

Bob Drum's widow, Marian Jane Drum, tells a tale about driving to Cleveland with Mr. and Mrs. Rooney for a Steelers game, only to find that he had no tickets. The guard allowed the party to enter because passersby needled the Steelers owner. Contrast that to the tale from Art Jr., who remembers his mother forgetting her tickets to a home Steelers game and trying to convince a guard she was the owner's wife.

Art Jr.: "The guard says, 'Yeah, and I'm Eleanor Roosevelt. There's the [ticket] office over there.'"

Rooney was celebrated for his long walks around Three Rivers, hands behind his back—and, as players later discovered, rosary in his hands.

On one such foray, he discovered a young man hiding in the seats trying to covertly watch practice. Offensive lineman Ted Peterson invited in a buddy who had just been released from his minor league baseball team and prepared to try to enter the NFL as a punter. After practice, they found the Chief in the Allegheny Club buying dinner for that guest, Jeff Gossett—who wound up punting for 15 years with four different AFC teams.

John Banaszak, defensive lineman 1975–1981:

He would always take his walk. And walk and walk and walk. One day he's taking his walk, and it's the first couple weeks of the season, it's my rookie year. You know how noisy it is inside that stadium with all the cleaning going on? He's walking, and Mike Collier takes a swing pass from Bradshaw, takes one step and just nails the Chief. Just freaking nailed him. Sent the Chief flying through the air. His face scrapes the real nasty turf of Three Rivers Stadium. Blood covering his face and all scratched up. He's laying on the ground. And you could hear a pin drop in that stadium. Mike Collier was mortified. There were only three rookies who made that team, and Mike Collier thought he was done. There were more people consoling Mike Collier than there were the Chief.

The next day, the Chief walks in, he's got scabs all over his face, he's limping. Our meeting room was right there, and George Perles saw him walk by: "Chief, Chief, how you feeling?" Chief says, "Boys, I got to tell you, that's the hardest hit I've had in a long time." He was about 74 at the time.

By the 1970s, the Chief ceded most of the club's control to sons Dan and Art. A decade earlier, he divided the sibling workload: The two eldest boys to the Steelers, the three youngest to the growing Rooney track empire. Tim and the twins, Pat and John, were placed in charge of Liberty Bell, Penn, and Yonkers (now back to its Empire City name) for harness and thoroughbred racing, West Palm for both horse meets plus dogs, and Pownal, Vermont.

Pat Sr.: "This sums up the attitude. John and I were working at Liberty Bell. We're at a Steelers game, and the Chief saw us. 'What are you doing?' 'We drove in from Philadelphia to see the game.' He said, 'Go home. You're racetrackers. You have nothing to do with this.'" The three youngest brothers, by this time thirtysomethings, were grateful for the distance away from the shadow that grew sizable through the 1970s. Still, the father didn't completely cut them off: He gave them Super Bowl rings. "I don't feel like I was a part of it. I bet that's exactly how John felt and exactly how Tim felt."

Tim Sr.: "If there ever was a vote on what we wanted to do, all five of us would've wanted to be with the football team. We were all football fans. We grew up with the football. We knew my father had horses; I used to go to the races with him all the time and to our farm, and enjoyed it a lot. We were all football people. Much more than racing."

The changing of the guard became official in 1975: The Chief booted himself up the flow chart to chairman of the board and promoted Dan from vice president to president. It wasn't announced. The media guide, which doesn't contain Rooney bios, merely changed titles. This came months after his admiring Steelers players became a tad misty when the Lombardi Trophy in New Orleans in January 1975 was handed to the old man—silver in his right hand, game ball in his left, and a satisfied 43-year-old smile on his 74-year-old face.

Gordon, recalling what Rooney came to find inside the Steelers offices upon his return from Mass the Tuesday after Super Bowl IX: "The operator answered, 'Good morning, World Champion Pittsburgh Steelers.' He walked over: 'That's not necessary. We're just the Pittsburgh Steelers. Everybody knows we're the champs.'"

Jack Butler, defensive back 1951–1959: "They treated everyone with respect and dignity. They paid as best they could. They can't give you what they don't have. I played nine years in the league. I made 72 [thousand]. Didn't care what anyone else made."

Frank Varrichione, offensive tackle 1955–1960: "Back in those days, they signed me to a three-year contract; I was making eight thousand. I had just made the Pro Bowl. He tore it up and gave me a three-year contract for ten thousand with a five-thousand bonus, which was a lot of money in those days. He was a man of his word. He did what he said he would do."

Star receiver Elbie Nickel is unable to gather this critical pass play in the end zone, with Russ Craft helping to break it up and Frank Reagan not far behind in this 1950 Eagles victory—by one touchdown, 17-10. Notice that the *Philadelphia Bulletin* identified "Nickel" in a box at his left hip. At the time, throwing around a nickel seems to have been an ironic nod to the perceived penurious owners. (Temple Urban Archives)

Dick Hoak, running back 1961–1970 and running backs coach 1972–2006, making him a forty-five-year employee: "1968, I made the Pro Bowl. We weren't very good as a team. We might have won two games, and I had a good year. In those days, you had to go to the Roosevelt Hotel every two weeks to get your check. [Business manager] Fran Fogarty was the one with the checks . . . , and he said, 'The Chief wants to see you.' The Chief said, 'We're not having a good year, but you are,' and he handed me an envelope. In it, there was a pretty good chunk of cash. And in those days you didn't have incentives and all that." After separating his shoulder in the season finale against New Orleans, he went back to the hotel and this time was sent to Dan Rooney's office. "I go in there, and Dan hands me an envelope, 'We want you to have this.' I opened it, and it was the same exact amount his dad gave me two weeks before. I told him that, and he said, 'I know, he wanted you to have this, too.'

"You hear the stories that Rooneys were cheap. That wasn't the whole story. They just didn't have the players. 'Cause I know there were other players that they did that for. I know guys who didn't quite make the incentives, and they gave it to them, anyway."

Radakovich: "We were probably the lowest-paid salary-wise in the league. But they gave us Christmas bonuses, which made it worth it. We could entertain sportswriters, and they would reimburse us. . . . We would stay at the Waldorf. . . . They were tight with salaries. But they were generous with bonuses and very generous with the expenses. The most generous of any team I was with—and I've been with *a lot* of teams."

Brown: "That's a big plus, when you start to build the relationship part of it. Having people feel like more than 'You're just a commodity.' You see them as a whole person."

Bono: "My memories are more of the loyalties that Webby and John [Stallworth] and Walter [Abercrombie] and Earnest [Jackson] and those guys had for the Chief. They crossed [the 1987 picket line] because of their loyalty not only to the Chief, but the Rooneys in general."

Jim Sweeney, guard–center 1996–1999: "My grandfather and Mr. Rooney used to pal around in the '20s. They used to hang together. They were great friends. He was an Irish Catholic cop. Him being a policeman I'm sure helped. My grandfather passed in 1951 before I was born.

"When I was drafted [in 1984], Mr. Rooney sent me a letter. He said, 'I wish you were around at No. 52 [he was chosen 37th overall], but Mr. Leon Hess and the Jets are a great organization.' They're just a great family. I still have it framed."

Times were a-changing, but the Chief stayed the same. Accorsi remembered a tale that Browns owner Art Modell told him. At the league meeting when NFL commissioner Pete Rozelle announced a new television contract worth a million . . . *per team* . . . the room went wild, owners exulting while standing on chairs. In the back of the room was the Steelers owner turning the cigar in his mouth. The man who kept alive his club through the Depression and plenty of bad football, Rooney already had crunched numbers and done the math: "Why aren't you happy?" Modell asked. Replied Rooney: "What do you think, we're going to get to keep it?"

Accorsi: "This from a guy who had trouble making payroll for years." Making payroll, yes. Making and keeping friends, never. This, after all, was a man with such a meticulous mind that he could remember names years after last meeting someone. This was a man whose kindness surprised even

The Chief. (Courtesy of the author)

those who knew him well. In 1987, after the Browns toppled the Steelers the day after Christmas and advanced to the playoffs, "Chief came to Modell—and I tell you what, I never would've believed anybody else in the league would've said it—'We've won a lot, I'm glad you have a chance.' I told Modell, 'Twelve other owners in the league would've told you that, but he's the only one who is sincere.'"

He was loyal not only to North Siders with crooked noses and even more crooked reputations, to panhandlers and beggars off the street, to his players and coaches and fans, but also to friends whose teams on the field represented enemies.

Gordon: "In the Chief, that was the quality he admired most in other people. And through that loyalty, he wanted Walt Kiesling [too often as coach] or would hang onto players. That was up and down the organization, from the janitor to the head coach."

McHugh: "It was more fun with Art Sr. He always said football was more fun before it became a business."

DAN ROONEY
Director of Scouting–Vice President–President–Chair

College: Duquesne • **Birthplace:** Pittsburgh • **Born:** July 20, 1932

Where the father played the ponies, the firstborn son was all business—the business of football.

Dan Rooney, the heir apparent, was born 354 days before the Pittsburgh football club and was reared along with it. When his time came, Art Rooney's firstborn transformed it from chump to champion, from laughingstock to prototype, from economic albatross to billion-dollar value. The five

Dan Rooney in 1987 on his desk at the Three Rivers Stadium that he helped to birth. (Vincent J. Musi)

Rooney brothers at various junctures of their lives served the family's team—ball boys, ticket sellers, you name it—but nobody had Steelers' hypocycloid gold, red, and blue blood coursing through them like the eldest.

Pat Rooney Sr.: "No one can run it better than Dan. What do you have to pay attention for [at Steelers family board meetings]? My brother John and I went outside to smoke. When I was on the board, nobody made any suggestions. There was no reason to tell Dan what to do.

"Dan worked at it harder than the Chief. The Chief had other interests. Where Dan, all of his interests were football."

Tim Rooney Sr.: "Dan is unbelievably more dedicated to football and the National Football League and the Pittsburgh Steelers. . . . That's the only interest that he has. The rest of us occasionally like to golf and other things.

"We'd have meetings, and some of them would be very serious meetings on [the family's horse] racing—and Danny wouldn't want to admit this, but he had as much stock in racing as the rest of us. We'd always come in for a football game [to meet]." Once, Dan excused himself from the meeting because a new goalpost was being erected. *A goalpost?* "Like they weren't going to put it up straight or put it in the right spot. We're having this meeting and making very important decisions, and Danny's out there making sure they're putting up the goalpost right.

"The success of the Steelers over the years wasn't the general manager or the business manager we had. The decisions were made by Dan, or at least with his okay. His decisions were always brilliant. He's been a miracle worker."

Pat Sr.: "Dan's idea was this thing would make money, we would pay players, and we can win championships. Dan was so far ahead of those other guys in the business. The Bears and the Giants were professional football operations. To a degree, Cleveland. The other guys . . . , they owned those teams, and they were a toy for them."

Joe Gordon, publicity director and vice president 1969–1998: "Dan came in and put it on solid business footing and knew what to do. Art gave him carte blanche."

Roy McHugh, sportswriter, columnist, and editor at the Pittsburgh Press: "He was a better administrator" than his revered father.

Tim Sr.: "Friendship entered into too many things for my father. He had a strong weakness for loyalty to people and loyalty to friends. Dan is all business."

McHugh: "Dan Rooney hired three coaches—Noll, Cowher, Tomlin—and all three won Super Bowls. He was as good at hiring coaches as his father was bad."

"He never had the charisma" of the Chief. His sons, Dan and Art Jr., "they were the ones who actually made the Steelers a winner, and the Chief got all the accolades. They handed [Art Sr.] the Lombardi Trophy, and Dan was sitting back in the corner, and nobody ever noticed."

Ed Kiely, publicity director and aide-de-camp for four decades: "I thought his old man was tough. But Dan? The pain and everything he puts up with?" After eighteen months of regular transatlantic flights back and forth, the U.S. ambassador to Ireland finally succumbed to the backache and stoop, and he underwent surgery. Days later, Dan got back on another six-hour flight to Dublin.

Pat Sr.: "He had a kidney stone removed without a cut or [anesthetic]. There ain't anything tougher than that. Toughest human being you'll ever meet in your life. No one is as tough as Dan Rooney."

McHugh: "He was tough. All business."

Dan is the boss who instituted a mandatory retirement age of sixty-five for Steelers employees, and that caused the departures of no less than his sister-in-law Mary Regan, longtime contract negotiator and revered employee Jim "Buff" Boston, and vice president Gordon.

He fired his own son John and nephew Mike.

And, in 1987, he fired his brother Art Jr.

Pat Sr.: "Dan had a vision of what he wanted things to be, and had the [guts] to do it. From a business standpoint, woo, was he tough! Where a lot of guys would hedge, he would have the guts to do it."

Art Jr., who, amid Dan's restructuring—Chuck Noll more involved in business operations, Dennis Thimmons promoted to second in command, and more—was replaced by Dick Haley and sent to the South Hills to oversee the family's local real-estate holdings in 1987: "It was tough on your family. It was like a state of shock. It was something I never thought would happen the way it would happen. Getting exiled with money, still being on the payroll." His father asked why Art Jr. didn't come to Three Rivers Stadium anymore, even though he was still a salaried employee. But the second son refused to return to St. Vincent College for twenty years, until they renamed it Chuck Noll Field. "I couldn't even talk about this stuff before. . . . It was like a narcotic being taken away from you."

Dan was born into the Steelers, but he assumed control gradually, over a half century.

He wasn't the firstborn son of royalty exactly, but he certainly made news: Next to the August 1, 1939, story in the *Pittsburgh Post-Gazette* about Johnny Blood retiring to drop the player half of his player-coach job description was a story about seven-year-old Danny Rooney breaking his wrist playing football. At age nine, he opposed his father's sale to Alexis Thompson, which was basically scuttled four months later when the Chief and co-owner Bert Bell swapped the Philadelphia Eagles to get Pittsburgh back.

At fourteen, while serving as waterboy in the 1946 camp, he watched Jock Sutherland ensure that every jock and sock was counted coming out in the laundry—a thorough accounting and accountability, indeed.

As a teenager, he was selected as the second-best quarterback in the Pittsburgh Catholic League. The first? Some kid named Johnny Unitas.

Dan attended Duquesne, learned accounting, and came out—as the Chief raised his boys—ready for management.

So he went into coaching.

Pat Sr. remembers Dan coaching him and twin brother John at the St. Peter's Church school's sixth- through eighth-grade football teams. Another kid coached by Dan: future General Michael V. Hayden. Dan also coached the neighborhood baseball team and brought son Art II to games.

Pat Sr.: "We'd drive around in the Steelers station wagon. I'm not kidding, this is true: It was taped together, with tape from the team [equipment room]. We'd have a game, and we'd be riding around the North Side trying to pick up players. We were in a league for seventeen-year-olds, and, who knows, we probably picked up twenty-five-year-old players.

"What kind of coach was he? Anything to win. Dan was anything to win.

"He coached for a while . . . until my dad told him he had other things to do."

Working for his father's team began to take on more formal roles for Dan. He tried to reroute coach Walt Kiesling in his path to taking Gary Glick as the Steelers' bonus first-overall pick in 1956, to no avail. He functioned as the vice president for almost a generation.

Still, he didn't wield enough power to pronounce the Steelers station wagon dead.

Tim Sr.:

My brother Danny got married [to Patricia Regan], and we were up at his house with the car. The junk truck . . . hit the back of the car. We were sitting on the stoop. The guy jumped out of his truck, and he looked at the car, which was a wreck, and he thought he'd done a lot of it. We laughed and told him, "You didn't do all that, keep going."

It was after one game, and the Steelers were really bad, and my father was really burned up about the game. We were dropping Kies off at the Carlton House, right off Grant Street, because he had an apartment there. The fastest way home was to cut across the Hill District. . . . We were going to pass Pitt Stadium. And my brother Dan, not saying anything to anybody, he puts it in reverse to start it up the hill. My father goes, "What are you doing? Why are you backing up this hill?" Danny says, "There's something wrong with this transmission. We don't have the power to go up the hill, so we have to go in reverse." This should've been recorded. My father says, "This is horrible. Our team stinks"—and the coach is in the back seat—"and we have a car that won't even go into drive." I think we got a new car that week.

The Chief became less and less involved in football, and he gave Buddy Parker authoritarian control starting in 1957. Parker wanted nothing to do with league business, so

Dan Rooney sitting in his spacious, spartan office in 1987 at Three Rivers Stadium, near the end-of-the-hall inner sanctum occupied by his father, the Chief. (Vincent J. Musi)

between that and his father's absence, such NFL's duties fell on Dan . . . for the next fifty years.

"He had a disdain for the league office, and I wound up getting involved," Rooney later said of Parker. "I would be in the office and I would get a call from the league, the commissioner. Other teams would call. They would all find out after awhile, 'Hey, the guy you can get is Dan Rooney. He'll get this done for you.'"

Gordon, interviewing in 1969 while working for the NHL's Penguins, remembers Three Rivers Stadium blueprints on Dan's desk: "Believe me, he was hands-on. All the time."

McHugh: "They had to get the right coach. They got the drafting straightened out, where Parker traded away the draft picks and Austin had his own ideas. Art Jr., he was glad to see Austin go. He was afraid they were going to hire another coach like Austin, though—a boss. He wasn't afraid to fight with Noll." Dan Rooney hired Noll in 1969, after a dalliance with Joe Paterno, after the Chief ceded the search and more control to his firstborn.

Gordon: Another of Dan's greatest accomplishments? "Giving Noll the time and patience. How many owners would have sat through 1-13, 5-9, 6-8. I bet there weren't more than three of four other owners who would have stuck with Noll."

Ralph Cindrich, former NFL linebacker, lawyer, and player agent: "Everybody loved the Chief, including me. But he wasn't the football guy that Dan and his brother Art [Jr.] were, putting together a championship team. You're looking at an organization that's the most successful in professional sports."

With Dan in charge, Art Jr. running the drafts, and Noll not only providing draft input but teaching and coaching and cajoling the players, the Steelers embarked on that unprecedented 1970s run:

- Four Super Bowls in six years
- A 67-20-1 regular-season record in that span
- A 13-2 postseason record
- A slew of drafts that from 1969 to 1974 produced nine Hall of Famers—excluding the coach, the Chief, and Dan, who also made Canton

Dan not only followed his father's footsteps to the Hall of Fame, he followed them to work.

After the Chief's death in 1988, Dan likewise assumed the position of family and Steelers patriarch. He moved into the North Side home where he was reared. He, like his father before him, walked to work at Three Rivers Stadium.

Gordon: "Dan inherited a lot from his dad. But the greatest characteristic was his mental toughness. When things really got tough, that's when those guys were at their best."

Dan was credited with helping settle not one but two NFL labor impasses. He worked with NFL Players Association Executive Director Gene Upshaw to construct the cap era. He founded the Rooney Rule. And those were his NFL issues beyond Stadium Circle.

After the glory days of the 1970s, there came times for retooling. In 1987, there was the front-office restructuring that bounced his younger brother. In 1988, he pressured Noll into firing some assistants and demoting Tony Dungy, who had been the league's youngest coordinator, to secondary coach. Dungy refused the move and resigned instead. In 2000, faced with a nettlesome decision, he and Art II forced the resignation of a former ball boy and scout, a man so close

Dan Rooney waves to a grateful Three Rivers Stadium crowd after his Steelers win the AFC championship game on January 14, 1996, and earn a spot in Super Bowl XXX . . . which would become the franchise's first loss on that giant stage. (Bill Amatucci)

he was almost related: Tom Donahoe. The rift between him and Bill Cowher had grown untenable.

What followed the last of those spasms? Three more Super Bowls in eleven years—well, six years if you start the clock with Super Bowl XL and Cowher, plus XLIII and XLV with Mike Tomlin.

The same as his father before him, Dan turned over the presidency to his heir apparent, Art II, officially in 2003. He didn't stop providing guidance, and didn't stop being tough, inimitable Dan Rooney.

Kevin Colbert, director of football operations and general manager 2000–present: "We're playing Indianapolis [in the playoffs en route to Super XL], and we get the sack that looked like we're going to close out the game. I jumped up and said, 'It's over!' And Mr. Rooney said [calmly], 'No, it's not.' Before I can get the second 'It's over' out of my mouth, Jerome Bettis fumbled. He was right again. He was the voice of reason. That was a great lesson."

Cindrich, relating how Dan chewed out a Steelers front-office type for ordering him a limo at one Super Bowl—an event where Dan and Pat Rooney normally take one of the NFL buses: "It fits in so well with the city."

Ralph Berlin, trainer 1968–1992: "Dan was more of a businessman. He was not a sportsman. He's honest to a fault. Still is. He's big on loyalty to his people. He's loyal to you and he expects you to be loyal to the organization."

Ernie Accorsi, general manager for Baltimore, Cleveland, and the Giants: "I went through the same thing with a son who succeeded a legend, in Wellington Mara and John [with the Giants]. You're never exactly like your father. But [in the Rooneys' case] those two are alike. Their integrity. Their word is their bond. A handshake is all you need from those guys. Dan's a product of a different generation. If you want to blueprint how to operate an organization . . . to me, if I bought a ball club, in the NFL or any [league], or launch any organization, you take the Steelers and Giants blueprint and you can't go wrong."

Joe Greene, defensive tackle 1969–1981, assistant, scout, foundation of a franchise: "The Chief, Dan, and Chuck, they all brought some great things to the table that have stood, really, since [1969]. That whole persona about the Pittsburgh Steelers, it still lives. It's a tribute to this organization that they found the formula, they keep playing by the formula.

Dan devoted considerable time and money to the American Ireland Fund and instituted the Rooney Prize for Irish Literature, among his many works in the Rooney family ancestral homeland and in Southwestern Pennsylvania. A Republican like his father, he was smitten by Democratic presidential candidate Barack Obama and the idea of becoming ambassador to Ireland. Funny thing, those family ties.

Art Jr.: Democratic majority leader and Speaker of the House "Tip O'Neill once talked to my dad about being the ambassador to Ireland. [The Chief] said, 'I'm old, I'm very happy in Pittsburgh, I got a wife, I got my family, I got my team. On top of all that, it costs a lot to be an ambassador. Plus, I'm a Republican.'

"He never got beyond the questioning point, where Dan was very interested in [pursuing] it."

Pat Sr.: "I think Dan has accomplished everything he's wanted to accomplish in life: Ambassador of Ireland and championships. It was a great ambassadorship, and Dan made it a job. I bet Dan is the greatest ambassador the United States has. They could have sent him to Russia, and he would have been great."

ART ROONEY II
Legal Counsel–Vice President–President

Colleges: Pitt, Duquesne Law • **Birthplace:** Pittsburgh
• **Born:** September 14, 1952

Welcome to the Pittsburgh Steelers' Ball Boy Hall of Fame:

Dan, Art Jr., Tim, Pat, and John Rooney

Art Rooney II. So that's two team presidents from the sidelines already.

General Michael V. Hayden, director of the Central Intelligence Agency

Bill Nunn Jr., actor from *Spiderman* films, *Do the Right Thing,* and more.

Judge Bernard McGinley, Commonwealth of Pennsylvania Court of Judicial Discipline

Tom Donahoe, former Steelers football operations director and Buffalo Bills president

Todd Haley, former Kansas City Chiefs head coach and Steelers offensive coordinator

Art Rooney II continues the family tradition. (Courtesy of the Pittsburgh Steelers)

Patrick Perles, assistant with Kansas City Chiefs, Los Angeles Rams, and several Canadian clubs

David Boreanaz, actor from *Buffy the Vampire Slayer, Angel,* and *Bones* television series

Richie McCabe, six-year NFLer and former assistant with Oakland Raiders and Denver Broncos

Jim "Buff" Boston, longtime Steelers contract negotiator

Who knew such a no-paying, low-hanging job was actually a highfalutin career-placement center?

In this particular case, a ball boy matured into a successful lawyer who nearly became a U.S. senator; a quarterback for the Heinz Field/amphitheater/North Shore project; a captain of the intricate, externally motivated sale of the Steelers franchise; and a 2011 peacemaker sitting on the same management council executive committee as his father, who twice before him helped to rescue the NFL from labor strife.

Ask the gentlemen who spent nearly the entire lifetime of the current president as a Steelers employee, and their memories of Art Rooney II are matter-of-fact and direct . . . much like the current president.

Dick Hoak, running back 1961–1970 and running backs coach 1972–2006: "He was the ball boy. They all were: him, Tom Donahue, the McGinleys . . ."

Art Rooney II, about his relationship with Bill Nunn Jr.: "That's where we first met. We were roommates for awhile up in St. Vincents in the summers."

Bill Nunn Sr., Pittsburgh Courier sports editor turned Steelers scout: "I kind of raised him."

Nunn's son became fast friends with his fellow ball boy Art II, born a year earlier. They were so close, they were in each other's wedding. When the actor joined the Steelers party for Super Bowl XL, he came more for his lifelong pal than his own father. Nunn Sr.—a part-time scout still despite trying to retire in 1987, what with Dan and Art II telling him since then to continually report to work—said not long after the Steelers won their fifth Lombardi Trophy that he informed his firstborn son in Detroit: "You act like you're affiliated more with the club than me. You were a ball boy. And you weren't a very good one."

It goes to show that more burbles under the guarded, stoic surface of Art Rooney II. Much more.

After all, he's best buds with Radio Raheem and Robbie Robertson, Jonah Jameson's right-hand man at the same *Daily Bugle* that employs Spiderman's alter ego, Peter Parker, as a photographer.

That's make-believe. This is reality: Art II appropriately is the latest in a continuing line of Rooneys participating in the family affair that is the Steelers.

Many ex–ball boys were the sons of owners, including a busload of McGinleys, who passed their one-fifth ownership slice from Barney to Jack to his children. Many more ball boys came from the kids of coaches and relatives, from North Catholic High friends. All ascended ladders. Yet no other ball boy reached a rung like Dan and Art II: steward of one of the world's iconic sports franchises.

One followed the other up to that rarified air—Art Rooney Sr., next Dan Rooney, then Art Rooney II.

Ernie Accorsi, general manager with Baltimore, Cleveland, and the New York Giants: "The apple doesn't fall far from the tree in either case."

Kevin Colbert, director of football operations 2000–2010 who in 2011 was given the title of general manager for the first true time in team history: "He accepts that he follows two Hall of Famers, but he's going to do it his own way. It's a tough act to follow. But it doesn't seem to hinder him at all. He goes about it [without affectation]. He's himself. Art II is a different personality from his father. Art is not as outgoing as his father, but he has the same type of values of family. And they all share that common truth that they're going to do the right things.

"The things you hear about [Art Rooney Sr.], they were passed down to his son and passed on to his grandson. They all share the same core values—with different personalities."

Pat Rooney Sr., one of his four uncles and, for years, on the Rooney empire's board: "Young Art is going to be a different type of operator than Dan. Art will be a manager who

delegates, and Dan would never delegate. We used to call Dan and tease him, 'Where were you, out checking the goalposts?' But that was his style of management."

Tim Rooney Sr.: "My father had a tremendously high regard for my nephew. All of us always did, too. He's a very capable person."

Colbert, with whom Art II meets after weekday practices—Mike Tomlin, too—and watches game tapes along with Nunn Sr. and other personnel department members: "Art is a lawyer by trade. He moves deliberately in the way he approaches things."

Art II graduated from Pitt in 1978 and his father offered him career advice: Go into law. So he graduated Duquesne Law, requiring four years because he attended night school. By day, he worked with the Steelers who, you know, were rather busy while tending a path to back-to-back Super Bowl victories from mid-1978 to early 1980.

Art Rooney II: "I didn't always know that [his future lay in the Steelers' front office]. It was always something I thought about. But it was nothing that was, say, a foregone conclusion. Both my dad and my grandfather encouraged me to have my own career.

"I always had somewhat of an interest in law and government. My dad encouraged me to go [into law]. Talked about the fact he was spending a lot of time with lawyers in our business, it might become relevant someday. It was a good decision. I enjoyed practicing law for 20-some years on my own."

Art II set up a law practice, staked a business in government relations among other things, and opened an office in Harrisburg, Pennsylvania. His firm, Klett Rooney Lieber and Schorling, fared so successfully that Governor Robert Casey took notice. When Senator John Heinz was killed in a plane-helicopter collision in 1991, Casey inquired if the young Rooney, then 38, wanted to be appointed to Heinz's seat. Art II talked it over with Casey's political advisors, which at the time included rising stars James Carville and Paul Begala. He begged off, because of the time and commitment away from

The Steelers' fifth Lombardi Trophy   the one ring for the thumb—is escorted by Jerome Bettis through the streets of Pittsburgh in a victory parade. (Courtesy of the Pittsburgh Steelers)

Art Rooney II and the house he helped to build, Heinz Field. (Courtesy of the Pittsburgh Steelers)

his family, his practice, his family's team: "The more I thought about it, it would have been a tough time for me to disappear."

So he continued to serve as legal counsel to the Steelers, having involved himself in ending the fifty-two-day stalemate a year earlier, in 1990, over tight end Eric Green's rookie contract. He assumed vice-presidential duties, took over Heinz Field stewardship—much like his father did with Three Rivers Stadium, and by 2000 was sitting down for a significant meeting with Donahoe—a fellow former ball boy. The result of their conversation: Amid a rift between Donahoe and a Bill Cowher with $6 million left on his contract, Donahoe officially resigned in an announcement delivered at a news conference he didn't attend.

Art Rooney II: "It was a tough decision. There's no denying that. Obviously, Tom had been somebody who had been around and connected to the organization in a number of different ways, including going back to when he was a ball boy. It was, no question, one of the more difficult decisions that I had to make, that's for sure."

Soon enough, the presidency was handed down in the same way as Art Rooney Sr. did without fanfare twenty-eight years earlier, in 1975: In the media guide, the elder Rooney's title was changed to chairman, and the son's to president. It was the third generation's turn to run the business of football. Art II laughed two years later, in 2005, when his father was quoted as saying the family torch wasn't passed to his son as much as "he grabbed it from my arm." Art II said to the *Pittsburgh Post-Gazette:* "I told him I was a chip off the old block."

Colbert: "They let you do your job in the manner it should be done, but under the rules they've established."

Hoak: "The Rooneys, they're good people. George Perles made a statement one day: You know what? In this league there are about six teams that can win. They're the teams where the front office isn't screwed up, and we're one of those teams. They let the coaches coach. They let the scouts scout."

Russ Grimm, offensive line coach and assistant head coach 2001–2006 and a head-coaching candidate before leaving for the Arizona Cardinals: "They treated everybody well in the organization. . . . Haven't talked to them since we played them in the Super Bowl [February 2009]. No, I have great respect for the Rooney family."

John Stallworth, receiver 1974–1987, on Art II: "You saw his development. We've talked a number of times over the years. I saw how Dan was bringing him along, and at the appropriate time Dan turned the reins over to him. He was more than ready for it. I think it's going to be good for him as time goes on that he grows in stature with the ownership group. And he's a lot like Dan: He's not going to be standing up a lot and talking about what he's doing. He's not going to be prancing the sidelines and being a visible part of the organization. He's going to be behind the scenes, gently and maybe at times forcefully, pushing the organization in the direction he thinks he needs it to go. That's part of the legacy of the Pittsburgh Steelers."

Such a family environment and foundation made the Steelers' sale all the more compelling and complex.

The NFL, overseen by the commissioner whom Dan Rooney helped to attain that office, Roger Goodell, sought changes in the Steelers' ownership structure. Then it sought wholesale divestiture of the ownership shares in the racing and casino businesses, meaning Tim Rooney Sr. (Empire City in New York) and Pat Rooney Sr. (West Palm Kennel Club in Florida). Each of the five brothers owned a 16 percent share of the Steelers, with the family of the late Jack McGinley holding the other 20 percent.

As one insider requesting anonymity put it, the NFL "kept moving the goalposts."

This, after all, was a family that lived for decades on the financial success of the racing business—from the Chief's wondrous wagering to their four-state track ownership—far more so than the Steelers.

Pat Sr.: "The racetracks were doing well. In the '60s, they paid the bills. In the '70s, they were responsible for our whole lifestyle. No money went out of the Steelers until '89 or '90. There was never a dividend paid until then."

Tim Sr.: "Racing was very good to all my brothers, even the ones that stayed with the football team completely. Because all of us had some stock in our racetracks. Even though it wasn't a lot of money, we did pay a dividend at the end of the year. But it would be $15,000, $20,000 on some occasion[s]. Living on the North Side, that was a pretty nice check to get at Christmas."

Art II: "First of all, it was a long process. It wasn't months; it was years, really. Anytime you're dealing with family, it's difficult; there are added emotions and complexity to the situation. It actually became more complicated by the fact the economy basically collapsed in the middle of us trying to get the deal done. That added some time and uncertainty to the process. It was a long and interesting road."

Dan Rooney formally was announced as U.S. ambassador to Ireland in July 2009, and less than three months later the sale was finalized. By then, the only Rooney resident left on the North Side was the club itself—or roughly half of it, anyway. In the end, Dan and Art II had to maneuver interest into a 30 percent share to meet the NFL's standard for controlling ownership. Two of Dan's other brothers, Art Jr. and John (who sold his racing interests), each retained an 8 percent share. The family of the late Jack McGinley likewise held onto shares. Pat Sr. and Tim Sr. sold their stakes and stayed in the racing business. New investors, new nonfamily owners were welcomed, among them Steelers Hall of Famer John Stallworth and movie mogul Thomas Tull, whose Legendary Pictures produced the *Dark Knight* episodes of the *Batman* series.

Yes, again, a comic-book connection.

But to the Rooneys this constituted serious and delicate stuff.

Tim Sr.: "I just find . . . one of the only things that I take offense to in the whole [sale] is being forced out of the team because of my involvement in Yonkers and Empire City because we have slot machines here. We're just a division of the lottery. After we agreed to sell—and I understood we had to sell because of being involved in this part of it—what happened was, the National Football League made deals with lotteries all over the country that they could use their image on lottery tickets. Which I thought was strange. I found that a little bizarre."

Amid this entire sale process, the Steelers advanced to Super Bowl XLIII and won in dramatic fashion: last-minute drive, Ben Roethlisberger pass into the end zone, Santonio Holmes toes-down touchdown catch. The Rooney brothers paused for a photograph on the floor of Raymond James Stadium afterward, and in the snapshot there were no smiles all around.

Tim Sr.:

It probably wasn't that we didn't want our picture taken. The funny thing is, our wives a lot of times say, in football,

we're not fans. My father surely wasn't. That was one of the things he put into us, and if he didn't put it into us, he would've ripped our heads off. You weren't allowed to show emotion. You could call a coach or a player a name for some mistake he made. Or an official. But there never was any outlandish celebration of wins or anything. You were extremely happy about it, I assure you. But it wasn't anything where you were jumping up and down and throwing things.

That was Tampa, on the sideline after the game. [Another] of the things that didn't make us [look] too happy is, we knew we were selling the team. We knew we had to get out. In order to make the deal go, [but] my other brothers kept some stock in the Steelers. The only ones who got completely out [were Tim Sr. and Pat Sr.]. That was just listening to orders.

The one good thing about that whole [sale] thing, when you're talking about the Rooneys and all the kids in this, the only way the Rooneys could've kept this was to keep it in one team. It really was wonderful that Dan could put together a situation where he and his family were able to run it and still get control of the team and have the chance of buying the team for themselves.

Pat Sr.: "As far as I'm concerned, the greatest thing about the Pittsburgh Steelers, and I don't know if anybody agrees or not, is that luckily the five of us basically transferred the ownership of it, and we did it without any embarrassment. If you think about other teams and other transfers . . . , it was a very, very unique thing.

"We were the [64 percent] owners, Timmy, Art [Jr.], John, and myself. It wasn't all easy. For the legacy, it was transferred. It was an absolutely unbelievable thing that we got done. Thank God it was the racetrackers, that we all had other interests, and we're involved in other things." It could have come apart at the seams in a mixture of ego and greed. "Which would have happened with most outfits. The important thing for me was Art Rooney [Sr.'s legacy], not the Pittsburgh Steelers. . . . It was important to me for us to have it [in the family]. It wasn't the same for me after he died as it was before. But it had to be done."

Stallworth, minority owner: "The first time I saw Joe Greene after the deal was done . . . , he referred to me as 'Boss.' It does feel a little bit [strange]. It was never something I thought about until the opportunity presented itself. I feel humbled in a way and feel honored in a way. You look over what the Rooneys have done over the years, the coaching, the performance, the quality of people in the organization. . . . I'm more than proud to continue to be part of what they've grown over the years."

Art II: "I'm pleased [how it turned out]. We were fortunate to find a great group of new partners who were really interested in joining the team with the idea that they liked the way things were and they wanted to invest with us and be partners. It wasn't like they wanted to come in and turn things around, do things differently. They were very supportive of what we were doing."

Generation Lost (1948–1968)

THE ANTIQUATED SINGLE-WING FORMATION that wouldn't go away. The slightly more modern T formation that wouldn't work, at least not with ragamuffin, sawed-off, or converted-safety quarterbacks.

The quarterbacks who got away: Johnny Unitas, Len Dawson, Jack Kemp, and Earl Morrall. The backfield that never was, but could've been, drafted: Lenny Moore and Jim Brown.

Coach Buddy Parker dealing away draft picks by the truckload, one of them turning into Dick Butkus.

Coach Buddy Parker quitting after almost every loss.

Coaches outnumbering winning seasons, six to five.

Quarterback Bobby Layne drinking. Quarterback Ed Brown giving up drinking.

Their one playoff being lost by such sobriety.

A wide receiver shot by a cannon—the cheerleaders did it.

There, in a nutshell, are the football follies that comprised the second generation of Steelers failure.

They lurched from the wretched to the mediocre, from the ridiculous to the entertaining, from Forbes Field to Pitt Stadium to both.

Chuck Cherundolo, who retired as a center in 1948 and coached and scouted through 1961: "The hardest part of being with the Steelers in those days? Getting in trouble and getting in a fight." For the players? "No, I'm talking about coaches. There was always at least one [who was difficult to deal with]."

Fans got testy, too.

Once during a St. Louis–Steelers game in the Parker years, the Rooneys tried to curry favor with the patrons by throwing miniature footballs into the stands as a freebie, a giveaway, a community nicety.

Pat Rooney Sr.: "And they threw the damn balls back."

This generation of losing all began with tragedy, the passing of a Pittsburgh icon in Jock Sutherland. Art Rooney turned the team over to Sutherland's protégé, Johnny Michelosen. The owner figured that all those season-ticket holders who wanted to watch Sutherland football would appreciate the same single wing and defense under his top lieutenant. Rooney pledged, He'll make good.

He didn't.

Next came Joe Bach for a second time, after his St. Bonaventure program was shuttered—and by Rooney's brother, Father Silas, the Bonnies' athletic director.

Then came Walt Kiesling for a third time.

The carousel was tossing off head coaches.

Steelers defensive back Richie McCabe shows his disgust at an Eagles touchdown pass in a 1955 loss in Philadelphia. (Temple Urban Archives)

Tim Rooney Sr.: "I remember going out to Forbes Field; we were playing the Redskins. I invited a lot of my friends; I could get them through the press gate without buying tickets. I'd just nod my head. I got 30 or 40 friends through. George Marshall, the owner of the Redskins, saw this was going on. He said [to the Steelers owner], 'No wonder you're not doing very well at the gate, there's some kid letting kids in for nothing.'

"The team wasn't real good, but the moments were fun for me."

In 1951, their leading receiver, Val Jansante, quit at midseason because of fans booing him.

In 1952, the Steelers played in front of their largest crowd to that point, 74,000 at Los Angeles' Memorial Coliseum. Rooney's take of the gate: $42,166.50, the franchise's biggest payday in his first 20 NFL seasons. Still, it showed they were a better road show than home theater.

Joe Walton, former Pitt All-American, NFL player, and coach: "At Pitt we used to sell out." The Steelers when they split time between Forbes Field and Pitt Stadium? "There was nobody there."

The best part of the 1950s for the Steelers was the threat of relocation. Art Rooney didn't make the threat; other cities tried to lure an NFL franchise. A November 14, 1956, Associated Press story circulated around the country reported that, despite "speculation" the franchise might relocate elsewhere, Rooney was staying put. Louisville, Denver, Minneapolis, and Buffalo made offers. Rooney was quoted as saying, "Actually, I have never wanted to leave this city. It's a good sports town and has been good to me." His friend the Pittsburgh mayor, and later Pennsylvania governor, David L. Lawrence entered the fray: "The answer is to form an authority to construct a huge stadium to serve all outdoor sporting events."

The idea for Three Rivers Stadium germinated a decade and a half before it opened.

Meanwhile, Joe Bach's contributions were minimally intrusive, at least. Heck, he fared slightly better the second time around (11-13 in 1952–1953) than the first (10-14 in 1935–1936).

It was on Walt Kiesling's watch that talent evaluation was, shall we say, a tad lacking. He kept Jim Finks, a converted safety, and tiny Ted Marchibroda at quarterback over a ninth-round pick and hometowner by the name of Johnny Unitas in 1955. The next year, awarded the bonus pick atop the first round, the Steelers nabbed cornerback Gary Glick and halfback Art Davis. Neither amounted to much—Davis, due to a creaky knee, lasted all of five carries for six yards in that one NFL season—compared to the Penn State halfback on whom the Steelers passed: Lenny Moore.

In 1957, with Buddy Parker arriving in August at Kiesling's behest, the Steelers drafted Len Dawson and passed on a Syracuse halfback of some repute: Jim Brown.

Art Rooney Jr., who soon after moved into scouting: "[They] didn't think much of him. He never did much against Pitt."

Hey, who needs arguably the greatest running back in NFL history when you have Billy Wells and Fran Rogel?

All together now: "Hey, diddle diddle, Rogel up the middle." That was the singsong chant before the first Steelers offensive play most every game under Kiesling, who was irritatingly predictable. If nothing else, his successor was far more creative.

Parker came from Detroit with a successful resume and a hothead history, and he flashed both with the Steelers. In fact, he left the Lions in a messy August and instantly steered the Steelers to a 6-6 record in 1957. Ah, mediocrity.

The best use Parker found for Dawson? He molded him into a kicker, albeit a failed brief experiment.

So Parker went back to his Detroit roots and . . . went back to his Detroit lineup. He traded for Bobby Layne, an aging

A smothered Ted Marchibroda (1953, 1955–1956) fumbles the ball—clearly marked by the *Philadelphia Bulletin*—and the only players around it are Eagles, of course. That's Fran Rogel on the ground in the foreground. No wonder that from 1945 to 1956 the Steelers went 5-16 against the Eagles. (Temple Urban Archives)

Bobby Layne, sans face mask, calls signals in an unspecified game against the New York Giants, likely 1961 or 1962, with Buzz Nutter at center. Notice that the Pitt Stadium stands aren't exactly filled, nor are the fans in attendance entirely rapt. (Courtesy of the Pittsburgh Steelers)

quarterback whom the Bears drafted—ahem—with a pick traded through the Lions and Steelers in 1948. He traded for running back Tom Tracy. He traded. And traded. And traded.

Over an eight-year period, he traded 49 draft picks, minimum.

The first-round pick that the Chicago Bears expended on Hall of Famer Dick Butkus? It was a multiple-picks deal that a year earlier netted Parker's Steelers a tight end from McKeesport, Pennsylvania, named Jim Kelly. Ten receptions and one season later, Parker got rid of him, too, before Butkus suited up for the Bears.

Parker was a wheeler-dealer, all right. Part of the deal to lure him to Pittsburgh included a percentage of Art Rooney's track winnings.

Art Jr.: "Tim or I would drive out to his house, and there'd be a sack."

The Steelers had become a sad-sack franchise. "The NFL's belly laugh," NFL Films once called the franchise.

Tim Sr., a ticket seller and team representative for his dad's club: "You'd go and take the highlights from the year before"—wait, there were actual highlights?—"and show them to these different groups. Then you'd have a question-and-answer program when it was over. . . . It was very, very interesting, the questions you got asked. The thing that was always remarkable was, how smart the people are. The only time I saw them make mistakes was when they thought a defensive back was really horrible. They were right, but what they didn't understand was the guy on the bench was worse than he was."

One of those defensive backs was cornerback Bill Daniels, who signed with the Steelers in 1961. His reason for leaving behind Mississippi and coaching high school football: irate parents. An angry father punched him in the nose over his son's playing time. So the Steelers were his asylum?

One, two, three, four . . . five Steelers defenders are in the vicinity but unable to stop Philadelphia's Billy Barnes from scoring a touchdown in 1960. It is the opening score of what becomes a 34-7 rout at Franklin Field. (Temple Urban Archives)

Pose of the 1964 Steelers linebackers, left to right: Max Messner, three-time Pro Bowl selection Myron Pottios, Rod Breedlove, Bob Schmitz, Bill Saul, Bob Soleau, and Robert Harrison. (Carnegie Library Archives)

Not with Parker roaming up and down the aisles of a team charter after a loss, it wasn't. Daniels smartly hid underneath a blanket once until Parker's miles-high rant evaporated and he exonerated the player after film study. Parker, when angry, was infamous for firing players and making heat-of-the-moment trades. Legend has it, other teams started calling him after losses to propose deals.

Believe it or not, amid this generation of losses came the winningest season in the franchise's history to this juncture. In 1962, with cheerleaders on their sidelines, with the American Iron and Steel Institute's hypocycloid Steelmark logo adopted and gracing only the right side of the helmet (not because of being cheap but rather because equipment manager Jackie Hart tried and liked it), Parker's team finished 9-5.

The most memorable part of that season, however, was weapon fire in the face of receiver Buddy Dial. He later told a reporter: "They'd fire off this cannon [on the sidelines] every time we scored, and it'd jump when they fired it. And we scored so often the thing was on the field by the fourth quarter. So they throw me a 50-yard pass, and I catch it, step into the end zone, score . . . and they fired off this cannon right in my face. And I mean, it scared me half to death! They show the film sometimes on the Carson show, in those funny highlights they run, you know? The smoke clears, and I'm sitting on my duff on the 8-yard line." Yeah, Parker eventually did deal Dial and, who knows, probably the cannon, too. And NBC swapped Jay Leno for a retiring Johnny Carson.

That 1962 season ended in something like the Steelers' second-ever postseason game. It wasn't a true playoff game because 14-1 Green Bay won the NFL championship a week earlier with a victory over the 12-3 New York Giants. The Steelers were granted a berth in the Playoff Bowl in Miami against Parker's old Detroit, the third annual consolation game

between the NFL's second-place finishers. Just the same, the Steelers took this rare opportunity seriously, what with it being their first after-the-regular-season date since Jock Sutherland and the 1947 NFL playoffs.

So serious was quarterback Ed Brown, wrote Myron Cope in *True Magazine,* that in the week leading to the game he stopped drinking—unlike the eventual Hall of Famer over whom he would start in that Playoff Bowl, Bobby Layne. So much for catching a genie outside the bottle. Brown went 5 for 12 and to the bench in the fourth quarter.

Andy Russell, outside linebacker 1963, 1966–1976: "1963, we almost won the championship. We had beaten the New York Giants in Pitt Stadium, I think, 31-nothing [the second week]. Really killed 'em. We go to the final game of the year, the New York Giants again. If we win that game, we're in the NFL championship game against the Chicago Bears [whom they tied three weeks earlier]. We were that close to a ring." The Giants got revenge, 33-17, and knocked the Steelers for a loop from which they didn't recover for two coaches and almost 10 years.

That 1963 season was the same year the club pulled up stakes at Forbes Field and moved to Pitt Stadium full-time. They couldn't practice on campus, so they set up shop at South Park. Proud, the owner remarked how his players relished having a practice home of their own.

Jack Butler, defensive back 1951–1959 turned assistant and scout: "It was terrible. The meeting room was just a room. It was an old house; I don't know what it was."

Dick Hoak, running back 1961–1970: "The hospital? It was awful. The showers were downstairs. There were six of them, and three didn't work."

Ralph Berlin, trainer 1968–1992: "People don't [understand]. There were three commodes, and two of them didn't have seats. We had nails; that's where you hung your stuff, on nails. I was shocked. I could not believe it when I came out of training camp that first year."

Hoak: "The field . . . it was always muddy. When it wasn't muddy, it had a track around it, and you always got dust in your nose.

"We would practice in the morning most times, 10 or 11 o'clock. Then, when you were done with practice, you had to go get something to eat. There were only two places to eat: bars. And sometimes guys would have a few beers at lunch. One time . . . we looked in the [defensive film study], the coaches and players were asleep, the film was done—going 'flip, flip, flip' [around the reels of the projector]."

Their indoor facility? The horse-training barn. You had to watch your step between irony and metaphor.

Berlin: "I thought I died and went to heaven when we moved to Three Rivers. And that thing on the South Side, that's the Taj Mahal."

How ugly was the end of this generation? Dan Rooney, trying to effect change, put triangles on the uniform shoulders—for the Golden Triangle. After washing the new unis in the preseason, the triangles faded. Dan admitted that the players felt they resembled Batman. They reverted to the style they wear today.

How cheap were the Rooneys? Not hardly, by comparison to their payroll. The *Pittsburgh Press'* Pat Livingston, once a Steelers scout, snagged a confidential document distributed to the players showing a $21,721 mean Steelers salary that was higher than that of Washington and Philadelphia and only slightly behind 1967 division winner Los Angeles.

How bad were they by 1968? The Nixon Administration—Mike, not Richard—and the gent recommended by Vince Lombardi himself, Bill Austin, were both flaming failures. Four days before Halloween 1968, the Eagles and Steelers waged an unofficial O.J. Bowl for the first-overall selection, which would become USC's Simpson. The two 0-6 teams, playing what was described as one of the worst games in NFL history, combined for 240 penalty yards (more than their combined rushing yards) and couldn't decide it until a field goal in the final seconds. It wound up 6-3, Pittsburgh. *Philadelphia Daily News* writer Bill Conlin likened it to a "Soviet beauty contest. Nobody won." Neither ended up with Simpson, either.

Although it eventually worked out for the Steelers, with one Mean first-round pick in that 1969 draft.

4

The Coaches

SIXTEEN MEN have coached the Pirates and Steelers, but it's a heavily tilted number. Thirteen of those fellows worked the franchise's first 36 seasons. Do the math: On the average, nobody made it to the end of their third season.

Those coaches included a co-owner, a college coach attempting to work two jobs at once, a Joe Bach twice, and a Walt Kiesling three times. Losers all.

What went so wrong for so long suddenly went so right. The Steelers have needed only three coaches over the past 40-plus years, and counting.

FORREST MCCREERY "JAP" DOUDS

College: Washington and Jefferson • **Years as Pirates coach:** 1933 • **Record:** 3-6-2

This tells you all you need to know about the Steelers' early years: Of the first 13 head coaches in club history, Jap Douds' .364 winning percentage ranked slightly above the middle of the pack—fifth overall, to be precise.

Douds was all of 28, barely four years younger than the owner of the fledgling franchise. He was, according to newspaper reports of the day, the only lineman-coach in the NFL, paid $5,000 to coach and $150 per game to play. Most of all, he was entrenched in Western Pennsylvania: from Rochester, Beaver County, and a former captain at Washington and Jefferson College, the small, liberal-arts school in neighboring Washington County with a Rose Bowl appearance and a considerable early 20th-century football pedigree. He was a decorated collegian, famed sportswriter Grantland Rice having named him to the 1927 and 1928 All-American teams in *Collier's Weekly*.

Still, he was one and done as a Steelers coach.

Forrest Douds' contribution: He played, and aligned with, the first African American player for Art Rooney's club, Ray Kemp, who was among the first African Americans to play in the NFL. His time with the club wasn't much shorter than Douds' stay: Kemp, a two-way tackle who interrupted law-school plans to play for Rooney's semipro teams the year before, was released after four games. This from the franchise that later gave the NFL its first African American starting quarterback in a season opener and the Rooney Rule, which requires teams to interview minorities in head-coaching searches, ultimately fostering more equality in hiring practices.

His team scored a field goal or less in more than half of its games, six. So that safety to start its inaugural-season scoring on a Wednesday night, September 20 against the New York Giants? It was an omen. For the season to come. For the first 40 seasons, mostly.

Oddly, Douds went back to playing tackle only—no more coaching—in 1934 and 1935, toiling for two different coaches who succeeded him.

ALBERT "LUBY" DIMEOLO

College: Pitt • **Year as Pirates coach:** 1934 • **Record:** 2-10

Art Rooney floated the name of DiMeolo—incorrectly listed for years as DiMelio in the Steelers' records—as potentially his inaugural coach as early as April 1933, some three months before being awarded the franchise. DiMeolo was officially named coach one year later, in April 1934.

This Coraopolis resident, born in Youngstown, Ohio, was a guard of distinction with Pitt and a captain of the 1929 Rose Bowl team. He was expected to install the Pop Warner system from Pitt, switching from the double wing under Douds to a single wing, and newspapers wrote breathlessly of his heralded passing attack. DiMeolo had served successful assistantships at New York University, where the celebrated college football of the day was a step above the National Professional Football League.

He was all of 30 years old.

By mid-December, with DiMeolo's Pirates getting shut out six times and never scoring as many as those 13 points after the opener (so much for that passing attack), Rooney had a list of three new coaching candidates: Joe Bach, future Hall of Famer Red Grange, and Pirates halfback Johnny "Blood" McNally.

Relieved of coaching duties, DiMeolo went back to Pitt in 1935 to get a master's degree while also returning to an assistant's post at Westminster College. In January 1942, he enlisted in the U.S. Navy reserves—and he was recommended by Lieutenant Commander Gene Tunney, the former boxer who also that same day recommended for reserve duty one Steve Belichick, a Detroit Lions player . . . and future father of Patriots head coach Bill.

Later, in the late 1950s and early 1960s, DiMeolo became president of Steelers Alumni Club, along with fellow officers Ted Marchibroda and the guy who replaced him, Joe Bach.

We're not quite sure why Johnny "Blood" McNally, who wore No. 15, is wearing a "27" shirt in this photograph. He played in 1934 and, while coaching, 1937–1939. (Courtesy of the Pittsburgh Steelers)

JOHNNY "BLOOD" MCNALLY

Colleges: Wisconsin–River Falls, Notre Dame, Dartmouth, St. John's (Minnesota) • **Years as Pirates coach:** 1937–1939 • **Record:** 6-19

After a previous stint as a Pirates player in 1934, the drawing card whom modern-day Steelers media guides label "John Blood" (one appellation by which he wasn't known), Johnny "Blood" McNally was hired by Art Rooney to replace Joe Bach when Bach left for Niagara University.

The Chief put it eloquently years later: "On most teams, the coach worries about where the players are at night. Our players worried about the coach."

Blood was a well-traveled 31 at the time, having played for five professional franchises already. The *Pittsburgh Press* in 1937 described him best: "Blood is a famed wanderer. . . . Suspended, with another Notre Dame student, for too-hilarious

observance of a certain March day dear to the Irish, McNally and the youth joined up with a semipro baseball team." That's when they grabbed pseudonyms, to protect their collegiate eligibility, from a theater marquee sign: Rudolph Valentino's 1922 *Blood and Sand.*

Luckily for Rooney, a petition to launch a franchise in Minnesota with Blood as coach never got off the ground, so the character Johnny Blood was expected to continue Bach's Notre Dame system of football. Blood had spent the previous two seasons as an assistant under another Damer disciple, Green Bay's Curly Lambeau. Given Blood's free-spirited nature, it was an interesting hire, nevertheless.

Legend has it that, in the 1937 season opener, the new player-coach scored the clinching touchdown over Philadelphia on a 92-yard kickoff return. He promptly returned to the bench and remarked, "Boys, that's how it should be done." In a 1974 interview, he told Philadelphia sports columnist Ray Didinger of the touchdown return: "That was an accident. If you saw our team, you would've known that."

In 1938, when Rooney paid Whizzer White a whopping $15,800, Blood got $3,500 to play halfback and coach. He was fired three losses into the 1939 season and nine in succession. Although on October 3, 1939 newspapers reported that Blood resigned moments after a 32-0 loss to the Chicago Bears, he talked in later years how his undoing was his own attitude—such as the time he went AWOL. Blood himself swore he attended a Green Bay–Chicago Cardinals game and unwittingly missed one of his own Pirates games. When the Pirates losing score was announced over the public address system, former Cardinals great Ernie Nevers "just looked at me and laughed . . . , 'Blood, you haven't changed.'" The *Pittsburgh Press* recounted that he indeed missed a November 20, 1938, game in Charleston, West Virginia, where his Pirates lost to Philadelphia, 14-7, without him. No other details were available.

Roy McHugh, Pittsburgh Press *sportswriter, columnist, and editor:* "One of the most irresponsible guys."

Blood, an intelligent fellow who graduated from college at 14, bounced around four colleges and later returned to St. John's in Collegeville, Minnesota, for a degree. He wound up writing a book on Malthusian economics and coaching the St. John's football team—he was replaced in 1953 by John Gagliardi, who became the winningest college football coach in history over the next half century and more.

Blood once ran for sheriff in Minnesota's St. Croix County, where his platform pledged honest wrestling. He was defeated.

Through the 1960s, Rooney kept three photographs of ex-Steelers on his office wall: White, Bill Dudley, and Blood.

BERT BELL

College: Penn • **Year as Steelers coach:** 1941, or 20 percent of it • **Record:** 0-2

What a 1941 Bert Bell had. He sold half of his Philadelphia Eagles to Art Rooney and exchanged the team with Alexis Thompson, who purchased the Pittsburgh club barely four months earlier. They renamed the club from Pirates to Steelers, after a name-the-team contest. And they installed the 47-year-old co-owner as coach when camp opened in Hershey, Pennsylvania.

It lasted two games.

Two losses.

One each by three points, to Cleveland in Akron and his old—and Thompson's new—Philadelphia club.

He announced in a resignation statement, "My deepest regret is that I did not produce a winner for the many well-wishers of the press, radio and loyal fans of Pittsburgh. My partner, Arthur J. Rooney, and my assistant, Walter Kiesling, gave me every cooperation that was humanly possible. I wish to further state that our losses to Cleveland and Philadelphia were no fault of anyone except myself."

Bell remained co-owner through 1946. Then his friend Rooney helped to push him into the NFL commissioner's chair—that's where he created the draft, saved the league from bankruptcy, negotiated national television contracts, founded sudden-death overtime and launched a pension plan with the new players' association.

Oh, and Bell's topsy-turvy 1941 season? It ended with the Japanese attacking Pearl Harbor, and the World War II years threw the Pittsburgh franchise into a flat spin.

He is the second-losingest Steelers coach all-time, behind the man who replaced him.

Chuck Cherundolo, Steelers center in 1941: "He wasn't afraid to tell you he didn't have any money."

Carl "Atom" Hughes, Pittsburgh Press Steelers beat writer in 1944 and 1945, was sharing a car with Art Rooney on a train to Cleveland for the Washington Redskins–Cleveland Rams championship game: "He asked, 'Atom, what do you think of Bert Bell as commissioner?' Bert was his partner, and I liked him very much. I said, 'Bert would be terrific, but you already have a commissioner, Elmer Layden.' He was trying to give me a story: The next day, Bell was named commissioner."

ALDO THEODORE "BUFF" DONELLI

College: Duquesne • **Year as Steelers coach:** 1941, or 50 percent of it • **Record:** 0-5

He's an answer to a trivia question: Name the only person to coach both a major college football team and a professional football franchise at the same time.

Buff Donelli worked the Bluff and the newly named Steelers at once.

For six weeks, anyway.

Art Rooney and partner Bert Bell, the coach for the first two months and two games of the season, devised a plan to name the popular coach from Duquesne University as their Pittsburgh boss at the same time. They offered a three-year, $30,000 deal. They gave carte blanche to the rising 34-year-old star.

The hiring of Donelli, wrote the *Pittsburgh Post-Gazette*, "is certain to revive interest in the Steelers at a time when many of their followers were about ready to toss in the sponge." He was 16-1-1 with Duquesne, which, coincidentally, was set the week of his Steelers debut to play Niagara and ex-Steelers coach Joe Bach.

Double-duty Donelli scrapped what the newspaper called Bell's "much-publicized flanker formation, which aroused considerable adverse comment." The Steelers brought aboard his brother Alan as a player along with Armand Niccolai and another player at Donelli's request, all without cutting a single

player. They moved practices from St. Vincent College, more than thirty miles east of Pittsburgh, and brought them to the city to accommodate him. They reached, according to the *Pittsburgh Post-Gazette*, an "understanding among all parties concerned that in the overpress of work, Duquesne, naturally, would come first in Buff's scheme of things."

Duquesne didn't lose and the Steelers didn't win during his job shares.

Duquesne was not only the school of Rooney and many of his family members, it was a spot where NFL Commissioner Elmer Layden earned some coaching chops. With Donelli's Duquesne taking a Tuesday morning train to San Francisco to play St. Mary's of California, Layden delivered an ultimatum to the double-duty coach: Stay with the Steelers, or be banned from the National Professional League, as it was called then.

Rooney announced at a luncheon that Donelli was being replaced. They had no idea Donelli had hopped a night-before plane—a "secret flight," the *Post-Gazette* labeled it—until his freshman coach and part-time Steelers scout, Lou Skender,

College football holds its high ground as King of the Hill—literally and figuratively—from such a perch as Pitt Stadium, shown here circa 1938. The professional Pirates became Steelers soon after, yet still they couldn't attract and enrapture crowds the same way as Pitt, then-Carnegie Tech, and Duquesne . . . from where Art Rooney tried to allow Buff Donelli to coach college *and* pro football at the same time in 1941. (Courtesy of University of Pittsburgh athletics)

called Steelers offices to inquire if he was still needed to scout the Brooklyn-Washington game since Donelli was flying to San Francisco against league orders.

A November 7, 1941, *Associated Press* account: "Aldo 'Buff' Donelli, the quick-change artist of the coaching profession this season, joined his first football love—Duquesne University—today but confusion still prevailed. Donelli stepped off a . . . plane after a cross-country dash starting in Pittsburgh last night and reiterated he had severed all connections with the National Professional League Steelers 'unless different arrangements are made next week.'" They weren't.

For the record, Donelli's Dukes won and Walt Keisling's Steelers forged a tie—against Philadelphia—that weekend. Predecessor and part-owner Bert Bell told the newspaper while at the game in Philadelphia, "If [Donelli] just doesn't want to buck up against tough pro competition anymore, that is up to him."

Chuck Cherundolo, Steelers center: "Buff was a hard guy to know."

WALT KIESLING

College: St. Thomas (Minnesota) • **Years as Steelers coach:** 1939–1940, 1941–1944, 1954–1956 • **Record:** 30-55-5

Before New York Yankees owner George Steinbrenner ever met Billy Martin, Art Rooney blazed the professional sports trail for hiring and firing the same coach, for naming and renaming, for applying and removing interim tags at the drop of a cigar ash.

Meet Walt Kiesling, the Chief's go-to coach.

Twice, he was named interim coach deep into the season. Twice, he shared coaching duties with another franchise's field boss during those amalgamations of the World War II years, the Steagles and Car-Pitts.

Twice he got to coach an entire season all alone.

Add it all up, and the man known as "Big Kies" directed the Steelers to a relatively respectable—for them—21-26 (.446) record when he was left to his own devices. He went 2-8-2 (.200) when cleaning up for other coaches. He went 5-14-1 (.263) when he shared duties with Philadelphia's Greasy Neale in 1943 and Chicago's Phil Handler in 1944.

Kiesling had been a burly guard for the Pirates from 1937 to 1939 when Johnny "Blood" McNally went AWOL and out the door. Kiesling pulled the player-coach double duty. He pulled considerable coaching duty with Rooney, with whom he was unquestionably close. Many anecdotes about the Chief include the phrase "Big Kies was in the backseat. . . ." A "family retainer to his buddy" Rooney, Arthur Daley of the *New York Times* called him. The coach enjoyed playing the horses with the franchise owner. He also enjoyed drab football, the reason for the Pittsburgh sing-song, "Hey, diddle diddle, [Fran] Rogel up the middle."

A Pro Football Hall of Famer because of his career as a lineman, Kiesling did have his moments in coaching. He directed the 1942 Steelers to their inaugural winning season, after nine clunkers, and contention for the Eastern Division title. Then the war decimated his roster by claiming Hall of Famer Bill Dudley, center Chuck Cherundolo, back Dick Riffle, and more. In both 1954 and 1955—his *third* go-round

with Rooney's club—Kiesling's Steelers started out 4-1. In fact, a few days after beating its cross-state rival in the fifth game of 1954, on October 23, the *Los Angeles Times*' Frank Finch was inspired to write: "When Pittsburgh clipped the Philadelphia Eagles the other night, rapturous Steeler fans carried their coach, Walt Kiesling, off the field on their shoulders. Which brings up a fair question: Just who in tarnation is Walt Kiesling?"

He was the one who suggested that Rooney hire the jobless Buddy Parker to replace him, upon Parker's falling out in Detroit after the 1956 season. Years later, the *New York Times*' Daley wrote that Parker wanted to run Rooney's offer past the affable Kiesling first, and when he did Kiesling supposedly responded: "Please take the job, Buddy. You'd be doing me a favor." When Parker called back to say he decided to take a hiatus from coaching, Kiesling moaned: "You can't do this to me. Rescue me, pal."

Al Wistert, a longtime Philadelphia tackle who played under Kiesling with the 1943 Steagles: "He was not a leader kind of guy. The kind who always took the backseat, you know. He didn't want anything to do with being the leader of the group."

Chuck Cherundolo, Steelers center 1941–1942 and 1945–1948, then an assistant coach 1948–1957: "I was good friends with Walt. We did all that stuff together. He still living? He's gone, too? I guess when you get to be ninety-four, they're all gone. [He had a] great memory. All you had to tell him anything was once, and you knew he knew it."

Frank Varrichione, tackle from 1955 to 1960 and a rookie witness to a 4-1 start that ended in seven consecutive losses:

Walt Kiesling, my first coach, I think he worked the players a little bit too hard early in the season. He kept the two-a-days going all summer long. We did a lot of contact, a lot of scrimmaging. I think that wore the players down a little bit. We would get off to a good start; we were in pretty good condition. But each player, especially the linemen, could've carried an extra 10, 15 pounds. You need that extra weight pushing up against the big guys.

When the weather got cold with Kiesling, teams would walk all over us. We would start [4-1], but we could get run over by better teams that had fresher legs and more weight than we did. We used to play six exhibition games, so by the time the season started, we were worn out, basically. That worked in college, but not in pros. He came from the old school; he believed in working players hard.

Dale Dodrill, nose guard–middle linebacker 1951–1959: "Even pregame warm-ups, the drills they put you through, it was almost like halftime [you were two quarters tired]. Other teams, you'd look down there, and they'd be doing stretching exercises and that. He'd have us up there running and running. Walt Kiesling, he was the only coach who was at the Steelers as long as I played. I think in the early years he coached for no money or what little money they had, so [Rooney] was loyal to Kies."

Jack Butler, defensive back 1951–1959: "He was the head coach every time a coach got fired. You talk about old school, holy mackerel. Very nice guy, but old school. He was a good friend of the Chief's. They'd go to the track together."

JIM LEONARD

College: Notre Dame • **Year coaching Steelers:** 1945
• **Record:** 2-8

"Big" Jim Leonard was a farmer-coach, possibly even in that order.

And, after one season as coach, he happily went back to the farm.

Well, maybe not so happily. First, he went back to college. After a playing career at Notre Dame and with the Philadelphia Eagles under coach Bert Bell, Leonard became a successful college coach at St. Francis in Loretto, joined the Steelers in 1942, and then returned to campus life by assisting with Holy Cross in 1943. Leonard again reverted to his roots after assisting on one of the worst teams in professional football history and then serving a one-year placeholder role as Steelers head coach before Art Rooney at long last bagged former Pitt coach Jock Sutherland.

Leonard then headed not to the 100-acre asparagus farm in Mullica Hill, New Jersey, but the college ranks.

He coached St. Francis again, applied for the vacant Duquesne job, and spent his final few years as Villanova's head coach.

How did his Steelers year go? Badly.

Walt Kiesling resigned soon after the 1944 Car-Pitts debacle—co-coaching a horrendous amalgamation of war-torn teams, going 0-10 and getting outscored 328-108—to accept a position on the Green Bay staff. With Sutherland still in the service, Rooney was left with the backfield coach and farmer "Big" Jim, whose claim to sideline fame was joining Green Bay's Curly Lambeau and Detroit's Gus Dorais in using a telephone to confer from the press-box perch with the players on the sideline.

Leonard's strapped '45 Steelers, with future Hall of Famer Bill Dudley rejoining the club in November after his three-year military hitch, lost their opening three games and their closing three. They were outscored almost 3-1, same as the Car-Pitts before them.

When he accepted Leonard's resignation in mid-December, Rooney offered: "Jim was a fine fellow, and I personally hate to see him leave our coaching staff. But he understood that we're trying to get Dr. Sutherland because we need a full-time coach. Jim has his farm in New Jersey and can't devote more than six months out of the year to football."

Carl Hughes, the Pittsburgh Press *beat writer:* "In '45, Jim Leonard was the Steeler coach, and they'd lost 14 straight games [over pieces of three seasons], as I recall. Probably still a Steeler record." Believe it or not, Chuck Noll lost 16 in a row—the 13 to end his inaugural, 1969 season and the opening three of 1970. "They were playing the New York Giants, and they ended their 14-game losing streak at the Polo Grounds." They won only once more in their next six games.

DR. JOHN BAIN "JOCK" SUTHERLAND

College: Pitt • **Years coaching Steelers:** 1946–1947
• **Record:** 13-9-1

This College Football Hall of Fame coach, the Scot who wound up compiling a 144-28-14 college record in a game

Jock Sutherland, known as Dr. for holding a degree in dentistry from Pitt, transforms the Steelers almost instantly into a credible team. . . and even a playoff participant for the inaugural time. (Courtesy of University of Pittsburgh athletics)

once foreign to him, the strict leader who guided Pitt to four Rose Bowls (they declined a fifth), was the big fish whom Art Rooney coveted for almost a decade.

Rooney wooed him when Sutherland left Pitt after the 1938 season, when the university made motions he considered to be deemphasizing football. The two men talked in private at the Fort Pitt Hotel because Sutherland preferred such secrecy. But the story got out, and Rooney's big fish wriggled away.

Rooney admitted to reporters in January 1940, according to the Associated Press, that he offered Sutherland "somewhat less than $15,000 a year" to coach the then-Pirates, replacing Walt Kiesling. Some reports quoted Rooney as being "confident and hopeful." However, Sutherland was headed for an interview with the Brooklyn Dodgers football team and, ultimately, World War II.

Finally, in late 1945, Rooney landed him.

Sutherland was everything the Chief had hoped.

A disciplinarian and a linear thinker, Sutherland meticulously constructed the Steelers by his second season into the franchise's winningest club to date, 8-4. He guided them to their inaugural playoff, a 21-0 loss to mighty Philadelphia in the 1947 semifinals.

How meticulously? He caused a part-time public-relations worker and supposedly the franchise's first scout, future Pittsburgh Press sports writer Pat Livingston, to quit over an argument about 25 cents in change for an errand Livingston ran to get Sutherland's dry cleaning. Sutherland also reputedly ran off future Hall of Famer Bill Dudley for failing to take the requisite amount of steps on an offensive play, as the late Livingston used to tell the tale.

Sutherland learned from the master. Glenn Scobey "Pop" Warner recruited to Pitt this burly wrestler who had relocated to Sewickley, walked a beat as a cop, and took classes at the local YMCA. He was 25 when he became a Pitt freshman. The first American football game he ever witnessed, the Scot started as a Pitt lineman.

Like many of his Pitt contemporaries, Sutherland studied in Pitt's dental school. He earned his D.D.S. and taught at the school, specializing in bridge and crown repair. He naturally found his way into coaching: from 1919 to 1938 in college, from 1940 to 1941 with the Brooklyn Dodgers, and from 1946 to 1947 with Rooney's Steelers. No less a source than coaching immortal General Bob Neyland of Tennessee, with whom Sutherland got into a drunken wrestling match once on a football field as grown men, summarized of him: "I considered Jock Sutherland the best all-around football coach who ever lived."

Carl Hughes, Pittsburgh Press *beat writer in 1944 and 1945, who shared a train car with Rooney to the Washington Redskins–Cleveland Rams championship game in Cleveland in 1945:* "That same trip, we met [Lieutenant Commander] Jock Sutherland in his naval uniform. And they signed him up to coach."

Tim Rooney, son of the Chief: "Sutherland was one of the great coaches of all time."

Roy McHugh, longtime Pittsburgh Press *sportswriter, columnist, and editor:* "Everybody called him 'Dr. Sutherland.' Even Art Rooney. And I don't think he ever pulled a tooth in his life."

Chuck Cherundolo, center in 1946 and then player-coach under Sutherland in 1947: "All he had to do was look at you— it scared the hell out of you. As a matter of fact, there were players scared to talk to him."

In hindsight, folks looked back at Sutherland's behavior in late 1947 and began to wonder. He was on a scouting mission in spring 1948 when he was found wandering a Kentucky field carrying a suitcase. Surgery back in Pittsburgh discovered a malignant brain tumor. He died the next day.

Cherundolo served as one of the pallbearers.

The Steelers careened another 14 years before reaching the playoffs again and attaining as many as eight victories.

It didn't happen a second time for a quarter century—until the Immaculate Reception.

JOHN MICHELOSEN

College: Pitt • **Years as Steelers coach:** 1948–1951
• **Record:** 20-26-2

Johnny Mike, as he was called almost everywhere but to his adult face, wasn't used to losing.

Under the famed Moe Rubenstein at Ambridge High, he lost only four games in his scholastic career.

Under Jock Sutherland at Pitt, he lost but twice in his collegiate career, all the while—alternating at quarterback with John Chickerneo in the "Dream Backfield" with Marshall Goldberg—winning the national championship as many times, including a 21-0 Rose Bowl shutout of Washington.

As an assistant under Sutherland the next season, he lost twice while coaching that Dream Backfield. He promptly quit Pitt when Sutherland did, amid concern the university was deemphasizing football. He followed him to the NFL Brooklyn Dodgers in 1940 and 1941, to the Steelers in 1946, to Kentucky when the ailing legendary coach was found wandering in a field. When Sutherland came home to Pittsburgh to die, he helped carry him on and off the plane.

So when John Michelosen was chosen to follow his mentor, idol, and friend as the Steelers coach, he could only lose.

Michelosen was 32 years and two months old a week after Sutherland's April 11, 1948, death when Art Rooney handed him the fragile franchise, one the good doctor—a dentist who taught but never practiced—hoisted to new heights the prior season: eight victories and the inaugural playoff berth.

In the post–World War II era, no other NFL coach was as young as Michelosen to open a season until Oakland's Lane Kiffin in 2007.

Johnny Mike was young, all right. But he clung to the single-wing formation and Sutherland's teachings in a modern, T-formation world.

Rooney felt somewhat safe giving the helm to Michelosen, a club-record 23,220 season tickets having been sold to 34,529-seat Forbes Field. After all, one potential replacement candidate floated was General Bob Neyland of Tennessee. The *Pittsburgh Post-Gazette* wrote at the time: "Rooney displayed a bit of sentiment rare in pro grid magnates by giving Michelosen a shot at the big job. . . . Numerous friends of the Steeler boss questioned the wisdom of risking the 32-year-old ex-Panther who has never even been head tutor of a high-school team nor played a pro game himself.

"I believe most of those fans who ordered 1948 tickets would want the Sutherland system to continue under Jock's first assistant," Rooney said. "It was Johnny who had to make the tough decision."

"And I think he will make good."

He lost, in order, eight, five (his only winning campaign at 6-5-1), six, and seven games in his four seasons. By all accounts, the Steelers were the last NFL club to still use the archaic single wing. A month from the end, after a three-touchdown loss to Philadelphia, he screamed at his players, "If we are going to lose and play poor football, we can do it with 22 [instead of] 32." Remember the old adage "You can't get rid of the whole team"? Or even one-third? Rooney fired the ninth coach in Steelers history in favor of the third coach, bringing back Joe Bach.

The *Post-Gazette* quoted Rooney on December 19, 1951: "I hated to let Johnny go. He's a good man, a very nice coach and one of the nicest fellows I've ever dealt with. But, in this business, we've got to look to the financial end of things and to what the future holds."

It quoted Michelosen: "I may quit coaching entirely and go into business."

For his next act, he returned to coach at Pitt, 1955–1965.

Bill Walsh, Pro Bowl center 1949–1955: "He followed a lot of stuff that Jock did. I liked him. He was a good man. He was a hard worker. And we worked very hard. We were single wing, the only team in the league doing that. I had played it [last] in high school. When I went to Notre Dame, we went to the T, naturally. The big thing was, it wasn't a spiral that you centered back to the tailback or the quarterback. You had to center it back end over end, 2½ revolutions. I was stunned how they centered the ball, but Chuck Cherundolo taught me how . . . and why they wanted it that way."

Dale Dodrill, a rookie nose guard in the 5–2 defense at the time:

That was the last year they played the single wing—last pro team to play the single wing. Teams didn't like to play against the single wing, because it was a little more physical offense than the T.

You never really saw anything of him other than practices and meetings, he seemed to be isolated on his own. Those were days when you didn't fraternize with coaches. The coaches and the players were two different groups altogether; you didn't associate with each other. Michelosen ran a good ball club, there was no problem with him . . . other than the two practices a day and two scrimmages [in camp]. Used to weigh in and weigh out each practice, and I think that first training camp I was down to 198 pounds. But I used to sweat a lot.

Jack Butler, a receiver turned into a defensive end turned into a Hall of Fame–caliber defensive back: "Everything was regimented—bang, bang, bang. We killed each other in camp. The ones who [made] the team survived; we scrimmaged every day with Johnny Mike."

JOE BACH

College: Carleton College (Minnesota), Notre Dame • **Years as Steelers coach:** 1935–1936, 1952–1953 • **Record:** 21-27 overall (10-14/11-13)

Art Rooney was ahead of his time: He began recycling coaches long before it became vogue in the NFL, NBA, NHL, and Major League Baseball.

Bach was older than his two Pirates coaching predecessors and an even older man than the club owner—he had a full 10 days on the Chief—when he first arrived in 1935.

He was the first Pittsburgh professional football coach from beyond Western Pennsylvania, having scrawled his name in history as one of Grantland Rice's "seven mules" blocking in front of the "Four Horsemen," one of whom he assisted previously at Duquesne, Elmer Layden. Bach found success at Rooney's old school, Duquesne, where his team scored a whopping 332 points a season earlier.

Bach's inaugural Pirates scored 100, about half the competition's total, en route to a 4-8 season . . . regarded as a success. His wins nearly equaled the five victories that Luby DiMeolo and Jap Douds collected cumulatively the two previous seasons. And when Bach went 6-6 in 1936, the franchise's first nonlosing season, it was a smash hit. He promptly returned to college coaching. On Christmas 1934 he had signed a three-year contract, and he lasted two.

He was a middle-aged man when he returned for his second go-round, replacing John Michelosen. St. Bonaventure gave up football on their two-year coach, and Bach switched employment from one Rooney brother (athletic director Father Silas) to another (the Chief). Maturity the second time around? Bach won one more game. He resigned after losing three exhibition games to start 1954, giving way to the more regular Rooney retread: Walt Kiesling.

Chuck Cherundolo, defensive coach 1948–1957: "He was one guy that never liked me. Just put in my time with him. He never talked to me. We didn't film our own guys back then. But we talked a lot about the other teams."

Jack Butler, defensive back 1951–1959: "The next coach came [after Michelosen], the practices dropped down to an hour and a half. No practice in the morning. Now we think we're not as sharp because we weren't banging the hell out of each other. He was great. Of course, we didn't win many games. In fact, we didn't win very many games at all. He never screamed. He'd come around and joke in practice, kid with you. And we threw the ball. Different things we never did before. He went to the T formation," more than a decade after most every other NFL team adopted it. Of course, Bach was so radically divergent, he even allowed beer in the team hotel. "We thought we were in a different world."

Dale Dodrill, nose guard–middle linebacker 1951–1959: "Joe, I think, he knew a lot of football. He seemed to have a problem with disciplinary [things], keeping control of the players—some of them didn't adhere to him too well as far as what he required. He was a little older at that time, even."

Pat Rooney Sr., who served as ball boy at Bach's last round of training camps and later worked in the Steelers ticket office for his father: "Hey, I have no idea how Joe Bach got through the second time. I heard stories [that] the defense made up [the defensive game plan] in the parking lot before the game. Bach, he couldn't hear. We were up at St. Bonaventure, watching film. Everybody in the room was farting, and he couldn't hear it. As the joke was, he got farted right out of the league."

In a tragic irony, Bach died in 1966 at a Pittsburgh Curbstone Coaches Hall of Fame luncheon where he was being inducted, moments after reading the Rice poem that helped to immortalize him at Knute Rockne's Notre Dame: "War, famine, pestilence and death. . . ."

RAYMOND KLEIN "BUDDY" PARKER

College: North Texas, Centenary • **Years as Steelers coach:** 1957–1964 • **Record:** 51-47-6

He quit in a huff after one season as co–head coach of the Chicago Cardinals.

He quit in a huff in the preseason, at a "Meet the Lions" banquet, when he told a roomful of Detroit fans that he just wasn't going to take losing anymore (in a Motor City where he previously won two NFL championships).

And Buddy Parker joined the Same Old Steelers days later?

Somehow, their marriage lasted eight, mostly successful years before—you guessed it—he quit in a huff in the preseason.

All that coaching business with Blood and retreads and legends and protégés, it certainly failed to match the color of Parker's period with the Steelers.

Buddy Parker squatting before a game. He was the Steelers' most successful, long-term coach . . . until Chuck Noll and the glory years began. (Courtesy of the Pittsburgh Steelers)

Start at their beginning. He was hired shortly after that infamous Detroit speech, agreeing to a five-year contract with an Art Rooney who at the time was . . . wait for it . . . in Atlantic City, New Jersey. Parker was recommended by his predecessor and friend, third-time head coach Walt Kiesling, who purportedly pleaded over the phone to Parker, "Rescue me, pal."

Perhaps it was an omen when, six months earlier, Parker and the Steelers had almost come to a contract after another of his Detroit fits, but the Lions signed him to a two-year contract . . . which they voided after his "Meet the Lions" meltdown.

Perhaps it was an omen when he told the *Pittsburgh Post-Gazette* that August 27 hiring night: "I have always said that one of the happiest seasons of my career was in 1944 when I was a Card-Pitt coach along with Kiesling, Phil Handler and Jim Leonard. We didn't win a game, either."

Parker fashioned a winner out of the losing franchise, all right—temporarily. He gave the Steelers their winningest team to date, the nine-game victors of 1962. He gave them their inaugural streak of consistent success, with five of his first seven seasons ending in a record of .500 or better. He gave them their second postseason date ever, though it was something known as the Playoff Bowl in which he received compensation for promoting Miami, Florida.

It was *how* he fashioned his Steelers that brought attention . . . and perhaps brought down the franchise for another half decade, at least.

Parker never met a rookie he liked.

Never met a trade he couldn't complete.

Never made any draft his priority or plan to build.

Legend has it that Parker manufactured so many trades when in a funk that other NFL teams would call him after losses to take advantage.

This was a man who would cut his own tie to shreds after a loss. A man who stomped and screamed about quitting after

preseason losses. A man who prowled up and down the aisles of the team flight—a sight the players came to dread—firing this one or demoting that one or declaring his intention to trade somebody, but only when the Steelers headed home from a loss.

In a 1958 loss to his former Chicago Cardinals, he fired five players over "lousy football."

In 1959 he fired defensive back Don Bishop who left the field with only 10 men for punt coverage so he could have his shoe taped. Wouldn't you know, Philadelphia's Art Powell returned it for a touchdown.

During his 1957–1965 tenure, he traded at least 49 draft picks. These included five first-round, five second-round, and five third-round selections in an eight-year period.

He traded away two quarterbacks, Hall of Famer Len Dawson and Earl Morrall (for Bobby Layne), and jettisoned another, Jack Kemp, who wound up winning championships elsewhere. He traded away Buddy Dial, one of the league's top receivers, for the rights to a young stud defensive lineman . . . who signed with Houston of the other league, the All-America Conference. (Some Steelers fans called Parker at home to voice their displeasure over that one.) He horded veterans a decade before George Allen made a living of it with his Washington Redskins "Over the Hill Gang."

Dale Dodrill, nose guard–middle linebacker 1951–1959, who asked Rooney to be traded—and was sent by the owner to the coach: "My conversation with Buddy Parker wasn't good. I knew there were a couple of teams that wanted my services, but he told me nobody was interested. I knew that he lied to me. I have a hard time getting along with somebody who lies to you. Buddy Parker showed favoritism to players, and I wasn't one of them."

Andy Russell, a rare rookie starter in 1963, a year when Parker traded away every draft choice Rounds 1 through 7: "The first speech he made . . . , it was in the Roosevelt Hotel, right down there [pointing to Liberty Avenue from his 31st-floor office]. I knew there were six *veteran* linebackers, and they were only keeping five. And Parker says, 'I hate rookies. If it was up to me, I wouldn't keep any of you. Makes you lose games. I might keep a couple of you, only because Mr. Rooney wants me to.'"

Some of the players selected with the draft picks that Parker gave away? Hall of Famer Dick Butkus of Chicago, defensive back Johnny Sample of the Super Bowl–winning New York Jets, and Pro Bowl running back Abner Haynes.

Parker later made a deal to acquire Sample, who topped the team in interceptions, punt returns, and kick returns in 1961 and in November of the next season was summarily "dismissed" or released by Parker ("hasn't been worth a damn all season") along with Harlon Hill, for whom the small-college Heisman Trophy is named.

Pittsburgh Post-Gazette columnist Al Abrams wrote in 1958, with still a half dozen good shopping years left, "As far as we can figure it out, the next Steeler draft choice must be in a kindergarten somewhere."

After a fourth of five preseason losses in 1965, Parker telephoned Dan Rooney to propose once again a trade with another team—reportedly defensive lineman Ben McGee and others for unproven youngsters. The Rooneys—Art and his team-president-in-the-making son, Dan—lay in wait to accept just such an angry offer to quit in a huff.

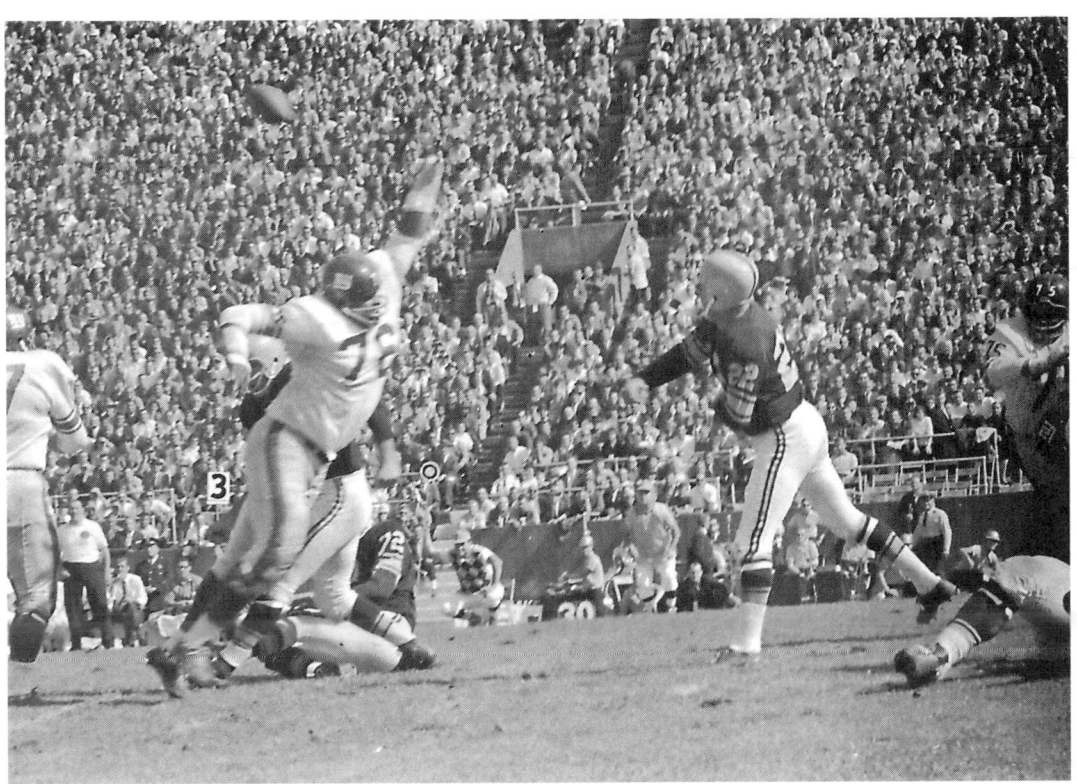

Bobby Layne launches a pass over mammoth New York Giants defensive tackle and future actor Rosey Grier, likely 1960 or 1961. The Steelers lost to the Giants five consecutive games in that period, and also dropped four consecutively in Pittsburgh. (Courtesy of the Pittsburgh Steelers)

Roy McHugh, longtime Pittsburgh Press *writer, columnist, and sports editor:* "Buddy Parker says, 'Are you questioning my judgment?' And Dan replied, 'I don't believe in making trades a few hours after a defeat.' 'I quit.'" Rooney the elder usually talked Parker out of resigning, but this time son Dan accepted it.

Pat Rooney Sr., one of the Chief's youngest twin sons and a Steelers ticket seller at the time: "When Parker came, that was a renegade period—him and the players. After the games we lost, he'd get in the cab and go to the airport. He was half cooked by the time the players' [bus] got there. The Chief was fed up with Parker. And Parker had a $25,000 contract, which was a lot of money in those days. The Chief told us, 'If Parker says he quit, you go find a newspaper guy and tell them. So I don't have to pay him.'"

Frank Varrichione, a Pro Bowl offensive tackle whom Parker—what else?—traded away: "When Buddy Parker took over, he saw the heavy [blocking] sleds we used, made us take our pads off, and had us walk through plays. I got along good with Buddy Parker." Even after his 1960 trade to Los Angeles.

Dick Hoak, running back under Parker 1961–1964: "Was a good offensive coach. The thing was, they traded all the draft picks. He liked a lot of those old-timers who were at the end of their careers. Trying to win right then and there. There was no plan for the future."

Jack Butler, assistant coach 1960–1962: "He was altogether different, too [than his predecessors]. He came from Detroit. He was a winner there. He was smart. He really knew football. His practices were good. But personality-wise, he was really introverted. All of the years I played for him, I think he talked to me one time, that I can remember. He knew football, but he had a hard time getting it [across]. [And folks like Bobby Layne and Tom Tracy who arrived in trade] had played well in Detroit, but they'd had it."

MIKE NIXON

College: Pitt • **Year as Steelers coach:** 1965 • **Record:** 2-12

He asked for it.

This former Pitt and 1935 Pirates running back, known as Mike Nicksick growing up around Burgettstown, Pennsylvania, informed Art Rooney that he wanted to succeed Buddy Parker as Steelers coach four games into the 1965 preseason.

The way Art Rooney Jr.—who was present at training camp in Rhode Island at the time—and longtime Pittsburgh Press sportswriter and editor Roy McHugh recalled it, the Chief flat-out advised Nixon against it. The boss reasoned: It's a lost season. There's no way you can win. Therefore, there's no way the owner can let you keep the job when the team fails.

Didn't matter.

Mike Nixon *had* to coach his hometown NFL team.

He signed a one-year contract a matter of hours after Parker's resignation.

The year lasted 113 days.

It contained the most losses in Steelers history to that point.

"How can you justify a 2-12 record?" Nixon admitted at his firing.

Nixon had gone 3-9 and 1-9-2 and out the door with Washington in 1958 and 1959, so he had the head-coaching experience to deserve a chance. He had Jock Sutherland roots, having served as a Steelers assistant from 1946 to 1951.

Star running back John Henry Johnson was injured and out for the year. Quarterback Bill Nelson was twenty-four, the owner of one full NFL game of experience, and playing on a gimpy knee. After Nixon's inaugural victory in week 6, he handed the game ball to defensive back Jim Bradshaw, who picked off three in that one-touchdown triumph at Philadelphia.

Nixon told McHugh at one point: "The ticket buyers are paying $6. They want a winner."

Dan Rooney, the team vice president, visibly began to exercise control over the franchise. His father wanted to wait through the holidays before announcing the end of this Nixon administration, but the son convinced him at a moment's notice that it was unfair to block the coaching staff from immediately looking for work. The Chief wound up apologetic with media for wearing a green flannel shirt to the presser instead of a white shirt and tie.

Dick Hoak, a running back under Nixon: "We were up in Rhode Island, where we went to camp. We played San Francisco [in preseason, though Hoak missed the game with a thigh bruise]. That night, I hear a lot of people in the halls chasing each other around. The next morning, I went down to get treatment in the training room and the guys were all there. I said, 'What's going on?' 'Didn't you hear? Buddy quit.'

"He quit all the time. . . . This time, Dan said, 'OK,' and took his resignation. We were six miles from the beach, so guys headed there. It was a shambles. That's the way they all were then. A lot of teams were like that team.

"Mike was a great person, a really good guy. All the guys liked him. I think we won maybe two games that year. He wasn't a head coach."

BILL AUSTIN

College: Oregon State • **Years as Steelers coach:** 1966–1968 • **Record:** 11-28-3

Word came from on high.

Vince Lombardi saith to Art Rooney: If you want to win a championship at long last, hire Bill Austin.

As it was written, so it shall be done.

And done badly.

Not that it was entirely Austin's fault, but his hiring turned out to provide a long list of Steelers lasts:

- Last coach for 40 years to wear a whistle to practice, until Mike Tomlin
- Last coach to fail to win regularly for a half century
- Last coach to fail to last
- Last coach to beat St. Vincent's Green Bay Packers

The final last was a quirk of fate. Austin's Steelers went to Wisconsin for the 1967 regular-season finale and toppled a resting bunch of Packers (Don Horn playing QB for Bart Starr and Zeke Bratkowski). The Packers never lost again that postseason on their way to a Super Bowl II victory. Lombardi stepped down from coaching Green Bay thereafter.

That royal road triumph aside, Austin's honeymoon period seemed already over by this end of his second season. Amid a 2-8-1 Steelers start—with the club on its way to a 1-6 home record—the final two 1967 games attracted to Pitt Stadium just 23,773 fans for the Vikings and 22,251 for the Redskins. The old bowl was 60 percent empty. It was a team that lost four games in the final quarter, half of those in the final two minutes.

Asked if Austin would return to see out the final year of his contract in 1968, vice president "Danny Rooney," as he was known then, responded to the question: "Sure, why not?"

Lombardi's Packers proved to be the last winning team Austin would defeat as the Steelers' head coach. The 1968 edition went 2-11-1 by beating woeful Philadelphia and Atlanta. The game against Philly, a 6-3 Steelers victory that Andy Russell later called "the worst pro football game ever" and the Associated Press classified as "a contest as dull as marshmallows at 30 paces," was billed as the O.J. Simpson Bowl. Neither club got him in the draft.

Austin, 39, got the door.

His was an interesting three-year period, to say the least. The Steelers held conversations with Notre Dame's Ara Parseghian and Nebraska's Bob Devaney, two of the most successful college coaches of the era if not of all time, but they chose to abide by Lombardi's recommendation instead. In 1967 training camp, Austin had to talk halfback-returner Jim "Cannonball" Butler into sticking around training camp instead of quitting. (Butler spent the next four seasons with Atlanta and one more with St. Louis.) Quipped Austin, "I should have been a psychologist as well as a coach in this business." First-round 1968 selection Mike Taylor, a USC offensive tackle, successfully hid from them until July that he had undergone knee surgery eight weeks earlier—a dicey procedure in the days before arthroscopy. How bad off was Taylor? The College All-Star team dropped him from its roster two weeks before playing the Super Bowl champion, Green Bay.

Perhaps the biggest contribution made by Austin and his Steelers: They were the NFL's first Astroturf guinea pigs. On the Saturday after Thanksgiving 1967, Austin and a half dozen Steelers flew to Terre Haute, Indiana. There they joined Charley Winner and a half dozen St. Louis Cardinals in testing the Astroturf at Indiana State University, according to United Press International and the *Pittsburgh Post-Gazette*. The new North Side stadium was going to get the same carpet three years hence. "I was skeptical, but I'm a believer now. We used pass plays, pass blocking . . . and had Jim Bakken punt and placekick. They tell me there have been no knee injuries there or on two similar fields. Nice part is that you can practice on it every day. And they have a vacuum-type machine to pull out the water. I was very impressed and believe it's sure to be widely used in the future." The Steelers and Pirates shared it for 31 years inside Three Rivers Stadium.

Austin, however, wasn't the coach to lead the Steelers into the new multipurpose concrete bowl.

Was . . . Joe Paterno?

The news accounts of Austin's firing contained the news that vice president Rooney had been in contact with the successful Penn State coach. Paterno had called him earlier seeking Steelers tickets for some of his players. Next thing anyone knew, Rooney was wooing Paterno.

In 1969, when Lombardi resurfaced with the Washington Redskins as general manager and coach, his first hire was Austin. When Lombardi was diagnosed with and later died from cancer, Austin guided the 1970 Redskins to a 6-8 mark—his last stint as an NFL coach.

Joe Gordon, longtime public-relations director: "When they hired Bill Austin, they did that on the advice of Vince Lombardi. They . . . got the word from the Gospel of Vince. And that turned out to be terrible."

Dick Hoak, who played running back for Austin and later played for and worked under the one who followed: "Austin tried to be a Vince Lombardi instead of being Bill Austin.

That's what happened to quite a few guys from the Lombardi staff. Bill knew football. But he wanted to be like Lombardi."

Ralph Berlin, longtime trainer: "Bill was in his last year of his contract when I came here. I forget how many games they won, but it wasn't many [two of 14, finishing on a five-game losing streak]. Bill got fired after the season."

CHUCK NOLL

College: Dayton • **Years as Steelers coach:** 1969–1991
• **Record:** 209-156-1

Joe Paterno slept on it. Or tried to sleep for days, anyway. It was a $250,000 offer to coach professional football. It was long-term security, a contract for a quarter of a million dollars for a fellow earning $20,000 a year. The erudite Penn State coach, who quoted Browning to his college boys, groped for the word to describe it: *staggering* was the best he could muster. When it came time to decide whether to up and leave Penn State after just four seasons as head coach, after an 11-0 and Coach of the Year 1968, he just couldn't do it.

So Paterno dialed up Dan Rooney around 11:30 P.M. on January 7, 1969, to say thanks, but no thanks to his offer to coach the Steelers.

Bad timing, they all agreed.

Suddenly, this coaching search was careening in the usual Same Old Steelers way: bad to worse.

Chuck Noll at the start of his final Steelers training camp of his Super Bowl era, Latrobe's St. Vincent College in 1991. (George Gojkovich)

Indiana University coach John Pont telephoned Rooney on January 24 to withdraw from consideration, hours before he was scheduled to come to Pittsburgh for an interview.

January 27, the day before the third annual NFL–AFL combined draft, Rooney got back on the phone. He called Colts secondary coach Chuck Noll about 8 A.M. Within moments, the job was offered and accepted. The plane from Baltimore was delayed, though. Instead of an 11 A.M. grand introduction in Pittsburgh's Roosevelt Hotel, the Steelers handed out a press release in the morning and then held a news conference with Noll present five hours later. A coach at long last.

Rooney announced a three-year contract, no financial terms divulged, and added, "We hope to keep him forever."

A reporter that afternoon brought up the Same Old Steelers tradition, the reputation of the Pirates, Pitt, and Penguins further rendering Pittsburgh a City of Losers.

Noll's reply was simple, pointed: "We'll change history."

Ernie Accorsi, later general manager of the New York Giants, Cleveland Browns, and Baltimore Colts, at the time a publicity director at Penn State: "I was nervous about [Paterno taking it], because I thought: 'What's going to happen to me.' But I was a nobody. Art [Modell] told me they talked to him about [former Steelers and then Browns assistant Nick] Skorich, but Modell was going to have to remove Blanton Collier. He told the Chief that he was going to keep Skorich, and the Chief—because they were such good friends—said, 'Okay, we won't talk to him.'" Legend has it, another Colts assistant also was considered, Don McCaffrey, who succeeded a gone-to-Miami Don Shula a year later. Ex-Steeler Ernie Stautner of Dallas, Giants assistant Jim Trimble, and the Jets' Walt Michaels also were considered. "But they got the best coach. Everybody around the Colts knew how smart Chuck was. His IQ was off the charts."

Art Rooney Jr., scouting director and second-oldest son of Art Rooney Sr., the Chief: "Shula was a good friend of my dad. Bert Bell Jr. and Upton Bell [sons of former Art Rooney co-owner and friend Bert Bell] worked with the Colts, and they really recommended him, too. [Colleagues] called him 'the Pope.' The Chief said [early in 1968], 'When you're on the road, ask about assistant coaches.' Noll's name always came up.

"He was the one who changed everything. Dan and I had the right philosophy, running it as a business. But, of course, Noll was phenomenal."

The first order of business for the new coach—at 37 years, 22 days, the third-youngest in the NFL behind San Francisco's Dick Nolan and Detroit's Joe Schmidt of Pitt—was the next day's draft. He huddled with the Rooney he already called Artie. Noll previously performed what at the time was labeled "talent scouting," so he came prepared. But he was taken by the Steelers' preparation, especially input from former *Pittsburgh Courier* sports editor Bill Nunn. In a funny aside, *Pittsburgh Post-Gazette* sports editor Al Abrams walked into Dan Rooney's office on Noll's introductory day at the same time as Dick Haley, then a scout with the Bears, Lions, Eagles, and Steelers Talent Organization (BLESTO), formerly a Pitt and Steelers player. Dan asked Haley point-blank: Georgia defensive tackle Bill Stanfill or the North Texas State guy? Take Joe Greene, Haley answered.

That inaugural draft netted the following: Greene, the building block for the rest of the franchise's history; homegrown backup quarterback Terry Hanratty, a choice that satisfied the rabble demanding his selection (in the first round, even); blindside offensive tackle Jon Kolb; and defensive end L. C. Greenwood, meaning they found half of the Steel Curtain in a matter of Noll's first few Steelers hours.

Was there enough time to redress the troops who went 2-11-1 the year before, redress the history that meandered to a 162-263-20 record over the franchise's previous thirty-six years?

Greene later recalled part of the inaugural camp address: "Our goal is to win the Super Bowl." There was sniggering in the room. And that delivery. He was more like a lecturer. A college professor. Just talking to them. Nothing like any football coach he'd ever seen.

Andy Russell, outside linebacker 1963, 1966–1976: "Noll walks in and says, 'I can tell you guys the reason why you were losing. You were losing because you weren't very good. You're not good enough. You're not fast enough. And I'm going to have to get rid of most of you.' And he did. One hundred guys in the room; five of us made it to the Super Bowl in 1974."

Dick Hoak, running back 1961–1970: "Coach Noll? You could see when he came in, he was completely different. He had a plan what he wanted to do. He was just honest with you, too. He told you if you would make the team, if you were going to play. 'You're going to have a tough time here.'"

John Banaszak, defensive lineman 1975–1981 and a fellow Clevelander: "Didn't have 43 rules that every player had to know. You know, be on time, do your job, and win. And that's the way he operated."

Chuck Noll barks late in the 1979 season. (Bill Amatucci)

Jack Ham, outside linebacker 1971–1982: "My first game . . . , I'm waiting for this big pep talk. Looking for Knute Rockne–type speeches. Chuck Noll gathers us all together. He says, 'We're introducing the defense. Let's go.'" And that was it.

Hoak: "Chuck didn't give a lot of speeches. But he knew what he wanted. He wanted his own players. He wanted *his* players. He didn't want someone coming from the outside saying, 'We did it this way in Chicago. . . .'

"It was difficult for some of the guys to accept Chuck; he was different. Some of the things he did. Roy Jefferson [who had back-to-back 1,000-yard receiving seasons, a rarity in those days] was going to test him. We went up to Montreal . . . played [the final 1969] preseason game. Roy came in late for bed check. Chuck got [business manager] Jim Boston out of bed and put Roy on the next plane back to Pittsburgh. Then Roy got traded. You knew he wasn't going to accept anything. Those old days were gone."

Ralph Berlin, trainer 1968–1992: "First off, Chuck really kept to himself. He was not open. Not like Mike [Tomlin]. Well, [Bill] Cowher, too. You know how they relate to the players? Chuck couldn't. I talked to him more after I retired than the entire time I was there."

Roy McHugh, longtime sportswriter, columnist, and editor of the Pittsburgh Press: "It was like going to school. He should have been a teacher." Knute Knowledge, other coaches called him. Or the Pope, "because he was infallible. I thought he was a very intelligent guy. You couldn't talk to him about football; he knew so much more about it than others, he got frustrated. I became a great admirer of Noll's. You had to be."

Kevin Kiely, ball boy and son of publicity chief and Chief aide-de-camp Ed Kiely: "You could talk to him about anything. But don't ask him about football."

Joe Gordon, publicity director and vice president 1969–1998: "Chuck came into my office every Saturday morning before the game . . . because I was always in the building then. We'd sit and BS. You couldn't talk to him about the game, though. Or football.

"The one thing that always impressed me about him from the very beginning: how serious he was."

Russell: "Coach Noll called and asked me to come to his office. I thought he was going to congratulate me for making a Pro Bowl [for the first time in 1968]. He says, 'Russell, I've been watching film since I took the job. I don't like how you play. You're too aggressive, you're too out of control, your techniques are flawed and you're trying to be a hero. I'll change the way you play. And you'll be a better player in your 30s than in your 20s.'

"And he was right. He always said, 'Success is in the details.' He taught me a lot. He was a wonderful teacher. He was a leader."

Hoak, who upon retirement spent a year coaching at Wheeling Central Catholic High before Noll brought him back to coach running backs in 1972: "He wanted to teach you his way, and he wanted his coaches to teach you a certain way, too. That's why he hired a lot of coaches who didn't play [pro football], a lot of college coaches."

George Perles, defensive assistant and coordinator 1972–1981: "He hired teachers. He wanted players to be taught, and that's why he went for so many college coaches—because of the teaching. And he was right."

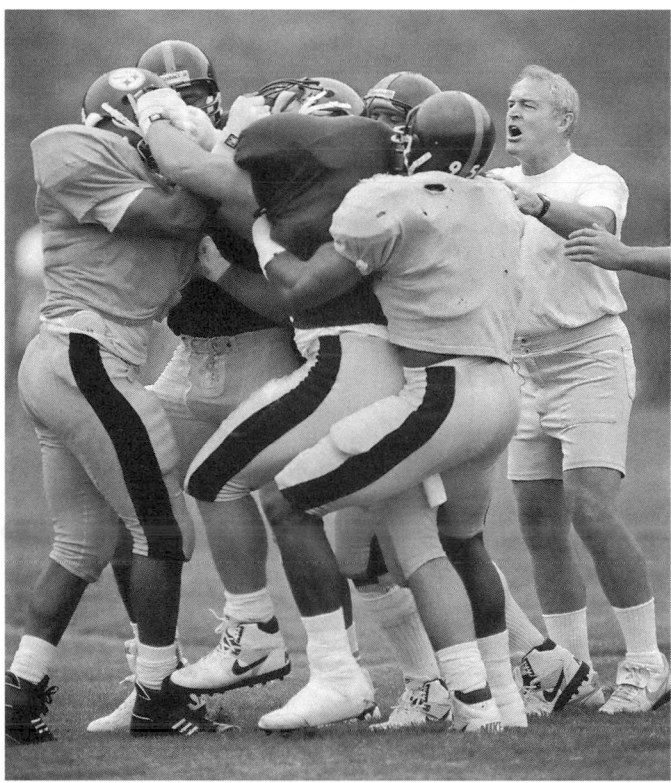

Chuck Noll tries to break up a scrum at St. Vincent College in 1991—his final training camp as Steelers head coach. St. Vincent's football stadium some 16 years later came to bear his name: Chuck Noll Field. (Vincent J. Musi)

Gordon: "He'd spend 15 minutes after practice with this guy . . . [who] had no chance of making the team. That was him."

Bubby Brister, quarterback 1986–1992: "Fundamentals. Balance. He taught us day after day."

Craig Wolfley, guard–tackle 1980–1989: "Taught everything. From A to Z. He coached everybody. Even the equipment manager. . . ."

Tunch Ilkin, tackle–guard–center 1980–1992: ". . . Even the mechanics on the plane in Philadelphia. Our plane sat on the runway for four hours after a game. And there was Chuck, looking over the mechanic's shoulder."

Banaszak: "Chuck would roam from one group to another group to another group. I can remember George Perles saying, 'Okay, here comes Chuck.' And he'd roll his eyes. And Chuck would say, 'I think your stance needs to be a little bit wider.' He'd say something to L. C. Then he'd move on to Joe Greene and have something that he saw on film the day before."

Berlin, recalling one positional practice session when the veteran Steel Curtain was plopped down on tackling dummies, taking five: "Chuck came over and said, 'What are you doing?' George said, 'What am I going to teach these guys about football?'"

Joe Walton, offensive coordinator 1990–1991: "He was a good judge of teaching. I thoroughly enjoyed my time. Chuck was not an easy guy to get to know."

Dan "Bad Rad" Radakovich, defensive line coach 1971, offensive line coach 1974–1977, and a former Penn State assistant: "Chuck let you coach. He liked new ideas. He was a lot like Paterno that way. He was all for doing it new and better. We had some new and different plays. The tackle trap and the flanker trap—people don't realize, the tackle trap beat Oakland and got us to the Super Bowl."

Perles: "Chuck and Shula were probably the smartest guys in coaching. Chuck could've been a surgeon."

Or a lawyer. Noll actually attended Cleveland State's Marshall Law School . . . even though he never fully intended to practice law. A Renaissance man, Myron Cope reveled in calling him—particularly in a Pittsburgh with a civic policy devoted to renaissance building projects where steel mills once belched dark clouds that caused noon to resemble midnight.

Charles Henry Noll, or the Emperor Chas as Cope came to affectionately call him on radio and television, was a Cleveland guy. It was an offense for which Pittsburghers came to forgive him.

He played guard and fullback at Benedictine High, tackle and linebacker at Dayton. In college, he played in what was for generations Dayton's only bowl game: no kidding, the Salad Bowl.

He was a 20th-round draft pick of hometown Cleveland, and the legendary Paul Brown made him a messenger guard for four years and a linebacker for three more between 1953 and 1959 (five interceptions *and* a safety in 1955 alone). Moving on with his life's work, to use his words, Noll served apprenticeships with Sid Gilman in San Diego, where the Chargers won five division titles in his six years there from 1960 to 1965, and with fellow brilliant Ohioan Shula in Baltimore from 1966 to 1968. Dan Rooney interviewed the Colts secondary coach the day after Joe Namath torched Noll's defensive backfield in a Super Bowl III upset for the ages. This time, Paul Brown was the messenger, telling the media: "This boy is a good one. Rooney deserves to have this thing go up."

All these masters under whom Noll trained, all this speckless gray matter, he was destined for immediate greatness, no?

No.

Jon Kolb, center–tackle 1969–1981 and assistant under Noll 1982–1991: "We beat Detroit in Pitt Stadium [16-13] . . . and then we proceeded to lose the next 13 in a row."

Gordon: "I was impressed by how he handled adversity. You never saw him panic. He always believed in what he was doing. Win or lose, he was the same guy Monday morning."

The Chief told Dave Anderson of the *New York Times* before Super Bowl IX in 1975: "The first year, we won the first game, then we lost the last 13, but he never lost his poise, he never lost the ball club. One of the biggest things about a coach is holding your ball club together, and he did that. I told [Dan and Art Jr.], 'You got yourself a football coach.' Chuck Noll became a football coach when he lost 13 in a row."

Russell: "Chuck was something. He said, 'We're not going to play a lot of gimmicks. I'm going to teach you how to play the game the right way. I'm going to teach you how to win.' Then the draft classes started getting really good."

Funny how Hall of Fame talent can make you look smart. Terry Bradshaw (thanks to a coin-flip victory over Chicago for the first-overall pick), Ron Shanklin (a fair starting receiver until a couple of dudes came in the 1974 draft), and Mel Blount arrived at the top of their 1970 draft. Nineteen seventy-one brought a rescue boatload: Jack Ham, Frank Lewis, Ernie Holmes, Dwight White (the Steel Curtain was set), Mike Wagner, Larry Brown, and Moon Mullins—seven future Super Bowl starters. Next was the offensive centerpiece,

Chuck Noll, dressed, alone in the coaches' dressing room, still unable to arise from a 1987 loss at Miami. (Vincent J. Musi)

Franco Harris in 1972, along with complementary pieces Joe Gilliam, Gordon Gravelle, John McMakin, and Steve Furness. In 1973, J. T. Thomas gave Blount a cornerback counterpart. And, of course, the 1974 draft caused Canton to tilt: Lynn Swann, Jack Lambert, John Stallworth, and Mike Webster in a once-in-a-millenium row.

Starting in 1974, the Emperor dressed in Super Bowl rings. Four times over the next six seasons came diamonds and delight like neither Pittsburgh nor the NFL witnessed before.

The Emperor remained silent, stoic. There were no advertisements or sponsorships for him. No grandstanding. Only matters cerebral, only the pursuit of knowledge, only teaching and getting it right floated his boat.

Oh, yeah, he learned boating. Piloting. Wine tasting. Ukelele playing. Knute knew it all.

Ed Kiely: "He even had season tickets for the symphony."

Banaszak: "Chuck was a man for all seasons. A pilot. A wine connoisseur. Knew a lot about everything." Banaszak wore a suit into Three Rivers Stadium one off-season day, and Noll quizzed him on it. Banaszak informed him that he got an off-season job in trucking. Why, Noll launched into yarns about *his* Cleveland off-season days in trucking. The conversation seemed to last an hour. Banaszak gave in: "Coach, I've only been on the job one day."

Perles: "'You want to talk about flying? Fine. I got all I can handle with that goddamned defense.'"

Kolb: "For some reason, he could not say my name. He would say, 'Greenwood, L-1 on kickoffs. L-3, K . . . Kah . . .' That's the only way I knew he even knew who I was." Then, one day in 1970 training camp, *Kahlb* got a rap on his St. Bonaventure Hall room door: "Coach wants to see you." "I've been there over a year, and he still hadn't spoken my name [correctly]. I'm getting madder and madder. I threw the playbook as hard as I could at that back wall, all 300 pages. And it scattered. I thought, 'Somebody's going to have a hard time picking that up.' I get to his room, and he had pictures in his hand. 'Hey, Jon, you like the outdoors. I was in Florida on vacation this year and thought you'd like to see some pictures.' And he starts explaining a master's thesis on the pileated woodpecker. Then I start getting this dissertation about the difference between crocodiles and alligators. 'Don't you like the pictures?' he asked me. 'I would if I wasn't getting cut!' 'Who said you were getting cut?'

"I was there for three days putting the playbook back together."

Dermontti Dawson, guard–center 1988–2000: "He was so philosophical, how he explained things to you. It wasn't just football that he was philosophical and versed on. He was versed on . . . everything. He had that soft voice. Never the kind of guy who got very excited. He was his usual self."

Russell: "He let me debate him—respectfully. He was flexible."

Banaszak: "Then there were times like Super Bowl XIV. We're behind, he's running off the field—it's a famous clip. He sees the camera and starts charging at [it]. Where'd that come from? That's not serious Chuck Noll."

Ilkin: "Chuck was different in that everybody was afraid of him. Chuck was the king of nonverbal communication. He would look at you and make you lose control of your bladder. But [to escape football moments] he loved to talk about other things. He loved to talk about his plane. He loved to talk about his boat. He loved to talk about fishing. He loved to talk about politics."

Now there was a land mine. In search of topics of conversation other than football, Art Rooney Jr. for a time became so embroiled in political discussions with Noll, his father made him stop—he could replace the scouting director, but not the fabulously successful head coach. The Noll–Kiely morning discussions at the coffee pot in the kitchen of the Steelers' Three Rivers offices likewise became infamous. Often, Noll walked away mumbling. Once, Kiely gave his youngest son, Kevin, tickets and a parking pass to a Pirates game that night. When the longtime ball boy parked and directed his friends toward the gate, he heard someone calling out his name. He turned to find Noll leaving the Steelers offices . . . still fuming eight hours later. *"And you tell your father another thing,"* Noll said to the kid, voice raised. *"To find that William F. Buckley article from May."*

Ed Kiely: "The other coaches used to say, 'How can you talk to him like that?' 'Cause he doesn't sign my check.'"

Chuck Noll and Terry Bradshaw hold one of their sideline debriefings. (John Beale)

What started all the Super Bowl success, all the diamond-encrusted excess in jewelry, were well-placed words from the Emperor.

One football talk resonated . . . for decades.

Remember, this was a man who spoke softly, spoke little. His pregame speech was unfailingly dry and numbingly repetitive: Sunday is fun day. You worked all week for this. Go out and have fun.

And that was about it.

Mike Wagner, safety 1971–1980: "Chuck Noll was, 'Don't poke your enemy. I want everybody on an even keel. I don't want any rah-rah stuff.' It was all analytical. If somebody was getting too loud . . ."

Larry Brown, tight end–tackle 1971–1984: "I remember the first time we went to the Super Bowl [1974]. Miami was playing well and prominent. So were the Raiders. They had a [playoff] game out in Oakland. A lot of commentators were saying, 'This is really the Super Bowl.' They felt the best two [NFL] teams were playing. He got us in a meeting room [hours later]: 'People are saying the two best teams played last week. They got it all wrong. The best team is sitting right here.'

"You couldn't break the confidence, the 'we-got-this' attitude that was in the room after that."

Joe Greene, defensive tackle 1969–1981, unquestioned leader, and later captain: "That was it. That was it."

Gordon: "What did the Raiders get, 21 yards rushing?" Twenty-nine yards on 21 carries, to be precise, was Oakland's output in that AFC championship game. The Vikings in Super Bowl IX assembled just 17 yards rushing on 21 carries.

Noll's Steelers were the best team for the rest of the decade.

Greene: "It was just a wonderful feeling to rise where we did. The journey. After that first Super Bowl, it felt so good. We all were driven to go back, for sure. Chuck, he wouldn't let you forget. Today is today; yesterday is gone. It's like, 'What have you done for me lately.' We all understood that. It wasn't a negative. I guess it's what a championship team needs: You can't forget how hard and difficult it was. We couldn't feel good about ourselves and not be able to get through the door because your head is so big. He had a way of keeping us grounded. Very special man. Very special man."

What followed also were a few gory days (the "criminal element" civil trial brought by Oakland's George Atkinson lawsuit stemming from Noll comments following the 1976 season opener; losing Harris, Rocky Bleier, and kicker Roy Gerela in the 1976 Baltimore playoff game; the 9-5 and one-and-done-playoff 1977). What ensued were rule changes seemingly aimed at Steelers defensive weapons: the head slapping by the Steel Curtain, the bump-and-run coverage favored by Blount, and linebackers Ham and Russell muscling receivers off routes. Into each reign, a little life must fall.

John Jackson, offensive tackle 1988–1997: "He always told some good stories. But he always told life stories. And I was always appreciative about that."

Mel Blount, cornerback 1970–1983, at a late-2011 North Shore public ceremony dedicating a street named Chuck Noll Way: "Chuck Noll was the first white coach I had. I must say this: That guy truly was a remarkable individual. I give all the credit to him. I came to this city naïve, somewhat sheltered. The things I've been able to do [in football] and the things I've been able to do in life are basically because of Chuck."

A bespectacled Tony Dungy coaches young cornerback Delton Hall in 1988, Dungy's final season with the Steelers before embarking on his journey to a championship head-coaching career. (Vincent J. Musi)

Tony Dungy, safety 1977–1978, was all set to launch his coaching career with Ray Perkins and the New York Giants until Wellington Mara told the Chief, who told Noll, who called Dungy and hired him instead: "It was the best thing that happened to me. I began to understand why we did things and why those things were important. I learned the why behind the what . . . and it was just special."

"He was a tremendous influence on me. Everything I did in coaching stemmed from that. I got there in 1977. I was an offensive player in college—actually, my whole life. Working with Chuck and Bud Carson and really learning the defensive side of the ball was huge. More than anything, it was his approach: Winning wasn't the most important thing in life to him; it was teaching us lessons. When we learned the lessons, we won. Instead of: . . . 'We gotta win, we gotta win.' That's what I learned more from him than anything; if you do the right things, we're gonna win."

Sure, even the Emperor made missteps.

Jackson: "The best story I have on Chuck Noll is, Chuck was always a fanatic about working out. He always coached on doing drills. And he's doing some drills on the treadmill. He slips and falls. The whole room goes silent. Chuck picks his pride up and walks out.

"All of a sudden, the room just busts out laughing. I know he had to hear it, I mean, he was just walking down the hallway."

Wagner, talking about how Noll never deviated from his norm, never displayed a spike in emotion or temperature . . . : "Except Cleveland [games]. He was like he wanted to go out and fight. He was all gnarly. If you were around him, it was like, 'Geez, Chuck, this was a little different. What got into him?' Something happened to him. There was always a fight or some shoving going on before the game, but it always looked like Chuck wanted to be in it."

Brister: "He was steady. He never went over the edge." Until . . . Jerry Glanville and the Oilers December 20, 1987. Television cameras captured Noll afterward at the midfield handshake wagging an accusing finger, *"Coming over and jumping people like that will get your ass in trouble. Know that."* "Houston was hitting me late. A lot of hitting us out of bounds. Chuck told their coach, 'I'm going to whip your ass.' And you saw it in his face. We all were right there. And I said, 'Damn, he *is* going kick his ass.' He wouldn't let go. It was like he was trying to hurt him."

Brown: "He was no-nonsense. You hear [today Mike] Tomlin talking about working with the guys who are here. Chuck is legendary for that. The show's got to go on. The expectations aren't wavering. Guys really bought into that."

Chuck Noll. (John Beale)

The guys who are here. That's the philosophy whence came some ugly moments in Steelers holdout history, when Noll uttered the absentees' names in forgettable (or is it forgotten) fashion:

Franco Who? 1982

Rod Who? 1987

Who's Tim Worley? 1989

You cannot instruct an absent pupil.

Noll maintained a degree of the same Steelers' success through the next decade, but the NFL endured spasms and change. Payrolls and egos mushroomed, both in boardrooms and on fields. Football styles altered.

The Emperor, after that wondrous Super Bowl spurt, ventured 96-96. He went 2-4 in the postseason. He guided the Steelers into the playoffs just once in his final seven years.

Dan Rooney attempted to effect change around the coach, firing his own brother Art and remodeling the organizational flow chart, forcing Noll to fire most of his assistants, giving Dick Haley control of scouting and then giving him a nudge in 1991 when it was apparent that the head coach would retire.

Brister: "For us to still compete with guys in the '80s, when we didn't have the payroll. . . . Our payroll was the lowest in the league, playing San Francisco and Houston with some of the biggest payrolls.

"I think as he got older and our team grew different, he changed with the times. They threw the ball a little more. He might have had to motivate a little bit more because they didn't have the talent. I always thought he was a great motivator for us."

Kolb, talking about the last Senior Bowl scouting mission in 1990, when the other assistants piled into the other rentals and left him with the head coach; Noll told him to throw on a sport coat and they'd go to dinner: "It was the only time I was around him in 23 years [that] he started talking about his son, Chris. It didn't have anything to do with a lesson."

The Steelers, in Noll's 1991 final season's final games, beat Cincinnati and, most fittingly, Cleveland. Both games were in Three Rivers. In the fourth quarter of that December 22 Cleveland finale, the big screen flashed a simple greeting: "Happy holidays from Chuck and Marianne Noll." The unspoken: And many happy new years.

Kolb, remembering the fateful telephone call to the assistants: "'Jon?'

"'Yeah?'

"'It's over.'"

A generation later, Kolb still marveled that his first reaction was to ask his longtime coach: "'What are you going to do?'"

Perles: "We're all phys-ed majors. You don't see any Ph.D.'s coaching. It's a simple game for simple people. And ours was all based on toughness, toughness, toughness.

"I visit him every year when I go to Florida. I told him once, 'Coach, we were tough.' He said, 'You made 'em tough.' That's one of the nicest compliments I ever had."

Sports Illustrated's Paul Zimmerman—who once walked into Joe Gordon's office hours before an AFC championship-game kickoff to find the future Hall of Fame coach on the floor, fixing Gordon's busted file cabinet—wrote a profile of the Emperor for a Steelers 75th-anniversary special edition. He relived conversations with Noll following his fourth and final Super Bowl. In that time, a remarkably candid Noll admitted to considerable angst and anxiety over Super Bowl XIV, facing ex-assistants Bud Carson and Dan Radakovich and Lionel Taylor, changing from defensive orientation to an offensive thrust, bearing the burden of greatness and legacy.

A smiling Chuck Noll in 1983. (Bill Amatucci)

"This whole area of historic evaluation bothers me. It's not so much that I dislike history, it's just the interpretation of it that screws everything up," Noll told Zimmerman. "It's the same in teaching. You think to yourself, boy, I did a great job teaching today, but it's no good if the words fall on infertile ground. It's teaching, plus the common repeated experiences, that make the whole thing work."

The story ended with these very words, with Noll's self-assessment: "Put down that I was a teacher."

Satisfactory answer.

Class dismissed.

BILL COWHER

College: North Carolina State • **Years as Steelers coach:** 1992–2006 • **Record:** 161-99-1

His wasn't merely a tale of Local Boy Makes Good. No, where Bill Cowher's outsized persona was concerned, there was, like the intersection of the three rivers, a confluence of story lines:

Local Boy Makes Faces.

Local Boy Makes Moisture.

Local Boy Makes Drama on a Football Field.

And, to the Steeler Nation, it was all good. He delivered only half as many Super Bowl trips—and one-fourth as many Super Bowl rings—as his predecessor. But Cowher's power

Bill Cowher's trademark grimace—hence his nickname "the Jaw"—in 2001. In his 10th Steelers coaching season, he orchestrated a revival. The team had gone 22-26 and missed the playoffs for three previous seasons. From 2001 on, his Steelers had a 63-32 record, three AFC Championship game appearances, and a Super Bowl XL victory in his final six seasons. (George Gojkovich)

lay in heart-palpitating and triumphant football (103-1-1 when leading by 11 points or more), blitzing and dominating defenses similar to the 1970s, and far, far more emotion than Chuck Noll. Where Noll was a stoically straight face, Cowher was foaming at the Jaw.

As this author wrote in the *Pittsburgh Post-Gazette* on January 21, 1992, the day when the Steelers officially hired a kid from Crafton, four miles from Three Rivers Stadium and 34 years removed from birth in what then was still the Steel City: "This is a Steelers coach you can reach out and touch, a Steelers coach who hardly restrains his feelings, a Steelers coach who isn't from Cleveland."

To fully appreciate what drives Cowher, you apparently need to play him in racquetball.

Larry Foote, inside linebacker 2002–2008, 2010– : "B.C.? He cheats at racquetball. I played him, just when I was starting [2002]. It was over very, very quick. I didn't score a point. He elbows you, forearms you. When you get in there with the head coach, you don't want to be physical with him. When he pisses you off, when he takes you to that limit, you got it in the back of your mind that he's the head coach. So you sit there and take it. I only played him once, but he beat up on Kevin Colbert like he stole something.

"He'd have Kevin Colbert coming in crying. Every day, you'd see Kevin Colbert coming in screaming. B.C. would be coming in smiling, that chin up in the air."

Bill Cowher on those postgame Monday and pregame Friday afternoons: "When Kevin and I played racquetball . . . , he was

the Generals, I was the Globetrotters. He probably felt that was part of his duties, to make sure I felt good on Fridays and Mondays."

Kevin Colbert, director of football operations 2000–2010 and general manager 2011– :

He was clearly better than I was. It was always a competitive game. For him, it was a diversion. For me, it was a competition because he was better. It was worth it for me to beat him when I could because it bothered him to lose. He was the same person on the racquetball court that you saw on the sideline.

Oftentimes, after we played, we'd sit and talk for 15, 20 minutes. Fridays, after all the work was put in that week, we talked about, "All right, what are we going to do this game?" He had a unique competitiveness about him. But he had a calmness and patience about him that if you didn't work with him you maybe didn't see. He was probably more patient with a young guy than I was. He was very good with making young players better. He had the . . . ability to stroke them when they needed stroked and to get after them when they needed someone to get after them.

That was William Laird Cowher. That also was Laird G. Cowher, his late father.

Dorothy Cowher, mother: "To me, he's Billy."

Dale Cowher, older brother: "Still is."

Dorothy: "Yes, I still call him Billy."

Dale: "Bill was an intense kid."

Dorothy: "Oh, yeah."

Shock. Surprise. Dick Butkus was his first football idol. Then came Jack Lambert.

Jim Sweeney, offensive lineman 1996–1999 and a fellow Local Boy: "I liked Bill. He was a Beechview guy. People always say he's a Crafton guy. He was in Beechview until the fifth grade. He went to Beechview Elementary," near Sweeney's roots.

Dale: "My dad coached Bill in Little League baseball. We were in Beechview then." The Cowhers moved to Crafton in 1967, when Dale was 16, Bill 10, and Doug 9. "My dad, everybody wanted to play for him. He was a motivator. And he knew the game. My dad would just sit in the dugout and not say much. He was intense. . . . I think Bill inherited a lot from our dad."

Dorothy: "He used to tell Bill in the car [after many an athletic event], 'Don't let them intimidate you.'"

Bill: "To some extent . . . , maybe other people have seen it more than I've seen it. I just know he was a very intense guy, very competitive. He was very thorough in everything that he did. Just wanted to make sure, whenever his kids went out, they did the best they could and never go out intimidated or not believing they could win or be good."

In 1992, the father related a tale of when his middle son was hired to coach the team for whom Laird Cowher once held season tickets at Pitt Stadium. Laird Cowher said then, "He used to lay in front of the TV set on days like this and say, 'That's what I want to do.' I'd say, 'What, fix TVs?' 'No, play football. I'm going to try.'"

Bill was bigger than most kids his age. No wonder he played linebacker and tight end. The Cowhers attended Carlynton High games on Friday nights. They drove to Raleigh, leaving Crafton at midnight, to catch North Carolina State games on

Saturdays. Then they'd awake Sunday mornings before 5 A.M. so they could get home in time to watch the Steelers.

Dale: "Pitt never offered him a scholarship. He only had two scholarship offers: North Carolina State and William and Mary."

Hey, didn't his successor go to school there?

Dale: "Bill ran into Lou Holtz flying back from a recruiting trip to William and Mary [and Holtz began recruiting him to N.C. State]. Lou came to our house and was talking to us when the lights went out. A fuse burnt out."

Dorothy: "He kept talking."

After college, in 1979, Bill was a late cut by Dick Vermeil in Philadelphia, so he returned briefly to N.C. State as a graduate assistant. He made the cut with Cleveland in 1980 and 1982. Then, in 1983 and 1984, he patrolled the field with Philadelphia's special teams.

Dale: "Had a couple of knee surgeries. If they had a 49-man roster, Bill was the No. 49 guy. Because of his special-teams play." In Cleveland, he made an impression on another fellow Western Pennsylvanian, defensive coordinator Marty Schottenheimer of McDonald.

Cowher became the Browns' special teams coach and defensive backs coach, at 31 just one year and three years older than Pro Bowl cornerbacks and Dawg Pound favorites Hanford Dixon and Frank Minnifield. In those Browns days, he would bring Browns friends to Crafton dinner: Dick "Bam Bam" Ambrose, Clay Matthews, Dave Logan. He followed Schottenheimer in 1989 to Kansas City, where he was defensive coordinator over Hall of Famer Derrick Thomas, Pitt's Bill Maas, Pro Bowler Albert Lewis, and Deron Cherry.

Dale: "When Bill was defensive coordinator in Kansas City, Tony Dungy was his defensive backs coach." In truth, Dungy left Noll in 1988 after Dan Rooney demanded that the coach demote Dungy from defensive coordinator back to secondary coach. Look where he ended up. Not just working *for* Noll's successor, Cowher. But on the Indianapolis sidelines standing between Cowher and Super Bowl XL. But that's getting ahead of the story.

Dorothy: "Oh, golly, I tell you, we could write a book."

Then the hometown team came calling.

Dorothy: "That's another story. It came down to him and Dave Wannstedt."

Dale: "It was Joe Greene, Wannstedt, Kevin Gilbride . . . he didn't think he could get it. 'Oh, I'll give it my best shot. If I don't [get it], I'll get the next one.'"

The year before, the former Browns special-teams player and coach—known for celebrating a special-teams play by leading the exultation in the Dawg Pound—was a finalist for Cleveland's head coach. The job went to some guy named Belichick, then 38. Cowher was 34. The NFL's youngest coach was David Shula, 32, then with the Cincinnati Bengals. The Steelers, with Houston offensive coordinator Gilbride in the minority, were looking at firm-handed men who spent most of their life in Pittsburgh: Wannstedt of Baldwin, Steelers legend and defensive line coach Greene, and the son of Laird and Dorothy Cowher.

Dorothy: "Kaye [Cowher] said, 'Be prepared, your son might be the coach of the Steelers.' He wasn't that sure."

Dan Rooney was.

The Beechview-Crafton kid was young enough to be a son to Noll, 60 years and 16 days old at the time. Legend has it, Rooney took to Cowher's blue-flame intensity and on-his-sleeve emotions, his commitment to the run and defense and

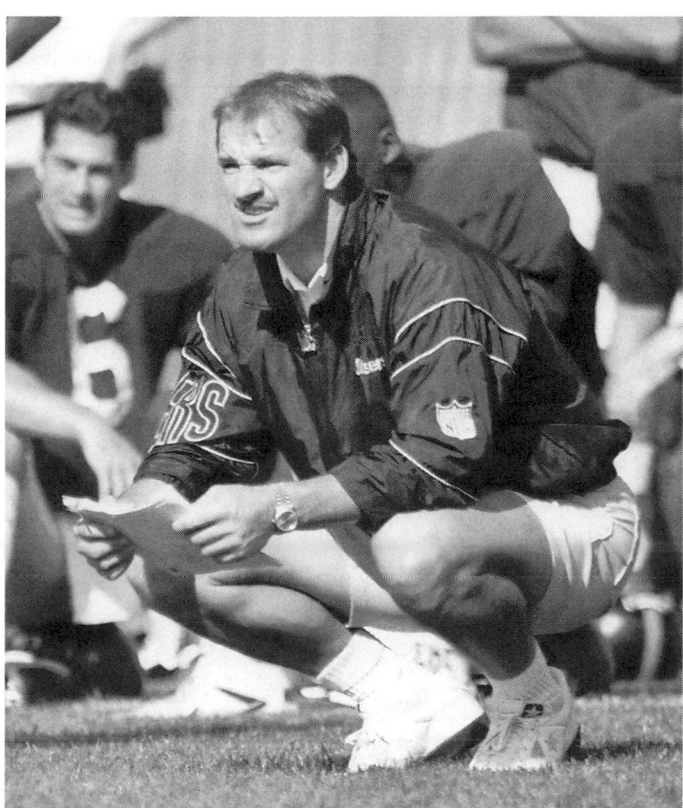

Bill Cowher squints into the summer sun to scrutinize his new club during his first Steelers training camp, 1992, at St. Vincent College. No. 6 in the background is quarterback Bubby Brister. (Bill Amatucci)

aggressiveness (not necessarily in that order), his Pittsburgh demeanor. Not to mention the fact he spoke in interviews in the plural "we."

Dick Hoak, who played under Noll and coached with him for 20 years: "He was different than Chuck. They wanted to do it different ways. Bill was more about motivating players. He would give them a lot more speeches than Chuck did. Whereas Chuck believed this was their jobs, you should be ready to go, Bill had a lot of individual one-on-ones with players in his office. Chuck didn't have any of that."

Ralph Berlin, trainer 1968–1992: "Whereas Chuck didn't relate to the players, this guy related to the players 'cause he wasn't that far removed from being a player himself. I really liked Bill Cowher."

Dom Capers, defensive coordinator 1992–1994: "I sensed it from the time I interviewed with him. We sat up to three o'clock in the morning talking football when I came in." Once the staff was assembled—three of whom later became NFL head coaches Cowher, Capers, and Dick LeBeau spent months putting together a 900-page binder about their defense. "There weren't any secrets with Bill. You knew what you were gonna have, day in and day out. Players, coaches, everybody felt that. They felt his sense of urgency and emotion. Felt his passion. You knew what he wanted. I think the players responded to him because he was a former player, an emotional guy. You know how this is a doggone emotional, passionate game, so you're going to feel and sense that emotion and urgency."

Dermontti Dawson, center–guard 1988–2000: "Hey, I loved Coach Cowher. He was a little bit younger, just starting out as a head coach. I think it was a little bit easier to relate to Coach Cowher. The game had evolved. Coach Cowher knew he had to adjust to the players. He was kind of a players' coach, he was right there, talking to you, joking around. He knew he could treat everybody the same. He knew how to touch and reach players of different levels."

From the jump, the local boy made the Steelers a winner again. It was quite an initial jump, too.

Trailing by 14-0 in the first quarter at rival Houston, the new coach went for, in order, a fake punt on fourth and 15 from a punter who never previously attempted an NFL pass (completed it for 44 yards), a fourth-and-four attempt for a first down (got it), and two reverses (including one on third and five late). Rod Woodson said of that fake punt 10 minutes into the opening game: "That's the first time we've ever had the turning point of the season in the first quarter of the first game."

They went 11-5 in his rookie season and won the division crown for the first time since 1984. Six Steelers made the Pro Bowl, the highest number in a decade. Cowher won the NFL-accepted award for Coach of the Year, something Noll could never manage in his 23 years.

They won, and they won, and they won. Six consecutive years from his start, Cowher nudged the Steelers into the playoffs. Only one other coach in pro-football history made six consecutive postseasons from the moment he stepped on an NFL coaching sideline. It was pretty heady company: The Jaw and Paul Brown.

LeBeau: "He did a great job, first, of organizing the football team and, second, managing the game. And address[ing] the things that came up over the course of the season."

Sweeney: "The one thing I remember most about Bill, come Wednesday, the game plan day, he'd come in with a three-ring binder about the team we were going to play."

There came a couple of wild-child moments by the young coach.

To the crowd's delight while running off the field, he angrily stuffed a photograph into the pocket of referee Gordon McCarter near midfield at halftime in early 1995. He had photographic evidence that line judge Ben Montgomery miscounted 11 men for 12 and wrongly penalized the Steelers, costing them a likely field goal. It proved costly, all right: Cowher was fined $7,500, McCarter and Montgomery each were suspended briefly, and the Steelers lost to Minnesota by a little more than three points, 44-24. It was their second loss in a row and dropped their record to 2-2.

They made Super Bowl XXX despite that start, despite playing without Rod Woodson every game but the first and the last.

In 1997, Cowher received heaps of criticism for straying too far afield, past the 35-yard line that stood as the NFL-mandated limit. In Jacksonville, on a Monday Night Football telecast, he stepped onto the field and lifted a forearm as Chris Hudson ran past the Steelers bench returning a blocked kick 58 yards for a touchdown. Instead of a 24-23 Steelers lead, it was a 30-21 Jaguars victory. Yes, Cowher admitted later, he briefly considered tackling Hudson.

"A . . . coach running out on the field all game just isn't right. Cowher doesn't belong there," Denver defensive end Alfred Williams told the *Denver Post* after the Steelers' December defeat of the Broncos in Three Rivers. "Anytime you're coming on the field as a player and you see their head coach is [almost] at the hash mark, it's aggravating. I don't see Mike Shanahan or Mike Holmgren or Marty Schottenheimer out there on the hash mark."

A bespectacled Bill Cowher congratulates Jerome Bettis, with Kordell Stewart, left, and an injured Mark Bruener nearby after Bettis rushes for 102 yards in a snowy 1996 playoff victory over Baltimore in Three Rivers Stadium. (Courtesy of the Pittsburgh Steelers)

Kevin Greene, outside linebacker 1992–1995: "I just enjoyed, you know, his intensity. That was a good thing to see as a player—that your coach has the same kind of intensity."

Dawson: "He could get excited about *everything.* He wasn't as reserved as Coach Noll. He got so fired up, like he was a player. Players feed on that as well. It was like having another player on the sideline who you could look up to—you wanted to do well by him."

Thanksgivings, Billy would come to the family home for dinner, but bring a notepad and scribble notes while games were on TV. His Thanksgiving Day 1998 loss in Detroit—you know, the Jerome Bettis overtime coin flip where the Steelers lost both the botched flip and the game—remained one of his lowest lows, a loss the family remembers him absorbing the worst in all his Steelers days. The players must've noticed: They lapsed into a five-game tailspin.

It turned into a three-year tailspin.

First, to think that Thanksgiving loss was worse than losing the AFC championship game at home, in his third Steelers year, on January 15, 1995, is a considerably hefty concept. Then, to think it was even worse than losing Super Bowl XXX and yet another AFC championship game at Three Rivers Stadium, on January 11, 1998, to a Denver team he beat barely a month earlier? Unconscionable. But the free-fall after that Detroit loss was pronounced.

The six-year playoff run crashed to earth.

Starting Thanksgiving Day 1998, Cowher's teams went 6-15 through the end of the 1999 season. They compiled back-to-back losing records, a five-game losing streak starting in Detroit and ending in a 7-9 record, then a 6-10 mark the next season. Noll had losing seasons in 1985 and 1986, but you needed to go back to the beginning to find three in a row: Noll's first three years, 1969–1971.

What if Cowher lost a third straight season?

A power struggle ensued. Personalities and work clashed at the franchise's football top. Rooney made the difficult choice of firing a former ball boy and scout, a man who was almost like family around the Steelers offices: Tom Donahoe, who had ascended to director of football operations two weeks before Cowher arrived. He was gone seven years, three AFC championship games, and one Super Bowl loss later, after that second losing season in 1999.

Cowher interviewed Colbert, another product of North Catholic (where the Rooney boys attended) and BLESTO by way of the Detroit Lions. A new Steeler dawn rose. Then the team went 9-7 and missed the playoffs for a third year.

It was the longest such drought since 1985–1988 under Noll. And 1969–1971 before that.

"Just because we don't make the playoffs one year doesn't mean that we'll make a change," Rooney said.

"Mr. Rooney is a football guy," Cowher said at the time. "He was very supportive through the three nonplayoff years, and I'm very appreciative of that, and will always understand that and appreciate that patience."

Dale: "There were some tough years. That was tough. We realized he just didn't have a quarterback. What, they had three losing seasons, which was unheard of. There was a minority of people who wanted him out. But I don't really think the majority wanted him to leave. I mean, you knew he was a good coach. They were just having a tough time. The first six years, you were in the playoffs. Nobody had done that since Paul Brown. Then . . . it was ugly. . . . Kaye, she was the one who raised the girls, did the shopping, walked down the aisles and heard the stuff."

Aaron Smith, defensive end 1999–2011: "My first year of starting was my second year. He comes to me and says, real quietly during the middle of practice, 'You know what, Aaron, you're playing really well. You just keep going. Keep doing what you're doing.' Real subtle. No one else knows you're talking.

"Being a young guy, I needed to hear that so badly."

Toward the close of the 2000 season, his Steelers won four of their final five as they shut down Three Rivers. The foundation for a decade started to fall into place: Aaron Smith, Casey Hampton, James Farrior, Alan Faneca, Hines Ward . . . A 23-8-1 combined 2001 and 2002, with a disappointing AFC championship game loss to New England in that first season, led to another dour year: a five-game losing streak, a departure from the run-first attitude, and a 6-10 season. So for 2004, Cowher brought back LeBeau and drafted . . . a quarterback? Make no mistake, Ben Roethlisberger was his choice, too.

The blitz and the bullish ground game returned with the vengeance of a Cowher sneer, important facets both to ease Ben Roethlisberger's transition once Tommy Maddox got hurt and to regain that Steelers mojo. They went 26-6 in Roethlisberger's inaugural two seasons. They handed him the ball in his second postseason, and let him wing them to four road victories and Lombardi Trophy No. 4.

Russ Grimm, offensive line coach and assistant head coach 2001–2006: "Before you get here, you definitely hear, 'Shoot, Bill's gonna be a tough guy to work for. He stays tough on his coaches.' But once you get here. . . . If you did a good job and you know what you're doing and your guys play hard, he . . . left you alone. Like if the guys made mental mistakes, offsides penalties, you were held accountable. . . . The demand for success. I mean, he always set the bar high."

Troy Polamalu, safety 2003– : "He really fought for his players. I thought he had a really good balance, being a players' coach as well as maintaining his superiority over everybody. He was both encouraging and coaching at the same time.

"One of the funny stories was during the Super Bowl year. He was talking about keeping your focus, your eyes on the prize. He was talking about how Christopher Columbus discovered America" on a journey people considered impossible, a metaphor for the Steelers' road to XL. "I had to correct him. 'Actually, he landed in, like, the West Indies.' 'Oh, you know what the hell I meant.' Yeah, I told him."

Max Starks, offensive tackle 2004– :

Here's the funny thing: I *saw* him at my Pro Day [at Florida], because he was the only head coach who was there. I'll never forget, I weighed in on the scale, and you're supposed to turn around and look at the scouts and everything after. And all I can see is Coach Cowher standing out in the crowd, the chin jutted out. He's nodding his head up and down. Then I don't see him the rest of the Pro Day. He left after that. So I definitely didn't think I was getting drafted here. Then I got that phone call, the first time I spoke to him.

Actually, when he first called me . . . , he asked me, "Do you like cold weather?" I said, "I'll play anywhere if you pay me." "Do you like being tough?" I'm like, "Uhh, I'm an offensive lineman." He said, "Good, 'cause we just drafted your ass." So that was my introduction to actually speaking to Coach Cowher for the first time ever.

On the Super Bowl XL victory podium: Hines Ward, son Jaden, Jerome Bettis with the Lombardi Trophy borne aloft, broadcaster Mike Tirico, Bill and Kaye Cowher. (Courtesy of the Pittsburgh Steelers)

Okay, this cannot wait any longer.

About, um, the proclivity to . . . you know . . . get excited and make someone else's face moist?

Dale: "The spitting."

"That's a family thing."

Dawson: "Oh, yeah, it happened to all of us. He would get so excited and passionate. He loved the game so much. He could spray you a little bit."

Kevin Greene: "I enjoyed him coming up and swearing in my face and getting in my grill. Not that I was doing anything wrong, just that 'Leeeeeeettt's go Greene, let's goooo.' He's spitting all over me with that jaw and chin and everything. I've been kind of known to spit, too. So we're spitting and slobbering all over each other. 'You're damn right, coach. Let's go. Let's go.'"

Dorothy: "Did you see the time his glasses fell off on the sideline?"

Dale: "That didn't work. Had to get laser surgery."

Dorothy: "They used to say, 'Here comes the Jaw.'"

Dale: "That was my dad. My dad had that jaw."

Dorothy: "He's the picture of his father."

Dale: "My dad? He might get a little upset with the umpires [when coaching youth baseball]. But not at kids. And nobody messed with him."

When any Steeler—player, coach, employee—got the Jaw and the projectile saliva, that wasn't good.

That meant pure, passionate, 212-Fahrenheit anger.

LeBeau, a Hall of Famer, remember, and the inventor of the zone blitz: "I don't know anybody who worked for him and didn't get the Jaw. That was a condition of employment."

Polamalu: "Oh yeah, he got angry at me. Big time."

Dawson, admitting that the spraying and excitement was acceptable, but . . . : "No-no-no-no, you didn't want the Jaw. 'Cause you knew then he wasn't happy with you."

Foote: "Being one of the young linebackers at the time, if Joey [Porter] and them were messing up, or Farrior, I was going to take the heat. He gave it to them. He evened it out. But I knew if we were having a bad game, I knew I better not mess up, 'cause I was going to get what I had coming to me—plus theirs."

James Farrior, inside linebacker 2002–2011: "We knew coming to that sideline, if he was fussing at you, you just walked the other way. [Breaking into a dandy Cowher impersonation.] 'Hey . . . I know you hear me! I know you can hear me!' Just keep on walking. Can't make eye contact with him."

Photographs around Dorothy Cowher's apartment offer a peek.

Super Bowl XL, when the parents stayed in Pittsburgh because Laird the old manager couldn't handle Ford Field and the travel, was a crowning moment.

Dale: "Ohhhhh, I was so happy for him. He worked so hard. And, finally, it paid off."

One season after the glory, the middle Cowher boy retired, reunited with his wife and the last of his basketball-playing daughters at their Raleigh, North Carolina, home. He worked as a CBS studio analyst and enjoyed the gig. Kaye died from cancer in July 2010. Cowher returned to Pittsburgh to coach one last time at Heinz Field—in fictional football, for the 2011 Batman production *The Dark Knight Rises,* the latest in the series from Steelers part owner and Hollywood mogul Thomas Tull. Colbert acted as one of Cowher's Gotham assistants. Roethlisberger and Ward were among the players. Old times. Drama, after all, was his forte.

Another photograph by the mother's door shows their old Crafton house and a street sign above a smiling Jaw.

Dale: "Of all the trophies and honors he got, the things that meant the most to him were the alley behind the house—Cowher Way—and when Carlynton retired his jersey."

Local Boy.

MIKE TOMLIN

College: William and Mary • **Years as Steelers coach:** 2007–
• **Record:** 60-28

The mentor's mentor was Chuck Noll. Noll's protégé's protégé almost became a lawyer, and Noll attended law school. More-over, the Steelers' third coach in almost a half century carried the same credentials as his predecessor, Bill Cowher: defensive coordinator, fiery gent, 34 years of age. Noll, of course, was 37 and a secondary coach. Interestingly, that was Mike Tomlin's previous calling, too.

So the third in this historic line of coaches wasn't so unlike the two celebrated men who came before him: He was a teacher, he was a motivator.

He was a winner.

He was indeed far more loquacious, far less of a jutting jaw, and African American—the first minority head coach in the Steelers' history. Even that innovation followed in Noll footsteps: Tomlin's mentor, Tony Dungy, was the first African American defensive coordinator in the NFL and certainly the youngest to that point, at age 28 when the 1984 Steelers season began.

Dungy, who hired him as Tampa Bay's secondary coach: "I interviewed him in 2001, and in 15 minutes you could tell he was going to be special. He was smart, he could communicate the game. He was at the University of Cincinnati at the time. To see him go full circle . . . and see him be successful, it is a gratifying feeling."

There's success, and then there's Tomlin's first four-year term: two Super Bowls, one championship, 12 victories per season on average.

Granted, he inherited players—and Hall of Fame defensive coordinator Dick LeBeau—from Cowher's Super Bowl XL victor. But only 13 of those starters were still around for Super Bowl XLIII and just 10 for XLV.

Troy Polamalu, safety 2003– : "I love Coach Tomlin. He's such a psychologist. Just the way that he prepares our team. The way he's constantly coming up with new ways to challenge us. He's probably my favorite head coach that I've ever had.

"Yeah, I know." The favorite over a player's coach, Cowher? The favorite over the rah-rah collegiate success that was Pete Carroll at USC? "Hall of Fame college coaches. Hall of Fame

Mike Tomlin peers onto the field at Cleveland Browns Stadium in one of his first few seasons as coach. (Courtesy of the Pittsburgh Steelers)

professional coaches. What else can you say about a coach. How long has he been here . . . , four years? So half the time he's been in the Super Bowl. I would definitely have to say he's the best coach in football."

Ben Roethlisberger, quarterback 2004– : "I just appreciate an open-door policy. I know all coaches say, 'Come talk to me whenever you want.' But I really feel he and I can talk about [anything]; we can laugh and joke and feel free."

Ryan Clark, safety who played for Hall of Fame coach Joe Gibbs in Washington before coming to the Steelers in 2006: "Most caring coach I've ever been around. Most understanding. A coach that relates to the players and also listens to the players. That's all you can ask for.

"A family-first guy. And the family includes the team. It's been a blessing to be able to play for him."

Kevin Colbert, director of football operations and general manager 2000– : "The competitiveness, the intelligence . . . , if you look at any successful coach, those factors are there. Mike's unique ability is he understands today's players—there are things that I don't recognize in the players that he sees right away. He can separate himself. He understands them. But he's not in that group. Mike understands the big picture."

Much like Cowher replacing an eventual Hall of Famer in Noll, Tomlin followed a fellow with some Canton credentials himself: two Super Bowls, six AFC championship games (one more than Noll), and a winning percentage better than even his legendary predecessor (.619 to Noll's .572). Tough act to follow there.

Tomlin didn't even try to act the same. Of course, that wouldn't have been Michael Pettaway Tomlin.

Bill Hillgrove, play-by-play announcer 1994– : "Two different people. Cowher kind of had to let you know who the boss was. Tomlin, that's not important to him. He knows you know. Sometimes, Cowher had to reaffirm that."

James Farrior, inside linebacker 2002–2011: "Mike T . . . . , he's a little different in that aspect. He doesn't fuss at his players, get all up in you. He lets the coaches pretty much be the coaches. But he's a fiery guy on the sidelines, too. He gets pumped up.

"Both great coaches, though."

Aaron Smith, defensive end 1999–2011: "The first sit-down with him, just talking to him, how personable, how impressive he was. A complete stranger, and you instantly felt comfortable with him. Like you've known him for a long time."

Colbert: "I think when he first came, he was very determined to establish who he was. . . . He understood he was following a Super Bowl–winning coach who left on his own terms. Usually, when you're a head coach coming in, the previous coach has failed. That wasn't the situation here. He set the standard he was going to follow. . . . But he was going to put his own stamp on it. Which he did right from the get-go. Which was difficult for the players: 'We have a routine, we've been successful, we know how to win.'"

"Obviously, success followed."

In February 2009, at 36, he became the youngest coach to win a Super Bowl. Age has been a factor with his Steelers. But it's a fine line they're careful not to cross.

Polamalu: "My favorite saying that he has is, 'I'm going to treat everybody fair, but I'm not going to treat everybody the same.' I love that saying. He's got a great discernment as a coach. He knows when to push players. He's really awesome at that."

Charlie Batch, quarterback 2002– : "He lets you know not everybody is on the same level. I like that. I have a different relationship with him because he's only three years older than I am. So me, Farrior, and Hines, all of us guys, we can talk to him a little differently than some of the rookies can. Similar in age."

Smith: "Coach T. always has a special spot with me. Obviously, when my son was diagnosed, he came to see us at the hospital that day." Elijah, then four, was diagnosed with leukemia in October 2008, Tomlin's second season. "He and I . . . we have a lot of moments. Those are genuine, real moments."

Tomlin keeps it real, all right. The potential lawyer—his receiver mate and best friend at William and Mary, Upper St. Clair (Pennsylvania) High graduate Terrence Hammons, went on to become a high-powered attorney—believes in the truth, the whole truth, and nothing but. As one of his Minnesota charges, defensive lineman Pat Williams, put it when he offered advice to the Steelers before Tomlin's first camp: "If you don't want to hear the truth, ask to be traded."

Tape sessions, entitled "News," could be downright eviscerating. His view remained, if it was the tale of the tape, it was a record of the play, of the performance, of the execution.

Farrior: "Oh, yeah, he's definitely honest. You don't want to get caught on tape; you don't want to be on the film study that Monday. In front of everybody, all of your peers. It can be brutal sometimes. But I think that's a good way for our team to be—up front and honest about everything."

Clark: "But you like that, though. The coaches that are hard to play for are the coaches that change on you from day to day. [There are] coaches you don't know what you're going to get. One day, you see me in the hall and say 'hello.' I play bad, you feel like you can't talk to me that next day? Those aren't the kind of people you want to be around, the kind of people you don't want to go out and fight for. Coach Tomlin's not like that. He's honest with everyone. He's honest with the positive, and he's honest with the negative."

He is exacting, and he exacts the same as Cowher before him. There is no coasting in these Steelers. There is no individual play, or if found it soon gets excised. There is no Buddy Parker publicly excoriating or firing players. There is no excuse for an injury necessitating a backup or even a backup's backup to play.

The standard is the standard.

Hillgrove: "One thing about Cowher's teams, and Tomlin has continued it: Players don't take snaps off. Like you see on other teams. And we're spoiled. Not going to the playoffs is the end of the world. Seven and nine is the end of the world. How could we handle 3-13? We couldn't; people would be jumping off the Sixth Street Bridge."

So how did the son of a single mother, a kid from Newport News, Virginia, and a bouncer whose Williamsburg, Virginia, tavern owner paid him in sandwiches, come to be the head coach of the Steelers?

Almost by accident. His career path found him late at William and Mary. An assistant coach advised him about a coaching opening at Virginia Military, and Tomlin wrote a letter to then-head coach Bill Stewart, who later wound up as West Virginia University's head coach. "I am extremely eager to pursue a career in coaching. . . . Very truly yours, Michael P. Tomlin." The newlywed worked for a stipend and barely $12,000 a year in 1995—the same year Cowher was steering the Steelers to Super Bowl XXX. Tomlin's mother, Julia Copeland, raised her voice in the retelling: "He told me he wanted to be a coach, and I just went ballistic. 'We sent you to William and Mary, and you want to *coach?*'"

The man plotted a course, though he probably never figured it would take him to Memphis, Tennessee-Martin (for a matter of days), Arkansas State, Cincinnati, and then Dungy, curmudgeonly defensive coordinator Monte Kiffin, and a Buccaneers secondary that included Ronde Barber and John Lynch.

Lynch, older than his new coach, went into the office for a chat and Tomlin produced a detailed breakdown of 63 plays on tape from that season, the techniques employed, the techniques unused. Lynch was sold.

After one season as the Minnesota Vikings' defensive coordinator, he began his interview pursuit of a head-coaching job. Atlanta, Arizona, Miami, and Pittsburgh were open. He told his mother he would land one of those four.

His mother told me six months later: "When he was interviewing for the Steelers' job, I was trying to prepare him because I really didn't think he was going to get it—you don't go from being a coordinator in one year to head coach. You know, and he's young. I said, 'Michael, look . . . learn all you can going through the process so the next time you get called, you'll be ready.'" She shrugged. "He got one."

Art Rooney II: "It's fair to say his interview was very impressive and probably something that we weren't expecting. We didn't know Mike. So it was a first-time meeting. It wasn't like we came out of that meeting saying, 'Here's our guy.' But we came out saying, 'This guy certainly is a candidate.' The first meeting was a real eye-opener for us. The process went on from there. He interviewed for the Miami job in the same time frame. He was being sought after by other teams as well."

Dungy: "So much of what he believes about the game and about life are similar [to the Steelers' way]. You could see it was going to be a great fit. I think that's what Dan saw." He remembers getting a call in the midst of playoff preparations, Dungy's Indianapolis Colts beating New England in the AFC championship game and en route to a Super Bowl XLI championship. "I got a call from Dan Rooney. I knew Dan wouldn't be calling me [so deep in the playoffs] if it wasn't an important question. 'Tell me about Mike Tomlin. We really like the guy.' I was really excited, 'cause I knew it was the perfect fit. I told him, 'You're going to the best situation. You're really going to enjoy it.'"

Ben Roethlisberger and Mike Tomlin confer during a 2010 rout over the Oakland Raiders, the Steelers' archrival so many decades earlier. (George Gojkovich)

STEELERS ASSISTANTS WHO BECAME HEAD COACHES

NFL—Gus Dorais (Lions), Joe Kuharich (Cardinals, Redskins, and Eagles), Buster Ramsey (AFL Bills), Nick Skorich (Eagles and Browns), Bud Carson (Browns), Rod Rust (Patriots), Tony Dungy (Buccaneers and Colts), Dom Capers (Panthers), John Fox (Panthers and Broncos), Mike Mularkey (Bills and Jaguars), Jim Haslett (Saints), Dick LeBeau (Bengals), Marvin Lewis (Bengals), Ken Whisenhunt (Cardinals), Chan Gailey (Cowboys and Bills).

Other pro leagues—Woody Widenhofer (United States Football League–Oklahoma), George Perles (USFL–Philadelphia), Rollie Dotsch (USFL–Birmingham), Charlie Sumner (USFL–Oakland), Babe Parilli (World Football League–New York/Chicago).

Major colleges—Carl DePasqua (Pitt), Perles (Michigan State), Joe Walton (Robert Morris), Widenhofer (Missouri and Vanderbilt), Ron Zook (Florida and Illinois).

The Golfing Assistant

Frank Souchek, a 1946 Steelers assistant under Jock Sutherland and an end on the 1939 Pirates, was better known with other clubs—golf clubs, that is.

Soucheck was an amateur golfer of some repute, particularly in Western Pennsylvania . . . where his bright and shining moment arrived. He shot a first-round 70 and wound up finishing as the low amateur—in a three-way tie for ninth overall—at the 1953 U.S. Open at Oakmont Country Club, where he was a member. (He would've won $325 were it not for his amateur status; Ben Hogan got $5,000 for the championship.) Frank's younger brother Mike Souchak was a 15-time winner on the PGA Tour and two-time Ryder Cup representative, and the siblings won the team competition at the 1967 Bing Crosby National Pro-Am.

The Band of Aides

It's a story line rarely noted, but the staffs under the past three Steelers' coaches alone have produced 11 NFL head coaches starting with Bud Carson in 1989 and him at the tender age of 58 years young.

The tally through roughly a quarter century: Bill Cowher seven, Chuck Noll four.

Granted, expansion and less-patient owners helped to swell Cowher's numbers a mite.

Some of the coaches who blossomed from the Noll tree served longer tenures in the college ranks, such as Rose Bowl–winning George Perles at Michigan State, Woody Widenhofer at Missouri and Vanderbilt, and Joe Walton at Robert Morris, a decorated Division I-AA program that he launched. Another handful coached in the fledgling rival pro leagues that came and went: Widenhofer, Perles (though he never got to game day there because Michigan State hired him), Rollie Dotsch, and Charlie Sumner in the United States Football League, Babe Parilli in the World Football League and Arena League. Noll did, however, send along to NFL head-coaching stops Carson with the Cleveland Browns, Rod Rust with the New England Patriots, and John Fox to a Super Bowl berth with the Carolina Panthers and later to a job with the Denver Broncos, plus Tony Dungy to a Super Bowl championship with the Colts and inaugural success with the Buccaneers.

Cowher's lucky seven all became NFL head coaches, some meeting with considerable success: Dom Capers with the Panthers, Jim Haslett with the Saints, Dick LeBeau and Marvin Lewis with the Bengals, Mike Mularkey with the Jaguars, Chan Gailey with the Bills, and the Cardinals' Ken Whisenhunt, who wound up losing to Mike Tomlin's Steelers in Super Bowl XLIII.

John Banaszak, Steelers defensive lineman 1975–1981 and later a college coach: "The best thing Chuck did was have those assistant coaches. And he let the coaches coach. That's why he hired them."

The avalanche of assistants started with tragedy. On April 24, 1971, while scouting Cal State–Long Beach, defensive line coach Walt Hackett, 47, collapsed and died. He was the first assistant Noll hired in 1969. He was the coach who formulated the company policy to give defensive linemen nicknames: Hollywood Bags, or Holly for short, to L. C. Greenwood, and so on. Two years into rebuilding, two and a half months from training camp, Noll started to rebuild his coaching staff with college coaches he first met in the interview process to replace the late Hackett.

Dan "Bad Rad" Radakovich, whose first of two Steelers stints came in replacing Hackett: "I was a linebackers coach. I called [Noll] on the phone. I was at the University of Cincinnati. I was the defensive coordinator going to law school." And the Steelers, his hometown team, suddenly needed a defensive line coach. "I couldn't live on my salary at Cincinnati. I got him right on the phone, and he didn't know me from Adam. I hung up the phone, 'There's no job there.' The next day, he called me back. He's all wired up. I'm talking to a different guy."

Noll had lined up five interviews before Radakovich threw in his own name. Radakovich offered to drive to Pittsburgh the next day for an interview, and a week later after completing the other interviews Noll hired him. "I'm sure Perles was one of them."

George Perles, assistant 1972–1981: "He was looking for a defensive line coach. I came in for an interview. It was interesting. I came in and interviewed; he was talking to one other guy. The other guy was Dan Radakovich. He called me Monday morning after I came back and said he was coaching the linebackers, he was going to hire Dan Radakovich to coach the defensive line then move him to linebackers after a year. So after the [1971] season, I came into Pittsburgh recruiting and went over to the Steelers offices. I came home and thought, 'Boy, I got fooled.' So one day I called him, 'Were you trying to call me coach? . . .' I heard from John McVay, who was the head coach at Dayton; [he] and Chuck Noll were good friends. McVay said, 'I think he's going to call you, he was just checking up on you.' He called; we were on the phone six minutes. He offered me a position, and I didn't know a car came with it." The offer: coach the defensive line in place of Radakovich, who's leaving for Colorado despite, he said, Noll offering him the defensive-coordinator job first. The salary was $19,000, a 50 percent raise over his Michigan State salary. He later recommended fellow Big Ten assistants Tom Moore, Rollie Dotsch, and Bob "Woody" Widenhofer, a former Michigan State graduate assistant under Perles. Radakovich, by the way, returned soon after: By 1974, he was coaching the Steelers' offensive line.

Banaszak: "There were legendary discussions in the coaches meetings. They would go at it pretty good."

Joe Walton, 1990–1991 offensive coordinator and later a college head coach with Banaszak at Robert Morris: "It was still that way when I got there [a decade later]."

Banaszak: "You'd take Woody and Bud and George, and they would hash it out. [Noll] would come to an agreement. And when the meeting was over, that's the way it was going to be. I remember the story about when they put in the stunt 4–3 defense before the playoffs in '74. Chuck said, 'You can't tilt the [defensive] tackle over the center like that.' I understand that meeting went for about three hours before they finally settled and George won: 'I'm going to put Joe Greene in a tilt position over the center.' They held the Raiders to 19 yards rushing and the Vikings to 17 yards rushing [in the next two games to win Super Bowl IX]. Because nobody knew how to block it. I think that's a sign of success, when you're able to listen and have everyone's opinion."

Radakovich: "When I was [offensive] line coach, I told everybody to play like linebackers. I taught them hands-on run and pass [showing punch blocking]."

Joe Greene and Jack Lambert, the leaders of the defense, chat with their leader—defensive coordinator George Perles—in 1975. (George Gojkovich)

Jon Kolb, center–tackle 1969–1981 and a Noll assistant 1982–1991: "Tunch [Ilkin] and Larry [Brown] had a season where they gave up only one sack. I gave up two a year for four years. [Bad Rad], he probably deserves more credit than I do. Chuck Noll and Dan Radakovich changed the game from where people ran into each other to a game where they hit each other. The same-foot, same-shoulder technique, Chuck started that. [Radakovich would keep the linemen in meetings and film watching until 10, 11 at night.] Rad and Chuck were such innovators."

Ralph Berlin, trainer 1968–1993: "It was the right fit at the right time. Bad Rad coached the offensive line. George was George. He was a tough son of B. And the players really loved him. George brought Woody, and Woody was a great linebacker coach."

Andy Russell, linebacker 1963, 1966–1976: "Bud Carson was a genius. It was unbelievable what he could do." One game against rival Cincinnati, Carson went through three separate defensive game plans, installing the last one in the tunnel during pregame introductions. "Years later, I was at a party in San Francisco, and I went over to talk with [then Bengals assistant and later 49ers head coach] Bill Walsh. I said, 'Coach, I don't know if you knew this, but when we played your Bengals, we wouldn't call a defense in the huddle.' He said, 'You gotta be kidding.' 'No, that's what Bud Carson asked us to do.' 'I couldn't figure out what defense you were running.'"

Mike Wagner, safety 1971–1980: "Chuck's usually not friendly. But on Sunday he would [get around to most of the guys in pregame]. He didn't talk to us a lot, but [this particular game day in Cincinnati] he said, 'Remember, Mike, when they come out in that formation, we check into this defense.' I said, 'No, Chuck, Bud just changed it. In the tunnel.' Bud would get a thought, or see something, or hear something, and decide, 'I want you to do something different.'

"Bill Walsh couldn't believe it. Every time they shifted their offense, we would change our defense. I thought offenses knew we did that. Particularly the Cowboys. Communication was key. We had all those hand signals. I used to be doing this with a 'V' [holding up his first two fingers]. And there was a newspaper once that wrote, 'Mike Wagner signals V for victory.' No, that was 'Cover-2.' You mean opponents didn't see it? When I had my fingers up, that signaled I was changing the defense."

Kolb: "Tony Dungy . . . there's the guy who taught me defense. I remember Tony and I were teammates. Then he was a coach. Then I was a coach, and we were roommates. Yes, I thought [he'd be a successful coach]. Tony's dad was kind of my mentor, too. He was a professor there in Detroit. I would bring my books on the road and meet with his dad."

Tony Dungy, Steelers assistant and coordinator 1981–1988: "That was Coach Noll's philosophy—you know offense, so you know how to attack a defense. So you can coach defense. That was the way he did things. [In 1984,] the USFL came in and we lost George Perles—George went to Michigan State [after the Philadelphia Stars] and Woody Widenhofer went to the [Oklahoma Outlaws]. He said, 'You know more about the defense than anybody I could find.' I was 29 at the time. He knew I understood the defense. Kind of like how you were expected to be the next person to go in at quarterback" even though you were a safety and both Terry Bradshaw and Mike Kruczek get hurt.

Gary Dunn, defensive lineman 1977–1987: "I was in the game when [Dungy] threw an interception [two, actually] and made an interception. That was in Houston. We ran out of quarterbacks. He might have well been a coach back then; he was in the film room all that time. All of us linemen, we thought, 'What are you doing in there so long?'"

Dom Capers, defensive coordinator 1992–1994: "I remember interviewing with Bill [Cowher]; we talked to the wee hours of the morning. Then he offered me the job. We hired Dick LeBeau. . . . Dick and I sort of roomed together at Allegheny Center until we could get permanent places. So we spent a lot of nights at Three Rivers Stadium putting that [900-page defensive] notebook together. He's a unique guy.

"We probably worked 2½, 3 months on it. Back then, we had no computers in the office. A lot of the drawings were done by hand. I have in my office in Green Bay the original notebook. . . . They were done with a template and pencil. And the secretary stayed in there until 11 o'clock at night typing.

"Amazing how things have changed. In 1992, we didn't have a computer on the football side of things for the Pittsburgh Steelers."

LeBeau: "I drew 'em all. Dom and Bill would get in a room and meet until about 2 A.M. I'd always try to go home because I knew the next day I'd always be drawing."

Gerald Williams, nose tackle–defensive end 1986–1994: "LeBeau was picking his brain, and vice versa."

Kevin Greene, outside linebacker 1993–1995: "It was really a unique time because of history. They were hanging out late at night, going at contests at the blackboard. They gave birth to the zone-blitz defense that rose to prevalence around the league. Showed quarterbacks different looks. They were just mapping that stuff out from square one. It was neat to be a part of that, in that place and that time period."

Ryan Clark, safety 2006– : "Coach LeBeau understands football. Coach LeBeau understands matchups. That's the confidence you have when you have a legend and a Hall of Famer as your defensive coordinator."

Capers, whose Green Bay Packers faced the Steelers in Super Bowl XLV: "It's amazing to me the continuity the Steelers have been able to have, especially on the defensive side of the ball. With Dick being there, a lot of the same things we started doing in 1992 there they're still doing now. That's one thing that's unique about the Steelers. They've been able to have a system, they've been able to draft to that system, they've been able to have more continuity than anybody else in the National Football League. You look around at franchises, there's a new coach every three years, a new system—that affects the salary cap, the whole deal."

5

Scouting

JOCK SUTHERLAND tried to bring the Steelers into modern times. In 1947, he hired what was believed to be the second full-time scout in the NFL. They had a falling out, but the idea was to be lauded, if not the execution. They replaced the fired scout, for the most part, with an undertaker.

Not until the mid-1960s did the Steelers seem to learn the scouting trade, and it took one of Art Rooney's sons to bring the club up to sea level.

ART ROONEY JR.
1960–1987

This was a franchise bereft of either effective talent evaluation or luck in affairs of the draft.

Their first pick was a William Shakespeare—we couldn't make this up. Better known as Bill, this Notre Dame end was the Steelers' No. 1 choice, third overall, in the inaugural NFL draft of 1936. Shakespeare declined to play for the woebegone franchise and instead accepted a job at the Cincinnati Rubber Company. Perhaps that in itself was an omen for a club that failed to reach the game's biggest stage for another thirty-eight years. Was it to be, or not to be?

They made Gary Glick the bonus pick, first overall in 1956. Pittsburghers still giggle over that one. Gary Glick the bonus pick—an NFL gift choice in an attempt to gain parity. No cornerback has been selected first overall in a half century since.

They hired as their first full-time scout a man, Pat Livingston, who soon after went onto his life's work as a sportswriter.

They used to compile information with the help of a mortician name of Digger Byrnes. He replaced the sportswriter.

Another sportswriter tale of the draft: In 1953, Jack Sell of the *Pittsburgh Post-Gazette* urged Art Rooney Sr. to select Pitt's Joe Schmidt. The Chief told him to shut up—he wanted Schmidt, too, and hoped his coaches wouldn't dismiss the chatter of a lowly sportswriter. As the story goes, the undertaker Byrnes jumped up in the seventh round and shouted down the Lions' choice as ineligible. The Lions, as rules allowed then, reneged on their pick and chose the player Rooney wanted. Schmidt became a Hall of Famer in Detroit.

Another tale of missed draft opportunities: Johnny Unitas (whom they selected in 1955 and summarily cut), Lenny Moore, and the great Jim Brown all could've played in the same Steelers backfield; they were ripe for plucking on the Steelers' draft turn.

No wonder the media and fans became so inured to the Steelers' evaluation foibles that, after the 1972 draft, the

Art Rooney Jr. sits in front of his stacks of scouting information, data that helped to produce two of the most acclaimed drafts in NFL history—producing five Hall of Famers and more than a dozen Super Bowl starters. (George Gojkovich)

Post-Gazette's esteemed Charley Feeney—inducted later into baseball's Hall of Fame—wrote: "Steelers scouts took lessons from the men who touted Custer." And that was the draft where they landed Franco Harris, he of the club's inaugural playoff triumph thanks to his Immaculate Reception (see Sidebar in Chapter 8, pp. 158–162) and the MVP of the club's inaugural Super Bowl.

Into this yawning void strode a burly fellow trained as an actor.

Rooney progeny, no less.

Art Rooney Jr: "I'm going to be really frank: It's pure, 100 percent nepotism. I got involved in ticket selling [1960–1961]. They liked my wife, . . . and they didn't want me to blow that one. So they gave me a job. We couldn't sell tickets. We stunk and we had a bad stadium [for football]. I got the job in the fervent thought, 'Well, nobody could ever say I'm lazy or stupid,' although I often wondered that myself. But I fell in love with the scouting department. Our scouts then were all assistant coaches, Jack Butler and those guys, I would hang around. I came up with a truism: 'You can lose with good football players, but you cannot win without them.'

"Good thing the old man owned the team, I could tell you that."

So the actor-come-scout evaluated college talent in the early 1960s, which was akin to working as a nurse at undertaker Byrnes' day job—utterly useless. Buddy Parker traded away most of his significant draft choices, he so despised rookies.

Roy McHugh, longtime sportswriter, columnist, and editor at the Pittsburgh Press: "Then Bill Austin wouldn't even listen. 'We're not drafting your ace from Grambling, we're drafting this guy. . . .'"

Jack Butler, defensive back 1951–1959 and assistant/scout before leaving for the Bears, Lions, Eagles, and Steelers Talent Organization in 1963: "Artic was a kid. Before BLESTO, I was doing some scouting for Pittsburgh. So was Ken Stilley. Art and I would go on the road for a week, two weeks. Chicago, New England, New York. Ask questions. Measure them. He did everything. He worked hard at it. Artie really worked hard at it."

Art Jr.: "I look back, I thought I knew about football, but I really didn't. Didn't know diddly about it."

He watched. He listened. He learned from Butler and Stilley, talent evaluators he considered his mentors.

It wasn't until Chuck Noll's arrival in 1969 that Art Jr. found a kindred scouting spirit on the Steelers coaching staff. The day after Noll arrived, they drafted Joe Greene, L. C. Greenwood, and Jon Kolb. The next year came Terry Bradshaw and Mel Blount, Hall of Famers in two of their opening three selections. In 1971 came Jack Ham, Mike Wagner, and the rest of the Steel Curtain—Dwight White and Ernie Holmes—among seven total Super Bowl starters.

That same 1971, he formally became the vice president of player personnel.

Bill Nunn Sr., the Pittsburgh Courier *sports editor whose Black College All-American teams led the Steelers to hire him as a scout:* "Artic had a top work cthic. The ability to listen. A great ability, really, to judge players—more so than he was given credit for. And his recall on things was really outstanding. When I'd go down to the Roosevelt Hotel [scouting office], which was the office next to the john . . . , we'd stay there until three or four in the morning getting ready for the draft."

Art Jr.: "Noll came in, and I couldn't stand him. He was like the toughest professor you ever had. But, of course, Noll was phenomenal. He was the one who changed everything."

The first two Noll–Rooney Jr. drafts built the Steel Curtain. An animated Joe Greene, with L. C. Greenwood on the ground behind him, wages yet another close game— a one-point loss at home—against the rival Cincinnati Bengals in 1980. (Bill Amatucci)

McHugh: "Art Jr. is much more personable than Dan—more like their father. Art Jr. was the sportswriter's friend; he was honest and forthcoming. He talked a lot. Dan, Art Sr., and Noll didn't like that."

Joe Gordon, publicity director and vice president, 1969–1998: "Certainly Art, he operated in the shadow of his dad and his older brother.

"If you look at the drafts before Art took control and after, it's no contest. He grew into the job. Became a very astute evaluator of talent. And probably really never got as much credit. Once you had the Chief, Dan, and Noll, all Hall of Famers, there wasn't room [for more credit].

"He was just so well organized. Going into those drafts, he knew exactly what they were going to do and rarely deviated."

George Perles, defensive assistant and coordinator 1972–1981: "The scouting department was super."

Noll suggested they bring aboard a pro-personnel scout, so Art Jr. one day at Villanova asked an assistant coach there—who just happened to be his cousin.

V. Tim Rooney: "He never let the coaches highjack the draft. That kept it [consistent]. He knew coaches as transitory [beings], either getting new jobs or getting fired, whatever the case may be.

"The basis of our system was BLESTO. Artie told me this: 'The system will make you.' It allowed you to have a [foundation] to begin to evaluate a player." It allowed them

That's a lot of names on the draft board behind Art Rooney Jr. in the Steelers scouting office in 1982. (George Gojkovich)

to speak the same language, rank and categorize and judge, even inject a measure of creativity. It provided structure in a liquid world.

Art Jr.: "I liked the coaches, but I didn't want to depend on them. I wanted our own scouts, somebody you could depend on, continuity."

The scouting boss compartmentalized the duties: Each scout had a geographic region, same as the BLESTO scouts. Each scout had the same scale, concept, philosophy as BLESTO. The Steelers were looking for a certain something—Noll preferred men with smarts, leverage, athleticism, and quickness, not necessarily in that order; and he didn't mind either a smaller fellow or even a tight end for an offensive lineman. They were looking for a certain personality and drive, too. And they were looking to utilize their resources the best way possible, mostly through joining BLESTO at the hip.

So Art Jr. opened a two-way relationship with Butler and BLESTO. First, by 1971, he hired a BLESTO scout who played at Pitt and for the Steelers, Dick Haley. He also began developing talent for Butler's service by using a Rooney form of nepotism: A pipeline from their old school, North Catholic High.

Kevin Colbert, whose old North Catholic coach, Ron Hughes, ascended through Art Jr.'s pseudo internship to BLESTO, later taking Colbert with him there and to the Detroit Lions: "In the personnel world, there are a lot of people from Pittsburgh and a lot with North Catholic connections. And it all goes back to Art. When he was in this position, he gave a lot of high school coaches part-time positions looking at film. What he was doing was scouting people for those positions.

"You can't underestimate the influence he had in the scouting world. Between him and Jack Butler . . . ," there followed: Haley, who later went to the New York Jets; Tom Modrak of the Philadelphia Eagles and Buffalo Bills; Chuck Connors of Miami Dolphins and Atlanta Falcons; and the Bushofsky brothers, Jack of the Carolina Panthers and Joe of Detroit. Art Jr. had his own NFL scouting tree.

Nunn Sr.: "Art helped to develop a lot of those guys . . . for Jack Butler."

The line stretched so deep that it lasted into the twenty-first century. In 1986, Art Jr. hired Tom Donahoe. So that meant he brought aboard his successors for much of the next decade and a half: Haley and Donahoe, who helped to select Bill Cowher to follow Noll.

V. Tim Rooney: "The Steeler system was probably not unlike some others; the key was continuity in the organization. By retaining very good head coaches over the decades, the team did not have to constantly adjust to new coaching philosophies and needs, did not have to deal with new coaching staffs who might bring their own various—and sometimes failed—ideas about what types of players were needed to fit their coaching concepts. The Steelers' scouts mostly had BLESTO backgrounds and shared common concepts . . . did not have to be reeducated, retrained. The coaches inherited a very good system and had the faith in the system to participate in it and not try to change it."

Dan "Bad Rad" Radakovich, defensive line coach in 1971 and offensive line coach 1974–1977: "He involved everybody. Even [trainer] Ralph Berlin went to see [players]. We weren't like other teams. We [assistant coaches] didn't just scout our positions. We scouted everybody. We all went out in the spring. I had the East. [Dick] Hoak had the Big Eight. [George] Perles and Woody [Widenhofer] had the Big Ten. [Bud] Carson [from Georgia Tech] had the South. And they used everybody's opinion.

"A lot of places, assistants were isolated from scouting. For example, I'm on the Jets. We're picking up a guy in a trade. I go up to the scouting director. I wanted to see the scouting report on this guy from college. 'Oh, noooo, you can't see that.' The Steelers, it was all open."

Well, the draft room wasn't completely open.

Given the transient nature of coaches, let alone Art Rooney Sr.'s guests to the Three Rivers Stadium offices, Art Jr. and Noll preferred to close the ranks a mite. However, through the Chief, one visitor was permitted: the Pirates manager from down the hall.

V. Tim Rooney, who spent six years with the Lions and fifteen years as the Giants pro personnel director after his 1972–1979 Steelers stint: "Anytime I begin to think I'm a smart guy in football, I think back. Danny Murtaugh was the only guy allowed in the draft room. But only for the last rounds." In those days, the Steelers hung two draft boards: one position by position, another by value accorded by Steelers scouts. "Danny was standing there, looking at the board, which was a large board. He called me over, ran his finger down the board and said, 'What about this kid? He's from my hometown [Chester, Pennsylvania], I know this kid. Played basketball. Pretty fast. Billy Johnson.' Murtagh never let me forget that." Yes, White Shoes was still on the board. He went to Houston, where he tortured the Steelers for years.

Oh, they made out that 1974 draft, anyway:

1. Lynn Swann, receiver, Southern Cal.
2. Jack Lambert, middle linebacker, Kent State
3. Traded to Oakland, who chose cornerback Maurice Spencer. No big deal.

   Received in trade for Ralph Anderson from New England, the pick that became

4a. John Stallworth, receiver, Alabama A&M
4b. Jimmy Allen, cornerback, UCLA
5. Mike Webster, center, Wisconsin

Four Hall of Famers in five picks.

V. Tim Rooney: "And I liked Jimmy Allen. A good player. I brought him up to Detroit.

"And don't forget the two free agents we got, [Randy] Grossman and [Donnie] Shell. Shell played linebacker at South Carolina State. Bill [Nunn] thought he would be a free safety."

That monumental draft paid immediate dividends.

The Steelers won the Super Bowl at the end of that season. And the next one. Then two more after the 1978 and 1979 seasons. The Super Steelers of the 1970s were all homegrown draft picks.

It was soon after that run of amazing fortune that the philosophy swerved.

McHugh: After the 1974 draft, Art Jr. "started accommodating Noll instead of . . . fighting him. From then on, he adapted his method to fit what Noll wanted. Noll was looking for great athletes who had flaws. He was a great coach who thought he could coach them out of it."

Dave Brown, Greg Hawthorne, Mark Malone, Keith Gary, Walter Abercrombie, and more proved to be nowhere close to the Hall of Fame's Greene, Bradshaw, Ham, Swann-Lambert-Stallworth-Webster drafts in the end.

FoxSports.com in 2011 ranked the greatest talent evaluators in NFL history. Bill Walsh of the San Francisco 49ers was third. Green Bay's Vince Lombardi was second.

And the winner was the actor who started out, thanks to that Rooney surname, in the Steelers ticket office before he took a shine to scouting.

Ernie Accorsi, general manager of Baltimore, Cleveland, and the Giants: "[He had] two or three of the greatest drafts in the history of the National Football League."

Colbert, about Art Jr.'s No. 1 ranking: "As it should be. No one has that kind of a record, no one has that kind of a class [as 1974]. Not only was he able to identify good players, but he was able to hire good evaluators."

Butler, who spent four decades overseeing BLESTO, on the Steelers' 1971 and 1974 pools: "Man, they were good drafts, that's all I know. I don't deserve any credit. He did it himself." With Nunn, Haley, V. Tim Rooney, and the coaches, that is.

Art Jr.: "Sixty-nine to '74, those six years. I don't know how anybody could dispute those drafts. We got Super Bowl winners. Hall of Famers."

BILL NUNN
1967–

Here was a sportswriter whom the Steelers smartly decided to hire. Actually, Bill Nunn Sr. was more than a mere sportswriter: He arose from sports editor to managing editor of the *Pittsburgh Courier*, one of the nation's most respected African American newspapers, if not *the* most respected. Among other things, Nunn Sr. had published a Black College All-America football team since 1950, and Steelers administrators were avid readers. They drafted defensive linemen Chuck Hinton, Ben McGee, and John Baker plus end Jack McClairen from Nunn Sr.'s list.

So it was a natural progression.

Art Rooney Jr.: "I like to take credit for hiring Bill Nunn, and I didn't. The Chief hired him. I met Nunn in the back offices of the Roosevelt [Hotel]. He's looking at me, and he's looking at me. We started talking. After about an hour, we realized we thought the same way.

"He opened all the doors. On the human things, he was always right. He cut through all the BS. He was a really great judge of character. He became a really good judge of talent. "

Nunn Sr.: "In '67, I was still with the paper. I covered some games every week. Then I started doing that, turning in stuff and working with Art. I'd be going down to the Roosevelt Hotel after work. Every week I was going to a different black college game. The Orange Blossom Classic, the Capital Classic in Washington, DC. So I was pretty well versed on black college football." In 1969, with Art Rooney Sr.'s approval, Dan asked Nunn to switch from part-time to full-time scouting. "I told Dan, 'I don't know if I'm ready for it. I'd like to give the paper a year's notice.' He said, 'A year?' But I was almost doing it full-time in 1969." Other journalism offers arose. "But I made the decision to come and try this. I think I was right moving on. And when I became full-time, I wasn't always seeing black programs. The one guy behind that was Chuck Noll."

He was, by *Sports Illustrated*'s accounting later, the sixth full-time African American scout in the NFL. But he proved to be the most important, the most influential. The Black College Football Hall of Fame placed Nunn Sr. among a 2010 inaugural class that included such superstars as Grambling coach Eddie Robinson, Florida A&M coach Jake Gaither, Jackson State halfback Walter Payton, Grambling defensive lineman Buck Buchanan, South Carolina State defensive end Deacon Jones, Morgan State linebacker Willie Lanier, and Mississippi Valley State wide receiver Jerry Rice.

other teams needed and planned. He long believed the most athletic player the Steelers ever drafted under his watch was Grambling's Frank Lewis in 1971's first round, though Lewis didn't begin to deliver on his promise until he was traded to Buffalo, what with Lynn Swann and John Stallworth needing to blossom. Lewis caught 269 passes in six Buffalo seasons, more than double his amount in seven Steelers years.

He remains happiest with what he calls the "down-the-liners," the latter-round picks who panned out well. That describes 7/11 of the defense, everyone but Joe Greene, Mel Blount, Jack Ham, and Jack Lambert.

Nunn Sr.: "Film can fool the hell out of you. There are a combination of things you need to see."

He saw racism, too. But he convinced folks outside football to see black *and gold.*

Nunn Sr. "The thing was, when I started going to white schools . . . I really got what I considered good assimilation even though there were places in the South where I had trouble moving into. Like hotels. They would accept blacks, and they would put you upstairs and in the back. But I would ask for downstairs facing the pool. Oh, yeah, they gave it to me. And part of it was, I was with the organization. I made it a point to have something with 'Steelers' on it. That would definitely open up doors. The places I would go to, football was high on the agenda."

Nunn Sr., by the way, adopted the Sr. when his former Steelers ball boy of a son, William G. Nunn Jr., became a Hollywood actor who eventually had seventy television and film titles to his credit.

DICK HALEY
1971–1991

A former Pitt player, Dick Haley bounced around Washington, the Steelers, and, for four games, Minnesota during his six-season NFL career. The former cornerback's mark in professional football, however, was made in picking football players who suited.

Haley was another of Jack Butler's BLESTO guys when Art Rooney Jr. plucked him for an opening created when Art Jr. was promoted to vice president of player personnel in 1971.

Haley contributed, along with Bill Nunn Sr., V. Tim Rooney, and their boss Art Jr., to the drafts that brought Franco Harris, Lynn Swann, Jack Lambert, John Stallworth, Mike Webster, J. T. Thomas, Ron Johnson, Matt Bahr, and other starters to the four-ring efforts of Super Bowls IX, X, XIII, and XIV.

When Art Jr. was pushed out the door, Haley ascended to the top of the scouting department and promptly set to drafting Rod Woodson, Greg Lloyd, Dermontti Dawson, John Jackson, Jerry Olsavsky, Carnell Lake, and Neil O'Donnell—key components to the Steelers' next contention for the ring, Super Bowl XXX.

Nunn Sr.: "Dick was a good appraiser of talent. I would like to think all three of us would have that ability. There would be disagreements, which was a healthy thing. There were times I thought I would be outvoted two to one. The one thing about scouting is, you're never going to be 100 percent right. Nobody wants to talk about their misses. I had my share of them. Everybody has.

"We got to the point that you felt we had such a good team that we drafted guys who we liked but we knew weren't

Bill Nunn, the former *Pittsburgh Courier* newspaperman whose black-college football expertise helped to make the Steelers' scouting so successful, shares a 1980 training-camp laugh with Chuck Noll. (George Gojkovich)

The schools were untapped wells. In the three drafts before Noll, the Steelers drafted two players from primarily black colleges. In Noll's first three drafts, they drafted sixteen—including players in successive rounds from Arkansas AM&N (one of them named L. C. Greenwood) and the entire Steel Curtain.

Ralph Berlin, trainer 1968–1992: "Back in those days, very few teams scouted the black schools. The Steelers were one of the few teams that did. And Bill Nunn did that. That's how they got all those players."

Jack Butler, BLESTO's boss for almost a half century: "That was some move. He worked all those guys. Oh, yeah, Bill did a good job. He's still down [at the Steelers facility working]."

Nunn Sr.: "I officially retired in 1987, and I'm still here. Every year I volunteer, and Art II says, 'Keep coming in.' I keep telling Dan all the time, 'The only reason I'm still around is, I'm older than you.'

"I've flown over two million miles. Unfortunately, that was before all the frequent-flyer [programs] and all that. That was one of the reasons I retired when I did." From full-time work. Not part-time.

Nunn's evaluation brilliance and personality assessments and black-college contacts were critical to the Steelers, but he and Dick Haley also were known for their feel for what

Dick Haley played for the Steelers from 1961 to 1964. But Haley—shown here in the 1990 training camp—made his greatest contribution as their director of player personnel from 1971 to 1990, working on the drafts that produced four Super Bowl champions in the 1970s. (George Gojkovich)

good enough to make our team. I feel if Dick had his own way, Dick would have traded some picks to move up higher in the draft."

George Perles, defensive assistant and coordinator 1972–1981: "Dick Haley was the leader there—he knew his stuff. He was a great player at Pitt and a great scout."

Joe Gordon, publicity director and vice president 1969–1998: "Very dedicated. Knew his business."

V. Tim Rooney, pro personnel scout 1972–1979: "A BLESTO-trained guy. Heavily influenced by Jack Butler, having some of the same experience—as a defensive back, a scout. . . . Dick was very good at the numbers. He could see through the reports. He knew the BLESTO scouts so well, he could read between the lines."

Twenty years after the father left the Steelers, his son, the former ball boy, returned to the Steelers' employ: in early 2012, Todd was named offensive coordinator.

Art Jr.: "A top guy, a wonderful guy, and a real good worker. Everybody started at BLESTO. A phenomenal number of people started out with them: [Dick] Haley, Donahoe, Colbert . . ."

KEVIN COLBERT
2000–

Far more than just racquetball roadkill for Bill Cowher, here was yet another North Catholic High kid, BLESTO alumnus, and member of the Art Rooney Jr./Jack Butler scouting tree. Kevin Colbert was the personnel architect of the second-greatest Super Bowl run in Steelers history: three in six years—XL, XLIII, and XLV.

Above all else, he was the first to attain a title heretofore formally unused in Steelers annals.

Kevin Colbert dressed up the roster to create the first of three Super Bowl teams in six years. The running backs: Jerome Bettis, Willie Parker, Verron Haynes, and Duce Staley. Parker's 75-yard touchdown run in the second half not only proved the difference in Super Bowl XL, it also marked the longest touchdown rush in Super Bowl history. (Courtesy of the Pittsburgh Steelers)

In 2011, in the same, inimitably quiet fashion as when the presidency shifted from a Rooney father to son, Colbert was awarded the inaugural franchise title of general manager.

This was the Pittsburgh native and Robert Morris University (née College) graduate who spent the previous ten seasons as the Detroit Lions' pro personnel director. When former ball boy and close associate Tom Donahoe came to constant loggerheads with Cowher—the man he helped to hire in 1992—Dan Rooney and Art II felt compelled to sit down with both; only the coach kept his chair. Next came Colbert, who arrived from the Lions, who went 27-33 collectively the previous four seasons.

With Colbert as director of football operations, the Steelers went 116-63-1 (.644) with three Super Bowls and two rings in his first eleven years on the job.

No problem with hiring a personnel chief from a losing team, right?

Ernie Accorsi, former Baltimore, Cleveland, and Giants general manager: "I remember I advised one club and recommended one general manager [from a less-successful franchise, and the club demurred]. 'You think Dan Rooney had a problem naming Kevin Colbert, coming from a losing organization?' If you have the right people and the stability they've had over the years . . . ? I'm sure there are ten clubs who'd love to have Kevin Colbert now."

Colbert:

You try to lend your own touch. I think what I try to do is try to find the right players for this organization, this team, this city. The right players who are going to fit in with this team. I'm trying to stay true to our standards with everything. Sometimes, it's difficult. But you know we've developed a successful pattern.

If you don't do any forward thinking and adapt your thinking, the game will pass you by. [But] we're always going to [examine] not only where we've succeeded but where we've failed. The things we often evaluate is a guy's heart or merits. The football part I don't want to say it's easy to figure out, but *easier.*

You want to do business this way. You want to stay true to core beliefs. For the most part, it has worked for us.

Bill Cowher: "Kevin was awesome. Kevin is selfless, really. He does so much. He's a great ear. He's a great judge of players, a great judge of situations, of where the state of team is. A great sounding board. I just think he's a great fit for the organization. He's a guy who does a lot and [seeks] little credit for it. Trust me, there's nobody who does as much as Kevin Colbert for that organization."

6

The Man and His Towel

MYRON COPE
Broadcaster–Writer–Icon

Height: 5-4 • **Weight:** "Stringy" • **College:** Pitt • **Years with the Steelers:** 1970–2005 • **Birthplace:** Pittsburgh • **Born:** January 23, 1929 • **Died:** February 27, 2008

TERRIBLE TOWEL
Flag

Height: 22.75 inches by 14.5 inches • **Weight:** "Stringy" • **College:** Philadelphia Textile (heh, heh) • **Years with the Steelers:** 1975– • **Birthplace:** Offices of WTAE-TV and WTAE-AM, Wilkinsburg, Pennsylvania • **Born:** December 27, 1975

They are, hmm hah, inexorably woven together.

This wee man and this symbol that stretches across a globe, not to mention that it reaches into space, are one. His name graces its top. His legacy—along with the Allegheny Valley School that he saw would benefit from each one, a tidy sum of $3 million and counting—is enwrapped in each twirling, black-on-gold flag. Born of bad times and good, embraced by a Steelers notion and Steelers Nation, each icon grew—thanks to the fortunes of a once-laughingstock football team—from diminutive stature to planetary celebrity.

Yoi. And double yoi.

Any dumbkopf between 1970 and 2005 within earshot of that unforgettable voice of Myron Cope, the one accidentally described by a Dallas Cowboy receiver from Pitt named Billy Davis as "anal," could offer a stranger a how-do, welcome to the store. You might share a hot toddy and spin tales of how a little radio station and a bumbling, fumbling NFL franchise adopted one of the country's most gifted writers. A writer whom *Sports Illustrated* sent across America (golfing with Lee Trevino even). A writer the magazine celebrated later in its 50th anniversary edition by reprinting his marvelous Howard Cosell profile and in its baseball book by republishing his incisive Roberto Clemente piece. A writer honored for the nation's best magazine sportswriting in 1963 and, in 1987, honored among such literary achievers as Jack London and Mark Twain. Okle dokle, indeed.

He authored *The Game That Was, Broken Cigars*, and *Double Yoi.* He worked from morning-drive as a radio sports announcer to nighttime news, when he delivered his

Myron Cope and his famous Terrible Towel, in front of the Steelers offices at Three Rivers Stadium in January 1980. Two enduring icons. (George Gojkovich)

"Myron Cope on Sports" television commentary. He served as the Steelers' colorful commentator for 35 years, his many catchphrases and dictionary-deep words helping him to spin some yarns. He will be remembered for perpetuity, however, for spinning the Terrible Towel.

As even he predicted, his obituary—after he died from respiratory illness at a South Hills nursing home where he used to push his wheelchair out the door, remove his oxygen feed, and light up one of his ever-present cigarettes—read something to this effect: Creator of Towel Dies.

Born Myron Sidney Kopleman, he didn't live merely to create a towel. It was more of a talisman. And, of course, he did all that other stuff.

Joe Gordon, Steelers publicity director and vice president 1969–1998: "On my list of Most Amazing People, the Chief [Art Rooney Sr.] is first, Franco Harris is second, and Myron is third. Myron by far is the most creative person I've known. The things he would come up with . . ."

Roy McHugh, longtime sportswriter, columnist, and editor with the Pittsburgh Press *and Cope's personal copy editor:* "I always thought he was a much better writer than a sportscaster. When he was writing for *Sports Illustrated,* nobody in Pittsburgh read it. When he did the broadcasts, he did something they liked. . . . He [became] even bigger than the players."

Gordon: "When we would travel, and when we would arrive at a hotel, and if the Steelers Nation was there in numbers—and most of them were—the hotel would rope that area off. There would be fans all over, behind those ropes. Bradshaw could walk by, Joe Greene. . . . Myron got the biggest crowds. He was their man."

Bill Hillgrove, longtime Pitt play-by-play announcer who succeeded Jack Fleming as Steelers' play-by-play announcer in 1994:

I was privileged, I was blessed, to work with him for 11 years. But people forget the 12th. Johnny Sauer got sick in 1983 [with a heart problem], and I had the joy of working with Cope that Pitt season. When he took the job, he was talking to Ted Atkins, the GM at the station [WTAE, where Cope long worked morning radio, nighttime radio talk shows, and TV, plus, of course, the Steelers' flagship broadcasts]. "I got a full enough plate." "Myron, your contract is coming up in January." "I'm all ears."

"There's one date here: Pitt's playing at Maryland. My favorite cousin is getting married, and the reception is at Rolling Rock [Country Club] in Ligonier. You got to get me from Maryland to Ligonier." "No problem. We'll get you a charter." Four minutes left in the game, he leaves. Meets his pilot, who's standing next to the plane in a leather helmet and goggles, at some airstrip. And off they go in a single-engine plane.

The pilot called the tower, and they said, "You can't land here, we've got an air show." "Tell 'em you've got a VIP." The pilot radios the tower. . . . "They want to know who is the VIP." "Tell 'em you've got Myron Cope." The pilot radios the tower again. . . . "I need four for the Cleveland game."

Everything stopped. The plane landed. That's the power of Cope.

Dan Torisky, executive director of the Autism Society of Pittsburgh, cofounder with Cope of the Pittsburgh Vintage Grand Prix, and longtime friend: "I used to bring coffee to a sports reporter named Kopelman. He didn't have a byline. He was a gall-danged cub reporter. A little stringy guy. Former boxer. Battered nose. Cauliflower ear. But he was moving up. I was 6-5, 6-6 [a wannabe basketball player and an unmotivated

Duquesne University student]. But I had respect for him because I wanted to become a reporter myself."

Frank Haller, an advertising exec, neighbor, and longtime friend who for years satirically portrayed spoiled ex-athlete "Lance Boyle" on Cope's radio shows: "When I met Myron, it was '52. I was graduating from Duquesne in the journalism department. One guy said, 'What we need to do is have a graduation dinner for ourselves. But get one of the TV stars and honor them.' 'No . . . , they're never going to come to that.' Somebody said, 'Let's get somebody [from the newspapers] who's the best new face in town.' Another guy said, 'Hey, Myron Cope.' We had it at a bar, I forget where. Drinks and burgers. We took up a collection among ourselves. But we got $21.55. And Myron was great."

After landing bylines at the *Erie Times-News* and the *Pittsburgh Post-Gazette,* after flashing creativity unseen in the dailies at that time, Cope quit and made out for freelance writing. A newspaper editor told him, "You'll starve."

In addition to *Sports Illustrated,* he wrote regularly for the *Saturday Evening Post* and *True Magazine,* somewhat equivalent to the *Vanity Fair* and *Rolling Stone* of the 1950s and 1960s. Once, owed roughly $150 for a story, he hitchhiked to New York to get his check. He had a wife, Mildred, and soon two children to feed: Danny, who was autistic, and Elizabeth. Another daughter died in infancy.

Hillgrove: "I was there when he began his broadcast career. I was a disc jockey at 'TAE, 1968. Don Shaffer was the program director. He called everybody in on the staff and said, 'We've got to spice up the morning; we're thinking of doing sports commentary. What do you guys think?' I thought for a minute, and said, 'I think one of the best writers in Pittsburgh is Roy McHugh.' I hardly got it out of my mouth, and Ron Rininger—a news guy who lived in the South Hills—says, 'I know a guy I loaf with, Myron Cope.'"

Haller: "When he first mentioned to [Mildred] the possibility about going on the radio, she told him not to do it. 'You'll embarrass us both.'"

The station set up Cope with the ability to broadcast from his Scott Township home. Haller used to walk across the street and sit down with him for those morning commentaries, which is where "Lance Boyle" was hatched.

In 1969, with the Steelers moving into Three Rivers Stadium the next season, with Chuck Noll attempting a huge reclamation project, with the franchise's flagship-radio deal with high-powered KDKA-FM drawing to a close, the NFL club's front office went looking for a platform, a buzz, a new twist.

Gordon: "Regardless of where the Pirates were in the National League standings, in September our games would get farmed out to WJAS. Obviously, we weren't comfortable with that, and we felt we could get more out of the radio rights if we left KDKA. We talked to WTAE, and they were interested." The Steelers sold four quarters of each game for $30,000 apiece for 1970. They tried to line up a young KDKA-TV sportscaster named Dick Stockton, but when they offered him a share of the play-by-play duties with Fleming—a famed West Virginia University broadcaster—Stockton demurred.

"So we had a meeting. We were still in the Roosevelt Hotel. Dan [Rooney], Ed [Kiely, Gordon's boss], and I. Being that Myron was doing commentaries on WTAE, [his name came up]. He was a huge fan. He was friendly with the players—

The Terrible Towel, extra-large edition, takes part in a halftime show at Three Rivers Stadium. (John Beale)

he used to drink with Bobby Layne and Ernie Stautner. Kiely thought it was a good idea."

Ed Kiely, publicity director since 1948 and right-hand man to Art Rooney Sr.: "Yes, I am the man to blame. I was the one who hired him. I hired him because he was a good football guy, he knew the game. I never thought he'd be the marketing man he turned out to be for us.

"Art asked, 'You know what you're doing?' I said, 'I'm not sure.'

"I never realized we were going to get 'Yoi' and 'Double yoi' . . . and the fans would love the 'Yoi' and 'Double yoi.'" Suddenly, Cope was a full-time radio and TV guy, no time for writing.

Hillgrove: "Morning commentary, TV commentary, afternoon stuff. . . . He would go back to the station and do it live [on TV] at 11 o'clock. That was a long day."

McHugh, his personal editor: "It was unfortunate when Cope left journalism. I thought it was terrible, awful. But he explained it. He was freelancing, he had an autistic son, and the radio station had health benefits.

"But that [move to radio] is what made him a celebrity. Made him lots of money, too."

Mike Wagner, safety 1971–1980: "I get here, and you got Chilly Billy Cardille [on WIIC-TV]; you got [Pirates famed broadcaster] Bob Prince and the Green Weenie. And Myron. I thought, 'Are you serious? I'm not sure this is the place I want to settle.'"

John Banaszak, defensive lineman 1975–1981: "You come to Pittsburgh and you hear that voice the first time. Who the hell . . . ?'"

Dan "Bad Rad" Radakovich, defensive line coach 1971 and offensive line coach 1974–1977, and a screamer whose voice became a scratchy rasp: "Even with that lousy voice, he overcame it."

Pittsburgh, which listened at previously unprecedented rates, and Steelers followers couldn't get enough of those nails *through* a chalkboard. The voice actually helped to get Cope heard, make him known.

Torisky: "In 1957 my son Eddie was born. A couple of years later Myron Cope's son was born." And, in 1965, as Torisky remembered it, he was among 62 fathers of challenged children banding together to launch the Autism Society of America. Torisky became its national secretary for 30-plus years. "We met him in my living room. We started the Autism Society of Pittsburgh. And Myron got us the grant. A thousand bucks. And a thousand bucks in 1967 was big money—that's maybe $8,000 today. We got an office started in a storefront in Monroeville. Myron Cope working with Dan Rooney got the thousand bucks from the Hearst Corporation, and that got the Autism Society of Pittsburgh started.

"He'd get a speaking fee and he'd send us a check. When Myron would go speak, he would not speak about autism. He would talk about sports and happy stuff. Myron admitted he didn't know [spit] about autism." Their wives became best friends. Torisky helped the Copes move Danny into the Allegheny Valley School, where the Toriskys' son later joined him.

As Torisky related in helping to write the Terrible Towel's lengthy Wikipedia entry, Atkins the WTAE GM called in Cope late in the 1975 season. They needed a gimmick to attract sponsors to his daily commentaries and talk show. Cope balked. "I am not a gimmick guy, never have been a gimmick guy." Once again, he was reminded that his contract was coming due. Cope replied, "I'm a gimmick guy."

Haller, the advertising guy: "I said, 'Hey, Myron, how about a Dollar Bill. The Steelers are a money team.' He loved that. He laid that on them. But the radio ad manager [Larry Garrett] suggested that everybody had to twirl it. I wanted to ask him when he was thinking of the terry-cloth towel, was Myron thinking of Terry Bradshaw? [Because] they got the 'Terry-bull Towel,'" as Cope always pronounced it. "He said, 'It's got to be something everybody has. They can pull it out and twirl it around, like a handkerchief.'"

Torisky: "In days of old, knights rode with their lady's handkerchief on their lance. Riding into battle at Waterloo. They were the holy cloth of attack. But the idea of naming it something as absurd as the Terrible Towel . . .'"

McHugh: "[Andy] Russell yelled at him, 'We don't go into that rinky-dink stuff.'"

Torisky: "Myron went around the locker room, he talked to this one and that one [trying to get an endorsement]. Terry Bradshaw went 'Hmmmph.' As Myron wrote in his book, he took that as an affirmation. WTAE promoted it like hell on the radio and all that. They were scared to death that nobody would have a yellow thing to wave. People were told to bring one. Come the day of the game [December 27, 1975, an AFC divisional playoff against the Baltimore Colts], after all the promotion, they had a trunk full of yellow towels to hand out. Andy Russell didn't like the idea. Joe Greene didn't like the idea. Ernie Holmes didn't like the idea. Jack Ham said it stinks. Myron had said this is going to benefit kids and people who are retarded and physically handicapped. [And WTAE officials] were scared to death.

"There they are, in the tunnel . . . and there's old Lynn Swann. Swann in that tunnel pulled this towel out of his belt. When they came out of the tunnel, he was the one waving the son of a [gun]. That caused the stadium to explode in those towels."

Banaszak: "Swann was the first one. We really didn't think too much of it. *No one* did at the outset."

Radakovich: "It wasn't a big hit until Swann started waving it. And you have to be winning for something like that to take hold."

Mike Wagner, safety 1971–1980: "Noll was always low-key, 'let's not create distractions.' But the message got to him: It was okay. The fans picked up on it."

So did the players. Interesting to note, the Steelers won that first playoff game, over the Colts. Russell the disbeliever wound up returning a fumble 93 yards for a touchdown—despite a knee that required surgery and two sprained wrists that prevented him from lateraling to a teammate. It's an NFL record that still stood 35 years later, and counting.

Behind the Towel, the Steelers won three Super Bowls and went 10-2 in the playoffs the rest of the 1970s. They were 4-4 in the postseason before, and 29-17 and winners of two more

Lynn Swann waving not one but two Terrible Towels after the "Ice Bowl" 1979 AFC championship victory, stirring up the Three Rivers Stadium crowd. (George Gojkovich)

Super Bowls (runners-up in another two) the first 35 years after. The players began to believe, all right.

Jackie Smith's wide-open drop in the end zone of Super Bowl XII? Wagner told reporters afterward: "When he broke free, I thought it was a touchdown. I just said, 'Get him, Towel.'"

John Stallworth, receiver 1974–1987: "The energy that they generated certainly propelled us to play better."

Haller: "It caught on. Boy, did it catch on."

Torisky: "The first year, 400 bucks Myron designated for us—the Pittsburgh chapter. After that, every cent went to the Allegheny Valley School. At the time the Towel started going big, Myron and I had a talk. Myron said, 'You and Connie, someday you're going to die. Mildred and I, too. You want this money to keep going somewhere, right?' We thought that would be a good way of ensuring the continuation of Allegheny Valley School." Connie died of cancer one year to the day after her best friend Mildred, in 1995.

Banaszak: "What it's turned out to be is . . . a multimillion-dollar enterprise for a great cause. If you don't have a Towel, you're not part of the Steelers Nation. That's his legacy. It's a heck of a tribute to the man who devoted his life to the Pittsburgh Steelers."

Haller: "Myron did a hell of a lot more stuff than the Terrible Towel, too. With his wallet and his time, he would spend for people. He'd get millions of requests. He just had a hard time saying no. Myron liked the floodlights. He liked getting up there. Sometimes, it could be a little organization having a dinner. Look back at '52, he came to our group of 12 bums" from Duquesne U. journalism.

Torisky: "The Grand Prix [every summer in Schenley Park since 1982] has raised $3 million. Half goes to the Autism Society, the other half goes to Allegheny Valley School. In 2011, for instance, it raised $200,000 to bring things the state won't give [the school]: wheelchairs, field trips, arts and crafts. . . ." The annual "Run to Pitt" or "Run from Pitt," an effort before the Backyard Brawl among Pitt and West Virginia University students, started with Cope and Gordon and a Pitt chapter of the Alpha Phi Omega service fraternity in a 1970 meeting at a jazz club. The Foge Fazio/Myron Cope Golf Tournament, later operated under Hillgrove's name, is another of his charities.

Towel in hand, Cope ascended to the radio booth—first in Three Rivers Stadium, then in Heinz Field—not only to lead a Nation but also to fill its airs with his shtick, his wit, his wordplay, his lexicon . . . and his knowledge of the players. The players enjoyed him as well. He was once boxed and given to Russell as a birthday present (though he kicked at the box's sides and complained). He staged dress offs for the players, though the impeccably dressed Frenchy Fuqua usually won. And he was known to share a libation or two on the road.

Gordon: "Smoking and drinking were his salvation."

Wagner: "We had a yuk about Myron in Washington one time. The media likes to go out and have a few pops. Myron had a few one night. So he took a cab back to the Marriott. Got in the elevator. Came back down. Walked out to the front desk. 'My room's on the sixth floor. Your elevator only goes up to the fourth floor.' He was in the wrong Marriott."

Radakovich: "I remember we all loved Myron. It wasn't World War II with Myron. It was a fun game. When he cut us up, he cut us up in a fun way. And Myron loved the fact that Chuck was a pain in the ass sometimes."

Noll liked Cope. When Cope moved to Upper St. Clair and the station continued to set up his home with broadcasting

On the edge with Myron Cope (wearing a sport coat and tie—yoi!) while he yakked his way through a 1988 Steelers broadcast alongside Jack Fleming, his partner from 1970 to 1993. Fleming, a decorated basketball announcer as well, started in the Steelers booth in 1958. (Vincent J. Musi)

equipment, Noll walked over and taped his Sunday pregame coach's show there.

Gordon: "Myron wasn't handy at all. So whenever the Copes were having a problem, like the refrigerator wasn't working, Myron would tell Mildred, 'Don't worry, Chuck's coming over.'"

Hillgrove: "One of Chuck Noll's shows, Marianne [Noll] heard it and said, 'Why do you let him ask you those kinds of questions?' Chuck just shrugged. He knew it was how he answered the question, it wasn't the question."

The question in the end was left to Gordon: Would you please tell me when it's time to retire? The PR guy who helped to hire him, Gordon was the one who advised him after the 2005 season: You've lost your fastball; it's time to hang it up. Tunch Ilkin, who followed Merril Hoge into the booth, moved from third fiddle to sidecar second seat.

That also meant an end to the pop-culture phenomena. The little old man with the cauliflower ear and the singing that sounded like gargling? He would do no more "Deck the Halls" ditties about the Broncos ("fug-uh-gug-uh-guh guh guh guh guh"?) or videos with him in a matador's costume (a "Macarena" takeoff) or MC Hammer pants ("Can't Touch This").

It was just as well, for Cope's health was beginning to turn. Back pain and surgery and endless trips to physicians didn't seem to help. Even though he had great fun writing in *Double Yoi* about it, his 2001 charge for driving under the influence was fodder for newscasts, followed later by a hospitalization and a five-car accident. He used to write the news, not make it.

Haller: "Myron would kill me if he knew I'd tell this story. He had peripheral neuropathy [a condition that afflicts limbs with abnormal sensations]. He had that accident [in 2005 on Interstate 279 near] Green Tree; I'm sure that's what happened, he was losing feeling in his feet. The state trooper later told me he had to write out a ticket, the news people were all there. Myron had to appear before a magistrate. We get to the magistrate, and the state trooper dismissed the charges. Myron says, 'Does that mean I'm not guilty?' The magistrate's name was Martini. Can you believe that? [Magisterial District Judge Randy C.] Martini. And he says, 'Yeah, Myron, we're not going to pursue charges.' Myron says, 'Can I give you my plea, anyway. I've prepared it.' So he did.

"He went through a lot there before he died."

His pallbearers included Russell and Franco Harris—not only two dear friends, but two Steelers closely aligned with memorable Myron moments.

Haller: "Franco told me a story at the funeral." His career, Harris said, was always closely aligned with the persona. "He said, 'We are sort of joined at the hip. Well . . . , his shoulder and my hip.'"

There are crucible moments in the Steelers history that involve Cope, that revolve around Cope.

The Immaculate Reception. (He first spread those words, though the name was coined that December 23, 1972, night by friends Michael Ord and Sharon Levosky, who called it into the WTAE-TV studios moments before Cope's 11 P.M. commentary.)

The Towel.

The voice equated with indelible plays—a scratchy Steelers' soundtrack.

To think that NFL Films, for using his commentary as part of the enduring audio accompaniment to many Steelers highlights of the 1970s, used to send him rights checks at the end of the year: $10.

Haller: "About a year before he died, Duquesne University had a night for him. They gave him a very nice lifetime achievement award. He insisted I come along with him. He got up, introduced me, and said, 'This isn't the first award I ever got from Duquesne. All you guys did tonight was confirm an award you gave me 50 years ago.'" The drinks-and-burgers affair with students that netted Cope that $21.55.

The man and his Towel were priceless.

Torisky: "My son Eddie cares little for possessions. But right beside his TV set is a Terrible Towel. It's his.

"You've got to realize, the Towel always brings awareness to autism and mental retardation.

"The legacy of Myron is remarkable. And, in my opinion, it's a case of using his celebrated position, his status in the community, to do more for the community and its most vulnerable population than he could have ever done in any other life choice. What he did behind the scenes . . . far outweighed anything he accomplished in the world of sports."

Gordon: "He's a legend."

Hillgrove: "I miss him every day."

In the manner in which Cope would conclude a conversation: Bye now.

The Players

IN THE GOOD, THE BAD, AND THE UGLY that has been Pirates and Steelers football—in inverse order, of course—there have been more than 1,400 individuals who played in regular-season contests wearing the black and gold and, for one wartime year, the Steagle green and white. They represented Pittsburgh, a socioeconomic region, an emotional attachment otherwise known as the Steelers Nation. They range alphabetically from the Walter Abercrombie who was supposed to be Franco Harris' replacement to a local Duquesne product named Frank Zoppetti. They came from such places as South Africa (Gary Anderson), Southern University (Mel Blount), and Southern California (Lynn Swann, Troy Polamalu). They reconnoitered from Korea (Hines Ward) and Bavaria (Ernie Stautner) and the military (too many to mention) and the paramilitary (Frenchy's Foreign Legion, Franco's Italian Army), but no guerrillas (just Gerela's Gorillas)

And they came to own a jewelry store of Super Bowl rings.

Here are the stories of 100 players vital to the Pittsburgh Pirates/Steelers history, much less the course of the NFL and professional football at large.

GARY ANDERSON
Kicker

Height: 5-11 • **Weight:** 193 • **College:** Syracuse • **Years with the Steelers:** 1982–1994 • **Birthplace:** Parys, South Africa • **Born:** July 16, 1959

Discarded by the Buffalo Bills in training camp, he became a fixture with the Steelers . . . and around the NFL. Anderson spent his first 13 seasons with Pittsburgh, but then 10 more seasons with Philadelphia, San Francisco, Minnesota, and Tennessee.

In 23 seasons, 353 games (second all-time), and 1,499 placement kicks—extra-point or field-goal attempts—he wound up running the ball just once. He gained three yards.

He topped the NFL in scoring once, in 1998, when he never missed a field-goal try in the preseason or regular season but muffed a critical one in the NFC championship game in which Minnesota lost at home in overtime.

Anderson finished his career second all-time in NFL points scored.

Jon Kolb, in 1982 in his first season as assistant coach after a 13-year career as an offensive lineman: "I remember sitting in the coaches meeting, and Dick Haley was there. They needed a kicker, and I remember Dick Haley said, 'Buffalo's got a kid. If they cut him, we need to pick him up. They're making a mistake.' It was Gary Anderson.

"I remember Gary got his teeth broken off in training camp and acted like he didn't notice. That was the smartest, greatest thing he could've done. 'Hey, he's not a kicker. He's a real player.'"

Ron Erhardt, offensive coordinator 1992–1995: "I used to kid him a lot: 'Are you going to kick anything 45 or 50? Or would you rather have chip shots?' He was a good kicker. Nothing wrong with him."

Dermontti Dawson, center 1988–2000: "Gary played for how many years, 20 years? Gary was kind of quiet. He was a nice guy. . . . You could always depend on Gary at the time. Gary was one of the most accurate kickers in Steeler history."

JOHN BAKER
Defensive End

Height: 6-6 • **Weight:** 279 • **College:** North Carolina Central • **Years with the Steelers:** 1963–1967 • **Birthplace:** Raleigh, North Carolina • **Born:** June 10, 1935 • **Died:** October 31, 2007

Big John Baker had four fumble recoveries in the 1963 season that fell one victory short of the playoffs. He was a steady defensive lineman who paired in 1961–1962 with Big Daddy Lipscomb. He played four seasons with the Los Angeles Rams, the team that drafted him, and one more with Philadelphia before finding his way to Pittsburgh and finding his niche.

He spent 1968 with Detroit before retiring, later becoming sheriff of Wake County, North Carolina, for 24 years.

Oh, and his one moment that endures? He was the hardhitting pass rusher who bloodied and beat up a certain 38-year-old Giants quarterback—bruised ribs, slumped on his knees, groggy, helmetless, career just about finished—and set the stage for one of the NFL's most memorable photographs, at Pitt Stadium in September 1964. Y. A. Tittle's pass landed in the arms of Steelers defensive tackle Chuck Hinton, who then rumbled 8 yards for a touchdown. It ended the Giants' three consecutive Eastern championships and effectively capped a 17-year career for Tittle.

"Heck of a way to get famous," Tittle, a two-time league MVP, joked years later. "That was the end of the road . . . the end of my dream."

Andy Russell, outside linebacker: "He was just becoming a pretty dominant player. He hit Y. A. Tittle in that famous photo."

JEROME BETTIS
Halfback

Height: 5-11 • **Weight:** 252 • **College:** Notre Dame • **Years with the Steelers:** 1996–2005 • **Birthplace:** Detroit • **Born:** February 16, 1972

He arrived as the Bus. He departed at the big bowl in his backyard.

In between, there was so much elation; there was Hines Ward and teammates crying over the prospect of premature retirement; and, en route to that Super Bowl finish, there was the fumble.

Jerome Bettis left smiles and storybook tales in his rumbling wake of a Pittsburgh decade.

A 14-day holdout and stigmas attached to him by new St. Louis Rams coach Rich Brooks—*bad attitude, selfish*—caused a 1996 draft-day exit by a two-time 1,000-yard rusher.

The Steelers sent second- and fourth-round selections to the Rams in return for Bettis and a third-rounder. Half of the deal was an immediate wash: The Steelers used St. Louis' third-round pick to take a fellow, linebacker Steve Conley, they hoped to choose in the second round.

So the deal boiled down to: The pick that produced a nice little tight end for the Rams in Ernie Conwell . . . and a likely future Hall of Famer for the Steelers.

No wonder Tom Donahoe, the Steelers director of player personnel, supposedly told Bettis on that draft day: "If you weren't already married, I'd kiss you."

Dick Hoak, running backs coach: "He had a falling out with some people in St. Louis, I guess. It was before the draft, we

Jerome Bettis runs against the Baltimore Ravens, a constant rival throughout his historic Steelers career. (Bill Amatucci)

Jerome Bettis and Joey Porter, left, share a laugh as they prepare for practice before Super Bowl XL in Detroit. (Courtesy of the Pittsburgh Steelers)

knew he was available. Bill [Cowher] came to Chan Gailey and me, 'Watch a tape of this guy.' After one reel, we said: 'Get him.'"

Dermontti Dawson, center 1988–2000: "We played against him when we played the Rams in LA; I knew how he was, 'cause he ran over us that game [76 yards on 16 carries in a 27-0 Rams triumph]. When he came to the Steelers, he fit right in. That was his kind of offense."

Jim Sweeney, center–guard 1996–1999: "We came in the same year. Another Hall of Famer. You don't know what the deal was in St. Louis, but he fit in here well. He made the most of it. Great guy, great teammate, great competitor."

Upon his arrival in Pittsburgh, he shared the halfback duties with Erric "Pee Wee" Pegram. He gained 57 yards in a season-opening loss, then thundered through Baltimore for 116. A celebrity vehicle was born.

Bill Hillgrove, Steelers play-by-play announcer: "We were playing a preseason game in Green Bay. It was Bettis' first year. Jay Hayes [of Bridgeville, Pennsylvania] was on the Pittsburgh staff and had been on the Notre Dame staff. We're in the lobby of the hotel. I heard him make a comment to Jerome and call him 'Bus.' After everybody broke up, I said, 'Jay, where did you get this Bus.'" 'We called him that at Notre Dame.' That night, I laid it on [Myron] Cope, and he took it and ran with it."

The Bus rolled to six consecutive 1,000-yard seasons, four Pro Bowls (to which he would bring his trusty escort, such as fullback Tim Lester), the 1996 NFL Comeback Player of the Year, and the 2001 Walter Payton Man of the Year.

Bill Cowher hitched his run-first offense and grind-it-out style to the Bus, and the Steelers—outside of a three-year hiccup in the late 1990s—remained an annual playoff participant for a decade. Problem was, Bettis couldn't transport them beyond the AFC championship game: 1997, 2001, 2004 all ended in failure.

After that last one, a halting, misting Bettis arose the next day in the locker room to inform his teammates that the loss to New England may well represent his final NFL game. Ward, meeting media later that day, broke up when mentioning that moment.

Ben Roethlisberger, quarterback 2007–, who made a pledge to Bettis on the sidelines at that AFC championship game loss:

"I felt horrible. 'Cause I knew he was getting close to the end, anyway. Everybody wanted to win one for him. I felt like I let him down, because I didn't play good. I remember [saying], 'Just give me one more shot. I'll get you there.' It's probably the dumbest promise I could have ever made, as a first-year guy. 'I promise I'll get you there, just come back for one more year.' Didn't know if it meant anything to him, but it meant something to me."

One year later, the Bus arrived at its appointed destination.

Roethlisberger had the biggest hand of all: After Bettis uncharacteristically fumbled in the Indianapolis end zone on what could have been the game-clinching play late, Roethlisberger retreated and tripped Colts cornerback Nick Harper midflight on a fumble return that could have defeated the Steelers.

Bettis: "If Charlie [Batch] had been back there . . ."

In that magical 2006 postseason, Bettis rushed for 180 yards in the four playoff games—a 180, indeed. The Steelers turned into a pass-first offense amid that postseason run and eight-game winning streak to complete that championship season. They allowed him, in Ford Field in his hometown of Detroit in his final NFL moment, to park the Bus as a world champion.

Dawson: "You talk about a jokester. Jerome is a guy who can light up a locker room with a joke and smile. Always playing around. Jerome . . . could crack on people, and if you tried to crack on him back and make fun of him, that would just fuel that fire. But you knew, come game day, he was going to punish people. [On Mondays, he'd be] in the trainer's room, ice on his hamstrings, his ankles, shoulder . . . hip, all over his body. I always just saw him limping in the locker room after the game."

Casey Hampton, nose tackle: "He was the best you could ever have as a teammate. He'd do anything for you. You don't find that often in this league. Some of the best feet I've ever seen. He was like a little guy with the light feet."

Hoak: "A lot of people didn't understand, he had great feet for a big guy. When you went to tackle him, you didn't know what he was going to do. A great player."

In both a shock and an honor, Jerome Bettis finds his teammates on the team charter decked out in editions of his green Notre Dame No. 6 jerseys. (Courtesy of the Pittsburgh Steelers)

Two favored halfbacks: Rocky Bleier with Jerome Bettis at Heinz Field. (Courtesy of the Pittsburgh Steelers)

Dick LeBeau, defensive coordinator 1996 and 2004–, and a competing coach in between: "Jerome [was] a rare bird. For a man that big to have the vision and cutting ability he had . . ."

Russ Grimm, offensive line coach 2001–2006: "The guy had fun playing. But he sure played the game hard."

Hoak: "Best run he ever made, he took the whole [Bears] team with him on a 4-yard run. Urlacher hit him around the 4-yard line, and he got rid of Urlacher. He knocked Urlacher into somebody else and took a lot of them into the end zone. That was the one that started the four-game winning streak that led to the Super Bowl [XL]. He was one easy guy to coach."

ROCKY BLEIER
Halfback

Height: 5-11 • **Weight:** 210 • **College:** Notre Dame • **Years with the Steelers:** 1968, 1970–1980 • **Birthplace:** Appleton, Wisconsin • **Born:** March 5, 1946

Impossible, his army doctor told him. A large chunk of his thigh was gone in the sniper fire and grenade attack in Vietnam. One hundred pieces of shrapnel pocked his right side, maiming his foot and rendering three toes essentially useless. Rocky Bleier wrote a letter to Art Rooney: I'll be back.

Joe Gordon, publicity director and vice president 1969–1998: [Pulling out his old media guides for reference—Bleier missed the '69 season for Vietnam and played one game in '70, the final one. Sidelined the rest of that time due to surgery.] "When he came out of Notre Dame, he was a marginal player at best. Then get shot up in Vietnam. I remember him coming out on Pitt Stadium [for a 1969 game], limping with a cane. Two years later, he was back on the team.

"Special guy, obviously. To overcome . . . and excel on four championship teams, that's a hell of a story. Sheer willpower. Nothing else could explain it. The first training camp [after Vietnam], I said, 'No way.' The guy couldn't run."

Rocky Bleier, ready to battle. (John Beale)

Dick Hoak, running back 1961–1970: "I saw him with a cane, limping on the field. I wasn't sure he'd come back. When I played with him [in 1968], he was a real good player. When he came back . . . , what he did, and I don't think I've ever seen any player do it, he made himself faster than [before].

Ralph Berlin, trainer: "There's a guy, I tried to talk him into retirement. If you could have seen his leg when he came back from Vietnam. If you saw him with shorts on, it would look like someone took a hatchet to his leg. And his foot was a lot worse." Long afterward, they would remove shrapnel that worked its way to the skin surface. "He would say, 'Ralph, I'm going to play professional football again.' I would take his toes and bend them backward. He almost died [in Vietnam]. They were going to cut him, and Chuck said, 'No, put him on IR.' Sixty-nine, '70, he did nothing; they just paid him. Seventy-two, when Franco came, we had Preston Pearson, and he didn't like to block."

Hoak, the running backs coach starting in 1972: "Whatever you wanted Rocky to do . . . Rocky was a very smart guy."

Bleier blocked. Bleier caught passes out of the backfield. Bleier, somehow faster than the marginal back of 1968 and earlier, made a nice halfback with Franco Harris officially running from the fullback position.

He gained 3,809 yards in the seven seasons between 1974 and 1980. He gained 56 in the six years between 1968 and 1973.

He caught 133 passes for 1,226 yards after. He caught three for 68 yards before.

Robert Patrick Bleier, 16th-round draft choice from Notre Dame in 1968, wasn't the same man after Vietnam. He was better, as a football player, as a story line.

Hoak: "The year the two of them gained 1,000 yards? I used to be upstairs in the booth. If we were beating somebody bad, Chuck would say, 'Come on down, the game's over.' We were playing somebody, I don't remember. Tampa? [Actually, it was at Houston a week later, the 1976 regular-season finale.] We took Rocky and Franco out. I feel a tap on my shoulder, and it's Franco. 'You know Rocky only needs a couple of more yards for a thousand.' That's how he got back in. If Franco hadn't told me . . ."

The 1976 season was when Terry Bradshaw's injury forced a rookie Mike Kruczek to play quarterback, forced Bleier and Harris to run incessantly and forced the defense to play at such a breathless level that it registered five shutouts and two games of a single field goal in a nine-game winning streak. When Bleier and Harris both fell injured in the Baltimore playoff victory, the amazing run screeched to an end in the AFC championship game, with just one healthy running back. They remained the backfield in the final three of the four Super Bowl seasons.

And that historic 1976, thanks to Harris' tap on Hoak's shoulder, made them the first NFL tandem to each rush for 1,000 yards.

Rocky Bleier, circa 1980. (Bill Amatucci)

MEL BLOUNT
Cornerback

Height: 6-3 • **Weight:** 205 • **College:** Southern • **Years with the Steelers:** 1970–1983 • **Birthplace:** Vidalia, Georgia • **Born:** April 10, 1948

From the beginning, he wasn't Supe. More like, he was in the soup.

Mel Blount wasn't starting. He wasn't starring. He was riding the pine—the bench, not to be confused with the safety Glen Edwards also known as Pine—for 10 games in 1970 and 1971 behind such cornerbacks as John Rowser and Lee Calland.

John Rowser.

And Lee Calland.

Dan "Bad Rad" Radakovich, defensive line coach 1971 and offensive line coach 1974–1977: "Mel Blount was thought by Chuck Noll and [secondary coach] Charley Sumner to have awesome potential. Six-four. Four-four [speed]. Coordinated. Who probably had a long way to go as a player as a rookie. They kept the faith with him. He made some costly mistakes in games, and they stayed with him. Tested the patience of some of the coaches. He ended up an awesome player. By the time we hit the Super Bowls, he hit his peak: '74, '75, '76. And he became without a doubt one of the best corners to ever play the game."

Melvin Cornell Blount was the youngest of 11 children from a tobacco and cotton farm in Vidalia, the south Georgia town famed for sweet onions. He came to the Steelers—raw, still growing—in the third round of the 1970 draft, a huge fellow who played both safety and cornerback at Southern University in New Orleans. Some football types considered him more of a safety prospect. After nine starts each in 1970 and 1971, he was still something of a suspect cornerback.

In 1971, the Steelers held a 21-3, first-half lead on Miami, and then Paul Warfield blew past Blount for the final three touchdowns of the game: 12, 86, and 60 yards. "I thought a whole lot about [quitting]," Blount admitted later. He credited Bud Carson, the defensive coordinator Noll brought from Georgia Tech in 1972, with showing him the ultimate confidence. No more kickoff-return work (18 for a 29.7-yard average as a rookie). No more benchings . . . at least for awhile.

Joe Gordon, publicity director and vice president 1969–1998: "He didn't start right away. The first year, he returned kickoffs. I think he returned a kickoff 91 yards and didn't score. That's when we needed points and wins. . . . He was inexperienced. He was green. Bud Carson did a great job with Mel."

Immediately, Blount responded. In 1972, he allowed zero touchdowns. None.

Not even when they played unbeaten Miami in the AFC championship game, when Paul Warfield caught two passes.

He intercepted three passes, picked up two fumbles, and ran back one of those fumbles for a touchdown. He became, at his own suggestion, known by a nickname.

Gary Dunn, defensive lineman 1977–1987: "Supe. Ever since I've been there, people called him Supe. L. C. was Hollywood. He was Supe."

Blount had four interceptions in 1973 and two more in 1974 . . . when there came one last stint on the bench. In the AFC championship game at Oakland, Blount got yanked by Carson and Noll after allowing a 38-yard touchdown pass for a 10-3 Raiders lead. Jimmy Allen replaced him, and the Raiders managed just one more field goal. Allen told reporters later that, once he went into the game, "They started to go back to the other side and the middle. They didn't pick on me. I didn't understand that at all."

Blount was, well, more blunt: "I really didn't think a smart coach would do something like that in a championship game. The touchdown pass to Branch was only the third I have given up all season, and the other two came in one game against Atlanta. Taking me out of the game was the worst thing he could have done." Noll banished him from the interview room.

But not from the Super Bowl IX lineup. Pine Edwards walloped Minnesota's John Gilliam as Fran Tarkenton's first-down pass arrived, and Blount intercepted at the goal line. That squashed the Vikings' first true drive and protected the Steelers' slim, 2-0, lead with 1:05 left before halftime.

After that first Super Bowl triumph, Blount came back a changed cornerback. He shaved his head. He snagged interceptions by the bagful. He grabbed two off the Jets' Joe Namath, giving him 10 with four games to go, and he announced his intent to equal or surpass Night Train Lane's NFL-record 14 in 1952. Alas, Blount got just one more.

Future Hall of Fame cornerback Mel Blount sits on the sideline in 1978. (George Gojkovich)

Still, his 11 interceptions in 1975 were a team record and topped the NFL. Only two Steelers ever led the league in picks: Blount and, in 1942, Bill Dudley with 10. Blount established a Steelers record with interceptions in six consecutive games that year.

Mike Wagner, safety 1971–1980: "Mel liked playing single coverage, which was amazing. Sometimes we'd double his man, and he'd say, 'Go help somebody else.' He would bait quarterbacks, he was sooo good. He'd hang back so he could come in and catch it."

There arose three more obstacles for Blount in roughly one year's time.

In training camp 1977, stemming from the brutal 1976 Oakland season opener that ended with Noll muttering something about a "criminal element," Lynn Swann and Dan Rooney and the head coach were among the witnesses called in Raiders cornerback George Atkinson's $2 million slander lawsuit against Noll. The head coach missed much of camp as a result.

Under questioning in the trial, Noll acknowledged that certain Steelers had gone beyond the rules in their roughness on certain plays: Joe Greene, Pine Edwards, Ernie Holmes . . . and Blount. Incensed at being lumped in as a "criminal," Blount vowed to never again play for Noll and filed a $6 million suit against the head coach claiming defamation of character.

At the same time, Blount—along with middle linebacker Jack Lambert—was embroiled in a holdout. It lasted eight weeks. He talked about becoming a tobacco farmer. Noll prepared to enter the season with Allen at cornerback. Eventually, both sides kissed, made up, signed, and withdrew the lawsuit. But . . .

Perhaps most impactful of all, the NFL continued their anti-Steelers legislative bent in 1978 by removing Blount's mode of coverage attack: the bump-and-run. The league couldn't stem his physicality, though.

Dunn: "He used to make all those big sticks."

George Perles, defensive assistant and coordinator 1972–1977: "Stronger than all get out. He'd stand back there and wait for them to catch the ball. He wasn't happy just to tackle them. He'd pick them up and throw them down."

Andy Russell, outside linebacker 1963, 1966–1976: "Mel Blount was 6-4½, 230. Could run like a deer. We didn't blitz at all those late years; Ham and I were covering. We were covering wideouts. We were trying to reroute them. Those Steelers defenses changed the way the NFL played. The NFL didn't like shutouts. I used to push the receiver from where they wanted to go. You could keep your hands on them, pushing them, before the ball was in the air. All of a sudden, the quarterbacks couldn't find the receivers. We had a lot of fun."

Undeterred, the game's best cornerback—with 23 interceptions total from 1975 to 1977—kept on dominating no matter where the goalposts were moved. He went to three of his five Pro Bowls after the rules change. He made another sizable pick on football's biggest stage.

After that 1978 season, with Super Bowl XIII tied at 14-14, Blount intercepted a Roger Staubach pass at the Steelers' 28. His return, plus a Dallas personal-foul penalty, gave the Steelers the ball at Dallas' 44. From there, they drove to the go-ahead touchdown and never were headed.

Blount and the Steelers won another Super Bowl after the 1979 season, and the thirtysomething cornerback continued to refuse to look his age.

Dunn: "After games, we used to sit in the sauna. He came in there, he's got to be six, seven years older than me. For a defensive back, he was just built. He came in there pounding on his chest, 'When you get old like me, I hope you [look] like me.' I looked at him and said, 'Shoot, Mel, we don't look like you now.' He's a freak."

Bill Nunn and Art Rooney Jr. worked out Olympic hurdler Renaldo Nehemiah one day at Three Rivers Stadium. Passing by, Blount gazed at Nehemiah's mark high up on the wall, a new Steelers record for the standing vertical jump, and promptly outdid it. He was wearing a three-piece suit and wing-tip shoes at the time. He was 33 years old. Ever the specimen. Supe.

He retired in 1983, at age 35, with a Steelers-record 57 career interceptions, 736 yards, and two touchdowns in returns, plus another two fumble returns for touchdowns among his 13 fumble recoveries.

While making his retirement announcement, Blount advised Dan Rooney on his way to owners' meetings: "You can tell them to change some of those rules back now that I'm leaving."

TERRY BRADSHAW
Quarterback

Height: 6-3 • **Weight:** 215 • **College:** Louisiana Tech • **Years with the Steelers:** 1970–1983 • **Birthplace:** Shreveport, Louisiana • **Born:** September 2, 1948

Tails.

That's how Terry Bradshaw came to the Steelers, to four Super Bowls, to Hall of Fame history.

The back-asset of a 1921 silver-dollar coin.

Chicago's Ed McCaskey, Papa Bear George Halas' son-in-law, called heads. The coin, after about a one-foot toss at a New Orleans hotel two and a half weeks before the 1970 draft, landed in favor of Dan Rooney, Chuck Noll and the 1-13, accursed-for-four-decades Steelers. Was their luck finally changing?

Shucks, not all of them were sold on him—not until the St. Louis Cardinals offered a busload of starters and their former Steelers star/assistant overseeing the BLESTO scouting service gave Art Rooney Sr. pause. The Chief didn't want to trade or toss away any more future quarterback stars: Johnny Unitas, Len Dawson, and Earl Morrall were *still* giving it to their old franchise.

Art Rooney Jr., scout and vice president of player personnel 1960–1987: "Jack Butler said it was once in a lifetime." The Chief didn't expect to have much lifetime left, either.

Joe Gordon, publicity director and vice president 1969–1998: "We were up in Dan's office on the eighth floor [in the Steelers headquarters at the downtown Roosevelt Hotel]. The Cardinals offered a . . . package for the No. 1 choice. I would say at least three or four of the players would have become instant starters. And Chuck said, 'Our goal is to win a championship. Those guys aren't going to get us any closer.' And Dan supported him. After Joe Greene, Bradshaw was the second connection."

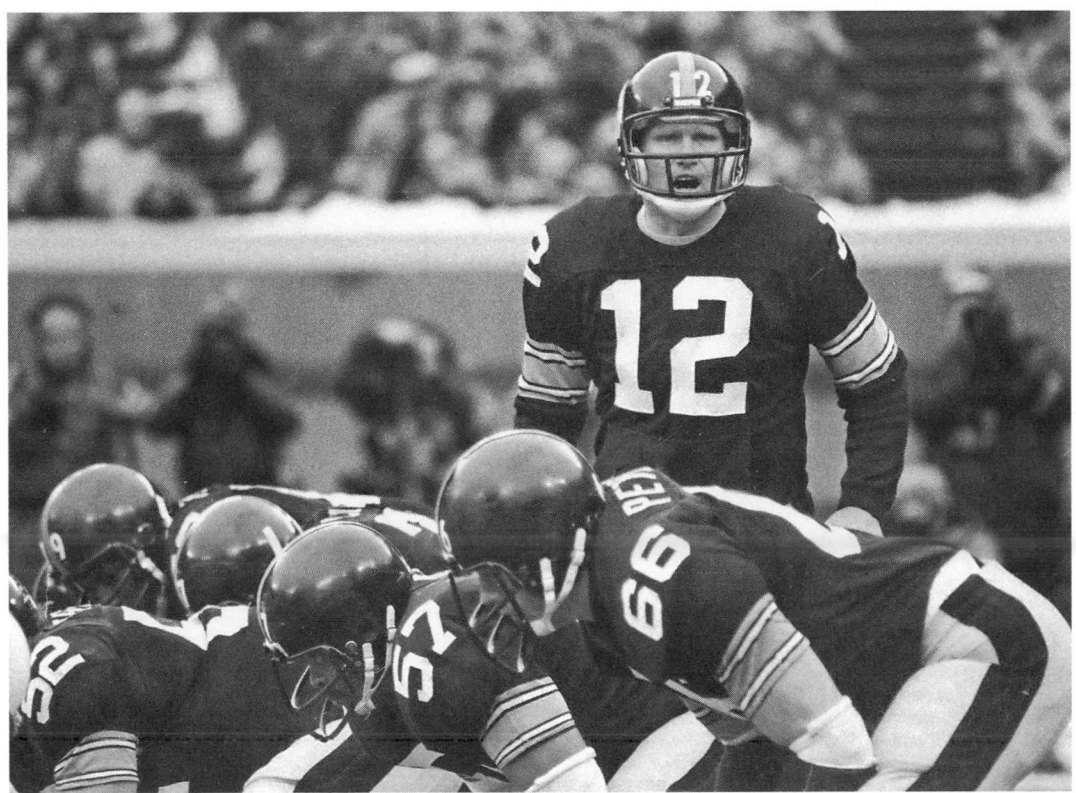

Terry Bradshaw barks out the call at the line of scrimmage. Oftentimes, center Mike Webster (52) took one look at the defensive alignment and advised him to change out of the play if necessary. (John Beale)

They ceremoniously signed Bradshaw to a contract in the middle of the construction site soon to become Three Rivers Stadium. Their luck *had* to be changing, right?

In the debut game of the savior—center Ray Mansfield in a 1970 *Newsweek* story likened him to Moses leading them from the desert—this 22-year-18-day-old quarterback went 4 for 16 with an interception and a loss. His second and third games were losses, too. Noll grabbed him by the face mask. Noll designated him the backup for most of the final six games. By rookie season's end, he threw four times as many interceptions, a league-leading 24, as touchdowns.

He threw 22 interceptions the next season, another loser for the Steelers.

In 1973, many of the home fans cheered when he suffered a separated shoulder against Cincinnati.

In 1974, after a strike and a benching where Noll anointed Joe Gilliam as the starter, Bradshaw had enough. "I'd love to be traded. I don't feel any allegiance toward the Steelers, that's for sure."

Roy McHugh, longtime sportswriter, sports columnist, and sports editor at the Pittsburgh Press: "Pittsburgh didn't like him at all. All that ballyhoo, and he was so erratic the first couple of years. 'Is this guy color blind? Can he not recognize our uniform?' And the people who said 'dahntahn' and ''n 'at' couldn't stand his accent. Or his cracker barrel humor. . . . [But] he's no dummy."

No matter how his coach truly felt about him (and he endured years of wondering about that), the fragile quarterback had two important people in his corner: Joe Greene and the Chief.

V. Tim Rooney, nephew and pro scouting director 1973–1979: "Matter of fact, Joe Greene and the Chief would take Terry out to dinner. Or have him over to the Chief's home."

Gordon: "Most people don't know, but [Greene] was very supportive of Terry Bradshaw. When he was going through his tough times, Joe Greene was there. Joe was the man."

Lou Riecke, strength coach 1970–1979: "Bradshaw, he wanted to complete every pass. He was trying to force them in. He didn't want any incompletions. So he struggled and lost a little confidence."

Larry Brown, tight end and offensive tackle 1971–1984: "Even though his first couple of years were rocky, people could see he was a diamond in the rough. You could see early on, with some patience and time and coaching, he could become the quarterback they thought he was."

Tony Dungy, teammate and, for one Houston game, No. 3 quarterback 1977–1978: "By the time I had gotten there, he had been through a lot of the trauma. People didn't realize how talented he was, how big, how strong his arm was, how accurate. He was fearless. He knew what he could do. He knew what that offense was capable of. Whether it was preseason, regular season, or the playoffs, he was the same way: 'I'm going to throw it in there, and they're going to catch it.'"

A crazy thing happened to that Li'l Abner, Ozark Ike, and Dumb Blond Bomber in his fifth Steelers year: He began to grow before their eyes into a Super Bowl winner. Smart move.

True, the surge of future Hall of Famers Lynn Swann and John Stallworth at wide receiver didn't hurt. Mid-1970s rules changes—stemming head-slapping pass rushers and bump-and-run defensive backs—weren't exactly an offensive hindrance, either. But there's no question Bradshaw made a giant stride, if not a canyon leap.

He finished 1974 with that Super Bowl IX triumph, his second of three postseason games with a completion percentage better than 60 and a passer rating above 100—after

Terry Bradshaw, then the backup quarterback to Jefferson Street Joe Gilliam, shares a laugh with his biggest ally in the Steelers locker room and organization, captain and conscience Joe Greene. (George Gojkovich)

dismissive linebacker, Hollywood Henderson. Bradshaw became one cool C-A-T, the word Henderson claimed that Bradshaw couldn't spell if you spotted him C-A.

The Monday morning after earning the MVP once again for his 309-yard, Super Bowl XIV winning performance, Bradshaw entered a news conference with a 10-gallon cowboy hat and 200-plus pounds of introspection. He admitted to depression.

"I've been through the whole thing. The boos, the injuries, sitting on the bench, being pulled out of games. . . . But it was part of a growth process, a maturity that took me longer than others. I had been thinking of calling it quits, but last night Joe Greene and some of the players told me they'd kick my bleeping bleep bleep if I didn't come back. I then decided it would be beneficial to my health to come back." He pledged to play two more seasons.

He tried three.

His muscle in his throwing elbow, the one he used for almost 4,000 game attempts and millions of practice throws, gave out at the end of 1982. It was an embittering period for him. Three Rivers booing rang in his ears long after a costly interception in a 1982 playoff loss to San Diego, the final such playoff appearance by a gent who remarkably crafted a 14-5 record in the postseason. He believed the Steelers weren't offering him much medical care, concern, and sympathy for his elbow, on which he tried surgery and a mynah bird (a Myron Cope thing) and an Electro-Acuscope (not the Miracle Machine it was nicknamed) and acupuncture. He was chased off the 1983 game day sidelines by Noll—"If he can't play quarterback . . . , he's not much use to us"—and sent home to Louisiana on weekends. Noll suggested the dread assessment: Perhaps it was time to get on with his life's work. The fragile quarterback went 11 months without

he had only six 100-plus-rating games in his previous 62. Then he reported to training camp that summer 24 pounds lighter, at 204. "Looking like a racehorse," was how Noll described it. Gordon's media-guide bio of Bradshaw referred to a "new maturity."

Onetime Steelers tight end Bob Adams likened witnessing the Louisiana kid quarterback play to "watching a rose bloom in slow motion." From calendar 1975, which he started with that inaugural Super Bowl and ended it with a Pro Bowl in Hawaii, Bradshaw blossomed. The seasons from 1975 through 1981, playing the equivalent of a 15-game schedule, he averaged 2,660 yards and 21 touchdowns. No wonder *Newsweek* made him the first athlete to grace its cover twice—and in the same decade, no less.

In January, he dazzled. He threw two touchdowns, had no interceptions, and crafted a 122.5 passer rating (third-highest of his career to date) in winning Super Bowl X. His first 300-yard game, in his 128th career game, came while winning the Super Bowl XIII MVP for his 318 yards and four touchdowns (yet another career high) against the Cowboys and their

Terry Bradshaw and Chuck Noll converse during a Thanksgiving-weekend 1979 date with the rival Cleveland Browns—a game the Steelers won in overtime, 33-30. Bradshaw compiled 407 yards of total offense that day, 364 passing. (George Gojkovich)

Terry Bradshaw tries to elude Baltimore's Mike Barnes and Greg Fields in a 1979 Steelers triumph. (John Beale)

playing in a game, though doctors advised him to take a longer hiatus for a recovery that came long afterward. "I panicked myself out of my career," he mused later.

In his final Steelers appearance on December 10, 1983, in the last NFL game at Shea Stadium, he completed five of eight passes. His final heave was, fittingly, a touchdown to Calvin Sweeney and enough impetus for a Steelers playoff-clinching victory. He put on his cowboy hat and rode off.

Tunch Ilkin, offensive tackle 1980–1992 and longtime broadcaster: "He came into the huddle after the opening kickoff, he hadn't thrown the ball in a year, and he says, 'Okay, boys, we're going to have fun.' We came out throwing it." And the game plan read simply: run away from New York Jets nose tackle Joe Klecko. "I said, 'Terry, I thought we were supposed to run the ball.' 'Shit, Tunch, you know me . . . , I'm a gunslinger.'"

Tom Beasley, defensive lineman 1978–1983 and 1984–1986 with Washington: "I saw something that happened a handful of times in training camp. Terry threw with such velocity, these [rookies] wouldn't know how to catch it. Terry would throw it, and it would rip the webbing between fingers. I was able to play for 10 years, and of all the quarterbacks I saw, Terry clearly had the strongest arm."

Brown: "I don't think Bradshaw gets enough credit: actually calling all the plays, being on top of things. He was an important player. A significant player. He was not somebody we could have won those Super Bowls without. There was nobody more significant playing in them."

LARRY BROWN
Offensive Tackle–Tight End

Height: 6-4 • **Weight:** 246 • **College:** Kansas • **Years with the Steelers:** 1971–1984 • **Birthplace:** Jacksonville, Florida • **Born:** June 16, 1949

Not many players catch a touchdown pass in one Super Bowl, compile another reception in the next . . . and then start the following two as a man in the trenches.

Welcome to the interior migration of Larry Brown, 48 catches and six seasons as a sleek tight end (1971–1976), followed by 90 games and one Pro Bowl as a stout offensive tackle (1977–1984).

It was a move that covered a few inches sideways and miles apart.

Brown on the subject of 1977: "I went into Chuck [Noll]'s office. I had knee surgery, was in a cast for most of the off-season. So I wasn't able to run coming into camp that year. He told me he wanted me to go with the tackles on offense. It was kind of an experimental thing. During the course of that training camp, watching and observing. As training camp was coming to an end, they traded away the starting tackle. So much for the experiment."

Gordon Gravelle, the starting right tackle in the first two Super Bowls (though replaced by Gerry Mullins in 1976), was shipped to New York. Brown at age 28 was the right tackle for the entire season and, injuries among them, the next seven seasons thereafter. Of his 167 career Steelers games, 86 of them were spent at starting right tackle and 34 starting at tight end.

Brown: "In retrospect, it was a good move for me. I played 14 years."

Joe Gordon, publicity director and vice president 1969–1998: "According to Chuck Noll, the most underappreciated offensive lineman in the NFL [at the time]. He came as a tight end. Caught a touchdown pass in Super Bowl IX." And finished as a punishing offensive lineman.

Andy Russell, linebacker 1963, 1966–1976: "The interesting thing about Larry Brown, he was the best basketball player on our team. A big, tall tight end. Maybe 235 pounds. Then they made him an offensive lineman. He got into weight lifting, all of a sudden he's 275 but with the athleticism of a tight end. I don't think he ever got his due. I think he was an All-Pro

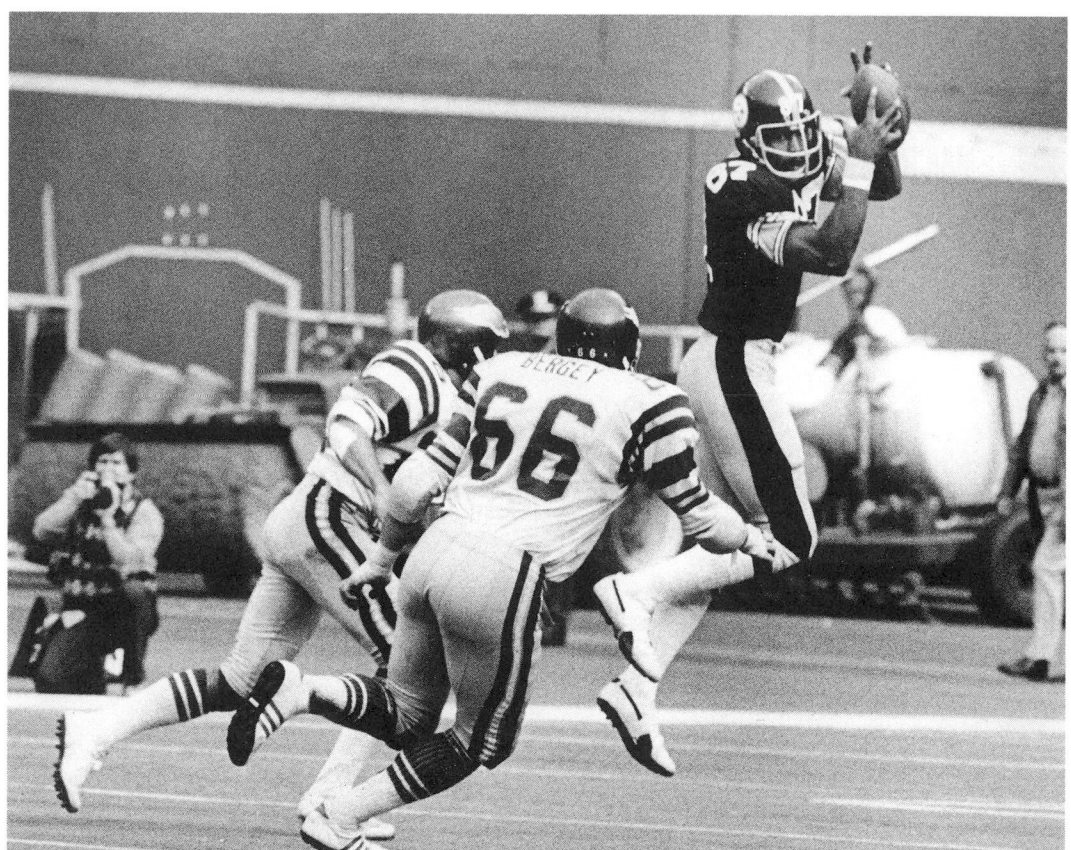

Before he became an offensive tackle that Chuck Noll considered one of his finest offensive linemen ever, Larry Brown played tight end. He caught a pass over Pro Bowl linebacker Bill Bergey in a 1974 Steelers victory over the Eagles at Three Rivers Stadium. (Temple Urban Archives)

player for quite a few years and never got the respect he should have. He'd neutralize Ed 'Too Tall' Jones [of Dallas] and Rams defensive end Jack Youngblood. Made them disappear."

Craig Wolfley, guard–tackle 1980–1989: "Bob Kohrs, who . . . knew him well, said Mark Gastineau [of the New York Jets] was crying after playing Larry once. Larry could punch so hard, they would stop rushing for the rest of the game."

Dan "Bad Rad" Radakovich, defensive line assistant 1971 and offensive-line coach 1974–1977: "I did two things with Larry Brown. He was there in 1971, when I was the defensive line coach. When I came back in 1974, he didn't play much the previous two years; John McMakin did. After 15 seconds of the first practice, I said, 'Larry, you're on first team.' He was a good player. Larry says to me, 'I'm at a disadvantage 'cause I got big arms.' I said, 'No, you're not.' The one guy Joe Greene was having trouble with was Larry Brown. An awesome blocker at tight end. Best in the league. In '76, I started putting him in at tackle. He became the full-time tackle in 1977. Players who came later, like Emil Boures [1982–1986], think he was the best tackle that ever lived."

Jon Kolb, teammate and line mate 1969–1981 and coach 1982–1991, still marveling that Brown could bench nearly 500 pounds with his thumbs touching: "I tell people when he walked in a room, his triceps came in five minutes later. Ask anybody on the team about Larry Brown lifting [6-4, 252-pound Hall of Famer] Claude Humphrey by the neck and pulling him into the air, his feet were off the ground. The little official, Tommy Bell, said, 'M-M-M-M-Mr. Brown, would you please put him down?'"

Brown: "He [Humphrey] certainly had a reputation as an intimidator. You're watching him all week [on film] and the

tactics that he used. And a lot of it was after a play. Things escalated." September 30, 1979, Brown was ejected. Allowed to stay was Humphrey—who admitted, "In all fairness to Larry, I would have hit me, too."

JACK BUTLER
Safety

Height: 6-1 • **Weight:** 200 • **College:** St. Bonaventure • **Years with the Steelers:** 1951–1959 • **Birthplace:** Pittsburgh • **Born:** November 12, 1927

A Pro Football Hall of Fame enshrinee in 2012, he should have been far more famous than merely the longtime director of the BLESTO scouting service or the name that Pittsburgh-born Michael Keaton chose for his main character in *Mr. Mom*—a 1983 flick the real Jack Butler still hasn't seen.

His 50 interceptions between his 1951 rookie season and 1958, his final full season before sustaining a career-ending broken leg, rank second in that time period between two Hall of Famers of that secondary generation: Emlen Tunnell's 57 and Night Train Lane's 47. Of the NFL's 50th Anniversary team, 43 of 45 were enshrined in the Hall—Butler was the last defensive starter left standing.

See, Butler was a stellar defensive back who played on forgettable Steelers teams. He had four coaches in nine seasons. He played on just one team that won more than a half dozen games—the 1958 entry won seven. The only teams that played above .500 were his final two. None made the playoffs.

The football gods resigned Butler to starring in obscurity, then scouting in obscurity.

Dale Dodrill, nose guard–middle linebacker the same years as Butler played: "Jack and I went into the Steelers the same year together. Jack was one of the great defensive backs. Covered a lot of ground, had a good feel for the game. He understood the game real well."

Frank Varrichione, offensive tackle: "The guys that kept that defense together were Jack Butler and Ernie Stautner."

Stautner, a Hall of Famer himself, once said of Butler: "Receivers did not want to go in his area. Not only was he a great cornerback, he'd flat-out knock the tar out of you."

How Butler even came to the Steelers is a typical Pittsburgh story.

This Munhall kid was told where to attend college by a friend of his father's: Art Rooney. He was a raw freshman walking around the St. Bonaventure campus when he was told to go out for football by the St. Bonaventure athletic director, Father Silas Rooney, Art's brother. He was an undrafted free agent when he reported to Steelers training camp at St. Bonaventure . . . and didn't expect to last long.

Butler: "They played the single wing. I didn't know what the hell it was. Never heard of it. The first day of camp, they're lining up, and I thought I was a receiver; I'm the smallest guy there. 'Why the hell don't we ever throw the ball?' . . . I finally went to him, 'Coach [John] Michelosen, I'll never make this team. I'm a wide receiver. You don't throw the ball that much. I want to quit and go to Detroit, 'cause I know this coach up there and I think I might have a chance to make that team.' He says, 'You can't go anywhere until I cut you.' I said, 'When are you going to cut me?' 'I'll let you know.'

"He changed me to defensive end. Now I'm the smallest defensive end."

Michelosen sent him out later that regular season to replace an injured player writhing on the field. He was positively giddy to find the afflicted player was not a defensive end, for once.

Butler: "Best thing that ever happened to me—I was a defensive back."

Chuck Cherundolo, defensive coach: "He was a great one. A great one until, what, he broke an ankle?"

Joe Walton, a Washington Redskins player at the time: "Jack—broke his leg, never played again. He was a very good player. "

Butler: "My knee pulled apart. We were playing the Eagles at Forbes Field. I'm playing left safety, and this receiver caught a quick little slant pass. He's falling, and I'm coming over. When he falls, his shoulder hit my knee. And that was it. I bet I had six or eight operations on it. It's been replaced and everything. I had a lot of infections in it."

Bill Walsh, center 1949–1955: "We lived about two, three blocks from each other. We drove back and forth to work. That was before people had two and three cars. He was the best. He came up as a rookie, took over a starting position, and played the rest of his career as the best safety in the game."

He tried coaching under Buddy Parker for a time from 1961 to 1963, but his heart wasn't in it. He moved into scouting. He served the rest of that career atop the NFL's leading scouting organization.

Butler: "I wasn't a coach. But we weren't allowed to do anything. I didn't like being a coach at all. One weekend, I told Parker, 'I quit. I don't want to come.'" He was given a scouting role. "Say we were going to play the Chicago Cardinals; I would go to their game and break it down. Then I got into more of the college scouting."

The Lions, Eagles, and Steelers formed a talent organization—presto, LESTO—in 1963, and Butler followed another Steelers scout, former Clairton mayor Ken Stilley, into that concern. The Bears joined the next season to create BLESTO. Butler scouted from New England to South Carolina. Soon after, he succeeded Stilley and served as BLESTO's director for 44 years, until his 2007 retirement. That's when the BLESTO office shuttered in Pittsburgh and moved south to Jacksonville.

The scouting reach of the man named to the Steelers' 75th Anniversary team! He introduced psychological and personality testing into the evaluation process. He

Jack Butler, elected to the Hall of Fame in 2012, makes a diving tackle of Eagles halfback Frank Ziegler in 1952. (Temple Urban Archives)

indoctrinated computerized scouting in the NFL. And he founded the NFL Combine.

It was there, in the 1990s, where they snapped a photograph of the Butler-BLESTO family tree: all the NFL front-office employees whom he gave their first nudge down that pro-football path.

There were some sixty men in that picture.

LYNN CHANDNOIS
Wingback–Halfback–Returner

Height: 6-2 • **Weight:** 198 • **College:** Michigan State • **Years with the Steelers:** 1950–1956 • **Birthplace:** Fayette, Michigan • **Born:** February 24, 1925 • **Died:** April 19, 2011

The eighth-overall selection in the 1950 draft, Lynn Chandnois came to the Steelers—at the advanced age of 25, after two years in the service—with considerable potential and promise. He left the same way, potential and promise largely untapped.

Oh, he was one of the great return men in NFL history. He topped the league in kickoff-return average in 1951 (32.5 yards per) and 1952 (35.2) and all-purpose yardage in 1953. His 1952 average was surpassed by only three players in the next 50 years, one of them Hall of Famer Ollie Matson. His 29.6-yard career kickoff-return average ranks second all-time in the NFL—behind only Hall of Famer Gale Sayers' 30.6.

He put up some numbers in his seven-year career: 1,934 yards rushing, 2,012 yards receiving on 162 catches, another 3,032 yards in total returns, and 256 yards passing in the 1951 season alone out of the single wing. And he was among the Steelers and Los Angeles Rams who committed fully to the formation of the NFL Players Association in February 1957.

Chuck Cherundolo, defensive coach at the time: "Never reached his potential. I don't know why."

Jack Butler, defensive back 1951–1959: "The guy had a lot of talent. You're practicing, you get in line. I'm next and he's right behind me. You turn around again, he's at the back of the line. He gave it to you at practice, but he never did [reach that potential]. He had size, he had everything."

Tim Rooney Sr., son of the Chief and ball boy/water boy at the time: "He was a tremendous athlete. From Michigan State. He really disliked Kiesling, who was very close to my father. And Kies hated Chandnois. In fact, Chandnois ran back two kickoffs against the Giants [in 1952]. The Giants won the toss and elected to kick off; they thought they'd hold us. And Chadnois ran the opening kickoff back for a touchdown." An offsides penalty negated the return. The Steelers were pushed back five yards. "They kicked off again, and he ran the second [one] back for a touchdown. Kies used to ride in the car after the games with my dad—Dan would drive, and I would sit in the back with Kies. Instead of complimenting Chandnois running back two kickoffs in a game—which doesn't happen very often—he called him a 'lucky stiff' for running it back."

Dale Dodrill, nose guard–middle linebacker 1951–1959: "He was really a flashy player. He seemed to have a problem with injuries, though. I don't think he ever played a full season [1954–1956] because of injuries. When Buddy Parker came and took over, that was one of the first players he removed. And Buddy removed a lot of players."

CHUCK CHERUNDOLO
Center

Height: 6-1 • **Weight:** 215 • **College:** Penn State • **Years with the Steelers:** 1941–1942, 1945–1948 • **Birthplace:** Old Forge, Pennsylvania • **Born:** August 8, 1916

To appreciate a former player and longtime Steelers assistant, it was best to visit a man who at the time was the fifth-oldest living NFL player.

Chuck Cherundolo lived with his daughter in Florida amid farms and low-slung houses, in a home dwarfed by deciduous trees. He sat in a lounger behind huge, wide, black-plastic glasses. He occasionally pushed himself up and into a wheelchair, so he could scoot himself to the fridge for a drink of iced tea from the container. He was 94 years old about to turn 95, though he continually called himself 91. At that age, what's three, four years? An eyeblink behind those glasses.

Cherundolo: "When I first got in the league, in 1937, I was with the Cleveland Rams. The coach didn't like me. Took me off the first team and put me on the second team. I was there for two years. I told him to go [expletive] himself. . . . Dutch Clark, used to be in Detroit. I put up with him for one year. At the end of the last year . . . , I told him in a meeting, 'You can take this team and shove it up your [posterior]; you just lost a football player.' That's when he traded me. . . . It's nice to be that tough. Wish I could be like that now."

After his 1937–1939 jaunt with the Rams and a 1940 stint with Philadelphia, he came to the Steelers in 1941 . . . and stayed. The only piece of business that interrupted his stay from 1941 through 1957 was World War II in 1943–1944. The captain, a former Penn State All-America, played through 1948. He was named to the 75th Anniversary Legends team, encompassing players from the pre-1970 era.

Tim Rooney Sr., son of the Chief and Steelers water boy: "He would have been one of the superstars [by today's standards]. He was one of the real, real top players. He competed with any other."

Cherundolo, on his reason for retirement: "Too old."

He moved instantly into coaching on defense, where Steelers players adored him. He coached from 1949 to 1957. Steelers records and newspaper accounts refer to Cherundolo, whose main vocation was the wine business, switching from scouting and back to coaching the defensive line in 1961. In 1962, he briefly joined the Eagles staff of former Steelers teammate and assistant Nick Skorich and later coached with the Redskins under one of his former defensive linemen, Bill McPeak, and with George Halas' Bears through 1969, when he left to become a head coach in the Continental Football League.

Bill Walsh, center 1949–1955: "Chuck Cherundolo was my coach, and he had just retired the year before. He got it across to me pretty quickly. But I was stunned how they centered the ball [in the single wing] . . . and why they wanted it that way.

"Chuck knew what he was doing all the time, as far as us young guys. He was a good man. I was able to see a lot of his films from the years before: He was a real great center. I used to stop at Chuck's house for coffee; it was that type of relationship."

Dale Dodrill, nose guard–middle linebacker 1951–1959: "They had me over on offense in a scrimmage once [in 1951, his rookie year]. I would go down the line and hit those big defensive tackles and ends, and Chuck yelled over there, 'Get that kid out of there; you're going to get him killed.' So they finally put me over on defense, and I finally found a place to play. He was hands-on, he knew all about it—he played the game long enough. He could communicate. I always enjoyed playing under him."

STEVE COURSON
Guard

Height: 6-1 • **Weight:** 274 • **College:** South Carolina • **Years with the Steelers:** 1978–1983 • **Birthplace:** Philadelphia • **Born:** October 1, 1955 • **Died:** November 10, 2005

Considered a yeoman lineman in his Steelers years, starting 48 of 73 games including half the 1979 season leading to Super Bowl XIV, Steve Courson's football legacy would've remained largely mundane—a brawny starter who liked his beer—had he decided to remain mum.

Courson couldn't stay silent about steroids, though.

He confessed. It shook the football world. And, ultimately, Courson helped to clear the air, but not the problem, in baseball and American youth sports.

Chuck Yesalis, a Penn State professor and a performance-enhancing drugs international expert who befriended Courson in 1985: "That's just the way he and I were wired. That was the truth, and the truth sets you free. We also believed most guys and gals don't want to do that stuff. To solve a problem, you first have to admit you have a problem.

"God has blessed me with five or six special friends. I was a pallbearer at his wife Cathy's funeral and at his funeral. We were both into military history. People said we must've been brothers in another life. Our whole ethos was the same."

Courson talked often how steroids were offered to him in college, at South Carolina, by a team doctor. They became an accepted football form when he was drafted in 1978's fifth round and, as he put it, he filled grocery bags for fellow Steelers along with other NFL players—trolling drugstore shelves for the proper steroids, needles, and such.

V. Tim Rooney, pro player scout 1972–1979: "When Courson was a rookie and nonstarter, he was sent onto the field by [Chuck] Noll with a play for Bradshaw [near the opponent's goal line]. Bradshaw knew that Courson had a play call, and was screaming at Steve for the call. But Steve was so happy and excited to be in the game, he forgot the call.

"Steve's strength and initial quickness gave a new definition for explosion in a way most of us had never seen before."

Dan "Bad Rad" Radakovich, assistant 1971, 1974–1977: "They talk about steroids, but I don't think the steroids came in until Courson. I never heard of them before him. The team the first two Super Bowls, they weren't on steroids."

Yesalis: "If you look at Steve's book [*False Glory: Steelers and Steroids*], my books [*Anabolic Steroids in Sport and Exercise* and *The Steroid Game*] . . . , that's a very fallacious statement. It started with the Chargers in the early '60s. When did steroids come to the Steelers? The team doctor gave [Courson] his first at South Carolina. It was extremely entrenched in professional football. That statement is laughable. I won't dignify it any more than that."

Jon Kolb, offensive tackle 1969–1981 and assistant 1982–1991: "I remember Steve being super strong. He would drive Rad nuts. Rad would teach [punch blocking]—the linebacker shuck is what it is. And Steve would do it like he was lifting weights. Here was a guy who weighed 275 and ran a 4.6[-second] 40. Vitamins don't make you fast. They can make you strong, but only God made you fast.

"I hear people like [former Buffalo LB Jim] Haslett say the Steelers' offensive line was taking steroids. Hey, wait a minute. Nobody talked about it while they were playing. It was all after the fact. If everybody knew what was going on, how come somebody next to you in the locker room didn't talk?"

Two years after being traded to lowly Tampa Bay, Courson came clean in the May 13, 1985, *Sports Illustrated*—for himself and others: "I use [steroids] to build up my strength in the off-season, but I never use speed to play. Guys are out there using speed. Why don't they outlaw that? Coaches say, 'Hey, steroids are no good for you.' Well, how good is taking a painkiller in the ankle or the knee? The whole thing is hypocritical.

"It's very easy for people on the outside to criticize. It's different when it's your livelihood, when it's your job to keep a genetic mutation from getting into your backfield."

Lest it be forgotten, former Dallas Cowboy offensive lineman Pat Donovan in that same *SI* issue said, "Steroids are very, very accepted in the NFL. In my last five or six years, it ran as high as 60 to 70 percent on the Cowboys on the offensive and defensive lines." So it existed on both sides of the lines of scrimmage.

Yesalis, on when they met doing a national television news show: "Steve was in Tampa, the year he got cut. If anybody wants to pursue blackballing in the NFL . . . , he gave up 1½ sacks all year, but he couldn't get a job anywhere? That was after the big *Sports Illustrated* story came out. Where he didn't squeal on anybody, but just said how it was. He never laid a dime on anybody.

"[Athletes today are bigger, stronger and faster,] but that's through better training techniques [and nutrition]. And I laugh my ass off as I say that. Being a former strength coach myself—oh, give me a break."

Courson suffered from cardiomyopathy and wound up on a heart-transplant list, his health worsened so quickly. On visits to Yesalis' State College home, Courson slept uncomfortably on the couch because he couldn't climb the stairs. Through healthy diet and exercise, together with moderation in his alcohol consumption, Courson developed into a fit fellow and wellness trainer who lived in rural southwestern Pennsylvania. He spoke to youngsters about a healthy lifestyle and avoiding performance-enhancing drugs. He spoke to Congress. He wrote letters to the editor and that book.

At one school appearance, he lay down on a bench and pressed 42 reps of 225 pounds.

Yesalis: "I believe the biggest stud at the Combine that same year did it 34 times. And [Courson officially] was still on the transplant list."

Only such stars as Rocky Bleier, telling the *Pittsburgh Post-Gazette* and later ESPN.com that he took Dianabol prescribed for him in 1973–1974 after his comeback from Vietnam-war injuries, and Terry Bradshaw, for medicinal purposes, openly admitted to using drugs that weren't illegal at the time. Jim Clack mentioned taking steroids to gain muscle and weight as part of Roy Blount's *Three Bricks Shy of a Load* book in 1973, though his comment created nary a ripple. Backup offensive lineman Rick Donnalley in 1982 told the *Cincinnati Post* that he used Maxibolin, Anavar, and Deca-Durabolin while some teammates took steroids for weight enhancement. Steel Curtain backup lineman Steve Furness' family members after his death said he tried steroids amid his playing career. Doctors for Mike Webster, in court papers as part of his victorious suit against the NFL pension plan, admitted that he experimented with steroids. And guard Terry Long, much later, in 1991, tested positive for them.

In 2005, chopping 5-foot-wide, 44-foot-high trees around his Farmington, Pennsylvania, home, he moved briskly to prevent one from falling on his beloved Labradors, Rufus and Rachel. The tree pinned and killed him.

When Steelers teammates came by bus to Courson's funeral in Gettysburg, friends and family felt pangs of Courson's disillusionment and the years where he believed former teammates turned their backs on a friend needing a heart transplant.

Yesalis: "The tremendous disappointment he had with his teammates. . . . 'Those guys, in their 50s, and they still [were reticent to talk about steroids].' Those guys were ostracized [at Courson's Gettysburg funeral], which I totally thought they deserved. That's just phenomenal, in this state.

"The NFL never really took me on, but they pilloried Steve. The NFL is a religion in this country. . . . We discussed this [numerous] times in later years: Our goal was to lift the rock up and let the light of truth shine forth on all those creepy, crawlies scurrying away. I think we totally succeeded."

Tight end Bennie Cunningham bleeds through gauze and adhesive strips after a particularly brutal game in 1980. (Bill Amatucci)

BENNIE CUNNINGHAM
Tight End

Height: 6-5 • **Weight:** 254 • **College:** Clemson • **Years with the Steelers:** 1976–1985 • **Birthplace:** Laurens, South Carolina • **Born:** December 23, 1954

The 1976 draft class produced perhaps the greatest defensive player in NFL history, Tampa Bay's Lee Roy Selmon at the top, along with fellow future Hall of Famer Mike Haynes and such NFL stars as Chuck Muncie, Joe Washington, Mike Pruitt, and Richard Todd throughout. At the end of that first round, for the two-time Super Bowl champions, came an oversized tight end who could run. Fast.

Nine of those fellow first-rounders had longer playing careers. Seven made more Pro Bowls than his zero.

But none of them outshined Bennie Cunningham in jewelry: two Super Bowl rings.

While he shared the tight end duties to a degree with Randy Grossman, who ranked as the Steelers' top receiver at that position in 1978 and 1980, every other year of his career Cunningham was the primary target there. His emergence allowed the Steelers to move Larry Brown from tight end to offensive tackle. All that blocking beef up front helped to create holes originally for Franco Harris and Rocky Bleier, later for Frankie Pollard and Walter Abercrombie.

Between 1979 and 1983, despite missing 10 games, Cunningham caught 151 passes for 2,037 yards and 14 touchdowns. Perhaps his most memorable score came in 1978 on a flea-flicker—which included a fake Lynn Swann reverse and pitch back to Terry Bradshaw—to beat Cleveland in overtime.

Perhaps part of his difficulty was unfulfilled potential. As Miami's Hall of Fame coach Don Shula was moved to remark in 1981: "I've seen him on film where he's done some unbelievable things. He should be All-Pro. But you never hear Cunningham mentioned with the likes of Ozzie Newsome or Kellen Winslow." Cunningham was named to the Steelers' 75th Anniversary team.

Mike Wagner, safety 1971–1980: "Bennie was kind of ahead of his time. A big guy, really fast, talented. Bennie thought he was a 5-10, fleet-footed running back instead of a 6-5, 240-pound man. He would try to tippy-toe and juke guys instead of running over people."

Tony Dungy, teammate 1977–1978 and defensive assistant and coordinator 1981–1988: "A good man, a good friend. The thing I remember about Bennie, he always wanted to be a wide receiver—he was just trapped in that big body. The first year I was there, he bought a Honda Prelude, 'cause it was sleek and sporty. We had to pry him in there. 'Bennie, you need a big man's car.' He always prided himself on getting the deep ball. Battled some injuries, but talent-wise he was special: size, speed, and hands."

DERMONTTI DAWSON
Center

Height: 6-2 • **Weight:** 288 • **College:** Kentucky • **Years with the Steelers:** 1988–2000 • **Birthplace:** Lexington, Kentucky • **Born:** June 17, 1965

The Pro Football Hall of Fame always looked so inevitable. For five consecutive seasons, Dermontti Dawson was a unanimous All-Pro. He was a seven-time Pro Bowl selection. He was among the first *pulling centers* to ever play the game, he was so nimble. He was so durable, he played 170 consecutive games, second-longest in club history—all in the middle of every play, snap after snap, game after game.

The man affectionately known as "Dirt" had only one Canton flaw: He played for Pittsburgh, the franchise with a wing full of enshrinees that caused voters to erect something of a wall—stay out, Steelers.

Time will show, there's no wall Dawson cannot knock down.

Ron Erhardt, offensive coordinator 1992–1995: "One of the finest linemen who has played this game. He was in the same league as John Hannah, who I had at the Patriots. He could do whatever you wanted as an offensive lineman. We could do some things scheme-wise that a lot of people weren't doing at that time. I mean, we could pull our center."

His career began alongside a Hall of Famer, Mike Webster, in his final Steelers season. Webster left the center position to Dawson, then joined the Kansas City Chiefs. An enshrined Dawson (in 2012) following an enshrined Webster placed them in the company of such other Hall of Famers following other Hall of Famers at the very same position as Dick Butkus and Bill George, Leroy Kelly and Jim Brown, Steve Young and Joe Montana.

Dirt paved the way for four of the top five rushing seasons in Steelers history. He set blocks for some seventy 100-yard rushing performances, involving nine different rushers. He was named among 33 players to the Steelers' 75th Anniversary team.

Dermontti Dawson: "After I became the starter the second year, I tried to emulate Mike [Webster] by being No. 1 in all the drills, being sure I wrote everything down, just the fine details. . . . You don't have to be a boisterous guy; you can lead by example. Guys recognize that. Accountability is everything."

Jim Sweeney, line mate 1996–1999, before the Canton vote: "He should be in the Hall of Fame. What's wrong with those guys? He'll be in there. He could pull. Dwight Stephenson [a Hall of Fame center from Miami] was the first guy I knew who could pull from center. Then Dirt. I mean, what a great thing."

Ralph Berlin, trainer 1968–1992: "Dermontti was bigger than Webster and, in his own right, just as good."

Jon Kolb, ex-lineman turned assistant 1982–1991: "I remember scouting Dermontti Dawson at the Senior Bowl and thinking how athletic he was. He would not touch a weight for a month or two months, lay down and bench press 400 pounds."

Kevin Greene, linebacker 1993–1995: "The Hall of Fame is a tricky deal; a lot of people deserve to be in the Hall of Fame. Absolutely, [Dawson] does. He was a good one. He was physical, quick, fast, violent. He was smart, tough, called out pressure, pointed out things to Mike Tomczak and Neil O'Donnell, had leverage. Everything you wanted a center to be, Dermontti was that guy. That's the thing, too: He had the ability to pull on the corner and actually reach an outside linebacker. From inside, three gaps removed. Amazing."

Sweeney: "A true sweetheart. A great friend. You know, game days when he stepped on the field, he was a different guy, man. He was like an animal. Come game day, what a competitor."

Bubby Brister, quarterback 1986–1992: "So athletic for a center, and so smart. I felt like I got one of the best centers, [so that] hopefully I can make a 10-year run. I didn't. But he did."

Hall of Fame Inductee Dermontti Dawson, shown here in 1983, carved a niche as a pulling center and an iron man at the position where he followed Hall of Famer Mike Webster. The Steelers had just two centers for more than a quarter century, from 1974 to 2000. (Bill Amatucci)

LEN DAWSON
Quarterback

Height: 6-0 • **Weight:** 190 • **College:** Purdue • **Years with the Steelers:** 1957–1959 • **Birthplace:** Alliance, Ohio • **Born:** June 20, 1935

First, a history lesson.

The Steelers/Pirates, from the 1933 start, had no luck, man. They had no luck at all with quarterbacks. They had no *need* for quarterbacks, with all that single-wing rot for their first generation.

On August 10, 1938, the Chicago Bears swapped Eggs Manske for the then-Pirates' first-round draft choice three months hence. The choice turned out to be the second overall pick. The pick turned out to be Sid Luckman, a T-formation specialist, which, of course, would have served no passing use to the Pittsburgh single wing. Luckman turned out to be a championship-winning quarterback and Hall of Famer for George Halas' Bears.

So it was in that same open vein from which dripped the Johnny Unitas deepest cut of 1955. Then late the next year—November 27, 1956, to be precise—came the 1957 draft and a gush over Len Dawson at No. 5 overall.

Publicist Ed Kiely long has told this draft story: When the Steelers selected Dawson, Paul Brown at a nearby hotel draft table slammed his fist and knocked books off, so angry was he that he couldn't nab Dawson for Cleveland. Thus the Browns, with the No. 6 overall pick, instead selected a guy named Jim Brown.

In August 1957, Buddy Parker was hired as coach, and he wanted some real quarterbacks. So he traded two future No. 1 picks to San Francisco for Earl Morrall, picked up Jack Kemp off the scrap heap, and inherited Dawson from his pal Walt Kiesling, the previous head coach who was more than glad to hand the Steelers' keys over to Parker. So the Dawson kid understudied Morrall for one season and, after another swap by the trade-happy Parker, Bobby Layne for two more.

The most productive place Parker found for him? In early 1957, after bonus pick Gary Glick failed to kick, he let Dawson dabble as placekicker. On October 13, Dawson missed two extra-point attempts. So much for that.

Dawson threw 17 passes in three Steelers years. He was traded to Cleveland New Year's Eve 1959. Hardly used there, he got released again two and a half years later. One tale had Dawson picking up the phone on Paul Brown's desk and promptly calling Hank Stram of the Dallas Texans, who previously promised him work. A wise move. It didn't mean an NFL end, after all. The Texans became the Chiefs, which became an NFL franchise and Super Bowl regular in two of the inaugural four such big games. He blossomed in Stram's moving pocket and skill-position talent: halfback Mike Garrett and wide receiver Otis Taylor.

Funny how things work out. In 1987, he was inducted into the Pro Football Hall of Fame in the same class as Steelers' greats John Henry Johnson, who was introduced by Art Rooney, and Joe Greene in front of a Pittsburgh-heavy crowd chanting "Dee-fense."

Chuck Cherundolo, an assistant through the 1950s: "At that time, you only needed one quarterback. You ever see one run out of halfback in the single wing? Christ, no, we didn't need [a passer]. I don't remember him throwing. Of course, I was defense at the time."

Joe Walton, fellow NFLer and Dawson's roomie at the 1957 college all-star game. "Lenny Dawson? Lenny was a real late bloomer. Didn't push himself forward. Quarterbacks in those days were take-charge guys . . . , had a commanding force about them. Lenny was laid-back, a quiet guy at that time. Finally got his chance, where? With Kansas City. And proved he was pretty damn good."

Pat Rooney Sr.: "There were loads of guys like that. I think the Chief got rid of them because he couldn't pay for them."

Frank Varrichione, Pro Bowl offensive tackle at the time: "They let these guys come in and let them go. I forgot about Lenny being there. That's remarkable. Lenny Dawson, Jack Kemp, Johnny Unitas, and one more . . . Earl Morrall [all of whom won at least one title elsewhere]. There were some great ones who passed through there."

BUDDY DIAL
Split End

Height: 6-1 • **Weight:** 194 • **College:** Rice • **Years with the Steelers:** 1959–1963 • **Birthplace:** Ponca City, Oklahoma • **Born:** June 20, 1935 • **Died:** February 29, 2008

Gilbert Leroy Dial was famous for two Pittsburgh events, neither of which was his fault.

1. He scored a touchdown, as he was wont to do, and had a male cheerleader immediately fire a cannon in his face.
2. He got traded by the mad swapper, coach Buddy Parker. Then again, who didn't Parker trade?

Thanks, Buddy, for those memories.

In between, he grew into one of the NFL's most productive receivers—he twice topped all league receivers in yards per catch, *averaged* 21.6 over his five Steelers years, and tallied 42 touchdowns in 66 games. So he deserved a rung somewhere not far from the Hines Ward, John Stallworth, Lynn Swann, Louis Lipps legacy in team history. Little does anyone know, but Dial ranks sixth all-time in Steelers receiving yards (4,723) right behind that quartet and Elbie Nickel . . . and those fellows played anywhere from three to nine seasons longer. His 42 scores rank behind two Hall of Famers and another potential one: Stallworth and Swann plus Ward. All that, and he left Pittsburgh at the tender age of 26.

In 1962, the male Ingots were launched with their own end-zone cannon filled with blanks. On October 21 that season, Dial turned a Bobby Layne pass into a touchdown against the Dallas Cowboys. And boom.

NFL Films voted it the No. 2 all-time member of their "Football Follies"—the epitome of dubious distinctions.

Wouldn't you know, the Steelers' leading receiver from 1960 to 1963—a choirboy, professional singer, and longtime Texas resident—was traded to Dallas after the 1963 season. Coach Tom Landry told reporters he was thrilled to land Dial because it meant two more Cowboys victories that season: "the two games he usually beats us." He retired from the Cowboys after the 1966 season, having caught 41 passes total there as opposed to the 45 he averaged per year in Pittsburgh.

Dick Hoak, halfback and teammate: "Buddy was a good player. We traded him [to Dallas] for the rights to Scott Appleton, and we didn't sign him. Appleton ended up going to the AFL [with Houston]."

Jack Butler, defensive back turned assistant coach turned BLESTO scouting director: "Buddy was a good receiver. He only played a couple of years. He wasn't a real blazer, but ran good patterns and had good hands."

A defender, believed to be Dale Dodrill tries to bring down a Philadelphia running back in a 1952 home Eagles victory. Bearing down in the background is big No. 70, future Hall of Famer Ernie Stautner. Notice that Stautner is wearing a face mask and the others are not. (Temple Urban Archives)

DALE DODRILL
Nose Guard–Middle Linebacker

Height: 6-1 • **Weight:** 215 • **College:** Colorado A&M • **Years with the Steelers:** 1951–1959 • **Birthplace:** Stockton, Kansas • **Born:** February 27, 1926

This man in the middle basically arose from 5–2 formation nose guard his first six seasons to 4–3 middle linebacker his final three. No matter where he aligned, he remained in the middle of it all.

Nine games into his rookie season, Dodrill sustained a broken jaw and nose when elbowed by Philadelphia's Bucko Kilroy and underwent season-ending surgery at Eye and Ear Hospital.

Dale Dodrill: "It must've been the last minute of the game, the last two minutes. The Eagles fumbled. I forget [what Steelers teammate] got the ball, but the defense becomes offense. Bucko was in the road, I was going to block him while we were returning the fumble, and I got one of his forearms into my face. I was all bandaged up. Some sportswriter came into the hospital room and got a picture of me. I must've been asleep, 'cause I don't remember him taking my picture. It got in the paper back home. My mother called me scared to death. . . . No face masks. You used to keep one arm up to protect your face."

He came back to play so well in 1952 that league coaches voted him to the Pro Bowl, but promoters left him off the squad—an omission that hacked off the Steelers.

Dodrill, described by *Pittsburgh Press* writer Pat Livingston in 1954 as the "hatchet-faced, 205-pound All-Pro," was the smallest nose guard in the league, though he claimed that he played closer to 220. He made the Pro Bowl four times (five

counting the omission) in his eight full seasons, and at both positions. He and Ernie Stautner were the first Steelers to earn a quartet of Pro Bowl invites.

Dodrill, named to the 75th Anniversary Legends (pre-1970) team, was something of a kick-blocking artiste, though records of blocks weren't officially kept until 1992. Ted "Mad Stork" Hendricks owned the unofficial NFL record at 25 blocked punts, point-after attempts, and field-goal tries.

Dodrill: "I blocked quite a few, I think—extra points and field goals. It used to cause a little excitement. I actually jumped over the center after he snapped the ball and before he got his head up."

Jack Butler, defensive back and teammate throughout 1951–1959: "There's a guy you look at, and you'd think, 'How the heck did he do it?' Just an ordinary looking guy, an ordinary build. But he played like a tiger. He could chase things down, make plays. He was a really good football player."

BULLET BILL DUDLEY
Halfback–Defensive Back–Returner–Punter–Kicker

Height: 5-10 • **Weight:** 182 • **College:** Virginia • **Years with the Steelers:** 1942, 1946 • **Birthplace:** Bluefield, Virginia • **Born:** December 24, 1921 • **Died:** February 4, 2010

No player may ever again lead the NFL in so many divergent categories—the rare triple crown of rushing, punt returns, and interceptions—and then summarily get run out of town the way William McGarvey Dudley left Pittsburgh following his MVP 1946 season.

Bullet Bill always was breathtakingly unorthodox.

He starred at his home state University of Virginia as a 17-year-old sophomore. He became the Steelers' inaugural first-overall pick in the NFL draft—Gary Glick and Terry Bradshaw were the other two—at the age of 20.

After just two Steelers games in 1942, coach Walt Kiesling remarked to reporters: "He's the best back we've ever had." Art Rooney was quoted as saying: "He looks better to me than Whizzer White, for whom we paid $15,000 last year." All Dudley did was put together a 44-yard touchdown run in his debut, then return a kickoff 84 yards for a score the next week—after being knocked out so badly in the first quarter that a *Pittsburgh Post-Gazette* photograph showed three teammates and the trainer carrying off a pained Bullet in their arms.

To show you the stepchild status of the NFL at the time, Rooney told the *PG* afterward: "Whizzer White couldn't carry this boy's shoes. His great comeback after being carried off the field in the first quarter would have made [head]lines in every sports section of the country had it happened in a college game."

1. He rushed for 696 yards and amassed 1,787 all-purpose yards that season. Then he went to war.
2. He missed the 1943 and 1944 seasons and most of 1945.
3. In 1946, playing in the single wing of meticulous Jock Sutherland, he

   - amassed 2,072 all-purpose yards and topped the NFL with 604 yards rushing

- added 10 interceptions and seven fumble recoveries
- kicked two field goals and 12 extra points
- averaged 40.2 yards per punt

Nice comeback: He won NFL MVP.

Nevertheless, there was friction between star player and legendary coach. Pat Livingston, one of the NFL's first full-time scouts at the time and later a longtime *Pittsburgh Press* writer and columnist, told the tale of Sutherland once bemoaning a Dudley run as being a mistake because the play was poorly executed. Tension escalated.

After two end-zone interceptions in a 1946 defeat of the Boston Yanks, Sutherland was moved to remark: "I wouldn't trade Bill Dudley today for any two backs in the league."

Not long after, Sutherland traded Dudley for two backs from Detroit, one still in college (the rights to Bob Chappuis, who never signed with Pittsburgh) and a draft choice. That choice, traded away in inimitable Steelers fashion, wound up being quarterback Bobby Layne—no matter, he ended up a Steeler a decade later.

Whatever the case, this "clash of personalities," as the front office publicly termed it, resulted in the trade to Detroit that "brought widespread opposition from Pittsburgh fans," reported the United Press.

McHugh: "[Sutherland told Dudley,] 'You're a great player, but I don't have to have great players to win.' And they had a better record in '47 without Dudley than they had before."

Tim Rooney Sr., a ball boy/water boy at the time: "He did have a run-in with Sutherland. He came back from the service. I don't know what Sutherland had against Bill Dudley. My father was very, very close to Bill Dudley, and Sutherland wanted to trade Dudley. My father—no matter as close as he was—in most cases, he let the coaches do what they wanted to do." So the Chief's friend Dudley was gone.

Chuck Cherundolo, a center in Dudley's Steelers days: "One of my good friends. He would never give in to injuries. He didn't look like a good runner. He was tall [5-10]. Hell of an athlete. Boy, he had a tough mind, too. He had that knack."

Dan "Bad Rad" Radakovich, a Steelers assistant and a hopeless Steelers fan as a youth: "The Chief took Bullet Bill Dudley as his guest to the Super Bowl [IX]. He caught [Roy] Gerela's kicks in warm-ups [at age 54]. Dudley was the best at everything. Like a smaller Jimmy Brown."

GLEN EDWARDS
Safety

Height: 6-0 • **Weight:** 185 • **College:** Florida A&M • **Years with the Steelers:** 1971–1977 • **Birthplace:** St. Petersburg, Florida • **Born:** July 31, 1947

He was affectionately called Pine, and he was known for bringing the wood.

Fact is, Glen Edwards may well rank as one of the hardest hitters—if not *the* hardest—in the physical history of the Steelers franchise. And that's a mouthful.

A free agent addition among the star-studded 1971 Steelers draft pool, Edwards replaced an injured Ralph Anderson in the 1972 Immaculate Reception playoff game . . . and stuck. He turned into a starter and star, winning the team's MVP award in 1974, the club's first Super Bowl season. The next

Steelers safety to win one? Troy Polamalu in 2010, the eighth Super Bowl season.

Edwards created national headlines and a hullaballoo in that 1974 season when he drilled Cincinnati quarterback Ken Anderson out of bounds, promptly getting ejected. He made the Pro Bowl in 1975, subbing for an ailing Jack Tatum of Oakland, and again after the defensive gem of a 1976 season—when all four Steelers defensive backs were selected.

Then it all began to come undone for Edwards in Pittsburgh.

Chuck Noll, on the stand at Oakland safety George Atkinson's civil trial over his "criminal element" remark, said under cross-examination that Mel Blount and Edwards similarly slipped outside the rules on occasion with their rough play. While Blount filed a $6 million lawsuit against Noll and the Steelers for defamation of character, Edwards basically shrugged and told reporters: "I can just say it didn't affect me."

He staged his own personal contract walkout, apparently against the advice of his agent, in November 1977. He stayed away four days and missed a loss in Denver before returning. The next training camp, 1978, he got traded to San Diego for a sixth-round pick who never lasted, tight end Bill Murrell.

Edwards endures. He ranks fifth all-time in franchise history for punt returns (99), punt-return yards (941), and interception-return yards (652), along with 10th in interceptions (25).

His Super Bowl contributions loom large. Edwards put a wallop on Minnesota receiver John Gilliam causing the ball to pop into Mel Blount's arms around the goal line in Super Bowl IX. And many fans—even authors—forget that Super Bowl X ended with Edwards intercepting Roger Staubach's desperation heave in the end zone, then opting to return it rather than accept a touchback in a dangerous play as time expired.

Mike Wagner, safety 1971–1980: "Glen started running out of the end zone, '*What are you doing? . . .*'"

Andy Russell, linebacker 1963, 1966–1976: "I would say he was the hardest hitter on those Steelers. A lot of people wouldn't know that. He made a big hit in Super Bowl IX. Toward the end of the first half, the Vikings tried a long pass; Glen made the hit and Mel intercepted it."

George Perles, defensive coach-coordinator 1972–1981: "Ohhh, he was [the hardest hitter]. But he didn't get too many [ball carriers] back that far."

V. Tim Rooney, pro player scout 1972–1979: "I just loved Glen Edwards. Everyone did. We called him 'Pine' because he was built like hard pine. They're in a game; a team started running the ball in chunks. After about the fifth or sixth gashing run, Edwards came in the huddle, 'Steel Curtain my ass. *My ass.*'"

Wagner: "The exact quote? 'Steel Curtain? Steel Curtain my ass.' Not many people remember, but after the 1976 season, all four Steelers defensive backs were in the Pro Bowl. The next year, all of a sudden, Glen is on the bench, I'm moved over to the weak side and they wanted to give Donnie [Shell] a chance. They told me, 'This will extend your career, Mike.'" Edwards, with four San Diego seasons, outlasted Wagner in the NFL by one year.

John Banaszak, defensive lineman 1975–1981: "Pine? Glen Edwards was one of those violent guys. He'd just time it up and tattoo somebody. [Jack] Ham would make a tackle, but you wouldn't hear it. Mike Wagner makes a tackle, but you wouldn't hear it. Glen Edwards makes a tackle, you're going to hear it."

ALAN FANECA
Guard

Height: 6-5 • **Weight:** 312 • **College:** LSU • **Years with the Steelers:** 1998–2007 • **Birthplace:** New Orleans • **Born:** December 7, 1976

Yet another Steelers lineman with worthy Hall of Fame credentials, Alan Faneca should make Canton someday soon, likely the next Steeler lineman to get inducted after center Dermontti Dawson.

The glut of Steelers busts already inside the Hall may cause voters to hold their ballots in abeyance for a while. But Faneca measures up for enshrinement. A first-round selection in 1998, taken 28th overall, he hastily moved into the starting lineup and refused to budge. He missed just three games over the next three seasons, zero over his final six in Pittsburgh, and nine overall. A modern-day iron man on the interior offensive line.

He made nine consecutive Pro Bowls. He made All-Pro a half dozen years. He played 158 games, and the Steelers had sixty 100-yard rushers in that span.

In his final Steelers' season, he was named to the franchise's 75th Anniversary team.

Russ Grimm, offensive line coach 2001–2006: You can have the Bettises, the Wards, the Roethlisbergers, the Polamalus . . . all potential Canton inductees. The best player he saw in a Steelers uniform from 2001 to 2007 was Faneca. "The guy's a hell of a player. Terrific person, too. He could've played in the '50s, '60s or '70s. He could have played anywhere."

Dermontti Dawson, center 1989–2000: "I knew Alan was going to be a player when he got drafted . . . , starting as a rookie. When Alan first came, you knew he had the skills. He was big, 6-5, over 300 pounds, good feet, good mobility. You knew Alan was going to be a heck of a player."

Max Starks, offensive tackle 2004– : "Big Red, geesh, he had so many funny moments. I'll never forget, my rookie year. I'm sitting on the sidelines in Buffalo. It's cold as hell. We're 14-1. Alan comes to the sidelines, takes his helmet off, and just looks at me, 'You're in. Good luck, rook.' And slaps me on the shoulder. I'm like, 'What? I play tackle.' 'Now you play guard. All right. Good luck.' And he sat there, unraveling his gloves, unlacing his shoes, like 'I'm not going back in.' Red gave me that christening and blessing in the NFL. I went in at guard. I thought it was a good idea until I saw who I was going against: Pat Williams and Sam Adams."

JAMES FARRIOR
Linebacker

Height: 6-2 • **Weight:** 242 • **College:** Virginia • **Years with the Steelers:** 2002–2011 • **Birthplace:** Richmond, Virginia • **Born:** January 6, 1975

The beloved Levon Kirkland was gone after nine years. Earl Holmes, who topped the team in tackles for three consecutive seasons, went out the door a year later. There existed a sizable hole in the middle of the Steelers defense, a canyon where fellows large and loud roamed previously. Before them, inside linebacker was home to Hardy Nickerson, David Little, Jack Lambert, and history.

Then the Steelers went out and signed an outside linebacker from the New York Jets, a former first-rounder—Bill Parcells' inaugural one there—who never quite seemed to fulfill his promise. And he came by way of free agency to Pittsburgh for about one-third the price Holmes got for fleeing to Cleveland, of all places.

Fan reaction: *"Say what?"*

Two years later, Farrior was second in the voting for NFL Defensive Player of the Year. Baltimore's Ed Reed beat him by four votes.

Dick LeBeau, defensive assistant 1992–1996 and defensive coordinator 2004– : "He should've been the Most Valuable Player in the league the year that he finished second. I've never seen a player have a better year than that. Whenever we needed a play, he made it. With an interception or a picked-up fumble or a caused fumble, he just was tremendous."

Farrior settled for other trinkets: defensive captain for a decade, two Pro Bowl berths, 93 consecutive starts until he had a calf injury midway through 2011, eight consecutive seasons of 100-plus tackles.

Farrior: "When I got here, I just tried to uphold the standard that was already set a long time ago as far as linebacker play. I just want those older guys, when I finish, to say: 'I could have played with him.' That's the biggest honor that I could probably receive." Jack Lambert, for one, not only sent word a few years ago that he appreciated Farrior's play; he also sent an autographed jersey.

Larry Foote, sidekick at inside linebacker 2002–2008 and 2010– : "Three Super Bowls. Been here 10 years. The numbers speak for themselves. But he should have his name on that [Hall of Fame] ballot, should get in there. One more Super Bowl definitely would solidify it.

"He loves to play. He's an old man, but he's a little kid at heart. He's always fired up. Always upbeat and ready to go. And everybody knows that's hard to do in this league; [the season is] so long; some games are meaningless."

LeBeau: "Unselfish. Tremendously unselfish. He has been a rock for all of my years here. He's an absolute joy to coach."

JIM FINKS
Defensive Back–Halfback–Quarterback

Height: 5-11 • **Weight:** 180 • **College:** Tulsa • **Years with the Steelers:** 1949–1955 • **Birthplace:** St. Louis • **Born:** August 31, 1927 • **Died:** May 8, 1994

Jim Finks was, by all accounts, an ordinary football player. He became an extraordinary football administrator.

He built the Minnesota Vikings and Chicago Bears into Super Bowl teams. He transformed the New Orleans Saints into a winner for their first time in history. When Pete Rozelle retired as commissioner in 1989, Finks was the first-ballot successor. But some owners changed their minds, and Paul Tagliabue assumed control. Soon after Finks died of cancer in 1994, he was posthumously enshrined in the Pro Football Hall of Fame in 1995.

As for his Steelers career, it would've been nondescript had it not been for a switch in positions . . . and a quarterback he beat out.

Finks played halfback in the single-wing offense that the Steelers refused to ditch, even though the rest of the NFL moved forward. Mostly, he was a capable defensive back until 1952, when the Steelers took the plunge into the modern era by installing the T formation, and switched him to starting quarterback.

He passed for more than 2,000 yards in 1952—when he topped the NFL with 20 touchdown throws and made the Pro Bowl—as well as 1954 and 1955. In the final season, when he led the league in attempts, completions, yards, and yards per game, he achieved what later became a piece of Steelers infamy by winning the starting quarterback job in the training camp where the Steelers summarily cast aside a future Hall of Famer, Johnny Unitas.

Chuck Cherundolo, defensive assistant 1948–1961: "Matter of fact, he was a defensive back." Better there than quarterback? "No question. He was just an ordinary football player but a pretty smart guy, though."

Jack Butler, defensive back 1951–1959: "Jim Finks was really something. He was a little guy. A leader, smart as hell. Took charge. Made it work. I knew he'd be something. He was organized. He got people to do things. He'd get the best out of you. Whatever it was, he really had it."

Frank Varrichione, offensive tackle 1955–1960: "A great guy. A leader, No. 1. He was in charge of the huddle. A little like Bobby Layne, but not as abrasive. He expected you to do your job. He was a great quarterback, I thought."

Dale Dodrill, nose guard–middle linebacker 1951–1959: "Conniving Jimmy, yeah. He always seemed to have more things going than maybe playing football. I remember [Walt] Kiesling had Jim Finks go down to Notre Dame to talk Bill Walsh into coming back and playing another year. Instead of Jimmy convincing Bill, Bill Walsh talked Jimmy into coming down to Notre Dame to coach, which he did [in 1956]. He went to Notre Dame to coach."

Tim Rooney Sr., son of the Chief and ball boy/water boy at the time: "My dad was so mad at Notre Dame. I don't think my dad ever rooted for Notre Dame again. It was one thing to take the two stars on our team, he said, but they took Finks after the draft and nearly before they went to training camp. It wasn't time enough to get a quarterback. He didn't think a Catholic school should be acting like that. He surely wasn't happy about it."

BARRY FOSTER
Halfback

Height: 5-10 • **Weight:** 223 • **College:** Arkansas • **Years with the Steelers:** 1990–1994 • **Birthplace:** Hurst, Texas • **Born:** December 8, 1968

Barry Foster proved to be as elusive off the field as on one.

He was selected as a junior—formally the first such in modern Steelers draft history—in the fifth round of 1990, the penultimate draft of the Chuck Noll era. Foster's rookie class became the offensive foundation for Bill Cowher's success through the early to mid-1990s: Foster, Neil O'Donnell, Eric Green, and Justin Strzelczyk. More than one-third of the unit.

Tim Worley's injuries and drug suspensions—first for part of 1991, then all of 1992—provided a hole through which barged this former college-wishbone fullback. Foster became perhaps the most critical component in Cowher's initial three playoff teams. He was the brutish ball carrier who enabled the

Barry Foster and the Steelers of 1994 don throwback uniforms for the franchise's 75th anniversary season. They matched outfits worn in the 1933 inaugural season. (Bill Amatucci)

Steelers to grind out the clock and allow the Dom Capers–Dick LeBeau Blitzburgh defense to wage its unrelenting attack.

He seemed a bit too driven by money and honesty: The only 1992 camp holdout with a contract, the oft-abrasive Foster told media that the Steelers were "screwing the players." Dan Rooney in return wasn't exactly giddy in December 1993 when Foster went against their wishes and underwent surgery, after which UPMC's Dr. Freddie Fu in an audiovisual news conference labeled Foster's ankle "a hostile environment." "He should try standing in front of Foster's locker," wrote Mike Prisuta—later of Steeler flagship station WDVE-FM—in the *Beaver County Times.* No wonder that, after an injury-abbreviated 1994, Foster was shipped to Capers' Carolina for a sixth-round draft choice (Bryan Stoltenberg, we hardly knew ye).

In five short seasons, Foster scrawled his name across the Steelers record books:

- His 1,690-yard, 390-carry odyssey of 1992 remains the high-water mark in those categories, along with his 2,034 total yards from scrimmage (rushing and receiving).
- Three of the top nine rushing performances in franchise annals were compiled by Foster—neither Hall of Famers John Henry Johnson (twice) nor Harris (once) ran for 168-plus yards as often as Foster, and they combined for 18 total seasons.

- His 4.31-yard average attempt falls behind only Hall of Famer Bill Dudley's 4.39 as the highest such career mark among Steelers running backs.

Ron Erhardt, offensive coordinator 1992–1995: "I don't think anybody thought of Barry Foster until we dug him out. We watched the tapes, and I told Dick [Hoak], 'There's a guy who could play.' I think it was a find. He did an outstanding job for us."

Dom Capers, defensive coordinator 1992–1994: "A guy who was hard to knock off his feet and always falling forward for positive yardage. Just the kind of guy you wanted for your offense. Very quiet, kind of introverted guy who didn't say a whole lot."

Dermontti Dawson, center 1988–2000: "Hey, I tell you what, boy. Barry, when he came to Pittsburgh . . . Of all the backs that I played with, Barry and Bam and Jerome, they were some of my favorite backs. Barry was just a hard-running back. Not very tall. I don't know; he just had a knack. We had our most success [average per carry] when Barry was running the ball. I'm really not sure why he quit. The one negative about Barry was that he wasn't a very social guy when it came to teammates. Never really let anybody know who Barry Foster was as a person. That helps to create a bond, when you allow people to know more personal things about you, who you are. I think when things started getting bad to Barry, he just kind of closed out everybody."

Although reunited with Capers in Carolina, between lingering ankle–foot problems from that 1993 surgery and clashing with the new head coach over exhibition play, Foster and his $2.5 million contract were let go before the 1995 season started.

Two months later, the Cincinnati Bengals signed him to a $1 million deal.

He quit the second day there.

John Jackson, offensive tackle 1988–1997: "Barry was a different guy. I mean, he didn't talk much. But I think Barry was a good guy. The interactions I had with him, Barry was one of the type of people who are misunderstood. Barry just wanted to win. He came to the right team. I know when he went to Cincinnati, he was there for a day. He gave the money back and went home. He figured that out *real* quick.

"No, they wouldn't let him back here; he burned too many bridges. That's one thing about Pittsburgh: You burn a bridge here, you won't be back."

RANDY FULLER
Cornerback

Height: 5-10 • **Weight:** 180 • **College:** Tennessee State • **Years with the Steelers:** 1995–1997 • **Birthplace:** Griffin, Georgia • **Born:** June 2, 1970

Remember the Immaculate Deflection? That was Randy Lamar Fuller.

He was a reserve cornerback they signed September 11, 1995, a month after he was released by the Broncos with whom he spent his 1994 rookie season. Funny thing about Fuller's timing: He not only missed the deadline for the Steelers' regular-season media guide . . . but team officials inadvertently neglected to place his bio in the 1995 postseason guide.

"That's the story of my career. At times, I have been forgotten," he told reporters a week later in Arizona. One of the public-relations officials who forgot him in the postseason guide: intern and future Arizona Cardinals offensive coordinator Mike Miller.

When it came to timing, though, the Steelers wouldn't have reached that Super Bowl XXX without Fuller.

Five seconds remained in the AFC championship game at Three Rivers Stadium. Colts quarterback Jim Harbaugh threw a jump ball into the right front corner of the end zone, where Indianapolis receivers Floyd Turner and Aaron Bailey were surrounded by such Steelers as Carnell Lake, Darren Perry, Willie Williams, Chris Oldham, and Fuller. Somehow, with Bailey falling on his back, the pass found him.

The ball bounced from his left hand to his chest and into the air—from where Fuller swatted it to the turf. Fuller joked later that, unless Bailey had a green stomach, he was sure the ball hit ground.

Bailey grabbed the ball with his other hand, which wasn't free previously amid the tangle of bodies, and snatched it off the end-zone turf. "When I turned around, I saw Bailey cradle it. I thought we lost another one," Lake said afterward.

Barry Foster opens 1994 against Dallas in his run to his second Pro Bowl . . . and toward the end of his flash of a five-year Steelers career. Foster, after a team-record twelve 100-yard games in 1992 and the fifth-most rushing touchdowns in franchise history, left as a free agent at the end of the '94 season. But he was traded to Carolina, wound up with Cincinnati, turned in his jersey, and never played another snap in the NFL. (Bill Amatucci)

In that same end zone a year earlier, San Diego linebacker Dennis Gibson tipped away a Neil O'Donnell pass meant for Barry Foster, and the Chargers advanced to the Super Bowl instead. Some called that the Immaculate Deflection. But all things Immaculate are supposed to benefit the Steelers, not betray them. Besides, Fuller's intervention occurred with Mr. Immaculate Reception himself, Franco Harris, standing half a field away as the honorary captain.

Fuller gathered 59 special-teams tackles in four years with the Steelers, then played one more year each with Seattle and Atlanta . . . with whom he also reached Super Bowl XXXIII.

Ron Erhardt, offensive coordinator 1992–1995: "He played his position well. He worked at it. He was ready when we needed him or called on him. That [AFC championship] game was as good as any played in the stadium there."

JOHN "FRENCHY" FUQUA
Halfback

Height: 5-11 • **Weight:** 205 • **College:** Morgan State • **Years with the Steelers:** 1970–1976 • **Birthplace:** Detroit • **Born:** September 12, 1946

Two questions follow him through life:

1. Did the Immaculate Reception pass really hit Oakland's Jack Tatum first?
2. Whatever happened to the goldfish in the heels of those platform shoes?

Comical and sartorial splendor abounded with John Fuqua, this vintage man of the 1970s better known as Frenchy. He was acquired from the New York Giants in a 1970 trade along with linebacker Henry Davis for the unfortunately named Dick Shiner. He used to boast about visits to a Detroit medium named Mama Haiti. He became a starting running back instantly and remained there through Franco Harris' inaugural three seasons, until Rocky Bleier unseated him and the Fuqua panache faded.

His 218 yards rushing in 1970 stood for nearly 40 years as the all-time Steelers single-game high.

Still, he was best remembered for a shoulder and heels. Not to mention the canes and capes, the peacock hats, the hard blocks for Harris.

Fuqua started his own mystique with banter about being the Count, a member of the Ruritanian royal family. Myron Cope made it into a team dress-off: Who could best the Frenchman?

Frenchy Fuqua: "It not only gave us that competitive spirit off the field, but we had a lot of fun. You should've seen guys: Rocky, L. C., Dwight, Mike Wagner. . . . Every city we went to, [they were] trying to get some kind of outfit to outdo my Count cape. I always prevailed.

"Could you believe a guy like a 6-6 L. C. going out in powder-blue hot pants and a cape that came down to his waist? And a little beanie hat? A fearsome defensive lineman wearing hot pants? [At least] it wasn't pink."

Valerie Miller, a Steelerette: "I remember walking up [Pitt Stadium's Cardiac] Hill behind Frenchy Fuqua, and he had that purple cape on. Those costumes he used to wear."

Marlene Pizutti, ditto: "The platform shoes with the goldfish in them!"

Dick Hoak, teammate in 1970 and running backs coach 1972–2006: "The goldfish? They died. 'Cause the water had no oxygen. Oh, he was crazy."

Fuqua: "I'll tell you one thing about it, I can barely walk today from some of the shoes I wore." The platforms with the fish? "I took them to a banquet, took my shoes off . . . and they were floating on their backs, dead. I went with tropical fish, freshwater fish. Goldfish, they all died. I had a little

Frenchy Fuqua, not pictured, rushed for 218 yards at Philadelphia in 1970—a team record that would stand for 36 years. But his Steelers' legacy remains wrapped around one teammate—the backfield mate for whom he blocked and his partner in the Immaculate Reception: Franco Harris, shown here in a 1973 preseason game. (Temple Urban Archives)

geranium plant put in them. But everybody still talks about the goldfish."

The Frenchman swore that he promised to Art Rooney Sr. never to reveal whether Terry Bradshaw's pass hit Oakland's Tatum, making it legal, or him, rendering it illegal. He maintained that he wanted to keep it truly Immaculate.

Hoak: "A character. He played middle guard in high school. He could catch and he could run. But we had Franco who could run and was way bigger than him."

Mike Wagner, safety 1971–1980: "Anytime we got guys from a team that was more successful than the Steelers, which was everybody, we thought they were like gods. If Joe Greene were here right now, he'd punch me. That was before we were good.

"Frenchy loved life. At the same time, he was a very tough, good running back."

JOE GILLIAM
Quarterback

Height: 6-2 • **Weight:** 187 • **College:** Tennessee State • **Years with the Steelers:** 1972–1975 • **Birthplace:** Charleston, West Virginia • **Born:** December 29, 1950 • **Died:** December 25, 2000

Becoming the first African American quarterback to start from an NFL season opener, Joe Gilliam found himself in a trail-blazing position like no other player in Steelers history, perhaps even Pittsburgh professional-sports history.

Upon Gilliam's shoulders later came to stand Steelers quarterbacks Kordell Stewart, homegrown Charlie Batch of Steel Valley High, and Dennis Dixon.

Yet it was a weighty burden for a 23-year-old man known as Jefferson Street Joe.

His father, Joe Sr., coached him at Tennessee State, from where the Steelers drafted him in the 11th round of the 1972 draft that, 260 selections earlier, brought them the half-black, half-Italian sensation of Franco Harris and, eventually, his Italian Army. Joseph Wiley Gilliam Jr. played pieces of seven games, attempting 71 passes, his first two years before he was thrust into the starter's role to open 1974.

During a 42-day player strike, Gilliam arose to No. 1 on the depth chart. The strike also gave Chuck Noll an opportunity to provide another dose of force-fed maturation to Terry Bradshaw, the top pick of the 1970 draft. Gilliam promptly went out and steered the Steelers to a shutout victory over Baltimore, a tie in Denver (where he went 31-for-50 for 348 yards), and a shutout loss to Oakland. He continued to start as the Steelers won the next three games, giving him a 4-1-1 record, but winning proved less and less to be a function of his passing. His numbers drooped precipitously: 14 for 36, 5 for 18. Two of the victories came by the sum total of seven points. Noll reverted to Bradshaw.

Jefferson Street Joe threw 14 more passes that 1974 season, which ended in a Super Bowl IX triumph and the jump-start to Bradshaw's Hall of Fame ascension.

Gilliam threw 48 more passes the next season, the same 1975 when he later admitted to experimenting with both heroin and cocaine. He spent five and a half months in a Virginia rehab facility. The next time anyone saw him, he was playing semipro football in 1978.

In 1974, Joe Gilliam became the first African American quarterback to start for an NFL team from the season's beginning. He earned the role after a strike-torn training camp and produced a 4-1-1 record plus a team leading 1,274 yards passing. After one more Steelers season, he was gone, a star that fizzled and fell as quickly as it rose. (George Gojkovich)

A crack addict as late as 46 years old, a desperate man who sold both Super Bowl rings to feed his habit, Gilliam vowed he was sober and settled, lecturing youth about drug-use dangers, writing a book he entitled *In Spite of Myself.* Four days short of his 50th birthday, he died of a cocaine overdose, as later reported by the medical examiner in Nasville, Tennessee.

Ray Kemp, the first African American Steeler and a former Tennessee State coach–administrator who taught Gilliam in a class, told the *Pittsburgh Press* for a November 28, 1979, story: "I knew Joe Gilliam when he was in college. I believe he could have quarterbacked any team in pro football had he not been saddled with his later [drug] problems. The black quarterback, that's a position of authority. It refutes all that people say about the lack of mentality of the black personality. A black quarterback has that racial badge to deal with as he attempts to cope with the usual things any player under pressure faces."

Kevin Kiely, son of team publicist Ed and a ball boy: "Bradshaw and Gilliam stayed after practice, and they both loved to try to test each other's arms—and they loved to torture us. The end of practice, I'd have a cross on my chest from catching them [the four-cornered nose of the ball leaving that distinct red mark]."

Mike Wagner, safety 1971–1980 and friend: "Joe had a slingshot for an arm, which was both a gift and a detriment. He had so much belief that he could deliver the ball, no matter the skill set of the people around him. I saw a lot of the struggles he went through, trying to become a quarterback in the NFL, trying to deal with racial discrimination issues, trying to deal with his own issues.

"I was with Joe the weekend before he died [at the reunion for the December 16 finale at Three Rivers Stadium]. Got a chance to spend some time with him. Really sad what happened."

GARY GLICK
Cornerback

Height: 6-2 • **Weight:** 195 • **College:** Colorado State (née Colorado A&M) • **Years with the Steelers:** 1956–1959 • **Birthplace:** Grant, Nebraska • **Born:** May 14, 1930

Halfback Lenny Moore? Lineman Forrest Gregg? Linebacker Sam Huff of nearby West Virginia University? Nah.

The Steelers didn't prefer any of those future Hall of Famers with the bonus pick, the first over-and-above-the-rest selection in 1956—a true reward for NFL futility. They poorly cashed in the bonus reward with a 26-year-old, ex-navy-base player and quarterback/cornerback named Gary Glick, guaranteeing further futility. Two years later, the league retired bonus picking.

Don't blame it all on Glick, though. The Steelers also held the selections at fifth overall (limping halfback Art Davis) and 17th overall (Joe Krupa). So they passed up Moore the first time around, then both Gregg and Huff and others in the second round, too.

Fifty-five drafts later and counting, no other cornerback has gone first overall since.

At least Glick could kick. He booted nine field goals (of 28 attempts) and 26 extra points in 1956–1957. He compiled four picks in as many Steelers years, too. Even then, his personal black-and-gold curse was at work.

When he played the next four seasons with the Redskins, Colts, and Chargers, he had *10* picks.

Frank Varrichione, tackle 1955–1960: "I remember Gary. In fact, my second year, he was the bonus pick. He was a great defensive player, great athletic ability, and a great guy."

Dale Dodrill, nose tackle–middle linebacker 1951–1959: "He kicked extra points and field goals, too. I know when he came up I told him, 'Gary, you better get a crossbar on that face mask.' He said, 'No, that will affect my vision.' I told him, 'You'll adjust.' Not long after that, I was visiting him in the hospital, and he says, 'I'm pretty lucky, they knocked out two teeth. Broke the jaw. . . . Now I drink through straws.' I still see Gary quite often. He lives in Fort Collins [Colorado], up here about 50 miles away. Gary played for, what, four different teams. That was another player that . . . got 'fired.' When Buddy [Parker] got there, he was [among] the first guys he got rid of. The last bonus pick, right?"

Joe Walton, a Redskins competitor and teammate 1959–1960, later a coach: "One of the jokes around at the time, too, was . . . Gary Glick the bonus pick. He never did much. I ended up playing with him with the Redskins. He couldn't play then, either."

ERIC GREEN
Tight End

Height: 6-5 • **Weight:** 280 • **College:** Liberty • **Years with the Steelers:** 1990–1994 • **Birthplace:** Savannah, Georgia • **Born:** June 22, 1967

A little-remembered fact about the big, memorable tight end: He could've been Emmitt Smith instead.

Jimmy Johnson's Cowboys, fearful the Browns at No. 18 would take a Florida halfback they coveted, swapped their first-round pick and a third-rounder (Craig Veasey) for the Steelers' 17th-overall spot. The Cowboys took Smith. History followed: Super Bowls, Hall of Fame, and so on.

The Steelers took Eric Green. An infamous rap-video project and NFL suspension followed.

It was a page of the Same Old Steelers circa 1933–1969.

This marked the inaugural first-round trade of the Chuck Noll era, 22 drafts into it. Perhaps that's why Noll reacted so angrily when Green ventured on a 52-day holdout, the second-longest by a Steelers rookie to that point. In 13 of the 16 games, Green caught 34 passes, third behind Louis Lipps and Merril Hoge, and seven touchdowns, second on the team. He had two touchdowns in his debut, five after the opening two games. One game, he blocked a nose guard so violently, their bodies rolled up on the ankle of guard Carlton Haselrig and the elbow of tackle Tunch Ilkin, injuring both.

Green gradually earned his ticket out of town, being suspended for six games in 1992 for violating the NFL's drug policy—the same as Tim Worley and Terry Long in 1991. He orchestrated a rap-video meeting before the 1995 AFC championship game, a fact from which the victorious Chargers took considerable glee. He criticized Neil O'Donnell for throwing the game's final pass toward halfback Barry Foster. When he signed with Miami the next year, he criticized director of football operations Tom Donahoe, a Pittsburgh media he labeled racist, and Penguins star Mario Lemieux for receiving special treatment. So, in the Steelers' end, he caught nothing but flak.

Kevin Greene, outside linebacker 1993–1995: "I mean, he was gifted. He would hurdle people."

Bubby Brister, quarterback 1986–1992: "I just wish I could have played with him longer."

John Jackson, offensive tackle 1988–1997: "Biggest tight end I ever saw with the greatest hands and great speed. Was always amazed he could get open, as big as he was. He's one of those people, he can't hide . . . but he could get open. A tremendous athlete. Always had some good jokes. Loved to tell them."

Gerald Williams, nose tackle–defensive end 1986–1994: "A phenomenal tight end. As far as a tight end that big, a 285-pound tight end? He was a guy [in practice] if he was on our side, get away from his as quick as you could. Because if you had him and that tackle on you? Battle lost."

JOE GREENE
Defensive Tackle

Height: 6-4 • **Weight:** 275 • **College:** North Texas State • **Years with the Steelers:** 1969–1981 • **Birthplace:** Temple, Texas • **Born:** September 24, 1946

Loved or loathed, followed or feared, chasing foes while wielding scissors or kicking them in the groin, mentoring potential replacements or motivating by his singular presence, his ends may not have justified his Mean Joe Greeneness early in his career, but the later result goes without debate: There would be no Super Bowl Steelers without him.

Jon Kolb, teammate and assistant coach who arrived in the same 1969 draft: "Joe, more than anybody else, set the example for the next 13 years."

Tony Dungy, teammate and later coaching colleague: "No question who the leader was. Who the driving force was. Who everybody followed. Joe was a dominant physical player, but also a dominant personality. Gave the team direction and toughness. Everything came from the way he approached things. Everybody fed off his energy and his emotions."

Larry Brown, tight end–offensive tackle 1971–1984: "And we had some significant players there."

George Perles, defensive line coach and later coordinator: "Joe was the easiest guy in the world to coach, [because] he wanted to win so bad."

Joe Gordon, publicity director and vice president, 1969–1998: "Dan Rooney credits Joe with much of the success of the Steelers. Chuck couldn't have made a better choice."

One day after the new coach came on the job, Greene became Noll's very first choice, unpopular though it was among the media and general public at the outset. Greene then wasted little time in burrowing underneath and attempting to hoist a laughingstock franchise on his shoulders. He needed more time, more help, in growing into that job.

Dick Hoak, a teammate in 1969–1970 and the running backs coach starting in 1972: "When Joe gets [to training camp after a holdout, Noll] lines up Joe against every offensive lineman we had, and he beat every stinking one. Ken Kortas and Frank Parker, the starters in '68, looked at one another and said, 'We might as well pack our bags.'

"You could tell. He was going to make a difference."

Ralph Berlin, trainer 1968–1992: "Probably the greatest player the Steelers ever had."

Roy McHugh, longtime sportswriter, columnist, and editor at the Pittsburgh Press: "My, God, Joe Greene, his first year, he was amazing. He tore through offensive lines. He'd wade right through them. They tripled-teamed him, they couldn't do anything with him.

"Joe Greene was the best defensive linemen I ever saw. To have one lineman who could have such an effect on a game . . ."

Gordon: "He was just so respected by the other players. And feared by the opposing players. He had a mean streak that you need in this business. When you're great and mean . . ."

John Banaszak, defensive lineman 1975–1982: "Joe Greene, he earned that nickname."

Against Cleveland in the early 1970s, he chased center Bob DeMarco across the field, punched and broke his jaw, and watched him get carried off on a stretcher. All because he contended that DeMarco gave him an illegal and unethical

The face on the Mount Rushmore of Pittsburgh sports, Joe Greene, from 1979. (George Gojkovich)

elbow to the throat. He then went over to the Browns bench and head coach Nick Skorich.

Perles: "He said, 'Nick, in case you want to know who did it, I did.' Took the whole team on.

"You talk about Bednarik and Butkus, you talk about Joe Greene. There wasn't anybody Joe wouldn't take on, and the whole league knew it. It was a violent game, and we had the most violent one: Joe. No one ever took advantage of us with toughness."

Butkus? Funny he should mention that name. Eight weeks into Greene's rookie season, the losing already was eating him from the inside. The Steelers opened that season with a 16-13 victory over Detroit, enthralling the sun-bathed Pitt Stadium crowd of 51,360 there for the start of the Noll era. And then they lost 13 in a dark, clammy row. The Bears were crushing them, 38-7, one November day in Wrigley Field, and Butkus took liberties—to Greene's way of thinking—when he speared fellow rookie L. C. Greenwood on a kickoff return.

Andy Russell, outside linebacker 1963, 1966–1976: "They're killing us. They had Gale Sayers. I mean, they're killing us. Joe runs out onto the field, grabs Butkus by the shoulders and lifts him to his eye level, and he spits in his face. Butkus turned and jogged off the field." Two weeks later, Greene went after a Minnesota Vikings player with a pair of shears. "My favorite story about Joe losing his temper is: We're playing Minnesota at their baseball field. You're on the same side of the field as the other team. As Joe Greene was coming off the field, two of their defensive linemen—[future Hall of Famer] Alan Page and Carl Eller—start making fun of him. Joe ran over to the Steeler medical box and he finds a pair of scissors. Biiiiiig scissors. He puts it up over his head and chased those guys. They ran up into the stands; they thought he was crazy. I don't know if he would have stabbed them or not, but it looked like he would.

Greene: "No, I didn't do that. I wouldn't do that—[Page and Eller]wouldn't run. It was an offensive guard holding me, and I got angry with him."

Russell: "He was so determined to turn the team around his rookie year. He hated to lose and would not accept it. He got into a lot of fights. He got thrown out of, like, four or five games his rookie year."

Joe Greene sacks Philadelphia quarterback Roman Gabriel, grimacing with only one hand on him, in a 1974 Steelers shutout in Three Rivers Stadium. The Eagles compiled 66 yards rushing on 22 carries and just 143 yards of total offense that dominating day—typical of the Steel Curtain of that period. (Temple Urban Archives)

He spat, he fumed, he carried on. And that was merely with his own teammates.

With opponents, he gradually lowered his attacks to mere punches and kicks. Denver's Paul Howard once informed the media that Greene kicked him so hard it tore his scrotum, but then Broncos coach John Ralston scrutinized the film and found no such kicking motion, so he exonerated Greene. A year later, when Howard held him, Greene retaliated with a Muhammad Ali uppercut to the solar plexus, and Howard had to be helped off the field. Cleveland lineman Bob McKay did indeed get a swift Greene boot in the groin for holding him. Greene's reaction for getting ejected for the kick? "What the hell should I do, break my hand on somebody's helmet?"

Greene: "Throwing my helmet in Chicago—I threw it about 50 yards. Hit the top of the goalpost. That I regret. And Philadelphia, I think we were, like, 21 points ahead [and lost that lead]. They came back, they were on our goal line. I picked up the football and threw it out of the stands, as far as I could throw it. Out of Franklin Field. That was the [1970] day Frenchy Fuqua set the team [rushing] record."

Jack Ham, outside linebacker 1971–1982: "He was crazy his first couple of years."

Banaszak: "Tough. Mean. He was a nasty football player." You can't spell dynasty without nasty, right?

Admittedly, Greene matured. He learned to control that rage.

Greene: "I'd get angry and go through my tantrums; we weren't playing good football. It affected my teammates. That's when I changed my attitude and approach." He continued with a chuckle. "I think that coincided with us starting to win some football games."

Ham: "When Chuck talked him into that stunt 4–3. . . . You don't make as many sacks. You face nothing but double-teams. That didn't let him freelance as much. Boy, that tells you a lot about Joe Greene. All he cared about was winning championships."

Gordon: "Probably more than anybody, he was determined to succeed. Through that, he developed great leadership qualities."

Dungy: "I remember I got to San Francisco [in 1979] when I got traded, and O. J. was there. O. J. told me a story about when he was young at Buffalo. They were playing Pittsburgh. And Joe told Buffalo's center, Mike Montler, not to snap the ball. 'You better not snap that ball.' Mike Montler was scared to snap it, and they got a delay of game." See, even opponents listened and obeyed.

Ralph Berlin, trainer 1969–1992: "Joe was the boss. If there were problems, Joe took care of them. If I had a problem, I didn't go to Chuck; I went to Joe."

Beasley: "Joe had such a knack for reading players' stances, running back signs, tendencies. I've heard Joe call out plays and how they're going to block even before the snap. I was drafted to replace Joe Greene. He knew it. Everybody knew it. Instead of shunning me, he took me under his wing. I learned more from Joe than all the other coaches in the time I played football. He was a real student. He shared things that certainly made me a much better ballplayer."

Greene was the player's shoulder on whom Terry Bradshaw leaned when he stumbled through his early Steelers years and remained at loggerheads with Noll. Greene was the one who derived the plan to send the Houston Oilers monogrammed leather briefcases after their 1977 upset of Cincinnati gave

Rookie defensive line coach Joe Greene in the 1987 opener celebrates with some of his defense after a Mike Merriweather interception off San Francisco's Joe Montana. Left to right: Donnie Shell, alongside whom Greene played all four Super Bowls, Merriweather, Tim Johnson, and Gary Dunn. Far right, John Stallworth heads back onto the field with the offense. (Vincent J. Musi)

the Steelers the division title and playoff berth. Greene was the key to the stunt 4–3 defense, him tilting into the center-guard gap and immovable. Greene was the spirit and the grit and the glue, even when Ernie Holmes and L. C. Greenwood surpassed him as consistent linemen. Greene was the tutor and the master to linemen who were tabbed as his eventual replacements or merely the new kid in camp whom he admired most.

It wasn't easy being Greene.

But it was natural to follow him.

Dungy: "I remember the year before I got there, watching on TV; I was a senior in college. They were playing Cincinnati in that snow game [in 1976]; it was 7-3. Cincinnati was at the goal line trying to score. It was snowing and Cincinnati couldn't get traction, and Joe took his shoes off and played in his socks. That was his personality. It's what Coach Noll taught, and he personified that. I asked him about that when I came in as a rookie [the next summer]. 'My cleats were all snowed up, and I couldn't get traction, so whatever it takes. The next step was taking the socks off.'

"The other thing that amazed me about Joe Greene when I got there: In Joe Greene's locker, there was nothing but shoulder pads. He didn't play with any other pads at all. He had no hand pads, no forearm pads, no hip pads, no shin pads, no knee pads. I was like, 'How could you play at that level in the trenches with no pads at all?' But that was the mentality. 'I want to be light, I want to be ready to go, and I don't need any type of protection to do what I need to do.' You look at some of those early pictures of Joe in the early '70s, you'll see—no pads."

Don't mistake his tenacity, his forceful nature for a lack of sensitivity. Fact is, therein lay the dichotomy of the man.

Deep down, he was a softie. That award-winning Coca-Cola commercial in 1979, adjudged one of the most memorable in American history? Or the Downy remake in 2012? Those may have come closer to showing the world the true heart of the man, Unseen Joe Greene.

Kolb remembered when Noll retired and his entire staff was let go, the end of the 1991 season. Guess who was the person who showed the most concern for an out-of-work friend, former coaching colleague, and longtime teammate?

Kolb: "Joe Greene called me every single day. 'Who did you talk to today? Do you need me to call somebody as a reference for you?' I'd known Joe Greene 23 years, but in those last two weeks . . ." He paused. "And he's calling every day. How impressive is that?"

Craig Wolfley, a guard–tackle who arrived in 1980: "The thing that always stood out to me: Joe Greene, what an incredible leader's personality he had. He truly was the conscience of that team."

The conscience's birth name is Charles Edward Greene, and how he arrived in Pittsburgh is a story in itself.

With USC's O. J. Simpson bound for Buffalo with the first-overall pick in the 1969 draft, Steelers media and fans—not that they were legion back then—foamed at the mouth for Butler's own Terry Hanratty of Notre Dame. Or even Penn State tight end Ted Kwalick of Montour High. They were primed for a name player at No. 4, an offensive star to give them reasons to attend, watch, hope.

Noll was introduced as the new coach the day before the draft, and he immediately huddled with scouting boss Art Rooney Jr. They admired the same defensive tackle from the team nicknamed the Mean Green—which, of course, represents the genesis of Greene's moniker.

Art Jr.: "I remember when I saw him play at Colorado State [September 28, 1968]. He was the greatest third-down player you ever saw in your life. I don't know what he was doing, but every third down he was like the Genie in the Bottle: He exploded."

Noll and Art Rooney Jr. selected Greene in the first round, and still got Hanratty in the second—to pacify Pittsburgh.

Art Jr.: "It was copacetic. We started off on the right foot."

Post-Gazette beat writer Jack Sell wrote: "The Steelers yesterday drafted a guy named Joe as their No. 1 choice. . . . That failed to send a single season-ticket buyer to the club's office in the Hotel Roosevelt."

The *Press'* story, without a byline, began: "Tackle Joe Greene, the Steelers' No. 1 draft choice whose selection raised eyebrows and triggered questions of 'Who's he?' among the local sporting set. . . ." The afternoon paper also ran a story containing fan reaction. Its headline: "Who's Joe Greene?"

Noll confronted the skepticism with a rather bold prediction for a gent who had been coach all of one day: "Greene is a good-sized defensive lineman who will play in the National League for the next 10 years. Pass defense begins with the rush on the passer."

Just as the Steelers success begins with Greene's rush to greatness.

Greene: "I knew the Steelers weren't a very good football team. I *hated* the uniforms, with the diamonds [on the shoulders]. I later learned it was the Golden Triangle [in honor of downtown Pittsburgh's nickname]. I learned even later that my boss [Dan Rooney] designed it.

"I was pleased to be drafted. But I was a little bit disappointed being drafted by Pittsburgh. The teams on my list that I didn't want: I didn't want Pittsburgh, I didn't want Buffalo, I didn't want to play for Green Bay. I'm glad they didn't leave the choice up to me."

KEVIN GREENE
Defensive End–Outside Linebacker

Height: 6-3 • **Weight:** 247 • **College:** Auburn • **Years with the Steelers:** 1993–1995 • **Birthplace:** New York City • **Born:** July 31, 1962

Captain Kevin D. Greene, the army-brat son of a Vietnam vet and globe-trotting colonel, was a tank man in the reserves and a tank of a man at left outside linebacker. He was Captain Crunch. He was Hulk Hogan, with whom he was photographed in a ring a few days before Super Bowl XXX. He was a hardwired military mind who reveled in putting quarterbacks in his cross-hairs, smelling spent artillery, idolizing the Hulkster and General George Patton, pumping iron, invigorating Blitzburgh.

Rams cornerback LeRoy Irvin, a teammate in Los Angeles before Greene left by way of that new bauble known as free agency, told me for a 1995 story: "To me, he's all about hitting the beach and dropping grenades and dropping napalm bombs on the opponent. He talks military all the time. He wears those fatigues. And he always talks about 0700 hours. He's not from here. He's not from Earth."

He was once a 185-pound weakling who walked on at Auburn as a punter. He grew into the first splashy free-agent signing by Steelers, a workout maniac who, when he came on

his recruiting visit, lifted weights at Three Rivers Stadium. The fans' favorite Greene since Mean Joe promptly went sackless in his opening three Steelers games and then topped them each season from there. The Captain, an armor officer in the U.S. Army Reserves, totaled 35.5 sacks in his three Steelers years and led the NFL with 14 in 1994, when he and Greg Lloyd were bookend first-team All-Pros at outside linebacker. Quiver and Quake, they were dubbed.

Dermontti Dawson, longtime center: "They had their salt and pepper when they were [together]. Two funny guys. Kevin was more of a jokester. But they fed off one another. They were inseparable. He wanted people to fear him as well [like Lloyd]. The difference was, Greg was always serious on the field. Kevin was more jovial. He could laugh and all that stuff. He got excited. 'Come on, baby, come on.'"

Dick LeBeau, Steelers secondary coach 1992–1994 and defensive coordinator 1995–1996, 2004– : "Tremendous competitor. Never was going to be outworked. He was going to outwork anybody, anything, any time. Tremendous strength. Excellent knowledge of the game. He and Greg Lloyd were a tremendous duo in that they challenged each other—neither wanted the other one to get one step in front of him."

Greene, on working in tandem with Lloyd: "It was a very competitive thing we had between us. 'I'm going to meet you there.'"

Dom Capers, Steelers defensive coordinator 1992–1994: "He's one of my favorite guys. Led the league in sacks in 1994. I brought him down to Carolina, and he led the league in sacks again. A very unique guy—he had a real passion for the game. He would leave Three Rivers with more tape than anybody else. He would know about the guy he was going against. Our calls were Hawk for pass and Rabbit for run. He could call out Hawk or Rabbit by reading the tackle and be right 90 percent of the time. He made guys around him better."

L. C. GREENWOOD
Defensive End

Height: 6-6 • **Weight:** 245 • **College:** Arkansas–Pine Bluff (née Arkansas AM&N) • **Years with the Steelers:** 1969–1981 • **Birthplace:** Canton, Mississippi • **Born:** September 8, 1946

He was Hollywood Bags. He was Bags. Or he was simply Holly.

Whatever the sobriquet, L. C. Henderson Greenwood rarely was identified by his appropriate designation: most prodigious rusher of the feared Steel Curtain. The sack leader of the NFL's most famous front four wasn't Mean Joe Greene. It wasn't Dwight White or Ernie Holmes, who combined for nearly as many as Greenwood's 73.5 in 13 seasons. The lead was in the Bags.

Greenwood graduated 10th in his high school class of 110 and went to Arkansas AM&N, where he graduated in the top 10 and was drafted in the 10th round in 1969 by Steelers who picked Mean Joe Greene in the first round.

In Pittsburgh, Greenwood became as colorful as his gold shoes, one of those size 18s gracing the Western Pennsylvania Sports Museum. He was as much a sight to behold as his goggles. He was all arms and sacks and nightmares for quarterbacks.

He batted down three Fran Tarkenton passes in Super Bowl IX. He sacked Roger Staubach three times in Super Bowl X.

He was waived in 1982 training camp . . . the last of the original 1969 Chuck Noll Steelers. Greenwood was named to the Steelers' 75th Anniversary team in 2007, but the largest honor eluded him: He was a Hall of Fame finalist in 2005–2006. He was born in Canton, Mississippi, but found it excruciatingly difficult to get into Canton, Ohio.

John Banaszak, fellow defensive lineman 1975–1981:

I can remember George Perles in the first meeting that we had as a defensive line my rookie year. "I don't want any of you guys to watch No. 68, 'cause there isn't one of you guys who can play that way." The more I watched him, there was no way I could swim like that, turn and not get blocked. He had arms that could turn a light switch off from here. Two hundred thirty-eight pounds.

Together, you can take the Purple People Eaters [of the Minnesota Vikings] and all those guys who were great defensive lines; there was nobody as good as these guys. L. C. should be in the Hall of Fame; that's a travesty. No question about it. His numbers are as good [as] or better than half of the Hall of Famers right now; maybe more than half. He single-handedly won Super Bowl IX. He should've been the MVP.

L. C. Greenwood relaxes on the bench with a cooling towel on his head in 1981. (Bill Amatucci)

Nice goggles, L. C. Greenwood. (John Beale)

Ralph Berlin, trainer 1968–1992: "Didn't like to practice. He'd be on crutches Wednesday or Thursday. Practice a little on Friday. He'd go out there on Sunday and play like hell."

George Perles, defensive line coach and defensive coordinator 1972–1981: "Well, they call 'em Sunday players. That means you can screw off all week. Nobody could do it—except L. C."

Larry Brown, tight end–offensive tackle 1971–1984: "What gets lost, though, I think people look at the game—the physicality of it. I gave so much more credit to the mental part of it. The reason they were so good . . . was their intelligence [and toil], students of the game. Joe, Dwight, L. C. . . . I played against L. C. I had good coaches, obviously. But I learned a great deal about playing offensive tackle from L. C. Greenwood. And he was quick to encourage and pump me up. I thought he was a terrific teammate."

Joe Greene, defensive tackle and sidekick on the left side 1969–1981: "L. C. and I talked; we were game-planning. Down and distance. Situation. Trying to figure out what the next call was going to be."

Dan "Bad Rad" Radakovich, defensive line coach 1971 and offensive line coach 1974–1977: "It's a shame that only one of the Steel Curtain is in the Hall of Fame. The Purple People Eaters have two, [Carl] Eller and [Alan] Page. You can't tell me Eller was as good as L. C. No way. If Greenwood doesn't get in, it's a freakin' shame."

RANDY GROSSMAN
Tight End

Height: 6-0 • **Weight:** 218 • **College:** Temple • **Years with the Steelers:** 1974–1981 • **Birthplace:** Philadelphia • **Born:** September 20, 1952

Undersized, underappreciated, underdog, Randy Grossman simply prevailed. He wasn't a dominating blocker, but he sufficed. He wasn't the Kellen Winslow of his time, but he caught enough passes and won enough Super Bowl rings to make most tight ends envious.

Not content to merely give Terry Bradshaw grief over the C-A-T spelling test, prior to Super Bowl XIII Dallas linebacker Hollywood Henderson also called out Grossman, who was subbing for starter Bennie Cunningham and his bad knee: "He's nothing but a backup. He only plays when somebody dies or breaks a leg. I'm not going to have any trouble covering him Sunday."

Grossman, whose 37 catches in 1978 were only a hair behind future Hall of Famer John Stallworth's second-best 41 on the Steelers, caught three passes in that Super Bowl triumph.

Ralph Berlin, trainer 1968–1992 and more: "I was the gopher. Dan [Rooney] would send me out, and I'd have a half dozen contracts in my bag. He said they wanted me to go to Temple and sign this tight end, Randy Grossman. . . . Randy walks in, and he's like 5-11. I asked [their] attorney, 'You have a phone I could use?' So I called Dan, 'You want me to sign this midget?' 'We got to have a tight end for camp.' He missed one game in 10 years." Two, actually. He started 43 of the 118 he played.

Mike Wagner, safety 1971–1980: "I [first] thought, 'How does this guy play football?' He was very undersized. Not the fastest. Tremendous hands, rarely dropped a ball near him. I'm sure other teams were shaking their heads, 'How could this guy do that?'"

JACK HAM
Outside Linebacker

Height: 6-1 • **Weight:** 225 • **College:** Penn State • **Years with the Steelers:** 1971–1982 • **Birthplace:** Johnstown, Pennsylvania • **Born:** December 23, 1948

In the war room of the Steelers' 1971 draft, home to perhaps the second-greatest draft in NFL history, a gaggle of assistants lobbied to expend their eighth-overall selection on Penn State linebacker Jack Raphael Ham Jr.

Instead, the consensus decided to nab Grambling wide receiver Frank Lewis.

Chuck Noll was comfortable with that, figuring this Ham fellow should still be available at 34th overall.

So when their second-round pick approached, one of those same assistants suggested an alteration.

Could you have imagined this Steelers linebacker corps for the ages, right to left: Andy Russell, Jack Lambert . . . and Phil Villipiano?

This Villapiano was a fine fellow, one inch taller and a shade beefier than Ham, with a nice resume from Bowling Green. In the end, the hated Oakland Raiders would select him 11 picks

Eight-time Pro Bowl selection and six-time All-Pro linebacker Jack Ham, in his customary hands-on-hips pose in 1982. He played one more season, his 12th, and enjoyed his first official regular-season sacks—three—after the Steelers switched to a 3–4 alignment. (George Gojkovich)

later. But, at such a critical moment, Noll and linebackers coach Charley Sumner sought the educated opinion of the new guy in the room, the recently hired defensive line coach who once tutored Penn State linebackers and laid claim to being the father of Mount Nittany's Lionbacker U. It was at Penn State where only defensive tackle Mike Reid became a starter earlier than Ham, and that by a mere two spring-scrimmage days faster as a second-semester freshman.

Dan "Bad Rad" Radakovich, coach of the defensive line in 1971 and offensive line from 1974 to 1977: "I said, 'He'll be a Steeler linebacker like you've never had before. He can do everything.'"

What a sage scouting report that proved to be.

To be fair, the relationship had a quizzical start. When a knock came at the Hilton Hotel door where the Steelers entertained their new draftees, scouting chief Art Rooney Jr. believed the lad standing there in a blue jacket to be a bellboy. Rather, it was their second-round pick.

Ham donned black-and-gold No. 59 and another 15 pounds, and wore both well for the next 12 years, eight Pro

Bowls (in succession from 1973 to 1980), six All-Pros, and four Super Bowls.

Ralph Berlin, trainer 1969–1982: "Jack was very intelligent, very bright. My favorite."

George Perles, defensive assistant and coordinator 1972–1981: "Jack Ham might be the nicest gentleman to ever play the game of football. He was smart and special."

Indeed, Ham was more a kindred spirit to Russell than with either Steelers middle linebacker, Henry Davis or the toothless smile who arrived in 1974, Jack Lambert.

Speaking of that position . . .

Ham, one of the greatest outside linebackers to ever play the game, almost got dumped in the middle.

Radakovich, who coached him in college and knew him well: "We were going to move him to middle linebacker, and Ham didn't want to. I just wanted to get him in the game. He didn't want to do it, but we were going to do it."

Jack Ham: "I went over to Rad's house, over in Mount Lebanon at the time. I played my freshman, sophomore, and junior years at Penn State on the outside [for Radakovich]. They moved me to middle linebacker my senior year, and it was my worst year. I didn't want to play the middle. And when I came here . . . , during the preseason, they wanted me to end up playing the middle. I didn't lobby for it, but I kind of knew my skills. Middle linebacker wasn't my forte. I lobbied with Rad, and then I had the three-interception game."

Radakovich: "Henry Davis got hurt [on the outside]. Ham started for Henry Davis in one preseason game, against [the New York Giants and Fran] Tarkenton. He had three interceptions, and that was it for Henry."

Ham: "Whether he liked me or not, [Tarkenton] threw me three interceptions in that game. After that, I was the starting left linebacker. Henry Davis wound up playing the middle."

History will note that the surly Davis was the one who got moved inside, and then got moved out. Davis became the next middle linebacker, and—with Ham and Russell on his wings—

was a pretty good one . . . until this kid Lambert replaced him after another Davis injury in 1974's camp.

Radakovich: "Henry was a really good player. But Henry got hurt twice, and got replaced by two Hall of Famers."

Ham started at left outside linebacker from the 1971 get-go. He was part of the defense that allowed Chicago eight first downs and 141 total yards in a 17-15 opening loss. He was among the unit that permitted 28 yards rushing on 18 Cincinnati carries the next week in victory, leaving the Three Rivers Stadium field to a mild standing ovation. In only his third NFL game, Ham intercepted John Hadl in the end zone on San Diego's second-to-last possession—his first of many critical career picks—then batted away a fourth-down pass in the end zone in the final seconds to help preserve a four-point Steelers triumph. Nice start, eh?

Ham captured a career-high seven interceptions his second season and started his string of Pro Bowls the next.

Then came 1974. He had five interceptions in the regular season. He had two in the AFC championship game that propelled the Steelers to their inaugural Super Bowl.

Joe Gordon, publicity director and vice president 1969–1998: "That was the over-the-hump game. Because everybody expected Oakland to win that game. And we dominated them. To me, that was the springboard to the four Super Bowls."

Gary Dunn, defensive lineman 1977–1987: "Ham, you know what? The guy was unbelievable. How a guy that size could take on those big blockers [50 pounds larger]. He'd take on those blockers and make them look silly. It was amazing. Those guys on the outside, you just felt confident we'd be able to stop somebody."

As intelligent and well spoken as he was, Ham didn't choose to play the media game. Sharing a locker room with the talkative likes of Terry Bradshaw, Lynn Swann, Joe Greene, Dwight White, Andy Russell, and more, there wasn't a crushing need. He chose to maintain a low profile—despite having his own fan club, *Dobre Shunka*, Hungarian for "good

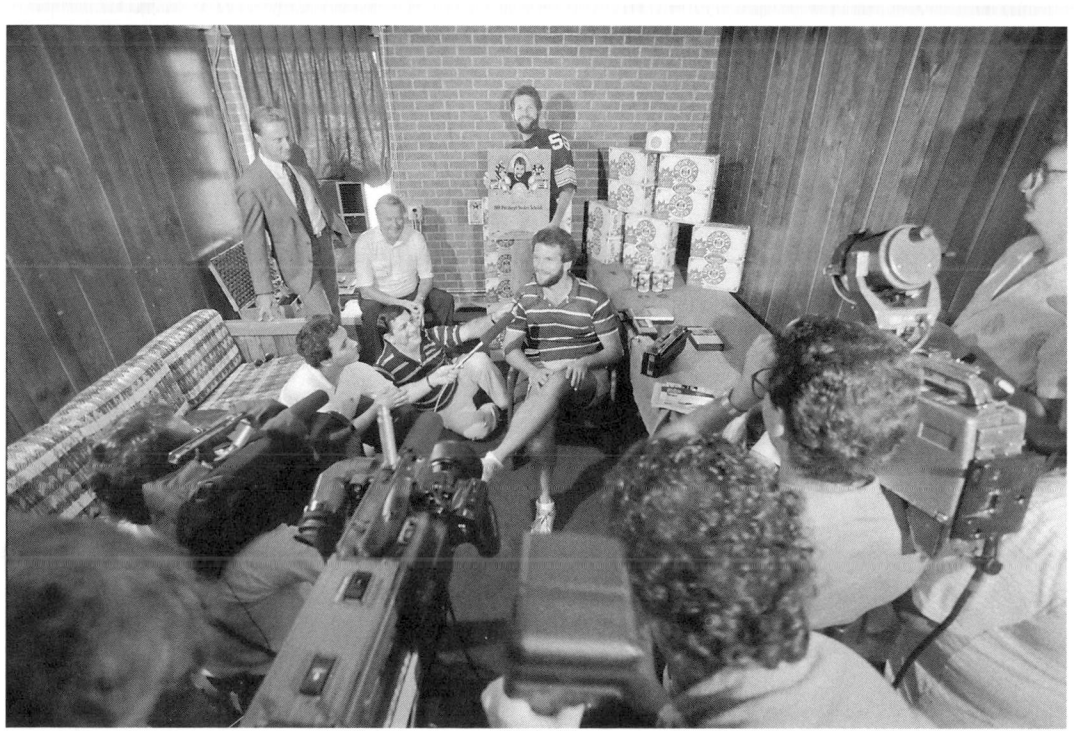

Jack Ham meets the media in the 1988 training camp at St. Vincent College to announce that hometown Iron City Beer is honoring him for his impending Pro Football Hall of Fame induction: Ham in a can. (Vincent J. Musi)

ham," and once getting selected for ABC's "Superstars" schlock competition with fellow ex–Penn Stater Franco Harris.

Or, as he once put it, "I'm not very good copy, am I?"

Phil Musick in 1978 in the *Pittsburgh Post-Gazette* perhaps described him best: "For Jack Ham, it was a typical Sunday afternoon. He wreaked quiet havoc, slipped unobtrusively into a telephone booth to shed his uniform and flew home to Metropolis."

He and his middle-linebacker teammate were quite the study. Where Lambert was vociferous and snarling and demonstrative, Ham was thoughtful and collected and unassuming. Yet they learned from one another.

Gordon: "George Perles used to say, 'There's a lot of Ham in Lambert, and a lot of Lambert in Ham.'"

Dunn: "He and Lambert were totally different in the huddle. They were both intense out on the field. But everybody had a different presence."

Mike Wagner, safety 1971–1980 and Ham's roommate and best friend: "He was a complete opposite of Lambert. Jack was very serious, businesslike on the football field. But Jack has a great sense of humor. He likes to gently agitate people—in a fun way.

"He used to get into these fights with Lambert. He'd be getting ready to intercept a ball, and Lambert would bump into him [and the pass would fall incomplete]. They'd be [swearing at] each other."

Pass coverage was his forte, his first priority.

He and Russell reveled in jamming and rerouting, a physical style that helped buy time for the Steel Curtain to draw to a close.

Russell, right outside linebacker 1963, 1966–1976: "We had a lot of fun doing that, Hammer and I."

By the same token, pass coverage grew into a territorial affair.

If no receiver strayed into Ham's area, he might sneak into someone else's. Wagner recalled covering a tight end once, only to find Ham fronting him.

Wagner: "I yelled at him, 'Play your coverage!'

"It was helpful for me to observe how he played. Jack was a Hall of Fame linebacker, but he prided himself more on stopping the pass than the run. Which was amazing—really a testament to him and the style we could play. He would cover running backs and tight ends, all over the field."

The AFC championship game to end the 1978 season, the one that was over in a 31-3 first half against Houston? Lambert at the time blamed it on Ham: "It was because everybody was in a hurry to get to Jack Ham's party. It's very seldom that he comes up with a freebie, and everyone wanted to take advantage of it."

In 1979, he dislocated a bone in his ankle in the second-to-last game of the regular season; Dirt Winston took his place in the playoffs. Ham played 1980 through pain. He broke an arm in 1981 training camp.

A durable sort who hardly missed games earlier in his career, he played half the time in 1982, and retired to the energy business and broadcasting on national radio. When he exited, his 32 career interceptions were third most by any NFL linebacker in history.

For all his plaudits—Steelers' 75th Anniversary team, NFL's 75th Anniversary team, all-time NFL team, Super Bowl Silver Anniversary team, Hall of Fame—Ham assessed himself harshly: "I'm my own worst critic."

He was the only one. You know, you don't tug on Superman's cape.

CASEY HAMPTON
Nose Tackle

Height: 6-1 • **Weight:** 320 • **College:** Texas • **Years with the Steelers:** 2001– • **Birthplace:** Galveston, Texas • **Born:** September 3, 1977

The visual is impossible to shake a decade later.

Two receivers grabbed the burnt-orange shorts with the University of Texas Longhorn logo, the tent-like pair belonging to the rookie nose tackle. Troy Edwards stood in one leg. Hines Ward stood in the other. And, in the middle of the Steelers locker room, they hiked up the shorts to their waists . . . and there was still room for another body in there. Maybe two.

The thighs of Texas, to be sure.

The bum of a steer.

Big Snack, Hamp, Case—Casey Hampton went by many a handle around these Steelers. One training camp, he reported over-overweight and promptly to Mike Tomlin's doghouse: the PUP list, for physically unable to perform. Yet his performance in the Steelers 3–4 was consistently remarkable and adjudged accordingly.

Five times, Hampton was named to the Pro Bowl. Yet he never recorded more than 2.5 sacks in a single season. He never recorded more than 43 tackles in a single season. The number important to Hampton, beyond the 340-pound threshold he wasn't supposed to cross?

The three blockers up the middle, that's the number he needed to tie up and keep from reaching his inside linebackers as long as possible.

Those sizable thighs and that ample anterior held their ground well enough to earn Hampton a spot on the Steelers' 75th Anniversary team.

Larry Foote, inside linebacker 2002–2008 and 2010– : "I have seen his butt for plenty of years. You can't miss it.

"He makes my job easier, you better believe that. One of the best in the game. When that guy pinches the line of scrimmage, it's automatic. You know the running back has to cut back."

James Farrior, middle linebacker 2002–2011: "Him and the other two defensive linemen have probably helped me out because they do a great job of keeping guys off me. It starts with Casey in the middle. That was one of the first guys I met when I got here. And that's what he said, 'I'm Casey Hampton. I'm going to keep people off you.' He stuck to his word. Big dude."

Dick LeBeau, defensive assistant 1992–1994 and defensive coordinator 1995–1996, 2004– : "He's a very unusual size/strength player who has better feet and athleticism than people realize. Casey has certainly been the anchor block for our 3–4 line. If you had to start building a 3–4 defense, Hampton is the guy you want to start with. He always has his position handled, and usually has two blockers strung out."

Aaron Smith, defensive end and sidekick 1999–2011: "I don't think people realize how good a person Casey is, how gentle he is, how loving and friendly he is. Just a good-natured guy. My kids' favorite guy, that says it right there. My three-year-old says [as Dad leaves for work], 'Are you going to see Casey?' It's hard *not* to like him."

FRANCO HARRIS
Running Back

Height: 6-2 • **Weight:** 230 • **College:** Penn State • **Years with the Steelers:** 1972–1983 • **Birthplace:** Fort Dix, New Jersey • **Born:** March 7, 1950

He could have been Robert Newhouse.

But could Robert Newhouse have been Franco Harris?

Chuck Noll was sold. This Newhouse fellow, all of 5-10 and 202 pounds, was a record-setting rusher at the University of Houston. He averaged three tear-away jerseys per game, broke five helmets in his career, and, for good measure, carried an A average in electrical engineering. At least one other of the Steelers draft hierarchy preferred the plug of a Texan, too.

Franco's war-room army for the 1972 draft consisted of player personnel director Dick Haley, scouting director Art Rooney Jr., and a Steelers assistant coach who had already accepted a job at the University of Colorado. Noll asked that

In his second-to-last regular-season game in a Steelers uniform, Franco Harris rushes for 103 yards in a 1983 victory over the host Jets to put the Steelers in the playoffs. It was the final Steelers game ever played by Terry Bradshaw. (George Gojkovich)

assistant to stay through the February 1 draft for this explicit purpose: Newhouse or Harris, Harris or Newhouse?

Art Rooney Jr., who moaned to future Giants General Manager George Young, then with the Colts, that Noll was convinced Newhouse would become the better player: "George said, 'You tell him that question was settled over 2,000 years ago when Socrates said, 'A good big man is better than a good little man any day.'"

Actually, the old Greek scout was referring to a "good man," period. But, ya know. Whatever it takes.

The same as he did with bringing together the Steel Curtain (he was the defensive line coach who put the four together in 1971) and with molding Mike Webster and blocking friends into tailored-jersey forces (he was the offensive line coach from 1974 to 1977), the then-outgoing coach accepts credit for breaking the tie in favor of Lydell Mitchell's former Penn State backfield caddy.

Dan "Bad Rad" Radakovich, in between Steelers and Colorado gigs at the time and a former Penn State assistant: "I was all for Franco. 'Cause I was the only one who knew Franco. I knew what kind of athlete he was. If we didn't get Franco, I was pushing to get Herb Orvis, a lineman out of Colorado. He ended up in Detroit. Newhouse was an engineering student. He was smart. He was short with good talent. Played 12 years. He would have been a good pick. Bill Nunn was for Newhouse. Dick Hoak [a fellow Penn Stater], Dick Haley, [Rooney Jr. and Radakovich were] for Franco.

"Chuck finally relented." So it was Radakovich's vote that swayed it? "Of course, I think so. Art Rooney Jr. thinks so. That's two guys."

With their first-round selection, the Pittsburgh Steelers drafted Franco Harris.

Twenty-three picks later, Dallas grabbed Robert Newhouse in the second round.

It turned out to be a lucky No. 13 overall.

With Harris, the Pittsburgh Steelers never had a losing record . . . after collecting just seven winning marks the previous 39 seasons. With Harris, the Steelers made the playoffs 10 of their 12 seasons . . . after playing in just one postseason game and one "Playoff Bowl." With Harris, the Steelers won four Super Bowls . . . including two against the Cowboys and Newhouse.

Roy McHugh, longtime sportswriter, sports columnist, and sports editor of the Pittsburgh Press: "I covered Penn State when he was there. The coaches thought he was lackadaisical and didn't work hard. I was at the Cotton Bowl, and they didn't put him in the whole game because he missed practices."

Hoak, explaining the Harris mentality that he evaluated early and embraced as a coach: "We could never time him [in the 40-yard dash]. He'd run about 32 yards and then glide in. He'd run 4.65. We'd ask, 'Franco, why don't you run there?' 'I don't want to pull a hamstring.' Franco was the type of guy, he was a hard worker. First on the field, last one off. Last one out of the training room. But you couldn't tell Franco, 'Go run through that wall.' He'd want a reason, 'Why?' That's the way Franco was. Franco would break everything down. You give him a reason why, he was all in."

Noll and the Steelers weren't completely all for their rookie, though. He played behind Frenchy Fuqua and a converted basketball player, Preston Pearson. In fact, they weren't quite sure what to do with him. He returned kicks (two for 42 yards total). He caught passes (six for 33). He rushed unsuccessfully

balled up his motivation and threw himself around NFL lots on a regular Pro Bowl basis from there.

He had played one game in his bits and pieces of two seasons. The first was spent on the 2002 practice squad, except for a December 29 date with, ahem, Baltimore. The second involved one month on the 2003 practice squad. After that early-2004 bad experience with Baltimore, Harrison went home to study for his CDL license, ready to get on with his life's work as a truck driver. Than Haggans snapped a couple of fingers, the Steelers signed him because they needed a healthy body, and Harrison made his move. He learned all four linebacker positions. He dazzled on special teams. He subbed capably against his hometown Cleveland Browns because Porter got ejected for inserting himself into harmless pregame warm-up jawing. Deebo's debut, James Farrior called it, invoking Harrison's nickname from a character he resembled in the movie *Friday*.

What followed were five Pro Bowls, three consecutive seasons of double-digit sacks, and a top-six spot among the sackers of storied Steelers history.

A couple of career highlights? A wrestling-style body slam of a drunken fan who ran onto Cleveland's field on Christmas Eve 2005, squatting on him until police arrived. And that improbable, exhausting 100-yard interception with 0:00 on the clock at halftime of Super Bowl XLIII.

Dick LeBeau, defensive assistant 1992–1994 and defensive coordinator 1995, 2004– : "I never saw James until I came here—his first year making it [as a regular] was my first year. Whatever the reason, the stars kind of aligned for us that we got him there. And what a great player he's been for us."

Tony Dungy, ex-Steeler and opposition coach in Tampa Bay and Indianapolis: "Unique guy. Fits the Steeler philosophy. Some people might look at him and say, 'Not big enough.' Coach Noll started that: Look at productivity. Don't typecast them. James Harrison is a dynamic player, powerful, never-say-die attitude. He would've fit in so well with the group I played with, the same mentality. Relentless, that's the word that describes him."

LeBeau: "To my way of thinking, he made the greatest football play I've ever seen [the 100-yard interception return in Super Bowl XLIII]. You ain't gonna see a play like that but once every 50 years . . . and we needed every point of it. Beyond that, there's not a linebacker in the league who could have made the run that he made and come back to play a really, really productive second half—James' conditioning was so high. You talk about all those situations falling in line for him to impact the game in that way. If you forgot all the other of millions of plays he made for us, that in itself would put him in the top 100 [Steelers]."

CARLTON HASELRIG
Guard

Height: 6-1 • **Weight:** 295 • **College:** Pitt-Johnstown
• **Years with the Steelers:** 1990–1993 • **Birthplace:** Johnstown, Pennsylvania • **Born:** January 22, 1966

He grappled his way to six NCAA heavyweight wrestling championships, a Division III behemoth beating all comers that included the baddest of the college sport's big boys. He leveraged a last-round selection by his home-area Steelers,

Carlton Haselrig, who rose from collegiate wrestling champion to NFL guard, was considered by Chuck Noll to be one of the finest offensive linemen he coached in Pittsburgh. Sadly, Haselrig became better known for off-field troubles. (George Gojkovich)

though their warbling radio announcer, Myron Cope, crowed about it happening only because he lobbied for the 12th-round pick. And he wrestled his way from developmental-squad nose tackle to Pro Bowl offensive guard to personal demons that landed him in prison and outside the NFL.

Carlton Haselrig contended with so much through the 1990s, pinning some, decisioned by others.

Jon Kolb, former lineman and assistant coach: "Carlton Haselrig, the tragedy of what could have been."

Dermontti Dawson, center 1988–2000: "One of the most gifted athletes I've ever seen, not just playing football. A guy who had all the talent in the world. One who could have accomplished great things for a long period of time."

Instead, after switching to the offensive line in 1990 and becoming a starter and star the very next season, Haselrig was gone from the NFL by late 1995.

A star that fizzled perhaps prematurely, he still performed remarkably for a fellow who arose from nowhere in 1989, having never played football before, to a Pro Bowler in 1992.

Kolb: "I took [son] Tanner to the NCAA wrestling championships. There was a guy there who won the Division III championship at heavyweight, won the Division II championship at heavyweight, and when I was there won the Division I championship at heavyweight. He was this wide [holding arms farthest apart]. That was my first year as [an assistant] coach. I went back and said, 'You guys want to sign a free agent? I guarantee he'd make a nose tackle.'"

Dawson: "Carlton made me better as a center. Carlton was signed and played nose guard. He had these wrestling moves. He would counter everything you could do. He could toss you and pin you like that. He made me much better with my feet and my balance—hone my skills, better myself."

Kolb: "He wound up a guard. And how that happened, he was blocking Joe [Greene, an assistant coach then] in practice" and stopped the eventual Hall of Famer cold.

Dawson: "I tell you who would talk some trash was Carlton Haselrig. [He and Leon Searcy,] they could talk some trash and back it up. Especially if they felt somebody was taking a pop shot at them. 'Hey . . . , we'll see who wins.' Carlton could grab you and toss you, and you wouldn't know what had happened."

Haselrig's '90s spiraled after making the Pro Bowl and first-team All-Pro in 1992.

1993: He missed four games after voluntarily checking himself into an alcohol and substance-abuse treatment center.

1994: He skipped off-season conditioning workouts—not exactly endearing himself to Bill Cowher—and drove his four-wheel-drive vehicle up the steps and onto the lawn at the Pittsburgh Theological Seminary. Two months later, he got arrested in a Strip District bar on a warrant for failing to appear on the seminary-ride charge—he originally denied to police he was Carlton Haselrig, they reported.

1995: He played for the Jets, where longtime Steelers scout Dick Haley signed him, but then disappeared that December more than a week after being suspended for violating league substance-abuse policy. That same week, an Allegheny County judge issued a warrant for his arrest after Haselrig missed a court date on a misdemeanor charge involving a drunken incident.

1996: Police said he raced through part of his hometown on a motorcycle, his helmet on backward—he was released to spend at least a year in an alcoholism treatment center.

1997: He got shot in the leg during a Johnstown dispute. And, as a result of the motorcycle incident, he was sentenced to prison for probation violation.

By 1998, he was playing in the National Minor Pro Football League and sharing the league's MVP with another Pittsburgh product, Major Harris. Haselrig wound up toiling as an assistant coach with the semipro Pittsburgh Colts in the early 2000s. Later in the decade, he tried his hand at mixed martial arts.

Dawson: "Carlton could run all day long; he was strong; he had a passion for the game. I think if he had kept that [passion] and not gotten into trouble, he could've been a perennial Pro Bowler *every* year. He just had that much talent. We all had vices that kind of get to us. He let that—family life or alcohol or whatever it may have been—affect him. So he didn't have any longevity whatsoever."

Kevin Greene, outside linebacker 1993–1995: "'Rig came and went for me fairly quickly. Just like this kid named Tim Worley out of Georgia. I hated for these kids. . . . They just did not have their mojo together. I've seen a lot of kids like that, a lot of kids come and go in the NFL who had the same problems. . . . He's grouped into that type of player who showed that type of potential, could have been a dominant player in this league for 10 years. It's unfortunate, but the NFL is littered with [such] people, past and present. And future."

DICK HOAK
Running Back

Height: 5-11 • **Weight:** 195 • **College:** Penn State • **Years with the Steelers:** 1961–1970 • **Birthplace:** Jeannette, Pennsylvania • **Born:** December 8, 1939

Dick Hoak arrived as a seventh-round draft choice about the time of the second Project Mercury flight, all 15 minutes, 37 seconds of it, and departed toward the end of the Space Shuttle program. Ten years as a running back. Thirty-five years as a running back coach. Nearly a half century around the same team, the same position, the same few yards of space.

No man other than a Rooney has gone deeper in modern Steelers history.

Tony Dungy, who arrived as a player in 1977 and exited as a coach in 1988, uttering what so many Steelers could: "Dick Hoak was there when I got there; he was there when I left."

The funny thing about it? Hoak figured he'd end up a high school coach.

Hoak, wearing Super Bowl XIII and XL rings (because "they're the nicest ones"): "Growing up, I really wasn't interested in pro football. I went to one game. My brother took me. It was the San Francisco 49ers against the Steelers. The Steelers got killed. . . . Even when I was in college, I didn't think a whole

Dick Hoak coaches running backs in the 1980 season. This photograph could have been taken anytime between 1972 and 2006, the three-plus decades he spent coaching Steelers running backs. Combined with his playing career, Hoak spent 46 years with his hometown franchise. (Bill Amatucci)

lot about playing pro football. I wanted to teach high school and coach football. No one in my family got the opportunity to go to college. I thought that was what I wanted to do."

He was a quarterback who became a halfback by accident, then returned to quarterback his senior year at Penn State—back when Joe Paterno still had five more years of toil as a Rip Engle assistant coach.

Hoak: "In those days, they didn't scout you. They sent you these little cards. They asked, 'Are you interested in playing pro football? How fast do you run?' I filled them out and sent them back."

Next thing he knew, he was commuting from home in Jeannette to Steelers practice in South Park.

For the next decade.

Then, once Three Rivers Stadium was built, he retired and found his dream job: teaching and coaching in high school at Wheeling (West Virginia) Central Catholic. Pitt's Carl DePasqua and Chuck Noll called on the same day to offer him a job. Fortunately for the Steelers, the interview with Noll was scheduled first. Hoak called DePasqua to inform the Pitt coach he was taking the Steelers running-backs position, where a half century later Hoak remained sixth in all-time rushing with 3,965 yards and fourth with 1,132 carries.

Hoak: "[DePasqua] said, 'You did the right thing.' I guess I did. 'Cause after that, all the guys from Pitt got fired."

Andy Russell, teammate 1963, 1966–1976: "It made sense that he would be a very good running back coach. He was a very smart guy. He went to a Pro Bowl; for a guy with his size and his speed that was pretty amazing. He was agile; he could make you miss. But he also could run over you."

Ron Erhardt, offensive coordinator 1992–1995: "And he was really a good coach. We had a good feeling together about the running game. He had a lot of running backs in his time. He knew what a running back should do."

Dungy, Steelers defensive assistant and coordinator 1981–1988 before becoming a head coach in Tampa Bay and Indianapolis: "Very soft-spoken. Knew as much football as anybody I've ever been around. A great way of communicating with guys. Running backs who came in there, no matter what their personality was, no matter what their challenges were, he got the most out of anybody. He loved living in Greensburg; he loved coaching in Pittsburgh. I tried to get him to Tampa when I became head coach there. 'As much as I'd love to be your offensive coordinator, I'm a Pittsburgh guy.'"

MERRIL HOGE
Running Back

Height: 6-2 • **Weight:** 225 • **College:** Idaho State • **Years with the Steelers:** 1987–1993 • **Birthplace:** Pocatello, Idaho • **Born:** January 26, 1965

How many Steelers running backs have rushed for 100 yards or more in consecutive conference playoff games?

Not Hall of Famer Franco Harris. Not potential Hall of Famer Jerome Bettis. Not Willie Parker, he of the longest run in Super Bowl history. Not Rashard Mendenhall. Just one: Merril Hoge. His home state of Idaho had a two-day celebration in his honor after his remarkable playoff run, but truly December 31, 1989, and January 7, 1990, were Merril Hoge's days.

Merril Hoge, the conscience of the Steelers as well as a critical offensive contributor from 1987 to 1993, stands stoically amid a preseason game in 1991—the start of Chuck Noll's final season. (Vincent J. Musi)

A running back with more want-to than wallop, with more giddyup than gallop, Hoge compiled four 100-yard games in his seven-year, 109-game Steelers career. Half of those 100s came in one playoff spurt. It was the end of the season that began ruggedly: with a confusing offense under new coordinator Joe Walton and an 0-2 start after drubbings at the hands of Cleveland and Cincinnati by a collective 92-10. By the playoffs, he was running through Jerry Glanville's Oilers for a New Year's Eve overtime upset and then the Broncos in a one-point heartbreaker.

This utilitarian fullback combined for more than 890 yards rushing and receiving for four consecutive years. He was the Steelers' leading rusher in three seasons. He was their second-leading receiver in two—and tied for the lead in yet another.

Hoge left an indelible mark on the NFL, not for his ESPN broadcasting career, but in relation to concussions: He was at the center of the seminal moment in neurocognitive testing history and the management of the injury that grew to epidemic proportions and congressional hearings almost two decades later. He wound up retiring and winning a lawsuit against the Chicago Bears over a career-ending concussion.

Later, he successfully battled non-Hodgkin's lymphoma, authored a book, and became a motivational speaker.

Jon Kolb, assistant coach 1982–1991: "He wrote a book, *Find a Way*. That talks [volumes] about Merril Hoge."

Bubby Brister, quarterback 1986–1992: "When he first came in, he was upstairs in a dorm room in Latrobe. I wound up getting a window-unit air conditioner, it was so hot. Merril asked, 'Can I throw a mattress on the floor?' He never left. He was lacking in confidence, and I probably had a little too much, so it worked out. 'Mutt and Jeff,' they called us. We wound up being roommates for several years."

Dermontti Dawson, teammate and center 1988–2000: "Hodgey, my man. When I first started out my rookie year in 1988, we had the trapping offense; Merril was the man. The workhorse. Big ol' thighs. Not a very big upper body. But when it came to running, Merril was one of the most efficient runners we had. Not the speed, but he could hurt you.

"He came to work *every day*. And just a great guy, a funny guy, joked around. Merril, I look at him breaking down the games on ESPN, he knows what he's talking about. He's got a presence. Not everybody has the ability to do it." And this from a former radio broadcaster.

Gerald Williams, nose tackle–defensive end 1986–1994: "He was the Rocky Bleier of our era. When he came to the table, same thing: Guts and glory. Believe it or not, he wasn't as talkative in the locker room as he is now. I guess he just came out of his shell when he got into the broadcasting business."

ERNIE HOLMES
Defensive Tackle

Height: 6-3 • **Weight:** 260-plus • **College:** Texas Southern • **Years with the Steelers:** 1972–1977 • **Birthplace:** Jamestown, Texas • **Born:** July 11, 1948 • **Died:** January 17, 2008

"How do you tell my story?"

Ernest Lee. Those were his given names, his apt description. The sincere soul and intense cauldron of an enigma that was Ernie Holmes, at one point the star and for years the most scarred of the Steel Curtain, still brought conflicted emotions to teammates and Steelers colleagues four decades later. How to describe him?

Ralph Berlin, trainer 1968–1992: "Fats was Fats. What you see. . . . With that arrow on his head, my Lord."

He was Fats indeed, and tales about his appetite were legendary.

He was the self-proclaimed Arrowhead, receiving help from friends and relatives in shaving an arrow where mohawks roam on scalps today. The reasons: to get attention, of course, but Holmes also claimed it kept him heading toward quarterbacks, moving forward.

Direction appeared to become a problem for him.

He arrived in the 1971 draft that brought the Steelers seven starters and Hall of Fame linebacker Jack Ham. Holmes was the last of three eighth-round selections, compensation for a center named Bob DeMarco. He spent a season on the taxi squad, as it was called then.

For the next half-dozen years, he was found most often in opposing backfields, at the buffet table, and in court.

Arrowhead Ernie Holmes in the 1975 season. It wasn't simply an ahead-of-its-time Mohawk. It really was an arrow. (George Gojkovich)

Joe Gordon, publicity director and vice president 1969–1998: "In his prime, in this period, he was as good as any defensive lineman in the NFL. He'd come in the office and say, 'Hey, Joe, get me some pub.'"

Holmes grabbed headlines on his own:

- His marriage failing, his finances a mess, he drove 1,300-plus miles nonstop to the Steelers offices seeking help in 1973. On the Ohio Turnpike, he pointed a revolver out his Cadillac window and shot tires of passing trucks. After a high-speed chase, he fired a shotgun at an Ohio State patrolman piloting a helicopter, wounding him in the leg. The Rooneys came to the Ohio jail holding him, put up his $45,000 bond, and brought him to Western Psychiatric at Pitt. He was convicted of assault and given three to five years probation plus psychiatric treatment. His Super Bowl X check went, under court orders, to pay the patrolman $25,000 in damages.
- In the cover story of the 1975 *Time* magazine carrying all four Steel Curtain faces, Holmes described himself as "stone crazy."
- From the September 12, 1976, Raiders-Steelers game in which the "criminal element" lawsuit sprang, four people were fined by NFL Commissioner Pete Rozelle: Chuck Noll

for that quotation, Oakland's George Atkinson and Jack Tatum for their brutal play . . . and Holmes.

- In 1977 he was acquitted of cocaine possession in Texas, where Noll, Dan Rooney, and a retired Andy Russell testified on his behalf. He was convicted of drunk driving that same year.

Holmes was traded in 1978, for 10th- and 11th-round picks, and summarily shipped to lowly Tampa Bay. The Buccaneers released him before he played in a regular-season game, and in his place they signed Randy Crowder, newly released from prison after serving almost a year for the sale of cocaine.

In a 1982 *Pittsburgh Press* story, Holmes admitted to alcoholism: "I drank so much cognac . . . , my head wasn't squared away." Chuck Noll remarked in the same article, "As problem players go, he was one of the larger ones."

Given all his personal demons, Holmes underwent a metamorphosis of sorts and became an ordained minister later in life.

At his 2008 funeral service, at his old high school, among the crowd of hundreds were a few folks who shaved their hair into an arrow, moving forward.

John Banaszak, defensive lineman 1975–1981: "Ernie Holmes took it down to a personal level. He was going to beat the snot out of the guy he was playing against. The NFL outlawed the head slap [in 1977] because of Ernie Holmes. And I'm here to tell you, I was the recipient of that head slap a number of times as a rookie. Especially when Ernie was hung over. Because as soon as I came off the ball simulating the offensive line against Ernie and smelled that breath, I knew I just hit Ernie too hard and gave him a headache. The next time I came off that ball, I'd get that head slap. And it just rings inside of your helmet. That was Ernie's downfall, [that] he didn't get the recognition."

George Perles, defensive line coach and defensive coordinator 1972–1981: "Ernie Holmes, my man. That's a story in itself. We're playing in Kansas City. He's waiting outside the meeting room for me. 'George, George, I don't get any recognition. You know why? I don't have a nickname. Mean Joe. Hollywood. Mad Dog. From now on, I'm Arrowhead.'" The haircut and persona were birthed.

"You talk about toughness. A lot of people were worried that maybe he'd fly off the handle. They were the easiest guys in the world to work with. We've already lost [the late] Dwight White, Steve Furness, and Ernie Holmes from that right side. But they were tough. They would knock your block off."

Larry Brown, tight end, draft of 1971 classmate, and friend: "Dwight said Ernie would come back to the huddle, 'I got him bleeding. I got him now.' . . . Despite everything, he was a good guy. To the people he knew and trusted, he was a gentle soul. He had a shell to protect himself."

Jon Kolb, center–tackle 1969–1981, who recalled Holmes asking for a salad for one team meal: "I know he had [polished off] 20 pieces of sausage and probably 10 pancakes on top of it. Chuck walks by—the salad was kind of smushed down—and Chuck says, 'I'm proud of you.' 'Thank you, Coach.'"

Gary Dunn, defensive lineman 1977–1987: "My rookie year, they had him on a diet of deviled eggs. There were like 80 of them. Ernie pulled the whole platter in front of him and ate every one. We were out on the [St. Vincent College] practice field; it must have been 95 degrees. All of a sudden, Ernie's in the huddle and he started gasping and gagging. He lets go with a mountain of deviled eggs. Bradshaw and the offense came out of the huddle, and there's this big pile of deviled eggs, steaming and everything. Chuck yells, 'Run the play.' 'You'd better come look at this.' 'Aw, geesh, let's go to the other field.' They had to move the [camera] tower and everything. All because of the deviled eggs."

Mike Wagner, safety 1971–1980: "Favorite Ernie story? There are so many.

"The real test with him, if you came back after curfew and you had a burger, if you didn't have two, you had none. Because Ernie would convince you to give him one. [Quarterback Terry] Hanratty once walked by Ernie's room with two pizza boxes. Ernie's on his bed, and all of a sudden you hear, 'Rat, it's Ernie—is that pizza?' Terry starts running down the hall, and Ernie is running after him." Up and down stairs, hoofing down Bonaventure Hall's tile floors. "Finally, 'Rat lets Ernie catch him. But there's nothing in the pizza boxes.

"He got over 290 for awhile, which was too much for him. At some '76, '77 point, he was probably the best lineman of the four. And this came from other people who watched closely.

"He came back to town for this one reunion, and he was 600 pounds. I could barely get my arms around his shoulders. As big and ferocious as he was on the football field, I thought he was a big teddy bear. He loved to talk. He ended up being a preacher. He was a piece of work. I loved him to death. I'm sad he's gone."

SANTONIO HOLMES
Wide Receiver

Height: 5-10 • **Weight:** 185 • **College:** Ohio State • **Years with the Steelers:** 2006–2009 • **Birthplace:** Belle Glade, Florida • **Born:** March 3, 1984

On February 1, 2009, he stood on his toes, reached into the night sky for a Ben Roethlisberger pass, and wound up with the world in his hands. Super Bowl XLIII MVP. Disney World parade. Leno, Letterman, ESPY. All at 24 years old.

It didn't last long.

Just 435 Steelers days, to be precise.

On April 12, 2010, one of the darkest days in franchise history—Roethlisberger's Milledgeville, Georgia, laundry was aired on live television by the district attorney even though he wasn't pursuing charges, Jeff Reed saw two of his four misdemeanor charges dropped, and Santonio Holmes was suspended four games for violating the league's substance-abuse policy—the club sent away the man whose gold-gloved hands snagged the Steelers a sixth Lombardi Trophy.

Steelers officials were fully prepared to release Holmes. But they finagled a fifth-round draft choice, which became the short-lived John Skelton, from the New York Jets in exchange for him.

That quickly, he was Steelers history.

Holmes caught four of his nine Super Bowl receptions on the game-winning drive, ending with the six-yarder in the back right corner with three Arizona Cardinals around him and 35 seconds left. All told, he grabbed 235 passes for 3,835 yards in his short Steelers career. That stood as the 11th-most catches and the ninth-most yardage.

Holmes, their 25th-overall selection in 2006 with the aim of replacing free-agent-to-be Plaxico Burress, endured a couple of legal entanglements after the draft and charges—later dropped—of marijuana possession early in that 2009 season.

Heath Miller, tight end 2008– : "I always remember him being a really good player. He helped us win a lot of games around here, not just Super Bowl XLIII. Being a beast at the backside of the formations, being the only receiver back there. Defenses had a lot of trouble with him."

Brice Arians, offensive assistant and coordinator 2004–2011: "Good kid. Loved him. Had him as a rookie in my room [as receivers coach]. Remember taking him to [a steakhouse] his first day in town. . . . We had a little motto that [2008 season]: consistency in each practice and game. I have a little picture on my wall of that Super Bowl catch, and he wrote 'consistency' on it. It's one of my treasures."

JOHN HENRY JOHNSON
Running Back

Height: 6-2 • **Weight:** 210 • **College:** St. Mary's (California) and Arizona State • **Years with the Steelers:** 1960–1965 **Birthplace:** Waterproof, Louisiana • **Born:** November 24, 1929 • **Died:** June 3, 2011

"John Henry Johnson was 200 pounds of hate," legendary *Los Angeles Times* columnist Jim Murray once wrote. "He went both ways, offense and defense, with equal skill, enthusiasm and malice. He was the fourth-greatest rusher in NFL history [when he retired], and he could play safety, corner or linebacker with such ferocity that some quarterbacks had to walk backwards for a week after John Henry hit them because that's the way their faces were pointing."

A second-round selection in the 1953 draft, Johnson chose the Calgary Stampeders of the Canadian Football League rather than, so he heard, the old-school single wing . . . which the Steelers at long last had tossed out a year earlier. Next, he joined the 49ers and their "Million Dollar Backfield," Detroit, and then the Pittsburgh that originally drafted him.

He was the first African American to play for the Detroit Lions, in 1957. The first 1,000-yard rusher for the Steelers—and for the first time of his career—in 1962, at age 33. The fourth all-time NFL rusher upon his retirement, after Jim Brown, Jim Taylor, and Joe Perry. "It just so happens," he told the *Pittsburgh Press'* Roy McHugh in 1966 upon convincing Art Rooney to let his star running back leave as a virtual free agent, "that everybody doesn't fall apart at the same age."

Roy McHugh: "Great blocker. Ever hear the story of how he pulled up a yard marker? Myron Cope tells the story." In 1961, Rams linebacker Ed Meador intercepted a Bobby Layne pass, and Johnson tackled Meador out of bounds and with great vigor. A row ensued, and Johnson already was smarting from earlier hits and tackles delivered to him. "He was so mad, he pulled the yard marker out of the ground." As teammate Clendon Thomas came to tell the tale, Johnson first pummeled tackler Bill Jobko with his fists, but when Rams tackle Urban Henry tried to come to Jobko's rescue down the sideline, Johnson yanked the yard marker from the ground and felled Henry with one swing. Incidentally, three years later, Henry became Johnson's Steelers teammate.

Dick Hoak, running back 1961–1970:

Matter of fact, that was the first game I started. It was the third game of the year. I'm in there; I don't know what the heck happened. A fight started. They're pushing and shoving. And at that time they had those wooden markers on the sidelines . . . they came to a point and had the 20, the 30, the 40 on it. John Henry Johnson picked that up. . . .

John was probably the best blocking fullback I've ever seen. He had a knack. He'd hide, then he'd pop out from behind those tackles and nail the linebackers right under the darn chin. I think that's what started that fight; he nailed [some Ram earlier] with one of those blocks. John was an excellent player. Actually when he came to Pittsburgh, he was on the way down—and he still played well for Pittsburgh.

GENE KEADY
Running Back

Height: 6-4 • **Weight:** 190 • **College:** Kansas State • **Years with the Steelers:** 0 (1958 training camp) • **Birthplace:** Larned, Kansas • **Born:** May 21, 1936

The Steelers' 19th-round pick of the 1958 draft lasted part of the summer. Good thing for college basketball, too.

Because he was cut too late to secure a high school football coaching job, Gene Keady landed with the Beloit (Kansas) High basketball team. From there he went to Hutchinson (Kansas) Junior College, Arkansas, Western Kentucky, Purdue, the U.S. Olympic team, and various hoops Halls of Fame.

He won 512 college games, a half dozen coach-of-the-year awards, and six Big Ten titles. Keady coached 27 years at Purdue and compiled the second-most victories in Big Ten history, with 262.

Another Division I basketball coach sprouted from the Steelers: 1968 defensive back Bob Wade. He wound up as the University of Maryland head coach, replacing Lefty Driesell after the Len Bias tragedy—the beloved Terrapins star and first-round NBA pick died of a cocaine overdose, and the Maryland program went into free fall. Wade earned both a 36-50 three-year record plus an NCAA probation before heading out the Terrapins' door.

JACK KEMP
Quarterback

Height: 6-1 • **Weight:** 201 • **College:** Occidental • **Year with the Steelers:** 1957 • **Birthplace:** Los Angeles • **Born:** July 13, 1935 • **Died:** May 2, 2009

This future vice-presidential candidate was part of a three-year pool of Steelers cast-off quarterbacks who combined to lead *other teams* to seven league championships.

Lump together 1957 quarterbacks Kemp, Earl Morrall, and Len Dawson plus 1955 camp cut Johnny Unitas, and you get some staggering numbers:

These four ex-Steelers combined to play in three Super Bowls, win seven NFL or AFL championships, compile a

17-10 playoff record, earn 25 Pro Bowl berths, and merit six MVPs or players of the year.

As Steelers quarterbacks, they reached nary a postseason and made just one Pro Bowl—Morrall's in 1957. (Morrall, by the way, also was the quarterback of record in 11 victories of the 1972 Miami Dolphins' 17-0 season.)

Kemp was acquired in mid-1957 by Steelers coach Buddy Parker, who apparently sent 1958 eighth- and ninth-round choices to Detroit—the team with whom Parker initially drafted Kemp. As the story goes, Parker summarily cut him in the 1958 preseason for countermanding an order to punt out of bounds, likely against Baltimore and Unitas.

The next two seasons after the Steelers released the third-stringer who completed eight of 18 passes in his black-and-gold, four-game career, Kemp combined for almost 5,700 yards passing and 35 touchdowns in leading the Los Angeles/San Diego Chargers to the AFL championship game each year. From there, he went on to a glorious career with the Buffalo Bills. In New York, he later dropped into politics and became a nine-term congressman, secretary of Housing and Urban Development, and Bob Dole's Republican running mate in the 1996 election.

Jack Butler, defensive back 1951–1959 and then an assistant coach: "Jack . . . I forget how many quarterbacks were here. He stayed here. He wasn't here but a short while. A nice guy and everything."

Frank Varrichione, offensive tackle 1955–1960: "You make mistakes on guys, it's amazing. They go someplace else, and they become great ballplayers. Kemp was that. We had Earl Morrall for awhile, too; he wound up winning a championship as a substitute [Miami's Super Bowl VII]. Went through a lot of quarterbacks in those days. They'd come in and leave."

Dale Dodrill, nose guard–middle linebacker 1951–1959: "Buddy Parker, there was something about never putting your hat on a bed, that was bad luck. Buddy was from *Kemp*, Texas, and they said that was the only reason Jack made the team—he was Buddy's good-luck charm. He never did get a chance to play, really. Oh, man, Jack took [the Bills] to championships. We had Teddy Marchibroda; we had Earl Morrall. They said the Steelers never had any quarterbacks. [Laughs.] They sure had the opportunity to have some good ones."

RAY KEMP
Tackle

Height: 6-1 • **Weight:** 215 • **College:** Duquesne • **Year with the Pirates:** 1933 • **Birthplace:** Cecil, Pennsylvania • **Born:** April 7, 1907 • **Died:** March 26, 2002

He started out a coal miner from Cecil, Pennsylvania, a Washington County burg where he was the first African American in his high school. He climbed out to play at Duquesne University for one of the famed Notre Dame "Four Horsemen" and later NFL commissioner, Elmer Layden.

In the April 27, 1978, *Pittsburgh Post-Gazette*, he said: "Art Rooney was a man of utter goodwill. But, through the years, Rooney has given complete authority to his coaches. The coach didn't want me on that team, and so I was let go. I was upset at the time. It wasn't the fact that I was going to be out of professional football that hurt. Back then, pro football was pretty loosely organized, and you could only make about

a hundred dollars a game. In fact, people used to look down at you for being a pro football player. What hurt me, though, was that I couldn't participate." He was paid between $40 and $70 a game in a league where almost everyone else got $100, as newspapers reported—in varying figures—over the years.

In the second game of that season, the Pirates played the Chicago Cardinals and the other African American NFLer of the day, running back Joe Lillard. In a January 11, 1998, column in the *New York Times*, Kemp was quoted as saying that Coach Jap Douds in a halftime speech used a racial slur to describe Lillard. Then, as the team filed out of the locker room, Kemp said, Douds grabbed him by the arm and offered: "You know, Ray, I didn't mean you."

Media reports vary, but he was released after either that game or the season's fourth game. He rejoined the team for the season finale—as affirmed by the November 27, 1933, *Pittsburgh Post-Gazette*. And that was the end of the African American presence in the NFL for another 13 years—and a year before Jackie Robinson integrated major league baseball. "They had a gentleman's agreement: no more blacks in professional football," he told the *Times*. Then, in 1946, the NFL welcomed several African Americans onto its rosters; among the notables was future Steelers running back Marion Motley in Cleveland.

The Steelers integrated anew in 1952, upon the drafting of Jack Spinks, a fullback from Alcorn State.

Kemp went on to become a coach, administrator, and teacher at predominantly African American colleges such as Lincoln University in Jefferson City, Missouri, and Tennessee State.

Tim Rooney Sr., son of the Chief and longtime Steelers worker/owner: "He was the first black player. Which we were always proud of. It took a long time to get another one."

LEVON KIRKLAND
Inside Linebacker

Height: 6-1 • **Weight:** 280 • **College:** Clemson • **Years with the Steelers:** 1992–2000 • **Birthplace:** Lamar, South Carolina • **Born:** February 17, 1969

Captain Kirk, by his own admission, was *big-boned*.

That's one way to describe how a fellow with light feet can play inside linebacker at 270 pounds. Or 274. Or 280. Or more, depending upon your scale.

Ron Erhardt, offensive coordinator 1992–1995 and a man whose offense practiced against him daily: "A lot of people probably would've used him as a nose tackle."

Levon Kirkland was cut essentially by his final three NFL teams for being heavy, brother. But that was his most amazing asset for so long: He could carry that weight. How else to describe his ability to start 131 consecutive NFL games at inside linebacker? How else to explain his durability in playing every single NFL game waged during his 11-year career, all 176?

Kirkland was the second pick of the Bill Cowher era, behind first-round tackle Leon Searcy, and replaced free-agent departee Hardy Nickerson with far more gentleness and pounds. He played in a 3–4 tandem during those mid-1990s heydays alongside the eccentric, the volatile, and the vociferous: snake charmer Chad Brown, hot-blooded Greg

Lloyd, and boisterous Kevin Greene. He played with a smile on his face, long before Hines Ward came along.

Kirkland finished his career as starting middle linebacker in Seattle and Philadelphia, one season apiece.

Kevin Greene, outside linebacker 1993–1995: "Levon Kirkland, as big as he was, he was athletic, physical, solid, always had good huddle command, good person. Gifted. Wanted to physically dish out punishment to whoever came out to block out. One of my true brothers. His playing weight, as I recall, was 265. Playing inside linebacker, carrying the tight end up the seam in cover-two, doing all the things. . . . He was a large man doing things 225-pound people could do."

Dom Capers, defensive coordinator 1992–1994: "He was a 260-pound Buck linebacker and tight-end side linebacker. I would have been kind in later years calling him 260 pounds. He was really a unique athlete at that size. Yet he could cover better than most of those guys. Levon was a class guy, very conscientious, try to do everything the way he was coached. Just a good team guy."

BRADY KEYS
Cornerback–Returner

Height: 6-0 • **Weight:** 185 • **College:** Colorado State • **Years with the Steelers:** 1961–1967 • **Birthplace:** Austin, Texas • **Born:** May 19, 1936

Brady Keys was the franchise's first full-time, long-distance threat as a punt returner. Problem was, he never scored.

Almost a half century later, Keys still held two of the top three spots for the longest punt returns in Steelers history: a 90-yarder against the Giants in 1964 and an 82-yarder against the same club a year earlier. He also had a 66-yarder to his credit and averaged more than 12 yards per return in three of his first four seasons. Just the same, he never reached the end zone. Never.

Ultimately, it was his secondary play that sent him packing—and not because he was among the first defensive backs to talk to receivers while covering them. Bill Austin, not normally a throw-under-the-bus coach, pronounced after Keys was beaten for a touchdown against the Giants and then the Cowboys: "It's a shame one man had to mess up the game when everybody else played well. The same guy fouled up things two weeks in a row." After a waiver claim, Dan Rooney traded him for a draft choice to ex-Steeler Jim Finks, the new general manager at Minnesota.

One of the first African American entrepreneurs among ex-athletes, Keys used an $8,000 gift from Rooney to seed his All-Pro Chicken takeout business. He later leveraged that into Kentucky Fried Chicken and A&W fast-food stores, among other businesses.

Roy McHugh, longtime Pittsburgh Press *sportswriter, columnist, and editor:* "Very savvy."

JON KOLB
Center–Tackle

Height: 6-2 • **Weight:** 262 • **College:** Oklahoma State • **Years with the Steelers:** 1969–1981 • **Birthplace:** Ponca City, Oklahoma • **Born:** August 30, 1947

Jon Kolb, shown here in his final season as a Steelers offensive tackle in 1981, spent the entire Chuck Noll era with the club. From 1969 to 1981, he toiled as a player. From 1982 to Noll's retirement in 1991, he worked as a coach. (Bill Amatucci)

So how did Jon Kolb come to the Steelers, a franchise he would represent for almost a quarter century?

Kolb, a physical therapist and wellness counselor in northwest Pennsylvania: "Did they send you up with that question?

"By my senior year, I heard from almost every team. The day before the draft, I got a form letter from the Pittsburgh Steelers; it wasn't signed. So I started answering when people asked, 'Where do you think you're going?': 'Anywhere but Pittsburgh.'" Never hearing from any team the day of the draft, he figured he went unpicked.

"I went into the stadium to work out, and somebody said, 'You have a call from a Mr. Rooney. He's old.' All my teammates were there, 'Who is it? Who is it?' I was convinced it was a joke. I thought it was a setup. I was just rude [to him]." That night, he heard it on the news: third round, Pittsburgh Steelers. "I was like, 'Oh my gosh.' I called Mr. Rooney [the next day] and told him the story, and he thought it was funny. Thirteen years later when I started coaching the Steelers, I was still apologizing. He was always so gracious."

In 1971, Kolb moved full-time to starting left tackle, from where he protected the blind side for Hall of Famer Terry Bradshaw and others for the next 11 seasons—never missing a start the first half dozen of those years. After his retirement at age 34 in 1981, he became a wherever-you-want-me assistant to the only Steelers head coach he ever knew, Chuck

Noll: strength coach, defensive line, special teams, offensive assistant, and conditioning and strength coordinator. In 2007, he was named to the 75th Anniversary team.

Dan "Bad Rad" Radakovich, offensive line coach 1974–1977: "The only reason he didn't make All-Pro every year [was that] for the first six years he wasn't a good pass blocker. I made him a good pass blocker in 15 minutes. With the hands. Then he became the best pass blocker in the NFL the next six years. I've got the film to prove it. He was undersized; he weighed 262. But he was the fastest and most coordinated in the league."

CARNELL LAKE
Safety–Cornerback

Height: 6-1 • **Weight:** 210 • **College:** UCLA • **Years with the Steelers:** 1989–1998 • **Birthplace:** Salt Lake City • **Born:** July 15, 1967

An accounting book sat on his locker shelf. A five-time Pro Bowl player, one of the most respected safeties, if not overall defensive players, in the league, and Carnell Lake was taking a night course at Duquesne University. One eye on the quarterback, the other eye on his future.

Lake converted from outside linebacker in college to an immediate starter and strong-safety star in the NFL. When Rod Woodson, one of the greatest defensive backs in NFL history, sustained a knee injury in 1995, who else would the coaches ask to replace him? Lake played so well, the Steelers got to Super Bowl XXX.

Two of his final three among his four Steelers Pro Bowls were similar corner-safety job shares.

Lake, named to the Steelers' 75th Anniversary team, returned to the franchise in 2011 as secondary coach, after Ray Horton left to become defensive coordinator in Arizona.

Jon Kolb, conditioning and strength coordinator then: "Class. Really just a classy guy. You loved to coach him. So it's not surprising he is a coach today. He's a guy who as a player knew all the positions, knew all the positions on special teams. Couldn't ever do enough. Never satisfied."

Dermontti Dawson, center 1988–2000: "He had the smarts, he knew how to play each position, whether it was safety or corner. I used to love to sit there and watch him come and put a lick on somebody. Those guys were beasts back there in the backfield—Lake, Woodson, all those guys. A phenomenal secondary."

Kevin Greene, outside linebacker 1993–1995: "One of the most talented guys I've seen. If we had a nick or injury, he would go from strong safety to corner, go out on the island and lock down people on the corner. What separated Carnell was, yes, his ability to cover man to man, his ability to be on the island . . . but Carnell would roll up in the box. There was no doubt in my military mind, if I follow Carnell Lake to the play, he's not only going to make that play, he was going to hit that ball carrier and hit that ball carrier hard. If they funnel to Carnell Lake, right then and there they die."

Dom Capers, defensive coordinator 1992–1994: "Another one of my favorite guys. He coached for us as an intern in Green Bay. Those guys, they were that way as players—they were cerebral. You knew they'd make great coaches someday, Carnell and Kevin [Greene]. I went out to UCLA to work out [1989 draft prospects]. I had one drill: I would have them

Carnell Lake, here at 1991 training camp, provided such a presence from 1989 to 1998 that the Steelers ultimately brought him back as secondary coach in 2011. (Vincent J. Musi)

backpedal 10 yards and then plant. Carnell was an outside linebacker, but he was the fastest guy I worked out that year. Carnell and Rod Woodson were the two fastest guys on our [Steelers] team, and in the nickel and dime we blitzed them a lot 'cause they created so many problems getting there."

JACK LAMBERT
Middle Linebacker

Height: 6-4 • **Weight:** 220 • **College:** Kent State • **Years with the Steelers:** 1974–1984 • **Birthplace:** Mantua, Ohio • **Born:** July 8, 1952

You got it all wrong.

John Harold Lambert was brilliant. He was a technician. He was "a sweetheart."

The toothless, scowling, foot-thumping creature? All show.

What a show it was, too. Jack Splat. Jack the Ripper. Dracula in Cleats.

Toothless rookie Jack Lambert, in the regular-season finale of the 1974 season that produced the franchise's first Super Bowl championship. (George Gojkovich)

That's what made Jack Lambert popular, what made him feared and famous and ferocious on a field.

But if that's all you saw, you didn't know Jack.

Andy Russell, right outside linebacker 1963, 1966–1976: "I think Lambert was misunderstood."

Mike Wagner, safety 1971–1980: Predecessor Henry Davis "was actually scarier than Lambert. Lambert, I was totally amused by him."

Tony Dungy, safety 1977–1978 and defensive assistant/coordinator 1981–1988: "I remember when I first got there; we were practicing, and Lambert told me, 'When we get in a game now, I'm not going to have my teeth in. If you don't [hear] anything clearly, I'll give you a hand signal.' I was like, 'Wow.' He was a different person on game day, with his teeth out. His whole personality changed."

Russell: "The reason Lambert was so good, he was technically sound. His technique was great. Didn't make any mistakes. His nasty attitude is what the fans loved, but that's not what made him good."

Jack Ham, left outside linebacker 1971–1982: "Boy, what a smart guy he was. A rookie calling signals through the Super Bowl? You normally don't have a rookie middle linebacker doing that. I was astonished. And you have a 6-4 guy in the

middle like that, especially in a cover-two situation? He was so good in the passing game, and that's what set him apart."

Larry Brown, tight end–offensive tackle 1971–1984: "Jack wasn't a prototypical middle linebacker at 215 pounds. What he had were tremendous toughness and smarts. He gets credit for being a maniac, but he was a smart player. A bunch of guys were, on those teams. You don't win without playing smart."

George Perles, defensive line coach and coordinator 1972–1981: "We put in a new pass defense. I'm standing at the door next to him [waiting to go onto the field for a game], and he said, 'George, we got a signal for that?' He had a knack for saying something to you and making you feel like a dummy."

Jon Kolb, center–tackle 1969–1981 and assistant coach 1982–1991: "Jack, I always thought, was a gentleman. He can be a sweetheart."

Roy McHugh, longtime sportswriter, columnist, and editor with the Pittsburgh Press: "Most athletes—professional athletes—don't [publicly acknowledge] writers. He spoke to you first. Very polite. I found him to be a gentleman in contrast to his image as a player."

Go back to the beginning.

Well, okay, birth was his very beginning. He was raised in football-crazed northeast Ohio, the product of divorce when he was two. He grew tall and lean, playing quarterback in high school—"a hander-offer," as he once described that duty—and, of course, defense. His high school coach talked Kent State into giving Lambert a scholarship when a recruit got married and stayed in New Jersey.

According to legend, Steelers scout V. Tim Rooney saw the Kent State captain running penalty laps, as a show of support, with the quarterback who incurred the coach's wrath. Art Rooney Jr., the head of the scouting department, drove to Kent the next day—only to find a sopping field and players practicing on the gravel parking lot. He watched Lambert dive onto the pavement. He watched him pick cinders from his epidermis. Rinse, lather, repeat. What was not to love?

Perles: "I remember when [Chuck Noll] sent Woody [Widenhofer] and I down to look at film on Lambert. Before we got back, he already made the decision to draft Lambert."

That 1974 spring, Lambert drove from Kent, Ohio, to Pittsburgh regularly to watch film and learn the playbook. Incumbent middle linebacker Henry Davis got hurt in camp, and the rookie Wally Pipped him. (Pipp, of course, was the Yankee first baseman replaced once by Lou Gehrig, who proceeded to play 2,130 consecutive games and fashion a Hall of Fame career.)

Ham, talking about that strange strike camp: "Lambert actually started as an outside linebacker. I think he was playing my side. Then they moved him to the middle [pretty quickly]. We had kind of musical chairs there for awhile."

Wagner: "I was already a veteran. He came in as this hotshot, and he was trying to motivate guys who'd already been to the championship [game]. 'You can play football your way. This is how we play football here, and it's pretty good football.'

"If you're going to be a middle linebacker, you have to be demonstrative. So the fans think you're intensely involved in the game. The outside linebackers, they aren't the ones pointing their fingers or challenging their teammates or challenging their manhood. But the middle linebacker is like that."

Dan "Bad Rad" Radakovich, defensive line coach in 1971 and offensive line coach 1974–1977: The stunt 4–3 "was the best defense in America for Lambert. He was a great linebacker

The Lambert's Brigade banner depicting Jack Lambert's infamous, fearsome image follows him from Three Rivers Stadium to his 1990 Pro Football Hall of Fame induction in Canton, Ohio. (Vincent J. Musi)

who floated. But he wasn't good off the low block. That was the best defense for it; it kept him free."

Perles: "The stunt 4–3 he was in the position behind Joe Greene; you couldn't get to him. He had a knack of hitting guys and punishing them and falling on them. He was tough and smart."

Nobody disputed his toughness, his fire, his pain. Lambert held a distinct spot in the pulpit of the Steelers' Sunday services.

Ham: "There was a play he made in the Oakland [1974 AFC championship] game. I bet he was 35 yards deep downfield in the two-deep package. He ends up making the tackle on Cliff Branch on that play. It's open field like that with Cliff Branch [the fastest man in the NFL]. I always kid Lambert; he probably closed his eyes and jumped after Branch."

He was outweighed by 50-plus pounds normally on the inside, he was surrounded by Hall of Fame talent, and still he topped the NFL's best unit in tackles every season through the 1970s. "Without Jack Lambert, I'm not sure we ever would've quite made it over the hump," the late defensive coordinator Bud Carson once told NFL Films. The guy made the Pro Bowl for nine consecutive seasons, every one between his rookie year and his part-time last year, not merely because of a toothless smile, pounding pre-snap feet, and a nasty image.

Take the Super Bowl X freeze-frame with Dallas safety Cliff Harris, for example.

When Roy Gerela missed a 36-yard field-goal attempt with 22 seconds left in a first half in which the Steelers trailed Dallas by 10-7, Harris for some inexplicable reason decided to pat the helmet of the little placekicker and thank him. Gerela started to push him away, but by that time Lambert intervened, spun Harris, and threw him to the ground as if steer wrestling.

A Steeler Nation stood up and cheered. Remember, though, he was 23 and making his maiden Super Bowl appearance. The rest of that Steelers defense, in which he was inarguably a catalyst, was chock full of more mature, experienced gents.

Russell: "I was the captain; I ran out and chewed Lambert out. 'You could be ejected for that!' The announcers said Lambert got us more fired up, which was total BS."

Such intensity seemingly became a burden.

Starting in 1978, he and Cleveland quarterback Brian Sipe began a dance of sorts: Lambert clobbered him, Sipe left the game in a heap, the referee called a penalty, Pete Rozelle called Lambert on the carpet in New York. By all accounts, it was after the first such instance that Lambert moaned to Howard Cosell on a *Monday Night Football* telecast, "Quarterbacks should wear dresses."

And that was before the 1981 and 1984 incidents with Sipe, referee Ben Dreith, and two ejections for thudding Lambert hits on the same quarterback—a six year tête-à-tête.

Having won four Super Bowls and moving to the less marquee position of inside linebacker in the 3–4 defense, Lambert's Steelers endgame began on the second play of 1984 when he dislocated a big toe trying to tackle a Kansas City running back named Theotis Brown. He limped away from football on his 33rd birthday. Art Rooney Sr., upon his retirement, offered: "Jack Lambert was a throwback to what people thought Pittsburghers were. This is a sad day not only for us but for Pittsburgh."

Fingers were bent, joints throbbed, the toe bothered him for a long time, but in retirement he enjoyed his peace and tranquility. He could hunt. He could work in the woods. And Jack Splat could always wear his bridge, which came from a basketball injury.

See, you didn't know Jack.

At least not the fellow in his tightie whities running down the St. Vincent College hallway screaming bloody murder.

Gary Dunn, defensive lineman 1977–1987: "You can retire on this one.

"Tom Beasley was a country boy. He knew Lambert hated snakes. . . ."

Tom Beasley, defensive lineman 1978–1983: "A friend of mine was coming back from a hunting trip from Garrett County, Maryland. I asked him, 'Can you do me a favor? When you come, can you bring me an extra snake box?' Jack knew Gary Bailey quite well; we hunted together. After dinner, I said, 'Jack, I got something I want to show you.' Gary's truck was right next to Jack's. He pulled out a snake box, opened the lid, and five or six rattlesnakes start climbing out—and Jack's scared to death of snakes. I said, 'Jack, remember when you spilled that drink on me last year? Be careful when you sleep tonight.' He actually pulled a 9-mm from his glove box and stuck it in my chest: 'I will shoot you nine times before you hit the ground.'" (By the way, Lambert's affinity for guns was somewhat legendary: He used to frequent the Pittsburgh Police No. 9 station and its basement shooting range, occasionally bringing his Thompson machine gun for, uh, practice.)

Dunn: "Jack was so miserable, we put him on the third floor by himself. So Beasley went up there and . . . put [the empty snake crate] in the middle of Jack's floor with the door open. All of a sudden, . . . here comes Lambert running down the hall with a cowboy hat on, his tightie whities on, his cowboy boots on. 'Beasley, Beeeeeeasley, this is attempted murder!'"

Beasley: "Two minutes before curfew, I heard a scream. Then 'attempted murder, call the police!' Then Chuck got involved."

Dunn: "Chuck comes out [of his room], and he's got his little nightgown on; everybody's scratching . . . whatever. Jack says, 'I want you to have Beasley arrested.' Chuck, he's so analytical, he says, 'Let's go see what you're talking about, Jack.' He goes to the room. There's no snake. 'Now Jack, did you actually see Tom put it in there?'"

Beasley: "Chuck and Jack strip-searched the room, one sock at a time. He was just emphatic that I had let out all these rattlesnakes in the room."

Well, Beasley did place one snake in the room.

A toy one, hidden between the two pillows where Lambert would lay his head.

Beasley: "Actually got it off Webster—a big rubber snake. At breakfast, Jack goes, 'Did you hear me scream in the middle of the night? I got up to go to the bathroom. I don't know what time it was; 3, 3:30. I slid my arm between my two pillows. . . . I felt this thing cold on my arm, then I raised my pillow. I thought you were going to have to pry me off the ceiling. I jumped straight off the bed and screamed like a girl.'"

Noll was so bothered, at the next morning's meeting he made a veiled threat about revoking the weekly camp night off "when you start attempting murder on each other."

All in fun. And don't misunderstand; Jack Splat certainly enjoyed some of that.

JOHNNY LATTNER
Running Back–Returner

Height: 6-1 • **Weight:** 195 • **College:** Notre Dame • **Year with the Steelers:** 1954 • **Birthplace:** Chicago • **Born:** October 24, 1932

The only Heisman Trophy winner to ever play for the Steelers, Johnny Lattner in the end hardly played for the Steelers.

As a rookie in 1954, the seventh-overall pick of that year's draft finished third in team rushing with just 237 yards and

Johnny Lattner, the only Heisman Trophy winner to ever play for the Steelers, collects some of his 237 yards rushing and 305 yards receiving against Philadelphia in his one and only season with the Steelers—and in professional football. The former Notre Dame star entered the Air Force in 1954 and suffered a career-ending knee injury. (Temple Urban Archives)

a 3.4-yard average per carry. He did, however, lead Steelers rushers with five touchdowns and rank second in team scoring behind the other halfback, leading receiver Ray Matthews.

Military football, however, wracked Lattner's knees. Upon his return to the Steelers in 1957, he was released that September and announced his retirement—one month before he turned 25.

Frank Varrichione, offensive tackle 1955–1960 and Notre Dame teammate: "Johnny was one of the great ballplayers . . . in my estimation."

Dale Dodrill, nose guard–middle linebacker 1951–1959: "The Notre Dame Flash. I don't know, if they drafted a player high, like Johnny was, they automatically had to keep them or they'd get bad publicity and all that. Johnny wasn't really a pro player. He only played the one year, I think. Never did see the potential that was supposed to be there. Lot of fun, the guy was. Good sense of humor. Full of life."

BOBBY LAYNE
Quarterback

Height: 6-1 • **Weight:** 201 • **College:** Texas • **Years with the Steelers:** 1958 1962 • **Birthplace:** Santa Anna, Texas • **Born:** December 19, 1926 • **Died:** December 1, 1986

Johnny "Blood" McNally, Ernie Holmes, and Terry Bradshaw were colorful in their own right. But they were paint-by-numbers compared to Bobby Layne, who refused to quit with time on the stadium clock and seconds left before closing time.

He was near the end of his hard NFL road by the time Buddy Parker traded Earl Morrall and two draft choices to the

Quarterback Bobby Layne was as beloved for his off-field style as on field. (Courtesy of the Pittsburgh Steelers)

Lions after two losses in early October 1958. That exchange was enough to bring Layne from Detroit, where Layne won two NFL championships in the early 1950s. Still combative as ever in his 30s, Layne refused to wear a face mask with the Steelers.

The day he threw for the sixth-most passing yards in NFL history to that point? It wasn't just snowy, icy, and cold on December 13, 1958, in Pitt Stadium. It followed a late-night session with *Pittsburgh Press* sports writer Bob Drum, the cowriter of Layne's biography, *Always on Sunday*. Drum was in such bad shape that he didn't get to the game until the second half, by which time Layne had passed for two scores and run for another.

Layne passed for 409 yards that day against the Chicago Cardinals, a team record that held firm for 44 years, until broken by Tommy Maddox. The Steelers' 692 yards of offense were the second-most in NFL history.

The old quarterback helped the Steelers to fashion winning records in three of his four healthy years in Pittsburgh—their best overall stretch until the 1970s.

Layne once told the Chief, "Don't give me a raise. Just give me a horse." To this, Art Rooney replied, "When I think I have a horse, I don't even tell my wife what horse it is."

Joe Walton, competitor with the Redskins and Giants: "He was crazy." On October 14, 1962, Layne engineered a 20–17 Steelers upset of the Giants, who went 12–2 that season. "We had a good team, then, too. And he beat us. Bobby Layne was

sitting there [at the Giants watering hole, P. J. Clarke's] waiting on us. 'The drinks are all on me.'

"Oh, shoot, was he good. First of all, he had a very good arm. Second, he was a great leader, tough guy. And he could run well, too—he was a good athlete. He wasn't young then, either, but he was getting around pretty good. A tough son of a bee."

Jack Butler, defensive back 1951–1959 and assistant coach afterward: "You talk about hard work: He'd stay out hours after practice. He'd stay out and throw passes to you as long as you wanted. A team guy. We had him when he was kind of over the hill. He didn't have the steam on the ball. Monday was payday; he'd arrange parties for the whole team. He liked to raise hell."

LOUIS LIPPS
Wide Receiver–Returner

Height: 5-10 • **Weight:** 190 • **College:** Southern Mississippi • **Years with the Steelers:** 1984–1991 • **Birthplace:** New Orleans • **Born:** August 9, 1962

Louuuuuuuuuuuu.

The first Steelers player upon whom fans could cascade a cacophony of boo-rhyming cheers, Louis Lipps brought a lot of cheer to Three Rivers Stadium.

He helped to guide a faltering 1980s club to the AFC championship game in his rookie 1984 and back to the playoffs in 1989. In his inaugural two seasons, he made the Pro Bowl primarily because of his returning ability. He had a team-record 53 punt returns as a rookie—even more work than his 45 catches—and topped the NFL with 656 yards. He topped the NFL again in 1985 with two punt returns for touchdowns.

From there, Lipps developed into a receiving threat, with five (of his eight) seasons with 50-plus receptions and four with 18.9 yards per catch, minimum. He ended up third in all-time Steelers receiving yards with 6,018 and receptions with 358.

Dermontti Dawson, center 1988–2000: "You could always depend on Louie making the catches. When it came to making first downs, he was one of the most dependable receivers. Louis was not afraid to hit you, either. He was almost a Hines Ward–type player. You knew he was going to be there for you."

John Jackson, offensive tackle 1988–1997: "I told Looie this: Whenever we were out in practice or getting into games, [offensive coordinator] Tom Moore would tell us, 'Keep holding them; Looie will get open.' He'd have triple coverage, and Louis would still get open—we'd just have to hold our blocks a little bit longer. But he was another guy [like Hall of Famer Mike Webster] that we really learned a lot from, as far as how to work, how to conduct yourself on and off the field. You had to take care of business."

Bubby Brister, quarterback 1986–1992: "He was the best receiver I had when I was in Pittsburgh, and I was there seven years. Back then there was that 46 defense—they'd send eight, you knew they'd hit the quarterback. So I looked for Looie. He was my go-to guy and one of the best receivers I ever threw to."

It only looks like Louis Lipps has extra hands—that's a defender directly behind him in this 1985 photo. (Bill Amatucci)

EUGENE "BIG DADDY" LIPSCOMB
Defensive Tackle

Height: 6-6 • **Weight:** 306 • **College:** None • **Years with the Steelers:** 1961–1962 • **Birthplace:** Detroit • **Born:** August 9, 1931 • **Died:** May 10, 1963

Two of his 10 NFL years were spent on the Steelers' defensive line, but Big Daddy Lipscomb left his mark across the landscape: three years with the Rams, five years—and the 1958 and 1959 championships—with the Colts, professional wrestling, carousing. . . . Steeler Bobby Layne didn't buy him drinks; he bought him bottles of whiskey.

A "fun-loving goliath," the Associated Press called him in the news account of his death—following a night on the town in Baltimore in his new yellow Cadillac convertible. A homemade needle was found next to the 31-year-old's body slumped on a friend's kitchen floor. Heroin overdose, the medical examiner ruled.

How popular was Big Daddy? Mourners stood four abreast waiting from 10 in the morning until 10 at night at the Baltimore funeral home. In Detroit, Big Daddy's hometown, a thousand mourners showed at his service. Hall of Famer John Henry Johnson, a Steelers teammate, served as a pallbearer.

Big Daddy was a gargantuan sunburst that blazed across the sporting sky, then fizzled almost as quickly. He went directly from a Detroit high school to the Marines in Camp Pendleton, California, where the Rams discovered him. The Colts claimed him for $100 and watched Big Daddy bloom. Amid off-field adventures that included three ex-wives and urban legends of nightlife, he was shipped to Pittsburgh on the first day of 1961 training camp with popular center Buzz Nutter for wide receiver Jimmy Orr and two others.

San Francisco end Clyde Connor used to tell a tale that a running back named Abe Woodson once emerged from a pile with Hall of Famer Ernie Stautner and line mate Lipscomb each holding Woodson upside down by his ankles: Lipscomb said, "All right, Ernie, make a wish."

Art Rooney Jr., scouting director: "They were in [camp]; one young guy tried to drill him. He gave him the head-on-home stare: 'Hey, take it easy. It's the preseason. We're only going to do this about 10,000 more times.' A gifted player. But he'd play one play, take off two."

Dick Hoak, running back 1961–1970: "My rookie year, that was the year they traded for Big Daddy. He really was the first big guy who could run. He would run sideline to sideline and make plays. And he was 6-8, 290. Good guy, Big Daddy. A lot of fun. We beat the Giants, and coming out [of Gotham] he said, 'This place is so big, they named it twice: New York, New York.'

"Oh, yeah, he was a game changer. That year, we came close [the 1962 Playoff Bowl between second-place teams]. After he was gone . . . , everything was downhill until Chuck came."

GREG LLOYD
Outside Linebacker

Height: 6-2 • **Weight:** 220 • **College:** Fort Valley (Georgia) State • **Years with the Steelers:** 1988–1997 • **Birthplace:** Miami • **Born:** May 26, 1965

Convention wasn't his thing.

Greg Lloyd made T-shirt statements such as "Real Men Are Black." He got fined for throttling quarterbacks, sometimes helmet first. He leveled a Jacksonville receiver, Keenan McCardell, and accused him of making threatening calls that week to Mrs. Greg Lloyd. A Jacksonville lineman accused Lloyd of kicking him in the groin. He accidentally swore on live television, celebrating a berth in Super Bowl XXX in front of a network locker-room camera.

But his play *was* the thing.

He ranked among the franchise's all-time top 10 in sacks (53.5) and fumble recoveries (14). He made the Pro Bowl five times and All-Pro three.

He sprained his right ankle against Philadelphia on November 23, 1997, endured a staph infection that hospitalized him for two weeks, and never played for the Steelers again.

Tony Dungy, defensive assistant and coordinator 1981–1988: "I remember Greg Lloyd, the very first game of the season, the 49ers I think it was. We had to take a time-out; we had 12 guys out on the field on the first play. I'm the defensive coordinator,

It only looks like ferocious Greg Lloyd is trying to remove the head of future Hall of Fame quarterback Warren Moon of the Houston Oilers in a 1988 Steelers victory in the Astrodome. The quarterback gets so abused by his AFC Central rivals over the years that his suffering gives credence to the musical phrase that Pittsburgh media invoke for all the times he picks himself up from the turf: Bad Moon Rising. (Vincent J. Musi)

and Coach Noll said, 'How can we have 12 guys on the field on the first snap?' It was Greg. I went up to him, and he said, 'Sorry, I've never been in a game where I wasn't the starter.' I said, 'Didn't you get an idea from practice when you were out there with the second team? Didn't you get an idea from introductions when you weren't introduced with the defense?' And he said, 'We kicked off. And I just ran out there. . . .'"

Dermontti Dawson, center 1988–2000: "Greg was one of the most aggressive players I've ever seen, whether it be practice or a game. He had a chip on his shoulder that he was going to beat you every play every game. He was a tae kwon do master, so he had those hand moves. Greg was the verbal leader when it came to the Steelers' defense. He willed other guys. And people feared Greg. He had that air about himself. He wanted guys to fear him."

Kevin Greene, fellow outside linebacker 1993–1995: "Greg Lloyd stories? Let me say this, Greg was one of the most physical players sideline to sideline I think I've ever seen. He had the hunt in him that was unique. He was really going to hit you as hard as he could, and if you got hurt, so be it. He was good to play opposite, the whole salt-and-pepper thing. If I made a play, it spurred him and got me to play harder."

Dom Capers, defensive coordinator 1992–1994: "Greg was one of the toughest guys, both mentally and physically, that I've ever coached. He was only about 227 pounds, so people didn't realize his size. He was a tae kwon do guy. He would stun people, he was so quick, then he was off them. That's the way he had to play, because he was always playing a bigger guy. I remember in '93 we closed out against the Cleveland Browns; we needed the game to get in the playoffs. At halftime, we were down. I remember him throwing a fit

Greg Lloyd after an AFC divisional playoff loss by 24-23 in Denver in 1990—when the Steelers well could've placed Chuck Noll in a fifth Super Bowl. Noll retired two seasons later. (Vincent J. Musi)

and going around to everybody in the locker room. He went out himself [in the second half], I can remember him hitting Bernie Kosar and knocking the ball out. And then Leroy Hoard [didn't see Lloyd] coming from the backside, and he knocked the ball out. He walked the walk. He challenged the team and then went out and made a couple of plays that helped us win the game."

John Jackson, offensive tackle 1988–1997: "That's what made us as a line so much better—because we had to compete against those guys in practice. When I was in Pittsburgh, practice was the hardest thing because we had so many good guys. We figured in the game it was a little easier."

TERRY LONG
Guard

Height: 5-11 • **Weight:** 272 • **College:** East Carolina • **Years with the Steelers:** 1984–1991 • **Birthplace:** Columbia, South Carolina • **Born:** July 21, 1959 • **Died:** June 7, 2005

Terry Long spent an NFL career prying open holes, then fell into some black ones.

What time may well forget: His death created a significant opening in football and medical science.

He was found, by a neuropathologist named Dr. Bennett Omalu in the Allegheny County coroner's office conducting his autopsy, to contain signs in his brain of what later became a buzzword—CTE, chronic traumatic encephalopathy.

Long blazed a way yet again.

Jon Kolb, assistant coach 1982–1991: "When you talk about Terry Long, it's kind of like Mike Webster—a tragic life. Terry was a guy, I'm not a psychiatrist, but I don't know if he didn't have [emotional issues] or was sensitive. I remember bringing Terry home. I began to kind of get to know him.

With the problems, I don't know, he seemed to bring upon himself."

He was a college power lifter, a strongman whom the Steelers drafted and placed on their offensive line as a rookie. Long remained a starter for seven seasons. Then, on July 23, 1991, less than two weeks after players at St. Vincent College training camp were drug-tested, Chuck Noll informed him: Long's testosterone levels tested at more than three times the limit to pass the NFL steroids test.

Long cried. He lapsed into shock. He grabbed a gun and considered shooting himself. He attempted to overdose on sleeping pills and followed that with rat poison.

Chuck Yesalis, Penn State professor and international expert on performance-enhancing drugs: "I'm in my house, I don't know what I'm doing. I get a call from Steve [Courson], and Steve and I talked multiple times a week. Pick up the phone. . . : 'Hi, Chuck, it's Steve. I'm over at Terry Long's house, and he just took rat poison. The EMTs are here, but he won't go with them. Would you talk with him?' And he just hands the phone to Terry. I tried anything I knew in a half hour, anything I could think of, to save this guy's life. I can't remember in detail, but he felt he disappointed the fans. . . . I was scrambling. But it worked."

Long underwent counseling, served a four-week NFL suspension, and started some in the 1991 season. He wasn't offered a new contract in 1992, when Bill Cowher replaced the retired Noll.

A postcareer business venture ran into legal difficulties. Long committed suicide in 2005, drinking antifreeze.

The coroner's office initially ascribed the cause of death to CTE, and gradually scientific study and increased awareness of concussions and sports-related brain injuries began to develop.

Dermontti Dawson, center 1988–2000: "Terry was a great guy, a great guy. Terry had this persona that he was mean and

Terry Long, middle, and Tunch Ilkin, on the turf, help to create a hole for Frank Pollard after he takes a handoff from David Woodley against Cleveland in 1985. (Vincent J. Musi)

all that. He used to bulge his eyes out and look at people crazy. That was just how Terry was. I used to always hang with Terry, go out to his house. Terry had some issues and things he was dealing with. But Terry was a heck of a guy.

"Terry wasn't the tallest guy. But Terry was just so massive and so strong, he could handle people that way. He was a heck of a player, quick, strong. He was a little technician when it came to blocking."

John Jackson, offensive tackle 1988–1997: "We used to get a kick out of Terry because Terry worked his butt off. We never tried to keep up with him. We figured . . . just trying to lift that much wasn't going to get you anywhere. You might want to be a little quicker."

Bubby Brister, quarterback 1986–1992: "Small, prototypical Chuck Noll guard. I remember him in the weight room all the time. That's a shame, what happened to him. Then you start thinking about all those guys," such as Long, Justin Strzelczyk, Mike Webster. . . .

RAY MANSFIELD
Center–Kicker–Defensive Tackle–Linebacker

Height: 6-3 • **Weight:** 250 • **College:** Washington • **Years with the Steelers:** 1964–1976 • **Birthplace:** Bakersfield, California • **Born:** January 21, 1941 • **Died:** November 3, 1996

Andy Russell, linebacker 1963, 1966–1976 and one of his best friends: "Well, you know, [Ray] Mansfield was the Dick Butkus of our class." The gent known as the Old Ranger was a college All-American, a future University of Washington Hall of Famer, and the 18th pick of the draft—by Philadelphia—between future Hall of Famers Bobby Bell and John Mackey. "Ray was a tough dude, old school. He played with a broken neck—he didn't let them x-ray it until the New Year."

On the same 1964 preseason day the Steelers traded kicker-defensive end Lou Michaels to Baltimore amid fan hullabaloo, they quietly purchased Mansfield from Philadelphia. Crazy thing about Mansfield: You couldn't get him out of the starting lineup. He started at defensive tackle in 1964 and 1965. After requesting a switch to offense, he started at center over veterans named Bob DeMarco and Bobby Maples, who made four Pro Bowls between them. Jim Clack was brought in to run off Mansfield, but Clack wound up a guard. Even Mike Webster, a future Hall of Famer, split time with Mansfield in his first two seasons and Mansfield's final two. And when Roy Gerela got hurt in the 1976 playoffs, the Old Ranger converted both extra-point tries.

Dan "Bad Rad" Radakovich, offensive line coach 1974–1977: "He was a bit of a character, liked to joke around. He gave the line the name 'The Seven Dwarves.' It wasn't public. But I had seven guys who were starters. And that's what he called them."

Mike Wagner, safety 1971–1980: "His whole career, he did it on guts and grit."

Russell: "We had five years together traveling the world [for postfootball business ventures]. I was the Abbott to his Costello. He was so funny. He could go in front of a roomful of Japanese and have them on the floor."

Not long after, the hail fellow Mansfield suffered a heart attack and died while hiking in the Grand Canyon; Dapper Dan Charities began a charity event in his honor.

TED MARCHIBRODA
Quarterback

Height: 5-8 • **Weight:** 178 • **Colleges:** St. Bonaventure and Detroit • **Years with the Steelers:** 1953–1956 • **Birthplace:** Franklin, Pennsylvania • **Born:** March 15, 1931

Ted Marchibroda was a wee fellow from Franklin, Pennsylvania, and St. Bonaventure College. So when Steelers coach Joe Bach expressed pleasure from a hospital bed that his new employers just spent the fifth-overall 1953 draft selection on his former St. Bonny signal caller, elsewhere incumbent quarterback Jim Finks was nonplussed. Finks told the *Pittsburgh Press:* "Well, I guess I'll have to make a career out of the insurance business." He didn't.

Marchibroda knew Bach's system well enough to give Finks an education on it. But playing the position in the NFL, where 5-8 is miniscule for a passer, his short stature proved to be a problem. Given his background with Finks, it was natural for the little quarterback to make a career move to coaching.

He rose to Baltimore Colts head coach when the Lydell Mitchell–Bert Jones crew became one of the AFC's best—though not better than the Steelers of the mid-1970s. His teams went 31-11 from 1975 to 1977, but lost all three playoff games. Marchibroda spent 12 seasons as an NFL head coach, all of them with the Colts or in Baltimore (with the Ravens 1996–1998). His record against his old team: 2-10, with three losses in the postseason. Among his assistants were future multiple Super Bowl winner Bill Belichick of New England, Super Bowl participant Ken Whisenhunt of Arizona, Cincinnati's Marvin Lewis, and Detroit's Jim Schwarz.

Jack Butler, defensive back 1951–1959: "Teddy was even smaller than Jim Finks. Teddy worked hard at it, but he didn't have what Jim had. I went to school with him at St. Bonny."

Dale Dodrill, nose guard–middle linebacker from 1951 to 1959: As a coach "he won the championship one year [1977 AFC East] and got fired [two seasons later]. I coached with the Broncos after I quit playing, and I don't know how these coaches today [do it]. I sort of classify the pro coach as: They tolerate the players more than they coach them. [Players] were more concerned with having a good time than anything."

PAUL MARTHA
Safety–Wide Receiver–Halfback

Height: 6-0 • **Weight:** 187 • **College:** Pitt • **Years with the Steelers:** 1964–1969 • **Birthplace:** Pittsburgh • **Born:** June 22, 1942

An All-American halfback at Pitt and a cover-boy athlete, first-round pick and star material Paul Martha took awhile to find his place in professional football. The Steelers tried him at returning punts, then returning kickoffs. They played him at split end, at wide receiver, at halfback his initial two seasons with little success: 17 catches, six carries for 15 yards.

At safety, Martha finally found a home. He intercepted 15 passes in his final four seasons with his hometown team. He ended up a starter with Denver in 1970, intercepting a career-high six passes.

Andy Russell, linebacker 1963, 1966–1976: "When I got back [from the military], he was . . . a good, strong defensive safety. Very athletic. You don't make All-America halfback if you're not a good athlete. We all struggled [with losing]. When your team has some holes in it, you overplay sometimes. To try to make the big play. To try to make something happen."

Martha retired, became a lawyer (he had gone to night school during his playing days), and then represented the DeBartolo family as CEO of the Pittsburgh Penguins, as executive vice president of the U.S. Football League Pittsburgh Maulers, and in the same position with the perennial Super Bowl champion 49ers.

Dick Hoak, running back 1961–1970: "He went off and worked for the DeBartolos, worked for San Francisco. He was the one who was instrumental when they started the other league [and brought the USFL Maulers to Three Rivers]. I went there for an interview, and they offered me the Pittsburgh job. I didn't take it. That was all through Paul. And he once tried to get me to come out to San Francisco."

Martha within a generation became the Steelers' John Mackey, a poster player whose history of concussions—10—and physical play took their toll on his brain function in his 50s and 60s. His family moved him into a dementia and Alzheimer's clinic in 2008, then an assisted living facility a short time later . . . at age 67. He told the *Pittsburgh Post-Gazette* in 2009: "I'm the youngest person in here."

RAY MATHEWS
Halfback–Wide Receiver

Height: 6-0 • **Weight:** 185 • **College:** Clemson • **Years with the Steelers:** 1951–1959 • **Birthplace:** Dayton, Pennsylvania • **Born:** February 26, 1929

The Same Old Steelers of the mid-1950s weren't exactly an offensive juggernaut, but in Elbie Nickel and Ray Mathews they unwittingly possessed two of the most dependable receivers in the NFL. Mathews ranked among the top eight pass catchers in the game with 40-plus receptions in 1954 and 1955.

His four-touchdown total in a 1954 Cleveland game constitutes the franchise record by a rusher or receiver, tying Roy Jefferson. His 43 career touchdowns rank seventh, his 3,919 receiving yards eighth.

Joe Walton, competitor with the Redskins: "Ray Mathews was the first speed guy. Most of those guys, Elbie Nickel and those guys, weren't very fast. Remember, the African American players didn't start playing for quite a while, until they started filtering in in numbers. I played defensive corner my first year in the league; there weren't just guys who could run. But Ray Mathews was a guy who could fly."

Jack Butler, a defensive back those same 1951–1959 years who practiced against Mathews: "Ray ran really good patterns. He'd set you up with his quickness. We never had [enough] real players like him. Good hands, smart. And he was tough; he'd go across the middle."

Dale Dodrill, nose guard–middle linebacker 1951–1959: "Great receiver, huh? I remember Ray used to catch balls, touchdown passes, circus-type catches. Great ability. [Then] he'd catch the ball and be running and drop it. I used to ask him: How come you drop the ball out there? He said, 'You catch all those touchdown passes, the fans forget about it. But if you drop the ball when you're open and had a touchdown, they'll remember that.' He was about right, too."

Ray Mathews (1951–1959) watches helplessly in a late-'50s game as Philadelphia's Lee Riley picks off a pass meant for Mathews in the end zone. Interestingly, both teams are wearing home dark jerseys for the game. (Temple Urban Archives)

JOHNNY "BLOOD" MCNALLY
Halfback–Kick Returner–Kicker

Height: 6-1 • **Weight:** 188 • **Colleges:** Wisconsin–River Falls, Notre Dame, Dartmouth, St. John's (Minnesota) • **Years with the Pirates:** 1934, 1937–1938 • **Birthplace:** New Richmond, Wisconsin • **Born:** November 27, 1903 • **Died:** November 28, 1985

There's so much material on the man they all called Blood, he cannot merely be captured in the coach category alone (see Chapter 4).

Upon his arrival in August 1934, the *Pittsburgh Post-Gazette* labeled him the "wandering quarterback purchased from Green Bay." A more apt description: peripatetic.

John Victor McNally graduated from high school at age 14 and worked for a time at the Minneapolis forerunner of the *Star-Tribune* newspaper, where his family owned an interest. He attended four colleges but didn't finish any of them until years later when he returned to St. John's. There, he ultimately earned a master's in and taught economics, wrote a book on the subject, and coached the football team.

Tim Rooney Sr., who served everywhere from ball boy to ticket office: "He was very, very smart."

McNally was suspended from Notre Dame, for something about stealing a motorcycle (he called it "borrowed"). He

A dashing Johnny "Blood" McNally during his Pittsburgh Pirates playing days, 1934, 1937–1938. (Courtesy of the Pittsburgh Steelers)

adopted the "Blood" surname to turn pro, with a year of college eligibility remaining, after the Notre Dame incident. He played for five different pro football teams, and in his final five seasons he bounced from Green Bay to Pittsburgh to Green Bay and again to Pittsburgh, finally.

Although Green Bay wrung some usage from him in between as a passer and receiver, Blood was toward the end of his playing days in both stints with the Pirates. He was Pittsburgh's leading scorer and receiver in 1937 as a player-coach. Then Byron "Whizzer" White—whom he convinced to skip his Rhodes Scholar year in Oxford to play for the Pirates—took the team rushing lead in 1938. Roy McHugh, the longtime *Pittsburgh Press* columnist and editor, heard tales of game officials occasionally refusing to allow him on the field as a substitute; they doubted his ability to play at ages 34 and 35.

Blood was through playing by 1939, when his coaching-only Pirates career ended after three games, all losses.

Yet few players in the NFL's first half century proved as colorful as Johnny Blood. Alex Hawkins, Alex Karras, Joe Namath, and their ilk merely followed in his devilish footsteps.

He ran across the top of moving train cars during a Packers journey to Chicago, but only because a teammate was chasing him. He once climbed a fire escape, inched along an eighth-floor ledge, and leaped some 6 feet through the air and into the coach's half-open window to try to convince his Packers coach to give him a salary advance. Good thing Curly Lambeau obliged and Blood survived the escapade; otherwise "Lambeau Leap" might have garnered a completely different connotation.

Blood once uttered: "They pay me to score touchdowns. The swagger, I give 'em for free."

Ollie Kuechle of the *Milwaukee Journal* wrote of him: "[Blood] won games with his brilliance and lost them with his capers. He could be with the riffraff on a waterfront one night, then recite Keats or Shakespeare by the hour in elite company the next."

Blood later told the media, "I didn't spend my whole career on fire escapes. I had fun, I broke a few rules, but I got the job done on game day."

HEATH MILLER
Tight End

Height: 6-5 **Weight:** 256 **College:** Virginia **Years with the Steelers:** 2005– **Birthplace:** Richlands, Virginia **Born:** October 22, 1982

Quietly, professionally, Earl Heath Miller stands poised to etch his name in Steelers history.

He passed Elbie Nickel, an end who by today's standard qualifies as a tight end, in late 2011 on the Steelers all-time receptions list. Hall of Famer Lynn Swann and Louis Lipps stood within his 2012 reach. In the end, Miller—as workmanlike as his name suggests—figures to toil his way into the top-three pass catchers in franchise history. Eric Green, Mark Bruener, and Nickel all were all-stars and splendid tight ends, but nobody took the position where Miller did. Perhaps even no one in his NFL time did.

James Farrior, inside linebacker 2002–2011: "He's the best tight end in the game. He's a great blocker. Catches anything that goes to him. He's got the total package as far as tight end goes. I think that's the thing that hurts him a little bit: He's really a quiet guy, doesn't really say too much. Sometimes he gets overlooked.

"I played with Eric Green—yeah, I played with EG [in 1999 with the Jets]. I remember watching him when I was in high school, or maybe middle school. 'Man, that's a tight end? How am I supposed to cover a guy like that?' He could move for a big guy; that was kind of unheard of back then. But, like I said, I still think Heath is the best tight end I've seen around in a long time, as far as the total package."

LaMarr Woodley, outside linebacker 2007– : "Heath Miller should go to the Pro Bowl every year. He gets overlooked sometimes because of where the [attention goes]. I'm not taking away from those guys, but they're more like receivers. Heath Miller is a total tight end; he blocks and he catches passes. . . . Another thing I like about Heath Miller, he doesn't talk. He gets the first down, and he flips the ball to the official."

BAM MORRIS
Running Back

Height: 6-0 • **Weight:** 244 • **College:** Texas Tech • **Years with the Steelers:** 1994–1995 • **Birthplace:** Cooper, Texas • **Born:** January, 13, 1972

Byron Morris lasted two seasons with the Steelers before he ran afoul of the law on a charge of marijuana possession, which caused the club to release him two days before his sentencing in Texas. He followed that with two productive seasons for the Baltimore Ravens. He was suspended twice for violating the NFL's drug policy. He was jailed for 89 days in 1998 for marijuana possession. After his final season, 1999, with Kansas City, he pled guilty to selling marijuana and laundering money and was sentenced to 10 years in prison.

The leading rusher on the Super Bowl XXX Steelers, Bam's career went bust in six short seasons. Done at 27.

Kevin Greene, outside linebacker 1993–1995: "Oh, Bam. Now Bam was a haaard, physical-running brother. He was fast, he had skill, he was a big man, he had the right attitude, he was a team player, he was a good kid inside his heart. And Bam now, he would hit you. He would absolutely hit you. We had an offensive line in those days; give him a crack, and Bam will hit it."

John Jackson, offensive tackle 1988–1997: "Bam was a great player, but Bam kind of really didn't understand it. You have to have a balance. You can't do things off the field that hamper you from doing things on the field."

MARION MOTLEY
Running Back

Height: 6-1 • **Weight:** 232 • **Colleges:** South Carolina State, Nevada • **Year with the Steelers:** 1955 • **Birthplace:** Leesburg, Georgia • **Born:** June 5, 1920 • **Died:** June 27, 1999

First of all, future Hall of Famer Marion Motley wasn't Marion Motley by the time he spent an eyeblink in a Steelers uniform. A freak knee-on-knee injury in a practice drill prohibited him from playing the entire 1954 season. When he wanted to make a comeback, coach Paul Brown exiled him to Pittsburgh.

The Steelers traded fullback Ed "Big Mo" Modzelewski, who gained 1,000 yards combined the next two seasons, for Motley, who officially gained eight yards on two carries with the Steelers. He served as a blocking back on field-goal attempts and punts. He was released on Halloween.

Motley told the *United Press International* in 1976: "I liked Pittsburgh. Mr. [Art] Rooney and I struck up a friendship that has lasted to this day. He always sends me a box of cigars."

Frank Varrichione, offensive tackle 1955–1960: "We didn't have many African Americans when I was there in the late 1950s, seven or eight." Motley helped significantly in bringing racial equality to the NFL. "I can remember him saying, 'I got a 35-year-old mind and 45-year-old legs. They just don't want to go.' In fact, that was his last year."

Jack Butler, defensive back 1951–1959: "I remember we were playing the Giants [in preseason]. He ran a quick trap; he went through nice and clean. He went 20 or 30 yards, and he couldn't go any farther. He was running as hard as he could, but he had nothing left. We had him at the end."

Dale Dodrill, middle guard: "It hurt you just to see him try to walk or run, his knees were so bad."

ELBIE NICKEL
Tight End

Height: 6-1 • **Weight:** 196 • **College:** Cincinnati • **Years with the Steelers:** 1947–1957 • **Birthplace:** Fullerton, Kentucky • **Born:** December 28, 1922 • **Died:** February 27, 2007

Elbie Nickel (1947–1957) grimaces as he catches the ball—clearly marked by the *Philadelphia Bulletin*—against the Eagles in the early 1950s. Nickel caught 175 of his 329 career passes after his 30th birthday, an advanced age for a player of that era. (Temple Urban Archives)

Elbert Everett Nickel wasn't all that big—by modern standards, anyway. Wasn't very fast. Wasn't overly strong. But he not only grabbed a bunch of passes at the position that amounted to tight end for the Steelers; he also played some defensive end while ranking among the league's leading receivers.

His 62 catches in 1953 were the ninth most in NFL history at the time, and he ranked second in league receptions that season. A year earlier, he finished third with 55 catches—while capping the season with 10 for 202 yards against the Los Angeles Rams and Hall of Fame cornerback Dick "Night Train" Lane, his longest covering only 45 yards (meaning the rest *averaged* better than 17 yards per). His career average of 15.6 yards per catch would be the envy of any modern-day wide receiver, forget about tight end. And his 329 career receptions remained the Steelers' record for a quarter century.

On the occasion of the Steelers' 50th Anniversary in 1982, he was chosen as their best tight end of all time. He and Bennie Cunningham were the only tight ends named to their 75th Anniversary squad.

Ed Kiely, longtime public-relations director: "He was fantastic. He would call the plays. Elbie was special. He and Stautner, you couldn't get any better."

Chuck Cherundolo, teammate and assistant with the Steelers: "One of the great ones. He could do everything. He didn't have much speed, but he looked like a burner. Good hands. He was a good leader, too. He'd never get to the point where he'd tell you to go [screw] yourself. Never could tell if the guy got mad. To me, that's important. When most guys get mad, they're doing things they shouldn't be doing."

Jack Butler, teammate and star defensive back: "Elbie was our tight end. A really good guy. He was a good football player, but he didn't have the great speed or great size. He could block well. He had good hands and would catch the little chintzy things."

Tim Rooney Sr., son of the Chief and ball boy/water boy at the time: "He was just a spectacular receiver. You think about all the passes that he caught, and the age that he played . . . it wasn't until Swann and Stallworth's era, he was still the leading receiver."

NEIL O'DONNELL
Quarterback

Height: 6-3 • **Weight:** 228 • **College:** Maryland • **Years with the Steelers:** 1991–1995 • **Birthplace:** Morristown, New Jersey • **Born:** July 3, 1966

Plug the phrase "Neil O'Donnell Super Bowl interception" into almost any search engine, and you find as many as 600,000 hits. Nearly a generation later, the hits keep coming.

Two passes. Too much blame?

Dallas Cowboys nondescript cornerback Larry Brown—the guy on the side opposite future Hall of Famer Deion Sanders—found two location passes that, for one, Steelers receiver Andre Hastings could not. They made both the Cowboys a 27-17 winner in Super Bowl XXX and Brown a wealthy man, after a $12.5 million free-agent contract with Oakland. Neil O'Donnell would never throw another pass for the Steelers, the native New Jerseyan signing a five-year, $25 million deal with the New York Jets. Each barely lasted two seasons in their new gigs. Too much burden?

Dermontti Dawson, center 1988–2000: "All I hear is about Neil and 1995. Neil was much more than those two bad passes in the Super Bowl. It was a miscommunication. I tell people, 'Don't judge Neil on those two throws, because we don't know. . . .'"

Ron Erhardt, offensive coordinator 1992–1995: "Basically one [interception] was his and the other was on the receiver, as far as being at fault. That's the way those go when you're doing a hot read."

Kevin Greene, outside linebacker 1993–1995: "He's taken heat for Super Bowl XXX, those two interceptions against Dallas. I disagree with the heat. We share in that. I had maybe two or three tackles, no inside plays; I am equally to blame for that loss. Two picks, I got that. Three points here, three points there. . . . When you go in that game, no matter what that adversity is, no matter what that situation is, you're a firefighter—it's your job to put it out no matter how big that fricking fire is. Defensively, we were not able to do that."

Gerald Williams, nose tackle–defensive end 1986–1994: "That was unfortunate. It wasn't even close" to O'Donnell's fault alone.

John Jackson, offensive tackle 1988–1997: "He suffers from one game, but I don't think you can judge a career off one game. Even though it's the Super Bowl, but . . . it was one of those things."

O'Donnell arrived in Pittsburgh in interesting times, a third-round pick in a 1990 draft where Chuck Noll's club needed more talent after a deceivingly uplifting ending to the 1989 season—two playoff games after an 0-2 start. Bubby Brister, partly due to injuries, gave way to O'Donnell in eight starts in 1991. New coach Bill Cowher handed the offense's keys to O'Donnell the next season, in 1992, though mostly that involved handing the ball to Barry Foster and passing cautiously, infrequently. The formula proved a success: O'Donnell went 37-16 as a regular-season starter over those four seasons.

Erhardt: "Neil could manage the game really well. There were a lot of things people got on his case about. When you look at his record, you got to look at it pretty good. He got us

Neil O'Donnell sets up in 1991, his second season . . . and Chuck Noll's last. (Bill Amatucci)

to the playoffs every year. He did a lot of good things and won a lot of games."

O'Donnell's last Pittsburgh season, 1995, new receivers coach Chan Gailey helped to install a passing offense that played to O'Donnell's strengths. The quarterback compiled the most touchdowns of his career (17) and tied the fewest interceptions (seven) and his most yards per game (247.5). And he got them to Tempe, Arizona, on January 28, 1996.

O'Donnell continued to tell reporters years afterward: "I took all the heat. That's fine, I can take it."

Erhardt: "I know he had the two passes in the Super Bowl; he'd like to have them back. It was too bad" so many judged him on two of his 2,144 Steelers passes and 3,504 in his 13-year career.

Dawson: "Neil was a great guy and a very consistent quarterback. It was a great fit for him."

For the record, O'Donnell threw for 2,283 yards in 1992, 3,208 on a career-high 486 attempts in 1993, 2,443 in 1994, and 2,970 in 12 games in 1995.

Greene: "It really did come together for him. I really liked Neil O'Donnell."

Dom Capers, defensive coordinator 1992–1994: "Neil was a very personable guy." O'Donnell played for three teams over eight post-Steelers seasons and ventured 16-23 as a starter in New York, Tennessee, and Cincinnati. "I think that's true; he never had the same success. The Steelers are unique—it's the right place for a number of guys because they fit the system."

Erhardt: "There were a lot of [other] teams he would struggle to play for."

Williams: "I tell you, Neil was probably the turning [point] of us having a decent quarterback. In those days, Bubby was wild. Either he would excel or . . . [laying hand flat on a chair]. You just didn't know. [O'Donnell] more resembled stability."

JERRY OLSAVSKY
Inside Linebacker

Height: 6-1 • **Weight:** 221 • **College:** Pitt • **Years with the Steelers:** 1989–1997 • **Birthplace:** Youngstown, Ohio • **Born:** March 29, 1967

By all accounts, he was possessed of too little heft, too little strength, too little speed to succeed in major college football, let alone the NFL. By all accounts, that is, except Jerry Olsavsky's.

He succeeded, all right. Olsavsky utilized instincts, presence, leverage, angles, everything a MacGyver of an inside linebacker could muster, and he started 37 of his 108 Steelers games. He started as a rookie for Hardy Nickerson. He started in the mid-1990s when Chad Brown and Greg Lloyd were hurt. But Olsavsky, the guy from nearby Youngstown, Ohio, by way of Pitt, did what Jerry-O excels at: He stood his inside-linebacker ground.

He came back from the football dead and the cadaver dead, too. In a game at Cleveland October 24, 1993, he dislocated and damaged a knee so badly that team orthopedic surgeon Dr. Jim Bradley talked about how years later he could still hear Olsavsky's scream as he maneuvered the joint back into place. Members of the vaunted Blitzburgh defense already had their backs turned, unable to watch.

With a ligament from a cadaver and a determination to prove detractors wrong—"people said. . . I'd never play football again"—Olsavsky rehabilitated to where he came back and not only played in a 1994 game but also started five games of the Super Bowl XXX season that followed and 13 more in 1996.

Dom Capers, defensive coordinator 1992–1994: "Unique guy. Very smart. Probably played football a lot better than he would test. Again, there's another guy who's coaching there now [same as Carnell Lake, joining the staff in 2011]. That's indicative of the kind of instincts he had. The one memory that stands out the most is when he got his knee hurt in Cleveland. He won the starting position for us, then we lost him—and it was a pretty good knee injury."

Gerald Williams, nose tackle–defensive end 1986–1994: "He was the epitome of that saying: It's not the size of the dog in the fight, but the fight in the dog. He just wasn't—or isn't—very big. But he had the will of a lion. You never could keep him down. And extremely smart."

PRESTON PEARSON
Halfback

Height: 6-1 • **Weight:** 205 • **College:** Illinois • **Years with the Steelers:** 1970–1974 • **Birthplace:** Freeport, Illinois • **Born:** January 17, 1945

He carved his own niche: Preston Pearson, perennial Super Bowl participant. In fact, he was the first NFL player to partake of five Super Bowls. He won only two of them—one being Super Bowl IX *with* the Steelers. *Against* the Steelers? He went 0-2 with the Dallas Cowboys.

Pearson started out as a defensive back in 1967 with the Baltimore Colts and young assistant Chuck Noll. The Steelers picked him up in 1970, and he became their second-leading rusher behind Frenchy Fuqua in 1970 and 1971. When Franco Harris entrenched himself and Rocky Bleier began to surge, Pearson grew expendable. So, by the time the Steelers and Cowboys met after the 1975 and 1978 seasons, Pearson wound up on the losing side. In Super Bowl X, in which MVP Lynn Swann caught four passes for 161 yards, Dallas' Pearson was actually the game-high receiver with five (for 108 yards fewer).

His other Super Bowl victory came in XII, when the Cowboys beat up Denver, and again Pearson was the game-high receiver with five.

That was just it: Pearson enjoyed catching passes more than blocking, the grunt work for a running back.

Dick Hoak, running backs coach: "He didn't play college football; he was a college basketball player. Preston was kind of a finesse player. His big thing was running pass routes."

DARREN PERRY
Safety

Height: 5-11 • **Weight:** 196 • **College:** Penn State • **Years with the Steelers:** 1992–1998 • **Birthplace:** Chesapeake, Virginia • **Born:** December 29, 1968

Darren Perry, an eighth-round pick in Bill Cowher's inaugural draft of 1992, stepped into the starting lineup as a rookie and never wavered.

His first six NFL seasons, he topped the Steelers in interceptions three times and finished no lower than second the other three. This was on a Blitzburgh defense starring perennial Pro Bowler Carnell Lake and future Hall of Famer Rod Woodson, considered one of the greatest defensive backs in pro-football history. Perhaps even more impressive: In his 123-game Steelers career, he missed only two games—in his final year, 1998, at age 30, due to a groin injury.

He spent one season starting in New Orleans, again without missing a game, and went into coaching. On the other sideline, he joined ex-Blitzburgh mates Kevin Greene and Dom Capers on the Super Bowl XLV–winning staff of Green Bay. It was his second Super Bowl ring, after working with Dick LeBeau and the Steelers on the Super Bowl XL victory.

Kevin Greene, outside linebacker 1993–1995: "I heard coming in this young kid from Penn State was a good kid, picking off all those balls [six as a rookie]. If it was his turn to rotate up there and hit somebody, you could rest assured that play was going to die right then and there, too."

Gerald Williams, nose tackle–defensive end 1986–1994: "Darren was an ambassador. He knew the whole lay of the land back there. He was the quarterback of the defense. Pretty much when he got in the huddle, what was said—it went."

TROY POLAMALU
Safety

Height: 5-10 • **Weight:** 213 • **College:** USC • **Years with the Steelers:** 2003– • **Birthplace:** Garden Grove, California • **Born:** April 19, 1981

Where to begin with the NFL player who gave new meaning—and even a rule—concerning the term "hair pull"? He became football's mane man, an amiable player who once reenacted to a degree Joe Greene's famous pop commercial. He tortured his old college roommate Carson Palmer, and he played a brand of safety no one else could dare.

Troy Polamalu, hair flowing, in the 2010 opener that he helped to secure with an interception that led to an overtime victory over Atlanta. (George Gojkovich)

Yes, that's the core of Troy Polamalu as an NFL player: There will be only one.

Polamalu: "I don't care about my legacy. I could be forgotten. . . ." Such concerns of self don't hold import to a man of religion and a player of external drive—his faith, his family, his team.

Dick LeBeau, defensive assistant 1992–1994 and defensive coordinator 1995–1996, 2004– : "Incomparable really. I've been lucky here with the Steelers. I had Rod Woodson and Carnell Lake in the same backfield when I came here. Troy's right there with them. They're three of the greatest defensive backs who have ever played."

Tony Dungy, Steelers safety 1977–1978, assistant 1981–1988, and opposition coach with Tampa Bay and Indianapolis: "I remember scouting him when he came out of USC. I thought he was going to be good, but I had no idea he would be as great and as dominant. You saw the relentlessness. But the instincts and ability to make the big play . . . ? In Dick LeBeau's system, you get to have a lot of creativity. It's really the perfect system for him to do what he does. He has been a tremendous player. Instinctive, that's the one word that comes to mind."

LeBeau: "Troy just has another gear. I think the reason he's so popular around the nation is that you can just be sitting in the stadium—you don't have to know anything about football—and you can see this guy is moving differently from the other guys. There's some magnetism there. He's produced so many great, great plays for us. I'll never forget the interception against Baltimore that sent us to [Super Bowl XLIII]—the game was *very much* in doubt; they had just scored; we needed to stop them there. Not only stopped them, he took it to the end zone and secured the victory."

To earn home-field advantage that helped the Steelers reach Super Bowl XLV, he blitzed and fashioned a strip sack of Baltimore's Joe Flacco that produced the game-winning touchdown.

To open 2009, he made five tackles, a breathtaking interception, and a touchdown-saving pass defense in barely a quarter and a half of the season opener against Tennessee. It was a performance on which alone he could have earned at least a seventh consecutive Pro Bowl, had he not been prevented from playing more than five games that season by a second-quarter knee injury.

LeBeau: "I've never seen a player make more plays than that [and in a quarter and a half]. But you can't start naming all the plays he's made" in his career.

Max Starks, offensive tackle 2004– : "Troy's a prankster, too. He gets it low key. Everybody thinks he's such a nice guy: 'Oh, he's so quiet.' Troy will sneak up on you. He likes to play practical jokes. Like, he'll do the shoulder tap from the opposite side. He had a whoopee cushion three years ago and put it under people's seats."

JOEY PORTER
Outside Linebacker

Height: 6-2 • **Weight:** 250 • **College:** Colorado State • **Years with the Steelers:** 1999–2006 • **Birthplace:** Bakersfield, California • **Born:** March 22, 1977

Envision Greg Lloyd with a motor mouth and a sense of humor, but without the tae kwon do and aggressive bent. Joey

Joey Porter in his Sunday finest at Ford Field for Super Bowl XL. (Courtesy of the Pittsburgh Steelers)

Porter was aggressive, mind you. It's just that it came with a healthy dose of trash talk and sarcasm, when they weren't one and the same.

Dermontti Dawson, center 1988–2000: "Almost like a mini–Greg Lloyd. He had that same mentality."

James Farrior, inside linebacker 2002–2011: "Man, that was certainly an experience, playing with him. He's a player that you never forget he's been in your locker room. Full of passion, full of energy. Always had an answer for everything. He's a guy you want in your foxhole."

Porter's mouth sometimes got him into the soup or media.

He used the Super Bowl XL podium to chop up a seemingly innocuous comment by Seattle tight end Jerramy Stevens and transformed it into kindling, primarily stoking Steelers fires. Stevens had three drops in the game, which, of course, the Steelers won.

He used a homophobic slur in discussing Cleveland tight end Kellen Winslow II in 2006.

He smooched Bill Cowher on the neck after a 2006 interception return for a touchdown.

There were other incidents, which teammates ascribed to *Joey being Joey.* Through no fault of his own, he got shot in the buttocks while in a fracas outside a Denver bar one off weekend in 2003. In 2006, his two dogs got loose and killed a neighbor's miniature horse. On the field, there was the time he shoved to the ground an already injured Todd Heap of Baltimore. And he was ejected in pregame warm-ups for

wading into some Cleveland–Pittsburgh trash talking that escalated into a fight.

Farrior: "I probably will remember that [ejection] for a long time. When he found out he wasn't going to be able to play, he was like a sad puppy. His whole demeanor fell. And that was Deebo's [starting] debut."

Indeed, November 17, 2004, became the coming-out party for James "Deebo" Harrison, who ultimately replaced Porter full-time at right outside linebacker and became the NFL Defensive Player of the Year. With a dose of health and fortune, Harrison may well surpass Porter's fourth-ranked 60 sacks in a Steelers career.

MYRON POTTIOS
Middle Linebacker

Height: 6-2 • **Weight:** 232 • **College:** Notre Dame • **Years with the Steelers:** 1961–1965 • **Birthplace:** Van Voorhis, Pennsylvania • **Born:** January 18, 1939

Long before No. 66 became famous in Pittsburgh, with Mario Lemieux putting it on ice and then in the rafters of Mellon Arena/Consol Energy Center, a local boy wore it for the Steelers.

There was a distinct local seasoning to that Steelers draft of 1961: Their opening two draft choices were second-rounder Pottios of Notre Dame and seventh-rounder Dick Hoak of Penn State. Hoak's Jeannette defeated Pottios' Charleroi in the 1956 WPIAL Class AA championship game at Latrobe in their senior years, 16-13. Not that it mattered to them five years later as teammates.

Dick Hoak, running back 1961–1970: "He was the second-round pick—the Steelers didn't have a first-round pick. I was the seventh pick—we didn't have a third, fourth, fifth, sixth pick. It was fun to play against him in high school; he played for us for a couple of years."

"He'll be another Joe Schmidt," assistant Chuck Cherundolo was quoted as saying in the *Pittsburgh Press.* Starting as a rookie at middle linebacker, Pottios made the Pro Bowl his first three seasons on the field, but not without turbulence. He separated a shoulder and missed half or more of both 1963 (when he was first-team All-Pro linebacker alongside fellow Western Pennsylvanians Joe Schmidt of Pitt and Bill George of Waynesburg) and 1964, and a broken arm sidelined him all of 1962. So frustrated was Pottios, he told his hometown newspaper in 1965 that he pondered quitting football. A year later he got traded to George Allen's Rams. Allen later took Pottios along to Washington, where he and the "Over the Hill Gang" lost Super Bowl VII to undefeated Miami.

Andy Russell, outside linebacker 1963, 1966–1976 of his ex-roommate: "Another local guy. Very tough guy."

GABE RIVERA
Nose Tackle

Height: 6-2 • **Weight:** 290 • **College:** Texas Tech • **Year with the Steelers:** 1983 • **Birthplace:** Crystal City, Texas • **Born:** April 7, 1961

Beside the 1948 tragic death of coach Jock Sutherland, perhaps no other moment in Steelers history brought to the playing

Gabe Rivera remains one of the sad stories in Steelers history. After six games of a promising rookie 1983 season, he became paralyzed after an automobile accident. (Bill Amatucci)

field as much sorrow and dread, as much change and disruption, as the loss of Gabe Rivera.

Rivera was their building block, the personality and player around whom they hoped to rebuild another stalwart defense using their tested 1969 blueprint.

After six games and two sacks, Rivera was paralyzed in an automobile accident—and the course of the franchise and their future Hall of Fame coach was altered.

Tony Dungy, defensive assistant and coordinator, 1981–1988: "We picked Gabe and passed on Dan Marino. Chuck saw Joe Greene in Gabe Rivera. He was big, physical, the guy everybody gravitated to. He was a special player. Obviously, nobody will ever know."

Tom Beasley, defensive lineman 1978–1983: "Probably one of the quickest defensive tackles I've ever seen. Just real explosive off the ball. A tremendous first three steps. Shorter guy, had great leverage. He certainly had strength, but coming into Pittsburgh he was undeveloped in that area. With their conditioning program, had it not been for the accident, he would have had an incredible career."

The No. 21 overall selection in the 1983 draft, Rivera remembers meeting the legendary defensive lineman he was supposed to follow.

Rivera: "Joe Greene retired two years before. But he was there in training camp, helping out. I learned a lot from him."

Soon after he notched his second sack in four weeks, between a home victory with Cleveland and a road trip to Seattle, Rivera got behind the wheel of his car after drinking. At 8:55 P.M., on October 20, 1983, at a difficult intersection on Babcock Boulevard in the North Hills, his car crossed the center line, skidded about 90 feet, and collided with an oncoming vehicle with such force that he was propelled through his rear hatchback window and roughly 20 feet. He was 22 years old.

He suffered a crushed spinal cord, three fractured neck vertebrae, a broken bone and nerve damage in his right shoulder, broken ribs, a bruised lung, a bruised heart. Operations were performed by trauma surgeons, neurosurgeons, orthopedic surgeons, and pulmonary specialists. He went on a ventilator.

And on November 11, in the same Allegheny General Hospital, his wife Kimberly gave birth to their firstborn, Timothy. Rivera noted later that his son "helped me through a lot of the state of depression at first."

The Steelers provided him with his full year's salary, even though they were under no obligation to do so because it wasn't a football-related injury. They offered him a scouting position, and he demurred.

More than passing on Jim Brown or Lenny Moore or even Dan Marino, this became the most lamentable incident for the team . . . and in its 50th Anniversary year.

Rivera: "One of the Rooneys had mentioned it to me not long ago, that [Noll] wanted to . . . build the defense around me. I got injured so. . . . They were still trying to put the defense together."

As the years mounted, Noll's teams from that moment went 65-73—not counting strike replacements—until his retirement. The Steelers never got past a second playoff in any postseason, which were few: three in Noll's final nine seasons. They spent five of the next eight drafts trying to re-create the blueprint, expending first-round selections (Daryl Sims, Aaron Jones, Huey Richardson) or second-round picks (Gerald Williams and Kenny Davidson) on defensive linemen. Only one truly stuck (Williams).

Dungy: "Chuck thought, 'This guy could be special.' You saw the natural ability, the speed, the power. And he was just learning the pro game. He had a chance, yeah. He had a chance to be one of those special defensive players like Rod Woodson or Joe Greene—an eight- or nine-year Pro Bowler. No question he had that kind of talent."

Beasley: "That certainly was everybody's expectation. It was absolutely tragic that Gabe had the accident."

Rivera, who struggles against bone infections to maintain his health, spoils his four grandchildren, and works with youth at a San Antonio center: "After the accident, I was kind of in a different world. Trying to get things going and stuff. But it was good [in Pittsburgh]. I really enjoyed the Rooneys. They took care of me; they took care of my family.

"I still sometimes think back and wonder. We'll never know if I would live up to my potential or flop. . . . But I don't dwell on it. I just try to take day by day."

BEN ROETHLISBERGER
Quarterback

Height: 6-5 • **Weight:** 247 • **College:** Miami University of Ohio • **Years with the Steelers:** 2004– • **Birthplace:** Findlay, Ohio • **Born:** March 2, 1982

Ben Roethlisberger signs autographs at training camp in St. Vincent College, Latrobe, Pennsylvania, 2008. (John Beale)

Newspaper archives retell his story: Ben Roethlisberger often found himself in print. In bandages, splints, X-rays, MRIs, operating rooms, trainer's rooms, and pain, too. Here is the unofficial Big Ben Boo-Boo List:

- Bruised rib, 2004
- Broken toes, 2005. Although Bill Cowher disputed that Roethlisberger claim, "We are unaware of any problems with his toes, okay?" And this came amid rumors that he earlier injured his thumb, too.
- Hyperextended knee and bone bruise, 2005
- Knee scope, 2005
- Motorcycle injuries, surgeries, and appendectomy, 2006
- Concussion, 2006
- Hip bruise, 2007
- Sore shoulder, 2007
- Sprained shoulder, 2008
- Concussion, 2008
- Two broken ribs, 2009, he said after Super Bowl XLIII
- Bruised Achilles tendon, 2009
- Fracture in fifth metatarsal of right foot, 2009
- Concussion, 2009
- Fractured bone in left foot and a broken nose requiring surgery, 2010
- Foot sprain, 2011
- Fractured right thumb, 2005 and 2011

All that—and the tote board reads three concussions, five surgical procedures minimum, 20 separate maladies, and counting—and he missed but six games total as a result of injury since his 2004 rookie year. The three-game hiatus from

his 2005 arthroscopic knee surgery that marked his career high? It's also half his career total of absences through 2011.

He faced a four-game NFL suspension in 2010 that nearly equaled those six injury absences of the previous seven seasons.

And about that suspension . . .

Roethlisberger over the years also received an abundance of newspaper, Internet, radio, television, and general national attention for incidents that remain in what may well be a more enduring archive: the public's memory.

There was his 2006 motorcycle accident that nearly killed a 24-year-old permitless man whose boss, Bill Cowher, a year earlier asked him to wear a helmet—and the rider had none when he crashed headfirst. There was a 2009 lawsuit filed in Nevada accusing him of sexually assaulting a hotel employee, with whom his side reached a settlement agreement in 2012. There was the 2010 incident in Milledgeville, Georgia, where the district attorney declined to bring charges against him after hundreds of police-report documents filled with accounts of his boorish behavior were released to the media and public.

NFL Commissioner Roger Goodell scolded Roethlisberger in announcing a six-game 2010 suspension that, after intervention and various actions, the quarterback got reduced to four: "In your six years in the NFL, you have first thrilled and now disappointed a great many people. I urge you to take full advantage of this opportunity to get your life and career back on track."

That same 2010 season ended with Roethlisberger in Super Bowl XLV, his third time on such a huge stage in six years. He reiterated to media there that he had grown, learned, changed. The one-score game came down to two minutes remaining and the ball in his hands. Unlike Super Bowl XLIII, unlike his previous 18 regular-season fourth-quarter comebacks to rank No. 25 all-time, this time Roethlisberger couldn't weave his winning-drive magic.

Roethlisberger: "There was so much stacked against us, from injuries and. . . . Everything that could've happened, happened. I mean, [2010] was crazy."

For a man approaching 30 and his career years, Roethlisberger tried to buff his public image. On a football field, if not winning back admiration, he continued to win games in that unique Roethlisberger passer persona: improvisation by extending plays with scrambling around; absorbing injurious blows in so doing; coming back for more comebacks, more victories.

Max Starks, offensive tackle 2004– , blind-side protector and close friend: "He just has a history of winning. He's a competitive guy. He knows how to move [defenders] with his feet and his eyes. That's a great combination to have."

Roethlisberger was the third of four quarterbacks selected in the 2004 first round. It was a bold choice by Steelers hierarchy after a 2-6 start leveled into a 6-10 season and holes seemed to exist all over the lineup. Quarterback wasn't one such spot. However, members of that hierarchy asked themselves if Tommy Maddox was the kind of quarterback to not just reach a Super Bowl, but win one.

Kevin Colbert, director of football operations and general manager 2000– : "When we drafted Ben, it wasn't out of need. Tommy was still a pretty successful quarterback for us. What Coach Cowher stated was, 'For the good of the organization, if the quarterback is there, we should take him.' There probably were other players who could have helped us win immediately."

Charlie Batch, backup quarterback 2002– : "The good thing is . . . you knew what you were getting, coming into it. How they were going to treat him in the offense."

Starks: "Every year, there's a new highlight, a new memory. Ben's been a tough, consummate competitor. His will to win and will to want to succeed are unmatched, I think, in any other professional athlete I've been around or seen. Michael Jordan might be the only one ever to compete with him on that. I mean, he wants to be the best. And he wants to make sure that everyone around him is just as successful. I think that's an attribute you want to have in your quarterback, a teammate and a friend."

Santonio Holmes, receiver 2006–2009: "Everything had to go well for him in practice. He played the way he practiced. He wanted everything to be on cue. He just wanted to have fun on the football field, and let's do a good job doing it."

Starks: "I think he came into the perfect system that allowed [him] to flourish. Look back, he got thrown into the game very quickly, the second game of the season, against Baltimore [after Maddox got hurt]. In 2004 we had a great run game and a very bruising offensive line. We commanded. We could run the same play three plays in a row and tell a team, 'We're running right here—there was nothing you could do to stop that.' So it wasn't purely dependent upon Ben throwing 30, 40 times a game. He was throwing 19, 20 times a game. He was allowed to get in a rhythm. Build up and develop."

Bill Cowher: "You knew he had qualities from Day One in that building, and when he stepped on that practice field, you could tell he was a special player. His resume spoke for itself.

"But nobody foresaw that he would go 15-1 his first year."

That 15-1 season perhaps constructed a false confidence in others about Roethlisberger, who was asked to be more caretaker than quarterback. The next season, the shackles were removed in the playoffs, when the Steelers won four consecutive road games—including Super Bowl XL. He completed 49 of 72 passes for 680 yards, seven touchdowns, one interception, a 124.75 passer rating, and three triumphs to reach Ford Field in Detroit.

Aaron Smith, defensive end 1999–2011: "How well he played in that AFC championship game in Denver [21 of 29 for 275 yards, two touchdowns, and no interceptions]. How

After an AFC championship flameout the previous January, Ben Roethlisberger, right, promised Jerome Bettis that he'd help him reach the Super Bowl if he gave the Steelers one more season. Bettis and Roethlisberger share a smooch with the Lombardi Trophy they snagged a year later. (Courtesy of the Pittsburgh Steelers)

much calmness he had. How he performed. How well he played *being so young*. That's when I really realized he was special."

Roethlisberger wound up directing the Steelers to Super Bowls at age 23, making him the youngest in NFL history to win one, and 26 and 28. Bradshaw, the black-and-gold standard, won rings at 26, 27, 30, and 31.

When Mike Tomlin succeeded Cowher in 2007 and offensive coordinator Ken Whisenhunt left to become Arizona's head coach, Bruce "BA" Arians landed atop a Steelers playbook that contained as much Wite-Out as original content. Cowher went through a waiting line of coordinators: Ron Erhardt, Chan Gailey, Ray Sherman, Kevin Gilbride, Mike Mularkey, and Whisenhunt. That's six in 15 seasons, or a new one every two and a half calendar years. With a refined playbook, what followed were far better statistical seasons for Roethlisberger in yardage, touchdowns, passer rating, even his most precious measure of all: one Super Bowl in the last three Cowher seasons compared to two in the first four under Tomlin.

Batch: "He took a lot of pride in, when Coach Tomlin took over," reworking the playbook. "Really, BA did a very good job sitting down with him in the off-season and breaking down the playbook. In years past, with Cowher hiring all the different coordinators, it was just [plays] stacked on top of each other. So you get to the point you're a new guy coming in like I was, asking 'Why are you calling it this?' 'I don't know; the coordinator before called it this.' Seriously?

"So it was hard for somebody to break it down. BA realized that when he was the receivers coach [2004–2006]. So in '07 when he realized he was going to be the coordinator, they really broke down that playbook and understood concepts. 'Okay, Ben, what do you like?' So they grew the playbook. Now the growth . . . , it's kind of fun to see."

Roethlisberger quickly compiled five seasons of 3,000-plus passing yards compared to Bradshaw's two.

He was poised in 2012 to surpass Bradshaw's team-record 27,989 career passing yards . . . and in five fewer years. There was a good chance he would beat Bradshaw's 212 career touchdown passes, and his passer rating likewise would top the Steelers' all-time best by far. Six of the Steelers' top 10 passing-yardage seasons, six of the top eight games, and eight of the top 10 completion-percentage seasons belonged to him already, too.

Yet again in a statistic vital to him: He was 2-1 in Super Bowls, far behind Bradshaw's 4-0.

Batch: "A lot of people talk about seeing a difference in him. I've always seen him; I've known him from his rookie year. I don't see any difference."

Roethlisberger, asked about his legacy as the Steelers' quarterback: "I hope it's not over yet. [Laughs.] Hard-nosed. Work. I think . . . I think . . . I hope I'm appreciated a lot more, from both the organization and the fans, for playing through the injuries, being tough. Where I don't know if I was playing for another team, if you were hurt and you played, I don't think [those fans] would appreciate it as much.

"You know, I want to be the guy that when they talk about the Pittsburgh Steelers and you think about the all-time teams—I know, it's a huge guy to overcome [in Bradshaw]—but . . . I want to be the guy that is on the 100th-year anniversary team. I want to be the guy that, when [people] think about the Pittsburgh Steelers, they think of me."

FRAN ROGEL
Fullback

Height: 5-9 • **Weight:** 203 • **Colleges:** California (Pennsylvania), Penn State • **Years with the Steelers:** 1950–1957 • **Birthplace:** North Braddock, Pennsylvania • **Born:** December 12, 1927 • **Died:** June 3, 2002

Strike up the chorus: "Hey, diddle diddle, Rogel up the middle."

Even the owner, Art Rooney, grew weary of hearing that refrain reverberate through Forbes Field and Pitt Stadium whenever the Steelers played. But that's a tale for another page in this book. . . .

Francis Stephen Rogel (pronounced roe-GAL) was a sight tougher than his name implied. He was the horse that coaches Walt Kiesling and others rode hard, rode often. He topped the Steelers in rushing five of six consecutive years from 1951 to 1956. He wasn't shifty, he wasn't fleet. All he was: utilitarian. Plow horses normally aren't pretty.

Rogel ranked among the Steelers' top-10 players in rushing yardage and attempts. He averaged 34.1 yards per game and 3.6 yards per carry for his career. He amassed the sum total of one 100-yard rushing performance (168 in 1953) in his 96 career games—and he never missed a game. That's a lot of use.

Chuck Cherundolo, assistant coach 1949–1957: "He was a tough apple."

Jack Butler, defensive back 1951–1959: "Hey, diddle diddle, and all that. Franny was one tough little dude. He was 5-9. Built. Tough as a boot. Had no moves. Nothing clever. No imagination. Just straight ahead."

Dale Dodrill, nose guard–middle linebacker 1951–1959: "What'd they used to say, pile of dust and two yards? Great guy. You won't find a guy any tougher than he was. He fit in the single wing."

Art Rooney Sr. once named a horse after him, Our Man Rogel. Friends wondered if his battering-ram style contributed to the Parkinson's that claimed his life in 2002, long before CTE or concussions became the rage.

ANDY RUSSELL
Outside Linebacker

Height: 6-2 • **Weight:** 225 • **College:** Missouri • **Years with the Steelers:** 1963, 1966–1976 • **Birthplace:** Detroit • **Born:** October 29, 1941

The savvy businessman and well-traveled fellow that is Charles Andrew Russell wrote not one, not two, but three books. So let's permit him to tell the tale of his own Steelers odyssey.

Andy Russell: "[While at Missouri,] my father called me and made me promise never to play professional football. 'It would be an embarrassment to the Russell family. You're going to work for a living.'" Russell already had his ROTC and military commitment, so that was a given in his future. At the time, NFL teams had gone to longer forms than what Dick Hoak recalled: asking only for speed and NFL interest. "The first question is 'Do you want to play professional football.' I wrote, 'No,' and didn't fill out the form . . . for 11 of those teams. The only team who didn't send me one was the Pittsburgh Steelers. That's how I got drafted." In January the Steelers drafted him and made him an offer: $12,000 with a $3,000 signing bonus.

He called up the corporate-executive father with Monsanto: "I'll never forget I had to call my dad in Brussels, Belgium: 'Dad, I have to break a promise.'" The signing bonus was important, given that "I was married and I was broke. 'Good idea, son.'" The idea was to play for pay, then go back for an MBA. "Then we got to Super Bowls. . . ."

The first two Steelers picks of that 1963 draft were *eighth-round* offensive tackle Frank Atkinson, who became his best friend, and Russell in the *16th round.*

Russell, who had one year in the NFL before completing his two-year military hitch: "The first game was Franklin Field against the Philadelphia Eagles. [Starting linebacker John Reger] made a tackle in the first quarter; he had a major concussion and he's swallowing his tongue. The doctor takes his scissors and knocks [Reger's] teeth out, pulling the tongue out. Bob Schmitz . . . , first play he's in there, tears his ankle up. 'Russell, go in there.' 'Well, I'm not sure I want to play professional football.'" Reger ultimately moved to right outside linebacker; Russell stayed at left outside linebacker. "You talk

Andy Russell, in cape, in 1974 shortly before his circuitous route—bad Steelers of 1960s, military service, good Steelers of early 1970s—produced the first of his pair of Super Bowl triumphs. (George Gojkovich)

about luck. If that hadn't happened, I would have played one year, got my MBA, and gone into business. I just got an enormous break.

"I joked that my most difficult job [in the army 1964–1965] in Germany was to drive my Porsche on the Autobahn."

Ralph Berlin, trainer 1968–1992: "Ask him where he was for the Tet Offensive. He was in a bathtub, hiding."

When Russell returned to the Steelers, he recalled that business manager Fran Fogarty gave him grief, believing Russell passed up the Reserve Unit duty in Western Pennsylvania that the Steelers had arranged for him. When he reported to training camp, the veterans he knew were all gone.

Russell: "The team had fallen apart."

Enter Chuck Noll.

The last half of Russell's 12-year career was history. Six of his seven Pro Bowls came under Noll.

Dan "Bad Rad" Radakovich, longtime linebacker coach elsewhere and Steelers assistant in 1971 and 1974–1977: "Watch a lot of film [of pre-1969 Steelers] . . . Andy Russell was impressive. Nobody else was. He should be in the Hall of Fame with Ham and Lambert. We had three of the smartest linebackers in the league. He was a great anticipator."

Upon retirement, Russell started a successful business career by toting the '74 highlight film overseas to show crowds. Soon after, he and Ray Mansfield were thrilling audiences across the Eastern Hemisphere.

RAY SEALS
Defensive End

Height: 6-3 • **Weight:** 296 • **College:** None • **Years with the Steelers:** 1994–1995 • **Birthplace:** Syracuse, New York • **Born:** June 17, 1965

Imagine his 1995: He anchored an end position for the Blitzburgh defense that advanced to Super Bowl XXX. He buried his cousin, best friend, and business partner, Jonny Gammage. He stemmed a wave of outrage.

"If I had said, 'Hey, just tear this city up,' they would have leveled the place," Seals told me for a *Pittsburgh Post-Gazette* story published Super Bowl Sunday. Instead, he attended a coroner's inquest and meetings with community leaders. He played and practiced through the torturous days for three months, then often answered the media by night. The word he spread: justice. "I wanted to make sure I didn't say the wrong thing. Justice in this case will do a lot of healing, even if it doesn't bring Jonny back."

Gammage, 31, was driving Seals' Jaguar through the South Hills of Pittsburgh the October 12, 1995, early morning he was killed. His hands were cuffed behind his back, his body face-down on the ground, five white policemen from the suburbs hovering around him—at least one, the coroner reported, responsible for compressing his chest. Three policemen involved in the traffic stop, handcuffing, and asphyxiation death were charged with involuntary manslaughter. Marches and civil unrest followed. *Civil* was the operative phrase. Seals, the son of a 30-year policeman, vowed justice, righteousness, change.

"Something weird happened [in] the Colts game," Seals said of the AFC championship game two weeks earlier, the wild Aaron Bailey end-zone finish. "The guy had the ball in his hands, but he couldn't close his arms. I thought, 'That's my cousin Jonny probably holding his arms open so we could go. That was our angel.' I go home, and I had calls from all over the country, six people, with the same thought. I think he's why we're at the point we are."

In football, Seals was a feel-good story. A doorman at the Hotel Syracuse, he played for the semipro Syracuse Express when Tampa Bay coach Ray Perkins took a flyer on him. Five years and 15.5 sacks later, he signed with the Steelers as a free agent—and brought his cousin with him to run their "60 Minute Men" clothing business. Seals got a trip to the desert for Super Bowl XXX and a city's attention at a time when Gammage's death constantly evoked the Rodney King beating of four years before.

An acquittal, a mistrial, and a hung jury ended the legal proceedings against the three officers. Although officials never admitted any guilt, the Pittsburgh Police Department later signed a Justice Department consent decree that instituted change.

Seals, after 15.5 sacks in two healthy Steelers years (a torn rotator cuff ended his 1996 season), finished his career in a 1997 reunion with Blitzburgh defensive coordinator Dom Capers in Carolina.

Gerald Williams, nose tackle and defensive end 1986–1994: "Played my last two years with Ray Seals. This was a guy, he was the Deion Sanders of the defensive line. He was not going to play run, but he was always rushing the quarterback. 'My contract says I need to get sacks; that's what I'm going to do.' Just as Deion boasted, 'They don't pay me to make tackles; they pay me to cover.'"

As Tom Donahoe, then the Steelers' director of football operations, put it at the time of Seals' 1995 incident: "When you think about it, how many people under the same circumstances would react the way he has . . . ? He's been able to deal with it, and he has dealt with it rationally and sensibly."

DONNIE SHELL
Safety

Height: 5-11 • **Weight:** 190 • **College:** South Carolina State • **Years with the Steelers:** 1974–1987 • **Birthplace:** Whitmire, South Carolina • **Born:** August 26, 1952

Talk about your defensive dichotomies. Donnie Shell the safety was also known as the Human Torpedo; Donnie Shell the Christian also was something of a football pacifist.

So in 1978, when he put out the indestructible Earl Campbell with a shot to the ribs that also separated the Houston Oilers star rookie from the football, Shell afterward went over to say he was sorry.

Ralph Berlin, trainer 1968–1992: "The one back there who didn't get enough credit was Donnie Shell. We're playing in Houston. Earl Campbell had, like, 100 yards in the first quarter. Donnie hit him and broke three of his ribs. We went on to win the game."

Neither the injury nor the yardage was quite that advanced, but the hit was one of the most memorable in Steelers history. Campbell had 41 yards with roughly one minute left in the first quarter, a pace for a 160-yard game. The brutish Campbell spun out from a Mike Wagner attempted arm tackle, and Shell pulverized him, sent him backward and flat on his back, and sent the football into the arms of rookie cornerback Ron Johnson. Campbell winced in pain as he was helped off the field. Soon after, he sent word to the press box to tell his mama, in attendance in the Astrodome, that he was all right. And, afterward, Shell apologized.

To think, Shell had contemplated retirement a year earlier.

First, go back to the Hall of Fame–rich class of 1974. After Lynn Swann, Jack Lambert, John Stallworth, and Mike Webster came a free-agent South Carolina State linebacker whom Bill Nunn lured through his connection with coach Willie Jeffries.

A regular scene through the mid-1980s: Donnie Shell blitzing and, with help from David Little, making life in the pocket relatively miserable for Cincinnati's Boomer Esiason in 1985. (Vincent J. Musi)

After two seasons as a special-teams standout, earning that Torpedo appellation, he was named by Chuck Noll as the first full-time special teams captain. Shell gave back that title in 1977 because he wanted to start, and Noll agreed that he "has to start somewhere for us." But after two games he had only a bruised knee and doubts about his future, contemplating whether to quit and put that newly earned master's degree in guidance and counseling to good use.

Suddenly, Wagner sustained a season-ending injury, and Shell commanded the platform. To open 1978, Shell was installed as a starter after two-time Pro Bowl safety Glen Edwards was traded to San Diego.

In the end, he didn't get to use the master's degree until 1988. He and John Stallworth used to ride to work together; after 14 seasons, they decided to ride into the sunset together. Shell's 51 interceptions were the NFL's most by a strong safety.

George Perles, defensive line coach–coordinator, 1972–1981: "He was great, he loved to press the tight end. That was a large part of his success. He was a good, straight-arrow, clean-cut guy. And that's a free agent."

Berlin: "Another one of Bill Nunn's guys. I'm sure he signed for the minimum [$10,000]. I'd let him use the Steelers phone so he could call his fiancée." Berlin overheard one conversation late in the 1974 season: Because of the NFL playoff money, Shell could get married.

Mike Wagner, safety 1971–1980: "Donnie was an extraordinary football player. A terrific athlete. Came up in the system. Spent his time with the special teams, certain situations, always did what he could for the team. We had a pretty good team when he came in 1974. A veteran team. I don't know why [the coaches opted to shake up a secondary with four Pro Bowlers in 1976], but obviously Donnie became a perennial All-Pro. Up for the Hall of Fame year after year [and a finalist in 2001]. He was all positive. He was probably a role model and mentor for a lot of people."

JERRY SHIPKEY
Linebacker–Fullback

Height: 6-1 • **Weight:** 213 • **College:** UCLA • **Years with the Steelers:** 1948–1952 • **Birthplace:** Fullerton, California • **Born:** October 31, 1925 • **Died:** November 28, 2009

Selected along with Elbie Nickel by Jock Sutherland in his final Steelers draft, adored by fans (maybe it was the California-beach kind of thing he had going on), Jerry Shipkey was a sturdy fullback at first and then a stout linebacker in the end.

Shipkey, picked to the 75th Anniversary Legends (pre-1970) team, actually quit on the club a couple of times, according to media accounts of the day. In training camp 1951, it was reported that he returned home to run his father's oil business (the *Pittsburgh Post-Gazette* later wrote that business was booming so well that he was "set for life"). He returned to football and ended both 1951 and 1952 as a Pro Bowler—the first in a long line of Steelers linebackers to receive that distinction.

There was another footnote in history: When Franco Harris in 1972 rumbled for 10 touchdowns, it was the most in a quarter century by a Steelers rookie since the eight in 1948 by . . . fullback Jerry Shipkey.

One last curiosity about that last Sutherland draft: Shipkey was a sixth-rounder, Nickel a 15th-rounder, and in between was an 11th-rounder who found glory elsewhere in football—future Notre Dame coach Ara Parseghian.

Dale Dodrill, nose guard–middle linebacker 1951–1959: "He was the only guy I ever knew who could do headstands on one arm. Great physical shape. He had a great physique. We played the 5–2 together."

Jack Butler, defensive back 1951–1959: "He played that left outside linebacker. He was a West Coaster. They're from a different country, those guys. He was a bodybuilder."

AARON SMITH
Defensive End

Height: 6-5 • **Weight:** 298 • **College:** Northern Colorado • **Years with the Steelers:** 1999–2011 • **Birthplace:** Colorado Springs, Colorado • **Born:** April 9, 1976

From the franchise that gave the pro-football world the Steel Curtain, Ernie Stautner, and rules changes designed to slow down their relentless rush, meet Aaron Smith: one of its greatest defensive linemen who may never receive his due credit.

He was officially elected to one Pro Bowl, he gathered enough sacks in a 13-year career to barely reach the top 10 in franchise history, but he could've achieved so much more were it not for a straitjacket of a zone-blitz, 3–4 defensive philosophy.

Dick LeBeau, defensive assistant 1992–1994 and defensive coordinator 1995–1996 and 2004– : "Our guys have a hard time in that [Pro Bowl category] because they go up against the 4–3 ends; our linebackers are going to be in that sack category. I always thought Aaron, Casey [Hampton], and Keis [Brett Keisel] should [compete] with the tackles for the all-star voting; those are the kinds of sack numbers they're going to get."

Smith had eight-sack seasons in 2001 and 2004, when he led the Steelers and made the Pro Bowl. But surgeries shortened his 2009–2011 seasons. Those came after the tumultuous 2008 when he, his wife, and family discovered that son Elijah, then 4, had leukemia. Treatment and care improved the boy to the point where his father could enjoy watching him play basketball. And Steelers Nation pitched in: a blood drive at Heinz Field brought enough donations to save 2,412 people.

James Farrior, inside linebacker 2002–2011: "A very underrated player. He's only made the Pro Bowl a couple of times. But the guy comes to work every day, works hard, never takes a day off. He's always in the right spot when he's out there playing the game. A guy you can always depend on. He's a great leader. Doesn't talk a whole lot. Lets his actions speak."

Would he almost double his sack total in a 4–3 instead of a 3–4?

Farrior: "Yes, he would. But I like him in our scheme."

LeBeau: "Aaron is one of the better defensive ends I've ever seen. He just never got blocked. Year after year, snap after snap, whatever assignment you gave him in the defense, he almost always took care of that and then went to help somebody else. At this level, against the people you're playing against, it's almost impossible to have the percentage of success that Aaron Smith had."

Smith: "I don't know if I ever really thought about [a legacy] too much. I guess just somebody who came to work, played hard every single down, was never scared to fight you on the field, never scared to compete, never gave up."

BILLY RAY SMITH
Defensive End

Height: 6-4 • **Weight:** 240 • **College:** Arkansas • **Years with the Steelers:** 1958–1960 • **Birthplace:** Augusta, Arkansas • **Born:** January 27, 1935 • **Died:** March 21, 2001

Here is another poster child of Steelers castoffs finding success elsewhere.

Funny, but quite a few of them helped to improve the Baltimore Colts in the mid-1960s.

Billy Ray Smith Sr. had just completed his rookie season with the Los Angeles Rams when coach Buddy Parker traded for him and rookie receiver Jimmy Orr. In a twist of irony, the acquisition came at the expense of quarterback Jack Kemp, who was cut—freeing him to lead the San Diego Chargers and Buffalo Bills to a handful of AFL championship games. Smith's presence was intended to free future Hall of Famer Ernie Stautner to move back to defensive tackle from defensive end, but Smith didn't exactly light up Pittsburgh. He reputedly didn't cavort with quarterback Bobby Layne, a fact that caused a rift. So at the January NFL meetings in 1961, Smith was shipped to Baltimore for a backup safety named Jackie Simpson, who never did much in his two Steelers seasons, 1961 and 1962.

Smith was moved to defensive tackle in Baltimore, where he teamed with fellow ex-Steeler Lou Michaels, Fred Miller, and Bubba Smith in creating a formidable Colts front four. Orr, who joined Smith in Baltimore after the July 1961 trade for Big Daddy Lipscomb, became a top target for yet another ex-Steeler, Johnny Unitas: Orr had 97 catches with the Steelers and 303 with the Colts—50 for touchdowns. Through the mid-1960s, the Colts went 57-15-3, won four division titles, and won the 1968 NFL championship before losing Super Bowl III to Joe Namath and the New York Jets.

Frank Varrichione, offensive tackle and teammate: "Billy Ray Smith was there when I was there. He ended up traded to the Colts, where he became a heck of a ballplayer. He was a good player. I have no idea why he was traded. Buddy Parker felt there was somebody ready to take his place. That's why I was traded. I thought I found a home the six years I was [in Pittsburgh], went to the Pro Bowl four times. Thought maybe I'd finish my career there. I got a call from Buddy Parker informing me that he traded me. But he explained, 'Frank, I didn't want to let you go, but I needed a placekicker and a defensive end, and they offered Lou Michaels.' . . . The following year, [the Rams beat the Steelers in LA's Memorial Coliseum], and they gave me the game ball."

DAVE SMITH
Wide Receiver

Height: 6-2 • **Weight:** 205 • **College:** Waynesburg, Indiana (Pennsylvania) • **Years with the Steelers:** 1970–1972 • **Birthplace:** New York City • **Born:** May 18, 1947

One moment, toward the end of the franchise's first 40 years of football follies, stands out. Chuck Noll, the coach who advised his charges to act like they've been in the end zone before, watched perhaps the worst and final embarrassing foible of his lengthy administration. Problem was, millions of Americans watched it on *Monday Night Football*, too.

The day after the Pirates won the 1971 World Series, wide receiver Dave Smith found himself all alone for the final few yards of an apparent 49-yard touchdown strike from Terry Bradshaw that night in Kansas City. He raised the ball aloft in his left hand, prematurely celebrating a touchdown. Three yards later, it slipped from his grasp—*at the two-yard line.* The ball bounded into the end zone, where Smith slipped trying to recapture his footing and give chase. Fellow receiver Jon Staggers likewise came in pursuit. The ball skittered through the end zone.

Touchback, Kansas City ball.

"It's out of 'Ripley's Believe It or Not,'" Bradshaw remarked later.

Smith flashed across the Steelers firmament quickly: 30 catches as a rookie eighth-round draft choice in 1970, then 47 catches for sixth in AFC receptions in that same 1971. After such success, he sought to renegotiate the third year of his contract. Without such satisfaction, he requested a trade. In late October 1972, he was accommodated.

This was a player who stayed so late doing a Myron Cope postgame interview that he missed the team bus; Cope jammed him, in full uniform and pads, into a cab bound for the airport to catch up. This was a player the *Pittsburgh Press* once described as blowing kisses to booing fans.

"Smith listened intently to his own drummer and left town with his ever-present candor intact," the *Press'* Phil Musick wrote.

Mike Wagner, safety 1971–1980: "It was a Monday night game. It was also the last time we wore our white-on-white uniforms. Which I liked. But the players didn't like the pants. They thought they were too stretchy.

"We've all done something. It's unfortunate Dave had that. A lot of people say to me about giving that hit on Mike Barber in that [1978 AFC] championship game. That's just a memory in the public's mind. Dave was a great athlete [he played basketball at IUP, too], and he was good enough to play on Chuck Noll's team while we were rebuilding. Hey, we've had receivers since then who have done worse." Plaxico Burress, remember, spiked it in the middle of the field and lost the ball to Jacksonville in 2000.

JOHN STALLWORTH AND LYNN SWANN

JOHN STALLWORTH
Wide Receiver

Height: 6-2 • **Weight:** 191 • **College:** Alabama A&M • **Years with the Steelers:** 1974–1987 • **Birthplace:** Tuscaloosa, Alabama • **Born:** July 15, 1952

LYNN SWANN
Wide Receiver

Height: 5-10½ • **Weight:** 178 • **College:** USC • **Years with the Steelers:** 1974–1982 • **Birthplace:** Alcoa, Tennessee • **Born:** March 7, 1952

The '70s were all about duos. Newman had Redford. Cheech had Chong. Peaches had Herb.

Swann had Stallworth. And Stallworth had Swann.

Lynn Swann focuses on an incoming pass in a 1981 game with the New York Jets. (Bill Amatucci)

The Steelers had both. The Hall of Fame has both.

Two routes to greatness, converging together yet separately.

Dick Hoak, running backs coach 1972–2006: "Fans always said we didn't throw enough to the backs. We got Lynn Swann and John Stallworth. Which one don't you want us to throw it to, so we can throw it to a back?"

Joe Gordon, publicity director and vice president, 1969–1998: "I don't know if any team ever had two receivers that good at the same time, who could make the big play, the great catches." Crazylegs Hirsch and Tom Fears of the 1949–1956 Los Angeles Rams, with eye-popping statistics for their generation, are both in the Hall of Fame together. After that . . .

Gary Dunn, defensive lineman 1977–1987: "They were two different guys, absolutely. But both were great."

They came in the same 1974 Steelers draft that was a one-way ticket to Canton. Swann was all West Coast, a television star, a diminutive jewel in John McKay's dazzling USC offense, a kid who pursued a real-estate license and planned his postfootball career. Stallworth was Deep South, from tiny Alabama A&M where the Steelers hid his game film and 40-yard dash time, a lanky and introspective fellow.

They reported to a running team, in the midst of a player's strike, and each ran his own route. The shorter one ran more with more deliberate speed, more flash, more pomp, and retired at age 30. The taller one loped, struggled through injuries, maintained a low profile, and matured in his 30s.

Larry Brown, tight end–offensive tackle 1971–1984: "It's hard for two individuals—even twins, I would guess—to progress and all be at the same place at the same time [in growth].

For whatever reason, these were extraordinary players, John and Lynn. One guy might have gotten an opportunity before another guy. And one may have [blossomed] before the other. It doesn't mean you're confident more with the other person, but there's a little more equilibrium, maybe. Each one of them, which you've got to give them credit for, achieved his potential . . . positioned at the top of their game as receivers. And they took advantage of making big plays. Balls that would have gone incomplete, they made receptions on. Each of those guys made plays, but not always in the same game."

Similar, but different.

Stars competing for attention, not so much from the public but from Terry Bradshaw.

John Stallworth: "That bond . . . it was there even when we were really hot and heavy, trying to catch more passes than the other. Looking back, it was kind of comical. The guys we played with [noticed], but I don't think either one of us—Lynn or myself—knew we were that obvious. We thought we were being discreet. And nobody was more conscious of it than Bradshaw himself. He played it well."

Bradshaw played it to four diamond rings and two Super Bowl MVPs, with Swann and Stallworth catching 439 of his 627 yards and five of his six touchdowns in those games.

Stallworth: "I think it was good not only for Lynn and I; it was good for the Steelers that we were competing. We both were on the field at the same time. Bradshaw's maturity, the rule changes [backing off bump-and-run cornerbacks], Swann and I developing—all that prompted us to throw the ball a little more than we had in the past."

Go back to the beginning and how they arrived in the same magnificent 1974 draft, and you begin to trace the career arcs—Swann from the right side of the offensive formation, Stallworth from the left.

Different duos danced in Chuck Noll's mind entering the 1974 first round. The coaches and scouting staff agreed on tight ends, so Colorado's J. V. Cain and Oklahoma State's Reuben Gant were the original objects of their affection. Both were gone by the No. 21 selection. Noll had grown enamored of Swann at the Senior Bowl, watching him make thudding blocks in practice and make aerial-trapeze receptions. So . . . the coach whittled his desires to Swann and Michigan State tight end Paul Seals.

See how luck enters into it more than science?

After Swann, the Steelers' draft war room rolled the dice: Stallworth or Jack Lambert?

V. Tim Rooney, Steelers scout at the time and later Detroit's and the Giants' pro personnel director: "There was even some discussion in the room about taking Stallworth second. As I remember it, in the development stages . . . , Bill Nunn was reasonably assured that Stallworth would be there in the fourth. And he liked Stallworth as much as anybody. A lot of teams didn't think Stallworth ran a good 40. Nunn did. He had it in his back pocket."

The "Stashing Stallworth" story: Nunn stood one Alabama day among a group of scouts at a Stallworth 40-yard dash. It didn't go too well. Nunn feigned illness, stuck around . . . and then told Stallworth they were driving to a Huntsville high school to run on a smoother track.

Stallworth: "I didn't know anything about the better time or the stashing until [later]."

Nunn: "The film we had on him, we held that, too."

Not only did Nunn keep Stallworth's faster 40 time tucked away; he never returned a one-game highlight film that Alabama A&M had loaned him.

Thus the Steelers nabbed Lambert with the 46th selection, sat impatiently through a third round in which they earlier traded that pick, and exhaled deeply upon snagging Stallworth in the fourth round. At 82nd overall. His number. (Don't forget, in the fifth round, at 125th, came Mike Webster.)

V. Tim Rooney: "If [Nunn] didn't do that . . . , the whole draft changes. 'Cause we don't take Lambert, and we don't end up getting both [him *and* Stallworth]."

Stallworth: "Bill never came to me and said, 'John, prior to the draft, we hid all your information.' It turned out to be ingenious, though. I'm glad he did. Four Super Bowls. Relationships with folks in Western Pennsylvania. I'm pleased as could be that he did that."

The two new receivers met at an orientation camp, though Swann was unsigned and unable to participate. Each went on to a strong preseason, catching passes from Joe Gilliam. Still, the veterans were on strike and absent.

Stallworth: "Lionel Taylor, our receivers coach, would tell us after a film session, 'Don't get too excited. You won't be able to do that when Mel Blount gets here.' He brought you back to reality.

"But Lynn and I formed a bond during that time. It was rookies versus vets. It was he and I versus Ron Shanklin and Frank Lewis. When they got there [after the strike], they'd start the game—they were the veterans, after all. And we played the second quarter. And we played the last quarter. That started in training camp and went on during the season. As it turned out, we'd run the ball in the first quarter and throw in the second. We'd run it in the third, and we'd throw in the fourth. I don't think Ron and Frank were too excited about it."

John Stallworth tries to shed future coach and broadcaster Herman Edwards in this 1979 Steelers loss at Philadelphia's Veterans Stadium. The Steelers go on to lose only three of their next 14 games as Stallworth and Company lead them to their fourth Super Bowl triumph in six seasons, his long touchdown catch helping to beat the Los Angeles Rams in the Rose Bowl. (Temple Urban Archives)

Another aspect of that 1974 fall was Stallworth's sight. A longtime glasses wearer, he had difficulties on overcast football days—far more of a problem in Pittsburgh than in Alabama. Sporting a new pair of specs at practice one day, Stallworth's vision caused Noll to scrunch up his face in confusion.

Stallworth: "Chuck walks up to me, 'I didn't know you wore glasses. Do you wear them in the game?' 'No.' 'Well, maybe you ought to wear contacts.' It was like a new day for me in the games, whether it was sunny or overcast. I could actually see the quarterback throwing the ball. Life was a lot easier."

The next season, Swann took off. His 11 touchdowns led the league. He started slightly more often and caught 49 passes to 20 for Stallworth. In the postseason, Swann launched himself into celebrity.

Swann's four catches for 161 yards, along with a record average of 40, earned him not only Super Bowl X MVP, but a berth in highlight-reel history. It wasn't only that 53-yard, juggling, falling wonder against Dallas' Mark Washington, on third down from the Pittsburgh 10. It wasn't only that 64-yard, graceful, over-the-shoulder catch for the touchdown that proved to be the winning difference. No, perhaps his best reception of a remarkable day might have been a 32-yarder down the right sideline, where his body seemed to hover out of bounds but he somehow stayed in play.

Tom Beasley, defensive lineman 1978–1983: "Lynn just had that knack of making acrobatic catches. So athletic. Had great balance. He just . . . made it look easy. And it obviously isn't."

Brown: "So a guy like Swann, who right away has a little more early success, attracts more attention. [Defenses] were accounting more for him. At some point, they had to account for both of them. We had a couple of Super Bowls where both of those guys made contributions and huge catches, in each one of those games."

To open 1976, Oakland's George "The Hitman" Atkinson turned out the lights on Swann with a forearm to the head of a receiver who wasn't even the target on the play. This Raiders safety gave Swann a concussion, prompting Noll to comment afterward about a "criminal element." Atkinson then brought a lawsuit against Noll and the Steelers, throwing the 1977 camp asunder.

Swann upon the defendants' victory: "Now that we have won the case, my reaction is complete ecstasy. It's not only a victory for the Steelers; . . . it's a victory for football. They have set some kind of limitation on unnecessary violence. Had the verdict come out in favor of George, it would have been tantamount to saying a defensive back or some other ballplayer can commit violent acts of that nature, then be rewarded by winning a lawsuit of $2 million." He then left reporters to attend a team meeting—while wearing a white Raiders T-shirt jokingly given him by tackle Gordon Gravelle.

Stallworth later to reporters: "Lynn is quotable. He's flamboyant. He always makes good print. Who wants to write about me? I'm a guy who stays home on Friday and Saturday nights to watch television . . . 'Perry Mason.'"

That 1977 season was the beginning of the Swann-Stallworth syncopated surge. The acrobat had 50 catches. The lanky guy had 44. The duo started to show its dynamic. They followed with 61 and 41 for a combined 20 touchdowns in 1978. Stallworth collected 113 yards in receptions in the first half against Dallas in Super Bowl XIII, but cramps pinned him to the sidelines through a vise-grip second half. This was an instance where Swann's other attributes shined: his savvy.

Stallworth: "My last game against the Dallas Cowboys, where I got the cramps and didn't play in the second half, Lynn saw something in the course of preparation that the Cowboys were doing. He thought we could fake that slant-in and then go by them. He convinced the coaches and we put that in, and we called it an I-takeoff. It was his suggestion. Then, in the game, we get down close and Bradshaw calls it, but he calls it to me [for their 28-yard opening touchdown]. . . . That probably didn't make him the happiest guy in the world. Later on in the game, in the fourth quarter, he calls that pattern for Lynn—and he catches it for a touchdown" that proved to be the winning points. Swann finished with seven receptions for 124 yards in that Super Bowl.

Swann: "I have retired." That was July 31, 1979.

He reported to camp 10 days later.

Holdouts, concussions, the brutality of the game all began to compile for him.

The future Hall of Famers had 41 and 70 catches in that 1979 season, Swann and Stallworth. The acrobat had five catches for 79 yards against the Rams in Super Bowl XIV, but the lanky one ruled the day with three catches for 121 yards and the game-sealing touchdown.

Stallworth: "To me, that's what you dream about—in the biggest games of the year, making the big catch to put your team ahead."

His dreams weren't close to realized, though. Stallworth played eight more seasons. Swann retired after 1982. Paths diverged again.

Dunn: "Stallworth made a couple of great catches over his head. So many times over on the sideline, Bradshaw would go back to pass . . . and Chuck would scream, 'Don't throw it, don't throw it.' And out through the middle comes Swann through two guys for a 30-yard gain, and Chuck goes, 'That-a-way.'"

Mike Wagner, safety 1971–1980: "If you didn't appreciate watching Johnny Stallworth working against Mel Blount every day. . . . He worked soooo hard. He became a great football player with his toughness and determination. He was even a better blocker. I can still remember him throwing key blocks for Franco in really big games. A lot of receivers didn't block in those days. A guy who wasn't expected to do a whole lot, didn't get a lot of hoopla, but quietly put together a Hall of Fame career."

Swann worked for more than a decade on ABC television announcing football, Olympics, and more. He toiled as a motivational speaker, board member, and businessman. He ran for governor of Pennsylvania. He became an owner of an Arena League football team.

Stallworth quietly retired to Alabama and started a company in software. He made millions. He became a minority owner of his old team. Yes, the employee became one of the employers.

Stallworth: "The first time I saw Joe Greene after the deal was done . . . , he referred to me as 'Boss.'"

Funny how, and where, paths come to an end.

ERNIE STAUTNER
Defensive Tackle

Height: 6-1 • **Weight:** 230 • **College:** Boston College • **Years with the Steelers:** 1950–1963 • **Birthplace:** Prinzing-by-Cham, Bavaria • **Born:** April 20, 1925 • **Died:** February 16, 2006

Before he became a decorated coach with the Doomsday Defense and Dallas Cowboys, Ernie Stautner was a blood-splattered, mud-sheathed trench mauler. He was a brute in a brutal game. He was, in short, a defensive lineman's defensive lineman.

Then again, most every other position on the field respected him immensely, too.

Andy Russell, outside linebacker 1963, 1966–1976: "The toughest Steeler who ever played the game. *Ever played the game.*"

Chuck Cherundolo, a former Steelers center who oversaw Stautner during his 1947–1961 Steelers coaching career: "He was tough. If you told him to break a wall down, he'd knock it down. God, he was tough."

Frank Varrichione, a Pro Bowl tackle who as a rookie played directly beside right-guard Stautner in a brief Stautner offensive experiment: "The guys that kept that defense together were Jack Butler and Ernie Stautner. Ernie was a hard-nosed guy. In fact, he would miss the first two weeks of the training camp because he owned a drive-in theater in Lake Placid, New York. He said the season would end Labor Day, so he would stay away the first few weeks. But he was always in great shape. He came to training camp, put the pads on, and started scrimmaging right away. Didn't bother him at all. One of the strongest men in the league."

Jack Butler, a defensive teammate throughout his 1951–1959 career: "Ernie was all gung-ho. He was strong. You'd be surprised by Ernie. Everything you read about the game today, they're 6-3, 6-4, 300 pounds. Ernie was no bigger than I was. I may have been taller; I'm not sure. He'd come to camp 230. In the season, I bet he'd play at 215, 220. He wasn't big. But he was strong for his size. He was quick off the ball, and he was a fireball every down."

He loafed at the popular watering hole called Dante's in Brentwood. Once, he told former Steelers scout turned *Pittsburgh Press* sports writer Pat Livingston that Pittsburgh fans had no right to boo a player the stature of Bobby Layne. As Livingston recalled in a 1983 column, Stautner called Pittsburghers "[expletive] fans," and the quote made the public prints. As a joke, Layne organized a Steelers movement so the rest of the players would lay back and let the criticizing captain run onto Forbes Field alone for the next game—a variation of Jerome Bettis' Super Bowl XL homecoming 40 years later.

The nationally syndicated *Parade Magazine* in 1961 asked Stautner, with coauthor Myron Cope of Pittsburgh fame, to write an article about the brutality of the NFL. They entitled it "Stop Short of Murder": "Nine years ago, when I was too brash to know better, I all but fractured a quarterback's jaw. As Tom Landry of the Giants drew back to pass, I whacked him across the jaw with an elbow. All I did was bloody his face and maybe loosen a few teeth, but the other players figured it wasn't necessary. . . . I was repaid in cracked ribs." In the piece, they wrote about how wrapped hands became weapons for NFL linemen.

Pat Rooney Sr., ball boy and later ticket salesman for his father's franchise: "I remember there was one rookie asking, 'How do you make this team?' Somebody told him, 'You pick a fight with the toughest guy.' He not only didn't make the team; he got the crap beat out of him by Stautner."

Russell, who started with him in 1963 as a wide-eyed rookie: "He was ferocious. I don't mean he would win a fight in the

Hall of Fame defensive tackle Ernie Stautner (1950–1963) drags down a Philadelphia running back by the back of his pants. Stautner was a Pro Bowl selection nine of his 14 Steelers seasons. (Temple Urban Archives)

parking lot—Joe Greene would kill him. But the toughest mentally. Forbes Field one game, Ernie came in the huddle and he's broken his thumb all the way back. Then I looked . . . he's got a compound fracture of the thumb, and he's not showing it to anybody. [He tucked in his thumb] and goes, 'What's the defense?' I've never seen a bone in the huddle." So Stautner taped it, made a mitt out of it, and resumed playing. "And I'm thinking, 'This is the NFL?'"

Varrichione, a rookie Pro Bowler in 1955 and a teammate before being traded to the Los Angeles Rams in early 1961: "I knew Ernie would make a career coach. Matter of fact, when I was with the Rams, there was some talk about Ernie becoming a head coach. Dan Reeves, the owner of the Rams, called me in his office and asked me about Ernie. I didn't have enough good things to say about Ernie, what a ballplayer he was and what a leader he is. Sometime at the end, he asked me, 'I heard he's a stutterer.' I said, 'Only a bit, but it was never a problem—that would never stop him from communicating his point.' I think that stopped him from getting a head coaching job."

JUSTIN STRZELCZYK
Offensive Tackle–Guard

Height: 6 6 • **Weight:** 301 • **College:** Maine • **Years with the Steelers:** 1990–1998 • **Birthplace:** Seneca, New York • **Born:** August 18, 1968 • **Died:** September 30, 2004

This affable, hockey-playing, guitar-strumming, bearded bear of a man has been transformed into a symbol of sorts.

Justin Strzelczyk, known as Jugs or Strells, in death joined former line mates Mike Webster and Terry Long in the scientific realm: ex-players found to have signs of chronic traumatic encephalopathy (CTE) in their damaged brains before they were 51. Strzelczyk was the youngest of the group at 36.

It was a tragic end. Strzelczyk, according to friends, appeared to suffer a psychotic episode. He even suspected he had bipolar disorder, his complicated post-NFL life felt as if it was closing in on him.

Strzelczyk believed demons were pouring through a hole in the roof of his home. He carried $2,800 in cash with him on a late-night trip from Pittsburgh to Buffalo but bypassed his hometown and kept heading east on America's deadliest toll road, the New York State Thruway, also known as Interstate 90. He offered cash and a crucifix to people. He told one mother to take her children to higher ground. He sped his pickup truck up to 100 miles per hour, disregarding the state-police cruiser chasing him, and switched into the other lanes—heading the wrong way, speeding east into westbound traffic. Ultimately, his vehicle collided with a tractor trailer.

He became a medical footnote after nine years, 75 starts, 133 games of reliability and levity as a lineman, teammate, friend.

John Jackson, offensive tackle 1988–1997: "Strells was a little different. I remember once at training camp . . . , Strzelczyk was too lazy to go back to the dorm. He had to mail a package. Dermontti Dawson picks up a worm and says, 'Listen, Jugs, I'll give you 20 bucks if you eat this worm.' He takes the worm, dirt and all, and swallows it whole. He says, 'Dirt, I want my 20.' He says, 'You got it when we go back to the locker room.' I was like, 'Wow, what you'd do for $20?' That's my worm story."

And the 20? "He went to the post office. He mailed the package with it."

Bubby Brister, quarterback 1986–1992: "Big mountain man with the beard and the motorcycle."

Gerald Williams, nose tackle–defensive end, 1986–1994: "Jugs stories that I can tell you? Put it like this: He was the epitome of what most defensive linemen think of offensive linemen. Nasty. . . . What I mean by nasty, he played the game that way. As far as the rules, played right up to the line. There wasn't anywhere where you can say he went over the line, but he was always up *to* the line."

J. T. THOMAS
Cornerback–Safety

Height: 6-2 • **Weight:** 196 • **College:** Florida State • **Years with the Steelers:** 1973–1981 • **Birthplace:** Macon, Georgia • **Born:** April 22, 1951

For four years, he was *the other guy.* He was the cornerback on that huge island opposite Mel Blount, future Hall of Famer.

Then he was sidelined for a season by a disorder, a victim of his own blood. He lost his starting job at left cornerback to a hotshot kid named Ron Johnson—the first rookie corner to start in a Super Bowl (XIII)—then later to a future judge, Dwayne Woodruff.

A team guy, J. T. Thomas moved to free safety upon his return in 1979. His career was spent in relative obscurity.

John Banaszak, defensive lineman 1975–1981: "J. T. is a guy who, because of a serious health issue, missed an entire

In 1980, J. T. Thomas plays cornerback in goggles, a look he borrowed from a fellow defensive mate known by his initials, defensive end L. C. Greenwood. (Bill Amatucci)

Super Bowl year. I can remember going from a Super Bowl [XIII] party with J. T. Thomas, with him saying, 'I just can't wait to get back.' He was still a part of that team. A very, very important part of that team."

Around the time of Super Bowl XIII, Thomas received a specialist's permission to launch his comeback for the 1979 season from the disorder then known as Boeck's sarcoid—today it's simply called sarcoidosis. He was first diagnosed with the disorder five years earlier, but doctors never advised him until 1978 to take a hiatus and recover. While on prescription medication, Thomas jogged, played racquetball, and stayed glued to the Steelers.

In 1979 he started for an injured Johnson at his old cornerback spot for part of the season, for an ailing Wagner at safety the rest. After his triumphant return, Thomas helped the Steelers overcome Houston—yet again—in the AFC championship game to reach Super Bowl XIV after he was absent the year before. He told reporters afterward: "There are some things you never get tired of tasting: pecan pie, chitterlings, collard greens, and going to the Super Bowl all taste the same, no matter how many times you taste them."

Here's a morsel to savor about Thomas: In his eight seasons on the Steelers' field, he never missed a game.

Mike Wagner, safety 1971–1980 and someone whom Thomas replaced at the position in 1979 after Wagner's hip surgery: "J. T. Thomas wanted to play man every play. Like quarterbacks and passing. Me, with my skinny legs, I wanted to play zone every play."

Joe Walton, an assistant coach who competed against the Steelers with the New York Giants and Washington Redskins: "Mel was in a class by himself. But I always thought J. T. Thomas was pretty damn good."

Banaszak: "He had to be, because of Mel. 'They're not going to throw Mel Blount's way. I had better be at my best.' And that made him a very good football player."

Thomas was traded to Denver during 1982 training camp, to clear the free safety spot for another converted cornerback: the same Johnson who replaced him in 1978.

TUNCH-N-WOLF

TUNCH ILKIN
Offensive Tackle–Guard–Center

Height: 6-3 • **Weight:** 263 • **College:** Indiana State • **Years with the Steelers:** 1980–1992 • **Birthplace:** Istanbul, Turkey • **Born:** September 23, 1957

CRAIG WOLFLEY
Guard–Tackle

Height: 6-1 • **Weight:** 265 • **College:** Syracuse • **Years with the Steelers:** 1980–1989 • **Birthplace:** Buffalo, New York • **Born:** May 19, 1958

They are a combo platter, a perpetual pair, less side by side than attached at the hip. Have been since 1980, when they arrived in Pittsburgh back to back: Craig Wolfley in the fifth round, Tunch Ilkin in the sixth.

Tunch Ilkin in 1984. (Bill Amatucci)

Craig Wolfley in 1981. (Bill Amatucci)

Rodney Carter, running back 1987–1989: "Him and Wolf, they were like partners back then. I know they're still the dynamic duo."

They played shoulder to shoulder in 1984, though for most of their Steelers years Wolfley aligned at left guard, next to Mike Webster or Dermontti Dawson, and Ilkin positioned at right tackle alongside Terry Long.

Wolfley remembered an early-season game against the Los Angeles Rams and defensive end Reggie Doss. The rusher one time performed a game/twist with a defensive line mate and sped past Ilkin, who was supposed to chip him and slow him down. Instead, a full-speed Doss "earholded" Wolfley and pushed him, right to left, through Ilkin's view and to the opposite sideline. It resembled something out of a cartoon: the character getting yanked off the stage. Back in the huddle, Webster teased Wolfley, "I didn't know you could run sideways that fast."

Wolfley: "I was hot. I yelled at Tunch, 'Do you think you could take a little off him?'"

They were part of "The Taping Club," offensive linemen—later joined by nose tackle Gary Dunn—who used two-sided tape to hold their jerseys tight so defensive linemen couldn't grab. Then came a slick addition. . . .

Wolfley: "It was mostly a cooking accident. Cooking omelets for the guys, [somebody] maybe got a little Pam spray on the jerseys. Then Chuck [Noll found out]; he was hacked off."

Ilkin: "He caught Ray Pinney doing it. 'What are you doing? We don't have to cheat. We are the Pittsburgh Steelers.'" Stallworth began blaming any of his drops on the linemen, whose cooking spray would rub off on his hands when he patted them on the back. If a ball squirted through his fingertips, he would yell on the field, "Oh, Ray!"

Dermontti Dawson, guard (alongside Ilkin for five starts in 1988) and center 1988–2000: "Tunch-n-Wolf, they were always together. Families always doing things together. They were the best of friends. Just two funny guys. Lots of people used to look at Tunch and say, 'He plays tackle?' He had those hands, those gloves on; he had them taped up. He just looked like a rock-'em-sock-'em robot, the way he punched guys. Tunch wasn't that big. But he was one of the best right tackles, 'cause he had a heck of a right punch on him. And Craig was the brawler, one of those guys you liked to have on your team 'cause he fought you tooth and nail every play. They have not changed whatsoever."

Ilkin went to two Pro Bowls. Wolfley left for Minnesota for two seasons, 1990 and 1991. Ilkin even went to the same NFC division, playing one game for Green Bay in 1993.

Upon retirement, they gravitated together, naturally. They did Pittsburgh television together; they did radio shows. Ilkin segued into the Steelers game-day radio booth in the mid-1990s, and by 2002 they were reunited on the radio—Ilkin in the game booth, Wolfley on the sideline, chattering away and having a blast the same as always.

JOHNNY UNITAS
Quarterback

Height: 6-1 • **Weight:** 194 • **College:** Louisville • **Years with the Steelers:** 0 (1955 training camp) • **Birthplace:** Pittsburgh • **Born:** May 7, 1933 • **Died:** September 11, 2002 **Elected to Hall of Fame:** 1979

Johnny U. was perhaps the biggest fish that got away, and, oh, the tales he spawned.

Those Same Old Steelers of the first 40 franchise seasons, the ones who traded off draft picks or failed to keep future stars or just couldn't avoid becoming football follies, they were the kings of the coulda-beens for too long.

They drafted Gary Glick the Bonus Pick in 1956 when they could've nabbed Lenny Moore. They drafted Len Dawson in 1957 over the fellow taken by Cleveland on the next pick, Jim Brown. (One reason: Brown was wholly unimpressive when he came to Pittsburgh, witness his 52 yards on 14 carries in a loss to Pitt two months earlier.) Of course, it was just the Steelers' luck back then that Dawson would become a Hall of Famer elsewhere, too.

Still, the popular Pittsburgh refrain of the late 1950s and early 1960s was "We coulda had a backfield of Lenny Moore, Jim Brown, and Johnny Unitas."

They had Unitas once, too. In the ninth round of the 1955 draft, with the 102nd overall pick, the hometown Steelers selected the buzz-cut kid from Brookline and St. Justin's High. They knew him well. He was the first-team all-Catholic League quarterback in Pittsburgh in 1949; second-team was North Catholic's Dan Rooney.

So the club went to training camp at St. Bonaventure College. The Steelers had Jim Finks, St. Bonaventure product Ted Marchibroda, and a part-time punter named Vic Eaton already playing quarterback. Unitas served as a camp rent-an-arm.

Apparently at the St. Bonaventure College training camp, Johnny Unitas was given No. 14 and no chance to make the Steelers. He later made No. 19 famous in Baltimore. (Courtesy of the Pittsburgh Steelers)

Chuck Cherundolo, a defensive coach at the time: "We always had two quarterbacks. You weren't going to keep him."

The Chief's youngest three boys—and others—considered it a shameless conspiracy perpetrated by coach Walt Kiesling and staff: Unitas never had a chance.

Pat Rooney Sr., a ball boy at that camp and one of the Chief's youngest sons along with John, his twin: "John, Tim, and myself, we'd catch passes from all of them. The fix was in for the vets [over] rookies. They'd make the vets look good and the rookies look like [spit]. So Unitas didn't get many reps. Marchibroda had the in."

Frank Varrichione, an offensive tackle who was the Steelers' first-round pick of the 1955 draft when Unitas came in the sixth round: "Oh sure, I remember. He wasn't there very long. They looked at him for a couple of weeks and let him go. They already had their mind made up on Jimmy Finks and Ted Marchibroda."

Pat Rooney Sr.: "The Chief was at a racetrack somewhere. Tim is the one who wrote Dad that famous letter, 'Keis is going to cut this guy, and he's way better.'"

Tim Rooney Sr., a college freshman at the time working camp with his younger brothers, the twins: "Oh, God, Unitas. I was in camp with Unitas. We were at St. Thomas College playing the Packers. I wrote my father a 22-page letter on Unitas. It was 11 pieces of paper, but I wrote the letter on both sides of the paper. I wrote about how good Unitas was, nobody was running for passes for him in practice. . . . There were other circumstances with Unitas: Marchibroda was our first pick [two years earlier]. I think they were a little afraid of our first pick getting run out for a local guy. My father opened it up and read the letter. He threw it in the wastepaper basket, 'That fresh punk.'"

Unitas recounted in his biography his affection for the Rooneys. He related a story about encouraging words from the Chief while driving down a road—each side suggested it was a different locale. To this day, brothers John and Dan debate over who was behind the wheel when this conversation took place.

Tim Rooney Sr.: "There was no doubt it was my brother John. How my brother Dan tried to take that story over is beyond me. [Laughs.] I guess that's what happens when you're in a position of authority."

Art Rooney Jr., picking up the tale: "They were going down West Liberty Avenue or something, to or from a funeral. John was driving, and the Chief was in the shotgun seat, and Big Kies was in the back. Chief had the window down, smoking and spitting. They drove to a stoplight. [John Rooney and Unitas waved and exchanged salutations.] Chief said, 'Who is that?' 'That's Johnny Unitas.' Chief said, 'Catch up to him.' At the next stoplight, the Chief yells through the window, 'John?' 'Yes, Mr. Rooney?' 'You hang in there. You'll be the greatest player who ever lived.'"

The rest is high-tops history.

Unitas played for the Bloomfield Rams semipro team in the Italian section of Pittsburgh, oil sprinkled on their field to prevent dust from rising (hence the high-tops became standard issue). Chuck "Bear" Rogers was the coach, general manager, and previous quarterback. He paid the local hero $6 a game to play quarterback, and the scrawny kid propelled them to a championship. Rogers wrote a letter to the Baltimore Colts asking for a tryout for one of his defensive linemen, Jim Deglau of Turtle Creek, Pennsylvania, and Wake Forest. The tale spun from there: Colts General Manager Don Kellett made an 80-cent call to Rogers, "Do you know a guy named Unitas from Pittsburgh?" Rogers responded, "Yeah, he's playing with us." Not for much longer, he wasn't.

Dale Dodrill, nose guard–middle linebacker 1951–1959: [laughs] "Everybody remembers him. No, he didn't look good in camp. That's why. A lot of coaches didn't understand his ability. He was very nonchalant. Nothing really riled him up. We never really had a good scrimmage unless a fight broke out. The coaches would say, 'Okay, break it up.' Johnny would be walking around in his own little circle; he wasn't worried about it. He never showed his potential, or maybe they never gave him a chance. We used to tell [Colts quarterback George] Shaw, 'You're going to roll out one time too many.' Sure enough, he did. That did him under. If George Shaw never got hurt, maybe you never would've heard of Johnny Unitas. That's when he went in and became a star."

Andy Russell, a linebacker who faced Unitas and Dawson often through the 1960s and early 1970s: "You heard about it constantly from fans and even the media."

Tim Rooney Sr.: "Johnny, we rooted for him like he was one of us. It did become a little embarrassing when he became so unbelievably good."

Pat Rooney Sr., in the army in 1962 and visiting Jacksonville for an exhibition between the Colts and Steelers: "I went under the stands, and Unitas was warming up there. He buzzed a pass right past my ear. 'Aren't you going to say hello to me?' He remembered me, which I never thought he would."

And bitter Steelers fans always remembered Unitas . . . at least for the next decade and a half, anyway, until a blond named Terry Bradshaw began to let them savor glory of their own.

FRANK VARRICHIONE
Offensive Tackle

Height: 6-1 • **Weight:** 234 • **College:** Notre Dame • **Years with the Steelers:** 1955–1960 • **Birthplace:** Natick, Massachusetts • **Born:** January 14, 1932

His name was raised anew in January 2011: When Maurkice Pouncey was named to the Pro Bowl, who was the previous Steelers rookie offensive lineman to receive such an honor? Frank Varrichione, 1955.

Varrichione (pronounced VERR-ick-ee-own-ee) offered himself as a different NFL trivia question: Have there ever been first-round selections in consecutive years from the same college and, as rookies, each made the Pro Bowl? He meant Notre Damers-come-Steelers Johnny Lattner in 1954 and Varrichione in 1955.

This sturdy right offensive tackle made four Pro Bowls in his six Steelers seasons. He also recovered seven fumbles, displaying either a nose for the ball or a knack for helping to bail out his underperforming teammates.

He came in the same 1955 draft as Johnny Unitas. In an act at Notre Dame that the legendary sportswriter Grantland Rice called "disgraceful," Varrichione feigned an injury to earn a time-out and allow the Irish to tie the score in what became a 14-14 deadlock with Iowa. He was known as "Fainting Frank" as a result during his junior and senior seasons. In the NFL, he was known for holding . . . which he admitted everyone did;

the art form was avoiding penalties. Hall of Fame defensive tackle Merlin Olsen, with whom he finished his career with the Los Angeles Rams, called him "the best hands in the business."

He was more than hands tucked inside the chest area and obscured from officials' view, though.

Varrichione, on teammate Bobby Layne: "He had Lou Creekmur with the Lions when they had some championship teams. He told me right to my face I'm a better blocker than Lou was, and Lou's in the Hall of Fame right now."

Coach Buddy Parker in 1957 placed two veterans at right tackle ahead of the third-year pro Varrichione the week of the November 3 date at the Baltimore Colts and All-Pro defensive end Gino Marchetti. The kid—and Parker despised youth for their propensity for youthful mistakes—won the job by game time, and he proceeded to suffocatingly block out the 11-time Pro Bowler and seven-time All-Pro.

Varrichione, on a rare moment when legendary coach Paul Brown was effusive about a competitor: "I was picked for the Pro Bowl. I ran into [Cleveland's] Mike McCormack at the airport. He told me, 'We were going to play [the Steelers] the following week. Everybody watches the game film of your opponent the next week. And Paul Brown told everybody . . . , 'Watch the right tackle, Varrichione. He'll put on an exhibition of what pass blocking is.' I was proud of that."

Jack Butler, teammate: "He had a *Bahstahn* accent. We used to make fun of him. We never won big-time. But he could've played for anybody, I don't care who."

MIKE WAGNER
Strong Safety–Free Safety

Height: 6-1 • **Weight:** 210 • **College:** Western Illinois • **Years with the Steelers:** 1971–1980 • **Birthplace:** Waukegan, Illinois • **Born:** June 22, 1949

An achiever, Mike Wagner was. Maybe even an overachiever.

He was cut as a freshman from his high school football team. He was a walk-on at Western Illinois. He played just six games his senior season at Western Illinois because of not one but two bad ankles.

A BLESTO scout had a pre-ankle clocking on Wagner. So Art Rooney Jr., acceding to Chuck Noll's late-round draft request to grab a defensive back, offered up this member of the Western Illinois Flying Leathernecks, Michael Robert Wagner.

At rookie camp, Jack Ham used to joke, Wagner went around clothes-lining ball carriers and hitting everyone that flinched—and that was when they weren't wearing pads.

Chuck Beatty blew out a knee the fourth snap of the opening exhibition game, and Wagner wound up a Steelers starter for most of a decade.

He was known to prey on Cincinnati quarterback Kenny Anderson, even going back to the days when Anderson's Augustana (Illinois) played Western Illinois. Six of Anderson's first 44 NFL interceptions—nearly one of every seven—fell into Wagner's hands. Anderson in 1976 even took to telling a joke on himself: "We're sending [wide receiver] Isaac Curtis to the Pittsburgh Steelers for Mike Wagner. Everybody knows Wagner catches everything I throw."

After the entire 1976 Steelers secondary made the Pro Bowl, Steelers coaches switched him from strong to free safety.

Tim Rooney, son of the Chief and ball boy/water boy: "One of the real top centers in pro football. He left and went to Notre Dame as a coach. Then Jim Finks left us." (See Finks profile.)

Dale Dodrill, nose guard–middle linebacker 1951–1959: "I was surprised; he could've played another five or six years. I guess he wanted to get into coaching."

HINES WARD
Wide Receiver

Height: 6-0 • **Weight:** 205 • **College:** Georgia • **Years with the Steelers:** 1998–2011 • **Birthplace:** Seoul, South Korea • **Born:** March 8, 1976

Between collecting 1,000 NFL receptions and 12,083 yards, and ranking among the top eight pass catchers of all time, between winning Super Bowl XL MVP and the *Dancing with the Stars* mirror ball, between achieving Pittsburgh popularity and earning United Nations acclaim for effecting change with biracial children in his native Korea, Hines Ward carved a distinction for himself in an area where few wide receivers tread:

Merciless, brutal blocking.

James Farrior, inside linebacker 2002–2011 and longtime defensive captain opposite Ward's offensive captaincy: "Hall of Famer. All the way. Everything. Definitely great as a pass catcher. He's been consistent."

Consistent, in that he clouted competitors and riled up the defenders who tried, and failed, to avoid his crushing blows. Baltimore's Chris McAlister, Bart Scott (who threatened to "kill" him), Ed Reed, Terrell Suggs ("Hines Ward is definitely a dirty player, a cheap-shot artist") . . . well, all the Ravens came to despise him. He had run-ins with Cleveland Browns, too. Heck, so many NFLers came to loathe him and his style that in 2009 he was voted the NFL's dirtiest player in *Sports Illustrated*.

Santonio Holmes, receiver 2006–2009: "He's a guy that always took pride in knocking somebody down. He would

MVP Hines Ward on the Super Bowl XL victors podium with Jerome Bettis, who holds aloft the Steelers' fifth Lombardi Trophy for a hometown Ford Field filled with Pittsburgh fans. (Courtesy of the Pittsburgh Steelers)

Hines Ward taking a moment to reflect late in the 2010 season . . . on his way to a third Super Bowl appearance and, later, a *Dancing with the Stars* championship. (George Gojkovich)

always tell me, 'You got to get them before they get you. And when you get them, that puts a fear into them.'"

And the hits kept on coming.

In 2008, he broke the jaw of Cincinnati Bengals linebacker Keith Rivers. After the season, the NFL passed what became known as the "Hines Ward Rule"—legislating a blindside block to a defender's head and neck area.

Farrior: "We already know he's a ferocious blocker. He's already proven that year in and year out." Best block? "It's got to be the Cincinnati hit. That hit, that was ferocious."

Max Starks, offensive tackle 2004– : "Definitely, the one against Cincinnati. Laying out Keith Rivers. He came flying in out of nowhere. Hines always has been a selfless guy. He would have been a good lineman; if he had the size, he definitely would have been a terror."

Heath Miller, tight end 2005– : "Nah."

Ward served not only as a leader and a tremendous pass catcher but also as a symbol for the franchise: he was a constant offensive threat as a blocker and receiver. His consistent contribution in receptions may get lost among all those crushing blocks. His career catches nearly doubled Hall of Famer John Stallworth's second-place 537—over a similar

14-year span. His touchdowns were almost 25 percent greater than Stallworth's 63 and fellow Hall of Famer Lynn Swann's 51. He had six 1,000-yard seasons and two more at 975.

How about this statistic: The most catches in a Steelers season were Ward's 112 in 2002, followed by Ward in second place with 95 (2003 and 2009), Ward in fourth place with 94 (2001), Ward in sixth place with 81 (2008), and, finally, Ward in seventh place with 80 (2004). Ward, Ward, Ward, Ward, Ward, Ward, six out of the top seven.

And, perhaps in the number most meaningful to the franchise's fans, his years of Steelers service placed him in the franchise's top eight, with such Hall of Famers as Mike Webster (15) and Stallworth, Mel Blount, Terry Bradshaw, and Ernie Stautner (14). His contributions dwindling and the Steelers' salary cap bloated, Ward was released in March 2012 along with linebacker James Farrior and defensive end Aaron Smith (both profiled earlier in this chapter). Ward soon after made a teary announcement about his retirement, with Jerome Bettis, James Harrison, Smith, and Brett Keisel in attendance at the news conference.

Ward, late in that final season, was asked to relate the legacy he hoped to leave behind: "That he was a helluva football player. Pretty simple. That he was a helluva football player. Tried to do good things, positive for the city of Pittsburgh. Tried to represent this organization as best as he could. The blocking? That's just me trying to go out and win, do whatever it takes to win ball games. I'm not trying to be compared to anybody."

Miller: "I'll remember him as being one of the best receivers in the history of this organization. And that's saying a lot, considering . . . *the history of this organization.* Not only one of the best receivers, but one of the best players. I think he embodies what this city and this team want to represent. That should be enough said about him."

MIKE WEBSTER
Center–Guard

Height: 6-1 • **Weight:** 255 • **College:** Wisconsin • **Years with the Steelers:** 1974–1988 • **Birthplace:** Tomahawk, Wisconsin • **Born:** March 18, 1952 • **Died:** September 24, 2002

Two factors turned a 218-pound kid from the Wisconsin hamlet of Tomahawk into one of professional football's greatest centers and most durable players: Iron work. Iron will.

Iron Mike Webster arrived in Pittsburgh in 1974, a fifth-round pick and the fourth eventual Hall of Famer of the classiest draft class in the history of any western hemisphere professional sport. He was the one of the four who got to wrap his hands around every snap, who got to start every offensive play—nobody was going anywhere without Webster. And he probably had the farthest to go to reach star status, much less Canton.

In fact, he acted as if he deserved to be back on the four-square-mile family farm in Harshaw, Wisconsin, and certainly not in the NFL.

That would explain climbing out of hospital beds and taking taxis to games, taping up lock-tight a knee that required the surgery he kept putting off, playing 177 consecutive games at the sport's most brutal position until a broken elbow just physically wouldn't let him do his job in a snap. Indomitable?

Mike Webster sports a look of bemusement in 1977 during a defeat of Seattle. (George Gojkovich)

That description hardly fits the bulging biceps of the man called Webby.

Andy Russell, outside linebacker 1963, 1966–1976: "Webster was amazing. He wasn't a big guy as a rookie, 235. He got into the weights. He was 280 in a few years."

Dan "Bad Rad" Radakovich, offensive line coach 1974–1977 after coming from the University of Colorado: "Well, first of all, I knew about Webster in college. We played them at Colorado [in early 1973]. He was the best center in the country. He was 6-1⅞, if you want to get real specific. And 218 pounds. Probably played as a rookie at 228. He could do all the skills. Very smart. Very tough."

Very very.

He put weights in his house and a blocking sled in his front yard.

Craig Wolfley, guard–tackle 1980–1989: "I pulled up one morning in the off-season to do something with him. It was 6:30 A.M. There he was, a middle-aged man—by NFL years—in a helmet, shoulder pads, and spikes, pushing a sled across the front lawn. *Six-thirty in the morning.* I said, 'Webby, do you know how crazy this looks? At least you should hook up the lawn mower to that sled.'"

Tunch Ilkin, tackle–guard–center 1980–1992: "Whoever ran the most stadium steps, he made sure he'd do more. He'd ask Walt Evans, our strength coach, 'Who ran the most steps today?' 'Tunch and Wolf ran 15.' 'I'm running 20.'"

John Jackson, tackle 1988–1997: "I can remember me and Dermontti Dawson were working out, running in Three Rivers Stadium. We were young guys trying to keep up with one of the greatest centers of all time. And we couldn't keep up with him. He just kept going. We went back down to the locker room, and Webby came down about 45 minutes later."

Gary Dunn, defensive lineman 1977–1987: "We called him the Hydraulic Man: You'd be on the way to breakfast in the morning [at training camp at St. Vincent College]; you'd hear clanging. He was doing squats in the weight room. Then you see him after practice; he'd be running up that hill. Make you dead tired [just to watch]."

Jon Kolb, center–tackle 1969–1981 and assistant coach 1982–1991: "You could go to the bathroom, and Mike would still be there doing squats. Mike just had knee surgery once. Was on crutches. And he came to the weight room to work out. It's a wonder that he didn't start bleeding."

Larry Brown, tight end–tackle 1971–1984: "A true wonder. You never saw anybody work harder than Mike. He was so invested. You always got the feeling that he felt like he shouldn't have been there in the first place."

Webster hunkered down in a good situation, With Ray Mansfield the wily veteran at center, he broke in at guard in 1974, rotated quarters with Mansfield in 1975, and became part of a starting five and a two-man rotation that Mansfield affectionately dubbed "the Seven Dwarves." Webster supplanted him in 1976, a passing of a center torch later reenacted to a degree with Dawson. Three centers in almost 40 years.

It wasn't indestructibility as much as it was resistance: Webster refused to miss even a practice snap.

Wolfley, recalling a viral infection that put Webster in Divine Providence Hospital, in traction, after 155 consecutive starts: "They wrote him off. He was done. And he played the whole game. Then took a cab back to the hospital."

Brown: "I remember him taping his knee in a certain place so it wouldn't move so he could play. Thinking, 'What are you doing? You don't have to play!' He had that will. He wanted to play so much."

Ralph Berlin, trainer 1968–1992: "I remember Mike tore a cartilage in his knee [in 1980]. It couldn't bend. I told him, 'Mike, you got a torn cartilage; we got to get it fixed.' He said, 'How far do I have to run? Once the season's over, I can get it fixed.' When he came back from the Pro Bowl, they did surgery. All they did was wash it out. He ground it to dust."

Wolfley, recalling Webster returning to the huddle after a brutal Rams collision in 1981: "'I think I broke my freakin' neck.' You got to remember: he had not missed a play, a practice play, in like four years."

Dermontti Dawson, guard–center 1988–2000: "He was always the first one in drills, lining up first. Even though he was in his 15th year, he wrote *everything* down. Whatever the coach said, he wrote it down in his notepad. Tell you what, he probably knew the offense better than the coaches. After I became the starter the second year, I tried to emulate Mike by being No. 1 in all the drills, being sure I wrote everything down, just the fine details."

Bubby Brister, quarterback 1986–1992: "I came in, and Webby was the center, and I was in awe of him. The first game I ever started was *Monday Night Football* at Cincinnati. I was a rookie. I didn't know I was going to start. Chuck Noll came up to me, 'I'm going to give you the start tonight.' I think I threw up all over the place. Webby goes, 'I got you. You do your reads, I got your protection.' He'd say, 'You're hot off 46.' I played pretty decent. Because of him."

Mike Webster not only makes calls at the line, he also offers audibles to quarterbacks. As line mate Craig Wolfley put it, "He was always coaching up the quarterbacks. The only thing he couldn't do was read coverages." (George Gojkovich)

Despite the look on his face, Captain Mike Webster is addressing the media after a victory—but one won after he crossed the picket lines to play alongside replacements in the first game of the 1987 strike, at Atlanta. Notice the space the media give him. The strike ended two games later. (Vincent J. Musi)

Wolfley, remembering the time Webster counseled Mark Malone to counter the Giants' Lawrence Taylor by throwing the ball quick: "He was always coaching up the quarterbacks. The only thing he couldn't do was read coverages."

His advice to Malone—and one of the NFL's greatest centers was positive the Steelers couldn't stop that Giants rush—sprang from the Webster personality. The negative intrigued him. A mudslide in Bangladesh? An incident where, no embellishment, someone got swallowed by a hippopotamus? The wide world Webby shared such matters in the locker room.

Ilkin: "He was always the news of doom and gloom."

Later in his career, long after the four Super Bowls and nine Pro Bowls, long after he turned his head and called audibles for Terry Bradshaw and Cliff Stoudt and Mark Malone and Bubby Brister, long after he was the last of the Mohicans, Webster couldn't give it up. He was pushed into a Steelers retirement, then joined the Kansas City Chiefs as a coach. He walked up to the general manager's office one day and advised him that the best place for Iron Mike Webster to contribute was snapping the ball again, and he played two more Chiefs seasons. Difficulties financial and physical proved that Iron fades.

Dunn:

Oh, God. I was playing the 4–3 front, I was playing the guards. Then they decided to move me to nose tackle. I wasn't happy about it. The year before I led the team in sacks, I thought I was going to be the pass-rush specialist. We had a scrimmage; it was my first real experience as a nose tackle. It was on a Saturday. Like, 25 plays. I talked to Mike before the thing: "Hey, Mike, you need to take it easy on me. You're All-Pro, Mr. Center. You got to take it easy on the new guy." He said, "You're fine; you don't need me to take it easy." The first play, he picked me up and dropped me on Lambert's feet. About five, six feet. "What in the world was that?" I realized he wasn't going to do the buddy deal. I was so discouraged after that scrimmage. I thought, "They're going to cut me."

I'm riding home in my Jeep. Here he comes on the Pennsylvania Turnpike in his Lincoln Continental. He goes by me, and I shoot him the bird. He pulls over, on the Pennsylvania Turnpike. "Dunnie, what's the matter?" "You made me look silly." He said, "Look, let me show you a few things." We're on the side of the Turnpike, and we're each in a three-point stance. I drove through him, put him against the bumper on his car, and he says, "That's it! You can do it!" He said, "Let's do this one more time." Then he picked me up and threw me over the guardrail. He said, "That's it, good night," and he got back in his car and drove off.

RALPH WENZEL
Guard

Height: 6-2 • **Weight:** 250 • **Colleges:** San Jose State, San Diego State • **Years with the Steelers:** 1966–1970 • **Birthplace:** San Mateo, California • **Born:** March 14, 1943 • **Died:** June 18, 2012

His playing career isn't what raises Ralph Wenzel's profile.

He came to the Steelers after failing to make the Packers roster and being waived by the Browns. He played Steelers games on and off from 1966 to 1970, Noll's second year. Mostly, he was on the roster, backing up Sam Davis and active for 43 of 70 Steelers games in that period.

What pushed Wenzel into the public consciousness, into the football conversation in the 21st century, and into the subject of congressional hearings, was what befell him—similar to Steelers teammate and former Pitt All-American Paul Martha—after his playing days.

They suffered heretofore in silence from a cognitive impairment afflicting several NFL alumni.

Eleanor Perfetto, his wife and a Pfizer senior director plus a board member with the Sports Legacy Institute in Boston studying contact sports' effects on the brain: "Now his condition has progressed severely enough where he's no longer able to walk. He's wheelchair bound. He really hasn't been able to communicate and speak for a number of years—not since 2006, but even then he . . . would jumble his words." He was fed pureed foods. He no longer recognized family members. "He doesn't really acknowledge people when you're talking to him. So he's pretty significantly debilitated.

"He started having these symptoms in the 1990s [in his 50s]. They were mild and sporadic. He started showing the signs of dementia, the cognitive problems, the math problems—balancing a checkbook—and confusion. At the time, the problems were early and minor; you don't really notice them. It wasn't until he was diagnosed in 1999 that we really did put it together." Cognitive impairment is a precursor to dementia and Alzheimer's—some don't progress to those points, but Wenzel did quickly. In early 2007, she had to place this former county parks and recreation worker into an assisted living facility, at age 64.

The NFL started the "88 Plan," after the late John Mackey, to help financially support such afflicted alumni and families: 150 were on the plan as of late 2011.

I think you have to factor that that's just the tip of the iceberg. Because there aren't a lot of guys who are just showing the symptoms. Or guys who already died.

There have been a few isolated cases that caused more media attention because of . . . some unusual behavior that happened. If you think about this as a progression of disease, if a guy starts having symptoms [in his 40s], some of the symptoms look like drug and alcohol abuse, because they self-medicate, or depression. . . . You see these things happen where they may be having a divorce, problems with their families, drug or alcohol abuse, people just chalk it up to [retiring] and that's the way it has been. Guys who have more of a support system in place, they're the ones getting by. They're not doing well, but they're not showing up on the front page of the newspaper. [Still,] they're progressing toward dementia.

He loved the Steelers. He loved the [Rooney] family that owned the Steelers and talked about those things. But that was about it.

BYRON "WHIZZER" WHITE
Halfback

Height: 6-1 • **Weight:** 187 • **College:** Colorado • **Years with the Pirates:** 1938 • **Birthplace:** Fort Collins, Colorado • **Born:** June 8, 1917 • **Died:** April 15, 2002

For all the grief Art Rooney endured for almost a half century about being cheap, he set the NFL's salary scale for players on its ear hole in his sixth year in the league by paying four times the usual top fee, $15,800, for a future U.S. Supreme Court justice.

Byron Raymond White, known as the Whizzer, was convinced by player-coach Johnny "Blood" McNally and Rooney to skip his Rhodes Scholar appointment with Oxford and play for the woebegone Pittsburgh Pirates, 15-37-2 prior to his arrival.

They went 2-9 with him, and he became the only rookie from a last-place team to lead the NFL in rushing, with 567 yards. No Steelers running back has topped the NFL in the nearly 75 years since.

Whizzer White, the first bonus baby that Art Rooney Sr. brought to Pittsburgh, 1938. He only lasted one season, then went to Oxford to complete his Rhodes Scholar work. (Courtesy of the Pittsburgh Steelers)

White was a quintuple threat: running, passing, punting, intercepting passes, returning kicks. For instance, in a victory over the Giants that Pirates season—accounting for half their victory total—he returned punts for 103 yards, rushed for 75, and returned an interception 17 yards.

Washington owner George Preston Marshall publicly complained, as *Washington Post* columnist Shirley Povich recalled in 1972, that "by such wanton prodigality Rooney was starting a trend that would break every team in the league." Rooney, a man adroit with numbers, got a return on part of his investment. When White returned from Oxford in 1940 and wanted to play a little pro football around his Yale Law School days, Rooney sold him to the Detroit Lions for $5,000 cash.

He spent 1940 and 1941 with Detroit, and the next celebrated bench for him was the Supreme Court. President John F. Kennedy named him to the nation's highest court in 1962.

Jim Klingensmith, the late Pittsburgh Post-Gazette *photographer:* "I used to go over to Art's office all the time and smoke a cigar. He told me a story one day. The first game at Forbes Field, the linemen were making $4,000 a year and [White] was making almost $20,000. They called his number and he hit the line—he didn't go anyplace, couldn't make any yardage. The second time, he hit the line and couldn't go anyplace. The next time they called his number to carry the ball, Art said, [White] asked the linemen, 'Could you please open a hole big enough for me to get through?' They said, 'We're making $4,000, you're making [$15,800]. Make your own hole.'"

Johnny "Blood" McNally, who had White serve as his Hall of Fame presenter, in a 1972 *New York Times* story: "As a football player, he was a slashing runner who won the ground-gaining championship with very little help from the rest of us. We were a bad team, winning only two games, and that is deeply significant. He did it alone."

DWIGHT WHITE
Defensive End

Height: 6-4 • **Weight:** 255 • **College:** Texas A&M–Commerce (née East Texas State) • **Years with the Steelers:** 1971–1980 • **Birthplace:** Hampton, Virginia • **Born:** July 30, 1949 • **Died:** June 6, 2008

He was a Mad Dog and a man of English.

This, after all, was the prescient player who noted in 1973 training camp that the Steelers were going to the Super Bowl "one of these years. I'm sure of that. Last year [after the Immaculate Reception and losing to undefeated Miami in the AFC championship game], I got a sip of paradise, and, man, I can still taste it."

Dwight White could turn a phrase, and reporters often gravitated to the right side of the Steel Curtain. He and Ernie "Fats" Holmes were the lesser lights as compared to the megawatt brightness of future Hall of Famer Joe Greene and sidekick L. C. "Hollywood Bags" Greenwood.

He arrived in the notable 1971 draft, from East Texas State (later Texas A&M–Commerce), where he earned the Mad Dog nickname and played with eventual Dallas Cowboys defensive end Harvey Martin. He was the last selection of the fourth round, five picks behind quarterback Joe Theismann and a gift of Roy Jefferson's recalcitrance. Because Jefferson ran afoul of Chuck Noll early in 1970, he was sent home before a preseason road game and bartered away. The trade of the lanky receiver—still the Steelers' 10th-all-time wideout in career yards—to Baltimore netted the next year's fourth-rounder, which became Dwight Lynn White.

White made Pro Bowls in 1972 and 1973, but thereafter his more celebrated line mates received the bulk of the accolades. Still, his talent, and his words, tumbled out. He snagged two interceptions in a single game in both 1973 and 1977: against Oakland's Daryle Lamonica and Houston's Dan Pastorini, respectively. (After one of the latter, he arose to offer a midfield rendition of a Billy "White Shoes" Johnson celebration jiggle.) He ranks eighth all-time with 46 Steelers career sacks.

His most famous moment, however, involved the Steelers' inaugural Super Bowl, a hospital sickbed (before and after), and the safety that marked the first score of a 16-6 triumph.

Ralph Berlin, trainer 1968–1992:

I remember 1974, when we went to the Super Bowl. He was complaining about pain in his back. I thought it was a muscle problem. We go down there . . . I got to my hotel room, and Joe Greene calls me: "Man, you got to get down here, Ralph, Dwight's really sick." I get to their room, and Dwight's on all fours. I said to the bellman, "Where's the closest hospital?"

Dwight called Wednesday and wanted to go to practice, and he couldn't do anything. So on Sunday, the day of the game, shoot, it was awful out. It was like a typhoon. Dwight calls me Sunday and says, "Come get me." He wanted to play, the [team internist Dave Huber] says absolutely not. [Team doctor] John Best said, "Look, Dave, let him go out there and walk around for pregame warm-ups. Who knows when they'll get here again?" Then, after warm-ups, Dwight wants to play. So John says, "He's been in the hospital all week, lost 20 pounds . . . how long can he play?" He played the whole damn game. We came back, and he spent a week in Divine Providence. Nearly died."

Dan "Bad Rad" Radakovich, defensive line coach in 1971, offensive line coach 1974–1977: "Smart player, good player, excellent player. He could talk, but he could back it up."

John Banaszak, backup and eventual successor at defensive end 1975–1981: "Dwight was the real character of that Steel Curtain. Dwight was emotional. He played the game at a high level of intensity. And you just didn't want to piss him off, because he was the guy who would just fricking lose it."

Dwight White in 1979, the last run to the Super Bowl by the aging Steel Curtain. (Bill Amatucci)

Mike Wagner, safety 1971–1980: "The left side of the defensive huddle was Greene, Greenwood, Ham, J. T. Thomas, then I was there. The right side, between Ernie [Holmes] and Dwight White . . . Dwight was always arguing with somebody. He and Ernie—they spent their time yelling at each other, yelling at the refs, yelling at the other team. I would look at L. C. and Ham, and we would shake our heads. No. 1, what are they arguing about? No. 2, we were just trying to catch our breath; where did they get the energy?"

Larry Brown, tight end, tackle, teammate: "Dwight had gone down to Ernie's funeral. He was profoundly moved—the way Ernie had endeared himself to the community [in Texas]. He was touched in a spiritual way, and I never heard him talk like that. And he was a good friend, too."

Six months later, White was gone as well. The right side of the Steel Curtain, closed shut.

DWAYNE WOODRUFF
Cornerback

Height: 5-11 • **Weight:** 198 • **College:** Louisville • **Years with the Steelers:** 1979–1990 • **Birthplace:** Bowling Green, Kentucky • **Born:** February 18, 1957

Where Carnell Lake attended night school for accounting, this defensive back went to law school at night.

Dwayne Woodruff, seen here in 1982, spent his Steelers career going to night law school. He eventually became a judge in Allegheny County. (Bill Amatucci)

Where Whizzer White sat on the highest bench in the land, only one other Steelers player was known to don a black robe regularly: Judge Dwayne D. Woodruff, Allegheny County Court of Common Pleas, Family Division.

As a cornerback, Woodruff also commanded respect. His 38 career interceptions ranked behind only four players, all of whom were finalists or enshrined in the Hall of Fame: Mel Blount, Jack Butler, Donnie Shell, and Rod Woodson. His 689 career return yards ranked behind only Butler, Woodson, and Blount.

He topped the Steelers in interceptions in five different seasons, the last three of his tenure while playing opposite a cornerback who made the NFL's 75th Anniversary team and rates as one of the best ever to play the game, Woodson. Then again, he also was once the team leader when the opposite corner was Blount, in 1982.

Woodruff sat out the 1986 season because of a knee injury but started full-time for eight seasons through the 1980s. He bridged a secondary gap between Super Bowl eras. When he retired in July 1991, he was the last of the ring-wearing Super Steelers still active in the NFL.

Dermontti Dawson, center 1988–2000: "Dwayne was always the . . . I can't say 'judge.' How can I describe Dwayne?"

Gary Dunn, nose tackle–defensive lineman 1977–1987: "Last time I was up there, I couldn't believe that. I asked if I could get out of jail free. He looked at me: 'The stuff you'd go to jail for, I don't know if I can help you.'"

ROD WOODSON
Cornerback

Height: 5-11 • **Weight:** 205 • **College:** Purdue • **Years with the Steelers:** 1987–1996 • **Birthplace:** Fort Wayne, Indiana • **Born:** March 10, 1965

One of Dan Rooney's great regrets, if not *the* greatest one, is letting one of the most gifted, if not *the* most gifted, cornerbacks in history get away.

Then again, nobody in the NFL ever was capable of corralling Rod Woodson.

The 10th draftee of Chuck Noll enshrined in Canton, Woodson was different, special, preeminent from the starting line of his career. Not many contract holdouts use the Olympics for leverage. Yet there was Woodson, the 10th-overall selection of the 1987 draft, flickering through the 110-meter hurdles in European track meets and posturing about ditching football awhile to train for the 1988 Summer Games.

He was no Seoul man. Woodson signed with the Steelers in early November, partly because his advisers wanted him to wait until the 1987 labor strife ended. He promptly went to work at hurdling NFL records.

Dom Capers, defensive coordinator 1992–1994: "I remember I was still the secondary coach in New Orleans, and he was the guy we wanted. I remember . . . Jim Mora walking in, and Rod Woodson's still on the board. He walked back in 15 seconds later, 'Pittsburgh just took him.' I didn't get to coach him in New Orleans, but I got to coach him in Pittsburgh" five years later.

Tony Dungy, defensive coordinator 1987–1988: "At that time, all the coaches went out [scouting]. You didn't have a Combine. You went out, got a report on guys. They said, 'Don't

Rod Woodson after an interception against Atlanta at Three Rivers Stadium in 1990. (Vincent J. Musi)

see kind of the nucleus of the next Steel Curtain defense, the late '80s, early '90s. And Rod was the ringleader, no question."

He scored his first defensive touchdown in his third NFL game. He wore no pads in his uniform pants; the lighter he felt, the faster he could motor. He returned punts, kickoffs, fumbles, and interceptions all for touchdowns. He went on to score 17 touchdowns—an NFL-record 12 on interceptions alone. Five of those came with the Steelers (the most in franchise history).

He intercepted 71 passes for the third most in NFL history—and 38 of those in his Steelers decade (fourth most in franchise history).

Seven of his 11 Pro Bowls, the latter a record for a defensive back, likewise came in his Steelers years. (It should be noted: He made the 1989 Pro Bowl as a returner, even though he allowed nary a touchdown at cornerback that season.)

All those Steelers baubles, and what did he have to show for it?

A Super Bowl XXX loss . . . though the mere fact that he played in the game was a testament to Woodson's ethereal ability. He tore an ACL in the 1985 season opener, on the second series, amid a simple swing pass. Something told Bill Cowher to avoid placing Woodson on the season-ending injured reserve. After an unprecedented recovery, Woodson played in special packages in the game at Sun Devil Stadium.

The injury put a halt to his returner career. The next year, 1996, he gathered up six interceptions for 121 yards and a touchdown, a fumble return for a touchdown, his seventh Pro Bowl in his last eight Pittsburgh seasons, and all his locker belongings.

When the Steelers—to Rooney's later regret—opted against spending excessive amounts for a future safety, Woodson hit the road. First, he played a year with San Francisco. With Baltimore . . . *Baltimore!* . . . he won a Super Bowl XXXV

even bother going to Purdue. We won't even have a shot at him.' We ended up drafting him, and you knew right away how special he was going to be.

"Rod, he held out for a long time. He got to us, I think, late October or early November. He was playing nickel back. Delton Hall was actually our rookie of the year. Rod, Delton Hall, Thomas Everett, Hardy Nickerson, and Greg Lloyd all came in that same 1987 class. You could

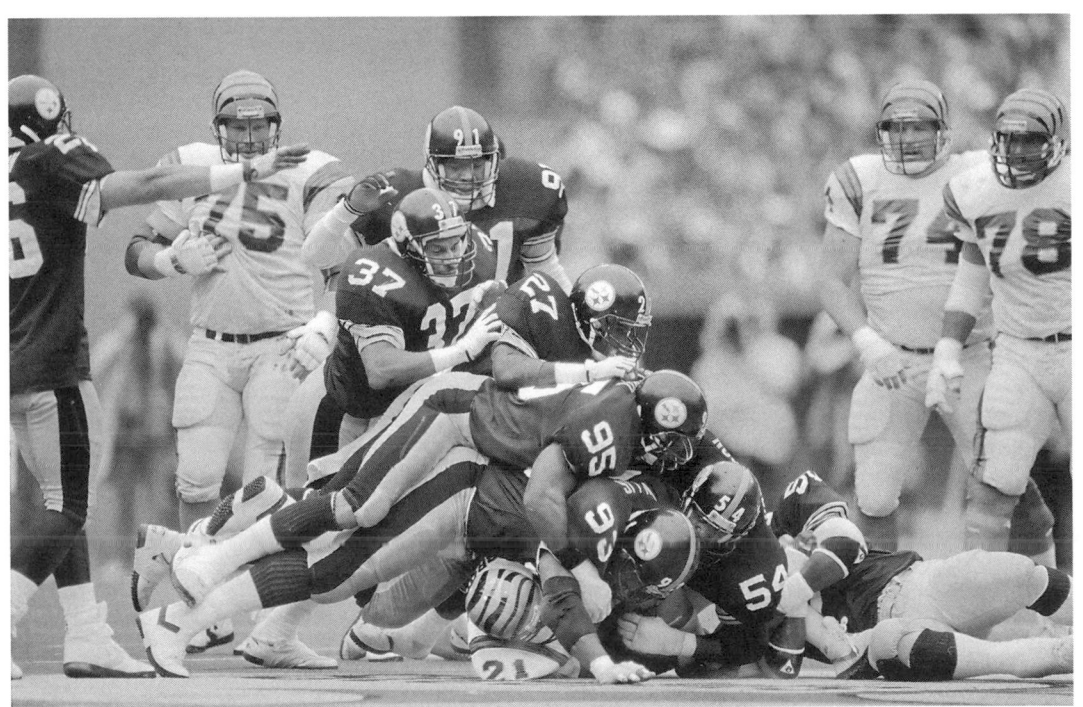

Rod Woodson signals first down, Steelers, after a smothering defensive stop of the Bengals in 1989: top to bottom, Jerrol Williams, Carnell Lake, Thomas Everett, Greg Lloyd, Keith Willis, and Hardy Nickerson. The obscured Steelers defender at the bottom right of the pile, wrapping up the legs of Cincinnati's 1,000-yard rusher James Brooks, is believed to be David Little. (Vincent J. Musi)

ring in 2000. And from there he went to Oakland, where his Raiders lost to Dungy and Tampa Bay in Super Bowl XXXVII.

His chronic knee didn't pass the Oakland physical in 2004, and that was it for a glorious career.

Gerald Williams, nose tackle–defensive end 1986–1994: "Rod was the beginning of the great Steeler teams of the last couple of decades. Wooooo. When Dom Capers came, we were just starting to build an impact defense, if you will. Rod was the beginning of the building blocks. Greg Lloyd . . . , Kevin Greene. . . . Things just fell in place. Rod was how the Jets are with [Aliquippa native and Pitt man Darrelle] Revis: you knew that one side of the field: covered. One word."

Kevin Greene, outside linebacker 1993–1995, on Woodson's 1995 comeback: "That was pretty amazing. His work ethic was second to none. He was somebody that, every day we practiced, he practiced at the level he played at. He inspired others to play at that level. And we had so many great leaders on that defense, between outside linebackers and inside linebackers, Rod on the corner, Carnell Lake. . . . We had so many strong-willed personalities pulling together and holding everybody responsible."

Jon Kolb, strength and conditioning coach at the time: "Rod was on the treadmill. I think it stuck at 20 mph and at a 21 percent grade. And I was talking to [team photographer] Mike Fabus. I heard [Rod] go, 'Coach?' Puh, puh, puh [laboring on treadmill], 'Coach?' Puh puh puh . . . and the thing hurled him off backward.

"Again, I think of two guys who had legs like I've never seen on a human being [before or since]: Mike Webster and Rod Woodson."

Ralph Berlin, trainer 1968–1992: "I always thought the greatest athlete here was Rod Woodson. He did things athletically that I didn't think were possible. He could've played anywhere. He could play wide receiver; he could play running back; he could play linebacker; he could even play tight end."

Bubby Brister, quarterback 1986–1992: "I wished he could have played some receiver. Tom [Moore, the offensive coordinator] and I talked about it. It was just that he was returning kicks, punts . . . he was doing as much as he could. Rod Woodson, he's a guy who could still play today. He's one of the best who ever played."

The Super '70s

A hauntingly familiar sight to opponents every NFL winter: snow, cold, darkness, dankness, a full Three Rivers Stadium (now Heinz Field), and nothing but the Steelers standing between you and the end zone. This scene comes from a December 1989 loss to the Houston Oilers, 7-6. (Vincent J. Musi)

THE SLOW CLIMB all started with Chuck Noll, Joe Greene, snowballs, and losses. Lots and lots of losses. All in a murderous row.

Nobody ever claimed that mountain climbing was quick and easy.

Nobody scaled a football mountain like this before, either: from the depths to the tallest peak.

Pat Rooney Sr., one of the owner's youngest twin sons who worked in ticket sales before departing to work in the family racetrack business: "It was very minor league. We got professional when Noll showed up."

The day after the coach and teacher arrived, the star pupil and franchise future was singled out, the fourth-overall selection in that 1969 draft.

So began the journey upward.

Jack Butler, ex-Steelers player and assistant turned scouting director with BLESTO (Bears, Lions, Eagles, Steelers, Talent Organization): "Everybody in Pittsburgh wondered: 'Who the hell is Joe Greene?' They couldn't block him. He clobbered people." Clobbered decades of horrible history, too.

Andy Russell, outside linebacker 1963, 1966–1976: "Noll walks in and says, 'I can tell you guys the reason why you were losing. You were losing because you weren't very good. You're not good enough. You're not fast enough. And I'm going to have to get rid of most of you.' And he did."

Their inaugural game together, they won.

Then they lost a record 13 consecutive games.

No NFL team lost as many games in a single season except one since the league's 1922 birth: the 1930 Frankford Yellow Jackets of Philadelphia had to toss in a couple of exhibitions to go 4-13, too. The 1969 Steelers' dubious distinction lasted until 1976, when the expansion Tampa Bay Buccaneers inaugurated their franchise with an 0-26 start. But, then, these Steelers started 1970 with three more losses, so the skein reached a 16-game losing streak before it got better.

Joe Gordon, who joined the club as publicity director five months after Noll's January 27 hiring: "At that point, the NFL was in a very rapid growth period. You could see it was going to get big. And bigger. And bigger.

"The timing couldn't have been better."

The next season, they would be moving into spanking new Three Rivers Stadium with a carpet for a field, a spacious locker room, and a weight room that, for once, wasn't a joke.

But in this brutal beginning, it was all bad times. Time after time after 13 and then 16 times in a row.

Is it possible to find more than one nadir in such an ugly run?

On December 7, 1969, the Steelers emerged from their Pitt Stadium locker room at halftime of an eventual 10-7 loss and had to dodge snowballs from their own stands.

On December 21 in New Orleans, they lost their third consecutive game by four points or fewer, but this time they allowed the Saints to score the game-winning touchdown in the final minute. They learned to do whatever it takes to lose before they understood how to fulfill whatever it takes to win. At game's close, the field erupted in a bench-clearing brawl. Not exactly the recipe for going down with a fight.

They would return to Tulane Stadium five years later a much different team.

With a flip of both a coin and new turnstiles, the sad-sack franchise's fortunes seemed to change. They possessed a brand-new playpen, a state-of-the-art Three Rivers Stadium.

They luckily won the flip with the Chicago Bears for the first-overall selection, *Newsweek* cover boy Terry Bradshaw. Owner and founder Art Rooney had gone from the semipro Hope Harveys to actual hope, in just 38 years' time.

Dick Hoak, running back 1961–1970 and running backs coach 1972–2006: "Once they moved there, things fell into place. Now you had a place to call your own."

Pat Rooney Sr.: "When we moved to Three Rivers, we had a $3 game-day ticket. I don't hear people remember that. People forget."

Bradshaw's struggles, they never forgot. Mel Blount's? Those got overlooked. Put it this way: He wasn't a Hall of Famer from the get-go, a rocky start that mirrored that of the No. 1 pick quarterback. Blount wasn't even a full-time starter until 1972, the season that changed all the others.

Bradshaw threw a league-leading 24 interceptions that rookie 1970 campaign. Blount grabbed only one interception, the fewest in any season of his career. Still, it was a start. More pieces fell into place.

In 1971, Noll and the scouting department added outside linebacker Jack Ham—whom they nearly changed into a middle linebacker—and several pieces: the right half of the Steel Curtain in Dwight White and Ernie Holmes, longtime safety Mike Wagner, and three more long-term starters for a total of seven. It just might be the second-greatest draft in NFL history. Second, that is. The other? It was coming.

Jack Ham, outside linebacker 1971–1982: "I played in the college all-star game. We scrimmaged the Chicago Bears; we were college players, and we killed them in their training camp. I came to Pittsburgh, my first game is against the Chicago Bears. I thought, 'Oh, we'll just kill this team. I've seen this team play.' We're leading, 15-3, the whole game. [Dick] Butkus hits two running backs, and we fumbled the ball twice. We lost, 17-15. I thought, 'You're kidding me. This is going to be one short career for Jack Ham.'"

Ex-Steelers quarterback Kent Nix completed the game-winning score, whereupon Greene flung his helmet toward the distant stands of Soldier Field. The helmet clanged off a goalpost instead.

Joe Greene, defensive tackle 1969–1981: "I threw it about fifty yards." Was he concerned they might turn him into a quarterback? "No accuracy."

Whether they realized it or not, the target was coming into focus.

Larry Brown, tight end and later offensive tackle 1971–1984: "There were people in your draft class replacing [veterans]. You can see the turnaround. The next year was the first year the Steelers made the playoffs" in a quarter century and the second of all time.

Hoak: "It was Joe, then Terry. Terry, you knew he would be a good quarterback, but he wasn't ready yet. Franco was a big part of it, too. Once we got Franco, we had a back where we could score from anywhere on the field."

The defense–running game combination matured in 1972, when Franco Harris came with the No. 13 pick in the first round. Sure, Noll was interested in University of Houston running back Robert Newhouse. But there was enough Nittany Lions intelligence in the draft room to convince him to opt for the fullback who had blocked for Lydell Mitchell at Penn State. Noll couldn't conceal his optimism, saying publicly that he had expected this group to win the AFC Central the year before, in 1971. Greene offered much the same line: "I got a feeling this is the year of the money."

Harris hardly got much work the first four games, failed to start until the sixth game, . . . and dashed off 976 yards in the final 10 regular-season games alone. He picked up 10 touchdowns, NFL Rookie of the Year, and his own militaristic fan group—Franco's Italian Army.

Even Jack Ham, a native of the nearby flood city of Johnstown, Pennsylvania, remarked that he noticed a sea change around the river city while he and the Steelers compiled that 11-3 record in 1972: "This whole city is reacting to the team's success. I've even heard sportscasters on television telling the people where they can drive to watch our home games on television. Imagine that in Pittsburgh."

Brown: "My second year, people always referenced to SOS, the Same Old Steelers. That was before my time. But to see all the new generation in the second year, that did a lot to raise the team's morale and the city's. It kind of gave its impetus for this."

Then this miracle happened, the Immaculate Reception.

The course altered abruptly.

A 1973 that began with Ernie Holmes shooting at a police helicopter and the Steelers getting run down in Oakland just made it seem that it wasn't their year. There still was something missing. Dan "Bad Rad" Radakovich, the defensive line coach who put the Steel Curtain components together on the field in 1971, returned in 1974 to coach the offensive line. And who else joined the Steelers that season? Oh, yeah, the greatest draft class in NFL history: four future Hall of Famers in the first five picks—Lynn Swann, Jack Lambert, John Stallworth, and Mike Webster. Each of them made a first-year impact.

Ham: "We were a good football team before that year. But when we got Swann, Stallworth, Lambert, and Webster, we knew."

"Especially Lambert."

From new techniques to new formations, from tailoring the offensive linemen's jerseys for both bulging-biceps looks and tight fits to limit defensive holding, these 1974 Steelers tried new wrinkles with peach-faced talent.

Ralph Cindrich, Houston linebacker 1973–1975: "I could stand there and call out every play they were running. Still, they would gain three or four yards. Every play. They were that good."

Radakovich: "I'm the guy that started the taping. Started in '74. The story's all in my book [*Bad Rad*]. I'm the guy who started the hands up [technique of blocking] and not Jim Hanifan. And it became a rule in '78. Maybe it was against the rules before. . . . Oh, and we didn't hold. I watch TV, other teams are taping now."

Jon Kolb, center–tackle 1969–1981: "Chuck Noll and Dan Radakovich changed the game from where people ran into each other to a game where they hit each other. The same-foot, same-shoulder [blocking] technique, Chuck started that. Rad and Chuck were such innovators."

The 10-3-1 season ended with a first-round playoff date against Buffalo and O. J. Simpson, the year after his 2,003-yard odyssey.

Time for more innovation.

Ham: "It's kind of like how rubber was invented: You get damn lucky."

Radakovich: "Joe Greene was screwing around. George looked at it and liked it. Really, it was an under-gap reduced defense. Against Buffalo in the playoffs, they went with the stunt 4–3, period. It worked so well, they played it exclusively in the playoffs."

George Perles, defensive line coach and later defensive coordinator: "The week before, O. J. had been running cutbacks and stretching the defense. They were killing people with it. I don't know why, I was doodling on a legal pad Monday night at home . . . and trying to keep O. J. [from cutting back]. Instead of over guard, I had Joe stunting between the guard and center, and Lambert stacked behind him—they couldn't get to him. [The Bills] were confused. You take Joe Greene and tilt him down, and he's aimed for the numbers on the center's head. The guard can't get to Lambert because Joe's in his way. It was a mess in there.

The Steel Curtain defense confronting Philadelphia's John Reaves in a 1973 preseason game: left to right, Joe Greene, L. C. Greenwood, Ernie Holmes, and Dwight White collapse the pocket around Reaves while Andy Russell, foreground, drops into pass coverage. A daunting sight, indeed. (Temple Urban Archives)

Immaculate Reception

"The Oakland Raiders have taken a 7-6 lead in a tough, tough football game that has featured nothing but staunch defense all afternoon. Hang onto your hats—here come the Steelers out of the huddle...."

Jack Fleming's voice still resonates.

The booth crew is no longer with us. Fleming, the decorated collegiate play-by-play announcer from his days doing West Virginia University football and basketball, then the Steelers additionally, passed away in 2001. Myron Cope, the little man with the gigantic legacy of his Terrible Towel and worse voice, signed off seven years later.

Thankfully for aural health in perpetuity, Cope's warble isn't available on the soundtrack of the Steelers' most compelling and imperative play in their history, on the play roundly hailed as the most memorable in American

Franco Harris, for whom things are looking up. (John Beale)

professional-sports annals. Cope, you see, descended the Three Rivers Stadium elevator seconds earlier to prepare for his postgame radio interviews. This colorful commentator, this gent with a lyrical lexicon if not voice, regretted that premature capitulation.

"Don't think I wouldn't have had a few words to say about it," he warbled later.

It took precisely 40 Steelers years to reach the Pittsburgh 40-yard line, fourth and forever.

So let's rewind the tape a moment.

The Same Old Steelers, as Art Rooney dubbed them during World War II, finally seemed to shed their laughingstock image. No longer were they football follies stock, shelf after shelf, for NFL Films. No longer were they lovable losers. Chuck Noll used draft building blocks Joe Greene, Terry Bradshaw, and a rookie that 1972 season named Franco Harris to catapult a heretofore accursed franchise. The Steelers, blasphemy, were a winner.

One week earlier, the Steelers were basking in the sun in San Diego, practicing toward a regular-season finale against the Chargers for their inaugural division title. Forty years after their birth, they finally won a flag and earned acclaim. Not only did Harris, the hard-charging lad from Penn State, find himself with a fan group, but also Franco's Italian Army stopped practice one of those San Diego afternoons so it could induct a new general: Frank Sinatra.

1972? It was a very good year.

Then came the playoffs.

For the second time in Steelers history, they officially merited a postseason berth. Jock Sutherland had steered the 1947 edition to what was then the most victories in club history, in an 8-4 season. There was a consolation Playoff Bowl for second-place finishers in 1963, but it remained the tangible fact that in their only previous one-and-done NFL playoff, the Steelers got shut out by Philadelphia, 21-0.

Here came the hated Oakland Ray-duhs, as Howard Cosell called them. The silver and black—against whom the Steelers opened their 11-3 season with a 34-28 victory that began to foster a bitter relationship between the two—descended upon Three Rivers two days before Christmas, December 23, 1972. It was a day that would live in infamy for their coach, John Madden.

Joe Greene, defensive tackle 1969–1981, captain and conscience of the Steelers: "The Raiders were our nemesis. The Raiders had a history of kicking your butt. Just beating you up. Beating you up pretty badly."

Frenchy Fuqua, running back and amateur historian of this inimitable NFL moment: "I'll tell you something about the Oakland Raiders: One of the worst beatings I ever had, we played them in 1970 or '71. It was played on September 12. They beat us 21-0." It was preseason 1970, and 20-6 Oakland, but the Frenchman was rolling. "You know what that was? It was my [24th] birthday. When I speak for myself, I think I speak for all of our guys, but I said that day, 'They will never beat us again.' I had never played a team that was as dirty. People tell you how dirty they were. 'When you get tackled, ball your fingers, because they'll try to break your fingers'—which they did. But I dislike them to this day."

After clinching home-field advantage with that victory in San Diego and taking that AFC Central crown back to Pittsburgh, Fuqua told reporters, "All I know is that right now Oakland is standing between me and $25,000 [in playoff money]. And I ain't gonna let a bunch of gorillas keep me from that."

The gorillas, and not Roy Gerela's, were winning. Gerela's two field goals had given the Steelers a tenuous 6-0 lead in this AFC Divisional playoff. But then Ken Stabler, Daryle Lamonica's partner in Madden's two-quarterback share, snaked around rookie backup defensive end Craig Hanneman and bolted 30 yards down the left sideline for the go-ahead touchdown with 73 seconds to go. It was the only touchdown of this defensive struggle. It was seemingly an omen. Still the Same Old Steelers? Still a lovable loser?

They were down to the final breath, fourth down and 10 from their own 40. NFL Films came to dub it "fourth and hopeless."

The game was blacked out under NFL rules of the day, so only 50,350 souls can lay claim to witnessing the event. Twenty-five miles away, listening to Fleming's voice on radio, this little Jewish kid called Dial-a-Prayer, which probably wasn't kosher.

Al Vento, pizza maker and cofounder of Franco's Italian Army: "The Immaculate Reception. Tony [Stagno] and I, we're on the 30. There were, I don't know, 22 seconds left in the game . . ."

Mike Wagner, safety: "So I'm sitting on my helmet. We're on the sidelines. Jack Ham and I are sitting next to each other, we're [disconsolate]. I thought we'd lost. 'I guess the off-season's here.' . . ."

Jon Kolb, left tackle:

We played San Diego the week before. The guy who did the chapel service . . . , he said, "What do you guys pray for before a game?" We've got to beat San Diego to play Oakland for the Immaculate Reception to happen, and Ray Mansfield goes, "That nobody gets hurt and may the best man win." And the guy goes, "Really? I'm not sure if God has any interest in a football game, but at least be honest with Him." So Ray says, "You think it's okay to pray to God for a win?"

As we're breaking the huddle [on that final play against Oakland], Ray says, "Somebody forgot to pray for a win."

I don't know if anybody else heard it. It's fourth down and forever. I don't know how many seconds on the clock. And Ray was a one-line guy. "Somebody forgot to pray for a win."

Fleming:

"Terry Bradshaw at the controls . . . 22 seconds remaining. And this crowd is standing.

"And Bradshaw back and looking again. Bradshaw running out of the pocket, looking for somebody to throw to . . . fires it downfield . . ."

Bradshaw's play selection, as sent in by Noll: 66 Circle Option.

Franco Harris, left, and Mike Webster, right, provide Hall of Fame blocking for Rocky Bleier in 1976—when he and Harris became the first 1,000-yard rushers from the same backfield in NFL history. (Bill Amatucci)

The play's design called for a pass over the middle to rookie receiver Barry Pearson.

Throw to a rookie on the most significant play in franchise history? A rookie playing his first NFL game? A rookie previously owning zero receptions, zero games, zero experience? Barry Lynn Pearson, 5-foot-11, 23 years old, had zero chance.

Especially against future Hall of Famer Willie Brown, Jimmy Warren, Nemiah Wilson, George "Hitman" Atkinson, and Jack "The Assassin" Tatum.

But it had to be a pass somewhere. The ground-oriented Steelers remained unable to dent the Raiders defensive front all day, Harris rushing for 64 yards on 18 carries and Fuqua 25 yards on 16 carries.

Fuqua, a veteran fullback playing halfback because of the presence of the burly Harris, circled out of the backfield and ventured about 30 yards downfield.

The NFL Rookie of the Year stayed in to block. It wasn't exactly his forte, but Fuqua possessed the better receiving skills even though Harris caught more passes during the regular season, 21 to 18. Harris had four receptions for 30 yards already that day compared to Fuqua's one reception for 11, so perhaps the Raiders were expecting that the rookie would be an intended target.

Kolb: "Frenchy and Franco really couldn't have done it if I hadn't set the play up. If you watch the film, my defensive end [Tony Cline, who had been flying upfield all day] on that play took two steps up and crosses underneath. I barely get a piece of the guy." Cline actually grabs a fistful of Bradshaw's jersey. "That causes Terry to reset. He took two steps to his right and fired the pass. If I had done my job, it never would have happened."

Fleming:

". . . And there's a collision and there . . ."

Fuqua milked the moment for decades.

He became a banquet regular, John William Fuqua and his yarns of 1972. He vowed he would never tell the truth (it leaked out). He promised that he made a pledge to the beloved Art Rooney Sr. that only the Chief knows for sure, besides Fuqua and Tatum, of course.

The Frenchman swore he would never tell if the ball hit him or Tatum first.

Wagner: "No matter how much he says, he doesn't know what happened. He had his eyes closed."

Fuqua: "Two years before he passed [in July 2010], Jack Tatum and I had a beer together. He said, 'All I know is, I was trying to tear your head off and I came at you.' 'Yeah, I felt it.'"

The sudden impact was undeniable.

Pearson was running a deep post, but Tatum left him to follow the ball underneath to the in-option route run by the running back who a year earlier tied for the Steelers receptions lead with 49. The Raiders safety and future author of the book *They Call Me Assassin* flung himself toward a Fuqua crossing underneath his coverage area.

Fuqua: "In those days, if Bradshaw looked at you, the ball was coming. I saw him looking at me. He cocked, and here comes the ball. I was going to be the hero to catch the pass that sets up the winning field goal."

"I could hear Tatum. I could hear footsteps: boom, boom, boom. And then I could hear him breathing: Hah-hah-hah. I knew there was going to be contact."

With 66 Circle Option breaking apart and his quarterback sidestepping the right arm of an oncoming Horace Jones and the likes of Pearson, Fuqua, and tight end John McMakin (one catch, nine yards all day) downfield, Harris took that opportunity to listen to Joe Paterno's teachings. At Penn State, they were imbued with the mantra "Go to the ball, go to the ball."

The ball arrived at the intersection of Fuqua and Tatum around the Oakland 34-yard line.

If the ball struck Fuqua first, no other Steelers could legally catch it. If it struck Tatum first, it was a live ball.

What if it struck both players?

Carnegie Mellon University even waded into the scientific question years later. John Fetkovich, an emeritus professor of physics at the respected Pittsburgh school, began bouncing a football off the wall, consulting Isaac Newton's laws of gravity, and watching football's Zapruder film. In 2004 he derived the conclusion: It hit Tatum.

Because slow-motion replay of the film clearly showed that the ball changed trajectory just *before* the collision, the ricochet indubitably was the result of Tatum's momentum. The Assassin and the football moved in the same direction. Ipso facto . . .

Ya know.

Fleming:

". . . And it's caught out of the air!"

"The ball is pulled in by Franco Harris! Harris is going for a touchdown for Pittsburgh! Harris is going. . . . Five seconds left on the clock. Franco Harris pulled in the football. I don't even know where he came from.

"Fuqua was in a collision. There are people in the end zone.

"Where did he come from?"

A miracle.

Vento: "Now, the Italian people are fierce believers in this little guy: Cornetto. It brings good luck to you and evil to the other guys. So here's the thing of this: Tony had a big red one, this big [spreads fingers 5 inches apart]. It [is at the end of a pendant and] looks like a hot pepper. You open it up to take out this little man, the Cornetto man.

"The ball bounces off Frenchy, and Tony drops the man. We bend down to pick it up. We stand up, and Franco's running down the field. Whether it was the little Cornetto man or Franco's ability, I don't know. That's as true as I'm sitting here."

Wagner: "All of a sudden, the ball bounces, Franco runs past us, and we start chasing Franco down the field."

Harris at his shoestrings at the Raiders' 42½-yard line made the catch of a lifetime, the catch of a century, the catch that grabbed a franchise and a city and a Steeler Nation. The footrace continues.

As for his touchdown run, it was rather droll Harris stuff. He rolled to the left sideline, stiff-armed Oakland's Warren between the 13- and 8-yard lines, and, while tiptoeing to keep his balance and stay in bounds, sauntered into the golden-painted end zone.

Bradshaw, decked by Kolb's man Cline, heard the roar of the crowd. It was a good roar. He knew.

Cope, somewhere in the end-zone throng that swelled with giddy fans pouring over the walls, was speechless for perhaps the first time in his life.

And where was the owner, the cigar-chomping Chief? In the Three Rivers elevator—there was only one for passengers—with the same Pirates announcer, Bob Prince, who went down too early and missed Bill Mazeroski's 1960 Game 7 homer, too.

Rooney to the *New York Times'* Arthur Daley hours later:

I didn't see the miracle. I missed the play. . . . I felt we had lost. I decided to go down to the dressing room and thank them in person.

Now, I don't ordinarily go to the dressing room. I remember doing it in New York the last time we had a shot at the championship. The touchdown that killed us that day was on a circus catch by Frank Gifford. It was better than any Willie Mays ever made. So with less than a minute to play, I headed for the elevator and just made it when Bob Prince, the [Pirates] broadcaster, held the door open for me.

Suddenly we heard a wild scream from the crowd. It could only mean one thing, but no one in the elevator dared believe it. When we reached the field level, I raced for the clubhouse. "What happened?" "We scored a touchdown." "But where are the players. The game must be over by now." "They're having a discussion about it." . . . My heart sank because I began to fear the worst. I started to suspect that whatever good had happened to us would be disallowed. The wait seemed endless.

When the door burst open, [punter Bobby Walden] . . . rushed over to me. He wrapped his arms around me, lifted me off the floor and spun me around. "We won! We won!"

Cope later dissected film shot by a cameraman at the WTAE-TV station where he did nightly commentaries. Frame by frame, it showed Bradshaw's pass finding Tatum first. It bothered the old newspaper guy turned broadcasting icon that the evidence would be lost in storage somewhere thereafter.

Fleming:

"Absolutely unbelievable. Holy moly."

The officiating crew was completely confounded.

Referee Fred Swearingen later recalled: "I have three 'I don't knows' and two 'I think but don't know.' And I have to make a decision." He went in the dugout to call NFL supervisor of officials Art McNally, who advised him to finalize the call on the field. Swearingen signaled touchdown.

Oakland's Madden, apoplectic, couldn't understand why Swearingen suddenly was sure it was a touchdown after one short call upstairs. A trailblazer, Madden later suggested that they used television replay to make the call; McNally denied the claim. No matter, as a lovely parting gift, Madden came away with the dugout phone as a lifelong souvenir.

He swears that not a day goes by without a brief moment of reflection—haunting?—of the play.

Wagner: "It takes a half hour until [NFL officials] decide. Then the defense has to go back in the game. I can't find my helmet. I think I grabbed Gerry Mullins' helmet, big old cage on it. I'm thinking, 'Great, I'll get my helmet turned around and get beat in coverage. I'll be the worst player ever.'" He didn't. Game over, 13-7 Steelers.

At game's end, Tatum chased down Fuqua, according to Fuqua: "'Tell them you touched the ball,' he screamed at me over and over. I ran down the tunnel to our locker room. And all the way Tatum's nagging me, 'Tell them it was you.'"

A security guard came to the Steelers' locker room afterward, having grabbed the helmet from a fan who partook of the Franco fandemonium on the field. The guard acted with as much formality as if it were the Holy Grail.

That night, shortly before the 11 P.M. news hit the air, a couple of fans after a few toddies called into the WTAE switchboard and got through to Cope. Michael Ord and Sharon Levosky happened upon a holiday nickname, and they just had to give it to him: the Immaculate Reception. Joy shot through Cope's diminutive body. Then fear: Can a Jewish fellow invoke such a phrase on television? Yoi. What the hell. And so Ord, Levosky, and Cope begat one of the most famous nicknames in American sports lore.

A kid knocked on the South Fayette door of Bradshaw the next day: He returned Dwight White's helmet.

The ball? Twenty-five years later, the fan who nabbed the prized football that day finally placed it back in the hands of the man who caught the pass, and Harris welled up.

The Steelers that next week played host to the undefeated Miami Dolphins, and gave them quite a go. A fake punt by Larry Seiple proved the turning point in the game, a 21-17 Dolphins victory. It was one of the Dolphins' closest games in that 17-0 season.

History didn't stop there. The Steelers hysteria was only beginning.

Four Super Bowls of the 1970s became a franchise half dozen before the Immaculate Reception turned 40.

Yet it keeps coming back to that one day, that one play, that one freeze-frame moment.

Fuqua: "I was at a [Morgan State] alumni reunion two years ago. [Oakland tight end] Raymond Chester says, 'You know you guys cheated.' I was very surprised that 30-some-odd years later, he still holds that grudge."

Wagner: "They didn't have videotape like they have today. It's a question about the call. [Shrugged.] People say, 'Oh, that ball hit the ground.' I say, 'Oh, no, that ball was this far off the ground [holding his hand 6 inches high]. It was a great catch. I saw. And someone out there is a disappointed fan who had a Mike Wagner helmet that the security people took from him."

Fuqua: "Every year on December 23, there is a phone call made. Either Franco calls me or I call Franco. The conversation is just short. 'Frenchy, happy anniversary.' 'Ah, you beat me to it. Happy anniversary, Franco.'"

Larry Brown, tight end: "You can go back and pull something out . . . of a historical time frame and say, This is really what generated or started something. I think it was

Terry Bradshaw, with Franco Harris and Jon Kolb protecting him from the rush, rears back to throw into the Seattle Seahawks defense in 1978. (John Beale)

significant; I don't know if it's overstated about where it fits because of what it meant at that time. That year was the first time the Steelers [won a division] and made the playoffs. One of the players involved was one of the cornerstones," Franco Harris, a biracial symbol adopted by two vital communities in Pittsburgh: African Americans and Italians. "That was significant that he was part of it, it . . . marked him as a part of the future. It was an extraordinary event and marked him as extraordinary. And it was against the Raiders." Brown smiled. "I think it started to [instill in the Steelers] self-esteem. I think the team really started to believe. I mean, you go so many years where it wasn't possible, you start to accept failure. But if you experience [success] and think . . . , 'It is possible.'"

Fuqua: "That was the trampoline that shot us up to the stars. There was a confidence that we had. And it stemmed from that one play."

Brown: "And for the community at large? One thing that's been a huge mystery to me, and I'm still trying to wrap my arms around it [four decades later], how a community could embrace a team in such a personal way. You didn't go unnoticed. You could be somewhere and somebody would tell you what you did well or what you did wrong in a game.

"That [AFC championship eight days later on New Year's Eve] was an important game, too. Even though it was a loss, [it] was against [vaunted] Miami. I don't think anybody who played that game didn't feel like that was a game we should have won. We played against a great, great team. We fell asleep on a punt. Everybody remembers we should have won the game. So I think that was just as important a game to play as that first one."

The Immaculate Perception?

"With Ernie Holmes at tackle or [Steve] Furness, we'd run a [twist] game, Ernie would stunt the gap, and Joe would run behind him. We were getting the same advantage as on a blitz—we didn't need the linebackers."

Next came the Raiders.

Armed with the talent, the techniques, the taut defense, the Steelers received the final ingredient from Noll in the week's opening meeting. He gave them reason to believe.

Gordon: "Chuck went into the first team meeting that week, which would have been on Tuesday, and said: 'I understand from reports that the AFC championship game was played last Sunday. But as far as I'm concerned, the best team in the AFC is sitting in this room right now.'"

Brown: "You couldn't break the confidence, the 'we-got-this' attitude that was in that room."

So confident were the Steelers that when a reporter happened upon L. C. Greenwood sitting outside their locker room moments before that AFC championship game in Oakland–Alameda County Coliseum as he was watching the NFC championship game on a portable television, Greenwood said, "Just watching to see who we play in the Super Bowl."

Ham: "You talk about a critical game, to win our first championship, to win on the road in Oakland . . .

The stunt 4–3—it made sense for all of us. It just made our defense so much sounder. And Ernie was just phenomenal that game against [Gene] Upshaw. It was just amazing."

Gordon: "What did the Raiders get, 21 yards rushing [that game]? That was the game Ernie Holmes really dominated Upshaw."

Perles: "The next week, we held the Raiders to 26 yards rushing, or something ridiculous."

It was 29, actually. On 21 carries.

No shame there: The Minnesota Vikings got 17 yards on the same number of carries in Super Bowl IX.

The Steelers' average age upon winning Super Bowl IX: 25.2 years.

A dynasty age.

John Banaszak, defensive lineman 1975–1981: "I had to do the old head butts every day against Joe Greene, L. C. Greenwood, Dwight White, and Ernie Holmes. That's the equivalent of being a ditchdigger on the Pittsburgh Steelers. Or the Porta-John cleaner of the Pittsburgh Steelers.

"Still, it was pretty nice to run into the huddle and see Joe Greene on my right, Jack Ham on my left, and Jack Lambert in front of us ready to call the signals. Surrounded by three [future] Hall of Famers, how bad could I play?"

Their horde of talent prevailed again in 1975, the season ending with victory in Super Bowl X, the season aided by the emergence of Myron Cope's Terrible Towel. After a 1-4 start

to 1976, admittedly due to a back-to-back Super Bowl hangover, let alone three of those losses coming by a field goal or less, the Steelers rebounded with defense and running. They had to, because Bradshaw was concussed after Cleveland's Joe "Turkey" Jones planted him head-first into the Municipal Stadium soil.

Rookie Mike Kruczek handed off mostly, Harris and Vietnam hero Rocky Bleier ran the ball mostly, and the defense pitched shutouts in five of the regular season's final nine games. Dan Rooney and many of the players and coaches steadfastly believe 1976 was the Steelers' finest team, but they lost the AFC championship game in Oakland after Harris, Bleier, and even kicker Roy Gerela got hurt in the victory at Baltimore.

Banaszak: "No question the best team. The Chief would tell you that. That was pretty cool. Twenty-seven points [allowed] in nine ball games. Mike Kruczek, he couldn't throw the ball from here to that wall. He won four games for us."

Hoak: "Probably was the best team. We probably made a mistake [preparing for Harris and/or Bleier to play against Oakland], hoping maybe they'll be ready, 'I think they'll be ready. . . .' I remember those guys running in warm-ups. We

Rocky Bleier, with help from excellent trap blocking and a run-first, run-second, run-third philosophy after an injured Terry Bradshaw gave way to an untested Mike Kruczek at quarterback, scoots to a 1,000-yard season, the same as backfield mate Franco Harris in 1976. They were the first running-backs tandem in NFL history to reach that plateau. (George Gojkovich)

would've been better off, 'Defense, we need you to do this; offense we need to do this.' We ran a one-back offense [for apparently the first time in NFL history]. That's one thing, too. Chuck never got the credit for all that he did. He never wanted it."

Russell: "In '76, we had five shutouts. That's incredible. I think the Oakland Raiders fooled us [in the AFC championship game]. All week, their coaches said they wouldn't run on us. They ran every play the first half. We changed everything at halftime. They threw every down the second half. I almost came back and played another year, because we lost that game the way we did."

Wagner: "I thought this was amazing. We were outplaying the Raiders in 1976 in the [AFC championship] game after we lost our three running backs. There were 30 seconds left, and there was no way [for the Steelers to win]. For whatever reason, the referee [Tommy Bell] walks into our huddle and starts saying, 'I just want to say, this is one of the greatest defensive units I've ever seen. This is my last football game, I'm retiring.' All of a sudden, Lambert says, 'What are you doing? Get the hell out of our huddle!' The ref jumped back. Just looked so terrified. [Steelers teammates said facetiously,] 'Oh, good job, Jack.'"

Radakovich: "No. Hell no it wasn't the best. We were 1-4. The defense got [complacent at first]. Lambert wasn't playing like he should. We were overconfident. We got straightened away, five shutouts. Awesome. The best team? No. Seventy-five was the best."

The most unsettled, and unsettling, season of the Super Bowl '70s had to be 1977.

It started with a $2 million lawsuit filed by Oakland's George Atkinson after that 1976 opening loss in Oakland, Atkinson concussing Lynn Swann and Noll remarking about a "criminal element" in the NFL. Clips of Greene, Holmes, Blount, and Glen Edwards were played in court. Noll testified in a San Francisco court, while missing training camp, that a few of his own players may qualify for that description as well. Blount filed a $6 million defamation of character suit against Noll. Lambert and Edwards were contract holdouts. It was a mess.

After a 4-4 start, longtime NFL reporter Vito Stellino in the *Pittsburgh Post-Gazette* wrote about the apparent dynastic demise: "A team that once won 20 of 22 games, including two straight Super Bowls, has fallen into decline. . . . If the Steelers collapse and miss the playoffs, a major overhaul may be in order."

Stallworth offered: "The whole town's against us."

They rallied to make the playoffs, but it was as if they almost preferred to escape 1977 than win in it.

Because the next year they seemed much more relaxed, much more Steelers-like . . . even if they were combating an NFL system that they felt became stacked against them.

In 1978, NFL owners—given the dominance of the Steelers and Raiders—enacted rules to prohibit defensive contact with receivers from the line of scrimmage.

Blount reacted angrily: "They legislated the game, in my opinion, to slow the Steelers down. They took away the head slap, the bump-and-run, and the blocking techniques."

Noll added, "They ganged up on us and are trying to win the championship through legislation."

What the rule changes also meant: Swann and Stallworth had more room to run and maneuver.

Even Bradshaw admitted that it was a transition period. The defense's sun was setting. The offense's was rising.

The fun was returning. But with a few new characters in the cast. J. T. Thomas, due to a blood disorder later known as sarcoidosis, sat out the season, and rookie Ron Johnson replaced him at the left corner opposite Blount. Glen "Pine" Edwards, whose interception had sealed a Super Bowl X triumph, was traded after his midseason 1977 holdout so Donnie Shell and Mike Wagner could share the safety duties. Gerry "Moon" Mullins replaced a traded Jim Clack at guard. Banaszak and Furness replaced a traded Steel Curtain defensive tackle Ernie Holmes.

Yeah, they'd miss Fats . . . perhaps off the field more than on one.

Gary Dunn, defensive lineman 1977–1987: "Fats, he'd fall asleep in meetings. One time, his elbow slipped off and he hit the cabinet. George [Perles] said, 'Ernie, why don't you lay on the floor before you hurt yourself?' So Ernie laid on the floor and took a nap.

"Another time, Joe and Fats got into it in the room, then they started getting into a wrestling match. George crawled out of the room on all fours. You could hear L. C. laughing down the hall, 'Bwah-ha-ha-ha-ha.'"

Of course, that was the same Greenwood who, during a film session once, tossed a lighted cigarette into a wastebasket and started a fire.

Dunn: "We all ran out of the room again. Chuck Noll's secretary sat right across from the room, and she said, 'You guys have the best meetings.'"

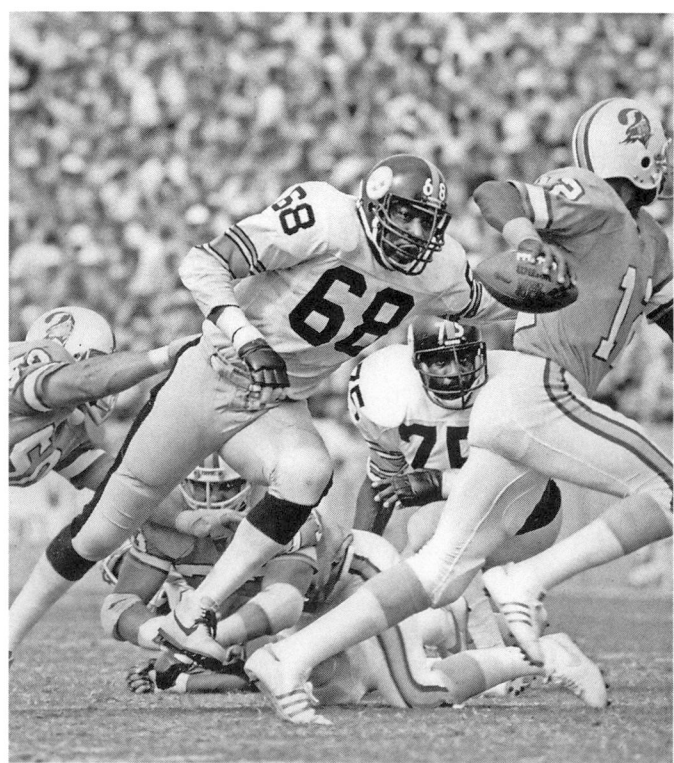

L. C. Greenwood, with Joe Greene on the ground, chases Tampa Bay quarterback Doug Williams in 1980. (Bill Amatucci)

The best talent made for practices as difficult as games, if not more so.

Brown: "It made you better. During training camp, all the time we were live. All the reps. And it was *endless.* [Laughing.] Seemed like we were out there seven to eight weeks. Maybe it wasn't that long. Live drills in the morning. Live drills in the afternoon."

Tony Dungy, safety 1977–1978:

That was the great thing about that team: the practices were so competitive. You were playing against good guys with a lot of pride. I remember Mel Blount telling me as a rookie: "I don't care what drill it is, you don't let anybody catch a ball." The defensive guys expected you to make plays no matter what the situation.

All those guys were able to play in the same system. When I got there, we were a running team, but they were starting to progress as a passing team. It took that time to develop. That's something guys don't get now. There was so much talent there: '76, '77, '78, '79. When I got there, 10 guys on defense had gone to the Pro Bowl the season before. In this day and age, I don't know if you can put that kind of team together; you wouldn't have that space under the salary cap. If those guys hit the free-agent market, you wouldn't have been able to keep them all. They all would've been the highest paid players at their positions.

Pat Rooney Sr., saying the family football enterprise never truly made money until about 1990, anyway: "The Steelers, even in the '70s, never paid anything off. The Steelers were never as big a financial thing as people always thought it was. The racetracks paid the bills."

Seasons of 14-2 and 12-4 ended in rousing AFC championship victories over Houston—so much for Oilers coach Bum Phillips promising Houston fans that his team would knock down that door to reach the Super Bowl. The Steelers closed out the decade wtih victories in Super Bowl XIII over Dallas and Super Bowl XIV over Los Angeles.

Four rings in six seasons. An unprecedented run of success. Maybe that explains why the bus trip home from that last one contained so much celebration that they had to pull over and let the fellows relieve themselves . . . on the streets of LA. These guys weren't kidding when they claimed that they never left each other's side.

Dungy: "That was the fun part of it. There was always something going on. Coach Noll fostered that atmosphere; you have to be close. And those guys were on and off the field."

Ralph Berlin, trainer 1969–1992, missing those Tuesday afternoon poker games: "Joe Greene, Franco, Swann, Mullins, [guard Sam] Davis, L. C. Bradshaw would come, drop a couple of hundred and leave. Stallworth came by, but he just came to eat. Tell you what, we had a good time in those poker games."

Wagner: "There's a core of about 20 Steelers who are very close and stay together. The personality of Dwight . . . I didn't realize how much I would miss Dwight. For fun, Mel and I play Jack and L. C. every year in a golf outing. That is the most serious blood match ever in the world—you would think a Super Bowl was going on.

"Those teams are extremely close when we get together. That, to me, is amazing. We all played together for years. The one thing you don't understand is, you don't necessarily grow up, you just grow older."

Berlin: "That miniseries *The Band of Brothers?* That's what those guys were."

9

The Super Bowls

SUPER BOWL IX
January 12, 1975
Tulane Stadium, New Orleans, Louisiana
Steelers 16, Vikings 6

With weak Dwight White climbing from his weeklong hospital bed to play, with four decades of demons awaiting exorcism, the Steelers made their inaugural moment on professional football's biggest stage a memorable one. And there were three more to come soon after.

In the city of jazz, it was all about having "sole."

Equipment manager Tony Parisi, a native Canadian and former goaltender for the minor league Pittsburgh Hornets hockey team, ordered 75 pairs of rubberized cleats from Montreal before the game. The shoes, which weren't even on the market yet, arrived the Wednesday prior. The Tulane Stadium Poly-Turf, combined with the weather forecast for wet, slick conditions, caused Parisi to remember an earlier

Terry Bradshaw opened the 1974 season as a stubble-strewn backup and ended it as a clean-cut Super Bowl champion. Here he and Chuck Noll confer with Joe Gilliam during Gilliam's only loss as a Steelers starter that season, to the Raiders at home in the third game. (George Gojkovich)

Miami game on the same surface, so he called Quebec to order the rain footwear. Outside linebacker Andy Russell told a reporter afterward, "God knows where he found those shoes. It was as if they came from heaven."

Third-year fullback Franco Harris rushed for a Super Bowl record 158 yards with a touchdown. Terry Bradshaw had to attempt only 14 passes, one of them a touchdown to a future offensive tackle, Larry Brown—who also had the longest play of the game, a 30-yard connection with Bradshaw.

White smothered a fumbling Fran Tarkenton for a safety—the franchise's very first score in 1933 was duplicated as their very first Super Bowl score. The Steel Curtain tipped five passes and harassed Tarkenton into an 11-for-26 showing for 102 yards and three interceptions, all computing to a lowly 14.1 passer rating. Chuck Foreman rushed 12 times for 18 yards into the fangs of the stunt 4–3 defense.

Brown, talking about Chuck Noll's stroke of genius in giving the Steelers their first two days in New Orleans without any curfew—or practice—at all: "The Minnesota coach [Bud Grant], he wouldn't even let his players use hand warmers. In Minnesota! Their coach was very strict. They had a hard curfew in New Orleans. We got down there, [Noll] gave us the first two days off. I mean, *off.* That allowed guys to *relax,* really. We went with Frank [Lewis] to Louisiana, where he was from. There were probably four or five of us. His hometown was throwing a day for him. Or we'd go down Bourbon Street. He let guys do that. He told us that; he knew that we understood. So when it was time to concentrate on football, we were more focused. You give guys respect . . . , and guys live up to that."

Ralph Berlin, trainer: "We were supposed to play in the [Super]dome, but they weren't finished. We had to play in Tulane Stadium, and it was condemned [seven months later]. We walked out of the locker room and saw this guy had a heart attack. George [Perles] stepped right over him. So did Joe [Greene]. We didn't know if the guy ever lived or not."

Perles, defensive line coach at the time: "Dwight doesn't practice one snap all week. And Steve Furness is going to start. He says to me, 'Dwight has been waiting his whole life for this, and I got plenty of more years to play.' Steve is trying to let me off the hook. Chuck and I are standing in the end zone, and Joe and Dwight are right in front of us. They're head butting, knocking the heck out of each other. Chuck says, 'What's going on?' 'He's just trying to prove he's ready to play.' I told Chuck, 'I'll just play him in the first series and take him out of there.'

I can still hear the pads hitting under the goalpost, those two guys warming up."

Mike Wagner, safety: "I was only nervous before the first Super Bowl game. . . . The defense is being introduced. We were in a line, inside a Cyclone fence. The Vikings offense is in one line along the Cyclone fence, and the Steelers defense is on the other. All of a sudden, Glen Edwards says to [Vikings tackle] Ron Yary, the biggest guy they have, 'We're going to kick your ass today.' I'm looking at Glen, 'What are you doing? You don't need to give anybody a reason to hit me harder.' [Yary] gave Glen a sleepy-eyed look, almost like batting an eye."

Perles: "I told [running backs coach] Dick Hoak to watch it. One bad play, I'm getting the hell out of that [stunt 4–3] defense, or it's my scalp. He would tell me from the press box, 'They're over on the sideline with the chalkboard, trying to draw the defense up.'"

Jack Ham, outside linebacker 1971–1982: "We're playing the stunt 4–3. I think I made one tackle the entire day. 'Cause Minnesota tried to run off tackle against the stunt 4–3—to this day, I don't know why they did that. I wanted to do more. I wanted to be more a part of this thing. Not that I didn't enjoy it afterward. But I wanted a couple more bruises, a couple badges of courage."

Russell: "The Vikings made a classic mistake: run at somebody's strength. A big mistake. They ran right at Joe Greene." Greene had one interception on a deflection and one fumble recovery. White, still so sick with pneumonia he was hospitalized again afterward, had four tackles according

to play-by-play accounts. Those same accounts credited Ham with three tackles—all in the first half.

Perles: "That stunt 4–3 was big for us. That was the beginning of the stunt 4–3 and the Steel Curtain."

Russell: "It's not something we could have imagined in the '60s. I can still hear Ray [Mansfield] on the sidelines after we just beat the Vikings, 'We just climbed the mountain.' And, later, he and I got into mountain climbing."

Art Rooney II: "I guess it's fair to say when I was younger it was hard for me to imagine our team would win a championship. For somebody like me who had been through a lot of that— obviously not as long as my dad or granddad—I had a feel for how things had been. There are a couple of moments that stand out. When we won the AFC championship game in Oakland to get to the Super Bowl, when we came home to the [Pittsburgh] airport at 1 or 2 o'clock, in the airport there was [a mob of happy fans who left] one single-file line for us to squeeze through. It was really one of the most remarkable things I've ever seen.

"It's funny, my dad . . . he's never been one to make sure everybody had their credentials and everything. All I had was a ticket to the game. After the game, I was determined to get into the locker room and be a part of the celebration. I got down to the locker room . . . I jumped over the fence, and these big Louisiana state troopers grabbed me. I told them who I was, and they weren't believing it. I showed them my driver's license and everything. Lucky for me [negotiator] Jim Boston came by" and got Art into the locker room.

"To see my grandfather be able to experience that after all he went through, it's something that always will be a good memory."

Dan "Bad Rad" Radakovich, offensive line coach at the time: "The end of the game, they gave [the Chief] a game ball. Mr. Rooney at that time was considered like God. The big thing was to win for Mr. Rooney."

Berlin, recalling the locker room ceremony: "The players picked [Art Rooney Sr.] up and put him on the podium, gave him the game ball. That showed the respect and the love the players had for him."

Ham: "In Art Rooney fashion . . . I can see him getting the Lombardi Trophy in the locker room . . . the typical unassuming Chief, he just said, 'Thank you.' That was probably the highlight to me."

SUPER BOWL X
January 18, 1976
Orange Bowl, Miami, Florida
Steelers 21, Cowboys 17

The weather was sunny, better. But there also was this movie crew around, shooting some terrorism flick involving an exploding blimp. The movie was called *Black Sunday*.

Even the trainer, Ralph Berlin, was so focused that he walked onto the field right past one of the movie's stars, Robert Shaw of *Jaws* fame.

Larry Brown, tight end at the time: "The national anthem was pretty cool. The blind folk singer, Tom Sullivan. I remember standing there and listening to that. I thought he did that song as well as I ever heard it."

Franco Harris looks for daylight in 1980. (Bill Amatucci)

Jack Lambert glowers. 'Nuff said. (Bill Amatucci)

but the pass was good for 64 yards, the game's longest play, and the deciding touchdown. It was 21-10, Steelers, with 3:02 to go.

Berlin: "He never even saw Swann catch the pass. A kid named [Larry] Cole. Really coldcocked him."

Bradshaw left with a concussion.

Staubach wasted precious little time. Within 74 seconds and five snaps, he put Dallas on the board with a 34-yard touchdown pass to Percy Howard, cutting the lead to 21-17.

Moon Mullins recovered the Dallas onside kick—wait, an offensive tackle on the "hands" team? Well, he was a converted tight end. The Steelers had the ball at Dallas' 42 with 1:48 left, but with backup Terry Hanratty of Butler, Pennsylvania, in there, Noll grew vest-tight with play selection.

Wagner: "That was the first year shoe companies gave you money to wear their shoes. You'd get $500, but you didn't know how they'd feel. . . . We looked at Hanratty, and he had two different brands on. He got paid by two different companies."

The Steelers' offense ran the ball once, twice, thrice . . . *four times.* Instead of asking for a pooch punt from Bobby Walden, who fumbled earlier in the game, Noll ran on fourth down . . . that gave the ball to the Cowboys on downs at the Dallas 39 with 1:22 on the clock.

In two plays, the Cowboys were at the Steelers' 38.

Wagner, about Staubach's game-ending deep throw into the end zone: "I tipped that. You go, 'Oh, spit . . .' I think about that play. At the time, I didn't think anything about it. If that ball had been a foot underthrown and Drew Pearson would have jumped up in front of me and caught it, or if I tipped it to a Dallas Cowboy [instead of Edwards], the whole thing

The best performance, the most dramatic actor on this stage, was all Lynn Swann. He made the 53-yard, falling, juggling, jaw-dropping midfield catch against Dallas cornerback Mark Washington. The reception not only rescued the Steelers from a third-and-six at their own 10-yard line, it put them in position for a field-goal attempt that provided some juice to the Steelers. That was the try where Roy Gerela missed, Dallas safety Cliff Harris patted him on the helmet, and Jack Lambert made Harris go splat.

Mike Wagner, safety: "That game was so serious. There was so much intensity on each play. One of the turning points was when Cliff Harris geeked Gerela, and Lambert threw him to the ground. Lambert, that was as stupid as can be. He could've been thrown out of the game. At the same time, I'm not sure that helped the Cowboys at all; was that really necessary? That was a stupid thing to do probably for a player of [Harris's] caliber."

The Steelers, in the form of Reggie "Boobie" Harrison, blocked a Mitch Hoopes punt for a safety. That cut the Dallas lead to 10-9, and Pittsburgh then drove the free kick into range for Gerela. After two misses, he gave them a 12-10 lead with 8:41 to go.

Former Steelers running back Preston Pearson fumbled and recovered the kickoff. Then, on first down from the Dallas 15, Roger Staubach was intercepted by Wagner. Soon enough, Gerela had another field goal and the Steelers a 15-10 advantage.

On third-and-four on the next Steelers' possession, the blond bomber went deep. Terry Bradshaw didn't even know it,

Lynn Swann. (Bill Amatucci)

could be completely different. Or there might not be six Super Bowls. Because Drew Pearson and Roger Staubach completed Hail Marys before. So I still kind of shudder about it every once in a while."

Russell: "Piney Edwards with the interception in the end of the game. Which could have been a disaster. That could've beat us." It was that close.

Wagner: "Glen started running it out of the end zone. 'What are you doing? If you fumble the ball . . .'" It was a legitimate concern. Late in a 1973 game against Washington, trying to preserve a narrow lead, Edwards fumbled an interception return . . . and Wagner fumbled it, too.

Even though Bradshaw passed for 209 yards and two touchdowns for a 122 passer rating, Swann was the MVP with four catches for 161 and a whopping 40.3-yard average. The most amazing catch was his second shortest: a 32-yarder in the first quarter down the right sideline. His body seemed to go out of bounds, but he exercised enough body control to keep his feet in bounds. Somehow.

Dan "Bad Rad" Radakovich, offensive line coach at the time: "Did we expect to win? Yeah, we expected to win. The whole season. We figured the only way we would lose the Super Bowl is if somebody got hurt. We won a close game. That game was closer than anybody realizes."

SUPER BOWL XIII
January 21, 1979
Orange Bowl, Miami, Florida
Steelers 35, Cowboys 31

Tony Dungy, nickel back and safety: "I remember walking out the field for warm-ups, I can't believe I'm not watching the ball game. I always watched it on TV."

Holy déjà vu, weren't these two teams just here: Same place, same stage, same brutes versus finesse?

This time, there were two major differences: Tony Dorsett's legs and Hollywood Henderson's mouth for Dallas. Both could move at amazing speeds.

Henderson flapped his jowls about Terry Bradshaw's intellect (the C-A- spelling business, as outlined in Chapter 7) and more. Dorsett flapped his flying feet for 96 yards, but on only 16 carries—a low total that should've forced Tom Landry to remove that chapeau and slap his forehead a couple of times.

By this time, amid rules changes and maturity, the Steelers' offense transformed into a dynamic unit. Four of the game's six longest plays? John Stallworth a 75-yard touchdown, and a 28-yard touchdown, Swann a 29-yard catch and a 26-yard catch. Stallworth, in fact, had three catches for 115 yards in the first half . . . then couldn't play in the second half because of leg cramps.

Dungy: "John Stallworth had this great game going. He was just killing [Cowboys cornerback] Aaron Kyle. He starts cramping up. I'm like, 'He'll get some fluids and come back.' The second half, they said, 'John can't play.' I went up to him, 'How about the Steelers' tradition, Dwight White came out of the hospital, and you got a cramp and can't play?' But Swann [seven total catches for 124 yards] took it over in the second half. It was that type of thing. It was a great offensive performance against a good defense. John was just on fire in the first half."

Terry Bradshaw in 1977. The next season, he directed the Steelers to the first of their last pair of back-to-back championships—winning Super Bowl MVP both times. (Bill Amatucci)

John Stallworth, receiver: "I look at a guy now having cramps, go to the locker room . . . and he's fine and he plays the rest of the game. I'm like, 'Where was that?' I had a really good first half, felt good, felt comfortable. I particularly had [Bradshaw's] eyes during the course of that game. It killed me. It got kind of close later on. And Joe Greene comes up to me, 'You *got* to get back in the game.' 'Joe, I wish I could.' I couldn't stand on my toes without my calves cramping up."

John Banaszak, defensive lineman, about how the power tilted from the Steelers' defense to offense: "It ended up going the other way, that's for sure, the last two Super Bowls."

Dungy: "The year before, Dallas had won, Dallas beat Denver. Harvey Martin and Randy White were co-MVPs. I remember Dwight White [a college teammate of Martin's] saying in the paper before the game, 'They won't touch our quarterback.' Jon Kolb said, 'Don't say that and get them mad.' But that's the confidence our guys had."

With the Steelers ahead by 21-17 late in the third quarter, Roger Staubach had third-and-three at the Steelers' 10. He threw into the end zone for an open tight end destined for the Hall of Fame. Jackie Smith played 15 seasons for St. Louis, that one last season for Dallas. In the end, this was his final game—one month before he turned 39 years old.

He dropped it.

Gary Dunn, defensive lineman: "Your heart dropped there. I saw him one place [later], first time I really met him. I busted his chops a little bit, just kidding around. He truly had a great career, and he said, 'All people remember me for is that ball.'"

Henderson, like Cliff Harris before him in Super Bowl X, only served to provide the Steelers with a little juice. Midway through the fourth quarter, he flung Bradshaw to the ground on a delay-of-game snap that didn't count. The five-yard penalty made it third-and-nine from the Dallas 22. Hardly a running down.

Mike Wagner, safety, about restraining his friend, outside linebacker Jack Ham: "I only saw Jack get agitated once [in a decade together]: Hollywood Henderson going after Bradshaw. Jack was very laid-back on the football field and very laid-back on the sideline. Henderson did something, pushing Bradshaw after a play. I've never seen Jack so irate. He tried to go out on the field; I had to grab him. That must've been the play right before Franco said, 'Give me the ball,' and they scored on that big touchdown."

The trap play resulted in a 22-yard, fourth-quarter touchdown that put the Steelers ahead for good. Bradshaw told reporters later of Harris, "I've never seen him run so hard."

Dungy hit Hall of Fame defensive tackle White on the next kickoff, and Dirt Winston recovered. The next play, Bradshaw found Swann for that lovely 18-yard touchdown.

Banaszak: "We really enjoyed playing the Cowboys. We knew we were a physical football team. We probably felt down

to a man they were a finesse team; we weren't going to let them beat us. We got up 35-17 on the Cowboys, and Roger Staubach's never going to quit. He marches them back and scores two quick touchdowns. Exciting games."

George Perles, defensive coordinator: "We were winning with six minutes and 30-some seconds. We were up by 16 or something. So I put the prevent in. Staubach gets hot. Boom boom boom, touchdown. Now we're up by 10. They get the ball, boom boom boom boom boom. Now we're up by three points."

Jack Ham, outside linebacker: "You talk about getting nervous in a game. We're ahead 35-17. They get a touchdown pass, and they get an onside kick. They get *another* touchdown. I can always remember Chuck Noll yelling at me. I'm never in on the onside team. He yells at me, 'Get in on the onside kick.' I think to myself, 'If they kick that ball to me, I don't recover, and they beat us, I might as well go to the Fort Pitt Bridge and jump off.' That was about as nervous as I've ever been in the Super Bowl. Then I saw Rocky fall on it."

Perles: "They onside kick, Rocky Bleier fell on the ball, and the game was over.

"I took a lot of heat on that one, putting the prevent in too early."

At the postgame news conference, the *Pittsburgh Post-Gazette*'s Vito Stellino mentioned that the Cowboys figured they would've won if there'd been a smidgen more time on the clock.

Perles: "I said, 'Bull. . . . If I don't put the prevent in so early, they couldn't beat us in a month of Sundays.'" When they opened the next season with these same Cowboys, Stellino reminded him of that quote.

Ever prescient, Noll said something to reporters afterward: "We haven't peaked yet."

SUPER BOWL XIV
January 20, 1980
Rose Bowl, Pasadena, California
Steelers 31, Rams 19

Larry Brown, by now a starting offensive tackle: "Obviously, the first one has its place. Until you go and do it. . . . But they each were significant. And the anxiety, the need to win, was just as strong in the last one as the first one."

John Banaszak, defensive lineman: "The Super Bowl XIV game was a very interesting game because of the Rams' coaching staff. With Bad Rad on it, Bud Carson, Lionel Taylor."

Mike Wagner, safety: "There was a lot of emotion going on, knowing Gordy [Gravelle, an ex-Steelers tackle] . . . , having Bud and Lionel and Bad Rad on the Rams. There were probably a lot of emotional issues. I sat in the stands [after surgery and being on injured reserve]. It was the worst experience of my life."

Dan "Bad Rad" Radakovich, Rams offensive line coach: "It was great playing against them. The Rams, we came from 4-5 to get to the Super Bowl. Then you get to play your old team. Nothing is bigger than a game against your friends. More important than a game against your enemy. Preparation is what wins games for you. [Playing friends] motivates you to prepare like a son of a bitch."

Tony Dungy, nickel back and safety: "If anybody knows us and knows how to attack us, [it would be those former

In a Super Bowl XIII rematch nine months later, Jack Ham and the Steelers sack Roger Staubach and the Dallas Cowboys . . . again. This time, Pittsburgh wins by 14-3. (Bill Amatucci)

Lynn Swann and John Stallworth twirl Terrible Towels together in the 1979 playoffs. There were at one time dark towels of the official Myron Cope brand, but it isn't known if the ones pictured were merely grabbed hastily at Three Rivers Stadium or vintage issue. (George Goikovich)

Steelers assistants]. And if you watch the game, the Rams had some good things in there. But these guys weren't going to be denied."

Stubborn Los Angeles answered each of the Steelers' first half scores, then grabbed a late field goal to enter intermission with a 13-10 advantage.

Then Bradshaw began to air it out. He tossed a 47-yard touchdown to Lynn Swann, a lead that once again lasted only seconds, and then a pair of interceptions. Less than three minutes into the fourth quarter, they went into the Emperor's bag of tricks.

Perles: "Chuck put in the winning touchdown pass the week of the game, the [60 prevent] hook and go. That's the one Stallworth caught way over his head. People were doubling him. Chuck knew." Indeed the defensive backs were confounded by the hook, and Stallworth made it go.

John Stallworth, receiver: "Initially, I thought [the pass] was going to be too long, that I wouldn't be able to get there." Long, tall Stall? Seventy-three yards, touchdown, and the Steelers had a 24-19 lead.

Bradshaw, in winning his second consecutive MVP, threw only four of his 21 passes for incompletions—three of them,

remember, landed in Rams hands—for two touchdowns and 309 yards, just nine yards shy of the Super Bowl record he established a year earlier. He told reporters afterward: "I ran the pass eight times in practice, and I didn't like it. But it worked today. This is my most satisfying Super Bowl. I felt more pressure than at any other time." Bradshaw wound up with such career Super Bowl records as most touchdowns (nine), most passing yards (932), most jewelry (four rings).

Yet Bradshaw and Stallworth still had one more bauble up their sleeves.

Gary Dunn, defensive lineman: "The defense was flat. I don't know why, we were just a little flat. Lambert said, 'We gotta make a play out here. Gotta make a play.' Right then, Jack made an interception in the second half."

Six minutes remained, with a 24-19 Pittsburgh lead, but the hometown Rams were driving. On first down at the Steelers' 32, Lambert picked off Vince Ferragamo.

Two plays later, the Steelers faced third-and-seven at their own 33.

Stallworth: "We had been back and forth with those guys. We needed something. The medium passing game for us, the 15- to 18-yard routes, were not working because of the coverage they were playing. They surged ahead. Maybe by virtue of them knowing so much about our defense, they were having success in that regard. Offensively we needed to do something, and that one sort of put us ahead. I think that was a blow to the Rams' psyche. 'God, what do we have to do to put the Steelers away?' Then the 45-yarder to me, the same pass pattern [as the 73-yard touchdown]. . . . We were able to score again." Ring time.

Perles about his old compatriots Carson, whom he replaced as coordinator, Radakovich, and Taylor: "I don't know why the guys ever left."

Brown: "I certainly feel fortunate to have played in four, and to have won four. Something that seemed so important before, later seemed like something you *had* to do. Losing wasn't an option. [Laughs.] So I feel fortunate to go there and not have lost."

Dunn: "Hear about the bus trip? The bus trip after winning Super Bowl XIV?

"Here we are the champs. We're staying in Newport Beach, California. I don't know, but it was about an hour and a half south of there. We got four buses lined up, we got the Rooneys, the wives, and the families. We're all pumped up. They got some beer on the bus. All of a sudden Lambert goes, 'Hey, Dunnie, where the hell is the bathroom on this bus?' There's no bathroom. We're on the wrong bus.

"He walks up to the bus driver. He calls the other buses, they don't have one either. [The driver] tells him he'll have to wait until we get to Newport Beach. He couldn't hold it. Jack tells the bus driver, 'I'm telling you right now, either you pull this bus over, or I'm peeing on the floor.' [The driver] pulls over to a gas station, but the problem is it's closed. We have the whole team out there, and everybody's out there trying to find a spot. And we just won the Super Bowl." Good thing there weren't cell-phone cameras back then.

Tom Beasley, defensive lineman: "I'm gonna tell you what, that bus driver would've drowned if he hadn't pulled over. Everybody running behind that gas station. . . . [Laughs.] The pavement was grated. It was just a river running under the bus and across the road."

The last podium for the Chief: left to right, Pittsburgh Mayor Dick Caliguiri; a hat-topped Chuck Noll; Art Rooney Sr. holding his fourth Lombardi Trophy; Dan Rooney; and one of the Chief's political protégés, county commissioner Tom Foerster, at a downtown celebration. (George Gojkovich)

SUPER BOWL XXX
January 28, 1996
Sun Devil Stadium, Tempe, Arizona
Cowboys 27, Steelers 17

A generation later, the brute and finesse football reconvened, for old time's sake. America's Team collided with Shot-and-a-Beer's Team in the desert, but with a very different cast of characters.

The Steelers had another stout defense, called Blitzburgh, a throwback to the 1970s. But the Cowboys were already two-time champions under the coach chased away by owner Jerry Jones, one Jimmy Johnson. This time, former University of Oklahoma coach Barry Switzer was running the asylum that was cornerback Deion Sanders, receiver Michael Irvin, quarterback Troy Aikman, and halfback Emmitt Smith—Hall of Famers all.

Ron Erhardt, offensive coordinator 1992–1995: "Actually should've beaten Dallas that day. We didn't. But we should've. We had their good runner down [Smith]. We did a good job getting ready for those people."

The Cowboys dominated much of the first half, staking themselves to a 13-0 lead after scoring on their opening three possessions: 47-, 75-, and 62-yard marches. Neil O'Donnell, Bam Morris, and Kordell "Slash" Stewart hadn't gotten their act together on football's biggest stage until late in the first half, when they put together a drive. O'Donnell, after a 5-for-12 start for 56 yards with two sacks, rallied with three consecutive completions for a Yancey Thigpen short touchdown catch 13 seconds before intermission, 13-7 Cowboys.

Dermontti Dawson, center: "My memory? Me snapping the ball over Neil's head. I remember that, the biggest game . . . , and I snapped it over Neil's head in a shotgun formation." It came at the Dallas 36-yard line, the Steelers' deepest

penetration of the first quarter, and effectively quashed that drive. "Luckily, Neil was able to recover it. But I complained to the refs the whole entire time. That's when guys . . . would put a substance on their jerseys; the league was starting to crack down on that stuff. I complained to the refs, 'Feel my gloves.' Then I had to take my gloves off, and my hands were like glass. I complained to the refs the whole game, 'They got something on their jerseys.'"

Kevin Greene, outside linebacker, who earlier in the week flew to Las Vegas to get in a wrestling ring with Hulk Hogan and Randy "Macho Man" Savage: "We were able to clamp down on the second half. Dallas, I don't know [if] they were all that good on third down. Our defense was awfully good on getting off the field on third down."

Erhardt: "We really had a good offensive team, or we wouldn't have gotten where we did. A 60-minute game, we wanted [to possess the ball] 40 and give them 20. [The philosophy] was good for us."

Blitzburgh—the mayorship firmly in Dick LeBeau's hands after Dom Capers left to coach expansion Carolina—harassed Aikman and put a lid on Smith. Meanwhile, the Steelers' offense methodically moved down field, reaching the Dallas 33 but punting on their opening possession. O'Donnell, throwing for Ernie Mills, sustained his first interception on a third-and-nine at midfield. Dallas' *other* cornerback, the one they wanted to attack, came up with the ball and a 44-yard return. Two plays later, Smith scored for a 20-7 Dallas advantage.

Cowher, trying to revive his side, went for a fourth-and-two at the Steelers' 47 . . . and failed. Blitzburgh held its ground. When they got the ball back, the Steelers marched to a Norm Johnson field goal. Special teams coach Bobby April immediately came up to Bill Cowher with a novel idea: onside kick. Energized, the Steelers grabbed the Deon Figures recovery at their own 48, and motored easily to another

Longtime assistant and defensive coordinator Dick LeBeau celebrates the Steelers winning the AFC championship game in January 1996 and advancing to Super Bowl XXX. It would be the first of four Super Bowls in his decade-plus with the Steelers. (Bill Amatucci)

touchdown. O'Donnell went five for five for 42 yards, and Morris did the rest. It was 20-17, Dallas.

Greene: "I thought the tide turned on the surprise onside kick. We went down and put points on the board. I really thought the tide was turning. For whatever reason, it didn't happen. Our defense didn't show up. Hold that offense to at least three points on at least one of those turnovers. . . . I blame myself."

The defense held on the next Dallas possession after the Morris touchdown. But Andre Hastings misread a route—and the *other* Cowboys cornerback didn't. A 33-yard return to the Steelers' 6 concluded in another Smith touchdown run, and a 27-17 lead with 3:43 left killed the Steelers' buzz. O'Donnell threw a third interception on the game's final play, and never wore a Steelers uniform again.

O'Donnell made his money in free agency, $25 million going home to the New York Jets, but never replicated his Steelers success: He threw just two playoff passes in his final eight seasons.

And *other* cornerback Larry Brown, the father whose prematurely born son, Kristopher, died earlier that year, wound up a Super Bowl MVP and an Oakland Raider with a new $12.5 million deal.

O'Donnell later offered, "I took all the heat. That's fine. I can take it."

Erhardt: "And basically one [interception] was his and the other was on the receiver, as far as being at fault. That's the way those go when you're doing a hot read and things like that. We had it worked out, but we just didn't execute.

"A lot of people never get to one of those [Super Bowls]. I had two with the Giants and one with the Steelers. It was very gratifying for me." Erhardt died, at age 81, barely three months after being interviewed for this book.

Bill Cowher: His memory? "The pregame walks you have out on the field. The efforts of so many months and years, to be honest with you, come back . . . and you're one game away from that championship. It's a long, long road to get there. And you try to savor every moment. It's a tremendous buildup—especially 'cause they're so late in the day."

Dawson: "It would've been nice to win that game. We had those two interceptions. . . . We just didn't have enough time. Once we established the run, they couldn't stop us. Just ran out of time.

"I know we were a footnote because we didn't win a Super Bowl; we didn't go down in history as being really good. But 1994–1995, we were *good.*"

SUPER BOWL XL
February 5, 2006
Ford Field, Detroit, Michigan
Steelers 21, Seahawks 10

This was the final Bus tour.

Russ Grimm, offensive line and assistant head coach then: "The year we won the Super Bowl, in '05, we had to win the last four games *just to get in.* Then we won all four on the road. I think that's the only time it's been done."

To arrive at this juncture, the story cannot be told without Ben Roethlisberger's hand and Nick Harper's ankle and a heap of defense and, yes, Jerome Bettis. It took some doing to get one for the Bus and one for the thumb.

Roethlisberger, in only his second season, was turned loose in the playoffs. In Cincinnati, Indianapolis, and Denver, the kid quarterback completed 49 of 72 passes for 680 yards, seven touchdowns, one interception, a 124.75 passer rating, and three triumphs. His biggest hand, however, came while retreating to catch a Colts cornerback, Harper, who earlier got stabbed in the leg by his own wife.

Roethlisberger, of the Immaculate Redemption: "I'm a tackling machine."

Harper getting caught by the kid quarterback cut deepest. There would be no Colts game-winning touchdown. Nor was there any overtime-forcing field goal by that "idiot kicker" (Peyton Manning's words), Mike Vanderjagt, who, after making every home field goal previously that season, missed from 46 yards. That three-point Steelers victory was followed by an AFC championship victory in Denver, the franchise's first such title on the road since the 1975 season and a rare triumph after losing five of the previous six conference finals.

The quarterback delivered on the pledge he made in losing the AFC championship game a year earlier.

Roethlisberger: "I remember [saying], 'Just give me one more shot. I'll get you there.' It's probably the dumbest promise I could have ever made, as a first-year guy. 'I promise I'll get you there, just come back for one more year.'"

Unbeknownst to Jerome Bettis, his teammates stayed behind and allowed him to enter his hometown field first and alone in the moments before Super Bowl XL. (Courtesy of the Pittsburgh Steelers)

Next Bus stop: Motown.

Gladys Bettis invited the fellas over to the family home for dinner.

Hines Ward, receiver: "We ate good. Took our whole team to his mom's house."

Throughout the week, Bettis was feted and honored, the kingpin of a bowling charity and king for a day.

King for Super Bowl Sunday.

Dick Hoak, running backs coach: "That was really a nice thing that they did."

Larry Foote, inside linebacker and another Detroit native honored that week at his old high school: "Joey Porter, he did it. Right when we were going through the tunnel, too. He made that suggestion so everybody would stay back. I know [Bettis] was surprised when he got out there. He didn't know he was going to get this big-time delay; he was out there by himself."

Casey Hampton, nose tackle: "Oh, it was a great idea. Plus, it was that guy. Everybody wanted it real bad for him."

Max Starks, tackle: "That's probably the best gift a team could ever give a player of his caliber, to be able to know that he's retiring . . . to be so fitting as to go back [home and] let that be your last memory playing football. He's just a selfless individual and such a consummate gentleman and professional. I mean, he's the epitome of what professional athletes should be. Plus, a local celebrity, too. I mean, I never thought I'd see the day I'd be blocking for a guy I'd seen in a *Living Single* episode on television."

The big run of the game wasn't by Bettis, but his successor, Willie Parker. His Super Bowl–record, 75-yard gallop on the second play after halftime presented the Steelers with a 14-3 lead and a significant shove.

Grimm, about the beautifully blocked play: "That was a pull. [Perennial Pro Bowl guard Alan] Faneca."

Seattle trimmed the Steelers' lead to 14-10 in the third quarter. It was in the fourth where referee Bill Leavy later admitted that he "kicked" two calls and erred. One, for a low block on quarterback Matt Hasselbeck's tackle, tackled 15 extra yards after Ike Taylor had already intercepted Hasselbeck at the Steelers' 5. The point proved moot four plays later on a gadget pass that would've scored from anywhere on Ford Field.

Hines Ward, the MVP with five catches for 123 yards, about this 43-yard pass hurled by a fellow receiver who played quarterback in college (and completed 17 of 21 of these tosses in his Steelers career): "Of course, my biggest memory is the pass from [Antwaan] Randle El going into the end zone to help our team seal the game. But that whole thing—I remember the whole game. It was so magical. A play I did make, a play I didn't make. Other guys. There were so many stories within the story. Not only winning it for yourself, but winning it for guys like Jerome Bettis. Started his career in Detroit and ended it in Detroit. For a guy who meant so much for our organization and city . . . , you can't even write a better script, how to go out."

Bruce Arians, receivers coach: "Just standing on the field in the confetti and not believing it ever happened. It was a great way to win it, going on the road all those games. Especially for Jerome, whom I loved to death."

Roethlisberger, who in Detroit suffered his worst statistical day of the entire postseason run: "Honestly, I felt that whole year there was a lot written on Alan Faneca about Tommy [Maddox] and myself, how he didn't want a young rookie playing [a year earlier]. He was good friends with Tommy, and that's why he said those things. I never held any ill feelings for him; when one of your best friends gets hurt, you don't want that to happen.

"Alan was always the consummate professional. Always did his job first and foremost. Your job as a football player isn't to be best friends with everybody; you don't have to do that. You just got to play your best. So Alan and I weren't exactly close; it was what it was. What I remember is, we were in the victory formation. I took a knee, I stood up, and he was the first person who hugged me. Kind of tears and happy. All I

Ben Roethlisberger dives for a touchdown against Seattle in Super Bowl XL, one of the many plays that led to disagreement from Seattle fans—and Steelers detractors—who claimed he fell inches short of the goal line. (Courtesy of the Pittsburgh Steelers)

could think about was, 'Wow, Alan Faneca turns and hugs me, of all people, first.' That just meant, you know, a lot."

Aaron Smith, defensive end: "I didn't enjoy a lick of it. No, too much pressure, too much anxiety. All you want to do is win. I didn't enjoy one bit of the week leading up to it. I mean, I enjoyed the game, but . . . I tell everybody, imagine your entire life is coming down to one moment. You may only get this one moment *ever* in your life. And I wasn't there to have fun. My wife thought we were going to need counseling, until the game was over. 'Oh, it's good to have you back.'"

Dick LeBeau, defensive coordinator back in the Detroit where he played cornerback to Hall of Fame levels: "I remember easily the first one, Detroit. Because I had been there [to the Super Bowl with Cincinnati and Pittsburgh] three times before and lost. I just kept staring at the scoreboard when the game was over. I just kept staring at the number, the zeroes on the clock. Ah, it's a moment that I'll never forget. I just was walking around the field telling everybody, 'We did it, we did it.' To no one in particular but to anybody who walked by. 'We did it.'"

Bill Cowher, coach: "It took so long to win the first one, I don't think you really realize the magnitude of it until two or three days later . . . , even the subsequent weeks after. At first, you recognize the joy, the multitude of what you've done. But the true essence doesn't sink in until days and weeks after."

Hines Ward, Jerome Bettis, the Lombardi Trophy, confetti, and smoke—a wild scene. (Courtesy of the Pittsburgh Steelers)

SUPER BOWL XLIII

February 1, 2009
Raymond James Stadium, Tampa, Florida
Steelers 27, Cardinals 23

One for the *other* thumb came with the most melodrama and the first comeback. That pair against the Cowboys in the 1970s required the Steelers to protect a padded lead on the final, last-ditch Dallas plays. This triumph required a Pittsburgh offensive rally in the final seconds. Ben Roethlisberger and Santonio Holmes didn't disappoint.

Then again, that entire taut drama in Tampa delivered one of the most electrifying Super Bowls in history—certainly from the last play of the first half until game's end.

Dick LeBeau, defensive coordinator: "The Arizona game, it was a tremendous catch and drive by Ben and the team, the offense there at the end. We played so well on defense until that last quarter, and then we kind of had a couple of bad plays. I was very thankful that the offense bailed us out. Like all close games between good teams, it usually comes down to that fourth quarter."

The greatest single play in Super Bowl history arrived, officially, on the final play of the first half. This was the situation for Arizona—or Pittsburgh West, as it was known with head coach Ken Whisenhunt, four assistants, four ex-Steelers players, and another four fellows with Western Pennsylvania ties, not least of all, magnificent receiver Larry Fitzgerald of Pitt. The Cardinals had 18 seconds before intermission, a chance to take the lead in their inaugural Super Bowl and the ball at the Steelers' one-yard line after a Roethlisberger interception.

To make a 100-yard mad dash, with the clock showing zeroes and every other player on the field either chasing you down or trying to escort you to the end zone while throwing blocks for you?

Welcome to James Harrison and the Immaculate Interception.

LeBeau: "He had a good thought process on that one. He knew the situation in the game. He knew the time left in the half. He knew in all probability they could not run, they could not risk a run—they didn't have any time-outs. They had to throw the ball. So once he engaged his guy and got the blitzer free, he just dropped. Was in the right spot for sure.

"I think that's the best football play I've ever seen. For me, and my football experience—and I've seen quite a few snaps—I've never seen a play that would outdo that one, for individual *and team* effort." Remember, too, this is a man with more than a half century of NFL experience. "After he caught the ball, he had some help going up that sideline. It was unbelievable the run that he made there. I mean, there just aren't many linebackers that can make that run and have the stamina to finish it. He's probably the best-conditioned athlete on the team. If that were not so, he wouldn't have been able to play so well in the second half, because a run like that takes a lot out of you. That was one right out of the Hollywood script writer right there." A 100-yard interception return for a touchdown, the longest in Super Bowl history.

And the Steelers needed every millimeter of it.

Fitzgerald had performed marvelously, perhaps even miraculously in leading the Cardinals from the desert—this

Troy Polamalu, perhaps the most revered Steelers defender since the glory 1970s, gave them a significant shove into the Super Bowl with an interception against the Baltimore Ravens. (George Gojkovich)

Chicago/St. Louis/Phoenix/Arizona franchise spent a longer exile in pro football's wasteland than even Pittsburgh. To reach its first Super Bowl, to obscure 80 years of nondescript-to-horrendous football, the Cardinals received record-setting performances from Fitzgerald to get to Tampa. Then, through three quarters, he was nowhere to be found. Fitzgerald had one catch for 12 yards, had been targeted one other time by Warner. Otherwise, cornerback Ike Taylor threw a blanket over him and tossed him in a trunk somewhere.

In the fourth quarter, though, Fitzgerald proved unstoppable. In fact, Warner completed all six passes he aimed in Fitzgerald's direction in the fourth quarter; he completed eight for 14 for 112 yards to everybody else. Those six receptions for 115 yards and two touchdowns will do a lot for a team, and for the Cardinals it gave them a 23-20 lead within five minutes' time and with 2:37 left. Too much time.

Roethlisberger found Holmes for 14, 13, then 40 yards down to the Arizona 6 with just 49 seconds remaining.

First and goal from the 6, Roethlisberger threw yet again for his 24-year-old receiver in his third NFL season, this time in the left corner. The pass slipped through Holmes' hands. Holmes described it later: "I took my eyes off it because I was trying to get my feet down . . . and just lost sight of the ball." He begged for a second chance.

Santonio Holmes: "At times, I can revert back to that, when conversing with a young guy and helping him cope with a situation—'just never lose focus.'"

Hines Ward, who had two catches while battling an MCL sprain: "Yeah, that's the thing; that's how history is made. That's what I always tell [young] guys: It's how you respond. People don't even talk about that. He could've had a catch before that . . . , so the other one wouldn't have had to add so much drama to it. Needless to say, he came through in a big way. We found a way to win."

Roethlisberger, on second-and-goal, waited, waited, then lofted a pass over three Cardinals defenders and into the golden gloves of Holmes, who touched both big toes to earth and fell into history. The drive covered 88 yards, including a holding penalty. Holmes personally handled 73 of it. The MVP—following Lynn Swann and Ward as Steelers receivers snagging such an honor—finished with nine catches for 131 yards, a Super Bowl–winning touchdown, a trip to Disneyworld, and a bedtime animated movie (*Madagascar II*) after midnight with his three kids.

Holmes: "No other bigger memory than sitting on the ground after the catch just soaking it all in. It was scripted in a way it couldn't have been scripted."

Ward: "To come back on the last drive and win it, have Santonio catch the ball in the end zone—I couldn't be more proud for him. Not only for making a great catch but winning us a second Super Bowl in three years. It was just amazing how we came together as a team to do it. Not too many guys . . . You can win one. But to win two? That's pretty special. You always cherish that. And cherish that ride we had together."

Heath Miller, tight end: "That whole last drive. Not only Santonio, but guys on the team who you remember throughout the whole year. More so for me [that's the memory]. You know, Nate Washington was a huge part of our team that year. He moved on in free agency soon after that. I remember him being a huge receiver—*huge* receiver—for us throughout the year on third down. And we came in together, so that sticks out. Justin Hartwig was the center. Darnell Stapleton stepped in and played guard for us that year. A lot of people you remember along the journey."

Roethlisberger: "[As memories go, the winning touchdown,] that was probably No. 1. No. 2 was standing up on that podium holding that trophy. So much was made of my offensive linemen, how they were terrible and couldn't block and this and that. I remember standing there and saying, 'Who's laughing now, O-line?' I looked down and they're all standing right there. I could still see all their faces, like they wanted to cry."

Bruce Arians, offensive coordinator: "The second one was even more special. I was receivers coach in Super Bowl XL, and I was calling the plays for the other one. The last drive. Santonio's catch. . . .

"It was bittersweet in Tampa, too, because of Kenny [Whisenhunt] and all the other guys on the other side."

Aaron Smith, defensive end, who discovered in October that his four-year-old son, Elijah, was suffering from acute lymphoblastic leukemia: "The second one I enjoyed, but the second one also my son got diagnosed that year. It was special. Yeah, that was a special one, for all of us. Got a picture of us—he has a bald head, everything."

SUPER BOWL XLV
February 6, 2011
Cowboys Stadium, Arlington, Texas
Packers 31, Steelers 25

Hard to tell who had it worse: The Steelers who lost the game or the Steelers fans who lost their seats.

Whether it was Aaron Rodgers passing precisely or the fire marshal refusing to permit fans in temporary bleacher seating, this wasn't a productive night for the Steelers. It wasn't normal for a Super Sunday night. After all, they lost only once in their previous seven.

The season opened with Ben Roethlisberger's four-game suspension for Roger Goodell's version of conduct unbecoming. It closed with the Steelers facing Green Bay without vital defensive end Aaron Smith, blind-side tackle Max Starks, Pro Bowl center Mike Pouncey, and an all-everything receiver Hines Ward nursing an MCL sprain.

Roethlisberger: "There was so much stacked against us, from injuries and . . . Everything that could've happened, happened. I mean, it was crazy." You know it's zany when TMZ "breaks" a story that the quarterback was seen cavorting late at night with his offensive linemen. On the Tuesday before the game. In a piano bar. Really, stop the presses.

Smith: "Personally, with the injury and trying come back and make it back [to play], it probably was the hardest year I've ever had. Rehab's so hard, anyway. To try to rehab at a pace to get back to be able to play football, to be able to do what you want to do and you can't do it, it's just. . . ." Frustrating.

Against that backdrop on a freezing, icy week around Jerry Jones' football emporium, Mr. Rodgers and the Packers ran up leads of 14-0 and 21-3. Amazingly, Rodgers' MVP day started out innocuously enough: 1 for 5. Didn't last long. Rodgers promptly completed 10 of his next 11 for 103 yards and a 21-10 halftime lead.

The Steelers whittled it to 21-17, Green Bay, and moved as close as the Packers' 29 midway through the third quarter. But Shaun Suisham, at a distance even Coach Mike Tomlin doubted, missed a 52-yard attempt at a field goal. On the opening play of the fourth quarter, the Steelers threatening again at the Green Bay 33, Rashard Mendenhall fumbled for only the third time all season. It was shades of Jerome Bettis in the Indianapolis end zone in the 2005 playoffs.

The Packers scored again, Rodgers tossing his third touchdown, but the Steelers rallied with a score of their own plus a two-point conversion. A 10-play, 75-yard, 5:27 drive resulted in a Mason Crosby field goal that prodded the Packers' lead to 31-25. Still, there were two minutes, seven seconds remaining when Roethlisberger started the offense from its own 13 on its comeback attempt, shades of Super Bowl XLIII when little more than two minutes remained and they got pushed back to their own 12.

There was no magic this time. No Magic Kingdom MVP.

Bruce Arians, offensive coordinator: "It doesn't feel good to lose one."

Dick LeBeau, defensive coordinator: "Daren Perry, Kevin Greene, Coach Capers—those were the only mitigating circumstances for not winning; you had some really good friends [on the Green Bay defensive staff]. It was their first Super Bowl win. I wish it hadn't been at our expense. But it was.

Ben Roethlisberger, with a tinted visor even though the game was indoors, drops back against the Green Bay Packers in Super Bowl XLV—the first loss of his inaugural three Super Bowl trips. (Courtesy of the Pittsburgh Steelers)

"It was a great game. A game that went down to the last quarter, the last play. I thought our guys played hard, for the most part played pretty well. A lot of their plays were plays they just made; their quarterback made some great throws. We'd like to go back and do it all over again, maybe change a few things. I'll be honest with you, the last two we were at before that, we won in very close, last-play kind of games. It's very hard to win them all. Philosophically, you're always going to have to look at that. I was proud of our team for getting there, beating Baltimore a couple of times and the Jets, who had beaten Indianapolis and New England."

Heath Miller, tight end: "Yeah, we're trying to wipe that one clean. You never want to be on that end of the big game. We learned what it tastes like to be on that side of the field."

Hines Ward: "Worst day of my life. You experience so much good times; you never experience the losing part of it. The worst feeling ever. I was seriously depressed. I couldn't watch TV. I couldn't eat. Lost weight. Every time you turn on the TV, you see the *Sports Illustrated* cover with them on

it. Very depressing. Thank God for me I had *Dancing with the Stars.* . . ."

Dom Capers, Packers defensive coordinator and mayor of Blitzburgh 1992–1994: "I felt when we played in the Super Bowl, probably a lot of the terminology would have been very similar to both teams. A lot of the elements were still similar. The defense we play in Green Bay has its origins there, from the defense we played in Pittsburgh in the early '90s."

Kevin Greene, Packers linebackers coach: "Believe it or not, that [Super Bowl XXX] game has kind of haunted me ever since I played in it. So . . . going to the Super Bowl, coaching linebackers against my old team the Pittsburgh Steelers, my outside linebackers having some critical plays to put us on the board—I think Frank Zombo had a critical sack on Roethlisberger. . . . Just having an impact . . . and winning my first Super Bowl, it kind of took the sting out of Super Bowl XXX, losing that. It's kind of ironic at the same time, looking back on it. The only two Super Bowls the Steelers ever lost, I had a hand in—one as a player, one as a coach. It's kind of ironic."

10

The Hall of Fame

BERT BELL
Co-owner/Head Coach

College: Pennsylvania • **Years with the Steelers:** 1941–1946 • **Birthplace:** Philadelphia • **Born:** February 25, 1895 • **Died:** October 11, 1959 • **Elected:** Inaugural 1963 class

Part of the Pennsylvania pair that got the Blue Laws repealed and launched new NFL franchises, Bert Bell opened the Philadelphia Eagles for business a month after Art Rooney opened his Pittsburgh Pirates in 1933. In December 1940, Rooney sold the Steelers to Alexis Thompson and bought half the Eagles from Bell. Their plan, according to newspaper accounts: Field one Pennsylvania team, playing in both Pittsburgh and Philadelphia. The NFL shot down the idea, though, as well as Thompson's wish to move the newly renamed Pittsburgh Iron Men to Boston. Four months later, they swapped with Alexis Thompson, a move that required player movement back and forth: 14 Steelers joined the Eagles, and 16 Eagles switched ends of the state. And in 1941, Bell started out as Steelers co-owner and head coach.

It lasted eight weeks and two losses. This from a coach who went 1-10 the season prior in Philadelphia and 10-44-2 in his five Eagles seasons. "My deepest regret is I did not produce a winner," he said in a September 24, 1941, statement after three-point losses to both Cleveland and his former Philadelphia Eagles.

Rooney helped to nudge Bell into the commissioner's position in 1946, replacing Elmer Layden and selling back his Steelers share. As commissioner from 1946 to 1959, Bell was credited with creating the modern draft, marshaling the NFL into the network-television age, recognizing the NFL Players Association, adopting an antigambling stance, and absorbing the All-America Football Conference.

Carl Hughes, Pittsburgh Press Steelers beat writer 1944–1945 and later Kennywood Park president: "The [Rooney-McGinley] boxing carried the football club in those days. And Art's [horse-track] winnings. Boxing carried the football club in those days, because they made money on boxing. It was the big thing then. It was second only to major league baseball. Pro football was nothing. I remember when Bert Bell came to town. He would have the [Fort Pitt] Hotel put a cot in the office that the boxing club and the football club shared." Jack Mintz was matchmaker, but Bert Bell could outshout him on another phone, forcing Mintz to carry on conversations under a desk.

Chuck Cherundolo, center for Philadelphia in 1940 and the Steelers 1941–1942 and 1945–1948: "He wasn't afraid to tell you he didn't have any money."

Rooney represented Bell when his old friend and co-owner was enshrined posthumously into the Hall.

MEL BLOUNT
Cornerback

Height: 6-3 • **Weight:** 205 • **College:** Southern • **Years with the Steelers:** 1970–1983 • **Birthplace:** Vidalia, Georgia • **Born:** April 10, 1948 • **Elected:** 1989

To see Mel Blount four decades later, appearing in his trademark white cowboy hat while representing his Mel Blount Youth Home or some other community interest, you are struck by how much he looks like he could still play. Looks like he could still intercept a bagful of footballs.

Even as a sixty-something man.

Mike Wagner, safety 1971–1980: "Quiet man. Heart of gold. Super man."

The man known as Supe credited defensive coordinator Bud Carson for working with him and captain Joe Greene for rooming with him.

Blount once noted of the difference in his 14-year, Hall of Fame career: "Maturity . . . I owe Joe Greene a lot for that. In 1977, when I came back from my holdout, we started rooming together. He really took me under his wing, like a big brother. We used to talk and talk and talk. Because of my country background, I hadn't been exposed to a lot of things, and Joe helped me understand them better."

Admittedly, he had growing to do when he arrived in 1970 from Vidalia, Georgia, by way of Southern University. Well, Pittsburgh had growing to do, too. Same for the Steelers. Or, as he put it during his Hall of Fame weekend in 1989, the franchise's image at the start of the 1970s was "a group of players who drank and got in bar fights and were losers in a dirty steel town." Look how they all turned out. Blount, for one, wound up a member of both the Steelers' and NFL's 75th Anniversary teams, a Hall of Famer, a community fixture.

Jon Kolb, center–offensive tackle 1969–1981: "Mel was a guy I got to know as we matured. Early on, we were trying to learn our trades. I see Mel still as a talented, talented guy. There's a

Bert Bell. (Pro Football Hall of Fame)

Mel Blount. (Pro Football Hall of Fame)

Terry Bradshaw. (Pro Football Hall of Fame)

word in the Bible, and it's the word 'authority.' The might and right to act in a situation."

Kolb and Blount remained close after their playing careers because of their love of horses. Blount in 2011, in fact, still attended quarter horse shows.

Wagner: "Mel was a real enigma for me. You look at Mel, 'What's going on here?' We had people playing corner [John Rowser and Lee Calland], and he was sitting on the bench. Some of those kids come in, they want to play man coverage. In pro football, coaches say, 'You've got to do run support; you've got to play coverages.' Obviously, the talent was there. He turned it. What a great career he had.

"It was interesting to hear Mel say later, 'At some point in my NFL career, I had to change the way I thought about football.' Thank God he did."

TERRY BRADSHAW
Quarterback

Height: 6-3 • **Weight:** 215 • **College:** Louisiana Tech • **Years with the Steelers:** 1970–1983 • **Birthplace:** Shreveport, Louisiana • **Born:** September 2, 1948 • **Elected:** 1989

He liked to act, all right. He performed in movies during his playing days (*Smokey and the Bandit II* and *Cannonball Run*) and long after (*Failure to Launch,* in which he showed his assets). He strummed a guitar and crooned "I'm So Lonesome I Could Cry," which, we would learn later, may have provided a glimpse into long-term personal issues.

But was Terry Bradshaw the drama queen of the NFL? Certainly, he had a Hall of Fame flair for theatrics:

- Browns defensive end Joe "Turkey" Jones attempted to plant Bradshaw headfirst into the Municipal Stadium turf

in Cleveland in 1976, and Bradshaw left the field on a stretcher.

Ralph Berlin, trainer 1968–1992: "Turkey Jones tried to make a fence post out of him in Cleveland. We came back on a plane, and Fats [Holmes] took him and carried him onto the plane" like a baby.

Amazingly, Bradshaw returned to start three weeks later.

- Bradshaw left a 1975 playoff game with Baltimore in the first half ("I thought I was out of the game [for good], I really did"). Then he got a slight concussion against Oakland in the AFC championship game.
- He got hurt in a 1977 game at Houston. Rookie safety and ex-college quarterback Tony Dungy, by default and injury the Steelers' No. 3 quarterback, was preparing to start the next week . . . but Bradshaw returned.

Dungy: "I remember him earlier in the year—and I guess that's why I didn't think too much about it—they carried him off. Dwight White told me, 'He'll be back in the second half.' And he was. Those guys were a little more used to it than I was as a rookie."

- St. Louis in 1979 had him on a stretcher, leaving the Busch Stadium field with what Bradshaw believed was a broken ankle. Cardinals defenders offered solace. He came back the second half to lead the Steelers to a come-from-behind victory.

Garry Dunn, defensive lineman 1977–1987: "He's going off on a stretcher. The [Cardinals] defense came over to him, 'Sorry, hope you come back.' He comes back the second half. Those guys were thinking, 'We probably should have knocked over the stretcher.'"

After his playing days, Bradshaw at first distanced himself from the organization and its faithful. Later, maybe due to the ADD medication and the therapies for depression and merely just a dose of modern maturity, Bradshaw began apologizing to fans, then Noll and the organization. He said he made a huge mistake allowing his selfishness, fears, and issues to prevent him from attending the 1988 funeral of Art Rooney Sr. He ventured 14 years without stopping in Pittsburgh for more than a few hours at a time. He went 19 years without taking the field on a Steelers game day, until 2002, when he was welcomed back in a Heinz Field halftime ceremony.

"It's great to be home. We've been through a lot, me and the fans. They've loved me, they've hated me, and I've driven them crazy. Through it all—what's that old song?—I've learned."

JACK BUTLER
Safety

Height: 6-1 • **Weight:** 200 • **College:** St. Bonaventure • **Years with the Steelers:** 1951–1959 • **Birthplace:** Pittsburgh • **Born:** November 12, 1927 • **Elected:** 2012

Along the same lines as Dick LeBeau, Jack Butler presented a threefold dilemma for the Seniors Committee: (a) Elect him as a standout defensive back? (b) Elect him for his contributions to the game after his playing days? Or (c) Both of the above?

After a Steelers career in which he nabbed interceptions at a rate between Hall of Famers Emlen Tunnell and Dick "Night Train" Lane, after polishing his star to the point where he was named to the NFL's 50th Anniversary team, Butler went on to a second career as the head of the BLESTO scouting service.

The NFL Combine? Jack Butler's doing.

Psychological testing? Computerized scouting? All started under his watch.

It took merely a half century after his playing days, but Butler was elected from the two-man Seniors Committee pool the day before Super Bowl XLVI, where the next evening he got to assist with the coin flip in Indianapolis—home to his Combine. He couldn't believe all this was happening.

Then again, he still couldn't believe he didn't make the NFL as a wide receiver, his college position and first football love. Perhaps that explains the 52 career interceptions that were the second most in NFL history when he retired.

Joe Walton, a Washington Redskins player at the time: "Jack—broke his leg, never played again. He was a very good player."

Butler: "My knee pulled apart. We were playing the Eagles at Forbes Field. I'm playing left safety, and this receiver caught a quick little slant pass. He's falling, and I'm coming over. When he falls, his shoulder hit my knee. And that was it. I bet I had six or eight operations on it. It's been replaced and everything. I had a lot of infections in it."

Dale Dodrill, nose guard–middle linebacker 1951–1959: "One of the great players. He might not have had the speed a lot of them had, but he was fast enough. Great guy."

Butler served for 44 years as the director of BLESTO—the Bears, Lions, Eagles, Steelers Talent Organization formed in 1963. He retired in 2007, when BLESTO closed its Pittsburgh office and the operation moved to Jacksonville.

DERMONTTI DAWSON
Center

Height: 6-2 • **Weight:** 288 • **College:** Kentucky • **Years with the Steelers:** 1988–2000 • **Birthplace:** Lexington, Kentucky • **Born:** June 17, 1965 • **Elected:** 2012

From Iron to Dirt, the Steelers poured a Hall of Fame foundation at center for a quarter century.

"Iron" Mike Webster's successor arrived in 1988 and aligned next to him.

Dermontti "Dirt" Dawson started out a guard.

Webster left for Kansas City in 1989, when Dawson bent over the football and stayed there for another remarkable dozen seasons. He made seven Pro Bowls. He was All-Pro six times.

Dawson played in 170 consecutive games (of 184 total). Webster, the only Steeler with a longer streak, played 177.

Kevin Greene, outside linebacker 1993–1995: "We had Dermontti Dawson, Justin Strzelczyk, Leon Searcy, Brenden Stai, John Jackson; they'd roll off the ball. They didn't have any problem getting dirty in the trenches. We really had some skill on that team [when Greene arrived]. I know we were a footnote because we didn't win a Super Bowl; we didn't go down in history as being really good. But 1994–1995 we were good.

"The Hall of Fame is a tricky deal; a lot of people deserve to be in the Hall of Fame. Absolutely, [Dawson] does. He was a good one. He was physical, quick, fast, violent. He was smart, tough, called out pressure, pointed out things to Mike Tomczak and Neil O'Donnell, had leverage. Everything you wanted a center to be, Dermontti was that guy. That's the thing, too: He had the ability to pull on the corner and actually reach an outside linebacker. From inside, three gaps removed from the outside linebacker position. He could block the outside linebacker and turn the corner on him so the toss or whatever [running play] could be outside. Amazing."

Jim Sweeney, line mate and backup center 1996–1999 (months before the Canton vote): "He should be in the Hall of Fame. What's wrong with those guys? He'll be in there. He could pull. Dwight Stephenson [a Hall of Fame center from Miami] was the first guy I knew who could pull from center. Then Dirt. I mean, what a great thing.

"A true sweetheart. A great friend. You know, game days when he stepped on the field, he was a different guy, man. He was like an animal. Come game day, what a competitor."

BULLET BILL DUDLEY
Halfback–Defensive Back–Returner–Punter–Kicker

Height: 5-10 • **Weight:** 182 • **College:** Virginia • **Years with the Steelers:** 1942, 1946 • **Birthplace:** Bluefield, Virginia • **Born:** December 24, 1921 • **Died:** February 4, 2010 • **Elected:** 1966

Bullet Bill Dudley. (Pro Football Hall of Fame)

Joe Greene. (Pro Football Hall of Fame)

Jack Ham. (Pro Football Hall of Fame)

Bill Dudley wasn't the fastest; hence his Bullet nickname was more akin to a tall gent being known as Shorty. He wasn't the biggest. But he was the hardest to catch.

He played his rookie Steelers season in 1942 as a 170-pound 20-year-old, and topped the league in rushing. He came back four years later, after two and a half years with the Army Air Corps, and won MVP.

His Steelers career indeed was abbreviated, no thanks to his icy relationship with Jock Sutherland. That was the reason he wrote an early 1947 letter to Art Rooney informing the club he no longer wanted to play for the Steelers . . . though soon after he signed a $25,000 deal after being traded to Detroit.

With the Lions and later Washington, he never rushed for the 600-plus yards he topped twice in his two Steelers seasons and change.

In those amazing two and a half Steelers seasons, Dudley crammed in numbers for the record books:

- The highest average per carry by a running back (4.39, ahead of Barry Foster's 4.31)
- The most all-time return yardage on interceptions, with 242 in 1946
- The second-most interceptions in a season, his 10 (1946) tied with Hall of Fame inductee Jack Butler (1957) and one behind Hall of Famer Mel Blount (1975)
- Sixth in all-time punt-return yardage (838), which he collected on the grand sum of 52 returns By contrast, leader Rod Woodson had 257 returns.

Little Bullet left quite a mark.

He also was the first player in NFL history to score touchdowns six different ways: rush, pass, interception, kick return, punt return, fumble recovery. The only other since: Deion Sanders.

Chuck Cherundolo, center and friend: "He wasn't fast. He was slow. I would always run with him. I don't know why they called him 'Bullet.' But he always did everything right."

Tim Rooney Sr., son of the Chief: "I remember when we got rid of him, and he went to the Redskins eventually. I was the water boy for the Steelers, standing on the sideline [December 3, 1950], and we punted to the Redskins. He caught the ball at the four-yard line [reputedly retreating 30 yards and reaching out of bounds to snag it]. He ran up the sidelines, and I don't think any of the [Steelers] saw me. I was yelling for him to run for a touchdown. And he did. He held that [96-yard] record for a long time." Sixty years, until 2010, in fact. "He was just a spectacular football player, both in college and the pros."

JOE GREENE
Defensive Tackle

Height: 6-4 • **Weight:** 275 • **College:** North Texas State • **Years with the Steelers:** 1969–1981 • **Birthplace:** Temple, Texas • **Born:** September 24, 1946 • **Elected:** 1987

Such an exemplary leader was Joe Greene that eight Steelers teammates followed him into Canton. Then his coach, Chuck Noll, and president, Dan Rooney, too. That's power.

Yet his style of play fostered criticism, created detractors, bred haters . . . until that image-softening cola commercial—the one that ended the same way as the 2012 remake—with Greene tossing his jersey to a much younger fan. Indeed, Greene was brutal, unforgiving, a player who skirted or approached the line of rules that were later altered to slow down the likes of him (no more head slaps, etc.). It's probably a good thing officials weren't the Hall of Fame voters, lest Greene never would've made it.

He kicked Cleveland lineman Bob McKay in the cup area. He punched Denver guard Paul Howard. Though, to Greene's mindset, Howard had it coming. Any lineman has it coming when they violate what a defensive lineman considers a cardinal rule.

George Perles, defensive line coach and coordinator 1972–1981: "If you ever held Joe. . . . That was another one. We were playing Denver. The guard [Howard] was holding him, so he slipped an uppercut with that fist that's like a ham. [Ex-Steelers coach and then-Denver assistant] Babe Parilli was coming off the field at halftime and said to Joe, 'I'm embarrassed for you.'" Perles lit into Broncos coach Red Miller about it, too.

At one point in that punching-kicking 1977, he essentially declared war on officials. He was fined for that Howard uppercut, originally $5,000, later amended to $4,000. The NFL assistant supervisor of officials back then? The same Nick Skorich whom, when he was Cleveland's coach, Greene once essentially challenged in a sideline skirmish.

Greene said after the Christmas Eve playoff punch: "If the man in front of me is impeding me illegally and the officials are not calling it a foul . . . , then I have to do something about it. Believe me, those punches I threw at Howard and then at center Mike Montler were retaliatory reactions. . . . I take more than I dish out."

He was fined $500 earlier that year after threatening to punch officials because he angrily reacted to three offside calls in a game. "I went off the handle and my language was way off base," he said. "I probably should have kept my damn mouth shut."

JACK HAM
Outside Linebacker

Height: 6-1 • **Weight:** 225 • **College:** Penn State • **Years with the Steelers:** 1971–1982 • **Birthplace:** Johnstown, Pennsylvania • **Born:** December 23, 1948 • **Elected:** 1988

His hallmark was consistency. In crucial games, Jack Ham was consistently excellent.

In the Steelers' first AFC championship date, he compiled eight tackles against the unbeaten Miami Dolphins of 1973.

In the Steelers' first AFC championship victory, he intercepted two passes against the 1974 Raiders and helped to propel his team to its inaugural Super Bowl.

In the 1975 playoffs, he leveled Bert Jones with the blitz sack that sealed the victory. . . .

Andy Russell, fellow outside linebacker 1963, 1966–1976: "My one NFL record, picking up a fumble against the Colts, they called a blitz. I got stuffed right at the line of scrimmage. Ham came free, reached the quarterback just as he was throwing, causes the fumble. The ball bounces right into my lap. I'm at the seven-yard line, 93 yards to go. I got a bad knee—I was going to get cut after the season. I'm the worst guy on the field to run it. I wanted to lateral it, but I had two sprained wrists and casts on my wrists. My guys knocked everybody down, I got to go 93 yards. The NFL record for the slowest and longest time of a single play. Bradshaw claimed NBC cut to a commercial and came back in time to catch the end of the run." It remained the NFL playoff record for the longest fumble return.

. . . In Super Bowl X, Ham made, well, X tackles.

In 1978, he intercepted two passes to help clinch a seventh consecutive playoff berth with a closer-than-anticipated victory over San Francisco. Mused Ham afterward: "I hate to play all these games we're supposed to win and the fans are upset if we don't beat the point spread."

In the 1978 AFC championship victory over Houston, in the ice and slick at Three Rivers Stadium, Ham pieced together a two-fumble, one-interception, one-sack, four-tackle masterpiece. The first play should've been a harbinger for Houston: Ham so forcefully threw a stout Earl Campbell for a three-yard loss on the opening play from scrimmage that he cracked and broke his face mask where it met his helmet. In the Super Bowl XIII ramp-up, Chuck Noll was asked if it was Ham's finest performance of his eight seasons to date. Noll, for once, was stupefied: "So we did some research, and it's difficult to say because he's so consistent." For the record, Ham—who retired with 32 interceptions, 25½ sacks, and 21 fumble recoveries along with memberships to the Steelers' and NFL's 75th Anniversary teams plus the Hall of Fame—humbly voted for his 1974 AFC championship effort as his personal best.

Joe Greene did the talking for Ham, who never sought the media spotlight: "Jack likes to play. He *really* likes to play. And he does it quietly, like a gentleman. He doesn't talk. He doesn't brag. He doesn't rub it in. He doesn't play dirty football. He just goes out there and plays, game after game. Ham probably hasn't had a penalty since he's been in the league."

FRANCO HARRIS
Running Back

Height: 6-2 • **Weight:** 230 • **College:** Penn State • **Years with the Steelers:** 1972–1983 • **Birthplace:** Fort Dix, New Jersey • **Born:** March 7, 1950 • **Elected:** 1990

Franco Harris continues to run hard. From civic event to civic event. From business meeting to business meeting.

It's all part of his postcareer transition. He went from the Hall of Fame to halls of power.

He still held, 40 years after his rookie debut, a vital place in Pittsburgh.

Joe Gordon, publicity director and vice president 1969–1998, who ranked Harris between Art Rooney Sr. and announcer Myron Cope as the three most amazing people he'd ever witnessed: "He's the only guy I know who probably has accomplished more since his career ended than in his career, which is remarkable. The things he has done off the football field, in business and in the community. That's why he's my No. 2 most amazing person."

Harris' football accomplishments are well known: a Super Bowl record of 354 career yards and 101 carries; 1,556 yards rushing in 19 playoff games; and 12,120 career yards rushing, which at the time of his 1984 retirement were the second most in NFL history.

His community achievements? To name-drop a few, besides his healthy-eating Super Bakery, of course: the Pittsburgh Promise scholarship program, the Western Pennsylvania Sports Museum, Special Olympics, United Way, Cystic Fibrosis, National Association for Retarded Children, Salvation Army, Multiple Sclerosis, Governor's Council on Physical

Franco Harris. (Pro Football Hall of Fame)

Cal Hubbard. (Pro Football Hall of Fame)

John Henry Johnson. (Pro Football Hall of Fame)

Fitness and Sports, Pittsburgh Children's Festival, Easter Seals, United Cerebral Palsy. . . .

In 2010, he even helped Pitt organize an African American athletic celebration—and this from a guy from rival Penn State.

The weekend before he sat down for an interview for this book, General Al Vento of Franco's Italian Army went out with the Harrises to a night at the opera and dinner at a tony downtown steakhouse. He recounted Harris telling him, "Al, this morning I had breakfast with the Korean consulate. At one I was at the stadium. At three I was at a concert listening to Jackie Evanchco sing. Now I'm having dinner with you. I never dreamed I'd be in this position."

Vento: "He's the best PR man that the City of Pittsburgh has. He's done more for Pittsburgh. . . ."

CAL HUBBARD
Tackle

Height: 6-2 • **Weight:** 253 • **Colleges:** Centenary, Geneva • **Year with the Steelers:** 1936 • **Birthplace:** Keytesville, Missouri • **Born:** October 31, 1900 • **Died:** October 17, 1977 • **Elected:** Inagural 1963 class

Like Marion Motley and too many other players, Robert "Cal" Hubbard came to the Steelers for the final season of his illustrious career.

His stay was even shorter than Motley's.

In fact, Hubbard's Steelers career covered the bare minimum: One game.

Then he retired.

But while playing for the 6-6 Pirates of Joe Bach in that 1936 season, Hubbard made a brilliant career move that changed his arc in sports history.

Hubbard began umpiring baseball games.

His football fame was equaled by his work around a baseball diamond. In 1958, he was named umpire-in-chief in the American League. He worked four World Series.

He became the first inducted into both Cooperstown (1976) and Canton. More than that, he also was enshrined in the College Football Hall of Fame (1962) and—because of his days at Geneva College, which once defeated Harvard—the Beaver County Hall of Fame (1976).

JOHN HENRY JOHNSON
Running Back

Height: 6-2 • **Weight:** 210 • **Colleges:** St. Mary's (California), Arizona State • **Years with the Steelers:** 1960–1965 • **Birthplace:** Waterproof, Louisiana • **Born:** November 24, 1929 • **Died:** June 3, 2011 • **Elected:** 1987

Even though he retired as the fourth-leading rusher in NFL history, in the same company as Jim Brown, folks around the NFL admired John Henry Johnson for his blocking. Feared him, too.

"I remember him hitting me upside the head with a forearm," Cleveland guard Chuck Noll (who was later replaced by future Hall of Famer Gene Hickerson) said of rushing a Pittsburgh punter once protected by Johnson. "He unloaded on me. . . . Those are the things you remember, how hard they hit you."

"He was one of the greatest blockers I ever saw in my life," Art Rooney Sr. told the *Pittsburgh Post-Gazette* shortly before serving as Johnson's presenter at the 1987 Hall of Fame ceremony—the final year of the Chief's life. "The other guys had one eye on John. I think they ducked. One time, we were playing an exhibition game in Atlanta, and we were punting. Some rookie came in, and John hit him from the blind side. His headgear flew off, and I didn't know if it was his head or his headgear. The kid never played again."

Even though he played with San Francisco's "Million Dollar Backfield" alongside Hall of Famers Joe Perry, Hugh McElhenny, and Y. A. Tittle, even though he rushed for 1,000-plus yards—the first to do so—with the Steelers as a 33- and 35-year-old man, even though he helped Detroit win the 1957 NFL championship, Johnson was known for how he could mete out pain. Whether it was a forearm block. Whether it was by an open-palm punch/stiff arm. Whether it was by run, block, or yard-marker swing.

Among John Henry's hit list:

- Calgary Stampeders teammate Bill Bewley, broken jaw, intrasquad scrimmage
- Rams linebacker Les Richter, broken jaw
- Cardinals eventual Hall of Fame safety Larry Wilson, concussion, unconscious
- Cardinals eventual Hall of Fame halfback Charlie Trippi, multiple facial fractures. One account reputed the collision to be so violent that it shattered Trippi's face mask and crushed his jaw and nose.

Upon making the Hall of Fame in 1987, where Rooney presented him, Johnson added, "I was confident someday I would be here, but then on the other hand, I thought I might be dead since it had taken so long. Today I feel that I finally have that respect, and I want to tell you, it makes me feel damn good."

WALT KIESLING
Guard

Height: 6-2 • **Weight:** 249 • **College:** St. Thomas (Minnesota) • **Years with the Pirates/Steelers:** 1937–1939, player; 1939–1940, 1941–1944, 1954–1956, coach • **Birthplace:** St. Paul, Minnesota • **Born:** May 27, 1903 • **Died:** March 2, 1962 • **Elected:** 1966

During his 34 years in professional football, Walt Kiesling devoted the first dozen, hard-charging seasons to stellar line play. He was an all-NFL selection in 1929, 1930, and 1932 with the Chicago Cardinals. He played a rugged two ways for Duluth, Minnesota; Pottsville, Pennsylvania; both the Chicago Cardinals and Bears; the Green Bay Packers; and the Pittsburgh Pirates. He went undefeated with the 1934 Bears and won a championship with the 1936 Packers. In a 1929 game with the Duluth Eskimos, he helped blaze a trail for Ernie Nevers to score six touchdowns.

However, his record as a coach wasn't as decorated: 30-55-5 in three different stints with the Pirates/Steelers.

Actually, he was better remembered for this: He was the coach of record when the Steelers cut Johnny Unitas in 1955, when the Steelers drafted the likes of Lloyd Colteryahn and Bob Goana and Tom Barton and John Alderton instead of homegrown future Hall of Famer Joe Schmidt of Pitt in 1953, when the Steelers drafted Gary Glick and Art Davis instead of Penn State's Lenny Moore and West Virginia's Sam Huff in 1956.

Nevertheless, Kiesling was considered a fine football body during his linemen days and a fine football mind as a coach.

Other body parts contributed, too. As assistant coach Nick Skorich, later the Browns head coach, commented in an Associated Press story after the nondescript 1954 Steelers started 4-1: "Football is 75 percent heart. We've got 80 percent heart. Kiesling's got the other 20 percent."

Chuck Cherundolo, Steelers center 1941–1942 and 1945–1948, then an assistant coach 1948–1957: "There's a real honest-to-God guy. He was one of the smartest guys you ever met. He knew everything about football.

"1942, we had a helluva year that year [going 7-4 and competing for the Eastern Division title]."

Roy McHugh, longtime Pittsburgh Press *sportswriter, columnist, and editor, about Art Rooney, who named Kiesling interim or full-time head coach on three different occasions (1939, 1941, and 1954):* "Every time he needed a coach at the middle of the season, he got Kiesling."

Joe Gordon, Steelers communications director 1969–1998: "He had a soft spot for Kiesling."

JACK LAMBERT
Middle Linebacker

Height: 6-4 • **Weight:** 220 • **College:** Kent State • **Years with the Steelers:** 1974–1984 • **Birthplace:** Mantua, Ohio • **Born:** July 8, 1952 • **Elected:** 1990

Earlier in his career Jack Lambert had what the Eagles put to music: a nasty reputation as a cruel dude. John Elway, in his NFL debut September 4, 1983, got caught in Lambert's life in the fast lane. "He had no teeth and he was slobbering all over, and I'm thinking, 'You can have your money back, just get me out of here.'" Maybe that explains why Elway went 1 for 8 and to the bench. Hell, maybe that explains why on his very first snap Elway lined up under guard, not center.

Doug Dieken of the rival Cleveland Browns contended for years that he would shake every other Steelers hand in postgames but Dwight White and Lambert, who would "kick your grandmother's cane away from her."

He didn't chew glass in front of his locker, but then he didn't remove his bridge until game days, either.

As coaches and teammates noted, there was a distinct method behind this perceived madman. He was certain his career highlight film would consist of the Cliff Harris throwdown at Super Bowl X, kneeing ex-Steelers teammate Preston Pearson in the groin, clouting Cleveland's Brian Sipe three times, pounding his feet, and scowling through missing teeth. It wasn't the complete picture, though.

Lambert called the defenses, and this in a complicated unit that would answer each and every Cowboys shift with a new play call.

Lambert covered tight ends and the first running back (instead of the second), and even receivers downfield.

Lambert made plays, leading the Steel Curtain in tackles every year through the 1970s. He had 10 tackles and a crucial Vince Ferragamo interception with 5:24 left in Super Bowl XIV. He had seven tackles in Super Bowl X.

Lambert attracted crowds. The more he gesticulated and scowled and screamed, the more the Steelers fans adored him and his shot-in-the-jaw-and-a-beer persona. That popularity would explain the pilgrimage to Canton, Ohio, that seemed to grow upon Lambert's induction and remained rather steady thereafter.

Walt Kiesling. (Pro Football Hall of Fame)

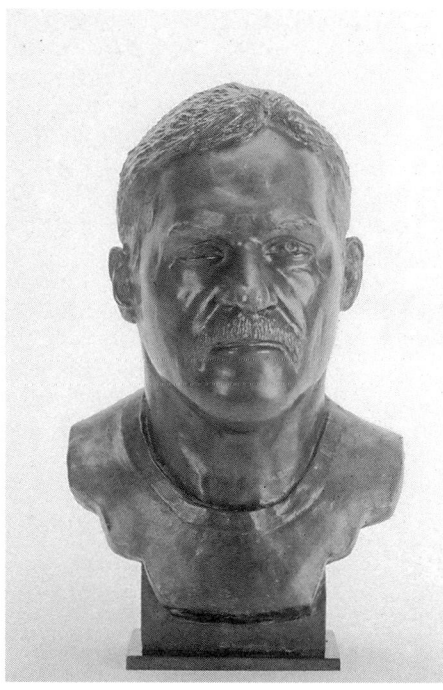

Jack Lambert. (Pro Football Hall of Fame)

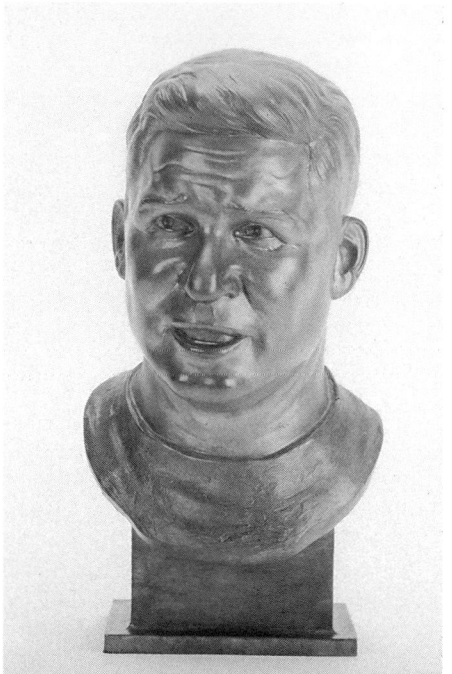

Bobby Layne. (Pro Football Hall of Fame)

Before he excused himself from their sight, becoming a wildlife ranger and a youth coach in a rural area 40 miles northeast of Pittsburgh, Lambert played to the crowd he attracted:

"If I could start my life all over again, I would be a professional football player, and you damn well better believe I would be a Pittsburgh Steeler."

BOBBY LAYNE
Quarterback

Height: 6-1 • **Weight:** 201 • **College:** Texas • **Years with the Steelers:** 1958–1962 • **Birthplace:** Santa Anna, Texas • **Born:** December 19, 1926 • **Died:** December 1, 1986 • **Elected:** 1967

If there were a Carousing Hall of Fame, a Tavern Patron Hall of Fame, and a Tall Texas Tale Hall of Fame, Robert Lawrence Layne would've been quickly enshrined in those as well. He indeed was a man for all . . . hours of the day.

Roy McHugh, longtime *Pittsburgh Press* sportswriter, columnist, and editor, remembered Bobby Layne being a jazz aficionado who would call home to friends in Lubbock, Texas, and have a famed trombonist on his end serenade them. Fellow *Press* writer Bob Drum was helping Layne write his autobiography, so Drum flew to Lubbock to spend time with Layne. First, upon arrival, McHugh said, Drum had to borrow $50 from the quarterback so he could tip the band. Layne up and took Drum to Colorado for several days, but by the time Drum returned to Pittsburgh he had lost one shoe and all his hand-written notes. Steelers' part owner Jack McGinley quipped, Layne ought to be writing a book about Drum.

Dick Hoak, running back 1961–1970:

All the stories you hear about Bobby were pretty true. He was a great guy. He took care of me. For some reason, he liked me. If you were a back and you didn't pick up a blitz, you were in his doghouse. We had Joe Womack, he was fast. He missed a blitz once, and the guy just destroyed Bobby. We were playing at Forbes Field. Bobby pulled him over to Buddy [Parker] on the sideline and said, "If you play this kid again, I'll quit."

When I got there [in 1961], he just about had it. You heard the story about him when he wrecked Tom Tracy's car? Buddy brought a lot of those guys from Detroit with him: Bobby, John Henry, Tom Tracy. . . . Tom Tracy worked for a car dealership in Detroit. So [every off Monday] he would fly to Detroit and drive back a car to sell. He had a big Bonneville. Bobby drove the car, and the night before a game he hits a streetcar. The next day, he came out and passed for 300 yards.

Playing the Eagles [sometime in 1961 or 1962]. Sonny Jurgensen and Bobby. They hooked up the night before the game. Neither one of them was having a very good game day. Going off the field at halftime, Bobby said to Sonny, "Having a hard time hitting 'em today." "Hit 'em? I can't even see 'em!"

DICK LEBEAU
Assistant/Defensive Coordinator

College: Ohio State • **Years as Steelers assistant:** 1992–1996, 2004– • **Birthplace:** London, Ohio • **Born:** September 9, 1937 • **Elected:** 2010

Dick LeBeau. (Pro Football Hall of Fame)

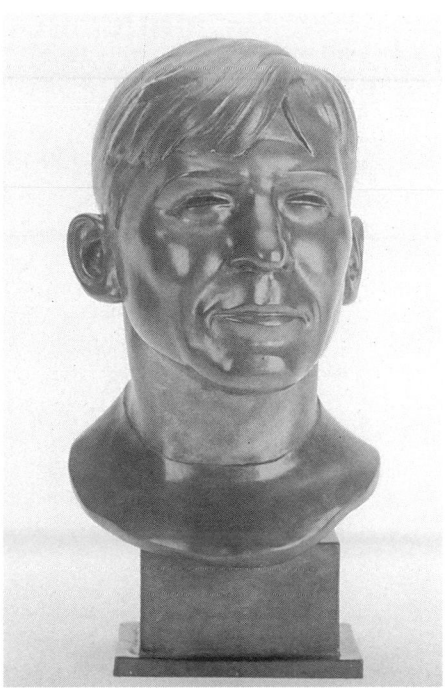

Johnny "Blood" McNally. (Pro Football Hall of Fame)

Marion Motley. (Pro Football Hall of Fame)

True, he grabbed 62 interceptions—the third most in league history upon his retirement as a player—and performed admirably as a defensive back for Detroit from 1959 to 1972. But to the defenders he mentored, to the Steelers fans who watched his defenses work for more than a decade, Dick LeBeau deserved a Canton bust for his coaching alone.

Ryan Clark, safety 2006– : "Coach LeBeau understands football. Coach LeBeau understands matchups. That's the confidence you have when you have a legend and a Hall of Famer as your defensive coordinator."

LeBeau fathered the zone blitz. He worked hand in hand with Dom Capers on Blitzburgh and then retooled the 900-page defensive playbook that they, along with Bill Cowher, devised in 1992. The Steelers' defense at the start of the 21st century propelled the franchise to three Super Bowls in six years, 2005–2010. It was the most remarkable Steelers Super Bowl run since some other Ohio-born coach went to four in six in the 1970s.

LeBeau is a soft-spoken gent who served as Michael Caine's stunt double in a 1970 movie retitled *Suicide Run,* which he jokes airs only on the late, late, late cable time slots. He not only reads opposing offenses well, but also reads "The Night before Christmas" to his teams every Christmas Eve, and they adore it. In fact, LeBeau's players adore him so much that they donned his throwback Detroit jersey for the Hall of Fame preseason game in 2007—he has that photograph hanging in both his office and home.

LeBeau, asked about his Steelers legacy: "I don't ever think in those terms. I've been blessed to be able to work with a great group of athletes and a great organization. Certainly the blessing and joy from that is plenty reward for me. I'm happy the good Lord, for some reason, brought me over here.

"When you've been in this business as long as I've been, you're going to have ups and downs. This is definitely life in the NFL. This is life. I don't keep score. I don't know whether the goods have outweighed the bads. It seems to me they have."

JOHNNY "BLOOD" MCNALLY
Halfback–Kick Returner–Kicker

Height: 6-1 • **Weight:** 188 • **Colleges:** Wisconsin–River Falls, Notre Dame, Dartmouth, St. John's (Minnesota) • **Years with the Pirates:** 1934, 1937–1938 • **Birthplace:** New Richmond, Wisconsin • **Born:** November 27, 1903 • **Died:** November 28, 1985 • **Elected:** Inaugural 1963 class

The bad boy of the NFL's early days? He was presented for enshrinement by none other than a Supreme Court justice, former Pirates star Byron "Whizzer" White.

"Some people have told me I'm really a frustrated priest. And a psychiatrist told my mother I should have been an actor," the star known as "Blood" told *Philadelphia Daily News* columnist Ray Didinger in 1974. "But I found my niche in football."

The *Miami News* in 1983 quoted him as saying: "I was half philosopher and half stud."

Blood admitted to gambling on games, such as betting the Bears he would make enough yardage for a critical first down. Of course he won. His biggest gamble? Parking a female acquaintance's car across railroad tracks to stop a team train so that he could avoid a fine for missing the Packers' departure.

His best season was 1931, when he scored 14 touchdowns for the Packers and was named all-league—the only other running back to receive that honor was Chicago's Bronko Nagurski.

Blood claimed that Cal Hubbard, a tackle who blocked for him in Green Bay and entered the Hall that same 1963 opening year, picked his all-time team once and asked if he could include a 12th player: Blood. White labeled him a "great teammate and player."

Art Rooney Jr., head of Steelers scouting: "[The Chief] always said a lot of the guys who played sandlot with him could play in the National Football League. All the guys who played at Pitt, Carnegie Tech, W&J . . . then they would take the train out to Canton and Akron and play there. Johnny McNally played at Notre Dame, but they headed to Chicago to [moonlight] for the NFL. They passed a movie house where Rudy Valentino's *Blood and Sand* was playing. He said, "I'll be Blood, you're Sand." He never liked the name 'Blood.'"

Tim Rooney Sr., who served everywhere from ball boy to ticket office: "The movie *Leathernecks* was supposed to be about him and [George] Halas and Mugsy Halas."

MARION MOTLEY
Running Back

Height: 6-1 • **Weight:** 232 • **Colleges:** South Carolina State, Nevada • **Year with the Steelers:** 1955 • **Birthplace:** Leesburg, Georgia • **Born:** June 5, 1920 • **Died:** June 27, 1999 • **Elected:** 1968

Marion Motley blazed an NFL trail through which thousands pass. He was among the four African Americans who integrated an NFL that had been almost completely white since the early- to mid-1930s. He and Bill Willis joined Paul Brown's Cleveland Browns, while Kenny Washington and Woody Strode joined the Los Angeles Rams.

Motley was the first of the four enshrined in Canton and the second African American—one year after Emlen Tunnell.

He dazzled in Cleveland from 1946 to 1953, averaging an all-time record 5.7 yards per carry and amassing 4,712 yards with the club. A knee injury effectively ended his career, though Cleveland traded him to Pittsburgh in 1955 for fullback Ed Modzelewski.

He gained eight yards on two carries with the Steelers.

He was released after seven games.

The NFL named him to its 75th Anniversary team and its 75th Anniversary two-way team—Motley played linebacker as well early in his career.

On his way to the 1950 NFL rushing title, he gained 188 yards and averaged 17.1 yards per carry in a victory over the Steelers.

Frank Varrichione, offensive tackle 1955–1960: "We didn't have many African Americans when I was there in the late 1950s, seven or eight." Motley helped significantly in bringing racial equality to the NFL. "I can remember him saying, 'I got a 35-year-old mind and 45-year-old legs. They just don't want to go.'" In fact, that was his last year.

Jack Butler, defensive back 1951–1959: "I remember we were playing the Giants [in preseason]. He ran a quick trap, he went through nice and clean. He was running down the middle of the field, and he had nothing left. He went 20 or 30 yards, and he couldn't go anything further. He ran out of gas. He was running as hard as he could, but he had nothing left. We had him at the end."

CHUCK NOLL
Head Coach

College: Dayton • **Years as Steelers coach:** 1969–1991 • **Record:** 209-156-1 • **Birthplace:** Cleveland • **Born:** January 5, 1932 • **Elected:** 1993

When listing Chuck Noll's contributions to the NFL, the discussion always starts with his unprecedented four Super Bowl championships (and in six years' time), his 11 division championships, his winning records in 16 of his 23 seasons.

But those are merely the superficial influences.

Noll, Art Rooney Jr., and their Steelers staff helped to change scouting and drafting, causing his NFL brethren to embrace small colleges, predominantly black colleges, and national evaluations. BLESTO went from a half dozen teams (the *S* stands for Steelers) to a league-wide initiative, with teams for the most part mimicking its philosophies and practices. And doggedness played a role, too: Noll once signed a punter after working him out at the Springfield, Ohio, airport—the kid never did beat out Craig Colquitt.

Noll made it mandatory for his offensive linemen to wear a fingerless form of boxing gloves, something that became a staple when NFL teams copied Dan "Bad Rad" Radakovich's style of punch-blocking, firing out their arm to meet defensive linemen.

Noll deciphered yards-per-attempt stats on both offense and defense before the NFL kept such a stat.

Noll even delivered the first major stage for the one-back offense, the 1976 AFC championship game. That was out of necessity, though: injuries to Franco Harris, Rocky Bleier, and Jack Deloplaine left Reggie "Boobie" Harrison as the last back standing, ergo . . . the one-back.

Jon Kolb, center–tackle 1969–1981 and assistant 1982–1991: "The same-foot, same-shoulder [blocking] technique, Chuck started that."

Noll also was the first successful coach to entrust a young assistant, much less a minority, with a coordinator's position. He installed Tony Dungy as defensive coordinator in January 1984, at the age of 29 years, three months and with just three years of coaching experience, after Woody Widenhofer left to coach the U.S. Football League Outlaws. Even if nobody wants to credit Noll for that, its reverberation continues throughout the league: Dungy's ascension to head coach gave rise to many more NFL opportunities for such folks as Lovie Smith, Leslie Frazier, and Mike Tomlin.

Unbelievably, Noll never won the NFL-recognized Coach of the Year award in his 23 years. The slight was ascribed to media bias, though Noll coexisted peacefully with the Pittsburgh media and other national journalists who dealt with him regularly. True, he loved to parry with questioners, relished the semantic skirmish. Sometimes, he had great fun with it. In 1987, when asked if this was a make-or-break season for anyone besides former first-round Darryl Sims, the coach replied, "Probably me."

Chuck Noll. (Pro Football Hall of Fame)

Art Rooney Sr. (Pro Football Hall of Fame)

Dan Rooney. (Pro Football Hall of Fame)

ART ROONEY SR.
Founder–President 1933–1975

Colleges: Indiana University of Pennsylvania (née Indiana Normal), Georgetown, Duquesne, Washington and Jefferson • **Birthplace:** Coultersville, Pennsylvania • **Born:** January 27, 1901 • **Died:** August 25, 1988 • **Elected:** 1964

When the Hall of Fame opened in 1963, Art Rooney presented posthumously his friend, former co-owner, and the commissioner he helped to install, Bert Bell.

Rooney could've been part of that inaugural class, too, but he declined the offer, according to a son.

Tim Rooney Sr.: "He turned it down because he thought there were other people who should've gone before him. They asked him, and he turned it down so somebody else could go in."

Seventeen somebodies were inducted in that first class, including George Halas and Curly Lambeau and Rooney's old track bookmaker, Tim Mara. Jim Thorpe, against whom the Chief said he competed and got one of his kicks blocked, and Bronko Nagurski and Sammy Baugh were enshrined at the outset. So was Johnny "Blood" McNally, Rooney's first star and the third coach of his Pittsburgh Pirates.

Records weren't kept in those days, and the selection process was far less sophisticated than the modern-day media committee, say Hall of Fame officials. So however it happened, the Chief ambled his way into Canton in the second year. It seems to fit the humility and affability of the man.

Folks from four-time Super Bowl champion quarterback Terry Bradshaw to Supreme Court Justice Byron "Whizzer" White extolled him—Bradshaw called him "the greatest man who ever walked."

The Steelers' founder, establishing the club in 1933, later helped to foster the formation of the NFL Players Association, and in the 1974 strike was seen handing over six-packs to Jack Lambert and Moon Mullins at the picket line.

Tunch Ilkin, offensive lineman 1980–1992 and player rep who visited Rooney in the hospital in 1988 while the NFL and its Players Association still hadn't reached agreement over issues that prompted the strike one year earlier: "'You and Danny'—and he was talking about my *boss* and his *son*—'you got to get the two sides together. I just said that at the NFL meeting, and they looked at me like I was passé.'"

Ed Kiely, publicity director and aide-de-camp for four decades: "He was sharp. He was good to the players. He went to bat for them. He fought very strongly for the union. The players got to know him. He treated everyone like friends."

He gave players unexpected bonuses, ripped up contracts when they deserved better, and brought players to the track with him. Elbie Nickel was a frequent guest to the Kentucky Derby. Did players get tips from the well-known winner who stole away just before post time or asked others to bet for him?

Chuck Cherundolo, center 1941–1947 and assistant 1948–1961: "He was pretty cagey."

In the February 27, 1964, announcement that he was named to the Hall, Rooney spoke about the honor and his impressive co-inductees, and added: "Gee, if I could only bring Steeler fans a championship."

DAN ROONEY
Front Office–Vice President–President–Chair

College: Duquesne • **Birthplace:** Pittsburgh • **Born:** July 20, 1932 • **Elected:** 2000

Only two father-son combinations have been enshrined in the Hall. Fittingly, they always were as close as family, with Art Rooney Sr.'s granddaughter and Dan Rooney's niece marrying into the family of Tim and Wellington Mara—the first such inducted family affair.

While Rooney the elder founded the franchise and stayed a difficult course, Rooney the son shouldered the Steelers into dominance and financial success. The firstborn also played a critical role in the league's rise.

He served on every influential committee, including being chair of the expansion committee when Tampa Bay and Seattle came aboard in 1976.

He instituted the Rooney Rule.

He was credited with bringing labor peace in 1982 and 1987, then brokering the agreement for tranquility and a $10 billion success with the cap era that he and NFL Players Association head Gene Upshaw forged almost by themselves.

He was presented by Joe Greene in his 2000 ceremony, this after Dan presented Chuck Noll in 1993 and Mel Blount in 1989. His father, for the record, presented John Henry Johnson in 1987 and Ernie Stautner in 1969, and posthumously Charles Bidwill and Bert Bell.

Tunch Ilkin, offensive lineman and player rep 1980–1992: "When Dan said, 'We have to do what's good for the game,' he meant it. It wasn't a sound bite.

"He was instrumental in getting the two sides together [by] '93, and you kept labor peace from '93 until [2010]. The depth of his commitment to do what's best for the game, that's something we players took for real. Mr. Rooney and Gene, they became partners. Give Gene some credit, too. It was the two of them. Dan and Gene trusted each other and they influenced [the rest].

"There were a majority of player reps who were worried for their jobs. I was never worried."

Joe Gordon, publicity director and vice president 1968–1998: "A consensus builder. He was, and probably still is, the most respected owner by the other owners. To this day, I think Dan knows more about the operation of an NFL team than any man in the world. Every detail. The uniforms. The medical. Dan was just amazing in his understanding of every detail."

JOHN STALLWORTH
Wide Receiver

Height: 6-2 • **Weight:** 191 • **College:** Alabama A&M • **Years with the Steelers:** 1974–1987 • **Birthplace:** Tuscaloosa, Alabama • **Born:** July 15, 1952 • **Elected:** 2002

They entered the league together, in 1974, as part of the greatest draft of all time. They combined to provide the Steelers a one-two receiver punch for the ages. The Hall of Fame doesn't work in such a poetic way, but at least Lynn Swann (2001) and John Stallworth entered Canton one after the other.

That sequence mirrored their careers.

Swann carved a place for himself first on the Super Bowl IX and X teams, leading the club in punt returns as a rookie and in receptions his second year—when he won game MVP.

By the second pair of Super Bowls, Stallworth was his equal—even leading the Super Bowl XIII team in receptions (70) and touchdowns (eight).

While he never won MVP those final two Super Bowls, Stallworth certainly boosted Terry Bradshaw's claim to the trophies he won. Stallworth caught three passes for 115 yards and two touchdowns . . . in the first half alone of Super Bowl XIII, sustaining a hamstring injury that wouldn't permit him to return. In Super Bowl XIV, Stallworth personally tortured the Rams secondary with three catches for 121 yards, including a 73-yard touchdown and a 45-yard pass.

His career yardage per Super Bowl catch: a gaudy 24.3.

Yet it wasn't singular accomplishments that carried either to success; it was the joint effort. Together, Swann and Stallworth caught 94 of Bradshaw's 162 completions and 14 of his 17 touchdown passes in the 1977 regular season. They collected 102 of 207 completions and 20 of his 28 touchdown passes in 1978. They had 111 of 259 completions and 13 of 26 touchdowns in 1979. Stallworth got hurt early in 1980. After the 1982 strike-shortened season, Swann retired at 30, and the one-two act split.

Amazingly, Stallworth surged when he went solo. He grabbed career bests of 80 passes for 1,395 yards and 11 touchdowns in 1984, with Mark Malone and David Woodley at quarterback. And in 1985 he had 75 receptions, the second most for his career, and the fourth most yards with 937.

He retired after the strike-shortened 1987 season.

ERNIE STAUTNER
Defensive Tackle–Offensive Lineman

Height: 6-1 • **Weight:** 230 • **College:** Boston College • **Years with the Steelers:** 1950–1963 • **Birthplace:** Prinzing-by-Cham, Bavaria • **Born:** April 20, 1925 • **Died:** February 18, 2006 • **Elected:** 1969

There is only one retired Steelers number: the No. 70 belonging to Ernie Stautner.

Oh, sure, Terry Bradshaw's No. 12, Joe Greene's No. 75, Jack Lambert's No. 58, Jack Ham's No. 59, and Franco Harris' No. 32 are among the numbers that the Steelers refuse to give out, even in training camp, to the never-will-bes. Someday, they'll get around to retiring those. Someday. For now, though, Stautner stands alone. As he did for the franchise's first four decades.

No wonder his presenter was the Chief, Art Rooney Sr.

As teammate Andy Russell noted elsewhere on these pages, Stautner was likely the toughest Steeler ever . . . which is akin to calling Everest a rather fair-sized hill. His statistics—beyond his nine Pro Bowls—weren't gaudy in an age long before the sack was monitored, but his games-played total shows only one game missed in his 173-game career—although Hall of Fame officials contend he missed all of six. (One absence, in 1958, was caused by a medical mix-up: A local anesthetic to allay shoulder pain put Stautner into such "deep sleep," the October 20 *Pittsburgh Post-Gazette* reported, that he could not be revived. He slumbered at the Cleveland Clinic through a loss to the Browns.) Those 173 games, as of his 1969 election, were the third most in league history.

Given that he likely played around 220 pounds, given that he stuck his face into scrums so often he retired among the NFL leaders in fumble recoveries (23) and safeties (three), his service record may well represent his most amazing number.

John Stallworth. (Pro Football Hall of Fame)

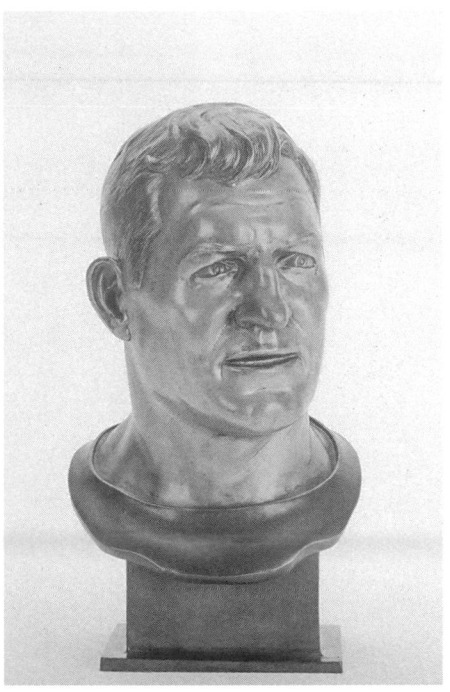

Ernie Stautner. (Pro Football Hall of Fame)

Lynn Swann. (Pro Football Hall of Fame)

Roy McHugh, Pittsburgh Press sportswriter, columnist, and editor: "In his day, he was a lot like Joe Greene."

McHugh remembers Stautner as a rookie assistant in 1963 talking to his defensive linemen and grabbing his forearms as an audiovisual: "You play football with these. If you could wear boxing gloves on your elbows . . . , I'd have been the heavyweight champion."

Stautner went on to become an acclaimed defensive-line coach with the Dallas Cowboys in 1966 and then defensive coordinator starting in 1973. Doomsday Defenses? That was Stautner. Many of his Dallas defenders joined him in Canton: Bob Lilly, Randy White, and Mel Renfro. Others carved memorable careers: Harvey Martin, Ed "Too Tall" Jones, John Dutton, Lee Roy Jordan. He remained a Cowboys coach until the Jerry Jones–Jimmy Johnson changeover in 1988, moving into scouting briefly before returning as a coach with Denver from 1991 to 1994. In the end, the Bavarian returned to Germany to coach in NFL Europe and steered the Frankfurt Galaxy to consecutive World Bowls, winning one.

LYNN SWANN
Wide Receiver

Height: 5-11 • **Weight:** 180 • **College:** USC • **Years with the Steelers:** 1974–1982 • **Birthplace:** Alcoa, Tennessee • **Born:** March 7, 1952 • **Elected:** 2001

The 14th time was the charm.

Lynn Swann was a finalist in Hall of Fame voting every year from 1988 forward. After retiring from the NFL following the 1982 season, he was considered one of the stars of his day, one of the finest receivers in the game. One of, that is. He topped the NFL only once in his nine NFL seasons, with 11 touchdowns in 1975. He also led the league in punt-return yardage as a rookie, with 577 in 1974, but that didn't much accentuate his viability as a Hall candidate.

No, Swann earned his Canton ticket on his consistency, on his aesthetic brilliance, on his domination of the game's biggest stage. He had 16 catches for 364 yards and three touchdowns in four Super Bowls. He was the MVP of Super Bowl X, the one with his highlight-for-the-ages juggling catch over Dallas' Mark Washington and his more-amazing sideline reception.

If it seemed fitting that the dramatic, first-round selection reached the Hall the year before the steady, fourth-round selection that was John Stallworth, it wasn't relevant. They were a combination, a pair of aces. Taken together, they provided the Steelers with the offensive thrust to win four Super Bowls and dominate the game—the ultimate standard for a Hall bust. Swann and Stallworth caught 27 of Terry Bradshaw's 49 Super Bowl completions. They accounted for 632 of his 932 Super Bowl yards, or two-thirds. They provided six of his seven Super Bowl touchdown passes. And they were responsible for half of the 22 longest offensive plays in those four Super Bowls.

So a sizable portion of Bradshaw's Super Bowl XIII and XIV MVPs belong to Swann and Stallworth, too.

Larry Brown, tight end–offensive tackle 1971–1984 and the pass receiver of that other Bradshaw Super Bowl touchdown: "We had a couple of Super Bowls where both of those guys made contributions and huge catches, in each one of those games."

In all, they ruled the postseason: Swann had 49 catches for 907 yards (18.5 average) with nine touchdowns in 16 playoff games; and Stallworth had 57 catches for 1,054 (the same 18.5 average) and 11 touchdowns—including at least one in nine of his final 10 postseason games.

Mike Webster. (Pro Football Hall of Fame)

Rod Woodson. (Pro Football Hall of Fame)

MIKE WEBSTER
Center–Guard

Height: 6-1 • **Weight:** 255 • **College:** Wisconsin • **Years with the Steelers:** 1974–1988 • **Birthplace:** Tomahawk, Wisconsin • **Born:** March 18, 1952 • **Died:** September 24, 2002 • **Elected:** 1997

Jon Kolb, center–tackle 1969–1981 and assistant coach 1982–1991: "Everybody thinks of Mike as a football player. I think of Mike as a man. We were in a car going to practice. We were going down the hill to Bridgeville [on Interstate 79], and he was talking about his brother . . . [who] had been in prison. At that point, he was kind of on top of the world [in football]. We all were. But I didn't know the turmoil that went on in his dad's side of the family. I think of Mike in that context. The people who played were people to me."

Mike Webster endured hardships physical and financial after his 17 NFL seasons, his 245 games, his 12,000-plus game snaps and collisions, his countless practices. He typed up notes at a lawyer friend's office. He told ESPN about being homeless and sleeping in his car, stories that were recounted in the days before his Hall of Fame induction. He admitted in public that he battled depression, admitted in court papers that he experimented with steroids as a player, called his teenaged son Garrett to ask for help finding his way home from, say, a wooded area he didn't recognize. The son confessed to looking after the father as much, if not more, than the father did the son.

He exhibited signs that his brain tissue later revealed, among the first in research that included fellow ex-Steelers Terry Long and Justin Strzelczyk. He won a landmark disability case against the NFL, or at least his estate did—Webster died more than four years before litigation ran its course. With similarly afflicted veterans receiving special payments

from the NFL, with concussion and brain research moving to the forefront of public consciousness and scientific efforts, Iron Mike once again was hunkered over the ball: It started with him.

His 220 games rank first in Steelers history. His 177 consecutive games remained a streak unlikely to be broken. Coincidentally, or not, behind Webster was the player who replaced him (Dermontti Dawson with 170) and the player he replaced (Ray Mansfield 168). He paid a price. Will others to follow learn from that transaction?

ROD WOODSON
Cornerback

Height: 5-11 • **Weight:** 205 • **College:** Purdue • **Years with the Steelers:** 1987–1996 • **Birthplace:** Fort Wayne, Indiana • **Born:** March 10, 1965 • **Elected:** 2009

Halfway through his career, not yet even 30 years old, Rod Woodson was chosen to the NFL's 75th Anniversary team. He was one of eight onetime Steelers on that prestigious lineup, along with Mike Webster, Mel Blount, Jack Ham, Jack Lambert, Joe Greene, Johnny Unitas, and Marion Motley.

He didn't make the first of his secondary-record 11 Pro Bowls until his third NFL season. At that, he made it as a returner. Chuck Noll groused about that. After all, the guy never yielded a touchdown at cornerback that season.

The star—who scored touchdowns on punt, kickoff, interception, and fumble returns—also proved highly durable. He missed three games during that seven-year span from his second season to the 1995 opener when he tore his ACL.

Ron Erhardt, offensive coordinator 1992–1995: "One of the outstanding football players who ever played the game back there."

Dom Capers, defensive coordinator 1992–1994: "One of the greatest defensive backs in NFL history. His stats speak for themselves. He's a rare guy. He was always going to be around the ball, get his hands on the ball. Football smart, football instinctive. A great athlete. He had a lot of interceptions and returned a bunch for touchdowns."

Dick LeBeau, defensive assistant 1992–1996, 2004– : "He's as good as there has ever been. Unquestionably [one of the greatest in NFL history]. He could do anything he wanted. He could run back kicks, he could block kicks, he could play corner, he could blitz, he could play safety, he's one of the all-time interceptors, he's in the Hall of Fame. . . . What more do you want a guy to do? He could've played [wide receiver in the NFL]. And at Purdue, he did. I went to scout him when he was coming out of college. In the Indiana game, I think he carried the ball [15 times for 93 yards, caught three passes for 67 yards], and made, like, 15, 16 tackles on defense [and forced a fumble for a touchdown]. He was a remarkable guy."

Dermontti Dawson, center 1988–2000: "One of the most gifted athletes I've ever seen. He could play receiver, he could play corner, safety—he could play anything. Just a phenomenal athlete. Track guy, Purdue. He could do it all. Of course we saw it on kickoff returns, punt returns. . . . The only thing about Deion [Sanders] was, he was so fast and quick. But Rod was so much bigger than Deion. Both of those guys, they were two of the best to play that position. Because he accomplished so much in a short period of time, before he left Pittsburgh . . . Rod should have been one of those guys who stayed there the whole career. I chose to stay there my whole career because that's where I had my success. It would've been nice to have Rod as a Steeler and not for several other teams as well."

The Super Second Generation (1980–)

DICK HOAK, *running backs coach 1972–2006:* "We won the four Super Bowls; [Chuck Noll] took us all on a trip after each one—all the coaches and our wives. The Bahamas. Went deep-sea fishing every day. The last two, we went to Acapulco. Every day, we'd meet in [Chuck and Marianne's] room at 5 o'clock for cocktails and then go to dinner."

Then the party was over.

The 1980s were unkind, if not cruel, to Chuck Noll and the Steelers. The stars of the '70s faded. Retrenching was needed.

Work didn't go so well.

The old guard retired or exited each year: Joe Greene in 1981, Jack Ham and Lynn Swann in 1982, Terry Bradshaw because of injury after a one-game 1983, Mel Blount and

The last of the Mohicans. John Stallworth, Mike Webster, and Donnie Shell, the final members of the four Super Bowl champions still playing at the time, in their final Steelers season together. Stallworth and Shell retired at the 1987 season's end; Webster left two years later. They had all come together in 1974: Stallworth in the draft's fourth round, Webster in the fifth round, and Shell as an undrafted free agent. (Vincent J. Musi)

Franco Harris that same year, Jack Lambert in 1984, John Stallworth in 1987, and Mike Webster in 1988. You just don't replace Hall of Famers. So Noll tried to keep pace with the game, in 1982 switching to a 3–4 defense . . . a move that stuck.

The NFL was undergoing changes, too. Two strikes and taking the field with replacement players didn't help the cause of Noll and the Steelers.

Tunch Ilkin, tackle and player representative 1980–1992: "We got our butts kicked so bad in the strike. The guys who were carrying 'No Football, No Freedom' sandwich boards were saying [with more vigor over those final few weeks]: 'Just get a little pension; forget free agency,' then . . . 'Take what they'll give us.'"

Craig Wolfley, assistant rep and guard 1980–1989: "We were like the Iraqi army looking to give itself up to the CNN camera crew."

Ilkin, watching the 1987 captains Stallworth, Webster, Donnie Shell, and Gary Dunn cross the picket line: "Each one of those guys, they were at the end. They were all close friends. You got to do what you think is right."

The Steelers, the little franchise that tried so hard to do right, couldn't make it work by the end of the 1980s. In the uneven financial landscape, at a time when they just couldn't draft as well as the past, they faced an additional problem they hadn't experienced in more than a decade: misfortune. Gabe Rivera, the defensive lineman whom Noll likened to a Joe Greene franchise foundation and selected over Dan Marino, got into an automobile accident that paralyzed him for life. In 1989, they rallied from losing the opening pair of games by a 92-10 collective margin—to Central rivals Cleveland and Cincinnati, to boot—and reached the AFC divisional playoffs, but a dropped pass cost them a trip to the championship game and a 24-23 loss at Denver. Terry Long was suspended for violating the league steroids policy and twice attempted suicide.

Bubby Brister, quarterback 1986–1992: "Our payroll was the lowest in the league, playing San Francisco and Houston with some of the biggest payrolls. For us to still compete with guys in the '80s, when we didn't have the payroll . . ."

Noll managed to prod the Steelers into the playoffs in seven of the 12 seasons between 1980 and 1991, but he made the AFC championship game once in those dozen years (1984), contrasted to six of the last eight seasons of the 1970s. Time passed. The time came.

Tunch Ilkin leaves the Mile High Stadium field after an excruciating 24-23 loss to Denver in the 1990 AFC Divisional playoffs. He later became the soundtrack to the Steelers of the 21st century, joining Myron Cope and Bill Hillgrove in the radio booth and ultimately taking Cope's seat upon his retirement in 2005. (Vincent J. Musi)

Bill Cowher: "I was on a flight with [Chuck Noll] one time and asked him about certain players. He was very guarded with his answers. What I took away from that was, he was allowing me not to prejudge people, not even the organization."

The road back to Super Bowls began with Cowher's open-eyed arrival in 1992, though it didn't completely unfurl in front of the Steelers' wheels for another decade.

Sure, he started his coaching career with a record-tying six playoff trips and pieced together a Super Bowl XXX run. But there were still pieces missing, as the franchise's first late-January loss evidenced.

Kevin Greene, outside linebacker 1993–1995 and a key free-agent acquisition for the Blitzburgh defense: "I remember looking in Jim Kelly's eyes. I know he's a Hall of Famer and a buddy of mine. But I remember looking in his eyes and seeing a look of bewilderment. Just trying to see where the pressure was coming from—it was overwhelming.

"I've been a part of some pretty good defenses with the Rams . . . , with the 49ers in 1997 . . . , with the Carolina Panthers—Dom [Capers] brought me there in 1996 and we went to the [NFC] championship game. But those three years in Pittsburgh, we had it rolling. We had the right mix of players. The right athletes. It was a special time, when I look back at my 15 years in the NFL.

"I know we're pretty much a footnote in NFL history, because we never did win a Super Bowl. But it was a special time."

While Greene, Dermontti Dawson, and Rod Woodson were Hall of Fame–worthy parts to the puzzle, a true contender

requires more. Once again, the same as in the early 1980s, the Steelers broke up the old gang and went back to remodeling.

Cowher: "It was done meticulously. It was done developing your own players. Not a whole lot of players were brought from the outside. I know we traded for Jerome Bettis [in 1996]. But when you look at the team, it was pretty much a team built in the system. To have long-term success, you have to build your own. If you look around, the people who acquire players,

Greg Lloyd pleads his case in 1997. (George Gojkovich)

it's not long-lasting. You might have short-term success. But in terms of building something for the long haul, having solid drafts, building with your own players is the recipe."

Big pieces arrived: Alan Faneca, Aaron Smith, Joey Porter, Hines Ward, Troy Polamalu . . .

Complimentary pieces came: Larry Foote, Chris Hope, Antwaan Randle El—the guy who threw the most important pass in Super Bowl XL came as a second-round wide receiver converting from college quarterback.

Then, after a 2003 season in which the Steelers sputtered to a 2-6 start and finished 6-10, the fourth nonplayoff year in six, Cowher stuck out that jaw and agreed to a bold draft decision: Ben Roethlisberger.

Cowher:

I thought in the long term this guy would have a chance to develop into a better quarterback. But I thought at the time it might be a pick for the future—for someone else—'cause we just had a losing season.

Kordell Stewart was solid. Tommy Maddox was solid at times. Neil O'Donnell [of the Super Bowl XXX period] was solid. But we never had anybody who could do what Ben did, make plays. With all the other guys when I was here, we had to be perfect. We had to play perfect defense. We had to play perfect special teams. We never had the player who has the special ability.

Sometimes, you have to be lucky. We did have a losing record in 2003. It allowed us to have the pick we had, No. 11. To be able to have that type of player still be there when we picked . . . , we were lucky. We had Tommy Maddox; we had some needs on offensive line. We were talking about getting the kid [lineman Shawn] Andrews from Arkansas; [he] wound up going to the Philadelphia Eagles. We talked about a lot of things there. When you have Eli Manning, Philip Rivers, and Ben Roethlisberger in the same draft, you're lucky. He was the missing piece we had been missing for years.

Baltimore's Gary Baxter blew out Maddox's throwing elbow in the third quarter of the second game, and the Ravens still rue that September 19, 2004, day.

Cowher: "You knew he had qualities from day one in that building, and when he stepped on that practice field, you could tell he was a special player.

"But nobody foresaw that he would go 15-1 his first year."

Heath Miller, Santonio Holmes, Willie Parker, Willie Colon. Pieces fell into place. By the end of Roethlisberger's second

Jerome Bettis starts his famous rumble—over Chicago's Brian Urlacher and through the Bears defense in the snow—in December 2005, the first steps of an eight-game winning streak that ended in the franchise's fifth Super Bowl triumph. In other words, the Bus started rolling toward Detroit here. (George Gojkovich)

season, 2005, he was throwing the ball all over the playoff lot and winning. In Cincinnati. In Indianapolis. In Denver.

The road to the Super Bowl didn't go through Pittsburgh anymore. It was a Rand McNally Atlas, a travelogue across football America.

The Lombardi Trophy returned to Pittsburgh, crowding the trophies that collected dust at Three Rivers Stadium for a generation, then moved to the South Side facility when Heinz Field opened in 2001. After 15 years as the head coach of his hometown team, with his wife and youngest daughter living in North Carolina, Cowher chose—as his predecessor used to say—to get on with his life's work. The Rooneys, Dan and Art II, selected another 34-year-old defensive coordinator and motivator as their new head coach: Mike Tomlin.

Cowher: "When Mike came in, I told him, 'I'll give you the same advice Chuck gave me: none.' [Laughs.]

"You've got to be your own person and have your own assessment. When you've been someplace 15 years, there are things you may want to change or think are outdated. But someone new comes in, and they may have fresher ideas and ideas about how things could be implemented. Like when Mike came in, I told him I was glad I had no preconceived notions about anybody or anything. I didn't want to take away from that opportunity for Mike to do the same."

Make no mistake, Tomlin was in a rush to grab a Lombardi with his own two hands. He told friends and family as much. He realized what the Steelers had in place.

Ralph Cindrich, former NFL player, agent, and university professor: "You have Art, Mike, Kevin, and Omar. There isn't an air of pretension about them. They just conduct themselves as if they're one of the guys. It's just typical Pittsburgh." Art Rooney II, Tomlin, Colbert, and business/football administration coordinator Omar Kahn are the leadership that propelled the franchise to two Super Bowls during 2007–2010. They are merely continuing the sound strategy and business tradition of Dan Rooney, a man so unpretentious he refused a Super Bowl limo and takes the media/VIP bus at Super Bowls.

What a ride, indeed.

Colbert: "You try to lend your own touch. I think what I try to do is try to find the right players for this organization, this team, this city. The right players who are going to fit in with this team. I'm trying to stay true to our standards with everything. Sometimes, it's difficult. But you know we've developed a successful pattern.

"We're always going to [examine] not only where we've succeeded but where we've failed. The things we often evaluate [are] a guy's heart or merits. The football part I don't want to say it's easy to figure out, but *easier.*"

Tomlin has grown, changed as well. He remains the same loquacious psychologist-coach, but four years and two Super Bowls and dozens of games with many of the same men provides a vast perspective. He knows his players, the buttons to push, the standards to raise.

His players appreciate his openness, his brutal honesty, his manner that's more lawyerly than coachspeak.

Mike Tomlin before the 2011 season opened: "I feel comfortable as I sit here today, but we proceed with the knowledge that things can change, and they usually do. That's the nature of this journey that we're embarking on and I think those of us that have any experience understand that."

Colbert: "I think when he first came, he was very determined to establish who he was. . . . He understood he was following a Super Bowl–winning coach who left on his own terms. Usually, when you're a head coach coming in, the previous coach has failed. That wasn't the situation here. He set the standard he was going to follow. . . . But he was going to put his own stamp on it. Which he did right from the get-go. Which was difficult for the players: 'We have a routine; we've been successful; we know how to win.'

"Obviously, success followed."

To be continued?

12

Steelers Nation

SUNDAY IS THEIR DAY to gather. Dressed in their finer-ies, prepared for fellowship, they congregate in the weekly meeting place. They chat for a spell, take a seat in their usual spot, grip their talisman, and turn their attention to the stage. They follow their Sunday chants, their Sunday rituals, their Sunday spirituals.

They root like holy hell for the Steelers.

It isn't a religion, a Pittsburgh wag related to a National Public Radio audience before Super Bowl XLIII.

It goes much deeper than that.

Goes much farther beyond Western Pennsylvania's borders, too.

This Sunday scene plays out across America. In Mexico, where Steelers television and radio broadcasts are beamed live. In Israel, where the Steelers Nation—InterNational?—convenes for Sunday nights live to watch games. In a Steelers bar in Italy. Across the globe. And beyond.

Colonel Mike Fincke, a Pittsburgh native with the longest logged time in the stars of any astronaut, pushed the envelope when he used NASA cameras to deliver good wishes to his hometown team before Super Bowl XLIII. He then allowed weightlessness to turn a Terrible Towel right side up in the space station he commanded. This goes beyond the Pittsburgh suburbs of Moon and Mars, too.

Welcome to the Steelers Galaxy.

Tim Rooney Sr.: "Everywhere you go, it's unbelievable."

He is the third-oldest son of the Steelers' founder, Art Rooney Sr. He is a former team ticket seller—mostly, he gave them away—and a septuagenarian old enough to have witnessed crowds of 20,000 or fewer at home games. Nowadays, that many people make pilgrimages to Steelers' Super Bowls in Detroit, Tampa, and Dallas and fail to scalp a ticket, thus get forced by local entrepreneurs to pay exorbitant cover charges just so they can continue their Sunday tradition of watching their team in a bar with fellow faithful, Terrible Towels a-twirling.

Rooney and his wife were in Palermo, Italy, in 2011 on vacation. They hailed a cab to go sightseeing. The question to the cabbie was an attempt at blank conversation: Do you follow much American sports? Without knowing the derivation or name of his customer, the driver replied: "I'm a big Steelers fan."

Let's venture to explain it.

Steelers Nation is a fanaticism that stirs in new hearts. . . .

Fans pour through the gates at Heinz Field. (John Beale)

The Kansas City Steelers Fan Club, in the heart of America, had roughly 270 members. Three-fourths of them had absolutely no ties to Western Pennsylvania.

Such worship from afar explains why there's a United Kingdom fans group that travels almost every year to catch a Steelers game, or a Steelers bar quaffing brews on game days in Rome. They fell for the decals on one side of the helmet, the rough-hewn style of American football, the 1970s rise, or the

Donald Durdan of Pawleys Island, South Carolina, at a well-known Steelers bar in Rome with owner Giovanni Poggi—who once posed in front of the Vatican, holding a "You're in Steelers Country" banner from his bar—for a photograph promoting the fan club that regularly convenes at his La Botticella establishment.

perpetual winning ways. Those exhibition games in Mexico City, Dublin, Barcelona, Tokyo, and Montreal over the past generation or so? The Steelers players admit to feeling right at home in those venues as much as Kansas City, Tampa, Jacksonville, and more.

Steelers Nation is a gripping skepticism, a constant concern that goes a tad beyond Pittsburgh. . . .

Roger Hunt, a onetime Steelers cheerleader, a fraternity so small (four) and so distant (last seen: 1962) that he couldn't be better concealed in witness protection: "I live in Hopwood; it's about three miles east of Uniontown," a highlands city 40 miles southeast of Pittsburgh. On his vacation, he pulled out a Steelers jacket to stay warm. "This guy comes up to me in the lobby of the Captain Cook Hotel. I'm in Anchorage, Alaska—4,000 miles away. And he says, 'So howdya think we're gonna do this season?' I know the Steelers Nation. This was the first time I ever experienced it."

Steelers Nation is a birthright. . . .

Russ Grimm knows. He was born in it, played in it with the Redskins, coached in it with the Steelers. Then lost to it in Super Bowl XLIII with Arizona.

Grimm: "I grew up a Steeler fan, went to the University of Pittsburgh, was at Pitt when it became the City of Champions. Western Pennsylvania football is totally different than anywhere else in the country. I said it in the Hall of Fame speech [in 2010]: I want to thank the people of Western Pennsylvania. Growing up, you would go with your father to a high school game on Friday night, you go to a college game Saturday, and Sunday was the Steelers, and you fed the hunger. It creates an atmosphere: This is what you want to be a part of. You buy into it." As a homegrown, it was buyer beware. "If you were playing bad and somebody threw something at you, you turned around and probably knew them."

Steelers Nation is an organized drinking game that's an amorphous 345 dates on the calendar, or fewer. . . .

There exist at least 850 taverns claiming to be Steelers bars in all 50 states plus the District of Columbia, as well as ports elsewhere around the globe, all rocking on game days and sometimes even draft days, but most certainly in January and February. The rest of that time, they make themselves seen and heard, particularly in cities wherever their football team plays.

Steelers Nation is an invasion. . . .

Dallas authorities caught fans climbing over fences trying to sneak into their previous stadium.

Indianapolis front-office types tried to block all ticket orders from the 412 and 724 area codes of Western Pennsylvania, a maneuver that spiked secondary sales and other means possible to limit interlopers to, oh, roughly 8,000 to 10,000 Steelers fans breaking into the Colts corral of 50,000.

Seattle types breathed a sigh of relief at Super Bowl XL that no more than 20 percent of their foes' fans could ever get inside. Too corporate an atmosphere, they surmised. Too tough a ticket. Then, come game day, with fans pouring into Detroit within the easy four-hour driving distance from Pittsburgh and points elsewhere, Ford Field was a Towel haven—easily 80 percent Steelers followers. An estimated 50,000-plus Steelers followers came to the Motor City that weekend; good thing Chicago lost to Seattle, or Bears fans could've made it one huge street fight.

Steelers Nation is not a modern-day phenomenon. . . .

In the 1972 regular-season finale, when the Steelers clinched their first AFC Central title and home-field advantage through the playoffs, some 1,200 Steelers fans were present . . . in San Diego.

Bubby Brister, quarterback 1986–1992 before playing in Philadelphia and Denver:

When I was on the Steelers—this is after the '89 season—I got asked to speak at a Black and Gold Brigade banquet in California. I was like, "You gotta be kidding me?" And it was packed. Thousands of people.

I saw it when we played out in California. Down in Tampa. A lot of fans. I knew a lot of people were in the stadium; when we were winning, you could hear them over the home crowd, for sure. There were Steelers fans everywhere. In abundance.

The Broncos were pretty good. Of course, when I got to Denver, they won two Super Bowls, so that helped. The Broncos have a great following. But they haven't been as big. There's nothing like the Steelers fans. My son is 11; we tried to tell him. We're at the [2011 Steelers–Patriots game in Heinz Field on Alumni Day], and he's swinging his Towel, and he said, "I get it."

Steelers Nation is more than traveling well, as football people call it, invoking a phrase from the collegiate level. . . .

For the most part, Steelers fans are already there. They are sons and daughters and nieces and nephews of folks with black and gold ruts, as the word "roots" is pronounced in some Western Pennsylvania burgs. Or they glommed onto a successful franchise in the Super Steelers age of the 1970s, or the resurgence of the 1990s and 21st century. Or they were the generation, or second generation, of the migration caused when the steel industry collapsed all around Chuck Noll and the fellas.

A

B

C

D

Gordon Dedman, who founded the Steelers fan chapter in the United Kingdom, poses with his Terrible Towel: **A,** On safari in Africa (the giraffes don't seem to care for his NFL affiliation); **B,** at the Great Wall in China—it's the other side of the world—hence the Towel is upside down; **C,** with the bridal party at the wedding of his daughter and son-in-law, Jodie and Jon Isherwood, at the Grand Roche Hotel, Paarl, South Africa; **D,** takes a photo of his close friend Karen Mayers (holding the Towel) and friends and family from Birmingham, England, in Lapland with, uh, Santa. (Courtesy of Gordon Dedman)

Don Galla, 55, of Hagerstown, Maryland, wears his favorite Steelers hat—the one with players' numbers written on each spike—to the 2008 training camp. (John Beale)

Rooney, who left his hometown in the 1960s to work in the family's horse-racing interests, winding up a New Yorker: "So many people lost their jobs when steel crashed, and they had to leave. Pittsburghers don't want to leave. But they left. And you keep that relationship with your team. A lot of that goes back to the 1970s; a lot of them were kids in the '70s, when the Steelers teams were so good."

Frenchy Fuqua, running back 1970–1976: "We had Frankie's Italian Army. I had my Frenchy's Foreign Legion. We had Gerela's Gorillas. We had all these groups. It was at a time when the city was coming together; they had something to root for. It was something that I never forget."

The steel bust in Western Pennsylvania stayed longer than just that Super Bowl decade. Between 1981 and 1984, some 120,000 steel and steel-related jobs were eliminated. Only three mills remained, none inside the city limits. Jones and Laughlin—where locals bragged that World War II was won and where former Bears and Dolphins coach Dave Wannstedt worked decades before he sat in Pitt's football facility on the very same grounds—gave way to football fields, medical complexes, and retail shops and restaurants. Pig iron was replaced by cheesecake. The Homestead Works that were the world's largest became, by the first decade of the 2000s, a shopping mall and a water park.

Health services and high-tech business became hallmarks, but still it was a demographic market in overall decline: Pittsburgh fell from the No. 6 television market in the United States in the mid-1980s to No. 23 in 2010. The city's population, hovering around 300,000, was less than half its size of two generations earlier.

The Steel City was no more.

It morphed in transplanted hearts and minds into a Steeler City, its boundaries for fanaticism stretching to the earth's poles.

One fan near the Arctic circle built an igloo every play-off January, a superstitious venue in which he kept his television, microwave, and all the modern-day amenities necessary to watch a 9 A.M. kickoff Alaska time. One Steelers club in Hawaii special-ordered Iron City and Yuengling beers for better viewing accoutrements. Hey, bartender, *Mahalo . . . 'n at.* In Arizona, one Steelers bar sells personal-seat licenses. In Italy, a couple of guys put on their Troy Polamalu and Ben Roethlisberger jerseys, then stretched a banner in front of the Vatican for a photograph: You're in Steeler Country.

A place in heaven, too? So many obituaries across the country contain the phrase "devout" or, inelegantly put, "die-hard Steelers fan." One Pittsburgh man, veteran John Henry Smith from the Garfield section, when he died of cancer in 2005 was laid out for a Steelers viewing—at his family's behest. He was in his favorite lounger, with a beer and cigarettes at his side, black-and-gold pajamas on and a remote in hand, and an HD television set running a highlights loop. Steelers faithful in perpetuity.

Steelers Nation is a heartbeat that thumps in unison not merely on game days or during the playoffs. . . .

Defensive end Aaron Smith deep into the 2008 season found out his then-four-year-old son Elijah was suffering from acute lymphoblastic leukemia, a cancer of the white blood cells. While the Steelers were making their Super Bowl XLIII drive, the Smith family was playing host to a blood drive at Heinz Field and bouncing from doctor visits to hospitals to vigils. The Nation by the thousands offered blood, cards, e-mails, online messages, gifts, prayers.

Smith, getting emotional: "It was unbelievable. It far exceeded anything I could possibly have [imagined]. I'm not a big ego guy, or feel very important or significant to this game. So when people rallied behind, it really, um, touched my heart. It really blew me away, the way the Steelers Nation [reacted]. I was shocked. For them to do that for me? . . . There's no way you could count [the cards and well wishes]. They would send my son stuff—my son would get boxes of stuff."

Steeler Nation is a symbol, a flag, a proud wardrobe. . . .

Actor Jake Gyllenhaal, a Patriots fan for crying out loud, became so enamored while filming in Pittsburgh that he left with a Steelers-logo tattoo on his lower back.

A champ stamp, of course.

Oh, and the movie he was shooting? The appropriately Steelers-named *Love and Other Drugs.*

No wonder, when ardent, lifelong fans desire to publicly show their devotion and connection, the Steelers franchise consistently ranks among the NFL's most-watched in game-television rankings, in merchandise sales, in the top of just about every meaningful league-business metric. So much for America's Team, the Dallas Cowboys of the 1970s and 1980s. Maybe it was wiped out by a special piece of cloth, roughly a million sold, and more Towel-themed trinkets in its "Myron Cope's Official . . ." name.

Dan Toritsky, longtime national officer with the Autism Society, and for 40 years an associate/friend of Cope: "It's my opinion that the Terrible Towel is the fabric of the Steelers Nation. It gives you a sense of belonging to the Steelers Nation. Other towels may come and other towels may go, but there's only one team that makes the Towel go."

Steelers fans enjoy the Super Bowl nostalgia of the 1990 Pro Football Hall of Fame inductions in Canton, Ohio, some 77 miles from Three Rivers Stadium: Jack Lambert and Franco Harris were enshrined in their first year of eligibility. Among their classmates was the Dallas Cowboys coach whom they twice tortured in the Super Bowl, Tom Landry. (Vincent J. Musi)

Whether the reasons behind these Towel-slinging legions of followers are genetic, generational, Gen-X, or engineered, however one defines The Birth of The Nation, truly it doesn't matter.

They are here; they are loyal; they are devout.

Which prompts the questions: Why, why, why?

Why such allegiance?

Why, sociologically and psychologically speaking, don't they find another to love?

Michael Tarr: "I've seen one live game in my life. It's expensive to go to games. And it's easier to watch on TV, more comfortable, and you see more. It's funny how we fans don't go to games. I've literally watched every game. I was famous for doing all my homework during games. No, it didn't hurt me too badly."

See, Dr. Michael Tarr, Ph.D., is a psychology professor and department codirector at the Center for Neural Basis of Cognition at Carnegie Mellon University. He is an Ivy League

man, a Cornell graduate. He received his Ph.D. from MIT. He taught at Brown for 14 years. He taught at Yale for six.

Then he moved back to his hometown, and he couldn't be happier.

It isn't all about the Steelers . . . but a vital, small part is.

Put it this way: The Tarrs prohibit their eight-year-old son, Ben, from watching television. Except, that is, for Steelers games. The little guy is such a big Steelers fan that in early 2010 he made a wager with his father: If the Steelers make Super Bowl XLV, you gotta buy me something. They made it. His wish: a 55-inch TV.

For a kid who watches three hours of TV only 20 or so weekends a year.

Tarr:

He and [*Sports Illustrated*'s] Peter King were the only two people who predicted that.

Why are we like the way we are? It would be a fun experiment to do, the Steeler area of the brain. The Steelers

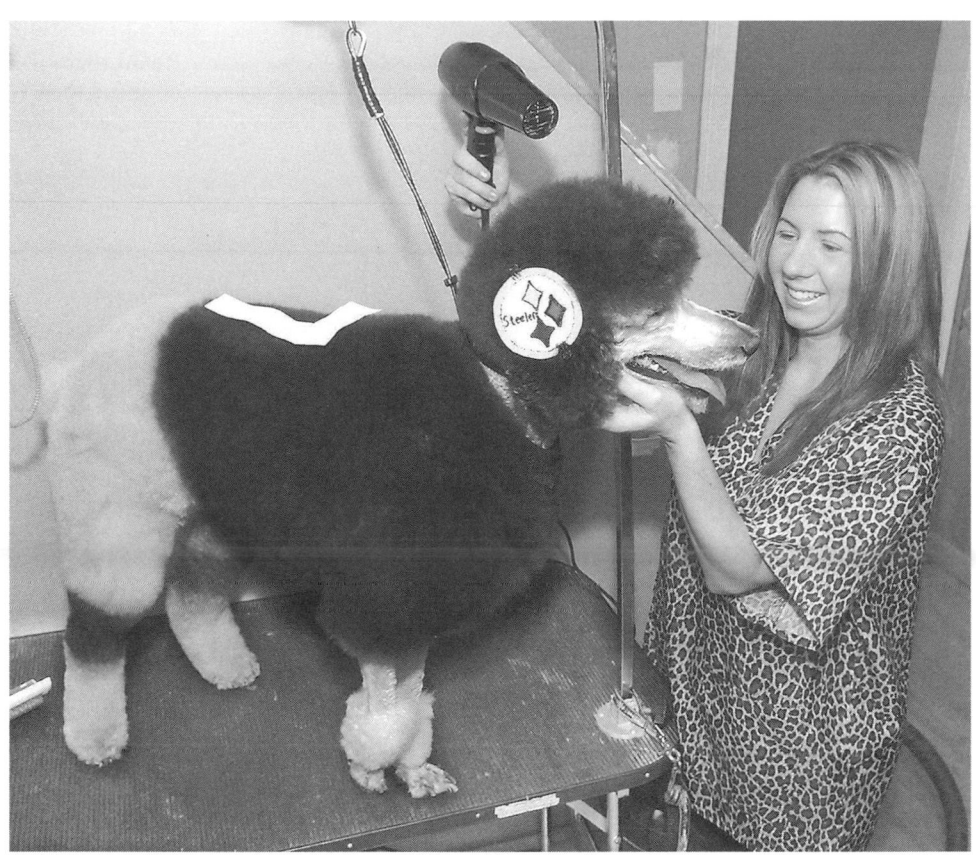

Professional groomer Justine Cosley turns her standard poodle Silas into Ben Roethlisberger in 2005 before Super Bowl XL. Silas won first place in a Hershey competition that year. Cosley operates Cat around Town Grooming in Dravosburg, Pennsylvania. (Robert J. Pavuchak)

versus the Cowboys or whatever, and see what areas of the brain light up.

What we have here [is], there's this wonderful reinforcement . . . like all that winning. I was in New England during the 16-0 season [in 2007]. I hate the Patriots, by the way. Just can't stand them. Their fans are annoying. They're unbelievably fair-weather. This irks Steelers fans. "How dare you? You need to take this stuff seriously."

The interesting thing is, it was really boring. The Patriots were ripping everyone up. So there's no good reinforcement [or] self-satisfaction. It's much more fun to have things like: the Bettis Fumble. [A Steeler fan] knows exactly what I'm talking about with the Bettis Fumble [of 2005]. Because that level of tension is reinforcement, that give-and-take where you get [both] positive and negative.

Tarr then launched into B. F. Skinner and the classic psychology theory of operant conditioning. Don't misunderstand, though: he wasn't likening Steelers fans to rats seeking juice.

The heart-in-the-mouth drama constantly displayed by the Steelers—12 of 19 playoff games between 1997 and 2010 decided by one touchdown or less—conditioned the Steelers Nation to come back for more, provided they survived these regular ordeals. The team's familiar personalities, with much of the defense intact for Super Bowls XL, XLIII, and XLV, helped to engender loyalty. And it carried weighty significance to have such consistency as three head coaches over XLIII years and counting (Chuck Noll to Bill Cowher to Mike Tomlin) and one family ownership since the franchise's 1933 start (Rooneys). Oh, it didn't hurt that they won, either, thereby undermining the future likelihood of a Los Angeles Clippers

Nation: 384-238-2 (.615) with six Super Bowl championships and eight Super Bowl appearances from 1974 to 2010.

Tarr: "There's something to the people of [and linked to] this city. People treat each other a different way here—everyone in it together. I think there's also something to the family-owned nature of the team. It's less corporate. No one likes [stuffed suits]. The Rooneys are beloved in this city. But if the team was crappy, maybe they wouldn't be so beloved."

THE SAVIOR

Jesus is a Steelers fan.

What else?

He wears a brown robe on Sundays and stands in the Heinz Field front row during warm-ups. He holds aloft signs with clever messages: Defeat Cin . . . My Dad Says: Run the Ball . . .

Matt Schmidt, a.k.a. Jesus: "That was actually my wife's idea."

Or . . . My birthday wish: Fire the Commish.

Schmidt: "That didn't make it into the game; they confiscated that. That was really my only negative one."

It is a fine line, all this Steelers worship, devotion, belief.

Schmidt is a Connecticut automobile technician who drives eight hours one way on Steelers home weekends, along with his wife, a native of Ellwood City, Pennsylvania, and a wonderful woman he married eight years ago—and not merely because she had second-row tickets. Jes . . . er, Matt, is a North Jersey guy, from the same town as the famed J-E-T-S fireman. He got to be a Steelers fan because his mother picked up a

Steelers white No. 88 at the Salvation Army, and it became a kick when the older kids congratulated him: "Lynn Swann, nice catch." He fell in with the Nation.

Schmidt: "There are Steelers bars everywhere. It wasn't difficult to find Steelers fans.

"My wife thinks I married her for her tickets. I have to say, she's the biggest fan I ever met, and I'm not saying that because she's my wife. We drive in literally every [home] game. [Against Jacksonville in 2011], the people two people behind us at the game—we are always the first people at Gate A; that's my wife, same security guard—drove in from Midland, Texas, 1,600 miles. The farthest I've heard someone coming from was Brazil; they took my picture. A lot of people from Mexico. Every game."

How he became Jesus is a relatively benign Halloween tale. With his long hair and beard, he always got kidded by his brother: "How's it going, Jesus." The Halloween 2004 game was against New England, a fan base covering segments of Connecticut. It would take a miracle to beat Tom Brady and that outfit, so he went the whole nine yards. He ordered a shepherd's costume online. Rush delivery. Wouldn't want to tempt fate, right?

The Steelers clobbered the Patriots and beat the Eagles the following week, the only NFL team to ever defeat undefeated teams back-to-back so deep into a season. Season-ticket holders around the Schmidts demanded that Jesus keep coming back. So on game days he'll hang with the Cowher Power guy and Super Dave the Super Steeler, these dress-ups being part and parcel of Steelers lore.

Schmidt: "Any time she sees a Steelers fan in a store, my mother breaks out these pictures—'My son's Jesus.' If they've never been to games, they don't know what she's talking about.

"What is a Steelers fan? They can't be a rah-rah person. They have to be critical. And they got to know who Chidi Iwouma is. When Brett Keisel was on special teams [with, by the way, Iwouma]. To me, that's what is a real Steelers fan."

"I know there were a lot of people who moved out of the area. But there are a lot of fans who weren't from there. It's who the team is. Blue collar. Rough and tough. Getting the job done. Don't have to be flashy; not about the glitter and glitz. That's what they love about them."

GERELA'S GORILLA

They adopted the kicker. Partly, it was out of jealousy. Dobre Shunka, Hungarian for good ham, was the name of the group that adopted future Hall of Fame outside linebacker Jack Ham. These were a bunch of guys sitting around the 19th Hole bar in Port Vue, yet another riverside steel town. They bought up front-row seats in Three Rivers Stadium because they were easy to land in those losing days. In 1972 the Steelers, for $100, picked up the kicker Houston waived, name of Roy Gerela. A few libations, a silly rhyme and—presto—you have a new fan group: Gerela's Gorillas.

Bob Bubanic:

We started renting the costume from a place down by Duquesne University. It cost us $50 a game. Then we ran a raffle, and we finally bought it. The lady finally gave it to us for a good price, like $250. 'Cause we were the only ones renting it. Some games, I lost 10 pounds in that. I had to put talcum powder in the hands. Sweating. It was hard to get aht.

And, one time, on New Year's, I wore a big diaper for Baby New Year. Another year, . . . with the Santa Claus suit over top the gorilla costume.

I went to all four Super Bowls [in the 1970s]. I had the distinction of wearing the gorilla suit on Bourbon Street. That first one, it was 80 degrees on Saturday; the Super Bowl was around 38. I had the suit on, and everybody

Terry Bradshaw comes through the cordon of fans at the opening of St. Vincent College training camp six months after his fourth and final Super Bowl championship with the Steelers. (George Gojkovich)

huddled against me. The next Super Bowl . . . I remember [original Riddler and actor] Frank Gorshen was appearing at our hotel. [A PBS documentary crew] wanted me to put on the suit, so they all followed me, and Frank Gorshen was like, "Who is that guy?" I didn't wear the suit to XIII and XIV. I was sitting with the players' wives and families; Roy got me tickets. I sat there where his girl was.

I have the costume sitting in a chair here. The only thing wrong with it, the head got messed up. I loaned it out once, and it lost its face at a high school rally.

Pittsburgh precedence, however, had long been set.

FRANCO'S ITALIAN ARMY

No other fan group ever dressed in military regalia, marched around a football stadium, and smuggled inside so much wine.

Or inducted Frank Sinatra into their army.

Franco Harris, a Hall of Fame running back who finished his career second only in rushing yardage to the inimitable Jim Brown, was best known for two factors: For getting his hands on the Immaculate Reception, and for being the half-black, half-Italian namesake of Franco's Italian Army.

His wild bunch invaded Three Rivers Stadium starting midway through Harris' rookie season of 1972.

Al Vento, pizza purveyor and four-star general: "Tony Stagno [a nearby baker] and myself were going to Steelers games for 11 years. First in Forbes Field, then at Pitt Stadium, then at Three Rivers. Now all those years we were going to Forbes Field and Pitt Stadium, the Steelers were . . ." He stuck his thumb upside down. ". . . very bad. They were so bad that we never had a winner. Occasionally, we cheered for the other side, so we had a winner. Occasionally. Broke our hearts. But made us feel good to have a winner.

"Then we went over to Three Rivers Stadium, and the Steelers drafted Franco Harris [two years later in 1972]. We were coming up with the Italian Stallion and all that. Tony and I were bumping around, and Tony came up with Franco's Italian Army. [Steelers guard] Sam Davis lived right behind the shop; we asked Sam Davis to ask Franco. He came back and said, 'Franco would be delighted.'"

Vento and Stagno, both from the East Liberty section of Pittsburgh known, in the local dialect, as S'Liberty, also sat on the board of the local armory, wouldn't you know. An old friend was a colonel. He supplied this army with helmets, a tank, you name it.

Vento: "We had planes flying over Three Rivers Stadium. We paid to have leaflets dropped, 'Beat the Raiders.' We don't know where the hell they went.

"And then Myron Cope joined. He was very instrumental in publicizing us on the air. Once, he was going on a two-week vacation, so we came up with kidnapping him. We marched in while he was on the air [doing his WTAE-TV nightly commentary] and carried him off.

"We would meet at the shop and make up 2,000 hoagies and bring them to the stadium. We had big bottles of Riunite wine. Sometimes, we would put more bottles in loaves of bread and bring them in. Or have the chaplain talk to the guard [to distract him during wine smuggling]. Myron would wave to us; we sat underneath the WTAE [radio] banner." They sit in the same numerical spot, Section 132 . . . where nowadays his good friend Franco stops by to say hello.

The army numbered about 15 officially, dressed and all. They were allowed to dance on the dugout roof. They held up signs: *Run Paisano Run.* They sold for a pittance almost 20,000 memberships and gave the money to charity. Banners sprouted around the concrete bowl of a home stadium: Franco soon had Black, Irish, and even Israeli armies. Was any stadium ever better protected by such an international force?

Vento: "How we met Sinatra. I get a phone call 2:30 in the morning. Myron. He called Tony and then me. He said, 'You guys meet me in San Diego. I made a date with Sinatra to meet us at practice.' How Myron met him was, they were at dinner and had a few toddies. He sent a note to Sinatra at his restaurant table in Palm Springs, where the Steelers were preparing for a playoff-implication game at the end of the magical 1972 season. 'Would you like to join the Army?'"

"We catch a plane and go to San Diego. The taxi leaves us off. We get into the stadium. We meet up with Myron and [Steelers traveling secretary and aide de camp] Jimmy Boston, and Boston looks at us, 'Where's your Frankie boy now?' Then there's a voice from behind us: 'When I make an appointment, I keep it!' Frank became a one-star general. So we marched up and down the field drinking wine and talking about it. And Chuck Noll wasn't too happy to let Franco get out of practice for a half hour."

In retelling the tale, Cope added a postscript about Stagno, the army's five-star general. Both Stagno and Vento came by his hotel room to freshen up for the flight home that night— Stagno was in the midst of Christmas-cookie season at his bakery, after all. He used the room phone to call his wife, and Cope overheard Stagno telling her about placing a peck on each of Sinatra's cheeks: "It was like kissing God."

Vento: In 2012, "the Immaculate Reception is going to be 40 years old and the Italian Army is going to be 40 years old. Franco says we're going to have a big bash."

WON, NOT LOST, IN SPACE

NASA declined to permit Colonel Mike Fincke to be interviewed for this book. The reason, wrote an official in an e-mail: It would place him "in a position that would infer endorsement of the Steelers [*sic*] . . . which is against NASA policy."

Presenting the Terrible Towel he displayed in space—as seen on YouTube—to the Steelers after they won Super Bowl XLIII?

Taking part in pregame ceremonies in the middle of Heinz Field as recently as the 2011 season?

A Sewickley Academy graduate from Ben Avon, an MIT man, Fincke is too bright a fellow to *endorse*, but he is also too Pittsburgh to conceal his heart. As he put it, patting his chest in that NASA-filmed message from the International Space Station where he wished both Super Bowl participants well, he must be true to his heart. He then, from off camera, snatched a Steelers cap and tugged it over his head, and he grabbed a Terrible Towel. Then, seeing in the monitor it was upside down, he allowed gravity to spin it right side up.

Message delivered.

After throwing the Super Bowl XLIII–winning touchdown to Santonio Holmes, Ben Roethlisberger did point into the heavens. . . .

Troy Polamalu gets hounded for signatures at the 2008 training camp. (John Beale)

Alma Fincke, his mother: "He's one of nine kids—seven boys and two girls. He's the oldest. So there was a lot of football watching going on. Not a great athlete, but he would've liked to have been. We didn't listen to baseball or watch it much. The Steelers were always fun. . . . He always wanted to be an astronaut.

"When he was in space, he started out that six-month stint . . . [and] he had no idea if the Steelers were going to be any good or not that year [2008]. So he planned to take a Terrible Towel [into the International Space Station] because you were allowed to take an item that's meaningful to you."

His greeting: "Hi, I'm Colonel Mike Fincke, NASA astronaut, and a native son of Pittsburgh, and also commander of the International Space Station more than 220 miles above our beautiful planet earth. Greetings to everyone at Raymond James Stadium in beautiful Tampa and Super Bowl XLIII. We'll be watching the game up here high above you and wish both teams the best of luck. But in my heart here aboard the International Space Station . . . it's . . . [grabbing hat, then towel] it's Steelers country. Go Steelers and good luck in pursuit of your sixth Super Bowl ring."

His mother: "Then he did what he felt like doing . . . because he's the commander of the space station, and he could. He even had a little 'hee hee' at the end. It was totally not planned. He just did what he thought was funny. It was all in good fun. But he was definitely rooting for them.

"So when the Steelers noted it, 'We're intergalactic,' it was kind of cool. He had it framed and presented it." It's in the Steelers headquarters' library along with the six Lombardi Trophies. At that presentation, "We were standing down on the field on the sidelines. We got to watch the ceremony. Mean Joe Greene was there. As they were coming off the field, they all shook hands."

Funny, but that famous video lasts the same number—in seconds—as Greene wore: 75.

13

Stadia

FORBES FIELD
1933–1957 Full-Time
1958–1962 Part-Time

Opened in 1909, the cozy confines sat in the Oakland neighborhood, on the University of Pittsburgh campus, and next door to the Carnegie Museum of History. More than a century later, all that remains of Forbes Field is the part of the outfield wall where Bill Mazeroski's 1960 World Series–winning home run—bottom of the ninth, Game 7—ignited history and hysteria.

World Series were played there in 1909, 1925, 1927, and 1960. Babe Ruth hit three home runs in his final-season swan song. Hank Greenberg hit homers there for the Pirates, who redesigned the cavernous outfield to provide him with an area they called Greenberg Gardens. That amazing '60 team. Good baseball memories.

Good football? Not so much.

Dan Rooney long said that the 33,000-seat park held about 10,000–15,000 good seats for football, meaning barely 33 to 45 percent of capacity.

Ed Kiely, publicity director for a half century: "And we froze to death."

Chuck Cherundolo, center in the 1940s and an assistant through the 1950s: "Used to fill that stadium up. The field would run from the first base side toward right field. That was a pretty good stadium for football. Pretty good field, anyway."

Joe Gordon, publicity director and vice president 1969–1998: "When I was a kid growing up in Oakland . . . when they started playing at Forbes Field, my brother and I went to games. There would always be 20 or 30 kids hanging around. Tim [Rooney] would come out and give [tickets] away. So I probably saw 10, 15 games at Forbes Field in that period.

"The field wasn't a good fit for the spectators."

Pat Rooney Sr.: "Besides, you couldn't go to a football game like this . . ." (craning his neck to the left, mimicking Forbes Field's made-for-baseball seating).

Frank Varrichione, offensive tackle 1955–1960: "It was a rickety old place. You could hear the shotguns going shooting the rats when we got there for practice. And you had to be careful when you went out on the field for [pregame warm-ups]; fans in the stands would throw beer cans at us—I'm exaggerating a little bit. We weren't doing very well. The steel worker or the factory worker, they were boisterous. You would hear from them. If you didn't do a good job, they would yell at us."

Buddy Parker standing at Forbes Field, where in the background looms the scoreboard and clock made famous less for football than for baseball and one particular moment: Bill Mazeroski's 1960 World Series–winning home run in October of Parker's fourth Steelers season—and first with a sub-.500 record. (Courtesy of the Pittsburgh Steelers)

Dale Dodrill, nose guard and middle linebacker 1951–1959: "Old Forbes Field that was sort of home. It was a baseball field. I liked playing in Pittsburgh. It was a tough field when you had wet weather. There'd be indentions and holes; then it would freeze. Then when you had to play on it the next week, man that was murder. The pitcher's mound was always a problem, to play a football game around. I don't know why they refer to it as the good old days. . . ."

Pitt Stadium offers a sweeping panorama of the Oakland neighborhood and Pittsburgh's east hills. It fails to offer the Steelers much of a view. Among Pittsburgh sports, Oakland was magical for generations. Just a few blocks to the right of the Cathedral of Learning tower in the background—that's where Forbes Field stood. The outfield wall where Pirates Hall of Famer Bill Mazeroski hit the 1960 World Series–winning home run remains intact there. (Courtesy of University of Pittsburgh athletics)

PITT STADIUM
1958–1962 Part-Time
1963–1969 Full-Time

The 56,000-seat bowl atop Cardiac Hill—so named for either its steep climb or the university-affiliated hospitals surrounding it, or both—opened in 1925. The legendary coach who demanded the construction of Pitt Stadium, Pop Warner, was weary of sharing Forbes Field with the baseball Pirates. During the 1909 World Series, after all, his football team had to start one game at 10 A.M. so as not to interfere. The kicker was, Warner left before the University of Pittsburgh played a game there; Jock Sutherland succeeded him. And that was a generation before Sutherland became coach of the Steelers and 33 years before professional football trod there.

It wasn't a very memorable "trod," to be sure. Most of the time, the Steelers were the ones bearing the tread marks afterward. Yet they played a hard-nosed game that was as much

black and blue as black and gold, and the belief remained that opponents would still feel the Steelers through the following Sunday.

Y. A. Tittle saw his Hall of Fame career end at Pitt Stadium for all intents and purposes, on his knees with his head bowed, bloodied, and probably concussed after a hard sack by the Steelers' John Baker—a famous snapshot. Tittle's New York Giants lost eight and tied two of the remaining dozen games. For once, some Pitt Stadium occupant was worse off than the Steelers.

Through the 1960s, most foes exited similarly bloodied and battered but still in overall better shape than the home side.

Chuck Noll even had bad times there: won his first game, lost his next six, got the heck out of the Oakland neighborhood.

The host Pitt Panthers had a tough decade there, too . . . even while employing former Steelers coaches John Michelosen and Carl DePasqua. Outside of that 1963 no-bowl Panthers bunch that went 9-1 while losing only to Navy and Heisman Trophy–winning Roger Staubach—with future Steeler Paul Martha in the Panthers' backfield—Pitt went 13-45 the rest of the final decade days they shared the bowl with the pro club.

Pat Rooney Sr.: "Pitt, they treated us like second-class citizens there. I'm not saying that being mean. The Pirates were big. Pitt was big. College football was big. We were a bunch of sandlotters. Our fans were a bunch of sandlotters."

Interestingly, the university ultimately went in with the Steelers on the University of Pittsburgh Medical Center Sports Medicine complex on the South Side and on Heinz Field. They shared the grounds of both upon the construction of Heinz Field in 2001.

THREE RIVERS STADIUM
1970–2000

Three Rivers Stadium was Dan Rooney's baby.

In October 1964 it was announced in a news conference in Mayor Joe Barr's office that the Steelers in writing committed to staying in Pittsburgh 13 years inside a yet-unnamed new stadium . . . "with a possible maximum of 40."

They made it to 30, but that was far in the future in 1964.

Barr said then, "The fact that the decision has been made in favor of Pittsburgh is a personal tribute to Art Rooney [Sr.]. For some time, we have known that the Steelers were being wooed by a number of cities seeking representation in the National Football League. He has demonstrated he is a devoted Pittsburgher, vitally interested in preserving this city's major league status."

It required another 5¾ years to get the concrete bowl up and running on the North Side, at the confluence of the (west to east) Ohio, Allegheny, and Monongahela rivers. The Pirates moved in first, playing that summer of 1970. In the Steelers' christening in the multipurpose facility that over its span grew from 50,000 to 59,000 seating for football, they lost to Houston, 19-7.

The Steelers went 61-12 through the 1970s at home and 118-46 there in the regular-season under Chuck Noll. Noll's teams went 8-2 in Three Rivers postseason games—though, amazingly, he never coached a home playoff game in a nonstrike season after 1979. (They lost to San Diego in the abbreviated 1982.)

Three Rivers Stadium.
(John Beale)

Aerial view of the Pittsburgh skyline, with Three Rivers Stadium on the North Side (top) across the Allegheny River from downtown. (John Beale)

Coach Marty Schottenheimer tried every home remedy imaginable—flying to Pittsburgh instead of busing; different hotels; sprinkling Cleveland Municipal Stadium dirt on the AstroTurf—trying to end Cleveland's jinx and losing streak the first 16 seasons of Three Rivers' existence. A radio station sent a witch to remove the spell. Cleveland only won in 1996 because the Steelers' Matt Bahr missed a late field goal from 24 yards—his first muff from inside 30 yards after 40 consecutive such makes. The Browns' special-teams coach that day? One Bill Cowher.

As Steelers head coach, by the way, he went 51-21 in Three Rivers in the regular season.

Remarkably, the Steelers suffered just one losing home record there: 1999, at 2-6.

Dick Hoak, running back 1961–1970 and running backs coach 1972–2006: "Once they moved there, things fell into place. Now you had a place to call your own. The meeting rooms were first-class. We had a weight room. . . ."

The oval held loud noise well. It held cold, ice, and snow well, too.

There were even a few memorable games played there during the 1970s and throughout the rise of the franchise, which went 182-72 there in the regular season and 13-5 in the playoffs. Bill Cowher went 5-3 in the postseason, but 1-2 in AFC championship games. Noll went 8-2 in the postseason, but won three consecutive AFC titles after losing in 1972 to the undefeated Miami Dolphins, who won by four points—their closest game in the final seven Dolphins triumphs.

Over the next generation, the place didn't age so well.

Aaron Smith, defensive end 1999–2011: "Playing on that turf was not fun. I liked the stadium, the way it was encircling you, how the crowd noise stayed in. I think my favorite game was the Washington game [the 24-3 victory and attendant alumni ceremonies that closed out Three Rivers December 16, 2000]. It was nice to be a part of that.

"Being a young guy at the time, it was a whole new experience. I had seen so many games they played on television. So much history. Anybody who played football knew Three Rivers Stadium. But I don't miss the AstroTurf.

"The one thing I remember: There were no windows [inside the Steelers offices]. It was like going into a cave. We didn't know what the weather was like until we went out to practice.

"Not too many of us left," he said wistfully in late 2011, "just me and Hines, huh?"

Not too many weeks later, both were gone—along with linebacker James Farrior. Like Three Rivers, they were deemed expendable because of age and costliness, their usefulness finished.

HEINZ FIELD
2001–

Heinz Field was Art Rooney II's baby.

In fact, for a while after it opened, the Steelers then–vice president maintained an office in Heinz Field while his father the president oversaw the Steelers from their South Side facility headquarters some—isn't this an interesting number?—5.7 miles away by vehicle.

The H. J. Heinz company was so enamored of the trademark digits illustrating their varieties of products that officials upon the 2001 opening of the field signed a $57 million naming rights deal for 20 years. Almost one-fourth of the fans on average congregate in the turn-back towers, end-zone veranda, or clubs rather than in the 65,050 or so mustard seats. Heinz Ketchup bottles (contents if real: 1.6 million ounces each) virtually pour on the scoreboard marking the Steelers' entry into the "Heinz red zone." It was a natch.

The political football that it became in the early going, the projects for where PNC Park and Heinz Field sprouted

Two young fans exchange chest bumps in celebration of a Steelers score at Heinz Field, with the panoramic view of downtown Pittsburgh through the open end zone between the umbrella-topped, turn-back towers. (John Beale)

from the outdated Three Rivers Stadium, was a drawn-out process with a distinct nadir: the rousing defeat of a 1997 public referendum. By the next year, city fathers formulated a "Plan B," arranging for $1 billion in construction for the two new stadia plus an upgrade to the outdated David L. Lawrence Convention Center—the sprawling building with the ski-slope roof across and up the Allegheny River a few blocks from PNC Park. Because the plan involved Pennsylvania state government funds, Philadelphia politicians used that opening to construct new football and baseball stadia.

Bill Cowher went 34-13-1 at Heinz Field, excluding 3-2 in the postseason—and 0-2 in AFC championship games (1-4 overall in those on the North Shore).

Mike Tomlin started out 31-9 in Heinz Field, not counting 4-1 in the postseason.

Hines Ward, who early on had a nice little T-shirt business about "Hines Field": "It was great. It was time. There were so many great traditions and histories in Three Rivers. Getting a new football field, Heinz Field and PNC Park, it brought a little excitement to the city of Pittsburgh. Now it almost seems like yesterday. A lot of these guys probably don't even know that Three Rivers ever existed. It's great for our fans. Our players love it. It's home for us.

"It's up-to-date. Stadium seating. Jumbotron. Look out and see the city of Pittsburgh. See Mount Washington. Just a great place to play."

14

Sidelines

PITTSBURGH GOES POP CULTURE

From the city that brought the world Gene Kelly and George Romero (zombies!), *Mr. Mom* (Michael Keaton) and *Mr. Rogers* (Fred Rogers), Wiz Khalifa and Billy Gardell and Jeff Goldblum, the Steelers have gone Hollywood and hit the musical charts as well.

In the movie category:

Black Sunday was filmed at Super Bowl X. Warren Beatty and the Rams waged a Super Bowl against the Steelers in *Heaven Can Wait,* which was released in 1978, a year before the Steelers–Rams Super Bowl XIV. *Smokey and the Bandit II,* a celluloid classic, included cameos by Terry Bradshaw and Joe Greene. *All the Marbles,* a 1981 female wrestling movie, included Greene on the bill—it did better overseas for some reason. The 2005 remake of *The Longest Yard* included fan boy Adam Sandler portraying Paul Crewe as a former Steelers quarterback. And in 2011, Ben Roethlisberger, Aaron Smith, Hines Ward, and several other Steelers joined former coach Bill Cowher and General Manager Kevin Colbert in a football scene in *The Dark Knight Rises,* shot in Pittsburgh by producer and Steelers co-owner Thomas Tull. The 34-year-old Ward scored on a kickoff return, so it had to be fiction, right?

On television:

Robert Ulrich starred as Rocky Bleier in 1980's *Fighting Back.* Ernie Holmes appeared in *The A-Team.* A Terrible Towel has made a cameo appearance on an episode of *Scrubs,* in Ward's hand on *Dancing with the Stars,* Khalifa's "Black and Yellow" video, and *Saturday Night Live* cast member Seth Meyers' twirling homage to Myron Cope's passing in 2008.

In TV football:

Cowher (CBS), Lynn Swann (ABC), and Merrill Hoge (ESPN) spent years working in studio or on sidelines. And Fred "the Hammer" Williamson, who also qualified in the movie category, worked a stint on *Monday Night Football*—not bad for a guy who started his NFL career as a rookie with the 1960 Steelers.

In commercials:

Greene's famous Coca-Cola spot, remade with Troy Polamalu a quarter century later, and redone in 2012 as a fabric- (and heart-) softener commercial. Polamalu's Head and Shoulders work, also starring Ward and Brett Keisel. L. C. Greenwood toiling in some Miller Lite beer commercials.

Terry Bradshaw. (John Beale)

In music:

Well, Bradshaw once crooned "I'm So Lonesome I Could Cry." In "In America," Charlie Daniels belted, "Just go and lay your hand on a Pittsburgh Steeler fan." Khalifa's "Black and Yellow" was adopted as a theme for the black and gold in their Super Bowl XLV rush. And there are way too many Steelers-themed songs out there to list.

STEELERS POLKA

Blame polkameister Jimmy Psihoulis, or, to use the musical handle by which the radio station executive was better known, Jimmy Pol.

He started all this Steelers noise.

From his polka tune also known as "The Steelers Fight Song," Pol spawned the advent of 50 Steelers songs, and counting. There have been odes to everyone from Troy Polamalu, to nasally announcer Myron—with apologies to U2—"In the Name of Cope." "We are the Steeler Nation who hail from near and far; want to win another ring for the man who said 'Hmm-hah.'" Double yoi.

Jimmy Pol, retired in Florida: "I know, I know. Yes, there are so many. When I was still [in Pittsburgh] and changing the words . . . , there were so many out. There was a Jewish one, an Italian one. Another was generic. But they were all about the Steelers, after mine. The last one, in 2003, I changed the words. After that, I didn't do it. From 1970, we're talking about 2000s, and we're still doing it. And I get calls, 'Oh, Jimmy. . . .'"

The fact that he came from Athens, Greece, explains the heavy accent in the songs. He endured Nazi occupation as a child in World War II; "People were dying on the street left and right." He had an uncle working and living in Pittsburgh, so he moved in. His first job was reading the news in Greek on radio for $5 a week.

Pol: "I started broadcasting first in sales; then I wound up in management. Everybody thought I was Polish because I had a five-hour program five days a week [at WZUM-AM] playing polkas and international music, and my name was Jimmy Pol.

"Ok, I give you the highlights. I started doing 10 seconds they put on the sportscasts. I think it was in 1969 or 1970, I remember because I put the line in one of my songs: 'It's been 40 years and coming, let the wheels keep humming.' You know how Steelers fans are . . . [Singing.] 'We're from the town with the great football team, the Pittsburgh Steelers.'"

He added a variation of his old polka tune for a second line, "It's been 40 years and coming, keep the Steelers machinery humming." They played it at WZUM as filler for sportscasts. Not for long, though.

Pol: "We're getting crazy calls here. 'Why don't you play this song? Why don't you make it a little longer?' That's when I wrote down, I think at that time: Bradshaw, Greene, Franco . . . and I made the first 'Steeler Fight Song.' I think it came out in '72 or whatever.

"They won the first Super Bowl and became a great team. Then as players were leaving and players were coming, I had to keep changing the names.

"I never even tried to push it. I never called a station and asked them to play it. I never called the Steelers: 'Hey, I wrote a song.' The song took off on its own. It was a political event, the grass roots with the voters.

"With my accent, it was always no problem. 'We like that.'" Accordion intro, please:

"Weer frum da tun wit da grate fuuut bawl tim, we cheer foor Peets-boig Stillers . . . .

"Eetz bin ford-ee yirs ind cuh-meen, letz keep da Stillers muh-sheen-a-ree hah-meen."

One mother told him her son came home from elementary school and informed her that he learned a song in class that day. He then launched into the "Steelers Fight Song"—replete with Jimmy Pol's steep Greek accent.

"Why are you singing like that?" she asked her boy.

"That's how the song goes."

STEEL CURTAIN

One of the most enduring nicknames in North American sports history had a father and a son.

The father: Dan "Bad Rad" Radakovich, the coach of the so-named defensive line.

The year was 1971. He had just joined the Steelers staff after the unexpected death of defensive-line coach Walt Hackett, who collapsed of a heart attack while scouting Cal State–Long Beach on April 24, 1971. Radakovich, a Pittsburgh-area native who was the defensive coordinator at the University of Cincinnati at the time, beat out George Perles—who got the job a year later—to coach a position where "Bad Rad" owned all of two weeks of coaching experience.

He inherited a two-year veteran named Mean Joe Greene. He moved around the three other starters, vets Chuck Hinton,

L. C. Greenwood, a Steelers Polka lyric and original member of the Steel Curtain, chills out on the bench, an ice pack on an ailing left knee and a towel over his head. (John Peale)

Lloyd Voss, and Ben McGee, and inserted swift youngsters L. C. Greenwood and Dwight White at defensive ends with Greene and either Hinton or McGee at defensive tackles. (Ernie Holmes, who joined the front four the next year, was on the taxi squad at the time.)

Radakovich: "How good were they right away? They played well. Well enough to get the nickname. People don't know this, but I'm the coach when they got the nickname 'the Steel Curtain.' It became famous three years later, when George was coaching them."

This is where the son comes into play, a freshman quarterback at Montour High School back in 1971.

Greg Kronz, a pastor in Hilton Head, South Carolina: "It's a funny story. I was in ninth grade. I was very small, but I did play football. I walked downstairs into our kitchen one morning, and I heard Myron Cope and Bill Hillgrove on the radio [WTAE-AM] announcing this contest to name the defensive line. I stood there for about 30 seconds. I said, 'Steel Curtain.' 'I'm going to send that in and win that contest,' I told my mother."

It was a variation on the Iron Curtain, as Communist Eastern Europe and Russia were known at the time. And Kronz wasn't alone in that thought.

Kronz: "It turns out, 17 people chose the same name. They threw us in a hat. And they pulled me out. It was a kick. So I was famous for a day. The prize: four days and three nights in Miami and tickets to a Steelers-Miami game [November 14]. Well, I was in ninth grade. I didn't want to go with my dad. And I didn't want to go with my mom. So I didn't have a choice. I let my parents go."

The kid who nicknamed one of the greatest front fours in NFL history went on to Pitt, seminary, San Antonio, and, since about the time Chuck Noll retired, Hilton Head. He raised a family. One of his boys went to the Citadel, where he played football. The grandson of the Steel Curtain?

Kronz: "He played defensive end, yes he did. His nickname was Big Daddy Kronz. And I'm 5-8. Go figure."

"ONE FOR THE THUMB"

Robert J. Pavuchak had a stealthy photo assignment July 24, 1980: Go to the locker-room back door at Steelers training camp and knock three times.

Joe Greene will be waiting for you.

The *Pittsburgh Press,* his employers at the time (he later retired from the *Post-Gazette*), wanted him to snap a quick photograph of Greene's four Super Bowl rings for a story about the club's jewelry.

Pavuchak, recalling his marching orders: "'And whatever you do, don't let coach Chuck Noll see you, as *Press* photographers aren't allowed in the training-camp locker room.'

"So I sneak into the hallway of the Steelers locker room, and knock three times on the door. Mean Joe Greene sticks his head out and says, 'Is that you, Bob?' He knew I was coming.

"I said, 'Yes, Joe. You got the rings?' He said, 'Right here, Bob, on my fingers.' I zoomed in with the lens on my camera, and got a tight shot of the rings on his fist. I said, 'Wow, that's really great, Joe!' Then he flipped out his thumb.

"He said, 'Yes, Bob, *all I need is one for the thumb!*'"

"Bingo!"

Joe Greene flashes four Super Bowl rings on his fingers in 1980 and devises a slogan: One for the Thumb. That digit doesn't get adorned, though, for another 25 years. (Robert J. Pavuchak)

ONE OF THE FIRST WITH CHEERLEADERS, ONE OF THE LAST WITHOUT

Robert Morris Junior College was a college without a football team. The Steelers were a football team without a college atmosphere. Bill Day, who worked a bit for both institutions, married the two somewhat out of convenience.

That was how the Steelers, after the Baltimore Colts inaugurated the idea briefly in 1954, became one of the first of the NFL franchises to regularly decorate their sidelines with cheerleaders.

The first to remove them, too.

And they remain one of the few NFL teams without pom-poms and circumstance still: the old-guard Steelers, Browns, Bears, Giants, Lions, and Packers have been among the last to disdain the practice.

Day was a vice president at the downtown Pittsburgh two-year school, long before it sprouted roots as a suburban university in Moon, near the airport. He doubled as something of an entertainment coordinator for the Steelers. So Day enlisted a Robert Morris stenography teacher, Garnet Glover, a former Penn State cheerleader, and the city's most famous cheerleader, Duquesne University alum and Dan Rooney friend Mossie Murphy. "He brought some insanity to this effort," Day told me for a 2007 *Pittsburgh Post-Gazette* story.

These folks gave birth to the Steelerettes.

The requirements were strict: short hair, single, a minimum 2.0 grade-point average, and a pristine image to go with the gold jumpers and skirts revealing scant traces of thigh.

Sportswriters crucified them for cheering "Go, Steelers, Go" while the Giants had the ball in the 1961 home opener, so they began taking a football test the next week.

Barbara Kruze, among the early 1960s class: "We were the first in the NFL." Precise dates are difficult to pin down, but the Cleveland Browns also launched their cheerleaders around the same 1961 time. They didn't last much longer than the Steelerettes, either.

Norreen Modry: "There were eight of us in '61 at Forbes Field. There were 10 of us in '62."

Valerie Miller: "The largest group was '64, when there were 16 of us. The second half of the year [when the weather chilled], we wore corduroy jumpers."

Modry: "Black leotards with a little pleated skirt. Looked like a [roller-]skating skirt. Gold cummerbund with a gold bowtie."

Jeanne Rattigan: "Those were the worst uniforms. Ugly. The bowties went right here [on the left side of the neck]. And they didn't have black tennis shoes in those days, so they dyed them black."

Modry: "And your feet would turn purply."

Miller: "I remember walking up [Cardiac] Hill behind Frenchy Fuqua, and he had that purple cape on. Those costumes he used to wear."

Marlene Pizutti: "The platform shoes with the goldfish in them!"

Kruze: "I don't know if it was '64 or '65 . . ."

Modry: "'65. 'Cause I was too tall, and he didn't want anybody 5-6 or taller."

Kruze: ". . . but [singer] Andy Williams was in town with Henry Mancini, and they were doing a concert at the Civic Arena. He wanted dancers behind him—shorter than him—for 'Girl Watcher.' They gave us costumes. That was a lot of fun."

Modry: "We did a Sears convention. We walked around trying to encourage them to sell. They gave us little green transistor radios as a gift."

Miller: "The Steelers . . . , we always cheered on the side of the visitors. The explanation for that was, . . . for the routines—the 'Hello Dolly' and 'The Stripper'—they wanted us to be beside Benny Benack['s band]."

"The Stripper?" The racy theme that goes, *Da-dunt-duh, du-du-dunt-duh* . . . ?

Modry: "That's the one on YouTube."

Pizzuti: "We were never allowed to talk to the players." Although a player or two did wind up fraternizing. . . .

Andy Russell, outside linebacker, remembers chasing a tight end out of bounds and running into a cheerleader, uh, hands first: "Did not intentionally do it. Did not want to do that. Some guy yelled, 'Get that sex maniac out of here.'"

Pizzutti: "We were playing the Giants in '65; they were the kindest team. They saw we were freezing; they brought us hot chocolate and hot dogs."

Miller: "We had no jackets, no coats. We were lucky we could use the bathroom."

Pizzutti: "The Steelers gave us footballs. Little footballs. We had to throw them into the stands. And there was hardly anybody in the stands. So we'd look for people we knew and threw it to them."

Rattigan: "The Steelers don't want to have anything to do with us now."

It didn't end well for the Steelerettes in 1970. As the story told by Art Rooney Jr. goes, one of the cheerleaders came to his father's office to complain about the puritanical uniforms. Nice girls, the Chief told his aide-de-camp Fran Fogarty, but fire the cheerleaders. Fogarty wondered about Murphy. The Chief responded, Fire him, too.

Kruze: "He didn't think the football team needed cheerleaders [around Chuck Noll's club in Three Rivers Stadium]. I'm surprised it lasted as long as it did."

The Steelerettes had a calendar, black-and-whites with a much less towering skyline in the background of their Mount Washington photo shoots. It was nothing like the bikini-or-less cheesecake . . . er, cheerleaders you see from, say, the world-celebrated troupe that started about the time the Steelerettes folded: the artists formerly known as the Dallas Cowboys CowBelles and Beaux. (Yes, they originally copied off the coed Steelers, too.)

Rattigan: "Gee, I wonder why they became famous. Compare our outfits to theirs."

Modry: "Look at our calendar compared to theirs."

Pizutti: "Those were the best years of our lives."

Rattigan, noting that the grandmotherly cheerleaders were about to celebrate their 50th reunion in October 2011 in Pittsburgh: "No, these are the best years. A lot of them didn't cheer together, but we all became such good friends."

Modry: "Keep the memories alive."

Rattigan, reaching out to clasp a hand with Modry: "For as long as we can remember."

MALE CHEERLEADERS: GONE IN A PUFF OF SMOKE

Start with the cheerleaders and the cannon.

Dick Hoak, a running back whose Steelers career spanned the entire tenure of the Steelerettes: "I remember them being there, that's all."

Okay, but how about them having male cheerleaders?

Hoak: "They did? I don't remember that."

The Ingots, they were called . . . apparently in private. Because even the four fellows themselves merely figured they were male Steelerettes. Male gymnasts, that was the preferred reference of their leader.

Blair Jury: "Mostly, what I remember was [1962] when they decided they were going to do this, I volunteered to put it all together. Bill Day, he was the public relations director [at Robert Morris Junior College]. And he was the guy in charge of the cheerleaders. The Steelers were discussing one day about putting some gymnasts on the field with them. Bill came into our class asking if anybody had any gymnastic experience. I couldn't believe that out of all the people in that school, I was the only one who had gymnastic experience. He told me I had 12 weeks to whip it together . . . and the interesting part was we had to do it in hard hats. Bona fide hard hats. And an orange T-shirt with 'Steelers' on it. I told him, nobody, nobody, does gymnastics with hard hats on. I told him here's the deal: first one to get hurt, the hard hats come off. Guess who was the first one to get hurt?"

Roger Hunt: "I was a student at Robert Morris, majoring in accounting. They already had the girls as Steelerettes. But they were looking for some guys to go on the squad. It said something about you would get to go to all the home games free. That interested me, that was my motivation for doing it. The Steelers weren't that good back then. Bobby Layne was the quarterback, Buddy Dial, John Henry Johnson was the running back, and Big Daddy Lipscomb was the big guy on the line.

"I was the guy in charge of the cannon."

Here came the Steelers' cheerleaders' blast into infamy, the shot heard 'round the cheerleader world.

NFL Films later voted it the second-wackiest moment in the league's wacky history.

This much Hoak remembers vividly: Against the Dallas Cowboys, receiver Buddy Dial made a reception around the three-yard line. He trotted in for a rare score. Kaboom.

On his third step into the Forbes Field end zone, he was met with a thunderous explosion and a puff of white smoke. He jump-stepped to a halt, his right leg kicking high in the air—as if he were a cheerleader. He spiked the ball behind his back and looked at the cannon, while one of the Steelerettes standing at that sideline corner also stared in disbelief at the cannon behind the end line. The official walked directly into the smoke signaling a TD. You can watch it here:

http://www.youtube.com/watch?v=iYReYzUYndg&feature=related

Hoak: "That was in Forbes Field [October 21, 1962]. Scored a touchdown, put a foot into the end zone . . . , they fired that cannon [in his face]. Scared him to death."

Hunt: "I was probably up around the 20- or 30-yard line talking to one of the players. Buddy went out for a pass, he was kind of running toward me when he caught this pass and went running into the end zone. One of the guys grabbed the lanyard—that thing shot 12-gauge shotgun blanks. He shot the cannon and, going back in my mind's eye now, it was a good five yards from [Dial]. Of course, there was a cloud of smoke.

"I went over to apologize to him, 'Aw shucks, it was nothing. Just startled me.' Which I'm sure it would. He wasn't nearly as upset as [Steelers and Pirates radio announcer] Bob Prince was. Bob Prince went on and on about it for several games."

Jury: "I didn't have too much trouble getting the volunteers. But when I saw what I had to work with? This ain't going to work. I guess we didn't get in trouble. None of us got fired. The cannon did."

Bill Day said in a 2007 Post-Gazette *story about the Steelerettes:* "I hear the film of that is in the Hall of Fame. It actually looked like Buddy had been shot with a cannon. Not only did Buddy disappear in a cloud of smoke, so did the Ingots."

TITTLE SHOT

The iconic photograph of New York Giants quarterback Y. A. Tittle became more famous than its subject.

Tittle played 17 years in the NFL and became a Hall of Famer. But the name likely means less to folks in the 21st century than the recognizable visual: a Google search for his name and "photograph" produces up to 500,000 results. You can go online and purchase copies of the snapshot showing a balding man bloodied and beaten to his knees—and possibly concussed—in the Pitt Stadium end zone after a September 20, 1964, sack by Steelers defensive end John Baker in a Steelers victory. He was a month shy of 38 and a couple of months from retirement.

Award-winning *Pittsburgh Post-Gazette* photographer Morris Berman turned in that photograph to the sports editor after the game.

Roy McHugh, longtime sportswriter, columnist, and editor at the Pittsburgh Press: "Al Abrams threw it [away]: 'No action.'

"Berman pulled it out of the garbage and sent it to *Life.* I think he got a thousand bucks for it, which was a lot of money in those days."

In later years, several other photographers emerged to claim they captured the same shot.

Associated Press photographer Dozier Mobley snapped it, and in the end his was the photograph used in Tittle's autobiography, not Berman's famous freeze-frame.

Pittsburgh Press photographers Al Hermann Jr. and Don Stetzer also said they had a similar photo. The late Stetzer apparently told coworkers for years he had a shot superior to Berman's.

Vincent J. Musi, former Press *photographer:* "One day, I got to my desk and there was his photo, sitting there. He was right. It was better."

Valerie Miller, a Steelerette nearby that freeze-frame moment: "When you're an 18-year-old watching that . . ."

Jeanne Rattigan, a cheerleading teammate: "That was scary. He took his helmet off. He was dazed. He had blood coming down his cheek."

Miller: "I was standing there with my mouth open. We were in awe."

Rattigan: "We all were."

CONCUSSIONS

Pittsburgh was the place and the Steelers were the team where neurocognitive testing and concussion policies originated.

Dr. Joseph Maroon, longtime team neurosurgeon plus a consultant to the NFL and others regarding mild traumatic brain injury, recalled that Chuck Noll suggested the doctor bring back "objective data." It all seemed to start about the time a concussed David Woodley had to sit out a game under doctor's orders. He was hospitalized in the 1984 season-opening week, then cleared to play four days later.

A second concussion sidelined him a month later, but Noll dressed him for a game in San Francisco as an "emergency" third quarterback. Noll said then: "We put him through every conceivable test—and then some—and couldn't find anything wrong. But the doctors want to make sure he doesn't get hit. It's a precautionary thing." Woodley added, "I don't like the idea of missing a game, but I'd rather miss one than 10."

They derived a pencil and paper test, and an acceptable formula and philosophy. Ex-Steelers running back Merril Hoge became the second player in modern NFL history believed to have retired because of concussions, and his retirement resulted from the Pittsburgh program. In the end, the NFL adopted neurocognitive testing as a form of concussion management, same as the NHL and Major League Baseball and many of the NCAA major-conference members as well as thousands of U.S. high schools and club teams.

The Steelers remain a much-discussed team with regard to brain trauma. Mike Webster, Justin Strzelczyk, and Terry Long were among the first NFLers found to contain chronic traumatic encephalopathy, a condition previously known as "punch-drunk syndrome," found in boxers after repeated blows to the head.

Andy Russell, outside linebacker 1963, 1966–1976: "I worry about it. I had 10 concussions that I can remember. And maybe 10 I can't remember. That's why I'm writing books now."

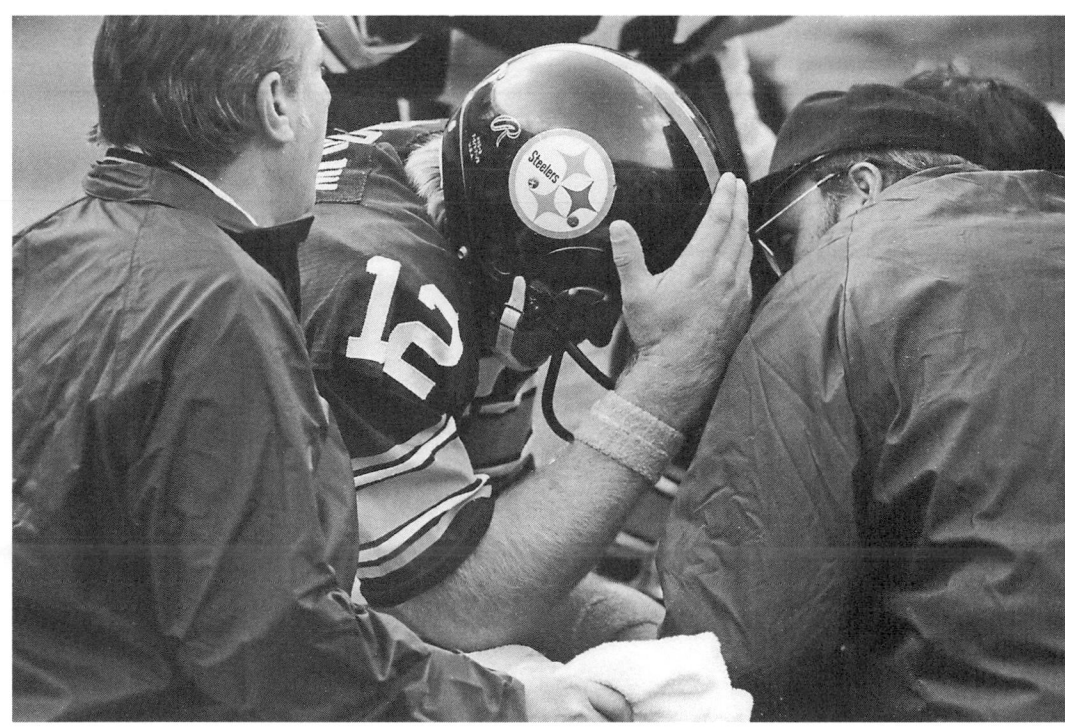

Yet another bump, bruise, or concussion for Terry Bradshaw. This one came in 1979. (George Gojkovich)

Mike Wagner, safety 1971–1980: "The public just doesn't realize what goes through a football player's head. You get the snot knocked out of you, then you come over to the sidelines and you'd be kind of like, what I call, 'daydreaming.' Does it worry me? No. As you get older, you start worrying about your mortality, period."

Dermontti Dawson, center 1988–2000: "I can tell you already I have short-term memory loss. Certain things I can't recall. If you were to ask me, I can't recall it. I know I suffer short-term memory loss. I've talked to a neurologist and stuff, went and got tested. I found out that I was ADD as well. It's amazing. But it didn't affect me playing football. I learned how to cope with it. To this day, I still write everything down. I keep a pad in my car. I put it in a certain order, to ensure that I'm on task each and every day. If not, I'd be all over the place."

Dale Dodrill, nose guard–middle linebacker 1951–1959: "I remember when the plastic helmet first came out, Chuck [Cherundolo the defensive line coach] took one in practice and said, 'Dale, they shouldn't allow these. These are a weapon.' I think they could eliminate a lot of all that if they brought back the old leather helmet. Then the player wouldn't lead with his head with a leather helmet. They would learn to use their arms and wrap up. The plastic helmet is nothing but a weapon. An awful lot of our friends as we get older, they have Alzheimer's and dementia and they didn't play football. I think they can attribute some of it to football [in many players of the "plastic-helmet" era]. I guess I've been fortunate in that area. To this point, I haven't had any problems, knock on wood."

DEATHS

More of a millstone than a milestone, the Steelers have raised wonders, if not suspicions, with around 50 ex-Steelers players dying since 2000. At least 17 of them were 59 or younger.

According to a *Los Angeles Times* survey in 2006, one fifth of the former NFL players from the 1970s and 1980s who died that year were former Steelers.

Some accounts found a causal link with heart disease or failures, but that isn't an uncommon death for former NFLers.

A handful of former Steelers have admitted to using steroids or have been tied postmortem to chronic traumatic encephalopathy (CTE), but neither has been found as leading to death.

Ralph Berlin, trainer 1968–1992: "Get a photo of that Super Bowl IX team. A lot of those guys are dead: Ernie Holmes, Mike Webster, Dwight White, Ray Mansfield, Joe Gilliam, Jim Clack, [defensive coordinator] Bud Carson, Steve Furness, [Ron Shanklin] . . . That scares you."

CRIMES AND MISDEMEANORS

In 2010 and 2011, considerable media attention was expended upon reported arrests and charges involving Steelers off the field of play. Granted, Ben Roethlisberger's much-publicized run-ins—sexual-assault accusations, in which Georgia authorities declined to prosecute, and a civil suit in Nevada, ultimately settled out of court—brought a harsh light on the franchise during that time. Yet other scrutiny was unwarranted.

Reports that characterized the Steelers as the NFL team with the longest rap sheet since 2000 are far from the truth.

According to a database operated by the *San Diego Union-Tribune,* as of New Year's 2012 there had been 17 cases of charges more meaningful than traffic tickets filed against the Steelers since 2000 (the same number as Washington and Carolina).

By contrast, in that same time period San Diego had 25, Kansas City 26, Denver 32, Cincinnati 35, and Minnesota 36.

Moreover, only three Steelers on that database list still remained on the roster as of Super Bowl XLV and the 2011

Mike Webster, the first modern-day Hall of Famer to pass away among the several Super Steelers' deaths, snaps the ball and arises to deliver a block by the time Matt Bahr's field-goal try is in the air. Twenty-five years later, Webster's family won a disability lawsuit against the NFL pension plan. (John Beale)

season. Those charges fell out thus: four citations, eight charges dropped, and one found not guilty in a jury trial. No probation was levied. Roughly $1,000 in fines were part of sentencing. And the community-service hours totaled 40, all falling on former kicker Jeff Reed.

Sentences were stiffer upon such teams as San Diego (one jail term, five probations, and 150-plus hours of community service), Kansas City (three jail terms, three probations, and 300-plus hours of community service), Minnesota (two jail terms, two probations, and 442 hours of community service), and Cincinnati (four jail terms, four suspended sentences, three probations, and 950-plus hours of community service).

Finally, the Steelers are second to last in the AFC North in this dubious category: Behind Cincinnati's 35 listed on the database come Cleveland with 22, the Steelers, and Baltimore one behind at 16.

JACKIE "ONE SIDE" HART

The Steelers' late equipment manager was the guy who deserved blame/credit for the logo on one side of the helmet.

It wasn't because then-owner Arthur Rooney was cheap. It wasn't because they ran out of stickers. Rather, in 1963 when the club switched from gold to black helmets, Jackie Hart merely affixed the logo to one side (the right) as an experiment—to see if everybody liked it.

George Perles, defensive line coach and coordinator 1972– 1981: "I asked Jackie, 'Why did you put the logo only on one side?' 'So you'd ask.'

"When I came to Michigan State [in 1982], I put the *S* only on one side."

Hart was a prankster. As one story went, overnight once he changed around all the nameplates in the locker room, just to watch the gridlock and confusion the next morning upon the players' arrival.

He once got so angry with scouting chief and boss' son Art Rooney Jr. for violating one of Hart's locker-room rules that he held Rooney's head in a cooler.

Art Rooney Jr.: "The old man [Art Rooney Sr.] didn't like that. Jackie Hart, we're at training camp, and he passed away. Chuck [Noll] and I come in from Latrobe for the wake. We all thought he was single; he had a wife and I don't know how many kids, and nobody knew it. He was born on the North Side and [the Chief] knew him the whole life, and he never really knew it, either."

CANTON VERSUS LATROBE

Art Rooney Sr. took an active role in the historic conflagration over where professional football all began.

When it came time in 1961 to vote and delineate funds to open a Pro Football Hall of Fame, Rooney held out for Latrobe—which laid a claim to playing host to the first professional football player and game in America.

When the vote reached 11-1 in favor of Canton, and he was the loan abstention, Rooney capitulated so the tally could become unanimous. It was the same meeting where the NFL adopted a disaster plan restocking a team's roster in case of a tragedy killing the entire squad, a reaction to the U.S. Olympic figure-skating team crash months earlier.

The Hall was opened in 1963 in Canton . . . and research soon after uncovered that the first professional player was not John Brallier in Latrobe on September 3, 1895. Actually, the inaugural pro earned his $500 for a game in *Pittsburgh,* of all places. William "Pudge" Heffelfinger, a Yale All-America from 1889–1891, accepted that cash to play one contest for the Allegheny Athletic Association on November 12, 1892. Pudge scored the only touchdown in a victory over the rival Pittsburgh Athletic Club, whose folks demanded it be called an exhibition so the ringers wouldn't affect the wagering.

Could you imagine the Hall of Fame in Pittsburgh?

ZEE PLANE, BOSS, ZEE PLANE

The Steelers were huddled in the visitor's locker room at Baltimore's Memorial Stadium, having just spanked the Colts in the 1976 AFC playoffs December 19. Chuck Noll had just started to deliver one of his usually brief postgame talks, but the players stopped paying attention. They were riveted to televisions in the room.

John Banaszak, defensive lineman 1975–1981: "We saw it. It scrolled on the bottom of the TV monitor, 'live from Baltimore' . . . as Chuck was talking after the game. Everybody's bumping each other, pointing at the TV, psss psss psss. Chuck's like. 'Come on, you guys, pay attention.' Finally, Chuck [saw the TV and] said, 'That's a plane in the stands.'" And Noll was a pilot, remember.

"Everybody ran out of the locker room . . . to check it out. Sure enough, there's a fricking plane up there. Chuck never got to finish his speech. And you know Chuck Noll's postgame speeches are 15 seconds long. So that's how quickly we were out of the locker room."

THE WEIGHT WORK

Art Rooney Jr., vice president of scouting: "Early on, that was one of the big reasons for success. [Chuck Noll] brought

Terry Bradshaw drops back to pass and deliver one of his trademark spirals, so hard and fast they were known to hurt the hands of unsuspecting catchers. (John Beale)

in Lou Riecke as weightlifting coach. Lou won an Olympic [Trials] medal."

Soon after, he had the Steelers winning silver—the Lombardi Trophy.

They were the strongest team in football, and they were made to look the part with the offensive linemen wearing jerseys that coach Dan Radakovich had tailored to fit tighter. It required mighty power to hoist the Lombardi four times in six years, to squat-thrust the burden of dynastic expectations, to clean and lift Western Pennsylvania and a burgeoning Steelers Nation.

Lou Riecke, strength coach 1970–1979: "I was at my office [in New Orleans] one day working when Chuck Noll called me. I said, 'What do you have in mind, coach?' 'Get yourself a plane ticket, first class, and we'll spend a few days here talking about it.' My first thought was, 'It had to be the Steelers, a last-place team. It couldn't be the Colts, a championship team. Wait a minute stupid, they got nowhere to go but up.' It was great.

"There was a fellow named Alvin Roy, he was the first strength coach [in the American Football League with the San Diego Chargers] when Chuck Noll was an assistant there. Chuck got to be the head coach of the Steelers, and he called Alvin . . . [who] said, 'Why don't you call Lou Riecke?'

"They won one game the year before, and they turned around and won four Super Bowls.

"Chuck was a brilliant guy, a great coach, a good guy."

Noll was also a staunch believer in weight training. So much so, he gave Riecke his own space in the new Three Rivers Stadium, stocked him with an abundance of free weights and allowed him to construct the specialized weightlifting machines he called Power Safe.

Riecke: "It wasn't exactly a machine. It was an apparatus. It enabled you to handle a lot of weight without catches, with no dangers of weights falling on you. I had built one for myself and used it. I told Chuck, 'I think this thing will really help.' Chuck said, 'Build 10 of those things.' I had a welder help me. It worked real well.

"As far as I know, [NFL] players hadn't done it much. San Diego had it, had a strength coach." The Chicago Bears, too. "When I went to the Steelers, Jon Kolb and Larry Brown and then Mike Webster, they were kind of the core guys. They were great examples for the other guys. As a matter of fact, Ray Mansfield told me one time, 'Louie, I got to thank you, you enabled me to play three more years than I thought I'd play.'"

Riecke put the Steelers on a regimen: Work with weights every day during training camp, in season on Mondays and Tuesdays only. The Steelers clank-clank-clanked their way to championship. Sometimes in their own garages.

Riecke: "Some of the guys worked on their own. After a few of them got to see how much it helped them, more and more did it."

When you're the strongman, people point and whisper. In the case of offensive tackle Steve Courson, he later admitted using steroids, buying them for Steelers teammates. He went to his grave disappointed that others from the 1970s weren't as open. The late Mike Webster in court documents for his family's NFL pension lawsuit was said by his doctors to have experimented with steroids. The family of the late Steve Furness said they suspected he tried them. Rocky Bleier told the *Pittsburgh Post-Gazette* he was prescribed small amounts

Steve Furness, first backup to the Steel Curtain and the sub who played for an injured Joe Greene throughout half of the four Super Bowl victories, was among the early group of South Hills-resident Steelers who lifted weights at the Red Bull Inn: Furness, Mike Webster, Jon Kolb, and more. Here Furness harries quarterback Vince Boryla in the 1976 preseason. One of the Eagles assistants was future Steelers defensive coordinator Dick LeBeau. (Temple Urban Archives)

of Dianabol once. Andy Russell talked about amphetamine usage, but that was a stimulant believed to affect performance when playing, not weightlifting.

Chuck Yesalis, a former college-team trainer turned Penn State professor and a performance-enhancing drugs international expert who befriended Courson in 1985: "Many people thought the bloom came off the rose [with Courson's confessions from 1985 on], but I don't agree. [NFL usage] was ubiquitous. The Steelers were the first team to be lean, strong, and fast, and Steve epitomized that.

"They were the ones who really worked their body right and hit the weights more than anybody else. People said [the reason for Super Bowl success] was more drugs for the Steelers, but they just did it in a more successful—if you want to use that term—manner."

In 1963 football's inaugural strength coach, Alvin Roy, gave cereal bowls of Dianabol to players, telling them it was a supplement. Noll was an assistant on that San Diego Chargers team.

Riecke, who was put on a 10-milligrams-a-day regimen of Dianabol as a competitive weightlifter but said he quit in 1964, long maintained that he was unaware of any Steelers steroid use. He added that he never saw it or recommended what he thought was dangerous.

Riecke: "Some of the players asked me about it; I said, 'Man, you guys don't need it.'"

Dan Rooney told the *Pittsburgh Post-Gazette* in 2005: "Chuck had that scientific mind. He knew about [steroids], and he was very strongly opposed to them. He told me what he told the players: There are no shortcuts. That stuff's no good for you. If you're on it, get off it. It's not going to do you any good. In fact, it'll hurt your sex life [by shrinking the testicles]. That was enough right there to convince the players."

Yesalis the expert admitted that by the early 1970s, steroids were an even playing field in the NFL. The Steelers prevailed by weightlifting, work ethic, fundamentals, and, yes, talent.

Gary Dunn, defensive lineman 1977–1987, on being part of a crowd gathering in the basement of a Washington County restaurant: "Those days, it was pretty cool. You'd go to the Red Bull [Inn], they had a gym downstairs. Mike Kruczek would go down there; he lifted with the linemen. Mike Webster, Larry Brown, Jon Kolb, Steve Courson, me, Steve Furness, John Banaszak . . . that was great. You look back on it. . . . Now it seems pretty normal, but back then it wasn't. Lou Riecke had those machines. He was big-time into the weightlifting. All those guys, all our offensive linemen, were into the weightlifting. It kind of rubbed off on you. But those guys, they really into it. It really helped the whole team." Those weights are on display at the Western Pennsylvania Sports Museum in Pittsburgh.

Art Jr., adding that he believes Noll's constant hands-on instruction in the weight room, showing his players lifting techniques, was the root cause for the coach's infirmities later in life: "How important was weightlifting? Good question. He said to me they had so much success in the American Football League with those undersized guys who had speed and quickness, and they would get them on to a good weightlifting program. He always told us, 'We don't want any midgets, but . . .'" don't be afraid of shorter, quicker linemen who could be taught and made taut.

Riecke: "You play football with your legs and your lower back; you don't play with your shoulders. If you could get underneath a guy and deliver that rising blow—that's what we worked on, both in technique and strength.

"You know what? I think [where] it helped them more than anything else, it gave them confidence. When you get strong, there's no way to know you're not strong. You've lifted more than anybody else. It gave you confidence you could get it done, and you did.

"To go from the worst team in the league to the best team of all time . . ."

FROM CURTAINS TO THE 3–4

Joe Greene was gone. The rest of the Steel Curtain had lifted: L. C. Greenwood, Ernie Holmes, Dwight White. So Chuck Noll decided to opt for a radical, but what he considered necessary, change.

To open the 1982 season, the Steelers' four-down-linemen alignment was gone, too.

Say hello to the 3–4—the formation that in Pittsburgh became the longest-running single style in the NFL. Three consecutive decades. And counting.

Three years after the fourth and final Super Bowl of the Noll era, not to mention the 1970s, the unit looked very different.

Dan Rooney vowed, "We're not in a year of transition."

The Steel . . . Tapestry was Tom Beasley (a converted tackle at end), Gary Dunn (a tackle converted to nose guard), and John Goodman (not the rotund comedian/actor). Jack Ham, in his final season, and Robin Cole were the outside linebackers with the inside manned by Loren Toews and Jack Lambert, who wasn't the same without that extra body in front of him, usually a tilting Greene, to keep his frame free of blockers.

Beasley, defensive lineman 1978–1983: "When Pittsburgh went from the four-man front to the three-man front, Jack was getting killed—200, 225 pounds; it was like asking me to guard Shaq, a total mismatch. Ain't gonna happen.

"I think it was probably one of the biggest mistakes Chuck made. We went from the four-man front to the three-man. You had Jack at the middle backer. You had Loren on the inside, and he was 210 pounds. Those guys were getting killed. I went to right defensive end, and in that defense you got to have 4.6 speed out there—certainly I didn't have that. Obviously, we weren't nearly as competitive."

Not nearly as dominating, anyway.

RIVALRIES: RAIDERS, OILERS, COWBOYS, AND BROWNS, OH MY

Of course, when you're king of the hill, everybody wants a piece of you. A certain few approached the Steelers' lofty perch through the 1970s—and the division-rival Baltimore Ravens in the early 2000s—but couldn't knock them off.

The Mike Renfro catch-or-no-catch ruling in the end zone. The Ice Bowl. The Pittsburgh pothole on the highway to history.

One Oail Andrew Phillips, for one, was still kicking his boots about it decades later.

George Perles, defensive assistant and coordinator 1972–1981: "That's what Bum Phillips said, you go to the Super Bowl through Pittsburgh."

The road was most often traveled in the AFC by Phillips' Houston Oilers, a Central Division foe and 1978–1979 championship-game punching bag, and the hated Oakland Raiders, who not only played the Steelers in three consecutive AFC championships from 1974 to 1976 but also took them to court.

Perles: "That was a good one. They had some tough, tough, tough kids, too."

Mike Wagner, safety 1971–1980, saying the heck with Oakland, the Pittsburgh PR guy was tough: "We're checking into the hotel [before 1974 AFC championship game]. There's a lot of jockeying going on. Joe [Gordon] is getting on people, 'Hey!' Pushing back. Getting forceful. If you think we were ready to play football, our publicity people were kicking ass the day before the game. If those guys were doing it, we had to, too."

The Raiders lost the AFC championships to the Steelers in 1974 and 1975, but everywhere else from the 1976 AFC championship game all the way until the 1983 regular season, they never lost to Pittsburgh once. Oakland prevailed in eight of 10 meetings between the 1973 postseason and the 1983 season . . . except for those two title games that led to the Steelers' first Super Bowls.

The Cowboys, after beating up on the Same Old Steelers seven consecutive times beforehand, lost to Noll's team five times in a frustrating row between 1975 and 1982—most important, including Super Bowls X and XIII.

Wagner: "Cowboys-Steelers, they became a cultural thing. The blue-collar versus the Dallas well-to-do. America's team versus . . . whatever. I think that overlapped on the players. That's the image that was created around those games. I don't think it helped those Cowboys."

Dwight White remarked after a 1979 regular-season meeting won by the Steelers, "They ought to just stay over

Jerome Bettis rumbles for another 100-yard game, this time against longtime-rival Oakland in Three Rivers Stadium. Giving chase, from right, are Regan Upshaw, Eric Allen, and No. 33, Anthony Dorsett—homegrown son of former Pitt Heisman Trophy winner Tony Dorsett. (Courtesy of the Pittsburgh Steelers)

there in the NFC with the Washington Redskins and the St. Louis Cardinals, and leave us alone."

The Bengals and Browns were street fights, plain and simple. AFC Central neighborhood rows.

Especially Cleveland, where Joe Greene broke a center's jaw, kicked at another lineman, got ejected with some regularity and watched angrily a Browns attempt to plant Terry Bradshaw headfirst into the soil.

Wagner: "There was always a fight or some shoving going on before the game, but it always looked like Chuck wanted to be in it. He was all gnarly. If you were around him, it was like, 'Geez, Chuck, this was a little different. What got into him?'"

Gerald Williams, defensive lineman, 1986–1994: "He loved to play Cleveland. And when we beat them, it was pure joy for him."

Say this for Noll: He coexisted peacefully with Cleveland coaches. For a time, he refused to shake the hand of Cincinnati's Sam "Wicky Wacky" Wyche. And he dressed down at midfield the new Houston coach, Jerry Glanville, whom he interviewed years before for a defensive-coordinator opening that Noll gave to Tony Dungy.

Bubby Brister, quarterback 1986–1992 of that Noll–Glanville confrontation: "I said, 'Damn, he *is* going kick his ass.'"

Houston was fun, though. After a 1978 victory in Houston's rattling Astrodome, the one where Donnie Shell put out Earl

Campbell and Oilers left injured all game long, Joe Greene noticed: "By the way, they didn't play that damn fight song very much, did they?" "Houston Oilers, Houston Oilers . . . ." That was the day Renfro, Dan Pastorini, Mike Barber, and Robert Brazile all left with injuries. Houston trainer Jerry Meins dubbed it "World War III." Phillips drawled: "It was the hardest-hitting game I've ever seen. I guess we just didn't have enough Band-Aids."

And this was a year after the Oilers did the Steelers a favor with a regular-season finale victory over Cincinnati, which sent the Steelers to the playoffs. In turn, Greene organized a movement where the Steelers sent each Oiler a monogrammed leather briefcase.

Jack Ham, outside linebacker 1971–1982: "Playing the Raiders, playing those Cowboys—it was so much fun playing those guys. There was always a dramatic play in those games."

Gary Dunn, defensive lineman 1977–1987: "All three—Cowboys, Raiders, Oilers. The early years, the Raiders and Cowboys. Then the Oilers, we had all those great playoffs with the Oilers. Bum Phillips: knocking on the door, breaking that door down. Worst field everywhere. The seams [in the Astrodome artificial turf] were split, like, five inches apart. Smoke throughout the place. And you had that Crazy George on the sidelines. I put my hand down, and it smelled like horse. . . . They had a rodeo there the day before."

Appendix

Statistics

1933 PITTSBURGH PIRATES: 3-6-2, LAST IN EAST, TIED FOR 8TH IN NFL
Head Coach: Jap Douds

Week	Day	Date	OT	Rec	Opp	Score Tm	Score Opp
1	Wed	September 20	L	0-1	New York Giants	2	23
2	Wed	September 27	W	1-1	Chicago Cardinals	14	13
3	Wed	October 4	L	1-2	Boston Redskins	6	21
4	Wed	October 11	W	2-2	Cincinnati Reds	17	3
5	Sun	October 15	L	2-3	Green Bay Packers	0	47
6	Sun	October 22	T	2-3-1	Cincinnati Reds	0	0
7	Sun	October 29	W	3-3-1	Boston Redskins	16	14
8	Sun	November 5	I	3-3-2	Brooklyn Dodgers	3	3
9	Sun	November 12	L	3-4-2	Brooklyn Dodgers	0	32
10	Sun	November 19	L	3-5-2	Philadelphia Eagles	6	25
11	Sun	December 3	L	3-6-2	New York Giants	3	27

	Pts	Yds	Ply	Y/P 1stD	Pass Cmp	Att	Yds	TD	Int	NY/A 1stD	Rush Att	Yds	TD	Y/A 1stD	TO	FL
Team Offense	67	1943	534	3.6	60	196	1029	3	40	5.3	338	914	4	2.7	40	0
Team Defense	208	2735	583	4.7	57	142	930	8	19	6.5	441	1805	16	4.1	19	0

Passing

	Age	Pos	G	GS	QBrec	Cmp	Att	Cmp%	Yds	TD	TD%	Int	Int%	Lng	Y/A	AY/A	Y/C	Y/G
Tony Holm	25	FB	9	9		17	52	32.7	406	2	3.8	13	25.0	0	7.8	−2.7	23.9	45.1
Walt Holmer	31		4	4		9	27	33.3	158	0	0.0	4	14.8	0	5.9	−0.8	17.6	39.5
Ed Westfall	24		6	4		8	26	30.8	100	0	0.0	5	19.2	0	3.8	−4.8	12.5	16.7
Angelo Brovelli	23	TB	8	8		8	25	32.0	114	0	0.0	3	12.0	0	4.6	−0.8	14.3	14.3
Elmer Schwartz	27	HB	10	5		5	22	22.7	103	0	0.0	3	13.6	0	4.7	−1.5	20.6	10.3
Frank Hood	25		3	1		6	18	33.3	45	0	0.0	4	22.2	0	2.5	−7.5	7.5	15.0
Bill Tanguay	24		3	0		5	17	29.4	101	1	5.9	5	29.4	0	5.9	−6.1	20.2	33.7
Harp Vaughan	30		8	1		2	8	25.0	2	0	0.0	3	37.5	0	−16.6	0.3	1.0	0.3
Ray Tesser	21	RE	11	10		0	1	0.0	0	0	0.0	0	0.0	0	0.0	0.0		0.0
Team Total	23.5		11			60	196	30.6	1029	3	1.5	40	20.4	0	5.3	−3.6	17.2	93.5
Opp Total			11			57	142	40.1	930	8	5.6	19	13.4		6.5	1.7	16.3	84.5

Rushing and Receiving

No.		Age	Pos	G	GS	Rush							Receiving							YScm
						Att	Yds	TD	Lng	Y/A	Y/G	A/G	Rec	Yds	Y/R	TD	Lng	R/G	Y/G	
	Angelo Brovelli	23	TB	8	8	60	236	2	0	3.9	29.5	7.5	6	137	22.8	0	0	0.8	17.1	373
	Tony Holm	25	FB	9	9	58	160	0	0	2.8	17.8	6.4	2	13	6.5	0	0	0.2	1.4	173
	Ed Westfall	24		6	4	44	61	1	0	1.4	10.2	7.3	4	79	19.8	1	60	0.7	13.2	140
	Elmer Schwartz	27	hb	10	5	38	94	0	0	2.5	9.4	3.8	2	20	10.0	0	0	0.2	2.0	114
	Harp Vaughan	30		8	1	26	74	1	0	2.8	9.3	3.3	6	101	16.8	0	0	0.8	12.6	175
	Bucky Moore			5	3	16	42	0	0	2.6	8.4	3.2								42
	Mose Kelsch	36		8	0	8	37	0	0	4.6	4.6	1.0								37
	George Shaffer	23	BB	5	5	5	6	0	0	1.2	1.2	1.0	1	11	11.0	0	11	0.2	2.2	17
	Walt Holmer	31		4	4	4	8	0		2.0	2.0	1.0								8
	Ted Dailey	25		10	4	1	1	0	1	1.0	0.1	0.1	7	66	9.4	0	0	0.7	6.6	67
	Jap Douds	28	rt	7	5	1	2	0	2	2.0	0.3	0.1								2
	Frank Hood	25		3	1	1	1	0	1	1.0	0.3	0.3								1
	Ray Tesser	21	RE	11	10	0	0	0			0.0	0.0	14	282	20.1	0	0	1.3	25.6	282
	Paul Moss	25	LE	10	7	0	0	0			0.0	0.0	13	283	21.8	2	30	1.3	28.3	283
	Bill Sortet	21		9	1	0	0	0			0.0	0.0	1	28	28.0	0	28	0.1	3.1	28

1934 PITTSBURGH PIRATES: 2-10-0, LAST IN EAST, MOST NFL LOSSES
Head Coach: Luby DiMeolo

Week	Day	Date		OT	Rec	Opp	Score	
							Tm	Opp
1	Sun	September 9	W		1-0	Cincinnati Reds	13	0
2	Sun	September 16	L		1-1	Boston Redskins	0	7
3	Wed	September 26	L		1-2	Philadelphia Eagles	0	17
4	Wed	October 3	L		1-3	New York Giants	12	14
5	Sun	October 7	W		2-3	Philadelphia Eagles	9	7
6	Wed	October 10	L		2-4	Chicago Bears	0	28
7	Sun	October 14	L		2-5	Boston Redskins	0	39
8	Sun	October 21	L		2-6	New York Giants	7	17
9	Sun	October 28	L		2-7	Brooklyn Dodgers	3	21
10	Sun	November 4	L		2-8	Detroit Lions	7	40
11	Sun	November 11	L		2-9	St. Louis Gunners	0	6
12	Sun	November 18	L		2-10	Brooklyn Dodgers	0	10

Rushing and Receiving

No.		Age	Pos	G	GS	Rush							Receiving							YScm
						Att	Yds	TD	Lng	Y/A	Y/G	A/G	Rec	Yds	Y/R	TD	Lng	R/G	Y/G	
	Warren Heller	24	TB	12	12	132	528	1	0	4.0	44.0	11.0	6	96	16.0	0	0	0.5	8.0	624
	Harp Vaughan	31	bb	11	7	58	196	0	0	3.4	17.8	5.3	2	56	28.0	0	0	0.2	5.1	252
	Peter Rajkovich	23		3	39	140	0	0	3.6	46.7	13.0									140
	Alex Rado	23	HB	8	4	38	210	0	0	5.5	26.3	4.8	5	93	18.6	0	0	0.6	11.6	303
	Angelo Brovelli	24	FB	5	5	37	112	1	0	3.0	22.4	7.4									112
	James Clark	21		9	3	31	84	0	0	2.7	9.3	3.4	1	28	28.0	1	28	0.1	3.1	112
	Silvio Zaninelli	24	BB	11	11	24	60	0	0	2.5	5.5	2.2	2	14	7.0	0	0	0.2	1.3	74
	Jack Roberts	28		6	0	24	55	0	0	2.3	9.2	4.0									55
	Jim Levey	24		1	1	9	69	0	0	7.7	69.0	9.0									69
	Pete Saumer	24		3	0	7	21	0	0	3.0	7.0	2.3									21
	George Kavel	25		1	1	5	5	0	0	1.0	5.0	5.0									5
	Buster Mott	31		1	0	5	24	0	0	4.8	24.0	5.0									24
	Johnny McNally	37	PR/P/ KR/K	5	1	3	3	0	0	1.0	0.6	0.6	1	10	10.0	0	10	0.2	2.0	13
	Mose Kelsch	24		8	0	3	11	0	0	3.7	1.4	0.4									11
	Cap Oehler	25	C	12	12	2	14	0	0	7.0	1.2	0.2									14
	Ben Ciccone	23		11	0	1	−5	0	−5	−5.0	−0.5	0.1									−5
	Ben Smith	23	LE	11	10	0	0	0	0		0.0	0.0	14	218	15.6	0	0	1.3	19.8	218
	Joe Skladany	22	RE	12	12	0	0	0	0		0.0	0.0	9	222	24.7	2	62	0.8	18.5	222
	Bill Sortet	22		12	1	0	0	0	0		0.0	0.0	7	93	13.3	1	21	0.6	7.8	93
	Ray Tesser	23.4		12	1	0	0	0	0		0.0	0.0	5	67	13.4	0	0	0.4	5.6	67
	Team Total			12		418	1527	2	0	3.7	127.3	34.8	52	897	17.3	4	62	4.3	74.8	2424
	Opp Total			12		517	2569	15		5.0	214.1	43.1	45	610	13.6	10		3.8	50.8	3179

	Pts	Yds	Ply	Y/P 1stD	Pass						Pass					
					Cmp	Att	Yds	TD	Int	NY/A 1stD	Att	Yds	TD	Y/A 1stD	TO	FL 1stPy
Team Offense	51	2479	604	4.1	58	186	952	4	23	5.1	418	1527	2	3.7	23	0
Team Defense	206	3179	650	4.9	45	133	610	10	20	4.6	517	2569	15	5.0	20	0

Passing

No.		Age	Pos	G	GS	QBrec	Cmp	Att	Cmp%	Yds	TD	TD%	Int	Int%	Lng	Y/A	AY/A	Y/C	Y/G	Rate
	Warren Heller	24	TB	12	12		31	112	27.7	511	2	1.8	15	13.4	0	4.6	−1.1	16.5	42.6	12.5
	Harp Vaughan	31	bb	11	7		19	42	45.2	262	2	4.8	5	11.9	62	6.2	1.8	13.8	23.8	42.1
	Alex Rado	23	HB	8	4		8	24	33.3	179	0	0.0	2	8.3	0	7.5	3.7	22.4	22.4	26.2
	Pete Saumer	24		3	0		0	3	0.0	0	0	0.0	1	33.3		0.0	−15.0		0.0	0.0
	James Clark			9	3		0	1	0.0	0	0	0.0	0	0.0	0	0.0	0.0		0.0	39.6
	Johnny McNally	31	PR/P/ KR/K	5	1		0	1	0.0	0	0	0.0	0	0.0	0	0.0	0.0		0.0	39.6
	Jess Quatse	26	LT	12	12		0	1	0.0	0	0	0.0	0	0.0	0	0.0	0.0		0.0	39.6
	Ray Tesser	22		12	1		0	1	0.0	0	0	0.0	0	0.0	0	0.0	0.0		0.0	39.6
	Silvio Zaninelli	21	BB	11	11		0	1	0.0	0	0	0.0	0	0.0	0	0.0	0.0		0.0	39.6
	Team Total	23.4		12			58	186	31.2	952	4	2.2	23	12.4	62	5.1	0.0	16.4	79.3	17.0
	Opp Total			12			45	133	33.8	610	10	7.5	20	15.0		4.6	−0.7	13.6	50.8	34.9

1935 PITTSBURGH PIRATES: 4-8-0, FINISHED 3RD IN EAST, 7TH IN NFL
Head Coach: Joe Bach

Week	Day	Date	OT	Rec	Opp	Score Tm	Score Opp	Offe 1stD	Offe TotYd	Offe PassY	Offe RushY	Offe TO	Defe 1stD	Defe TotYd	Defe PassY	Defe RushY	Defe TO
1	Fri	September 13	W	1-0	Philadelphia Eagles	17	7										
2	Sun	September 22	L	1-1	New York Giants	7	42										
3	Sun	September 29	L	1-2	Chicago Bears	7	23										
4	Sun	October 6	L	1-3	Green Bay Packers	0	27										
5	Wed	October 9	L	1-4	Philadelphia Eagles	6	17										
6	Sun	October 20	W	2-4	Chicago Cardinals	17	13										
7	Sun	October 27	W	3-4	Boston Redskins	6	0										
8	Sun	November 3	L	3-5	Brooklyn Dodgers	7	13										
9	Sun	November 10	W	4-5	Brooklyn Dodgers	16	7	6	187	84	103	3	10	174	68	106	4
10	Sun	November 24	L	4-6	Green Bay Packers	14	34										
11	Sun	December 1	L	4-7	Boston Redskins	3	13										
12	Sun	December 8	L	4-8	New York Giants	0	13	2	67	52	15	4	14	333	134	199	1

Passing

No.		Age	Pos	G	GS	QBrec	Cmp	Att	Cmp%	Yds	TD	TD%	Int	Int%	Lng	Y/A	AY/A	Y/C	Y/G	Rate
	Johnny Gildea	25	TB	12	10		28	105	26.7	529	2	1.9	20	19.0	0	5.0	−3.2	18.9	44.1	14.8
	Warren Heller	25		12	1		9	41	22.0	88	0	0.0	8	19.5	0	2.1	−6.6	9.8	7.3	0.0
	John Turley	23	BB	10	9		12	27	44.4	144	1	3.7	6	22.2	0	5.3	−3.9	12.0	14.4	34.1
	Heinie Weisenbaugh	21	hb	5	5		1	11	9.1	14	0	0.0	1	9.1	14	1.3	−2.8	14.0	2.8	1.7
	John Doehring	26		2	1		4	8	50.0	83	2	25.0	1	12.5	0	10.4	9.8	20.8	41.5	87.0
	Buzz Wetzel	25	fb	9	5		2	8	25.0	21	0	0.0	1	12.5	0	2.6	−3.0	10.5	2.3	0.0
	Silvio Zaninelli	22	FB	11	6		1	8	12.5	4	0	0.0	2	25.0	4	0.5	−10.8	4.0	0.4	0.0
	Swede Ellstrom	29		3	1		6	7	85.7	68	0	0.0	0	0.0	0	9.7	9.7	11.3	22.7	107.1
	Glenn Campbell	31		1	0		2	5	40.0	38	0	0.0	0	0.0	0	7.6	7.6	19.0	38.0	67.1
	Cy Casper	23		9	4		1	4	25.0	3	0	0.0	0	0.0	3	0.8	0.8	3.0	0.3	39.6
	Jim Levey	29		8	1		1	4	25.0	4	0	0.0	0	0.0	4	1.0	1.0	4.0	0.5	39.6
	Mike Nixon	24		3	0		0	3	0.0	0	0	0.0	1	33.3	0	0.0	−15.0		0.0	0.0
	Art Strutt	23	HB	9	5		0	2	0.0	0	0	0.0	0	0.0	0	0.0	0.0		0.0	39.6
	Mike Sebastian	25		2	0		0	1	0.0	0	0	0.0	0	0.0	0	0.0	0.0		0.0	39.6
	Team Total	24.0		12			67	234	28.6	996	5	2.1	40	17.1	14	4.3	−3.0	14.9	83.0	12.4
	Opp Total			12			68	209	32.5	1208	13	6.2	21	10.0		5.8	2.5	17.8	100.7	34.4

Rushing and Receiving

No.		Age	Pos	G	GS	Rush Att	Yds	TD	Lng	Y/A	Y/G	A/G	Receiving Rec	Yds	Y/R	TD	Lng	R/G	Y/G	YScm
	Cy Casper	23		9	4	56	102	1	0	1.8	11.3	6.2	5	94	18.8	1	0	0.6	10.4	196
	Johnny Gildea	25	TB	12	10	49	1	0	0	0.0	0.1	4.1	4	61	15.3	0	0	0.3	5.1	62
	Art Strutt	23	HB	9	5	46	111	0	0	2.4	12.3	5.1	7	112	16.0	0	0	0.8	12.4	223
	Jim Levey	29		8	1	42	61	2	0	1.5	7.6	5.3	7	112	16.0	2	34	0.9	14.0	173
	Warren Heller	25		12	1	37	112	0	0	3.0	9.3	3.1	2	16	8.0	0	0	0.2	1.3	128
	Silvio Zaninelli	22	FB	11	6	22	15	0	0	0.7	1.4	2.0	1	7	7.0	0	7	0.1	0.6	22
	Heinie Weisenbaugh	21	hb	5	5	21	11	0	0	0.5	2.2	4.2	6	67	11.2	2	0	1.2	13.4	78
	Buzz Wetzel	25	fb	9	5	19	41	1	0	2.2	4.6	2.1	4	18	4.5	0	0	0.4	2.0	59
	Swede Ellstrom	29		3	1	10	14	0	0	1.4	4.7	3.3	1	12	12.0	0	12	0.3	4.0	26
	Mike Nixon	24		3	0	7	5	0	0	0.7	1.7	2.3								5
	Mike Sebastian	25		2	0	4	3	0	0	0.8	1.5	2.0								3
	John Turley	23	BB	10	9	4	−3	0	0	−0.8	−0.3	0.4								−3
	Thomas Cosgrove			1	0	3	18	0	0	6.0	18.0	3.0								18
	John Doehring	26		2	1	3	−6	0	0	−2.0	−3.0	1.5								−6
	Al Arndt	24	PR/P/KR/K	7	2	1	21	0	21	21.0	3.0	0.1								21
	Glenn Campbell	31		1	0	1	6	0	6	6.0	6.0	1.0								6
	Henry Hayduk	22		8	0	1	3	0	3	3.0	0.4	0.1								3
	Vic Vidoni	23	LE	11	8	0	0	0	0		0.0	0.0	11	111	10.1	0	0	1.0	10.1	111
	Ben Smith	24	re	11	6	0	0	0	0		0.0	0.0	9	166	18.4	0	0	0.8	15.1	166
	Bill Sortet	23	RE	12	8	0	0	0	0		0.0	0.0	7	178	25.4	0	0	0.6	14.8	178
	Cliff Dolaway	22		4	0	0	0	0	0		0.0	0.0	2	42	21.0	0	0	0.5	10.5	42
	Armand Niccolai	24	RT	12	10	0	0	0	0	0	0.0	0.0	1	0	0.0	0	0	0.1	0.0	0
	Team Total	24.0		12		326	515	4	21	1.6	42.9	27.2	67	996	14.9	5	34	5.6	83.0	1511
	Opp Total			12		543	1957	12		3.6	163.1	45.3	68	1208	17.8	13		5.7	100.7	3165

1936 PITTSBURGH PIRATES: 6-6-0, 2ND IN EAST, 5TH IN NFL
Head Coach: Joe Bach

Week	Day	Date	OT	Rec	Opp	Score Tm	Opp	Offe 1stD	TotYd	PassY	RushY	TO	Defe 1stD	TotYd	PassY	RushY	TO
1	Sun	September 13	W	1-0	Boston Redskins	10	0										
2	Wed	September 23	W	2-0	Brooklyn Dodgers	10	6	10	178	62	116	1	8	202	28	174	2
3	Sun	September 27	W	3-0	New York Giants	10	7	9	184	61	123	1	11	327	86	241	2
4	Sun	October 4	L	3-1	Chicago Bears	9	27										
5	Wed	October 14	W	4-1	Philadelphia Eagles	17	0										
6	Sun	October 18	L	4-2	Chicago Bears	7	26										
7	Sun	October 25	L	4-3	Green Bay Packers	10	42										
8	Sun	November 1	W	5-3	Brooklyn Dodgers	10	7	12	211	211	2	6	206	206			
9	Thu	November 5	W	6-3	Philadelphia Eagles	6	0										
10	Sun	November 8	L	6-4	Detroit Lions	3	28										
11	Sun	November 15	L	6-5	Chicago Cardinals	6	14										
12	Sun	November 29	L	6-6	Boston Redskins	0	30	2	32	34	−2	3	10	237	10	227	6

Passing

No.		Age	Pos	G	GS	QBrec	Cmp	Att	Cmp%	Yds	TD	TD%	Int	Int%	Lng	Y/A	AY/A	Y/C	Y/G	Rate	Sk	Yds
	Ed Matesic	29	TB	12	11		64	138	46.4	850	4	2.9	16	11.6	0	6.2	1.5	13.3	70.8	36.5		
	Johnny Gildea	26	BB	12	9		9	29	31.0	147	1	3.4	5	17.2	0	5.1	-2.0	16.3	12.3	21.0		
	Max Fiske	23		11	0		6	15	40.0	64	0	0.0	3	20.0	0	4.3	-4.7	10.7	5.8	13.6		
	Silvio Zaninelli	23		12	3		1	6	16.7	2	0	0.0	1	16.7	2	0.3	-7.2	2.0	0.2	0.0		
	Warren Heller	26	HB	12	4		0	5	0.0	0	0	0.0	1	20.0	0	0.0	-9.0		0.0	0.0		
	Bull Karcis	28	FB	12	12		0	4	0.0	0	0	0.0	2	50.0	0	0.0	-22.5		0.0	0.0		
	Art Strutt	24	hb	10	5		1	1	100.0	15	0	0.0	0	0.0	15	15.0	15.0	15.0	1.5	118.7		
	Team Total	25.6		12			81	198	40.9	1078	5	2.5	28	14.1	15	5.4	-0.4	13.3	89.8	27.7		
	Opp Total			12			52	164	31.7	907	13	7.9	25	15.2		5.5	0.3	17.4	75.6	38.4	0	0

Rushing and Receiving

No.		Age	Pos	G	GS	Rush Att	Rush Yds	Rush TD	Rush Lng	Rush Y/A	Rush Y/G	Rush A/G	Rec	Rec Yds	Rec Y/R	Rec TD	Rec Lng	Rec R/G	Rec Y/G	YScm
	Warren Heller	26	HB	12	4	106	332	0	0	3.1	27.7	8.8	12	1601	3.3	3	0	1.0	13.3	492
	Bull Karcis	28	FB	12	12	89	272	2	0	3.1	22.7	7.4	8	71	8.9	0	0	0.7	5.9	343
	Art Strutt	24	hb	10	5	84	180	1	0	2.1	18.0	8.4	11	166	15.1	0	0	1.1	16.6	346
	Max Fiske	23		11	0	58	92	0	0	1.6	8.4	5.3	7	96	13.7	0	0	0.6	8.7	188
	Ed Matesic	29	TB	12	11	46	58	0	0	1.3	4.8	3.8	1	13	13.0	0	13	0.1	1.1	71
	Johnny Gildea	26	BB	12	9	35	31	0	0	0.9	2.6	2.9	5	70	14.0	0	0	0.4	5.8	101
	Silvio Zaninelli	23		12	3	31	61	1	0	2.0	5.1	2.6	2	12	6.0	0	0	0.2	1.0	73
	Jim McDonald	25		5	0	9	18	0	0	2.0	3.6	1.8	1	8	8.0	0	8	0.2	1.6	26
	Dick Sandefur	24		8	0	7	13	0	0	1.9	1.6	0.9								13
	Jim Levey	30		4	0	4	3	0	0	0.8	0.8	1.0								3
	Bill Sortet	24	re	12	5	1	47	0	47	47.0	3.9	0.1	14	197	14.1	1	55	1.2	16.4	244
	George Kakasic	24	RG	12	7	1	-8	0	-8	-8.0	-0.7	0.1								-8
	Bill Lajousky	23	rg	11	5	1	1	0	1	1.0	0.1	0.1								1
	Ed Skoronski	26	LE	12	6	0	0	0	0		0.0	0.0	8	95	11.9	1	19	0.7	7.9	95
	Jeep Brett	22		8	4	0	0	0	0		0.0	0.0	7	139	19.9	0	0	0.9	17.4	139
	Vinnie Sites	24	RE	12	7	0	0	0	0		0.0	0.0	2	22	11.0	0	0	0.2	1.8	22
	Vic Vidoni	24		2	2	0	0	0	0		0.0	0.0	2	35	17.5	0	0	1.0	17.5	35
	Ed Karpowich	24		11	3	0	0	0	0		0.0	0.0	1	-6	-6.0	0	-6	0.1	-0.5	-6
	Team Total	25.6		12		472	1100	4	47	2.3	91.7	39.3	81	1078	13.3	5	55	6.8	89.8	2178
	Opp Total			12		543	2150	11		4.0	179.2	45.3	52	907	17.4	13		4.3	75.6	3057

1937 PITTSBURGH PIRATES: 4-7-0, 3RD IN EAST, 7TH IN NFL
Head Coach: Johnny McNally

Week	Day	Date	OT	Rec	Opp	Score Tm	Score Opp	Offe 1stD	Offe TotYd	Offe PassY	Offe RushY	Offe TO	Defe 1stD	Defe TotYd	Defe PassY	Defe RushY	Defe TO
1	Sun	September 5	W	1-0	Philadelphia Eagles	27	14										
2	Sun	September 19	W	2-0	Brooklyn Dodgers	21	0	15	302	163	139	2	4	92	12	80	5
3	Sun	September 26	L	2-1	New York Giants	7	10	5	117	17	100	9	8	191	96	95	1
4	Mon	October 4	L	2-2	Chicago Bears		0	7									
5	Sun	October 10	L	2-3	Detroit Lions		3	7									
6	Sun	October 17	L	2-4	Washington Redskins	20	34										
7	Sun	October 24	L	2-5	Chicago Cardinals	7	13										
8	Sun	October 31	W	3-5	Philadelphia Eagles	16	7										
9	Sun	November 7	L	3-6	New York Giants	0	17	4	80	54	26	6	13	239	129	110	
10	Sun	November 14	W	4-6	Washington Redskins	21	13										
11	Sun	November 21	L	4-7	Brooklyn Dodgers	0	23										

Passing

No.		Age	Pos	G	GS	QBrec	Cmp	Att	Cmp%	Yds	TD	TD%	Int	Int%	Lng	Y/A	AY/A	Y/C	Y/G	Rate	Sk	Yds
	Johnny Gildea	27	TB	11	8		14	47	29.8	288	2	4.3	9	19.1	0	6.1	−1.6	20.6	26.2	27.2		
	Max Fiske	24		7	1		17	43	39.5	318	4	9.3	4	9.3	0	7.4	5.1	18.7	45.4	58.1		
	Johnny McNally	34		9	2		10	25	40.0	115	1	4.0	2	8.0	0	4.6	1.8	11.5	12.8	34.6		
	Bill Davidson	22	HB	11	10		8	24	33.3	81	0	0.0	5	20.8	0	3.4	−6.0	10.1	7.4	4.3		
	Tuffy Thompson	23		7	4		6	14	42.9	100	1	7.1	4	28.6	39	7.1	−4.3	16.7	14.3	51.8		
	By Haines	23		5	1		1	6	16.7	14	0	0.0	1	16.7	14	2.3	−5.2	14.0	2.8	0.0		
	Bull Karcis	29	fb	6	2		1	3	33.3	2	1	33.3	1	33.3	2	0.7	−7.7	2.0	0.3	42.4		
	Stu Smith	22	FB	10	6		0	2	0.0	0	0	0.0	1	50.0	0	0.0	−22.5		0.0	0.0		
	Team Total	25.2		11			57	164	34.8	918	9	5.5	27	16.5	39	5.6	−0.71	6.1	83.5	33.1		
	Opp Total			11			60	185	32.4	902	9	4.9	17	9.2		4.9	1.7	15.0	82.0	27.4	0	0

Rushing and Receiving

No.		Age	Pos	G	GS	Rush Att	Rush Yds	Rush TD	Rush Lng	Rush Y/A	Rush Y/G	Rush A/G	Rec	Rec Yds	Rec Y/R	Rec TD	Rec Lng	Rec R/G	Rec Y/G	YScm
	Bull Karcis	29	fb	6	2	127	513	3	0	4.0	85.5	21.2	2	18	9.0	0	0	0.3	3.0	531
	Bill Davidson	22	HB	11	10	101	293	1	0	2.9	26.6	9.2	4	169	42.3	2	0	0.4	15.4	462
	Stu Smith	22	FB	10	6	66	211	0	0	3.2	21.1	6.6								211
	Johnny Gildea	27	TB	11	8	49	65	1	0	1.3	5.9	4.5	3	47	15.7	0	0	0.3	4.3	112
	Tuffy Thompson	23		7	4	43	80	0	0	1.9	11.4	6.1	6	126	21.0	1	55	0.9	18.0	206
	Izzy Weinstock	24	fb	11	6	30	88	0	0	2.9	8.0	2.7								87
	Max Fiske	24		7	1	28	44	0	0	1.6	6.3	4.0	1	0	0.0	0	0	0.1	0.0	44
	By Haines	23		5	1	24	29	0	0	1.2	5.8	4.8	2	17	8.5	0	0	0.4	3.4	46
	Bill Breeden	24		9	3	10	25	0	0	2.5	2.8	1.1	6	59	9.8	0	0	0.7	6.6	84
	Johnny McNally	34		9	2	9	37	0	0	4.1	4.1	1.0	10	168	16.8	4	0	1.1	18.7	205
	Silvio Zaninelli	24	BB	10	5	4	14	0	0	3.5	1.4	0.4	2	12	6.0	0	0	0.2	1.2	26
	Ed Karpowich	25		9	4	1	15	0	15	15.0	1.7	0.1								15
	John Perko	23	RG	10	8	1	5	0	5	5.0	0.5	0.1								5
	Bill Sortet	25	RE	9	6	0	0	0	0		0.0	0.0	9	121	13.4	1	26	1.0	13.4	121
	Jeep Brett	23	LE	10	7	0	0	0	0		0.0	0.0	8	135	16.9	1	0	0.8	13.5	135
	Mac Cara	23		10	4	0	0	0	0		0.0	0.0	2	36	18.0	0	0	0.2	3.6	36
	Vinnie Sites	25		7	1	0	0	0	0		0.0	0.0	2	10	5.0	0	0	0.3	1.4	10
	Team Total	25.2		11		493	1419	5	15	2.9	129.0	44.8	57	918	16.1	9	55	5.2	83.5	2337
	Opp Total			11		405	1311	7		3.2	119.2	36.8	60	902	15.0	9		5.5	82.0	2213

1938 PITTSBURGH PIRATES: 2-9-0, LAST IN EAST, TIED FOR LAST IN NFL
Head Coach: Johnny McNally

Week	Day	Date	OT	Rec	Opp	Score Tm	Score Opp	Offe 1stD	Offe TotYd	Offe PassY	Offe RushY	Offe TO	Defe 1stD	Defe TotYd	Defe PassY	Defe RushY	Defe TO
1	Fri	September 9	L	0-1	Detroit Lions	7	16										
2	Sun	September 11	L	0-2	New York Giants	14	27	6	251	73	178	3	13	223	135	88	1
3	Fri	September 16	L	0-3	Philadelphia Eagles	7	27										
4	Fri	September 23	W	1-3	Brooklyn Dodgers	17	3	13	371	235	136	4	6	205	152	53	3
5	Mon	October 3	W	2-3	New York Giants	13	10	10	216	50	166	2	7	186	104	82	3
6	Sun	October 9	L	2-4	Brooklyn Dodgers	7	17										
7	Sun	October 23	L	2-5	Green Bay Packers	0	20										
8	Sun	November 6	L	2-6	Washington Redskins	0	7	4	178		178		13	351		351	
9	Sun	November 20	L	2-7	Philadelphia Eagles	7	14										
10	Sun	November 27	L	2-8	Washington Redskins	0	15	13	309	180	129		9	362	252	110	
11	Sun	December 4	L	2-9	Cleveland Rams	7	13										

Passing

No.		Age	Pos	G	GS	QBrec	Cmp	Att	Cmp%	Yds	TD	TD%	Int	Int%	Lng	Y/A	AY/A	Y/C	Y/G	Rate	Sk	Yds
	Frank Filchock	22		6	3		30	74	40.5	392	3	4.1	7	9.5	0	5.3	1.9	13.1	65.3	32.0		
	Whizzer White+	21	TB	11	11		29	73	39.7	393	2	2.7	18	24.7	0	5.4	−5.2	13.6	35.7	27.2		
	Max Fiske	25		10	2		11	37	29.7	121	0	0.0	4	10.8	0	3.3	−1.6	11.0	12.1	1.1		
	Tuffy Thompson	24	HB	10	3		0	7	0.0	0	0	0.0	3	42.9	0	0.0	−19.3		0.0	0.0		
	Bill Davidson	23		10	2		2	2	100.0	10	0	0.0	0	0.0	0	5.0	5.0	5.0	1.0	87.5		
	Tom Burnette	23		6	1		0	1	0.0	0	0	0.0	0	0.0	0	0.0	0.0		0.0	39.6		
	Team Total	24.6		11			72	194	37.1	916	5	2.6	32	16.5	0	4.7	−2.2	12.7	83.3	21.7		
	Opp Total			11			74	185	40.0	1213	13	7.0	14	7.6		6.6	4.6	16.4	110.3	54.6	0	0

Rushing and Receiving

No.		Age	Pos	G	GS	Rush Att	Yds	TD	Lng	Y/A	Y/G	A/G	Rec	Yds	Y/R	TD	Lng	R/G	Y/G	YScm
	Whizzer White+	21	TB	11	11	152	567	4	79	3.7	51.5	13.8	7	88	12.6	0	0	0.6	8.0	655
	Stu Smith*	23	FB	11	11	80	241	0	0	3.0	21.9	7.3	3	30	10.0	0	0	0.3	2.7	271
	Scrapper Farrell	23		5	2	46	176	0	0	3.8	35.2	9.2								176
	Tuffy Thompson	24	HB	10	3	39	139	1	0	3.6	13.9	3.9	9	55	6.1	0	0	0.9	5.5	194
	Bill Davidson	23		10	2	33	52	0	0	1.6	5.2	3.3	12	229	19.1	0	0	1.2	22.9	281
	Max Fiske	25		10	2	29	83	0	0	2.9	8.3	2.9								83
	Frank Filchock	22		6	3	17	20	0	0	1.2	3.3	2.8								20
	Bull Karcis*	30		3	0	16	31	0	0	1.9	10.3	5.3								31
	Swede Hanson	31		5	1	15	50	0	0	3.3	10.0	3.0	1	2	2.0	0	2	0.2	0.4	52
	John Oelerich	22		3	1	12	21	0	0	1.8	7.0	4.0	2	23	11.5	0	0	0.7	7.7	44
	Eggs Manske	26	LE	6	4	5	29	0	0	5.8	4.8	0.8	9	113	12.6	1	23	1.5	18.8	142
	Bob Douglas			2	0	4	10	0	0	2.5	5.0	2.0								10
	George Platukis	23		5	2	3	6	0	0	2.0	1.2	0.6	4	82	20.5	0	0	0.8	16.4	88
	Johnny McNally	35	BB	10	4	2	−5	0	0	−2.5	−0.5	0.2	2	5	2.5	0	0	0.2	0.5	0
	Bill Sortet	26		8	3	1	−5	0	−5	−5.0	−0.6	0.1	11	166	15.1	4	50	1.4	20.8	161
	Mac Cara	24		9	3	1	−1	0	−1	−1.0	−0.1	0.1	4	18	4.5	0	0	0.4	2.0	17
	Tom Burnette	23		6	1	1	0	0	0	0.0	0.0	0.2	1	3	3.0	0	3	0.2	0.5	3
	Izzy Weinstock	25		2	2	1	0	0	0	0.0	0.0	0.5								0
	Paul McDonough	22		6	3	0	0	0	0		0.0	0.0	6	86	14.3	0	0	1.0	14.3	86
	Jess Tatum	24	RE	5	4	0	0	0	0		0.0	0.0	1	16	16.0	0	16	0.2	3.2	16
	Team Total	24.6		11		457	1414	5	79	3.1	128.5	41.5	72	916	12.7	5	50	6.5	83.3	2330
	Opp Total			11		425	1368	7		3.2	124.4	38.6	74	1213	16.4	13		6.7	110.3	2581

1939 PITTSBURGH PIRATES: 1-9-1, TIED FOR LAST IN EAST, TIED FOR 9TH IN NFL
Head Coaches: Johnny McNally and Walt Kiesling

Week	Day	Date	OT	Rec	Opp	Score Tm	Opp	Offe 1stD	TotYd	PassY	RushY	TO	Defe 1stD	TotYd	PassY	RushY	TO
1	Thu	September 14	L	0-1	Brooklyn Dodgers	7	12	11	215	106	109	3	12	250	100	150	1
2	Sun	September 24	L	0-2	Chicago Cardinals	0	10	9	287		287		5	195		195	
3	Mon	October 2	L	0-3	Chicago Bears	0	32	10	54	39	15	2	18	441	193	248	1
4	Sun	October 8	L	0-4	New York Giants	7	14	14	246	78	168	6	9	183	108	75	2
4	Sun	October 15	L	0-5	Washington Redskins	14	44	19	260	150	110	4	13	395	173	222	
6	Sun	October 22	L	0-6	Washington Redskins	14	21	9	345	175	170	2	13	413	105	308	2
7	Sun	October 29	T	0-6-1	Cleveland Rams	14	14	8	177	80	97	2	9	249	18	231	7
8	Mon	November 6	L	0-7-1	Brooklyn Dodgers	13	17	13	252	186	66	5	11	284	52	232	
9	Sun	November 19	L	0-8-1	New York Giants	7	23	5	99	36	63	7	11	260	153	107	3
10	Thu	November 23	L	0-9-1	Philadelphia Eagles	14	17	7	294	165	129	6	6	248	208	40	3
11	Sun	November 26	W	1-9-1	Philadelphia Eagles	24	12	8	210	44	166	2	14	199	173	26	2

Passing

No.		Age	Pos	G	GS	QBrec	Cmp	Att	Cmp%	Yds	TD	TD%	Int	Int%	Lng	Y/A	AY/A	Y/C	Y/G	Rate	Sk	Yds
	Hugh McCullough	23	TB/P	10	6		32	100	32.0	443	2	2.0	12	12.0	0	4.4	−0.6	13.8	44.3	14.3		
	Lou Tomasetti	23	HB	11	6		13	47	27.7	140	1	2.1	7	14.9	0	3.0	−3.3	10.8	12.7	7.1		
	Coley McDonough	24		7	0		15	38	39.5	292	2	5.3	6	15.8	0	7.7	1.6	19.5	41.7	45.0		
	Ernie Wheeler	24		5	3		3	13	23.1	59	1	7.7	6	46.2	30	4.5	−14.7	19.7	11.8	32.1		
	Boyd Brumbaugh	24		6	4		3	7	42.9	121	2	28.6	1	14.3	17	17.3	16.6	40.3	20.2	89.9		
	Bill Davidson	24		7	2		1	7	14.3	8	0	0.0	0	0.0	8	1.1	1.1	8.0	1.1	39.6		
	Dick Nardi	24		3	2		2	5	40.0	12	0	0.0	1	20.0	0	2.4	−6.6	6.0	4.0	8.3		
	Bob Masters	28		4	1		1	3	33.3	9	0	0.0	1	33.3	9	3.0	−12.0	9.0	2.3	2.8		
	Jack Lee	22		5	0		0	1	0.0	0	0	0.0	0	0.0	0	0.0	0.0		0.0	39.6		
	Team Total	25.3		11			70	221	31.7	1084	8	3.6	34	15.4	30	4.9	−1.3	15.5	98.5	21.4		
	Opp Total			11			88	193	45.6	1368	10	5.2	11	5.7		7.1	5.6	15.5	124.4	63.1	0	0

Rushing and Receiving

No.		Age	Pos	G	GS	Rush Att	Rush Yds	Rush TD	Rush Lng	Rush Y/A	Rush Y/G	Rush A/G	Rec	Rec Yds	Rec Y/R	Rec TD	Rec Lng	Rec R/G	Rec Y/G	YScm
	Boyd Brumbaugh	24		6	4	86	282	2	0	3.3	47.0	14.3	4	90	22.5	1	0	0.7	15.0	372
	Hugh McCullough	23	TB/P	10	6	60	96	1	0	1.6	9.6	6.0	4	57	14.3	0	0	0.4	5.7	153
	Swede Johnston	29		8	2	59	220	2	0	3.7	27.5	7.4								220
	Sam Francis	26		5	3	55	171	1	0	3.1	34.2	11.0	1	5	5.0	0	5	0.2	1.0	176
	Lou Tomasetti	23	HB	11	6	49	86	1	0	1.8	7.8	4.5	4	22	5.5	0	0	0.4	2.0	108
	Carl Littlefield	23	FB	10	4	39	141	0	0	3.6	14.1	3.9	1	18	18.0	0	18	0.1	1.8	159
	Coley McDonough	24		7	0	23	63	0	0	2.7	9.0	3.3	1	3	3.0	1	3	0.1	0.4	66
	Bill Davidson	24		7	2	21	27	0	0	1.3	3.9	3.0	6	27	4.5	0	0	0.9	3.9	54
	Ernie Wheeler	24		5	3	15	8	0	0	0.5	1.6	3.0								8
	Bob Masters	28		4	1	9	39	0	0	4.3	9.8	2.3	2	12	6.0	0	0	0.5	3.0	51
	Dick Nardi	24		3	2	8	10	0	0	1.3	3.3	2.7								10
	Karl Schuelke	25		1	0	2	2	0	0	1.0	2.0	2.0								2
	Rink Bond	22	BB	11	11	1	4	0	4	4.0	0.4	0.1								4
	Jack Lee	22		5	0	1	−11	0	−11	−11.0	−2.2	0.2								−11
	Sam Boyd	25		11	4	0	0	0	0		0.0	0.0	21	423	20.1	2	0	1.9	38.5	423
	Bill Sortet	27	RE	11	8	0	0	0	0		0.0	0.0	16	196	12.3	1	0	1.5	17.8	196
	George Platukis	24	LE	11	6	0	0	0	0		0.0	0.0	7	170	24.3	3	63	0.6	15.5	170
	Bernie Scherer	26		9	3	0	0	0	0		0.0	0.0	2	49	24.5	0	0	0.2	5.4	49
	Frank Souchak	24		4	0	0	0	0	0		0.0	0.0	1	12	12.0	0	12	0.3	3.0	12
	Team Total	25.3		11		428	1138	7	4	2.7	103.5	38.9	70	1084	15.5	8	63	6.4	98.5	2222
	Opp Total			11		440	1701	18		3.9	154.6	40.0	88	1368	15.5	10		8.0	124.4	3069

1940 PITTSBURGH STEELERS: 2-7-2, 4TH IN EAST, TIED FOR 9TH IN NFL
Head Coach: Walt Kiesling

Week	Day	Date	OT	Rec	Opp	Score Tm	Score Opp	Offe 1stD	Offe TotYd	Offe PassY	Offe RushY	Offe TO	Defe 1stD	Defe TotYd	Defe PassY	Defe RushY	Defe TO
1	Sun	September 8	T	0-0-1	Chicago Cardinals	7	7	3	129	64	65	3	9	192	128	64	4
2	Sun	September 15	T	0-0-2	New York Giants	10	10	8	197	60	137	3	9	215	111	104	2
3	Sun	September 22	W	1-0-2	Detroit Lions	10	7	11	209	37	172	1	13	231	44	187	4
4	Sun	September 29	L	1-1-2	Brooklyn Dodgers	3	10	7	188	111	77	3	14	315	56	259	2
5	Sun	October 6	L	1-2-2	Washington Redskins	10	40	15	188	93	95	4	14	333	186	147	1
6	Sun	October 13	L	1-3-2	Brooklyn Dodgers	0	21	12	213	76	137	3	8	240	121	119	2
7	Sun	October 20	L	1-4-2	New York Giants	0	12	7	148	108	40	4	14	300	142	158	6
8	Sun	October 27	L	1-5-2	Green Bay Packers	3	24	9	95	34	61	5	13	296	120	176	3
9	Sun	November 3	L	1-6-2	Washington Redskins	10	37	10	289	194	95	1	11	371	204	167	1
10	Sun	November 10	W	2-6-2	Philadelphia Eagles	7	3	8	171	26	145	2	8	129	59	70	1
11	Thu	November 28	L	2-7-2	Philadelphia Eagles	0	7	5	130	65	65	6	8	120	67	53	1

Passing

No.		Age	Pos	G	GS	QBrec	Cmp	Att	Cmp%	Yds	TD	TD%	Int	Int%	Lng	Y/A	AY/A	Y/C	Y/G	Rate	Sk	Yds
	Billy Patterson	22	TB/P	11	9		34	117	29.1	529	3	2.6	15	12.8	0	4.5	−0.7	15.6	48.1	14.9		
	Tommy Thompson	24		11	2		9	28	32.1	145	1	3.6	3	10.7	31	5.2	1.1	16.1	13.2	22.8		
	Merl Condit*	23		10	2		2	15	13.3	33	0	0.0	2	13.3	0	2.2	−3.8	16.5	3.3	0.0		
	Coley McDonough	25		4	0		8	14	57.1	92	0	0.0	3	21.4	0	6.6	−3.1	11.5	23.0	37.5		
	Boyd Brumbaugh	25		8	4		2	7	28.6	46	0	0.0	1	14.3	0	6.6	0.1	23.0	5.8	14.9		
	Lou Tomasetti	24	HB	10	9		3	6	50.0	30	0	0.0	2	33.3	0	5.0	−10.0	10.0	3.0	25.0		
	George Kiick	23	FB	11	4		0	2	0.0	0	0	0.0	1	50.0	0	0.0	−22.5		0.0	0.0		
	Team Total	24.9		11			58	189	30.7	875	4	2.1	27	14.3	31	4.6	−1.4	15.1	79.5	14.4		
	Opp Total			11			83	192	43.2	1231	9	4.7	8	4.2		6.4	5.5	14.8	111.9	63.1	0	0

Rushing and Receiving

No.		Age	Pos	G	GS	Rush Att	Rush Yds	Rush TD	Rush Lng	Rush Y/A	Rush Y/G	Rush A/G	Rec	Rec Yds	Rec Y/R	Rec TD	Rec Lng	Rec R/G	Rec Y/G	YScm
	Billy Patterson	22	TB/P	11	9	87	171	0	0	2.0	15.5	7.9								171
	Lou Tomasetti	24	HB	10	9	68	246	1	0	3.6	24.6	6.8	6	129	21.5	1	26	0.6	12.9	375
	George Kiick	23	FB	11	4	66	212	0	0	3.2	19.3	6.0	3	22	7.3	0	0	0.3	2.0	234
	Merl Condit*	23		10	2	52	205	0	0	3.9	20.5	5.2	4	30	7.5	1	0	0.4	3.0	235
	Swede Johnston	30		10	3	41	113	0	0	2.8	11.3	4.1								113
	Tommy Thompson	24		11	2	40	39	0	0	1.0	3.5	3.6	4	55	13.8	0	0	0.4	5.0	94
	Boyd Brumbaugh	25		8	4	32	79	0	0	2.5	9.9	4.0	1	0	0.0	0	0	0.1	0.0	79
	Coley McDonough	25		4	0	15	33	1	0	2.2	8.3	3.8								33
	John Noppenberg	23		9	4	2	4	0	0	2.0	0.4	0.2	4	74	18.5	0	0	0.4	8.2	78
	George Platukis	25	LE	11	11	0	0	0	0		0.0	0.0	15	290	19.3	2	45	1.4	26.4	290
	Bill Sortet	28	RE	11	8	0	0	0	0		0.0	0.0	7	112	16.0	0	0	0.6	10.2	112
	Hank Bruder	33	BB	8	7	0	0	0	0		0.0	0.0	5	49	9.8	0	0	0.6	6.1	49
	Walt Kichefski	24		11	3	0	0	0	0		0.0	0.0	4	26	6.5	0	0	0.4	2.4	26
	John Klumb	24		4	0	0	0	0	0		0.0	0.0	3	76	25.3	0	0	0.8	19.0	76
	Ev Fisher	26		4	0	0	0	0	0		0.0	0.0	2	12	6.0	0	0	0.5	3.0	12
	Team Total	24.9		11		403	1102	2	0	2.7	100.2	36.6	58	875	15.1	4	45	5.3	79.5	1977
	Opp Total			11		438	1491	12		3.4	135.5	39.8	83	1231	14.8	9		7.5	111.9	2722

Defense

No.		Age	Pos	G	GS	Sk	Def Int	Def Yds	Def TD	Def Lng	Def PD	Fumb FF	Fumb Fmb	Fumb FR	Fumb Yds	Fumb TD	Tack Tkl	Tack Ast	Sfty
	Tommy Thompson	24		11	2		3	23	0	0	0								
	Merl Condit*	23		10	2		2	7	0	0	0								
	Armand Niccolai	29	RT/K	11	11		1	5	0	5	0								
	John Noppenberg	23		9	4		1	27	0	27	0								
	Frank Sullivan	28		9	2		1	0	0	0	0								
	Team Total	24.9		11			8	62	0	27	0								
	Opp Total			11									0	−15					1

1941 PITTSBURGH STEELERS: 1-9-1, LAST IN EAST AND NFL

Coaches: Bert Bell, Aldo Donelli, and Walt Kiesling

						Score		Offe					Defe				
Week	Day	Date	OT	Rec	Opp	Tm	Opp	1stD	TotYd	PassY	RushY	TO	1stD	TotYd	PassY	RushY	TO
1	Sun	September 7	L	0-1	Cleveland Rams	14	17	8	199	58	141	7	10	194	125	69	3
2	Sun	September 21	L	0-2	Philadelphia Eagles	7	10	7	169	45	124	3	8	192	65	127	3
3	Sun	October 5	L	0-3	New York Giants	10	37	7	177	113	64	6	9	207	131	76	3
4	Sun	October 12	L	0-4	Washington Redskins	20	24	9	190	163	27	3	5	156	83	73	1
5	Sun	October 19	L	0-5	New York Giants	7	28	5	214	114	100	4	13	206	56	150	2
6	Sun	October 26	L	0-6	Chicago Bears	7	34	9	159	42	117	4	17	410	129	281	3
7	Sun	November 2	L	0-7	Washington Redskins	3	23	4	47	24	23	5	16	340	132	208	7
8	Sun	November 9	T	0-7-1	Philadelphia Eagles	7	7	5	155	10	145		10	248	75	173	1
9	Sun	November 16	W	1-7-1	Brooklyn Dodgers	14	7	5	205		205		9	278	175	103	3
10	Sun	November 23	L	1-8-1	Green Bay Packers	7	54	11	266	56	210	10	13	271	116	155	
11	Sun	November 30	L	1-9-1	Brooklyn Dodgers	7	35	5	112	25	87	7	8	313	123	190	4

Passing

No.		Age	Pos	G	GS	QBrec	Cmp	Att	Cmp%	Yds	TD	TD%	Int	Int%	Lng	Y/A	AY/A	Y/C	Y/G	Rate	Sk	Yds
	Boyd Brumbaugh	26	TB/KR	10	7		13	41	31.7	260	2	4.9	8	19.5	72	6.3	−1.5	20.0	26.0	31.6		
	Coley McDonough	26		6	1		12	41	29.3	200	1	2.4	7	17.1	59	4.9	−2.3	16.7	33.3	16.0		
	Dick Riffle*	26	FB	10	7		8	39	20.5	88	1	2.6	9	23.1	22	2.3	−7.6	11.0	8.8	8.5		
	Art Jones*	22	WB/PR/P	11	9		6	23	26.1	86	0	0.0	3	13.0	19	3.7	−2.1	14.3	7.8	3.1		
	Les Dodson	25		2	0		1	8	12.5	7	0	0.0	3	37.5	7	0.9	−16.0	7.0	3.5	0.0		
	Al Donelli	24		7	0		2	8	25.0	13	1	12.5	3	37.5	10	1.6	−12.8	6.5	1.9	39.6		
	John Noppenberg	24		4	2		0	3	0.0	0	0	0.0	0	0.0	0	0.0	0.0		0.0	39.6		
	Ben Starret	24		4	0		0	2	0.0	0	0	0.0	1	50.0	0	0.0	−22.5		0.0	0.0		
	Elmer Hackney	25		11	4		0	1	0.0	0	0	0.0	0	0.0	0	0.0	0.0		0.0	39.6		
	Joe Hoague	23		10	1		0	1	0.0	0	0	0.0	0	0.0	0	0.0	0.0		0.0	39.6		
	Frank Zoppetti	25		4	0		0	1	0.0	0	0	0.0	0	0.0	0	0.0	0.0		0.0	39.6		
	Team Total	24.7		11			42	168	25.0	654	5	3.0	34	20.2	72	3.9	−4.6	15.6	59.5	13.6		
	Opp Total			11			84	189	44.4	1168	10	5.3	19	10.1		6.2	2.7	13.9	106.2	42.9	0	0

Rushing and Receiving

No.		Age	Pos	G	GS	Rush							Receiving							YScm
						Att	Yds	TD	Lng	Y/A	Y/G	A/G	Rec	Yds	Y/R	TD	Lng	R/G	Y/G	
	Dick Riffle*	26	FB	10	7	109	388	1	54	3.6	38.8	10.9	2	24	12.0	1	14	0.2	2.4	412
	Boyd Brumbaugh	26	TB/KR	10	7	68	114	2	8	1.7	11.4	6.8	1	1	1.0	0	1	0.1	0.1	115
	Elmer Hackney	25		11	4	63	253	1	31	4.0	23.0	5.7	1	10	10.0	0	10	0.1	0.9	263
	Art Jones*	22	WB/PR/P	11	9	62	239	4	34	3.9	21.7	5.6	4	121	30.3	1	59	0.4	11.0	360
	Joe Hoague	23		10	1	33	112	1	29	3.4	11.2	3.3	2	21	10.5	1	14	0.2	2.1	133
	Coley McDonough	26		6	1	20	64	0	28	3.2	10.7	3.3								64
	Al Donelli	24		7	0	15	20	0	7	1.3	2.9	2.1	2	25	12.5	0	14	0.3	3.6	45
	John Noppenberg	24		4	2	10	21	0	8	2.1	5.3	2.5								21
	Ben Starret	24		4	0	7	9	0	15	1.3	2.3	1.8								9
	Jay Arnold	29		10	4	2	4	0	4	2.0	0.4	0.2	1	5	5.0	0	5	0.1	0.5	9
	Les Dodson	25		2	0	2	−4	0	6	−2.0	−2.0	1.0								−4
	Rocco Pirro	25		11	1	1	1	0	1	1.0	0.1	0.1	2	31	15.5	0	19	0.2	2.8	32
	Dick Dolly	24		9	4	1	2	0	2	2.0	0.2	0.1								2
	Don Looney	24		9	0	0	0	0	0		0.0	0.0	10	186	18.6	1	66	1.1	20.7	186
	Joe Wendlick	26	RE	10	6	0	0	0	0		0.0	0.0	7	84	12.0	0	19	0.7	8.4	84
	Walt Kichefski	25	re	11	5	0	0	0	0		0.0	0.0	5	111	22.2	1	72	0.5	10.1	111
	George Platukis	26	LE	11	7	0	0	0	0		0.0	0.0	2	15	7.5	0	11	0.2	1.4	15
	Dick Bassi	26	RG	11	11	0	0	0	0		0.0	0.0	1	6	6.0	0	6	0.1	0.5	6
	Elmer Kolberg	25		4	0	0	0	0	0		0.0	0.0	1	2	2.0	0	2	0.3	0.5	2
	John Patrick	23	BB	11	8	0	0	0	0		0.0	0.0	1	12	12.0	0	12	0.1	1.1	12
	Team Total	24.7		11		393	1223	9	54	3.1	111.2	35.7	42	654	15.6	5	72	3.8	59.5	1877
	Opp Total			11		426	1556	17		3.7	141.5	38.7	84	1168	13.9	10		7.6	106.2	2724

Defense

No.		Age	Pos	G	GS	Sk	Int	Yds	TD	Lng	PD	FF	Fmb	FR	Yds	TD	Tkl	Ast	Sfty
	Art Jones*	22	WB/PR/P	11	9		7	35	0	12	0								
	Dick Riffle*	26	FB	10	7		6	93	0	29	0								
	Jay Arnold	29		10	4		1	0	0	0	0								
	Chuck Cherundolo*	25	C	11	9		1	13	0	13	0								
	Al Donelli	24		7	0		1	18	0	18	0								
	John Patrick	23	BB	11	8		1	25	0	25	0								
	Rocco Pirro	25		11	1		1	2	0	2	0								
	John Schiechl	24		4	2		1	0	0	0	0								
	Team Total	24.7		11			19	186	0	29	0								
	Opp Total			11									17	9					1

1942 PITTSBURGH STEELERS: 7-4-0, 2ND IN EAST, 4TH IN NFL
Head Coach: Walt Kiesling

Week	Day	Date	OT	Rec	Opp	Tm	Opp	1stD	TotYd	PassY	RushY	TO	1stD	TotYd	PassY	RushY	TO
1	Sun	September 13	L	0-1	Philadelphia Eagles	14	24	15	193	75	118	2	14	328	169	159	2
2	Sun	September 20	L	0-2	Washington Redskins	14	28	13	165	34	131	3	10	205	108	97	1
3	Sun	October 4	W	1-2	New York Giants	13	10	13	209	41	168	2	9	150	27	123	1
4	Sun	October 11	W	2-2	Brooklyn Dodgers	7	0	9	167	167	2	7	129	43	86	4	
5	Sun	October 18	W	3-2	Philadelphia Eagles	14	0	9	221	13	208	1	11	207	106	101	2
6	Sun	October 25	L	3-3	Washington Redskins	0	14	14	247	134	113	11	193	126	67	1	
7	Sun	November 1	W	4-3	New York Giants	17	9	12	235	40	195	4	10	216	80	136	3
8	Sun	November 8	W	5-3	Detroit Lions	35	7	15	315	48	267	1	6	189	77	112	4
9	Sun	November 22	W	6-3	Chicago Cardinals	19	3	8	266	40	226	1	12	258	183	75	7
10	Sun	November 29	W	7-3	Brooklyn Dodgers	13	0	5	181	7	174	2	7	100	100		
11	Sun	December 6	L	7-4	Green Bay Packers	21	24	17	340	254	86	3	17	414	260	154	2

Passing

No.		Age	Pos	G	GS	QBrec	Cmp	Att	Cmp%	Yds	TD	TD%	Int	Int%	Lng	Y/A	AY/A	Y/C	Y/G	Rate	Sk	Yds
	Bill Dudley*+	23	TB/PR/KR	11	11		35	94	37.2	438	2	2.1	5	5.3	38	4.7	2.7	12.5	39.8	37.5		
	Andy Tomasic	23		11	0		11	54	20.4	174	0	0.0	5	9.3	41	3.2	-0.9	15.8	15.8	1.9		
	Dick Riffle	27	FB	11	11		3	8	37.5	64	0	0.0	1	12.5	27	8.0	2.4	21.3	5.8	27.1		
	Curt Sandig	24	P/HB	11	8		2	4	50.0	10	0	0.0	0	0.0	8	2.5	2.5	5.0	0.9	56.2		
	Joe Hoague	24		11	0		0	1	0.0	0	0	0.0	0	0.0	0	0.0	0.0		0.0	39.6		
	Team Total	24.3		11			51	161	31.7	686	2	1.2	11	6.8	41	4.3	1.4	13.5	62.4	21.9		
	Opp Total			11			100	211	47.4	1183	9	4.3	21	10.0		5.6	2.0	11.8	107.5	39.6	0	0

Rushing and Receiving

No.		Age	Pos	G	GS	Rush Att	Yds	TD	Lng	Y/A	Y/G	A/G	Receiving Rec	Yds	Y/R	TD	Lng	R/G	Y/G	YScm
	Bill Dudley*+	23	TB/PR/KR	11	11	162	696	5	66	4.3	63.3	14.7	1	24	24.0	0	24	0.1	2.2	720
	Dick Riffle	27	FB	11	11	115	467	4	44	4.1	42.5	10.5	3	50	16.7	0	31	0.3	4.5	517
	Joe Hoague	24		11	0	65	168	1	42	2.6	15.3	5.9	168							
	Andy Tomasic	23		11	0	60	214	0	34	3.6	19.5	5.5	1	27	27.0	0	27	0.1	2.5	241
	Curt Sandig	24	P/HB	11	8	50	116	3	39	2.3	10.5	4.5	6	103	17.2	0	38	0.5	9.4	219
	George Gonda	23		5	1	17	147	2	68	8.6	29.4	3.4	1	7	7.0	0	7	0.2	1.4	154
	John Binotto	23		7	1	16	57	0	30	3.6	8.1	2.3								57
	Al Donelli	25		4	1	2	−4	0	0	−2.0	−1.0	0.5								−4
	Hubbard Law	21		11	0	1	6	0	6	6.0	0.5	0.1								6
	Walt Kichefski	26	RE	11	11	0	0	0	0		0.0	0.0	15	189	12.6	0	26	1.4	17.2	189
	Don Looney	25		3	1	0	0	0	0		0.0	0.0	7	59	8.4	1	14	2.3	19.7	59
	Vern Martin	22	BB	11	11	0	0	0	0		0.0	0.0	7	64	9.1	1	24	0.6	5.8	64
	Tom Brown	21		9	0	0	0	0	0		0.0	0.0	4	69	17.3	0	30	0.4	7.7	69
	Tony Bova	25	LE	11	10	0	0	0	0		0.0	0.0	3	37	12.3	0	17	0.3	3.4	37
	Russ Cotton	27		11	0	0	0	0	0		0.0	0.0	2	58	29.0	0	41	0.2	5.3	58
	John Woudenberg*	24	RT	11	11	0	0	0	0		0.0	0.0	1	−1	−1.0	0	−1	0.1	−0.1	−1
	Team Total	24.3		11		488	1867	15	68	3.8	169.7	44.4	51	686	13.5	2	41	4.6	62.4	2553
	Opp Total			11		366	1205	6		3.3	109.5	33.3	100	1183	11.8	9		9.1	107.5	2388

Defense

No.		Age	Pos	G	GS	Sk	Def Int	Yds	TD	Lng	PD	Fumb FF	Fmb	FR	Yds	TD	Tack Tkl	Ast	Sfty
	Curt Sandig	24	P/HB	11	8		5	94	0	42	0								
	Dick Riffle	27	FB	11	11		4	59	0	51	0								
	Bill Dudley*+	23	TB/PR/KR	11	11		3	60	0	25	0								
	Andy Tomasic	23		11	0		2	75	0	41	0								
	Tony Bova	25	LE	11	10		1	16	0	16	0								
	Chuck Cherundolo*	26	C	11	11		1	3	0	3	0								
	Russ Cotton	27		11	0		1	0	0	0	0								
	George Gonda	23		5	1		1	37	0	37	0								
	Joe Hoague	24		11	0		1	15	0	15	0								
	Hubbard Law	21		11	0		1	13	0	13	0								
	Jack Sanders	25	LG	9	9		1	8	0	8	0								
	Team Total	24.3		11			21	380	0	51	0								
	Opp Total			11									19	12					

1943 PHI/PITT EAGLES/STEELERS: 5-4-1, 3RD IN EAST, 5TH IN NFL
Co-coaches: Walt Kiesling and Greasy Neale

Week	Day	Date	OT	Rec	Opp	Score Tm	Opp	Offe 1stD	TotYd	PassY	RushY	TO	Defe 1stD	TotYd	PassY	RushY	TO
1	Sat	October 2	W	1-0	Brooklyn Dodgers	17	0	10	300	98	202	1	8	93	126	−33	4
2	Sat	October 9	W	2-0	New York Giants	28	14	14	303	112	191	8	6	92	50	42	3
3	Sun	October 17	L	2-1	Chicago Bears	21	48	12	298	181	117	3	17	396	186	210	3
4	Sun	October 24	L	2-2	New York Giants	14	42	12	242	178	64	2	10	199	127	72	
5	Sun	October 31	W	3-2	Chicago Cardinals	34	13	16	241	74	167	3	9	206	175	31	5
6	Sun	November 7	T	3-2-1	Washington Redskins	14	14	10	169	89	80	3	11	209	147	62	6
7	Sun	November 14	L	3-3-1	Brooklyn Dodgers	7	13	18	249	52	197	2	5	176	74	102	
8	Sun	November 21	W	4-3-1	Detroit Lions	35	34	17	358	96	262	2	12	379	194	185	5
9	Sun	November 28	W	5-3-1	Washington Redskins	27	14	19	390	82	308	3	10	269	211	58	2
10	Sun	December 5	L	5-4-1	Green Bay Packers	28	38	10	318	176	142	8	8	278	103	175	2

Passing

No.		Age	Pos	G	GS	QBrec	Cmp	Att	Cmp%	Yds	TD	TD%	Int	Int%	Lng	Y/A	AY/A	Y/C	Y/G	Rate	Sk	Yds
	Roy Zimmerman	25	QB/P/K	10	9		43	124	34.7	846	9	7.3	17	13.7	60	6.8	2.1	19.7	84.6	44.0		
	Allie Sherman	20		9	0		16	37	43.2	208	2	5.4	1	2.7	49	5.6	5.5	13.0	23.1	68.3		
	Johnny Butler	25	PR/LH	10	9		6	13	46.2	84	0	0.0	1	7.7	26	6.5	3.0	14.0	8.4	35.4		
	Ernie Steele	26	KR/lh	10	1		0	1	0.0	0	0	0.0	1	100.0	0	0.0	−45.0		0.0	0.0		
	Team Total	24.9		10			65	175	37.1	1138	11	6.3	20	11.4	60	6.5	2.6	17.5	113.8	41.5		
	Opp Total			10			102	221	46.2	1393	15	6.8	22	10.0		6.3	3.2	13.7	139.3	49.8	0	0

Rushing and Receiving

No.		Age	Pos	G	GS	Rush							Receiving							YScm
						Att	Yds	TD	Lng	Y/A	Y/G	A/G	Rec	Yds	Y/R	TD	Lng	R/G	Y/G	
	Jack Hinkle	26	RH	10	9	116	571	3	56	4.9	57.1	11.6	1	3	3.0	0	3	0.1	0.3	574
	Johnny Butler	25	PR/LH	10	9	87	362	3	69	4.2	36.2	8.7	3	63	21.0	0	37	0.3	6.3	425
	Ernie Steele	26	KR/lh	10	1	85	409	4	47	4.8	40.9	8.5	9	168	18.7	2	60	0.9	16.8	577
	Bob Thurbon	25		10	1	71	291	5	25	4.1	29.1	7.1	6	100	16.7	1	43	0.6	10.0	391
	Roy Zimmerman	25	QB/P/K	10	9	33	−41	1	12	−1.2	−4.1	3.3								−41
	Ben Kish	26	FB	10	9	22	50	0	11	2.3	5.0	2.2	8	67	8.4	1	17	0.8	6.7	117
	Allie Sherman	20		9	0	17	−20	1	5	−1.2	−2.2	1.9								−20
	Charlie Gauer	22		9	1	12	69	0	25	5.8	7.7	1.3	2	18	9.0	0	14	0.2	2.0	87
	Ted Laux	25		4	0	9	23	0	12	2.6	5.8	2.3	2	19	9.5	0	15	0.5	4.8	42
	Steve Sader			2	0	3	5	0	16	1.7	2.5	1.5								5
	Bob Masters	32		3	0	2	6	0	0	3.0	2.0	0.7								6
	Tony Bova	26	LE	10	6	1	11	0	111	1.0	1.1	0.1	17	419	24.6	5	51	1.7	41.9	430
	Dean Steward	20		6	0	1	−6	0	−6	−6.0	−1.0	0.2								−6
	Larry Cabrelli	26	RE	10	9	0	0	0	0		0.0	0.0	12	199	16.6	1	49	1.2	19.9	199
	Tom Miller	25		8	1	0	0	0	0		0.0	0.0	3	60	20.0	1	32	0.4	7.5	60
	Bill Hewitt	34		6	4	0	0	0	0		0.0	0.0	2	22	11.0	0	11	0.3	3.7	22
	Team Total	24.9		10		459	1730	17	69	3.8	173.0	45.9	65	1138	17.5	11	60	6.5	113.8	2868
	Opp Total			10		312	793	15		2.5		79.3	31.2	102	1393	13.7	15		10.2	139.3	2186

Defense

No.		Age	Pos	G	GS	Sk	Def					Fumb					Tack		
							Int	Yds	TD	Lng	PD	FF	Fmb	FR	Yds	TD	Tkl	Ast	Sfty
	Ben Kish	26	FB	10	9		5	114	1	86	0								
	Roy Zimmerman	25	QB/P/K	10	9		5	19	0	10	0								
	Jack Hinkle	26	RH	10	9		4	98	0	91	0								
	Larry Cabrelli	26	RE	10	9		1	24	1	24	0								
	Enio Conti	30		10	1		1	0	0	0	0								
	Charlie Gauer	22		9	1		1	0	0	0	0								
	Ray Graves	25	C	10	9		1	15	0	15	0								
	Ted Laux	25		4	0		1	24	0	24	0								
	Tom Miller	25		8	1		1	0	0	0	0								
	Bob Thurbon	25		10	1		1	3	0	3	0								
	Al Wukits	26		10	1		1	7	0	7	0								
	Team Total	24.9		10			22	304	2	91	0								
	Opp Total			10									20	12					

1944 CHI/PITT CARDINALS/STEELERS: 0-10, LAST IN WEST, TIED FOR LAST IN NFL
Head Coaches: Walt Kiesling and Phil Handler

Week	Day	Date	OT	Rec	Opp	Score Tm	Score Opp	Offe 1stD	TotYd	PassY	RushY	TO	Defe 1stD	TotYd	PassY	RushY	TO
1	Sun	September 24	L	0-1	Cleveland Rams	28	30	11	310	182	128	5	6	232	136	96	4
2	Sun	October 8	L	0-2	Green Bay Packers	7	34	8	187	126	61	6	15	388	241	147	3
3	Sun	October 15	L	0-3	Chicago Bears	7	34	4	115	26	89	4	13	285	154	131	3
4	Sun	October 22	L	0-4	New York Giants	0	23	10	215	103	112	7	15	333	109	224	6
5	Sun	October 29	L	0-5	Washington Redskins	20	42	19	367	180	187	6	8	351	211	140	2
6	Sun	November 5	L	0-6	Detroit Lions	6	27	13	284	112	172	9	12	277	194	83	5
7	Sun	November 12	L	0-7	Detroit Lions	7	21	17	338	177	161	5	8	119	41	78	1
8	Sun	November 19	L	0-8	Cleveland Rams	6	33	12	210	120	90	5	9	331	196	135	2
9	Sun	November 26	L	0-9	Green Bay Packers	20	35	5	157	138	19	4	11	277	190	87	1
10	Sun	December 3	L	0-10	Chicago Bears	7	49	10	94	96	−2	2	12	412	104	308	1

Passing

No.		Age	Pos	G	GS	QBrec	Cmp	Att	Cmp%	Yds	TD	TD%	Int	Int%	Lng	Y/A	AY/A	Y/C	Y/G	Rate	Sk	Yds
	John Grigas	24	FB/KR	9	9	−50	131	38.2	690	6	4.6	21	16.0	72	5.3	−1.0	13.8	76.7	31.5			
	John McCarthy	28	P	7	2	−20	67	29.9	250	0	0.0	13	19.4	38	3.7	−5.0	12.5	35.7	3.0			
	Tony Bova	27	LE	9	8	−6	30	20.0	96	0	0.0	1	3.3	34	3.2	1.7	16.0	10.7	26.5			
	Coley McDonough	29		−2	0	−10	23	43.5	208	2	8.7	4	17.4	67	9.0	3.0	20.8	104.0	65.4			
	Walt Masters	37		−3	0	−1	7	14.3	13	0	0.0	2	28.6	13	1.9	−11.0	13.0	4.3	0.0			
	Team Total	27.3		10		258	87	33.7	1257	8	3.1	41	15.9	72	4.9	−1.7	14.4	125.7	21.2			

Rushing and Receiving

No.		Age	Pos	G	GS	Rush Att	Rush Yds	Rush TD	Rush Lng	Rush Y/A	Rush Y/G	Rush A/G	Rec	Rec Yds	Rec Y/R	Rec TD	Rec Lng	Rec R/G	Rec Y/G	YScm
	John Grigas	24	FB/KR	9	9	185	610	3	29	3.3	67.8	20.6	2	33	16.5	0	36	0.2	3.7	643
	Bob Thurbon	26	RH	10	7	69	185	4	25	2.7	18.5	6.9	7	134	19.1	1	37	0.7	13.4	319
	Johnny Butler	26	HB	3	3	20	48	0	14	2.4	16.0	6.7	3	109	36.3	2	67	1.0	36.3	157
	George Magulick	25	LH/PR	9	6	17	102	0	49	6.0	11.3	1.9	6	50	8.3	0	2	0.7	5.6	152
	Bernie Semes	25	HB	8	2	17	38	0	3	2.2	4.8	2.1	3	22	7.3	0	10	0.4	2.8	60
	Ed Rucinski	28	LE	10	6	16	72	0	22	4.5	7.2	1.6	22	284	12.9	1	40	2.2	28.4	356
	Tony Bova	27	LE	9	8	14	−22	0	3	−1.6	−2.4	1.6	19	287	15.1	2	46	2.1	31.9	265
	John Popovich	26	HB	6	1	8	29	0	9	3.6	4.8	1.3	3	−1	−0.3	0	1	0.5	−0.2	28
	John McCarthy	28	P	7	2	6	−49	0	−8	−8.2	−7.0	0.9								−49
	Walt Rankin	25	QB	10	8	4	13	0	6	3.3	1.3	0.4	4	18	4.5	0	8	0.4	1.8	31
	Coley McDonough	29		2	0	3	7	0	4	2.3	3.5	1.5								7
	Walt Masters	37		3	0	1	−14	0	−14	−14.0	−4.7	0.3								−14
	Don Currivan	24		10	0	0	0	0	0	0.0	0.0	7	163	23.3	2	72	0.7	16.3	163	2
	Walt Kichefski	28	RE	10	8	0	0	0	0	0.0	0.0	6	85	14.2	0	34	0.6	8.5	85	0
	Clint Wager	24		8	0	0	0	0	0	0.0	0.0	5	73	14.6	0	38	0.6	9.1	73	0
	Team Total	27.3		10		360	1019	7	49	2.8	101.9	36.0	87	1257	14.4	8	72	8.7	125.7	2276
	Opp Total			10		366	1381	23		3.8	138.1	36.6	98	1575	16.1	22		9.8	157.5	2956

1945 PITTSBURGH STEELERS: 2-8-0, LAST IN EAST, 5TH IN NFL
Head Coach: Jim Leonard

Week	Day	Date	OT	Rec	Opp	Score Tm	Opp	Offe 1stD	TotYd	PassY	RushY	TO	Defe 1stD	TotYd	PassY	RushY	TO
1	Tue	September 25	L	0-1	Bos/Bkn Yanks/Tigers	7	28	12	135	113	22	6	10	331	117	214	4
2	Sun	October 7	L	0-2	New York Giants	6	34	12	134	28	106	5	14	337	246	91	
3	Sun	October 14	L	0-3	Washington Redskins	0	14	6	119	33	86	2	22	376	227	149	2
4	Sun	October 21	W	1-3	New York Giants	21	7	10	224	128	96		11	222	128	94	3
5	Sun	October 28	L	1-4	Bos/Bkn Yanks/Tigers	6	10	11	193	133	60	5	3	73	59	14	2
6	Sun	November 4	L	1-5	Philadelphia Eagles	3	45	5	141	108	33	5	12	425	225	200	2
7	Sun	November 11	W	2-5	Chicago Cardinals	23	0	4	171		171	1	5	83	26	57	4
8	Sun	November 18	L	2-6	Philadelphia Eagles	6	30	13	194	52	142	2	15	277	106	171	3
9	Sun	November 25	L	2-7	Chicago Bears	7	28	9	131	9	122	3	14	525	243	282	2
10	Sun	December 2	L	2-8	Washington Redskins	0	24	10	156	46	110	1	10	320	211	109	5

Passing

No.		Age	Pos	G	GS	QBrec	Cmp	Att	Cmp%	Yds	TD	TD%	Int	Int%	Lng	Y/A	AY/A	Y/C	Y/G	Rate	Sk	Yds
	Buzz Warren	29	PR/KR/tb	8	4		36	92	39.1	368	0	0.0	10	10.9	47	4.0	−0.9	10.2	46.0	11.8		
	Bill Dudley	26	TB	4	4		10	32	31.3	58	0	0.0	2	6.3	32	1.8	−1.0	5.8	14.5	14.6		
	Ed Stofko	25		2	1		7	17	41.2	94	0	0.0	4	23.5	26	5.5	−5.1	13.4	47.0	19.9		
	Toimi Jarvi	25		1	0		4	10	40.0	50	0	0.0	3	30.0	21	5.0	−8.5	12.5	50.0	16.7		
	Al Postus	25		2	0		2	5	40.0	73	0	0.0	1	20.0	52	14.6	5.6	36.5	36.5	47.9		
	Jackie Lowther	23		2	2		0	4	0.0	0	0	0.0	1	25.0	0	0.0	−11.3		0.0	0.0		
	Paul Duhart	25		2	2		1	3	33.3	1	0	0.0	0	0.0	1	0.3	0.3	1.0	0.5	42.4		
	Tony Bova	28	HB	10	5		0	1	0.0	0	0	0.0	0	0.0	0	0.0	0.0		0.0	39.6		
	John Petchel	26		9	2		1	1	100.0	8	0	0.0	0	0.0	8	8.0	8.0	8.0	0.9	100.0		
	Team Total	25.1		10			61	165	37.0	652	0	0.0	21	12.7	52	4.0	−1.8	10.7	65.2	9.8		
	Opp Total			10			103	187	55.1	1617	14	7.5	13	7.0		8.6	7.0	15.7	161.7	80.0	0	0

Rushing and Receiving

No.		Age	Pos	G	GS	Rush Att	Yds	TD	Lng	Y/A	Y/G	A/G	Rec Rec	Yds	Y/R	TD	Lng	R/G	Y/G	YScm
	Buzz Warren	29	PR/KR/tb	8	4	95	292	2	75	3.1	36.5	11.9	1	−1	−1.0	0	−1	0.1	−0.1	291
	John Lucente	23	FB	10	5	82	242	1	18	3.0	24.2	8.2	11	45	4.1	0	23	1.1	4.5	287
	Bill Dudley	26	TB	4	4	57	204	3	32	3.6	51.0	14.3								204
	Art Jones	26		7	2	16	64	0	20	4.0	9.1	2.3	5	8	1.6	0	6	0.7	1.1	72
	George Kiick	28		6	3	15	45	1	9	3.0	7.5	2.5	1	−2	−2.0	0	−2	0.2	−0.3	43
	Jackie Lowther	23		2	2	15	54	0	17	3.6	27.0	7.5								54
	Pepper Petrella	25		3	1	15	33	0	11	2.2	11.0	5.0								33
	Ed Stofko	25		2	1	13	−16	0	6	−1.2	−8.0	6.5								−16
	Paul Duhart	25		2	2	11	7	1	0	0.6	3.5	5.5								7
	Allen Nichols	29		1	1	10	5	0	9	0.5	5.0	10.0								5
	Toimi Jarvi	25		1	0	9	24	0	11	2.7	24.0	9.0								24
	Tony Bova	28	HB	10	5	6	11	0	5	1.8	1.1	0.6	15	215	14.3	0	52	1.5	21.5	226
	Leon Pense	23	BB	10	8	6	1	0	1	0.2	0.1	0.6	1	32	32.0	0	32	0.1	3.2	33
	Sid Tinsley	25	P	9	0	5	3	0	4	0.6	0.3	0.6								3
	Jack Itzel	21		10	0	4	11	0	5	2.8	1.1	0.4	1	4	4.0	0	4	0.1	0.4	15
	John Popovich	27		1	0	4	−8	0	4	−2.0	−8.0	4.0								−8
	John Petchel	26		9	2	2	2	0	15	1.0	0.2	0.2	2	25	12.5	0	21	0.2	2.8	27
	Al Postus	25		2		0	2	4	0	12	2.0	2.0	1.0							4
	John Naioti	24		6	1	1	−17	0	−17	−17.0	−2.8	0.2	2	14	7.0	0	8	0.3	2.3	−3
	Morgan Tiller	27		10	0	0	0	0	0	0.0	0.0		10	146	14.6	0	35	1.0	14.6	146
	Dick Dolly	28	LE	10	9	0	0	0	0	0.0	0.0		8	122	15.3	0	47	0.8	12.2	122

No.		Age	Pos	G	GS	Rush							Receiving							YScm
						Att	Yds	TD	Lng	Y/A	Y/G	A/G	Rec	Yds	Y/R	TD	Lng	R/G	Y/G	
	Frank Kimble	28		9	3	0	0	0	0		0.0	0.0	2	16	8.0	0	13	0.2	1.8	16
	Al Olszewski	25		1	0	0	0	0	0		0.0	0.0	2	28	14.0	0	22	2.0	28.0	28
	Team Total	25.1		10		368	961	8	75	2.6	96.1	36.8	61	652	10.7	0	52	6.1	65.2	1613
	Opp Total			10		363	1374	16		3.8	137.4	36.3	103	1617	15.7	14		10.3	161.7	2991

Defense

No.		Age	Pos	G	GS	Sk	Def					Fumb					Tack		Sfty
							Int	Yds	TD	Lng	PD	FF	Fmb	FR	Yds	TD	Tkl	Ast	
	John Lucente	23	FB	10	5							0	8	6	16	0			
	Leon Pense	23	BB	10	8		3	39	0	30	0	0	1	3	0	0			
	Buzz Warren	29	PR/KR/tb	8	4		1	19	0	19	0	0	4	2	9	0			
	Tony Bova	28	HB	10	5							0	1	3	−4	0			
	Elmer Merkovsky	28	LG	10	10							0	0	4	−2	0			
	Bill Dudley	26	TB	4	4		2	47	0	26	0	0	1	0	0	0			
	John Perko	31	RG	10	10		0	1	2	0	0								
	Pepper Petrella	25		3	1		1	8	0	8	0	0	2	0	0	0			
	Sid Tinsley	25	P	9	0		1	−2	0	−2	0	0	1	1	−3	0			
	Ted Doyle	31	RT	10	10		1	50	1	50	0	0	0	1	0	0			
	Art Jones	26		7	2		1	17	0	17	0	0	1	0	0	0			
	John Naioti	24		6	1							0	1	1	−17	0			
	Allen Nichols	29		1	1							0	1	1	0	0			
	John Popovich	27		1	0							0	1	1	−10	0			
	Ed Stofko	25		2	1							0	1	1	−16	0			
	Al Wukits	28		3	1							0	2	0	0	0			
	Chuck Cherundolo	29	C	6	5		1	17	0	17	0								
	Joe Coomer	27	lt	9	5							0	0	1	0	0			
	Jack Itzel	21		10	0		1	13	0	13	0								
	Toimi Jarvi	25		1	0							0	0	1	−17	0			
	John Petchel	26		9	2		1	4	0	4	0								
	Joe Pierre	25	RE	10	7							0	0	1	0	0			
	Glen Stough	24	LT	10	5							0	0	1	0	0			
	Morgan Tiller	27		10	0							0	0	1	23	0			
	Si Titus	27		9	3							0	0	1	11	0			
	Team Total	25.1		10			13	212	1	50	0	0	26	32	−10	0			
	Opp Total			10									40	26					

1946 PITTSBURGH STEELERS: 5-5-1, TIED FOR 3RD IN EAST, TIED FOR 7TH IN NFL
Head Coach: Jock Sutherland

Week	Day	Date		OT	Rec	Opp	Score		Offe					Defe				
							Tm	Opp	1stD	TotYd	PassY	RushY	TO	1stD	TotYd	PassY	RushY	TO
1	Fri	September 20	W		1-0	Chicago Cardinals	14	7	8	137	25	112	2	11	186	79	107	4
2	Sun	September 29	T		1-0-1	Washington Redskins	14	14	14	231	122	109	1	18	324	165	159	2
3	Sun	October 6	L		1-1-1	New York Giants	14	17	17	369	218	151	6	10	249	41	208	1
4	Sun	October 13	W		2-1-1	Boston Yanks	16	7	15	317	100	217	3	16	223	93	130	3
5	Sun	October 20	L		2-2-1	Green Bay Packers	7	17	11	213	59	154	2	24	382	94	288	2
6	Sun	October 27	W		3-2-1	Boston Yanks	33	7	13	281	121	160	1	14	190	64	126	5
7	Sun	November 3	W		4-2-1	Washington Redskins	14	7	5	108	8	100	2	14	277	139	138	5
8	Sun	November 10	L		4-3-1	Detroit Lions	7	17	12	202	174	28		7	293	182	111	1
9	Sun	November 17	W		5-3-1	Philadelphia Eagles	10	7	6	122	53	69	3	9	190	29	161	5
10	Sun	November 24	L		5-4-1	New York Giants	0	7	10	139	53	86	3	10	154	39	115	2
11	Sun	December 1	L		5-5-1	Philadelphia Eagles	7	10	9	158	37	121	5	14	225	14	211	1

Passing

No.		Age	Pos	G	GS	QBrec	Cmp	Att	Cmp%	Yds	TD	TD%	Int	Int%	Lng	Y/A	AY/A	Y/C	Y/G	Rate	Sk	Yds
	Bill Dudley	27	TB/PR/P/ KR/K	11	11		32	90	35.6	452	2	2.2	9	10.0	37	5.0	1.0	14.1	41.1	20.5		
	Johnny Clement	27		11	0		16	47	34.0	345	1	2.1	3	6.4	52	7.3	4.9	21.6	31.4	41.5		
	Andy Tomasic	27		4	0		4	12	33.3	53	0	0.0	1	8.3	20	4.4	0.7	13.3	13.3	13.5		
	Bill Dutton	28		11	3		4	6	66.7	31	0	0.0	0	0.0	11	5.2	5.2	7.8	2.8	79.2		
	Merl Condit	29	HB	9	8		2	4	50.0	89	1	25.0	0	0.0	80	22.3	27.3	44.5	9.9	135.4		
	Steve Lach	26		11	3		0	1	0.0	0	0	0.0	0	0.0	0	0.0	0.0		0.0	39.6		
	Cullen Rogers	25		5	0		0	1	0.0	0	0	0.0	0	0.0	0	0.0	0.0		0.0	39.6		
	Team Total	26.4		11			58	161	36.0	970	4	2.5	13	8.1	80	6.0	2.9	16.7	88.2	31.8		
	Opp Total			11			64	162	39.5	939	6	3.7	14	8.6		5.8	2.6	14.7	85.4	35.5	0	0

Rushing and Receiving

No.		Age	Pos	G	GS	Rush Att	Yds	TD	Lng	Y/A	Y/G	A/G	Rec	Receiving Yds	Y/R	TD	Lng	R/G	Y/G	YScm
	Bill Dudley	27	TB/PR/P/ KR/K	11	11	146	604	2	41	4.1	54.9	13.3	4	109	27.3	1	80	0.4	9.9	713
	Tony Compagno	25	FB	10	8	67	217	1	23	3.2	21.7	6.7	8	101	12.6	0	36	0.8	10.1	318
	Bill Dutton	28		11	3	53	169	2	38	3.2	15.4	4.8	2	68	34.0	0	52	0.2	6.2	237
	Merl Condit	29	HB	9	8	46	141	1	23	3.1	15.7	5.1	4	33	8.3	0	23	0.4	3.7	174
	Johnny Clement	27		11	0	43	60	1	13	1.4	5.5	3.9	1	22	22.0	0	22	0.1	2.0	82
	Steve Lach	26		11	3	42	111	5	14	2.6	10.1	3.8	3	22	7.3	0	11	0.3	2.0	133
	Ernie Bonelli	27		3	0	6	7	0	4	1.2	2.3	2.0	1	26	26.0	0	26	0.3	8.7	33
	Cullen Rogers	25		5	0	6	-8	0	4	-1.3	-1.6	1.2								-8
	Val Jansante	26	LE	11	7	2	5	0	5	2.5	0.5	0.2	10	136	13.6	1	34	0.9	12.4	141
	Max Kielbasa	25		2	0	2	-2	0	1	-1.0	-1.0	1.0								-2
	Walt Gorinski	27		6	1	1	3	0	3	3.0	0.5	0.2								3
	Charley Mehelich	24		10	4	0	0	0	0		0.0	0.0	10	116	11.6	0	35	1.0	11.6	116
	Tony Bova	29		11	0	0	0	0	0		0.0	0.0	6	171	28.5	0	37	0.5	15.5	171
	Charlie Seabright	28	BB	10	7	0	0	0	0		0.0	0.0	4	77	19.3	1	33	0.4	7.7	77
	Bill Garnaas	25		10	3	0	0	0	0		0.0	0.0	3	56	18.7	1	30	0.3	5.6	56
	Bob B. Davis	25	RE	11	11	0	0	0	0		0.0	0.0	1	13	13.0	0	13	0.1	1.2	13
	Sam Gray	27		6	0	0	0	0	0		0.0	0.0	1	20	20.0	0	20	0.2	3.3	20
	Team Total	26.4		11		414	1307	12	41	3.2	118.8	37.6	58	970	16.7	4	80	5.3	88.2	2277
	Opp Total			11		466	1754	9		3.8	159.5	42.4	64	939	14.7	6		5.8	85.4	2693

Defense

No.		Age	Pos	G	GS	Sk	Def Int	Yds	TD	Lng	PD	FF	Fumb Fmb	FR	Yds	TD	Tack Tkl	Ast	Sfty
	Bill Dudley	27	TB/PR/P/KR/K	11	11		10	242	1	80	0	0	8	7	30	0			
	Tony Compagno	25	FB	10	8		1	40	0	40	0	0	7	5	4	0			
	Merl Condit	29	HB	9	8							0	6	5	4	0			
	Johnny Clement	27		11	0							0	4	2	0	0			
	Val Jansante	26	LE	11	7							0	2	4	12	0			
	Steve Lach	26		11	3		1	10	0	10	0	0	4	0	0	0			
	Cullen Rogers	25		5	0							0	3	1	0	0			
	Bob B. Davis	25	RE	11	11							0	1	2	32	1			
	Jack Wiley	26	LT	11	8							0	0	3	15	0			
	Max Kielbasa	25		2	0							0	1	1	0	0			
	Charlie Seabright	28	BB	10	7		1	3	0	3	0	0	1	0	0	0			
	George Titus	24		11	0							0	0	2	2	0			
	Ernie Bonelli	27		3	0							0	0	1	4	0			
	Tony Bova	29		11	0							0	1	0	0	0			

No.		Age	Pos	G	GS	Sk	Def					Fumb					Tack		Sfty
							Int	Yds	TD	Lng	PD	FF	Fmb	FR	Yds	TD	Tkl	Ast	
	Ray Bucek	24	RG	11	11							0	0	1	0	0			
	Chuck Cherundolo	30	C	11	11		1	0	0	0	0								
	Joe Coomer	28		7	3							0	0	1	0	0			
	Walt Gorinski	27		6	1							0	0	1	0	0			
	Frank Mattioli	23		11	2							0	0	1	15	0			
	Art McCaffray	25	RT	11	10							0	0	1	0	0			
	Charley Mehelich	24		10	4							0	0	1	6	0			
	Elmer Merkovsky	29		4	1							0	0	1	0	0			
	Team Total	26.4		11			14	295	1	80	0	0	38	40	124	1			
	Opp Total			11									28	11					

1947 PITTSBURGH STEELERS: 8-4-0, TIED FOR FIRST IN EAST, TIED FOR 2ND IN NFL
Head Coach: Jock Sutherland

Week	Day	Date	OT	Rec	Opp	Score		Offe					Defe				
						Tm	Opp	1stD	TotYd	PassY	RushY	TO	1stD	TotYd	PassY	RushY	TO
1	Sun	September 21	W	1-0	Detroit Lions	17	10	14	283	194	89	6	14	278	165	113	5
2	Mon	September 29	L	1-1	Los Angeles Rams	7	48	10	149	74	75	6	20	455	258	197	1
3	Sun	October 5	L	1-2	Washington Redskins	26	27	16	373	167	206	1	15	384	275	109	3
4	Sun	October 12	W	2-2	Boston Yanks	30	14	19	403	127	276	3	8	112	86	26	1
5	Sun	October 19	W	3-2	Philadelphia Eagles	35	24	25	406	177	229	1	16	343	168	175	3
6	Sun	October 26	W	4-2	New York Giants	38	21	14	313	155	158	4	14	250	130	120	5
7	Sun	November 2	W	5-2	Green Bay Packers	18	17	14	261	128	133		12	290	165	125	1
8	Sun	November 9	W	6-2	Washington Redskins	21	14	15	260	89	171	2	16	316	183	133	2
9	Sun	November 16	W	7-2	New York Giants	24	7	13	239	94	145	2	6	82	35	47	3
10	Sun	November 23	L	7-3	Chicago Bears	7	49	17	316	92	224	5	26	522	242	280	2
11	Sun	November 30	L	7-4	Philadelphia Eagles	0	21	6	120	45	75	3	15	251	32	219	2
12	Sun	December 7	W	8-4	Boston Yanks	17	7	13	235	68	167	2	8	186	108	78	4
		Playoffs															
Division	Sun	December 21	L		Philadelphia Eagles	0	21	7	154	52	102	2	17	255	131	24	2

Passing

No.		Age	Pos	G	GS	QBrec	Cmp	Att	Cmp%	Yds	TD	TD%	Int	Int%	Lng	Y/A	AY/A	Y/C	Y/G	Rate	Sk	Yds
	Johnny Clement	28	TB	10	4		52	123	42.3	1004	7	5.7	9	7.3	68	8.2	6.0	19.3	100.4	59.8		
	Walt Slater	27	PR/KR/tb	11	8		18	39	46.2	215	1	2.6	5	12.8	37	5.5	0.3	11.9	19.5	32.5		
	Gonzalo Morales	25		8	1		8	27	29.6	78	1	3.7	4	14.8	23	2.9	-3.0	9.8	9.8	12.3		
	Bob G. Sullivan	23		3	1		3	9	33.3	52	0	0.0	1	11.1	24	5.8	0.8	17.3	17.3	14.4		
	Steve Lach	27	FB	12	8		2	5	40.0	12	1	20.0	0	0.0	6	2.4	6.4	6.0	1.0	87.5		
	Bob Cifers	27	P	10	4		2	3	66.7	28	0	0.0	0	0.0	22	9.3	9.3	14.0	2.8	96.5		
	Paul White	26		11	1		1	3	33.3	21	0	0.0	0	0.0	21	7.0	7.0	21.0	1.9	59.0		
	Team Total	26.0		12			86	209	41.1	1410	10	4.8	19	9.1	68	6.7	3.6	16.4	117.5	42.6		
	Opp Total			12			98	244	40.2	1847	20	8.2	18	7.4		7.6	5.9	18.8	153.9	63.7	0	0

Rushing and Receiving

No.		Age	Pos	G	GS	Rush Att	Rush Yds	Rush TD	Rush Lng	Rush Y/A	Rush Y/G	Rush A/G	Rec	Receiving Yds	Receiving Y/R	Receiving TD	Receiving Lng	Receiving R/G	Receiving Y/G	YScm
	Johnny Clement	28	TB	10	4	129	670	4	43	5.2	67.0	12.9	1	6	6.0	0	6	0.1	0.6	676
	Steve Lach	27	FB	12	8	120	372	8	19	3.1	31.0	10.0	11	77	7.0	1	24	0.9	6.4	449
	Bob Cifers	27	P	10	4	87	356	0	41	4.1	35.6	8.7	3	58	19.3	0	37	0.3	5.8	414
	Walt Slater	27	PR/KR/tb	11	8	46	167	0	19	3.6	15.2	4.2								167
	Tony Compagno	26		12	4	34	126	2	13	3.7	10.5	2.8	9	190	21.1	1	39	0.8	15.8	316
	Gonzalo Morales	25		8	1	29	96	0	18	3.3	12.0	3.6								96
	Paul White	26		11	1	22	85	1	52	3.9	7.7	2.0	2	55	27.5	0	55	0.2	5.0	140
	Bob G. Sullivan	23		3	1	21	61	0	14	2.9	20.3	7.0	4	72	18.0	1	50	1.3	24.0	133
	Paul Davis	22		5	0	4	5	0	6	1.3	1.0	0.8								5
	Gene Hubka	23		1	0	2	4	0	3	2.0	4.0	2.0								4
	Charlie Seabright	29	BB	12	12	1	4	0	4	4.0	0.3	0.1	7	16	2.3	0	10	0.6	1.3	20
	Joe Glamp	26	K/HB	12	5	1	2	0	2	2.0	0.2	0.1								2
	Val Jansante	27	LE	12	8	0	0	0	0		0.0	0.0	35	599	17.1	5	46	2.9	49.9	599
	Bob B. Davis	26	RE	11	11	0	0	0	0		0.0	0.0	5	145	29.0	0	44	0.5	13.2	145
	Bill Garnaas	26		10	0	0	0	0	0		0.0	0.0	5	144	28.8	2	68	0.5	14.4	144
	Charley Mehelich	25		11	4	0	0	0	0		0.0	0.0	3	38	12.7	0	13	0.3	3.5	38
	Elbie Nickel	25		11	1	0	0	0	0		0.0	0.0	1	10	10.0	0	10	0.1	0.9	10
	Team Total	26.0		12		496	1948	15	52	3.9	162.3	41.3	86	1410	16.4	10	68	7.2	117.5	3358
	Opp Total			12		403	1622	11		4.0	135.2	33.6	98	1847	18.8	20		8.2	153.9	3469

Defense

No.		Age	Pos	G	GS	Sk	Def Int	Def Yds	Def TD	Def Lng	Def PD	FF	Fumb Fmb	Fumb FR	Fumb Yds	Fumb TD	Tack Tkl	Tack Ast	Sfty
	Tony Compagno	26		12	4		4	163	2	64	0	0	6	0	0	0			
	Walt Slater	27	PR/KR/tb	11	8		4	38	0	38	0	0	2	3	7	0			
	Johnny Clement	28	TB	10	4							0	7	1	0	0			
	Paul White	26		11	1		2	22	0	15	0	0	2	3	0	0			
	Charlie Seabright	29	BB	12	12		3	80	1	39	0	0	2	0	0	0			
	Bob Cifers	27	P	10	4		1	32	0	32	0	0	3	0	0	0			
	Val Jansante	27	LE	12	8							0	1	3	7	0			1
	Frank Sinkovitz	24		9	0		3	57	1	47	0								
	Bob G. Sullivan	23		3	1							0	2	1	7	0			
	John Mastrangelo	21	rg	11	5							0	0	2	0	0			
	Charley Mehelich	25		11	4							0	0	2	13	0			
	Red Moore	25	LG	12	12							0	0	2	5	0			
	Gonzalo Morales	25		8	1		1	5	0	5	0	0	1	0	0	0			
	Nick Skorich	26	RG	12	6							0	0	2	0	0			
	Jack Wiley	27	LT	11	11							0	0	2	0	0			
	Ralph Calcagni	25		9	0							0	0	1	0	0			1
	Paul Davis	22		5	0							0	1	0	0	0			
	Al Drulis	26		10	2							0	0	1	0	0			
	Bill Garnaas	26		10	0							0	0	1	0	0			
	Steve Lach	27	FB	12	8							0	1	0	0	0			
	Joe Repko	27		8	0							0	0	1	48	1			
	Paul Stenn	29	rt	11	5							0	0	1	0	0			
	Team Total	26.0		12			18	397	4	64	0	0	28	26	87	1			3
	Opp Total			12									34	20					

1948 PITTSBURGH STEELERS: 4-8-0, TIED FOR 3RD IN EAST, TIED FOR 6TH IN NFL
Head Coach: John Michelosen

Week	Day	Date	OT	Rec	Opp	Tm	Opp	1stD	TotYd	PassY	RushY	TO	1stD	TotYd	PassY	RushY	TO
						Score		**Offe**					**Defe**				
1	Sun	September 26	L	0-1	Washington Redskins	14	17	23	344	111	233	3	18	399	257	142	1
2	Sun	October 3	W	1-1	Boston Yanks	24	14	24	339	48	291	5	5	137	31	106	2
3	Sun	October 10	W	2-1	Washington Redskins	10	7	17	210	113	97	2	15	243	121	122	6
4	Sun	October 17	L	2-2	Boston Yanks	7	13	11	205	113	92	7	9	242	162	80	4
5	Sun	October 24	L	2-3	New York Giants	27	34	14	287	204	83	5	13	336	192	144	1
6	Sun	October 31	L	2-4	Philadelphia Eagles	7	34	15	254	144	110	6	20	334	177	157	3
7	Sun	November 7	W	3-4	Green Bay Packers	38	7	19	301	80	221	3	13	250	152	98	3
8	Sun	November 14	L	3-5	Chicago Cardinals	7	24	14	327	186	141	5	18	368	184	184	1
9	Sun	November 21	L	3-6	Detroit Lions	14	17	22	288	86	202	5	11	192	68	124	
10	Sun	November 28	L	3-7	Philadelphia Eagles	0	17	12	200	113	87	2	15	350	167	183	5
11	Sun	December 5	W	4-7	New York Giants	38	28	23	431	165	266		31	463	363	100	3
12	Sun	December 12	L	4-8	Los Angeles Rams	14	31	16	277	166	111	3	20	321	113	208	2

Passing

No.		Age	Pos	G	GS	QBrec	Cmp	Att	Cmp%	Yds	TD	TD%	Int	Int%	Lng	Y/A	AY/A	Y/C	Y/G	Rate	Sk	Yds
	Ray Evans	26	TB/PR	9	8	64	137	46.7		924	5	3.6	17	12.4	66	6.7	1.9	14.4	102.7	41.7		
	Johnny Clement	29		5	1	18	58	31.0		281	3	5.2	7	12.1	39	4.8	0.4	15.6	56.2	25.8		
	Joe Gasparella	21		9	3	23	57	40.4		294	0	0.0	4	7.0	43	5.2	2.0	12.8	32.7	28.0		
	Bob Cifers	28	P/KR/HB	12	7	0	4	0.0		0	0	0.0	1	25.0	0	0.0	-11.3		0.0	0.0		
	Gonzalo Morales	26		10	3	3	4	75.0		30	0	0.0	0	0.0	14	7.5	7.5	10.0	3.0	95.8		
	Charley Mehelich	26	LE	12	6	0	2	0.0		0	0	0.0	0	0.0	0	0.0	0.0		0.0	39.6		
	Norm Mosley	26		5	1	0	2	0.0		0	0	0.0	0	0.0	0	0.0	0.0		0.0	39.6		
	Joe Glamp	27	K	12	2	0	1	0.0		0	0	0.0	0	0.0	0	0.0	0.0		0.0	39.6		
	Charlie Seabright	30	BB	12	11	0	1	0.0		0	0	0.0	0	0.0	0	0.0	0.0		0.0	39.6		
	Team Total	25.7		12			108	266	40.6	1529	8	3.0	29	10.9	66	5.7	1.4	14.2	127.4	30.3		
	Opp Total			12			149	279	53.4	1987	18	6.5	13	4.7		7.1	6.3	13.3	165.6	78.4	0	0

Rushing and Receiving

No.		Age	Pos	G	GS	Att	Yds	TD	Lng	Y/A	Y/G	A/G	Rec	Yds	Y/R	TD	Lng	R/G	Y/G	YScm
						Rush							**Receiving**							
	Bob Cifers	28	P/KR/HB	12	7	112	361	1	21	3.2	30.1	9.3	4	55	13.8	0	29	0.3	4.6	416
	Ray Evans	26	TB/PR	9	8	99	343	2	24	3.5	38.1	11.0	7	93	13.3	0	36	0.8	10.3	436
	Johnny Clement	29		5	1	67	261	2	28	3.9	52.2	13.4								261
	Jerry Shipkey	23	FB	12	4	64	199	8	16	3.1	16.6	5.3	10	106	10.6	0	43	0.8	8.8	305
	George Papach	23		10	3	60	324	2	42	5.4	32.4	6.0	4	72	18.0	1	31	0.4	7.2	396
	Joe Glamp	27	K	12	2	28	167	1	55	6.0	13.9	2.3	9	138	15.3	2	39	0.8	11.5	305
	Jerry Nuzum	25		10	1	26	109	0	20	4.2	10.9	2.6	2	37	18.5	0	32	0.2	3.7	146
	Tony Compagno	27		12	1	24	101	0	20	4.2	8.4	2.0	1	4	4.0	0	4	0.1	0.3	105
	Gonzalo Morales	26		10	3	13	29	0	8	2.2	2.9	1.3								29
	Norm Mosley	26		5	1	13	39	1	8	3.0	7.8	2.6								39
	Paul Davis	23		6	3	2	-1	0	1	-0.5	-0.2	0.3								-1
	Val Jansante	28	le	12	5	1	-3	0	-3	-3.0	-0.3	0.1	39	623	16.0	3	66	3.3	51.9	620
	Joe Gasparella	21		9	3	1	5	0	5	5.0	0.6	0.1								5
	Elbie Nickel	26	RE	12	7	0	0	0	0		0.0	0.0	22	324	14.7	1	35	1.8	27.0	324
	Charlie Seabright	30	BB	12	11	0	0	0	0		0.0	0.0	8	63	7.9	1	16	0.7	5.3	63
	Bob B. Davis	27		12	4	0	0	0	0		0.0	0.0	2	14	7.0	0	11	0.2	1.2	14
	Team Total	25.7		12		510	1934	17	55	3.8	161.2	42.5	108	1529	14.2	8	66	9.0	127.4	3463
	Opp Total			12		434	1648	7		3.8	137.3	36.2	149	1987	13.3	18		12.4	165.6	3635

Defense

No.		Age	Pos	G	GS	Sk	Def					Fumb					Tack		Sfty
							Int	Yds	TD	Lng	PD	FF	Fmb	FR	Yds	TD	Tkl	Ast	
	Tony Compagno	27		12	1		7	179	1	82	0	0	5	4	0	0			
	Ray Evans	26	TB/PR	9	8							0	9	4	7	0			
	Jerry Nuzum	25		10	1		1	3	0	3	0	0	4	4	0	0			
	Bob Cifers	28	P/KR/HB	12	7							0	4	3	−2	0			
	Johnny Clement	29		5	1							0	5	2	0	0			
	Jerry Shipkey	23	FB	12	4							0	4	3	−2	0			
	Paul Davis	23		6	3		1	7	0	7	0	0	2	3	5	0			
	Elbie Nickel	26	RE	12	7							0	2	3	5	0			
	Joe Gasparella	21		9	3							0	1	3	0	0			
	Val Jansante	28	le	12	5							0	2	1	5	0			
	Steve Suhey	26		12	4							0	1	2	0	0			
	Bill Cregar	23	RG	12	6							0	0	2	0	0			
	Joe Glamp	27	K	12	2							0	1	1	0	0			
	Bryant Meeks	22		10	3							0	0	2	0	0			
	Gonzalo Morales	26		10	3		1	17	0	11	0	0	0	1	36	1			
	Carl Samuelson	25		11	0		1	33	0	33	0	0	0	1	0	0			
	Charlie Seabright	30	BB	12	11		1	16	0	16	0	0	1	0	0	0			
	Frank Wydo	24	RT	12	9							0	0	2	0	0			
	Bob B. Davis	27		12	4							0	1	0	0	0			
	Norm Mosley	26		5	1							0	1	0	0	0			
	George Papach	23		10	3							0	0	1	0	0			
	Hubert Shurtz	25		12	1							0	0	1	0	0			
	Frank Sinkovitz	25		9	3		1	65	0	65	0								
	Jack Wiley	28	lt	12	7							0	0	1	0	0			
	Team Total	25.7		12			13	320	1	82	0	0	43	44	54	1			
	Opp Total			12									29	11					

1949 PITTSBURGH STEELERS: 6-5-1, 2ND IN EAST, TIED FOR 4TH IN NFL
Head Coach: John Michelosen

Week	Day	Date	OT	Rec	Opp	Score		Offe					Defe				
						Tm	Opp	1stD	TotYd	PassY	RushY	TO	1stD	TotYd	PassY	RushY	TO
1	Sun	September 25	W	1-0	New York Giants	28	7	18	372	149	223		13	259	154	105	2
2	Mon	October 3	L	1-1	Washington Redskins	14	27	19	303	110	193	2	17	410	182	228	
3	Sat	October 8	W	2-1	Detroit Lions	14	7	18	272	66	206	4	17	262	210	52	3
4	Sun	October 16	W	3-1	New York Giants	21	17	13	194	63	131	2	14	244	99	145	3
5	Sun	October 23	W	4-1	New York Bulldogs	24	13	24	402	46	356	3	19	315	244	71	3
6	Sun	October 30	L	4-2	Philadelphia Eagles	7	38	14	224	143	81	3	21	365	128	237	3
7	Sun	November 6	L	4-3	Washington Redskins	14	27	20	319	89	230	2	16	383	208	175	3
8	Sun	November 13	T	4-3-1	Los Angeles Rams	7	7	7	138		138		23	362	167	195	3
9	Sun	November 20	W	5-3-1	Green Bay Packers	30	7	19	449	154	295	4	16	287	99	188	2
10	Sun	November 27	L	5-4-1	Philadelphia Eagles	17	34	6	196	134	62		26	486	190	296	1
11	Sun	December 4	L	5-5-1	Chicago Bears	21	30	14	347	207	140	6	19	355	201	154	4
12	Sun	December 11	W	6-5-1	New York Bulldogs	27	0	17	289	135	154	1	9	162	146	16	4

Passing

No.		Age	Pos	G	GS	QBrec	Cmp	Att	Cmp%	Yds	TD	TD%	Int	Int%	Lng	Y/A	AY/A	Y/C	Y/G	Rate	Sk	Yds
	Joe Geri	25	TB/P	12	1		31	77	40.3	554	5	6.5	5	6.5	63	7.2	5.6	17.9	46.2	60.2		
	Jim Finks	22		11	0		24	71	33.8	322	2	2.8	8	11.3	35	4.5	0.0	13.4	29.3	19.0		
	Bob Gage	21	PR	12	4		17	36	47.2	329	2	5.6	4	11.1	52	9.1	5.3	19.4	27.4	58.4		
	Don Samuel	25		5	1		7	21	33.3	67	0	0.0	1	4.8	13	3.2	1.0	9.6	13.4	23.3		
	Joe Hollingsworth	24		11	2		0	1	0.0	0	0	0.0	0	0.0	0	0.0	0.0		0.0	39.6		
	Jerry Nuzum	26	HB	12	3		1	1	100.0	21	0	0.0	0	0.0	21	21.0	21.0	21.0	1.8	118.7		
	George Papach	24	FB	12	9		0	1	0.0	0	0	0.0	0	0.0	0	0.0	0.0		0.0	39.6		
	Charlie Seabright	31	BB	12	11		1	1	100.0	17	1	100.0	0	0.0	17	17.0	37.0	17.0	1.4	158.3		
	Team Total	25.6		12			81	209	38.8	1310	10	4.8	18	8.6	63	6.3	3.3	16.2	109.2	40.6		
	Opp Total			12			161	337	47.8	2043	9	2.7	22	6.5		6.1	3.7	12.7	170.3	48.9	19	152

Rushing and Receiving

No.		Age	Pos	G	GS	Rush Att	Yds	TD	Lng	Y/A	Y/G	A/G	Rec	Yds	Y/R	TD	Lng	R/G	Y/G	YScm
	Jerry Nuzum	26	HB	12	3	139	611	5	64	4.4	50.9	11.6	4	81	20.3	2	63	0.3	6.8	692
	Joe Geri	25	TB/P	12	1	133	543	5	25	4.1	45.3	11.1								543
	George Papach	24	FB	12	9	99	407	0	25	4.1	33.9	8.3	6	18	3.0	0	11	0.5	1.5	425
	Bob Gage	21	PR	12	4	46	228	3	97	5.0	19.0	3.8	1	8	8.0	0	8	0.1	0.7	236
	Don Samuel	25		5	1	39	163	1	31	4.2	32.6	7.8	1	2	2.0	0	2	0.2	0.4	165
	Jim Finks	22		11	0	35	135	1	38	3.9	12.3	3.2	1	17	17.0	1	17	0.1	1.5	152
	Jerry Shipkey	24		12	4	26	93	5	14	3.6	7.8	2.2	2	32	16.0	0	21	0.2	2.7	125
	Bob Hanlon	25	hb	12	7	6	13	0	7	2.2	1.1	0.5	1	4	4.0	0	4	0.1	0.3	17
	Joe Hollingsworth	24		11	2	6	13	0	7	2.2	1.2	0.5								13
	Joe Glamp	28	K	8	0	3	−8	0	2	−2.7	−1.0	0.4	1	14	14.0	0	14	0.1	1.8	6
	Bill Long	23		10	0	2	6	0	10	3.0	0.6	0.2	2	21	10.5	0	13	0.2	2.1	27
	Frank Minini	28	KR/bb	12	7	1	5	0	5	5.0	0.4	0.1								5
	Val Jansante	29	LE	12	10	0	0	0	0		0.0	0.0	29	445	15.3	4	47	2.4	37.1	445
	Elbie Nickel	27	RE	12	10	0	0	0	0		0.0	0.0	26	633	24.3	3	52	2.2	52.8	633
	Charlie Seabright	31	BB	12	11	0	0	0	0		0.0	0.0	4	4	1.0	0	5	0.3	0.3	4
	Frank Wydo	25	RT	12	11	0	0	0	0		0.0	0.0	2	21	10.5	0	12	0.2	1.8	21
	Jack Wiley	29	LT	12	10	0	0	0	0		0.0	0.0	1	10	10.0	0	10	0.1	0.8	10
	Team Total	25.6		12		535	2209	20	97	4.1	184.1	44.6	81	1310	16.2	10	63	6.8	109.2	3519
	Opp Total			12		463	1862	17		4.0	155.2	38.6	161	1891	11.7	9		13.4	157.6	3753

Defense

No.		Age	Pos	G	GS	Sk	Def Int	Yds	TD	Lng	PD	Fumb FF	Fmb	FR	Yds	TD	Tack Tkl	Ast	Sfty
	Bob Gage	21	PR	12	4		5	58	0	16	0	0	7	7	20	0			
	Don Samuel	25		5	1		1	4	0	4	0	0	6	2	0	0			
	Jerry Nuzum	26	HB	12	3							0	5	3	0	0			
	Joe Geri	25	TB/P	12	1							0	4	3	0	0			
	Howard Hartley	25		12	0		6	63	0	41	0								
	George Papach	24	FB	12	9							0	3	3	0	0			
	Jerry Shipkey	24		12	4		3	76	0	50	0	0	2	1	0	0			
	Bob Hanlon	25	hb	12	7		3	29	0	19	0	0	1	1	0	0			
	Darrell Hogan	23		12	2		1	5	0	5	0	0	0	2	0	0			
	Jim Finks	22		11	0		1	14	0	14	0	0	0	1	0	0			
	Joe Hollingsworth	24		11	2							0	1	1	−2	0			
	Bill Long	23		10	0							0	1	1	0	0			
	Carl Samuelson	26		12	0							0	0	2	26	1			1
	Joe Glamp	28	K	8	0							0	0	1	0	0			
	Bill McPeak	23		12	2							0	0	1	0	0			
	Frank Minini	28	KR/bb	12	7							0	1	0	0	0			
	Leo Nobile	27		12	0		1	7	0	7	0								
	Charlie Seabright	31	BB	12	11							0	0	1	0	0			
	Frank Sinkovitz	26		12	3		1	54	0	54	0								
	Jack Wiley	29	LT	12	10							0	0	1	0	0			
	Team Total	25.6		12			22	310	0	54	0	0	31	31	44	1			1
	Opp Total			12		13							26	17					

1950 PITTSBURGH STEELERS: 6-6-0, TIED FOR 3RD IN AMERICAN, 6TH IN NFL
Head Coach: John Michelosen

						Score		Offe					Defe				
Week	Day	Date	OT	Rec	Opp	Tm	Opp	1stD	TotYd	PassY	RushY	TO	1stD	TotYd	PassY	RushY	TO
1	Sun	September 17	L	0-1	New York Giants	7	18	10	138	104	34	9	10	197	30	167	2
2	Sun	September 24	L	0-2	Detroit Lions	7	10	8	176	122	54	2	24	372	107	265	5
3	Sun	October 1	W	1-2	Washington Redskins	26	7	15	238	137	101	2	12	289	157	132	2
4	Sat	October 7	L	1-3	Cleveland Browns	17	30	19	345	131	214	6	15	266	75	191	1
5	Sun	October 15	W	2-3	New York Giants	17	6	17	328	178	150	4	12	173	76	97	5
6	Sun	October 22	L	2-4	Philadelphia Eagles	10	17	13	306	205	101	6	17	362	175	187	4
7	Sun	October 29	L	2-5	Cleveland Browns	7	45	19	349	220	129	8	22	533	195	338	1
8	Sun	November 5	W	3-5	Philadelphia Eagles	9	7	13	217	10	207	1	19	258	146	112	7
9	Sun	November 12	W	4-5	Baltimore Colts	17	7	15	229	96	133	2	20	316	206	110	1
10	Thu	November 23	W	5-5	Chicago Cardinals	28	17	19	357	131	226	5	16	283	169	114	4
11	Sun	December 3	L	5-6	Washington Redskins	7	24	12	243	124	119	8	12	250	167	83	1
12	Sun	December 10	W	6-6	Chicago Cardinals	28	7	17	408	211	197	5	19	367	274	93	5

Passing

No.		Age	Pos	G	GS	QBrec	Cmp	Att	Cmp%	Yds	TD	TD%	Int	Int%	Lng	Y/A	AY/A	Y/C	Y/G	Rate	Sk	Yds
35	Joe Geri*+	26	TB/P/K	12	0		41	113	36.3	866	6	5.3	15	13.3	78	7.7	2.8	21.1	72.2	42.4		
77	Bob Gage	22	PR	10	0		21	58	36.2	294	1	1.7	5	8.6	42	5.1	1.5	14.0	29.4	23.2		
48	Joe Gasparella	23	bb	11	0		23	54	42.6	383	3	5.6	5	9.3	51	7.1	4.0	16.7	34.8	47.1		
7	Jim Finks	23		9	0		5	9	55.6	35	0	0.0	1	11.1	19	3.9	-1.1	7.0	3.9	25.0		
44	Shorty McWilliams	24	LDH	10	0		5	8	62.5	113	0	0.0	1	12.5	63	14.1	8.5	22.6	11.3	66.7		
14	Lynn Chandnois	25	WB/S/KR	12	0		1	6	16.7	5	0	0.0	2	33.3	5	0.8	-14.2	5.0	0.4	0.0		
27	Fran Rogel	23		12	0		3	4	75.0	30	0	0.0	0	0.0	11	7.5	7.5	10.0	2.5	95.8		
33	Charlie Seabright	32	BB	10	0		1	3	33.3	3	0	0.0	0	0.0	3	1.0	1.0	3.0	0.3	42.4		
	Team Total	25.8		12			100	255	39.2	1729	10	3.9	29	11.4	78	6.8	2.4	17.3	144.1	36.5		
	Opp Total			12			146	300	48.7	1801	10	3.3	22	7.3		6.0	3.4	12.3	150.1	48.2	46	369

Rushing and Receiving

No.		Age	Pos	G	GS	Rush							Receiving							YScm
						Att	Yds	TD	Lng	Y/A	Y/G	A/G	Rec	Yds	Y/R	TD	Lng	R/G	Y/G	
35	Joe Geri*+	26	TB/P/K	12	0	188	705	2	47	3.8	58.8	15.7	1	33	33.0	1	33	0.1	2.8	738
27	Fran Rogel	23		12	0	92	418	3	40	4.5	34.8	7.7	24	304	12.7	1	64	2.0	25.3	722
14	Lynn Chandnois	25	WB/S/KR	12	0	71	216	0	17	3.0	18.0	5.9	7	158	22.6	0	51	0.6	13.2	374
22	Jerry Nuzum	27		12	0	57	154	1	32	2.7	12.8	4.8	6	142	23.7	1	68	0.5	11.8	296
77	Bob Gage	22	PR	10	0	39	106	3	18	2.7	10.6	3.9	6	127	21.2	2	48	0.6	12.7	233
49	Jerry Shipkey*	25	LLB/FB	12	0	18	17	3	11	0.9	1.4	1.5								17
44	Shorty McWilliams	24	LDH	10	0	10	39	0	12	3.9	3.9	1.0								39
7	Jim Finks	23		9	0	1	2	0	2	2.0	0.2	0.1								2
42	Joe Hollingsworth	25		10	0	1	2	0	2	2.0	0.2	0.1								2
54	Val Jansante	30	LE	12	0	0	0	0	0		0.0	0.0	26	353	13.6	0	40	2.2	29.4	353
81	Elbie Nickel	28	RE	12	0	0	0	0	0		0.0	0.0	22	527	24.0	4	65	1.8	43.9	527
33	Charlie Seabright	32	BB	10	0	0	0	0	0		0.0	0.0	3	37	12.3	1	13	0.3	3.7	37
11	Howard Hartley	26	RDH	12	0	0	0	0	0		0.0	0.0	2	27	13.5	0	24	0.2	2.3	27
55	Charley Mehelich	28	LDE	12	0	0	0	0	0		0.0	0.0	2	18	9.0	0	10	0.2	1.5	18
48	Joe Gasparella	23	bb	11	0	0	0	0	0		0.0	0.0	1	3	3.0	0	3	0.1	0.3	3
	Team Total	25.8		12		477	1659	12	47	3.5	138.3	39.8	100	1729	17.3	10	68	8.3	144.1	3388
	Opp Total			12		460	1889	12		4.1	157.4	38.3	146	1432	9.8	10			119.3	3321

Defense

No.		Age	Pos	G	GS	Sk	Def					Fumb					Tack		Sfty
							Int	Yds	TD	Lng	PD	FF	Fmb	FR	Yds	TD	Tkl	Ast	
35	Joe Geri*+	26	TB/P/K	12	0							0	12	3	0	0			
27	Fran Rogel	23		12	0							0	7	3	0	0			
77	Bob Gage	22	PR	10	0		4	64	0	23	0	0	5	0	0	0			
11	Howard Hartley	26	RDH	12	0		5	84	0	38	0	0	3	1	0	0			
22	Jerry Nuzum	27		12	0							0	7	0	0	0			
88	George Nicksich	22	MG	12	0		3	31	0	18	0	0	0	3	5	0			
49	Jerry Shipkey*	25	LLB/FB	12	0		2	34	0	30	0	0	2	1	0	0			
14	Lynn Chandnois	25	WB/S/KR	12	0							0	3	1	0	0			
57	Frank Sinkovitz	27	MLB	11	0		2	24	0	17	0	0	0	2	0	0			
7	Jim Finks	23		9	0		3	24	0	24	0								
44	Shorty McWilliams	24	LDH	10	0		2	31	0	27	0	0	1	0	0	0			
28	Bob B. Davis	29		10	0							0	0	2	0	0			
73	Darrell Hogan	24	RLB	12	0		1	3	0	3	0	0	0	1	0	0			
40	George Hughes	25	RG	12	0							0	0	2	0	0			
63	Ernie Stautner	25	LDT	12	0							0	0	2	0	0			1
46	Bill Walsh*	23	C	12	0							0	0	2	0	0			
79	Frank Wydo	26	RT	12	0							0	1	1	0	0			
54	Val Jansante	30	LE	12	0							0	0	1	2	0			
84	Bill McPeak	24	RDE	11	0							0	0	1	19	0			
86	Carl Samuelson	27		8	0							0	0	1	0	0			
89	Walt Szot	30	RDT	11	0							0	0	1	0	0			
	Team Total	25.8		12			22	295	0	38	0	0	41	28	26	0			1
	Opp Total			12		10							30	14					3

1951 PITTSBURGH STEELERS: 4-7-1, 4TH IN AMERICAN, 8TH IN NFL
Head Coach: John Michelosen

Week	Day	Date	OT	Rec	Opp	Score		Offe					Defe				
						Tm	Opp	1stD	TotYd	PassY	RushY	TO	1stD	TotYd	PassY	RushY	TO
1	Mon	October 1	T	0-0-1	New York Giants	13	13	12	251	155	96	3	11	303	133	170	2
2	Sun	October 7	L	0-1-1	Green Bay Packers	33	35	16	247	96	151	2	17	393	252	141	3
3	Sun	October 14	L	0-2-1	San Francisco 49ers	24	28	20	326	192	134	5	18	374	216	158	4
4	Sun	October 21	L	0-3-1	Cleveland Browns	0	17	12	201	96	105	4	17	243	46	197	4
5	Sun	October 28	W	1-3-1	Chicago Cardinals	28	14	11	287	159	128	1	23	392	227	165	6
6	Sun	November 4	L	1-4-1	Philadelphia Eagles	13	34	14	187	68	119	3	15	242	123	119	3
7	Sun	November 11	W	2-4-1	Green Bay Packers	28	7	21	324	148	176	5	16	218	159	59	5
8	Sun	November 18	L	2-5-1	Washington Redskins	7	22	5	115	45	70	1	19	321	50	271	2
9	Sun	November 25	W	3-5-1	Philadelphia Eagles	17	13	17	323	167	156	3	18	300	136	164	5
10	Sun	December 2	L	3-6-1	New York Giants	0	14	14	199	120	79	4	10	171	34	137	3
11	Sun	December 9	L	3-7-1	Cleveland Browns	0	28	13	209	118	91	5	15	251	91	160	2
12	Sun	December 16	W	4-7-1	Washington Redskins	20	10	17	411	288	123	7	9	215	97	118	7

Passing

No.		Age	Pos	G	GS	QBrec	Cmp	Att	Cmp%	Yds	TD	TD%	Int	Int%	Lng	Y/A	AY/A	Y/C	Y/G	Rate	Sk	Yds
49	Chuck Ortmann	22	tb	12	0		56	139	40.3	671	3	2.2	13	9.4	37	4.8	1.1	12.0	55.9	24.0		
35	Joe Geri*	27	TB/P/K	12	0		29	90	32.2	506	2	2.2	7	7.8	77	5.6	2.6	17.4	42.2	27.4		
14	Lynn Chandnois	26	WB	12	0		16	43	37.2	256	2	4.7	4	9.3	49	6.0	2.7	16.0	21.3	34.6		
44	Ray Mathews	22	KR	12	0		15	31	48.4	208	2	6.5	0	0.0	39	6.7	8.0	13.9	17.3	91.9		
7	Jim Finks	24	RDH	12	0		14	24	58.3	201	1	4.2	1	4.2	40	8.4	7.3	14.4	16.8	82.1		
23	Joe Gasparella	24		4	0		0	2	0.0	0	0	0.0	1	50.0	0	0.0	-22.5		0.0	0.0		
27	Fran Rogel	24	FB	12	0		0	1	0.0	0	0	0.0	0	0.0	0	0.0		0.0	0.0	39.6		
	Team Total	25.6		12			130	330	39.4	1842	10	3.0	26	7.9	77	5.6	2.6	14.2	153.5	35.4		
	Opp Total			12			136	266	51.1	1687	12	4.5	30	11.3		6.3	2.2	12.4	140.6	46.6	25	201

Rushing and Receiving

No.		Age	Pos	G	GS	Att	Yds	TD	Lng	Y/A	Y/G	A/G	Rec	Yds	Y/R	TD	Lng	R/G	Y/G	YScm
								Rush								**Receiving**				
27	Fran Rogel	24	FB	12	0	109	385	3	51	3.5	32.1	9.1	10	59	5.9	0	24	0.8	4.9	444
14	Lynn Chandnois	26	WB	12	0	108	332	2	34	3.1	27.7	9.0	28	440	15.7	4	55	2.3	36.7	772
35	Joe Geri*	27	TB/P/K	12	0	90	252	3	17	2.8	21.0	7.5	3	59	19.7	1	49	0.3	4.9	311
49	Chuck Ortmann	22	tb	12	0	59	327	0	32	5.5	27.3	4.9	4	62	15.5	0	22	0.3	5.2	389
22	Jerry Nuzum	28	fb	11	0	27	56	1	9	2.1	5.1	2.5	2	43	21.5	0	39	0.2	3.9	99
44	Ray Mathews	22	KR	12	0	21	37	0	15	1.8	3.1	1.8								37
37	Joe Hollingsworth	26		10	0	7	11	0	6	1.6	1.1	0.7								11
7	Jim Finks	24	RDH	12	0	3	27	0	22	9.0	2.3	0.3								27
40	Truett Smith	27	BB	11	0	1	1	0	1	1.0	0.1	0.1	4	71	17.8	0	24	0.4	6.5	72
37	Henry Minarik	24	le	11	0	0	0	0	0		0.0	0.0	35	459	13.1	1	37	3.2	41.7	459
81	Elbie Nickel	29	RE	12	0	0	0	0	0		0.0	0.0	28	447	16.0	3	77	2.3	37.3	447
54	Val Jansante	31	LE	6	0	0	0	0	0		0.0	0.0	15	194	12.9	1	46	2.5	32.3	194
86	Tom Jelley	25		5	0	0	0	0	0		0.0	0.0	1	8	8.0	0	8	0.2	1.6	8
	Team Total	25.6		12		425	1428	9	51	3.4	119.0	35.4	130	1842	14.2	10	77	10.8	153.5	3270
	Opp Total			12		499	1859	13		3.7	154.9	41.6	136	1486	10.9	12		11.3	123.8	3345

Defense

No.		Age	Pos	G	GS	Sk	Int	Yds	TD	Lng	PD	FF	Fmb	FR	Yds	TD	Tkl	Ast	Sfty
								Def					**Fumb**				**Tack**		
11	Howard Hartley	27	PR/LS	12	0		10	69	0	23	0	0	1	2	0	0			
14	Lynn Chandnois	26	WB	12	0							0	7	2	0	0			
35	Joe Geri*	27	TB/P/K	12	0							0	5	4	2	0			
33	Jerry Shipkey*+	26	RLB	10	0		6	113	1	58	0	0	0	2	0	0			
44	Ray Mathews	22	KR	12	0		1	0	0	0	0	0	3	2	0	0			
49	Chuck Ortmann	22	tb	12	0		1	62	0	62	0	0	5	0	0	0			
27	Fran Rogel	24	FB	12	0							0	4	2	0	0			
80	Jack Butler	24	LDH	12	0		5	142	1	52	0								
7	Jim Finks	24	RDH	12	0		3	46	1	25	0	0	1	0	0	0			
57	Frank Sinkovitz	28	LLB	12	0		2	6	0	6	0	0	0	2	0	0			
75	George Hays	27	LDT	12	0							0	0	3	15	0			
37	Joe Hollingsworth	26		10	0							0	1	2	0	0			
40	George Hughes*	26	RG	12	0							0	0	2	0	0			
22	Jerry Nuzum	28	fb	11	0							0	2	0	0	0			
78	Carl Samuelson	28		12	0							0	1	1	0	0			
68	John Schweder	24		12	0		1	20	0	20	0	0	0	1	0	0			
65	Lou Allen	27	LT	12	0							0	0	1	0	0			
60	Dale Dodrill	25	MG	7	0							0	0	1	3	0			
63	Darrell Hogan	25	RS	12	0		1	3	0	3	0								
86	Tom Jelley	25		5	0							0	0	1	0	0			1
55	Charley Mehelich	29	LDE	5	0							0	0	1	0	0			
70	Ernie Stautner	26	RDT	12	0							0	0	1	0	0			
79	Frank Wydo	27	RT	12	0							0	1	0	0	0			
	Team Total	25.6		12			30	461	3	62	0	0	31	30	20	0			1
	Opp Total			12		40							30	14					

1952 PITTSBURGH STEELERS: 5-7-0, 4TH IN AMERICAN, 8TH IN NFL
Head Coach: Joe Bach

						Score		Offe					Defe				
Week	Day	Date	OT	Rec	Opp	Tm	Opp	1stD	TotYd	PassY	RushY	TO	1stD	TotYd	PassY	RushY	TO
1	Sun	September 28	L	0-1	Philadelphia Eagles	25	31	20	320	190	130	4	18	394	275	119	1
2	Sat	October 4	L	0-2	Cleveland Browns	20	21	15	258	183	75	1	19	459	401	58	4
3	Sun	October 12	L	0-3	Philadelphia Eagles	21	26	8	178	140	38	4	14	301	188	113	1
4	Sun	October 19	L	0-4	Washington Redskins	24	28	19	311	123	188	2	14	270	133	137	3
5	Sun	October 26	W	1-4	Chicago Cardinals	34	28	13	313	199	114	3	19	417	208	209	2
6	Sun	November 2	W	2-4	Washington Redskins	24	23	12	175	41	134	2	22	389	230	159	3
7	Sun	November 9	L	2-5	Detroit Lions	6	31	15	192	195	−3	3	25	391	70	321	
8	Sun	November 16	L	2-6	Cleveland Browns	28	29	18	379	329	50	3	25	410	209	201	2
9	Sun	November 23	W	3-6	Chicago Cardinals	17	14	14	226	122	104	3	19	278	94	184	3
10	Sun	November 30	W	4-6	New York Giants	63	7	20	415	292	123	5	8	162	147	15	9
11	Sun	December 7	W	5-6	San Francisco 49ers	24	7	15	275	133	142	1	14	302	232	70	6
12	Sun	December 14	L	5-7	Los Angeles Rams	14	28	18	353	244	109	6	27	516	358	158	6

Passing

No.		Age	Pos	G	GS	QBrec	Cmp	Att	Cmp%	Yds	TD	TD%	Int	Int%	Lng	Y/A	AY/A	Y/C	Y/G	Rate	Sk	Yds
7	Jim Finks*	25	QB	12	12	5-7-0	158	336	47.0	2307	20	6.0	19	5.7	60	6.9	5.5	14.6	192.3	66.2		
25	Ray Mathews*	23	PR/LH	12	0		3	13	23.1	104	0	0.0	1	7.7	69	8.0	4.5	34.7	8.7	28.4		
17	Gary Kerkorian	22	K	12	0		5	11	45.5	79	1	9.1	3	27.3	27	7.2	−3.3	15.8	6.6	60.		
28	Pat Brady	26	P	12	0		1	3	33.3	14	0	0.0	0	0.0	14	4.7	4.7	14.0	1.2	49.3		
49	Lynn Chandnois*	27	RH/KR	12	0		0	2	0.0	0	0	0.0	0	0.0	0	0.0		0.0	0.0	39.6		
	Team Total	25.4		12		5-7-0	167	365	45.8	2504	21	5.8	23	6.3	69	6.9	5.2	15.0	208.7	61.7		
	Opp Total			12			167	369	45.3	2765	24	6.5	27	7.3		7.5	5.5	16.6	230.4	62.2	28	220

Rushing and Receiving

						Rush							Receiving						
No.		Age	Pos	G	GS	Att	Yds	TD	Lng	Y/A	Y/G	A/G	Rec	Yds	Y/R	TD	Lng	R/G	Y/G	YScm
49	Lynn Chandnois*	27	RH/KR	12	0	97	298	1	25	3.1	24.8	8.1	28	370	13.2	2	48	2.3	30.8	668
34	Fran Rogel	25		12	0	84	230	3	14	2.7	19.2	7.0	12	140	11.7	0	26	1.0	11.7	370
39	Ed Modzelewski	23	FB	10	0	82	195	3	14	2.4	19.5	8.2	11	109	9.9	0	23	1.1	10.9	304
25	Ray Mathews*	23	PR/LH	12	0	66	315	0	36	4.8	26.3	5.5	33	543	16.5	5	50	2.8	45.3	858
7	Jim Finks*	25	QB	12	12	23	37	5	20	1.6	3.1	1.9								37
37	Jack Spinks	22		10	0	22	94	0	42	4.3	9.4	2.2	2	22	11.0	0	23	0.2	2.2	116
35	Tom Calvin	26		12	0	7	14	0	11	2.0	1.2	0.6	2	4	2.0	0	6	0.2	0.3	18
17	Gary Kerkorian	22	K	12	0	2	20	0	20	10.0	1.7	0.2								20
33	Jerry Shipkey*+	27	LLB	12	0	1	1	0	1	1.0	0.1	0.1								1
81	Elbie Nickel*	30	RE	12	0	0	0	0	0		0.0	0.0	55	884	16.1	9	54	4.6	73.7	884
25	Dick Hensley	25		11	0	0	0	0	0		0.0	0.0	12	217	18.1	2	60	1.1	19.7	217
88	George Sulima	24	LE	9	0	0	0	0	0		0.0	0.0	9	176	19.6	1	69	1.0	19.6	176
80	Jack Butler	25		12	0	0	0	0	0		0.0	0.0	3	37	12.3	2	20	0.3	3.1	37
	Team Total	25.4		12		384	1204	12	42	3.1	100.3	32.0	167	2504	15.0	21	69	13.9	208.7	3708
	Opp Total			12		460	1744	8		3.8	145.3	38.3	167	2545	15.2	24		13.9	212.1	4289

Defense

No.		Age	Pos	G	GS	Sk	Int	Yds	TD	Lng	PD	FF	Fmb	FR	Yds	TD	Tkl	Ast	Sfty
							Def					**Fumb**					**Tack**		
7	Jim Finks*	25	QB	12	12							0	7	2	0	0			
25	Ray Mathews*	23	PR/LH	12	0							0	6	3	0	0			
80	Jack Butler	25		12	0		7	168	0	41	0	0	0	1	14	0			
20	Howard Hartley	28	LS	9	0		4	51	0	24	0	0	1	1	0	0			
63	Darrell Hogan	26		12	0		4	50	0	21	0	0	1	0	0	0			
14	Ed Kissell	23	RS	6	0		5	71	0	37	0								
50	George Tarasovic	22		12	0							0	1	4	14	0			
49	Lynn Chandnois*	27	RH/KR	12	0							0	3	1	0	0			
33	Jerry Shipkey*+	27	LLB	12	0		2	15	0	9	0	0	0	2	0	0			
24	Claude Hipps	25	LDH	12	0		3	48	0	17	0								
57	Frank Sinkovitz	29	RLB	11	0		1	5	0	5	0	0	0	2	0	0			
35	Tom Calvin	26		12	0							0	2	0	0	0			
78	Lou Ferry	25	LDT	12	0							0	0	2	71	1			
39	Ed Modzelewski	23	FB	10	0							0	2	0	0	0			
37	Jack Spinks	22		10	0							0	0	2	10	0			
60	Dale Dodrill	26	MG	12	0							0	0	1	0	0			
82	George Hays	28	LDE	11	0		1	1	1	1	0								
65	George Hughes	27	RT	12	0							0	0	1	0	0			
17	Gary Kerkorian	22	K	12	0							0	1	0	0	0			
84	Bill McPeak*	26	RDE	12	0							0	0	1	0	0			
81	Elbie Nickel*	30	RE	12	0							0	1	0	0	0			
34	Fran Rogel	25		12	0							0	1	0	0	0			
68	John Schweder	25	LG	12	0							0	0	1	0	0			
70	Ernie Stautner*	27	RDT	12	0							0	0	1	10	0			
88	George Sulima	24	LE	9	0							0	1	0	0	0			
56	Bill Walsh	25	C	12	0							0	0	1	0	0			
	Team Total	25.4		12			27	409	1	41	0	0	27	26	119	1			
	Opp Total			12	39								26	13					2

1953 PITTSBURGH STEELERS: 6-6-0, 4TH IN EAST, 7TH IN NFL
Head Coach: Joe Bach

						Score			Offe				Defe				
Week	Day	Date	OT	Rec	Opp	Tm	Opp	1stD	TotYd	PassY	RushY	TO	1stD	TotYd	PassY	RushY	TO
1	Sun	September 27	L	0-1	Detroit Lions	21	38	18	319	223	96	3	20	432	375	57	1
2	Sat	October 3	W	1-1	New York Giants	24	14	14	208	102	106	2	8	205	156	49	5
3	Sun	October 11	W	2-1	Chicago Cardinals	31	28	24	354	268	86	5	16	233	161	72	5
4	Sat	October 17	L	2-2	Philadelphia Eagles	7	23	12	168	114	54	3	17	326	259	67	1
5	Sat	October 24	W	3-2	Green Bay Packers	31	14	24	351	69	282	2	11	125	91	34	1
6	Sun	November 1	L	3-3	Philadelphia Eagles	7	35	15	262	207	55	5	19	422	256	166	1
7	Sun	November 8	L	3-4	Cleveland Browns	16	34	22	356	209	147	2	16	422	218	204	4
8	Sun	November 15	W	4-4	New York Giants	14	10	8	247	142	105	1	18	323	216	107	2
9	Sun	November 22	L	4-5	Cleveland Browns	16	20	17	288	72	216	3	13	235	175	60	1
10	Sun	November 29	L	4-6	Washington Redskins	9	17	16	285	242	43	4	17	216	77	139	3
11	Sun	December 6	W	5-6	Chicago Cardinals	21	17	18	210	63	147	3	14	212	165	47	4
12	Sun	December 13	W	6-6	Washington Redskins	14	13	18	351	139	212	2	15	230	107	123	7

Passing

No.		Age	Pos	G	GS	QBrec	Cmp	Att	Cmp%	Yds	TD	TD%	Int	Int%	Lng	Y/A	AY/A	Y/C	Y/G	Rate	Sk	Yds
7	Jim Finks	26	QB	11	9	4-5-0	131	292	44.9	1484	8	2.7	14	4.8	77	5.1	3.5	11.3	134.9	49.8		
13	Bill Mackrides	28		4	3	2-1-0	48	94	51.1	453	1	1.1	5	5.3	36	4.8	2.6	9.4	113.3	46.1		
17	Ted Marchibroda	22		4	0		9	22	40.9	66	1	4.5	2	9.1	16	3.0	-0.2	7.3	16.5	25.9		
49	Lynn Chandnois*	28	RH/PR/KR	12	0		1	3	33.3	11	0	0.0	0	0.0	11	3.7	3.7	11.0	0.9	45.1		
25	Ray Mathews	24	LS/LH	12	0		0	2	0.0	0	0	0.0	0	0.0	0	0.0	0.0		0.0	39.6		
18	Pat Brady	27	P	12	0		0	1	0.0	0	0	0.0	0	0.0	0	0.0	0.0		0.0	39.6		
27	Jim Brandt	24		12	0		0	1	0.0	0	0	0.0	0	0.0	0	0.0	0.0		0.0	39.6		
33	Fran Rogel	26	FB	12	0		0	1	0.0	0	0	0.0	0	0.0	0	0.0	0.0		0.0	39.6		
	Team Total	25.1		12		6-6-0	189	416	45.4	2014	10	2.4	21	5.0	77	4.8	3.1	10.7	167.8	47.1		
	Opp Total			12			193	372	51.9	2413	22	5.9	21	5.6		6.5	5.1	12.5	201.1	68.5	20	157

Rushing and Receiving

No.		Age	Pos	G	GS	Rush Att	Yds	TD	Lng	Y/A	Y/G	A/G	Rec	Receiving Yds	Y/R	TD	Lng	R/G	Y/G	YScm
33	Fran Rogel	26	FB	12	0	137	527	2	58	3.8	43.9	11.4	19	95	5.0	0	19	1.6	7.9	622
49	Lynn Chandnois*	28	RH/PR/KR	12	0	123	470	3	38	3.8	39.2	10.3	43	412	9.6	0	55	3.6	34.3	882
25	Ray Mathews	24	LS/LH	12	0	65	260	2	31	4.0	21.7	5.4	27	346	12.8	4	77	2.3	28.8	606
27	Jim Brandt	24		12	0	42	106	3	9	2.5	8.8	3.5	2	15	7.5	0	11	0.2	1.3	121
39	Leo Elter	24		12	0	26	81	0	10	3.1	6.8	2.2	3	29	9.7	0	15	0.3	2.4	110
35	Tom Calvin	27		10	0	13	65	0	15	5.0	6.5	1.3	4	28	7.0	0	16	0.4	2.8	93
13	Bill Mackrides	28		4	3	13	25	1	4	1.9	6.3	3.3								25
7	Jim Finks	26	QB	11	9	12	0	2	4	0.0	0.0	1.1								0
17	Ted Marchibroda	22		4	0	1	15	0	15	15.0	3.8	0.3								15
81	Elbie Nickel*	31	RE	12	0	0	0	0	0	0.0	0.0		62	743	12.0	4	40	5.2	61.9	743
89	Ed Barker	22	LE	6	0	0	0	0	0	0.0	0.0		17	172	10.1	1	22	2.8	28.7	172
88	George Sulima	25	le	10	0	0	0	0	0	0.0	0.0		10	131	13.1	0	17	1.0	13.1	131
80	Jack Butler	26	RDH	12	0	0	0	0	0	0.0	0.0		2	43	21.5	1	33	0.2	3.6	43
	Team Total	25.1		12		432	1549	13	58	3.6	129.1	36.0	189	2014	10.7	10	77	15.8	167.8	3563
	Opp Total			12		366	1125	9		3.1	93.8	30.5	193	2256	11.7	22		16.1	188.0	3381

Defense

No.		Age	Pos	G	GS	Sk	Def Int	Yds	TD	Lng	PD	Fumb FF	Fmb	FR	Yds	TD	Tack Tkl	Ast	Sfty
80	Jack Butler	26	RDH	12	0		9	147	1	28	0	0	0	3	0	0			
49	Lynn Chandnois*	28	RH/PR/KR	12	0							0	9	3	0	0			
25	Ray Mathews	24	LS/LH	12	0		1	17	0	17	0	0	5	3	1	1			1
26	Art DeCarlo	22	LDH	12	0		5	83	0	27	0	0	1	1	0	0			
13	Bill Mackrides	28		4	3							0	3	3	0	0			
60	Dale Dodrill*	27	MG	12	0		1	3	0	3	0	0	0	3	16	1			
7	Jim Finks	26	QB	11	9							0	3	1	0	0			
57	Dick Flanagan	27	LLB	12	0		2	23	0	23	0	0	0	1	0	0			
56	Marv Matuszak*	22	RLB	12	0		1	0	0	0	0	0	0	2	0	0			
33	Fran Rogel	26	FB	12	0							0	2	1	0	0			
27	Jim Brandt	24		12	0							0	1	1	0	0			
24	Claude Hipps	26	RS	5	0		2	0	0	0	0								
66	John Schweder	26	LG	12	0							0	0	2	0	0			
61	Lou Tepe	23		10	0							0	1	1	0	0			
75	Nick Bolkovac	25	K	12	0							0	0	1	14	1			
63	Darrell Hogan	27		12	0							0	0	1	0	0			
63	George Hughes*	26	RT	12	0							0	1	0	0	0			
81	Elbie Nickel*	31	RE	12	0							0	1	0	0	0			
88	George Sulima	25	le	10	0							0	1	0	0	0			
82	George Tarasovic	23	LDE	12	0							0	0	1	3	0			
	Team Total	25.1		12			21	273	1	28	0	0	28	28	34	3			2
	Opp Total			12		21							29	15					

1954 PITTSBURGH STEELERS: 5-7-0, 4TH IN EAST, 8TH IN NFL
Head Coach: Walt Kiesling

Week	Day	Date	OT	Rec	Opp	Score Tm	Opp	Offe 1stD	TotYd	PassY	RushY	TO	Defe 1stD	TotYd	PassY	RushY	TO
1	Sun	September 26	W	1-0	Green Bay Packers	21	20	23	444	316	128	2	9	252	91	161	4
2	Sat	October 2	W	2-0	Washington Redskins	37	7	26	429	277	152	1	18	253	132	121	4
3	Sat	October 9	L	2-1	Philadelphia Eagles	22	24	18	231	132	99	2	17	288	178	110	6
4	Sun	October 17	W	3-1	Cleveland Browns	55	27	22	441	257	184	1	23	436	269	167	8
5	Sat	October 23	W	4-1	Philadelphia Eagles	17	7	11	213	149	64	3	15	278	157	121	5
6	Sun	October 31	L	4-2	Chicago Cardinals	14	17	15	251	206	45	4	18	311	140	171	2
7	Sun	November 7	L	4-3	New York Giants	6	30	20	311	229	82	8	20	382	137	245	3
8	Sun	November 14	L	4-4	Washington Redskins	14	17	15	246	180	66	3	24	414	156	258	1
9	Sat	November 20	L	4-5	San Francisco 49ers	3	31	13	202	84	118	3	25	472	210	262	1
10	Sun	November 28	W	5-5	Chicago Cardinals	20	17	22	339	174	165	2	13	437	218	219	7
11	Sun	December 5	L	5-6	New York Giants	3	24	10	177	94	83	8	14	383	303	80	6
12	Sun	December 12	L	5-7	Cleveland Browns	7	42	10	171	75	96	6	25	464	186	278	3

Passing

No.		Age	Pos	G	GS	QBrec	Cmp	Att	Cmp%	Yds	TD	TD%	Int	Int%	Lng	Y/A	AY/A	Y/C	Y/G	Rate	Sk	Yds
7	Jim Finks	27	QB	12	12	5-7-0	164	306	53.6	2003	14	4.6	19	6.2	78	6.5	4.7	12.2	166.9	63.4		
17	Paul Held	26	K	8	0		24	73	32.9	305	1	1.4	6	8.2	37	4.2	0.8	12.7	38.1	17.2		
25	Ray Mathews	25	LH	12	0		0	4	0.0	0	0	0.0	1	25.0	0	0.0	−11.3		0.0	0.0		
49	Lynn Chandnois	29		11	0		1	3	33.3	13	0	0.0	0	0.0	13	4.3	4.3	13.0	1.2	47.9		
	Team Total	26.2		12		5-7-0	189	386	49.0	2321	15	3.9	26	6.7	78	6.0	3.8	12.3	193.4	52.8		
	Opp Total			12			167	295	56.6	2458	18	6.1	30	10.2		8.3	5.0	14.7	204.8	64.7	35	281

Rushing and Receiving

No.		Age	Pos	G	GS	Rush Att	Yds	TD	Lng	Y/A	Y/G	A/G	Receiving Rec	Yds	Y/R	TD	Lng	R/G	Y/G	YScm
33	Fran Rogel	27	FB	12	0	111	415	1	16	3.7	34.6	9.3	18	51	2.8	1	16	1.5	4.3	466
25	Ray Mathews	25	LH	12	0	80	242	2	24	3.0	20.2	6.7	44	652	14.8	6	78	3.7	54.3	894
41	Johnny Lattner*	22	RH/PR/KR	12	0	69	237	5	17	3.4	19.8	5.8	25	305	12.2	2	43	2.1	25.4	542
49	Lynn Chandnois	29		11	0	45	147	1	15	3.3	13.4	4.1	22	176	8.0	0	23	2.0	16.0	323
27	Jim Brandt	25		12	0	19	82	1	20	4.3	6.8	1.6	1	9	9.0	0	9	0.1	0.8	91
39	Leo Elter	25		11	0	13	54	0	12	4.2	4.9	1.2	4	16	4.0	0	26	0.4	1.5	70
35	Tom Calvin	28		6	0	12	57	0	8	4.8	9.5	2.0	1	19	19.0	0	19	0.2	3.2	76
7	Jim Finks	27	QB	12	12	9	17	0	6	1.9	1.4	0.8								17
37	Burrell Shields	25		6	0	7	28	0	13	4.0	4.7	1.2	1	22	22.0	0	22	0.2	3.7	50
17	Paul Held	26	K	8	0	3	3	0	3	1.0	0.4	0.4								3
81	Elbie Nickel	32	RE	12	0	0	0	0	0		0.0	0.0	40	584	14.6	5	52	3.3	48.7	584
88	George Sulima	26	LE	12	0	0	0	0	0		0.0	0.0	30	439	14.6	1	37	2.5	36.6	439
80	Jack Butler	27	RDH	12	0	0	0	0	0		0.0	0.0	1	12	12.0	0	12	0.1	1.0	12
26	Dewey McConnell	24		9	0	0	0	0	0		0.0	0.0	1	2	2.0	0	2	0.1	0.2	2
89	Jack OBrien	22		7	0	0	0	0	0		0.0	0.0	1	9	9.0	0	9	0.1	1.3	9
	Team Total	26.2		12		368	1282	10	24	3.5	106.8	30.7	189	2321	12.3	15	78	15.8	193.4	3603
	Opp Total			12		466	2193	14		4.7	182.8	38.8	167	2177	13.0	18		13.9	181.4	4370

Defense

| No. | | Age | Pos | G | GS | Sk | Def | | | | | Fumb | | | | | Tack | | Sfty |
							Int	Yds	TD	Lng	PD	FF	Fmb	FR	Yds	TD	Tkl	Ast	
34	Paul Cameron	22	LS	12	0		7	118	0	33	0	0	1	3	0	0			
49	Lynn Chandnois	29		11	0							0	4	3	0	0			
7	Jim Finks	27	QB	12	12							0	4	2	0	0			
61	Lou Tepe	24		12	0		3	67	0	29	0	0	1	2	0	0			
80	Jack Butler	27	RDH	12	0		4	75	2	41	0	0	0	1	10	0			
60	Dale Dodrill*+	28	MG	12	0		3	28	0	16	0	0	0	2	66	0			
25	Ray Mathews	25	LH	12	0							0	5	0	0	0			
57	Dick Flanagan	28	LLB	5	0		3	0	0	0	0	0	0	1	0	0			
41	Johnny Lattner*	22	RH/PR/KR	12	0							0	4	0	0	0			
26	Dewey McConnell	24		9	0		3	117	0	30	0	0	0	1	0	0			
33	Fran Rogel	27	FB	12	0							0	4	0	0	0			
70	Ernie Stautner	29	RDT	12	0		1	3	0	3	0	0	0	3	5	0			
83	Dewey Brundage	23	LDE	11	0							0	0	3	0	0			
24	Russ Craft	35	LDH	11	0		3	120	1	81	0								
39	Leo Elter	25		11	0							0	1	1	0	0			
78	Lou Ferry	27	LDT	11	0							0	0	2	0	0			
17	Paul Held	26	K	8	0							0	1	1	0	0			
65	George Hughes	29	RT	12	0							0	0	2	0	0			
81	Elbie Nickel	32	RE	12	0							0	1	1	0	0			
37	Burrell Shields	25		6	0		1	8	0	8	0	0	1	0	0	0			
27	Jim Brandt	25		12	0							0	0	1	0	0			
35	Tom Calvin	28		6	0							0	1	0	0	0			
28	Ed Kissell	25	RS	7	0		1	15	0	15	0								
84	Bill McPeak	28	RDE	12	0							0	0	1	5	0			1
50	Stan Sheriff	22	RLB	12	0		1	18	0	18	0								
56	Bill Walsh+	27	C	12	0							0	0	1	0	0			
	Team Total	26.2		12			30	569	3	81	0	0	28	31	86	0			1
	Opp Total			12		19							31	11					1

1955 PITTSBURGH STEELERS: 4-8-0, LAST IN EAST, 10TH IN NFL
Head Coach: Walt Kiesling

| Week | Day | Date | OT | Rec | Opp | Score | | Offe | | | | | Defe | | | | |
						Tm	Opp	1stD	TotYd	PassY	RushY	TO	1stD	TotYd	PassY	RushY	TO
1	Mon	September 26	W	1-0	Chicago Cardinals	14	7	23	355	236	119	5	8	86	25	61	2
2	Sun	October 2	L	1-1	Los Angeles Rams	26	27	16	258	103	155	3	20	346	190	156	3
3	Sun	October 9	W	2-1	New York Giants	30	23	26	459	297	162	4	11	290	225	65	3
4	Sat	October 15	W	3-1	Philadelphia Eagles	13	7	17	306	105	201	3	6	148	140	8	5
5	Sun	October 23	W	4-1	New York Giants	19	17	22	359	212	147		16	284	189	95	2
6	Sun	October 30	L	4-2	Philadelphia Eagles	0	24	11	176	119	57	3	18	245	86	159	1
7	Sat	November 5	L	4-3	Chicago Cardinals	13	27	21	466	321	145	6	12	261	78	183	1
8	Sun	November 13	L	4-4	Detroit Lions	28	31	26	451	367	84	5	12	234	169	65	2
9	Sun	November 20	L	4-5	Cleveland Browns	14	41	16	238	173	65	5	18	267	68	199	2
10	Sun	November 27	L	4-6	Washington Redskins	14	23	15	308	243	65	6	20	300	−32	332	1
11	Sun	December 4	L	4-7	Cleveland Browns	7	30	8	123	97	26	5	19	343	70	273	1
12	Sun	December 11	L	4-8	Washington Redskins	17	28	10	172	114	58	2	16	305	87	218	6

Passing

No.		Age	Pos	G	GS	QBrec	Cmp	Att	Cmp%	Yds	TD	TD%	Int	Int%	Lng	Y/A	AY/A	Y/C	Y/G	Rate	Sk	Yds
7	Jim Finks	28	QB	12	12	4-8-0	165	344	48.0	2270	10	2.9	26	7.6	62	6.6	3.8	13.8	189.2	47.7		
18	Ted Marchibroda	24		7	0		24	43	55.8	280	2	4.7	3	7.0	47	6.5	4.3	11.7	40.0	62.2		
12	Vic Eaton	22	PR/P	12	0		0	2	0.0	0	0	0.0	0	0.0	0	0.0	0.0		0.0	39.6		
49	Lynn Chandnois	30	RH	8	0		0	1	0.0	0	0	0.0	1	100.0	0	0.0	-45.0		0.0	0.0		
	Team Total	25.9		12		4-8-0	189	390	48.5	2550	12	3.1	30	7.7	62	6.5	3.7	13.5	212.5	47.9		
	Opp Total			12			123	242	50.8	1530	19	7.9	10	4.1		6.3	6.0	12.4	127.5	79.7	29	235

Rushing and Receiving

No.		Age	Pos	G	GS	Rush Att	Yds	TD	Lng	Y/A	Y/G	A/G	Rec	Yds	Y/R	TD	Lng	R/G	Y/G	YScm
33	Fran Rogel	28	FB	12	0	168	588	2	19	3.5	49.0	14.0	24	222	9.3	0	28	2.0	18.5	810
49	Lynn Chandnois	30	RH	8	0	105	353	5	23	3.4	44.1	13.1	27	385	14.3	0	36	3.4	48.1	738
25	Ray Mathews*	26	LH	12	0	57	187	1	23	3.3	15.6	4.8	42	762	18.1	6	61	3.5	63.5	949
7	Jim Finks	28	QB	12	12	35	76	4	9	2.2	6.3	2.9								76
39	Sid Watson	23	KR	12	0	29	31	0	15	1.1	2.6	2.4	19	223	11.7	1	62	1.6	18.6	254
28	Leon Campbell	28		12	0	18	42	0	27	2.3	3.5	1.5	9	76	8.4	0	36	0.8	6.3	118
18	Ted Marchibroda	24		7	0	6	−1	1	8	−0.2	−0.1	0.9								−1
36	Marion Motley	35		7	0	2	8	0	8	4.0	1.1	0.3								8
81	Elbie Nickel	33	RE	12	0	0	0	0	0		0.0	0.0	36	488	13.6	2	30	3.0	40.7	488
83	Ed Bernet	22	LE	12	0	0	0	0	0		0.0	0.0	22	276	12.5	1	38	1.8	23.0	276
89	Jack OBrien	23		12	0	0	0	0	0		0.0	0.0	9	105	11.7	2	38	0.8	8.8	105
87	Jack McClairen	24		12	0	0	0	0	0		0.0	0.0	1	13	13.0	0	13	0.1	1.1	13
	Team Total	25.9		12		420	1284	13	27	3.1	107.0	35.0	189	2550	13.5	12	62	15.8	212.5	3834
	Opp Total			12		494	1814	11		3.7	151.2	41.2	123	1295	10.5	19		10.3	107.9	3109

Defense

No.		Age	Pos	G	GS	Sk	Def Int	Yds	TD	Lng	PD	FF	Fmb	FR	Yds	TD	Tkl	Ast	Sfty
39	Sid Watson	23	KR	12	0							0	7	1	0	0			
50	John Reger	24	RLB	12	0		2	11	0	9	0	0	0	5	4	0			
7	Jim Finks	28	QB	12	12							0	5	1	0	0			
33	Fran Rogel	28	FB	12	0							0	5	0	0	0			
60	Dale Dodrill*	29		12	0		2	25	0	25	0	0	0	2	0	0			
24	Richie McCabe	22	RS	12	0		3	29	0	25	0	0	0	1	76	1			
49	Lynn Chandnois	30	RH	8	0							0	2	1	0	0			
18	Ted Marchibroda	24		7	0							0	3	0	0	0			
61	Marv Matuszak	24		4	0		1	7	0	7	0	0	1	1	0	0			
72	Bob Gaona	24	LT	12	0							0	0	2	0	0			
42	Jim Hill	26	LDH	10	0		1	9	0	9	0	0	0	1	11	0			
76	Willie McClung	25	RDT	12	0							0	0	2	0	0			
70	Ernie Stautner*	30	RG	12	0							0	0	2	0	0			
61	Lou Tepe	25	C	12	0							0	0	2	0	0			
83	Ed Bernet	22	LE	12	0							0	1	0	0	0			
80	Jack Butler*	28	RDH	12	0							0	0	1	0	0			
28	Leon Campbell	28		12	0							0	1	0	0	0			
41	Dick Doyle	25	LS	12	0		1	4	0	4	0								
78	Lou Ferry	28		12	0							0	0	1	0	0			
57	Dick Flanagan	29	LLB	12	0							0	0	1	9	0			
25	Ray Mathews*	26	LH	12	0							0	1	0	0	0			
84	Bill McPeak	29	RDE	10	0							0	0	1	2	0			
82	Ed Meadows	23	LDE	12	0							0	0	1	0	0			
85	Joe OMalley	22		10	0							0	0	1	0	0			
74	Frank Varrichione*	23	RT	12	0							0	0	1	0	0			
	Team Total	25.9		12			10	85	0	25	0	0	26	28	102	1			
	Opp Total			12		20							35	16					

1956 PITTSBURGH STEELERS: 5-7-0, TIED FOR 4TH IN EAST, TIED FOR 7TH IN NFL
Head Coach: Walt Kiesling

						Score		Offe					Defe				
Week	Day	Date	OT	Rec	Opp	Tm	Opp	1stD	TotYd	PassY	RushY	TO	1stD	TotYd	PassY	RushY	TO
1	Sun	September 30	W	1-0	Washington Redskins	30	13	17	225	83	142	1	10	192	117	75	4
2	Sat	October 6	L	1-1	Cleveland Browns	10	14	14	245	153	92		17	336	122	214	
3	Sun	October 14	L	1-2	Philadelphia Eagles	21	35	17	324	247	77	3	12	265	168	97	2
4	Sun	October 21	L	1-3	New York Giants	10	38	10	182	91	91	1	25	460	213	247	
5	Sun	October 28	W	2-3	Cleveland Browns	24	16	18	358	219	139	3	11	284	108	176	4
6	Sun	November 4	L	2-4	New York Giants	14	17	18	255	118	137	3	18	229	110	119	2
7	Sun	November 11	L	2-5	Philadelphia Eagles	7	14	14	149	95	54	3	13	252	130	122	4
8	Sun	November 18	W	3-5	Chicago Cardinals	14	7	15	280	39	241	4	15	254	103	151	6
9	Sun	November 25	L	3-6	Chicago Cardinals	27	38	25	352	206	146	6	19	370	128	242	4
10	Sun	December 2	W	4-6	Los Angeles Rams	30	13	16	264	134	130	3	7	163	63	100	2
11	Sun	December 9	L	4-7	Detroit Lions	7	45	9	129	104	25	6	15	296	166	130	6
12	Sun	December 16	W	5-7	Washington Redskins	23	0	11	253	177	76	1	5	85	15	70	6

Passing

No.		Age	Pos	G	GS	QBrec	Cmp	Att	Cmp%	Yds	TD	TD%	Int	Int%	Lng	Y/A	AY/A	Y/C	Y/G	Rate	Sk	Yds
18	Ted Marchibroda	25	QB	12	11	4-7-0	124	275	45.1	1585	12	4.4	19	6.9	75	5.8	3.5	12.8	132.1	49.4		
12	Jack Scarbath	26		7	1	1-0-0	12	41	29.3	208	2	4.9	5	12.2	47	5.1	0.6	17.3	29.7	24.9		
26	Lou Baldacci	22	P	10	0		0	1	0.0	0	0	0.0	0	0.0	0	0.0	0.0		0.0	39.6		
49	Lynn Chandnois	31	rh	5	0		0	1	0.0	0	0	0.0	0	0.0	0	0.0	0.0		0.0	39.6		
	Team Total	25.6		12		5-7-0	136	318	42.8	1793	14	4.4	24	7.5	75	5.6	3.1	13.2	149.4	44.4		
	Opp Total			12			128	234	54.7	1646	14	6.0	18	7.7		7.0	4.8	12.9	137.2	64.9	25	203

Rushing and Receiving

No.		Age	Pos	G	GS	Rush							Receiving							YScm
						Att	Yds	TD	Lng	Y/A	Y/G	A/G	Rec	Yds	Y/R	TD	Lng	R/G	Y/G	
33	Fran Rogel*	29	FB	12	0	131	476	2	40	3.6	39.7	10.9	23	88	3.8	0	13	1.9	7.3	564
39	Sid Watson	24	RH	12	0	112	298	4	18	2.7	24.8	9.3	12	138	11.5	0	37	1.0	11.5	436
49	Lynn Chandnois	31	rh	5	0	44	118	4	28	2.7	23.6	8.8	7	71	10.1	1	17	1.4	14.2	189
18	Ted Marchibroda	25	QB	12	11	39	152	2	26	3.9	12.7	3.3								152
26	Lou Baldacci	22	P	10	0	31	140	0	29	4.5	14.0	3.1	5	62	12.4	0	22	0.5	6.2	202
35	Charlie Shepard	23		12	0	30	91	0	14	3.0	7.6	2.5	1	31	31.0	0	31	0.1	2.6	122
24	Henry Ford	25	PR/LS	12	0	12	26	2	16	2.2	2.2	1.0	3	7	2.3	0	8	0.3	0.6	33
44	Art Davis	22		9	0	5	6	0	9	1.2	0.7	0.6	1	9	9.0	0	9	0.1	1.0	15
12	Jack Scarbath	26		7	1	4	19	0	21	4.8	2.7	0.6								19
25	Ray Mathews	27	RE	12	0	3	−11	0	2	−3.7	−0.9	0.3	31	540	17.4	5	64	2.6	45.0	529
41	Lowell Perry	25	LE	6	0	2	37	0	23	18.5	6.2	0.3	14	334	23.9	2	75	2.3	55.7	371
81	Elbie Nickel*	34	LH	12	0	0	0	0	0		0.0	0.0	27	376	13.9	5	47	2.3	31.3	376
89	Jack OBrien	24		12	0	0	0	0	0		0.0	0.0	6	71	11.8	0	25	0.5	5.9	71
87	Jack McClairen	25		7	0	0	0	0	0		0.0	0.0	5	56	11.2	0	18	0.7	8.0	56
80	Jack Butler*	29	RS	12	0	0	0	0	0		0.0	0.0	1	10	10.0	1	10	0.1	0.8	10
	Team Total	25.6		12		413	1350	14	40	3.3	112.5	34.4	136	1793	13.2	14	75	11.3	149.4	3143
	Opp Total			12		468	1743	14		3.7	145.3	39.0	128	1443	11.3	14		10.7	120.3	3186

Defense

No.		Age	Pos	G	GS	Sk	Int	Yds	TD	Lng	PD	FF	Fmb	FR	Yds	TD	Tkl	Ast	Sfty
							Def					**Fumb**					**Tack**		
80	Jack Butler*	29	RS	12	0		6	113	0	34	0	0	0	2	6	1			
39	Sid Watson	24	RH	12	0							0	4	1	0	0			
42	Dick Alban	27	RDH	12	0		2	21	0	21	0	0	0	2	0	0			
64	Marv Matuszak	25		9	0		2	28	0	26	0	0	1	1	0	0			
33	Fran Rogel*	29	FB	12	0							0	4	0	0	0			
53	George Tarasovic	26	LLB	12	0		3	60	0	31	0	0	0	1	0	0			
24	Henry Ford	25	PR/LS	12	0		1	17	0	17	0	0	1	1	0	0			
75	Joe Krupa	23		12	0							0	0	3	0	0			
18	Ted Marchibroda	25	QB	12	11							0	3	0	0	0			
50	John Reger	25	RLB	12	0		2	33	0	33	0	0	0	1	0	0			
26	Lou Baldacci	22	P	10	0							0	1	1	0	0			
41	Fred Bruney	25	KR	5	0		1	39	0	39	0	0	0	1	0	0			
27	Gary Glick	26	LDH/K	8	0							0	0	2	0	0			
85	Joe OMalley	23	LDE	12	0							0	0	2	5	0			
12	Jack Scarbath	26		7	1							0	1	1	0	0			
70	Ernie Stautner*	31	RDT	12	0							0	0	2	0	0			
49	Lynn Chandnois	31	rh	5	0							0	0	1	0	0			
60	Dale Dodrill	30	MG	12	0		1	1	0	1	0								
87	Jack McClairen	25		7	0							0	0	1	4	0			
76	Willie McClung	26	LDT	12	0							0	0	1	0	0			
61	Marv McFadden	26	RG	12	0							0	0	1	0	0			
86	Bob ONeil	25	lg	12	0							0	0	1	0	0			
35	Charlie Shepard	23		12	0							0	1	0	0	0			
57	Jim G. Taylor	22	C	12	0							0	0	1	3	0			
74	Frank Varrichione	24	RT	12	0							0	0	1	0	0			
	Team Total	25.6		12			18	312	0	39	0	0	16	28	18	1		1	
	Opp Total			12		16							39	17					

1957 PITTSBURGH STEELERS: 6-6-0, 3RD IN EAST, TIED FOR 6TH IN NFL
Head Coach: Buddy Parker

Week	Day	Date	OT	Rec	Opp	Tm	Opp	1stD	TotYd	PassY	RushY	TO	1stD	TotYd	PassY	RushY	TO
						Score		**Offe**					**Defe**				
1	Sun	September 29	W	1-0	Washington Redskins	28	7	16	301	228	73		13	242	153	89	6
2	Sat	October 5	L	1-1	Cleveland Browns	12	23	14	236	173	63	4	12	240	134	106	1
3	Sun	October 13	W	2-1	Chicago Cardinals	29	20	12	231	79	152	4	15	315	126	189	5
4	Sun	October 20	L	2-2	New York Giants	0	35	10	172	118	54	4	17	340	212	128	1
5	Sun	October 27	W	3-2	Philadelphia Eagles	6	0	15	334	227	107	3	5	70		70	5
6	Sun	November 3	W	4-2	Baltimore Colts	19	13	12	271	256	15	1	17	255	87	168	4
7	Sun	November 10	L	4-3	Cleveland Browns	0	24	18	276	186	90	4	11	291	168	123	4
8	Sun	November 24	L	4-4	Green Bay Packers	10	27	11	167	108	59	7	15	253	102	151	3
10	Sun	December 1	L	4-5	Philadelphia Eagles	6	7	13	258	87	171	2	10	220	67	153	2
10	Sat	December 7	W	5-5	New York Giants	21	10	12	189	47	142	1	16	260	194	66	3
11	Sun	December 15	L	5-6	Washington Redskins	3	10	7	158	78	80	2	15	209	65	144	4
12	Sun	December 22	W	6-6	Chicago Cardinals	27	2	19	297	129	168		10	96	58	38	4

Passing

No.		Age	Pos	G	GS	QBrec	Cmp	Att	Cmp%	Yds	TD	TD%	Int	Int%	Lng	Y/A	AY/A	Y/C	Y/G	Rate	Sk	Yds
10	Earl Morrall*	23	QB	12	11	6-5-0	139	289	48.1	1900	11	3.8	12	4.2	64	6.6	5.5	13.7	158.3	64.9		
7	Jack Kemp	22		4	0		8	18	44.4	88	0	0.0	2	11.1	21	4.9	-0.1	11.0	22.0	19.9		
16	Len Dawson	22		3	1	0-1-0	2	4	50.0	25	0	0.0	0	0.0	15	6.3	6.3	12.5	8.3	69.8		
41	Jug Girard	30	P/LE	12	0		0	1	0.0	0	0	0.0	0	0.0	0	0.0	0.0		0.0	39.6		
	Team Total	25.8		12		6-6-0	149	312	47.8	2013	11	3.5	14	4.5	64	6.5	5.1	13.5	167.8	61.8		
	Opp Total			12			112	234	47.9	1523	12	5.1	19	8.1		6.5	3.9	13.6	126.9	52.4	20	157

Rushing and Receiving

No.		Age	Pos	G	GS	Rush Att	Rush Yds	Rush TD	Rush Lng	Rush Y/A	Rush Y/G	Rush A/G	Rec	Rec Yds	Rec Y/R	Rec TD	Rec Lng	Rec R/G	Rec Y/G	YScm
24	Billy Wells	26	PR/LH/KR	10	0	154	532	0	51	3.5	53.2	15.4	14	89	6.4	0	17	1.4	8.9	621
33	Fran Rogel	30	FB	12	0	68	232	1	23	3.4	19.3	5.7	20	128	6.4	0	18	1.7	10.7	360
33	Dick Young	27		11	0	56	153	2	14	2.7	13.9	5.1	4	38	9.5	0	12	0.4	3.5	191
10	Earl Morrall*	23	QB	12	11	41	81	2	35	2.0	6.8	3.4								81
43	Bill Bowman	26		5	0	28	76	0	13	2.7	15.2	5.6	11	107	9.7	0	21	2.2	21.4	183
27	Dean Derby	22		8	0	18	49	1	7	2.7	6.1	2.3	4	79	19.8	0	36	0.5	9.9	128
39	Sid Watson	25		11	0	12	21	0	12	1.8	1.9	1.1	3	24	8.0	0	11	0.3	2.2	45
25	Ray Mathews	28	RE	12	0	3	-1	0	6	-0.3	-0.1	0.3	15	369	24.6	4	64	1.3	30.8	368
16	Len Dawson	22		3	1	3	31	0	27	10.3	10.3	1.0								31
7	Jack Kemp	22		4	0	3	-1	0	2	-0.3	-0.3	0.8								-1
41	Jug Girard	30	P/LE	12	0	2	-5	0	0	-2.5	-0.4	0.2	21	419	20.0	4	46	1.8	34.9	414
24	Dick Hughes	25		1	0	2	6	0	4	3.0	6.0	2.0								6
87	Jack McClairen*	26		12	0	0	0	0	0		0.0	0.0	46	630	13.7	2	48	3.8	52.5	630
81	Elbie Nickel	35	RH	12	0	0	0	0	0		0.0	0.0	10	115	11.5	1	31	0.8	9.6	115
86	Perry Richards	23		7	0	0	0	0	0		0.0	0.0	1	15	15.0	0	15	0.1	2.1	15
	Team Total	25.8		12		390	1174	6	51	3.0	97.8	32.5	149	2013	13.5	11	64	12.4	167.8	3187
	Opp Total			12		412	1425	7		3.5	118.8	34.3	112	1366	12.2	12		9.3	113.8	2791

Defense

No.		Age	Pos	G	GS	Sk	Def Int	Def Yds	Def TD	Def Lng	Def PD	Fumb FF	Fumb Fmb	Fumb FR	Fumb Yds	Fumb TD	Tack Tkl	Tack Ast	Sfty
10	Earl Morrall*	23	QB	12	11							0	12	0	-2	0			
24	Billy Wells	26	PR/LH/KR	10	0							0	7	6	0	0			
80	Jack Butler*+	30	LS	12	0		10	85	0	20	0	0	0	1	0	0			
26	Gary Glick	27	LDH/K	12	0		2	0	0	0	0	0	0	5	26	0			
50	John Reger	26	LLB	12	0							0	0	5	14	1			
42	Dick Alban	28	RDH	12	0		1	35	0	35	0	0	2	1	0	0			
68	Ed Beatty	25	C	12	0							0	0	4	0	0			
22	Fred Bruney	26	RS	12	0		1	0	0	0	0	0	1	2	0	0			
27	Dean Derby	22		8	0							0	3	0	0	0			
60	Dale Dodrill*	31	MLB	12	0		2	50	0	44	0	0	0	1	0	0			
25	Ray Mathews	28	RE	12	0							0	3	0	0	0			
43	Bill Bowman	26		5	0							0	2	0	0	0			
24	Dick Hughes	25		1	0							0	1	1	0	0			
84	Bill McPeak	31	RDE	12	0							0	0	2	1	0		1	
64	Bill Priatko	26		2	0							0	0	2	0	0			
86	Perry Richards	23		7	0							0	1	1	0	0			
62	Mike Sandusky	22	LG	12	0							0	0	2	0	0			
52	George Tarasovic	27		12	0		2	21	0	11	0								
39	Sid Watson	25		11	0							0	2	0	0	0			
16	Len Dawson	22		3	1							0	1	0	0	0			
41	Jug Girard	30	P/LE	12	0							0	1	0	0	0			
82	Bob Gunderman	23		1	0							0	0	1	0	0			
7	Jack Kemp	22		4	0							0	1	0	0	0			
75	Joe Krupa	24	LDT	12	0							0	0	1	0	0			
72	Herman Lee	26	lt	8	0							0	0	1	0	0			
76	Willie McClung	27	LT	12	0							0	0	1	0	0			
33	Fran Rogel	30	FB	12	0							0	1	0	0	0			
66	Aubrey Rozzell	25	RLB	7	0		1	4	0	4	0								
70	Ernie Stautner*	32	RDT	12	0							0	0	1	0	0			
33	Dick Young	27		11	0							0	1	0	0	0			
	Team Total	25.8		12			19	195	0	44	0	0	39	44	49	1		1	
	Opp Total			12		37							39	16					1

1958 PITTSBURGH STEELERS: 7-4-1, 3RD IN EAST, 6TH IN NFL
Head Coach: Buddy Parker

						Score		Offe					Defe				
Week	Day	Date	OT	Rec	Opp	Tm	Opp	1stD	TotYd	PassY	RushY	TO	1stD	TotYd	PassY	RushY	TO
1	Sun	September 28	L	0-1	San Francisco 49ers	20	23	10	217	100	117	4	18	322	234	88	3
2	Sun	October 5	L	0-2	Cleveland Browns	12	45	12	269	169	100	9	20	411	219	192	5
3	Sun	October 12	W	1-2	Philadelphia Eagles	24	3	19	286	72	214	2	16	207	148	59	7
4	Sun	October 19	L	1-3	Cleveland Browns	10	27	14	259	172	87	4	19	409	145	264	3
5	Sun	October 26	L	1-4	New York Giants	6	17	10	239	194	45	4	12	175	29	146	1
6	Sun	November 2	W	2-4	Washington Redskins	24	16	20	398	252	146	2	15	296	216	80	4
7	Sun	November 9	W	3-4	Philadelphia Eagles	31	24	15	386	290	96	2	23	322	197	125	2
8	Sun	November 16	W	4-4	New York Giants	31	10	17	297	168	129	2	13	191	103	88	1
9	Sun	November 23	W	5-4	Chicago Cardinals	27	20	18	458	374	84	2	18	315	242	73	3
10	Sun	November 30	W	6-4	Chicago Bears	24	10	12	396	202	194	3	19	270	143	127	5
11	Sun	December 7	T	6-4-1	Washington Redskins	14	14	20	385	287	98	5	19	188	−28	216	1
12	Sat	December 13	W	7-4-1	Chicago Cardinals	38	21	35	683	472	211	3	17	277	244	33	7

Passing

No.		Age	Pos	G	GS	QBrec	Cmp	Att	Cmp%	Yds	TD	TD%	Int	Int%	Lng	Y/A	AY/A	Y/C	Y/G	Rate	Sk	Yds
22	Bobby Layne*	32	QB	10	10	7–2–1	133	268	49.6	2339	13	4.9	10	3.7	78	8.7	8.0	17.6	233.9	80.4		
10	Earl Morrall	24		2	2	0–2–0	16	46	34.8	275	1	2.2	7	15.2	66	6.0	−0.4	17.2	137.5	23.6		
30	Tom Tracy*	24	RH	12	0		6	16	37.5	270	2	12.5	2	12.5	72	16.9	13.8	45.0	22.5	85.4		
16	Len Dawson	23		4	0		1	6	16.7	11	0	0.0	2	33.3	11	1.8	−13.2	11.0	2.8	0.0		
	Team Total	25.6		12		7–4–1	156	336	46.4	2895	16	4.8	21	6.3	78	8.6	6.8	18.6	241.3	66.5		
	Opp Total			12			173	334	51.8	2136	11	3.3	24	7.2		6.4	3.8	12.3	178.0	52.9	31	244

Rushing and Receiving

						Rush							Receiving							
No.		Age	Pos	G	GS	Att	Yds	TD	Lng	Y/A	Y/G	A/G	Rec	Yds	Y/R	TD	Lng	R/G	Y/G	YScm
30	Tom Tracy*	24	RH	12	0	169	714	5	64	4.2	59.5	14.1	32	535	16.7	4	56	2.7	44.6	1249
35	Tank Younger	30	FB	12	0	88	344	3	36	3.9	28.7	7.3	16	188	11.8	0	51	1.3	15.7	532
20	Dick Christy	23	KR	12	0	38	101	0	19	2.7	8.4	3.2	7	73	10.4	0	26	0.6	6.1	174
34	Leo Elter	29		7	0	37	104	2	18	2.8	14.9	5.3	6	68	11.3	0	22	0.9	9.7	172
22	Bobby Layne*	32	QB	10	10	37	153	3	21	4.1	15.3	3.7								153
46	Billy Reynolds	27	PR	12	0	10	29	1	11	2.9	2.4	0.8	1	1	1.0	0	1	0.1	0.1	30
25	Ray Mathews	29	LH	12	0	4	24	0	14	6.0	2.0	0.3	25	525	21.0	4	65	2.1	43.8	549
31	Larry Krutko	23		6	0	4	6	0	5	1.5	1.0	0.7								6
10	Earl Morrall	24		2	2	4	39	0	22	9.8	19.5	2.0								39
16	Len Dawson	23		4	0	2	−1	0	1	−0.5	−0.3	0.5								−1
86	Jimmy Orr	23	P/LE	12	0	1	8	0	8	8.0	0.7	0.1	33	910	27.6	7	78	2.8	75.8	918
87	Jack McClairen	27	RE	12	0	0	0	0	0		0.0	0.0	29	491	16.9	1	35	2.4	40.9	491
83	Dick Lucas	24		4	0	0	0	0	0		0.0	0.0	4	47	11.8	0	17	1.0	11.8	47
85	Don Bishop	24		12	0	0	0	0	0		0.0	0.0	3	57	19.0	0	29	0.3	4.8	57
	Team Total	25.6		12		394	1521	14	64	3.9	126.8	32.8	156	2895	18.6	16	78	13.0	241.3	4416
	Opp Total			12		403	1491	14		3.7	124.3	33.6	173	1892	10.9	11		14.4	157.7	3383

Defense

No.	Name	Age	Pos	G	GS	Sk	Int	Yds	TD	Lng	PD	FF	Fmb	FR	Yds	TD	Tkl	Ast	Sfty
30	Tom Tracy*	24	RH	12	0							0	10	1	0	0			
80	Jack Butler*+	31	RS	12	0		9	81	0	19	0								
27	Dean Derby	23	LDH	12	0		4	0	0	0	0	0	1	2	0	0			
42	Dick Alban	29	RDH	12	0		5	25	0	16	0	0	0	1	17	0			
26	Gary Glick	28	LS	12	0		2	60	0	26	0	0	0	3	37	1			
22	Bobby Layne*	32	QB	10	10							0	5	0	0	0			
20	Dick Christy	23	KR	12	0							0	4	0	0	0			
71	Joe Lewis	22	LDT	12	0		1	8	0	8	0	0	0	3	0	0			
87	Jack McClairen	27	RE	12	0							0	1	3	13	0			
46	Billy Reynolds	27	PR	12	0							0	2	2	0	0			
66	Dick Campbell	23		12	0		1	58	0	58	0	0	0	2	0	0			
86	Jimmy Orr	23	P/LE	12	0							0	1	2	0	0			
35	Tank Younger	30	FB	12	0							0	3	0	0	0			
34	Leo Elter	29		7	0							0	2	0	0	0			
61	Ted Karras	24	LT	12	0							0	0	2	7	0			
62	Mike Sandusky	23	LG	12	0							0	0	2	0	0			
74	Frank Varrichione*	26	RT	12	0							0	0	2	0	0			
60	Dale Dodrill	32	LLB	12	0		1	13	0	13	0		0	0	0	0			
64	Billy Krisher	23		8	0							0	0	1	0	0			
75	Joe Krupa	25	RDT	12	0							0	0	1	0	0			
31	Larry Krutko	23		6	0							0	1	0	0	0			
24	Richie McCabe	25		5	0							0	0	1	0	0			
10	Earl Morrall	24		2	2							0	1	0	0	0			
65	John Nisby	22	RG	12	0							0	0	1	7	0			
50	John Reger	27	RLB	12	0		1	3	0	3	0		0	1	0	0			
77	Billy Ray Sr. Smith	23		12	0							0	1	0	0	0			
70	Ernie Stautner*+	33	RDE	12	0							0	0	1	0	0			1
52	George Tarasovic	28	LDE	12	0							0	0	1	0	0			
	Team Total	25.6		12			24	248	0	58	0	0	32	31	81	1			1
	Opp Total			12		18							34	16					

1959 PITTSBURGH STEELERS: 6-5-1, 4TH IN EAST, 8TH IN NFL
Head Coach: Buddy Parker

Week	Day	Date	OT	Rec	Opp	Score Tm	Opp	Offe 1stD	TotYd	PassY	RushY	TO	Defe 1stD	TotYd	PassY	RushY	TO
1	Sat	September 26	W	1-0	Cleveland Browns	17	7	18	323	202	121	2	20	274	135	139	1
2	Sun	October 4	L	1-1	Washington Redskins	17	23	23	381	268	113	3	14	322	238	84	1
3	Sun	October 11	L	1-2	Philadelphia Eagles	24	28	15	269	203	66	2	18	281	172	109	2
4	Sun	October 18	W	2-2	Washington Redskins	27	6	13	187	53	134	3	12	182	−13	195	6
5	Sun	October 25	L	2-3	New York Giants	16	21	9	243	210	33	6	10	279	199	80	4
6	Sun	November 1	L	2-4	Chicago Cardinals	24	45	20	329	154	175	6	20	336	70	266	3
7	Sun	November 8	T	2-4-1	Detroit Lions	10	10	14	189	123	66	4	16	314	131	183	3
8	Sun	November 15	W	3-4-1	New York Giants	14	9	20	322	167	155	3	9	187	109	78	3
9	Sun	November 22	W	4-4-1	Cleveland Browns	21	20	21	338	156	182		16	387	261	126	
10	Sun	November 29	W	5-4-1	Philadelphia Eagles	31	0	24	393	165	228	2	9	225	196	29	4
11	Sun	December 6	L	5-5-1	Chicago Bears	21	27	18	314	166	148	1	24	391	230	161	3
12	Sun	December 13	W	6-5-1	Chicago Cardinals	35	20	12	307	185	122	1	11	164	114	50	4

Passing

No.		Age	Pos	G	GS	QBrec	Cmp	Att	Cmp%	Yds	TD	TD%	Int	Int%	Lng	Y/A	AY/A	Y/C	Y/G	Rate	Sk	Yds
22	Bobby Layne*	33	QB/K	12	12	6-5-1	142	297	47.8	1986	20	6.7	21	7.1	48	6.7	4.9	14.0	165.5	62.8		
30	Tom Tracy	25	RH	12	0		3	12	25.0	159	0	0.0	2	16.7	68	13.3	5.8	53.0	13.3	39.6		
16	Len Dawson	24		12	0		3	7	42.9	60	1	14.3	0	0.0	32	8.6	11.4	20.0	5.0	113.1		
24	Bobby Luna	26	P	12	0		1	1	100.0	55	0	0.0	0	0.0	55	55.0	55.0	55.0	4.6	118.7		
25	Ray Mathews	30	LH	12	0		1	1	100.0	38	0	0.0	0	0.0	38	38.0	38.0	38.0	3.2	118.7		
86	Jimmy Orr*	24	RE	12	0		0	1	0.0	0	0	0.0	0	0.0	0	0.0	0.0		0.0	39.6		
	Team Total	26.3		12		6-5-1	150	319	47.0	2298	21	6.6	23	7.2	68	7.2	5.3	15.3	191.5	63.2		
	Opp Total			12			128	285	44.9	2014	12	4.2	22	7.7		7.1	4.4	15.7	167.8	50.8	22	172

Rushing and Receiving

No.		Age	Pos	G	GS	Rush Att	Yds	TD	Lng	Y/A	Y/G	A/G	Receiving Rec	Yds	Y/R	TD	Lng	R/G	Y/G	YScm
30	Tom Tracy	25	RH	12	0	199	794	3	51	4.0	66.2	16.6	23	273	11.9	5	45	1.9	22.8	1067
39	Larry Krutko	24	FB	12	0	75	226	4	12	3.0	18.8	6.3	13	100	7.7	0	27	1.1	8.3	326
43	Tom Barnett	22		12	0	75	238	1	19	3.2	19.8	6.3	7	52	7.4	1	14	0.6	4.3	290
22	Bobby Layne*	33	QB/K	12	12	33	181	2	21	5.5	15.1	2.8								181
34	Leo Elter	30		8	0	8	25	0	9	3.1	3.1	1.0	3	31	10.3	0	28	0.4	3.9	56
86	Jimmy Orr*	24	RE	12	0	5	43	0	29	8.6	3.6	0.4	35	604	17.3	5	43	2.9	50.3	647
16	Len Dawson	24		12	0	4	20	0	10	5.0	1.7	0.3								20
20	Jack Call	24		4	0	3	9	0	4	3.0	2.3	0.8	1	0	0.0	0	0	0.3	0.0	9
24	Bobby Luna	26	P	12	0	3	3	0	10	1.0	0.3	0.3								3
25	Ray Mathews	30	LH	12	0	1	4	0	4	4.0	0.3	0.1	13	182	14.0	0	56	1.1	15.2	186
88	Pete Brewster	29		9	0	0	0	0	0		0.0	0.0	22	360	16.4	2	42	2.4	40.0	360
83	Buddy Dial	22	fl	12	0	0	0	0	0		0.0	0.0	16	428	26.8	6	68	1.3	35.7	428
84	Gern Nagler	27	LE	12	0	0	0	0	0		0.0	0.0	14	222	15.9	2	35	1.2	18.5	222
87	Jack McClairen	28		1	0	0	0	0	0		0.0	0.0	3	46	15.3	0	20	3.0	46.0	46
	Team Total	26.3		12		406	1543	10	51	3.8	128.6	33.8	150	2298	15.3	21	68	12.5	191.5	3841
	Opp Total			12		405	1500	10		3.7	125.0	33.8	128	1842	14.4	12		10.7	153.5	3342

Defense

No.		Age	Pos	G	GS	Sk	Def Int	Yds	TD	Lng	PD	Fumb FF	Fmb	FR	Yds	TD	Tack Tkl	Ast	Sfty
27	Dean Derby*	24	LDH	12	0		7	127	0	24	0								
30	Tom Tracy	25	RH	12	0							0	7	0	0	0			
42	Dick Alban	30	RS	12	0		6	119	0	46	0								
24	Bobby Luna	26	P	12	0		3	53	0	32	0	0	1	2	42	0			
82	George Tarasovic	29	LDE	12	0							0	1	5	57	1			
39	Larry Krutko	24	FB	12	0							0	4	0	0	0			
22	Bobby Layne*	33	QB/K	12	12							0	2	2	0	0			
43	Tom Barnett	22		12	0							0	3	0	0	0			
80	Jack Butler+	32	RDH	7	0		2	16	0	16	0	0	0	1	8	0			
68	Mike Henry	23	MLB	12	0		2	42	0	33	0	0	0	1	0	0			
57	Ed Beatty	27	C	12	0							0	0	2	0	0			
34	Leo Elter	30		8	0							0	1	1	0	0			
26	Ron Hall	22	LS	2	0		1	0	0	0	0	0	0	1	0	0			
70	Ernie Stautner*	34	RDE	12	0							0	0	2	0	0			
66	Dick Campbell	24	LLB	12	0		1	6	0	6	0								
16	Len Dawson	24		12	0							0	1	0	0	0			
60	Dale Dodrill	33	mlb	12	0							0	0	1	0	0			
35	Rudy Hayes	24		12	0							0	0	1	19	0			
61	Ted Karras	25	LT	12	0							0	0	1	0	0			
25	Ray Mathews	30	LH	12	0							0	0	1	0	0			
65	John Nisby*	23	RG	12	0							0	0	1	0	0			
86	Jimmy Orr*	24	RE	12	0							0	1	0	0	0			
62	Mike Sandusky	24	LG	11	0							0	0	1	0	0			
20	Don Sutherin	23	PR/KR	6	0							0	1	0	0	0			
74	Frank Varrichione	27	RT	12	0							0	0	1	0	0			
	Team Total	26.3		12			22	363	0	46	0	0	22	24	126	1			
	Opp Total			12	31								22	10					

1960 PITTSBURGH STEELERS: 5-6-1, 5TH IN EAST, TIED FOR 9TH IN NFL
Head Coach: Buddy Parker

Week	Day	Date	OT	Rec	Opp	Score Tm	Opp	Offe 1stD	TotYd	PassY	RushY	TO	Defe 1stD	TotYd	PassY	RushY	TO
1	Sat	September 24	W	1-0	Dallas Cowboys	35	28	20	475	353	122	1	17	395	323	72	4
2	Sun	October 2	L	1-1	Cleveland Browns	20	28	18	406	296	110	2	17	428	296	132	
3	Sun	October 9	L	1-2	New York Giants	17	19	16	312	143	169	4	18	323	246	77	5
4	Sun	October 16	W	2-2	St. Louis Cardinals	27	14	12	237	146	91		20	295	154	141	6
5	Sun	October 23	T	2-2-1	Washington Redskins	27	27	21	384	265	119	2	18	367	250	117	2
6	Sun	October 30	L	2-3-1	Green Bay Packers	13	19	16	308	189	119	5	20	343	180	163	2
7	Sun	November 6	L	2-4-1	Philadelphia Eagles	7	34	11	212	108	104	3	24	487	320	167	
8	Sun	November 13	L	2-5-1	New York Giants	24	27	16	330	203	127	3	20	365	233	132	3
9	Sun	November 20	W	3-5-1	Cleveland Browns	14	10	18	323	174	149	2	24	413	292	121	
10	Sun	November 27	W	4-5-1	Washington Redskins	22	10	20	394	186	208	3	9	181	115	66	3
11	Sun	December 11	W	5-5-1	Philadelphia Eagles	27	21	21	484	209	275	6	16	308	274	34	3
12	Sun	December 18	L	5-6-1	St. Louis Cardinals	7	38	9	180	150	30	4	21	379	108	271	1

Passing

No.		Age	Pos	G	GS	QBrec	Cmp	Att	Cmp%	Yds	TD	TD%	Int	Int%	Lng	Y/A	AY/A	Y/C	Y/G	Rate	Sk	Yds
22	Bobby Layne	34	QB/K	12	11	5-6-0	103	209	49.3	1814	13	6.2	17	8.1	70	8.7	6.3	17.6	151.2	66.2		
10	Rudy Bukich	28		12	1	0-0-1	25	51	49.0	358	2	3.9	3	5.9	51	7.0	5.2	14.3	29.8	60.7		
30	Tom Tracy*	26	HB	12	0		9	22	40.9	322	4	18.2	1	4.5	70	14.6	16.2	35.8	26.8	108.9		
40	Preston Carpenter	26	TE/PR	12	0		1	2	50.0	2	0	0.0	0	0.0	2	1.0	1.0	2.0	0.2	56.2		
35	John Henry Johnson	31	FB	12	0		1	1	100.0	15	1	100.0	0	0.0	15	15.0	35.0	15.0	1.3	158.3		
	Team Total	26.5		12		5-6-1	139	285	48.8	2511	20	7.0	21	7.4	70	8.8	6.9	18.1	209.3	72.1		
	Opp Total			12			184	361	51.0	3075	20	5.5	16	4.4		8.5	7.6	16.7	256.3	80.0	36	284

Rushing and Receiving

No.		Age	Pos	G	GS	Rush Att	Yds	TD	Lng	Y/A	Y/G	A/G	Receiving Rec	Yds	Y/R	TD	Lng	R/G	Y/G	YScm
30	Tom Tracy*	26	HB	12	0	192	680	5	28	3.5	56.7	16.0	24	349	14.5	4	65	2.0	29.1	1029
35	John Henry Johnson	31	FB	12	0	118	621	2	87	5.3	51.8	9.8	12	112	9.3	1	26	1.0	9.3	733
34	Charlie Scales	22		12	0	26	81	0	9	3.1	6.8	2.2	1	−2	−2.0	0	−2	0.1	−0.2	79
22	Bobby Layne	34	QB/K	12	11	19	12	2	13	0.6	1.0	1.6								12
40	Preston Carpenter	26	TE/PR	12	0	17	36	0	20	2.1	3.0	1.4	29	495	17.1	2	70	2.4	41.3	531
39	Larry Krutko	25		7	0	17	99	0	18	5.8	14.1	2.4	1	8	8.0	0	8	0.1	1.1	107
86	Jimmy Orr	25	FL	12	0	8	57	0	19	7.1	4.8	0.7	29	541	18.7	4	51	2.4	45.1	598
43	Tom Barnett	23		12	0	6	25	0	16	4.2	2.1	0.5								25
28	Rex Johnston	23	KR	12	0	4	12	0	17	3.0	1.0	0.3								12
10	Rudy Bukich	28		12	1	3	−8	0	0	−2.7	−0.7	0.3								−8
84	Buddy Dial	23	SE	12	0	1	8	0	8	8.0	0.7	0.1	40	972	24.3	9	70	3.3	81.0	980
88	Pete Brewster	30		12	0	0	0	0	0		0.0	0.0	2	26	13.0	0	18	0.2	2.2	26
87	Jack McClairen	29		1	0	0	0	0	0		0.0	0.0	1	17	17.0	0	17	1.0	17.0	17
	Team Total	26.5		12		411	1623	9	87	3.9	135.3	34.3	139	2511	18.1	20	70	11.6	209.3	4134
	Opp Total			12		414	1493	13		3.6	124.4	34.5	184	2791	15.2	20		15.3	232.6	4284

Defense

No.		Age	Pos	G	GS	Sk	Def Int	Yds	TD	Lng	PD	Fumb FF	Fmb	FR	Yds	TD	Tack Tkl	Ast	Sfty
30	Tom Tracy*	26	HB	12	0							0	6	1	0	0			
47	Dicky Moegle	26	RS	12	0		6	49	0	31	0								
35	John Henry Johnson	31	FB	12	0							0	5	0	0	0			
28	Rex Johnston	23	KR	12	0							0	5	0	0	0			
10	Rudy Bukich	28		12	1							0	3	1	0	0			
40	Preston Carpenter	26	TE/PR	12	0							0	2	2	0	0			
27	Dean Derby	25	LS	12	0		3	40	0	25	0	0	0	1	0	0			
34	Charlie Scales	22		12	0							0	2	2	0	0			
22	Bobby Layne	34	QB/K	12	11							0	1	2	0	0			
86	Jimmy Orr	25	FL	12	0							0	2	1	0	0			
50	John Reger*	29	RLB	12	0		1	18	0	18	0	0	0	2	5	0			
26	Joe Scudero	30	LCB	4	0							0	1	2	13	0			
77	Billy Ray Sr. Smith	25	RDE	12	0							0	0	3	13	0			
74	Frank Varrichione*	28	RT	12	0							0	0	2	0	0			
42	Junior Wren	31	RCB	12	0		2	0	0	0	0								
88	Pete Brewster	30		12	0							0	0	1	0	0			
66	Dick Campbell	25	MLB	12	0		1	5	0	5	0								
84	Buddy Dial	23	SE	12	0							0	0	1	0	0			
36	Rudy Hayes	25	LLB	12	0							0	0	1	0	0			
75	Joe Krupa	27	RDT	12	0							0	0	1	0	0			
71	Joe Lewis	24		12	0							0	0	1	0	1			
44	Bert Rechichar	30		6	0		1	10	0	10	0								
70	Ernie Stautner*	35	LDT	12	0							0	0	1	0	0			
20	Don Sutherin	24		4	0		1	0	0	0	0								
82	George Tarasovic	30	LDE	12	0		1	8	0	8	0								
46	Fred Williamson	23		11	0							0	0	1	5	0			
	Team Total	26.5		12			16	130	0	31	0	0	27	26	36	1			
	Opp Total			12		11							25	12					1

1961 PITTSBURGH STEELERS: 6-8-0, 5TH IN EAST, 10TH IN NFL
Head Coach: Buddy Parker

Week	Day	Date	OT	Rec	Opp	Score Tm	Opp	Offe 1stD	TotYd	PassY	RushY	TO	Defe 1stD	TotYd	PassY	RushY	TO
1	Sun	September 17	L	0-1	Dallas Cowboys	24	27	15	342	237	105	4	20	403	307	96	2
2	Sun	September 24	L	0-2	New York Giants	14	17	19	252	128	124	4	18	278	136	142	1
3	Sun	October 1	L	0-3	Los Angeles Rams	14	24	14	218	124	94	8	17	258	216	42	3
4	Sun	October 8	L	0-4	Philadelphia Eagles	16	21	19	281	140	141	1	14	227	103	124	5
5	Sun	October 15	W	1-4	Washington Redskins	20	0	12	185	90	95	5	13	191	126	65	7
6	Sun	October 22	L	1-5	Cleveland Browns	28	30	17	309	222	87	3	21	378	149	229	4
7	Sun	October 29	W	2-5	San Francisco 49ers	20	10	8	204	48	156	1	12	216	164	52	3
8	Sun	November 5	W	3-5	Cleveland Browns	17	13	18	356	196	160	2	14	252	104	148	2
9	Sun	November 12	W	4-5	Dallas Cowboys	37	7	22	371	204	167	1	8	185	122	63	2
10	Sun	November 19	L	4-6	New York Giants	21	42	20	305	187	118	4	21	425	304	121	2
11	Sun	November 26	W	5-6	St. Louis Cardinals	30	27	19	347	187	160	7	12	224	165	59	7
12	Sun	December 3	L	5-7	Philadelphia Eagles	24	35	20	361	200	161	7	12	284	192	92	3
13	Sun	December 10	W	6-7	Washington Redskins	30	14	20	324	214	110	3	21	343	247	96	3
14	Sun	December 17	L	6-8	St. Louis Cardinals	0	20	16	238	155	83	6	15	245	111	134	1

Passing

No.	Name	Age	Pos	G	GS	QBrec	Cmp	Att	Cmp%	Yds	TD	TD%	Int	Int%	Lng	Y/A	AY/A	Y/C	Y/G	Rate	Sk	Yds
10	Rudy Bukich	29	qb	11	7	4-3-0	89	156	57.1	1253	11	7.1	16	10.3	88	8.0	4.8	14.1	113.9	67.0		
22	Bobby Layne	35	QB	8	7	2-5-0	75	149	50.3	1205	11	7.4	16	10.7	53	8.1	4.7	16.1	150.6	62.8		
30	Tom Tracy	27	HB	14	0		4	12	33.3	73	0	0.0	0	0.0	38	6.1	6.1	18.3	5.2	55.2		
18	Terry Nofsinger	23		5	0		7	11	63.6	78	0	0.0	0	0.0	23	7.1	7.1	11.1	15.6	84.7		
42	Dick Hoak	22	FL	14	0		1	3	33.3	13	1	33.3	1	33.3	13	4.3	−4.0	13.0	0.9	47.9		
35	John Henry Johnson	32	FB	14	0		0	2	0.0	0	0	0.0	1	50.0	0	0.0	−22.5		0.0	0.0		
89	Bobby Joe Green	25	P	14	0		0	1	0.0	0	0	0.0	0	0.0	0	0.0	0.0		0.0	39.6		
	Team Total	26.2		14		6-8-0	176	334	52.7	2622	23	6.9	34	10.2	88	7.9	4.6	14.9	187.3	62.1		
	Opp Total			14			201	420	47.9	2780	22	5.2	25	6.0		6.6	5.0	13.8	198.6	62.2	42	334

Rushing and Receiving

No.	Name	Age	Pos	G	GS	Rush Att	Yds	TD	Lng	Y/A	Y/G	A/G	Rec	Yds	Y/R	TD	Lng	R/G	Y/G	YScm
35	John Henry Johnson	32	FB	14	0	213	787	6	44	3.7	56.2	15.2	24	262	10.9	1	51	1.7	18.7	1049
30	Tom Tracy	27	HB	14	0	147	402	2	26	2.7	28.7	10.5	14	133	9.5	1	38	1.0	9.5	535
42	Dick Hoak	22	FL	14	0	85	302	0	22	3.6	21.6	6.1	3	18	6.0	0	7	0.2	1.3	320
34	Charlie Scales	23		14	0	50	184	0	27	3.7	13.1	3.6	7	43	6.1	0	16	0.5	3.1	227
10	Rudy Bukich	29	qb	11	7	14	4	2	12	0.3	0.4	1.3								4
22	Bobby Layne	35	QB	8	7	8	11	0	9	1.4	1.4	1.0								11
40	Preston Carpenter	27	TE	13	0	7	9	0	13	1.3	0.7	0.5	33	460	13.9	4	40	2.5	35.4	469
26	Brady Keys	25	RCB	12	0	6	14	0	11	2.3	1.2	0.5								14
18	Terry Nofsinger	23		5	0	6	6	0	3	1.0	1.2	1.2								6
84	Buddy Dial*	24	SE	14	0	3	6	0	15	2.0	0.4	0.2	53	1047	19.8	12	88	3.8	74.8	1053
89	Bobby Joe Green	25	P	14	0	2	37	0	33	18.5	2.6	0.1								37
88	Steve Meilinger	31		4	0	1	6	0	6	6.0	1.5	0.3	8	103	12.9	0	17	2.0	25.8	109
46	Bob Coronado	25		5	0	1	−7	0	−7	−7.0	−1.4	0.2	3	32	10.7	0	14	0.6	6.4	25
88	Bob Schnelker	33		8	0	0	0	0	0		0.0	0.0	18	331	18.4	3	59	2.3	41.4	331
23	Red Mack	24		11	0	0	0	0	0		0.0	0.0	8	128	16.0	2	39	0.7	11.6	128
28	Henry Clement	22		14	0	0	0	0	0		0.0	0.0	5	65	13.0	0	19	0.4	4.6	65
	Team Total	26.2		14		543	1761	10	44	3.2	125.8	38.8	176	2622	14.9	23	88	12.6	187.3	4383
	Opp Total			14		396	1463	11		3.7	104.5	28.3	201	2446	12.2	22		14.4	174.7	3909

Defense

No.	Name	Age	Pos	G	GS	Sk	Def Int	Yds	TD	Lng	PD	FF	Fmb	FR	Yds	TD	Tkl	Ast	Sfty
10	Rudy Bukich	29	qb	11	7							0	7	3	0	0			
35	John Henry Johnson	32	FB	14	0							0	7	3	0	0			
24	Johnny Sample	24	PR/LCB/KR	14	0		8	141	1	42	0	0	0	2	0	0			
20	Bill Butler	24	LS	10	0		3	103	1	71	0	0	1	1	0	0			
26	Brady Keys	25	RCB	12	0		2	21	0	12	0	0	2	1	0	0			
22	Bobby Layne	35	QB	8	7							0	4	1	0	0			
44	Willie Daniel	24	RS	14	0		3	76	0	41	0	0	0	1	3	0			
34	Charlie Scales	23		14	0							0	4	0	0	0			
70	Ernie Stautner*	36	RDE	14	0							0	0	4	0	0			
84	Buddy Dial*	24	SE	14	0							0	3	0	0	0			
37	Mike Henry	25		10	0		1	8	0	8	0	0	0	2	0	0			
75	Joe Krupa	28	RDT	14	0							0	0	3	0	0			
66	Myron Pottios*	22	MLB	14	0		2	40	0	22	0	0	0	1	0	0			
50	John Reger*	30	RLB	14	0		1	17	0	17	0	0	1	1	0	0			
47	Jackie M. Simpson	27		8	0		2	46	0	27	0	0	0	1	11	0			
71	Charlie Bradshaw	25	LT	12	0							0	1	1	0	0			
23	Red Mack	24		11	0							0	1	1	0	0			
68	Ron Stehouwer	24		14	0							0	0	2	0	0			
82	George Tarasovic	31	LLB	12	0		1	16	0	16	0	0	1	0	0	0			
40	Preston Carpenter	27	TE	13	0							0	1	0	0	0			
27	Dick Haley	24		8	0		1	0	0	0	0								
42	Dick Hoak	22	FL	14	0							0	1	0	0	0			
64	John Kapele	24		14	0							0	0	1	0	0			
79	Lou Michaels	26	LDE/K	14	0		1	30	0	30	0								
65	John Nisby*	25	RG	13	0							0	0	1	0	0			
30	Tom Tracy	27	HB	14	0							0	1	0	0	0			
	Team Total	26.2		14			25	498	2	71	0	0	34	31	14	0			
	Opp Total			14		36							36	16					

1962 PITTSBURGH STEELERS: 9-5-0, 2ND IN EAST, TIED FOR 4TH IN NFL
Head Coach: Buddy Parker

Week	Day	Date	OT	Rec	Opp	Score Tm	Opp	Offe 1stD	TotYd	PassY	RushY	TO	Defe 1stD	TotYd	PassY	RushY	TO
1	Sun	September 16	L	0-1	Detroit Lions	7	45	10	173	129	44	2	26	395	236	159	
2	Sun	September 23	W	1-1	Dallas Cowboys	30	28	22	354	144	210	1	19	351	225	126	2
3	Sun	September 30	L	1-2	New York Giants	27	31	23	317	142	175	3	19	427	332	95	1
4	Sat	October 6	W	2-2	Philadelphia Eagles	13	7	18	368	132	236	2	11	197	153	44	3
5	Sun	October 14	W	3-2	New York Giants	20	17	16	322	72	250	1	18	291	194	97	3
6	Sun	October 21	L	3-3	Dallas Cowboys	27	42	21	373	250	123	4	19	402	295	107	3
7	Sun	October 28	L	3-4	Cleveland Browns	14	41	17	205	41	164	4	21	354	154	200	2
8	Sun	November 4	W	4-4	Minnesota Vikings	39	31	29	439	227	212	1	15	319	240	79	2
9	Sun	November 11	W	5-4	St. Louis Cardinals	26	17	16	253	59	194	1	17	335	220	115	5
10	Sun	November 18	W	6-4	Washington Redskins	23	21	18	347	251	96	6	14	271	174	97	3
11	Sun	November 25	L	6-5	Cleveland Browns	14	35	18	288	144	144	3	24	418	263	155	2
12	Sun	December 2	W	7-5	St. Louis Cardinals	19	7	23	412	174	238	2	14	271	213	58	4
13	Sun	December 9	W	8-5	Philadelphia Eagles	26	17	16	268	138	130	4	16	283	218	65	3
14	Sun	December 16	W	9-5	Washington Redskins	27	24	14	283	166	117	2	17	311	289	22	5

Passing

No.		Age	Pos	G	GS	QBrec	Cmp	Att	Cmp%	Yds	TD	TD%	Int	Int%	Lng	Y/A	AY/A	Y/C	Y/G	Rate	Sk	Yds
22	Bobby Layne	36	QB	13	11	7-4-0	116	233	49.8	1686	9	3.9	17	7.3	62	7.2	4.7	14.5	129.7	56.2		
15	Ed Brown	34	P	14	3	2-1-0	43	84	51.2	726	5	6.0	6	7.1	50	8.6	6.6	16.9	51.9	70.8		
42	Dick Hoak	23	FL	14	0		0	1	0.0	0	0	0.0	0	0.0	0	0.0	0.0	0.0	0.0	39.6		
30	Tom Tracy	28		4	0		1	1	100.0	7	0	0.0	0	0.0	7	7.0	7.0	7.0	1.8	95.8		
	Team Total	26.9		14		9-5-0	160	319	50.2	2419	14	4.4	23	7.2	62	7.6	5.2	15.1	172.8	60.1		
	Opp Total			14			223	438	50.9	3490	34	7.8	28	6.4		8.0	6.6	15.7	249.3	77.0	36	284

Rushing and Receiving

No.		Age	Pos	G	GS	Rush Att	Yds	TD	Lng	Y/A	Y/G	A/G	Receiving Rec	Yds	Y/R	TD	Lng	R/G	Y/G	YScm
35	John Henry Johnson*	33	FB	14	0	251	1141	7	40	4.5	81.5	17.9	32	226	7.1	2	18	2.3	16.1	1367
32	Joe Womack	26	HB	11	0	128	468	5	28	3.7	42.5	11.6	6	57	9.5	0	33	0.5	5.2	525
42	Dick Hoak	23	FL	14	0	117	442	4	39	3.8	31.6	8.4	9	133	14.8	0	23	0.6	9.5	575
30	Tom Tracy	28		4	0	20	116	0	35	5.8	29.0	5.0	2	11	5.5	0	6	0.5	2.8	127
46	Bob Ferguson	23		13	0	20	37	0	13	1.9	2.8	1.5	1	6	6.0	0	6	0.1	0.5	43
22	Bobby Layne	36	QB	13	11	15	25	1	17	1.7	1.9	1.2								25
87	Harlon Hill	30		7	0	7	72	0	24	10.3	10.3	1.0	7	101	14.4	0	25	1.0	14.4	173
86	John Burrell	22		14	0	6	38	0	18	6.3	2.7	0.4	8	193	24.1	0	42	0.6	13.8	231
48	Gary Ballman	22		3	0	3	7	0	3	2.3	2.3	1.0								7
23	Red Mack	25		14	0	2	-2	0	7	-1.0	-0.1	0.1	8	203	25.4	2	40	0.6	14.5	201
15	Ed Brown	34	P	14	3	2	-8	0	-2	-4.0	-0.6	0.1								-8
40	Preston Carpenter*	28	TE/PR	13	0	1	-3	0	-3	-3.0	-0.2	0.1	36	492	13.7	4	43	2.8	37.8	489
84	Buddy Dial	25	SE	14	0	0	0	0	0		0.0	0.0	50	981	19.6	6	62	3.6	70.1	981
88	John Powers	22		14	0	0	0	0	0		0.0	0.0	1	16	16.0	0	16	0.1	1.1	16
	Team Total	26.9		14		572	2333	17	40	4.1	166.6	40.9	160	2419	15.1	14	62	11.4	172.8	4752
	Opp Total			14		363	1419	13		3.9	101.4	25.9	223	3206	14.4	34		15.9	229.0	4625

Defense

No.		Age	Pos	G	GS	Sk	Def					Fumb					Tack		Sfty
							Int	Yds	TD	Lng	PD	FF	Fmb	FR	Yds	TD	Tkl	Ast	
22	Bobby Layne	36	QB	13	11							0	7	2	0	0			
28	Clendon Thomas	27	LS	14	0		7	48	0	15	0								
42	Dick Hoak	23	FL	14	0							0	3	3	4	0			
44	Willie Daniel	25	RS	13	0		5	85	1	49	0								
35	John Henry Johnson*	33	FB	14	0							0	5	0	0	0			
46	Bob Ferguson	23		13	0							0	3	1	0	0			
27	Dick Haley	25	LCB	14	0		4	26	0	18	0								
50	John Reger	31	RLB	9	0		1	0	0	0	0	0	0	3	0	0			
82	George Tarasovic	32	LLB	14	0		4	55	0	37	0								
26	Brady Keys	26	RCB/KR	14	0		3	16	0	13	0								
62	Mike Sandusky	27	LG	14	0							0	0	3	0	0			
67	Bob Schmitz	24	MLB	9	0		3	65	1	24	0								
70	Ernie Stautner	37	RDE	14	0		1	2	0	2	0	0	0	2	0	0			1
32	Joe Womack	26	HB	11	0							0	3	0	0	0			
65	Tom Bettis	29		11	0							0	0	1	0	0			
15	Ed Brown	34	P	14	3							0	1	0	0	0			
37	Ken Kirk	24		14	0							0	0	1	0	0			
75	Joe Krupa	29	RDT	14	0							0	0	1	0	0			
72	Ray Lemek	28	RG	14	0							0	0	1	0	0			
76	Gene Lipscomb*	31	LDT	14	0							0	0	1	3	0			
23	Red Mack	25		14	0							0	1	0	0	0			
79	Lou Michaels*	27	LDE/K	14	0							0	1	0	0	0			
34	Bob Simms	24		3	0							0	0	1	0	0			
	Team Total	26.9		14			28	318	2	49	0	0	24	20	7	0			1
	Opp Total			14		44							21	11					

1963 PITTSBURGH STEELERS: 7-4-3, 4TH IN EAST, 7TH IN NFL
Head Coach: Buddy Parker

Week	Day	Date	OT	Rec	Opp	Score		Offe					Defe				
						Tm	Opp	1stD	TotYd	PassY	RushY	TO	1stD	TotYd	PassY	RushY	TO
1	Sun	September 15	T	0-0-1	Philadelphia Eagles	21	21	21	315	206	109	2	14	353	295	58	4
2	Sun	September 22	W	1-0-1	New York Giants	31	0	18	286	63	223	1	7	175	116	59	5
3	Sun	September 29	W	2-0-1	St. Louis Cardinals	23	10	14	217	38	179	1	13	303	166	137	5
4	Sat	October 5	L	2-1-1	Cleveland Browns	23	35	23	400	303	97	2	19	357	138	219	1
5	Sun	October 13	L	2-2-1	St. Louis Cardinals	23	24	14	321	215	106	1	23	525	408	117	3
6	Sun	October 20	W	3-2-1	Washington Redskins	38	27	24	349	219	130	1	23	397	300	97	5
7	Sun	October 27	W	4-2-1	Dallas Cowboys	27	21	19	484	370	114	3	22	416	290	126	3
8	Sun	November 3	L	4-3-1	Green Bay Packers	14	33	17	278	155	123	5	24	399	151	248	2
9	Sun	November 10	W	5-3-1	Cleveland Browns	9	7	23	382	195	187	1	14	227	93	134	1
10	Sun	November 17	W	6-3-1	Washington Redskins	34	28	22	390	246	144	3	22	442	404	38	4
11	Sun	November 24	T	6-3-2	Chicago Bears	17	17	19	291	125	166	1	19	328	241	87	3
12	Sun	December 1	T	6-3-3	Philadelphia Eagles	20	20	22	374	215	159	5	8	221	107	114	3
13	Sun	December 8	W	7-3-3	Dallas Cowboys	24	19	19	426	215	211	2	15	263	112	151	1
14	Sun	December 15	L	7-4-3	New York Giants	17	33	17	400	212	188	5	21	423	280	143	4

Passing

No.		Age	Pos	G	GS	QBrec	Cmp	Att	Cmp%	Yds	TD	TD%	Int	Int%	Lng	Y/A	AY/A	Y/C	Y/G	Rate	Sk	Yds
15	Ed Brown	35	QB/P	14	14	7-4-3	168	362	46.4	2982	21	5.8	20	5.5	85	8.2	6.9	17.8	213.0	71.4		
12	Terry Nofsinger	25		2	0		2	3	66.7	46	0	0.0	0	0.0	27	15.3	15.3	23.0	23.0	109.7		
14	Bill Nelsen	22		2	0		0	2	0.0	0	0	0.0	0	0.0	0	0.0	0.0		0.0	39.6		
30	Tom Tracy	29		6	0		0	1	0.0	0	0	0.0	0	0.0	0	0.0	0.0		0.0	39.6		
	Team Total	26.8		14		7-4-3	170	368	46.2	3028	21	5.7	20	5.4	85	8.2	6.9	17.8	216.3	71.2		
	Opp Total			14			191	384	49.7	3400	21	5.5	25	6.5		8.9	7.0	17.8	242.9	71.5	34	299

Rushing and Receiving

No.		Age	Pos	G	GS	Rush							Receiving							YScm
						Att	Yds	TD	Lng	Y/A	Y/G	A/G	Rec	Yds	Y/R	TD	Lng	R/G	Y/G	
42	Dick Hoak	24	HB	12	0	216	679	6	17	3.1	56.6	18.0	11	118	10.7	1	23	0.9	9.8	797
35	John Henry Johnson*	34	FB	12	0	186	773	4	48	4.2	64.4	15.5	21	145	6.9	1	26	1.8	12.1	918
33	Theron Sapp	28	fb	10	0	96	431	1	27	4.5	43.1	9.6	3	41	13.7	0	22	0.3	4.1	472
46	Bob Ferguson	24		5	0	43	171	1	19	4.0	34.2	8.6	3	7	2.3	0	9	0.6	1.4	178
15	Ed Brown	35	QB/P	14	14	15	20	2	7	1.3	1.4	1.1								20
30	Tom Tracy	29		6	0	10	11	0	5	1.1	1.8	1.7	1	21	21.0	0	21	0.2	3.5	32
85	Gary Ballman	23	KR/FL	14	0	8	59	0	18	7.4	4.2	0.6	26	492	18.9	5	67	1.9	35.1	551
23	Red Mack	26	TE	14	0	2	1	0	1	0.5	0.1	0.1	25	618	24.7	3	85	1.8	44.1	619
40	Preston Carpenter	29		14	0	1	-3	0	-3	-3.0	-0.2	0.1	17	233	13.7	1	28	1.2	16.6	230
14	Bill Nelsen	22		2	0	1	-6	0	-6	-6.0	-3.0	0.5								-6
84	Buddy Dial*	26	SE	14	0	0	0	0	0		0.0	0.0	60	1295	21.6	9	83	4.3	92.5	1295
86	John Burrell	23		14	0	0	0	0	0		0.0	0.0	2	27	13.5	0	14	0.1	1.9	27
25	Roy Curry	24		6	0	0	0	0	0		0.0	0.0	1	31	31.0	1	31	0.2	5.2	31
	Team Total	26.8		14		578	2136	14	48	3.7	152.6	41.3	170	3028	17.8	21	85	12.1	216.3	5164
	Opp Total			14		419	1728	14		4.1	123.4	29.9	191	3101	16.2	21		13.6	221.5	4829

Defense

No.		Age	Pos	G	GS	Sk	Def					Fumb					Tack		Sfty
							Int	Yds	TD	Lng	PD	FF	Fmb	FR	Yds	TD	Tkl	Ast	
28	Clendon Thomas*	28	LS	13	0		8	122	0	32	0	0	0	2	0	0			
27	Dick Haley	26	LCB	14	0		6	65	1	37	0	0	1	0	0	0			
42	Dick Hoak	24	HB	12	0							0	4	3	0	0			
35	John Henry Johnson*	34	FB	12	0							0	5	2	0	0			
15	Ed Brown	35	QB/P	14	14							0	5	1	0	0			
36	Andy Russell	22	RLB	14	0		3	20	0	10	0	0	1	1	2	0			
78	John Baker	28	RDE	14	0							0	0	4	0	0			
66	Myron Pottios*	24	MLB	14	0		4	78	0	38	0								
24	Jim Bradshaw	24		14	0		1	0	0	0	0	0	0	2	0	0			
84	Buddy Dial*	26	SE	14	0							0	2	1	5	0			
26	Brady Keys	27	RCB/PR	11	0							0	1	2	0	0			
33	Theron Sapp	28	fb	10	0							0	3	0	0	0			
85	Gary Ballman	23	KR/FL	14	0							0	2	0	0	0			
43	Glenn Glass	23	RS	14	14		1	29	0	29	0	0	0	1	0	0			
79	Lou Michaels*	28	LDE/K	14	0		1	0	0	0	0	0	0	1	0	0			
14	Bill Nelsen	22		2	0							0	1	1	0	0			
62	Mike Sandusky	28	LG	13	0							0	0	2	0	0			
63	Art Anderson	27		13	0							0	0	1	0	0			
73	Frank Atkinson	22	LDT	14	0							0	0	1	0	0			
71	Charlie Bradshaw*	27	LT	14	0							0	0	1	0	0			
75	Joe Krupa*	30	RDT	14	0							0	0	1	0	0			
23	Red Mack	26	TE	14	0							0	0	1	0	0			
88	John Powers	23		14	0							0	0	1	0	0			
50	John Reger	32		9	0		1	16	0	16	0								
70	Ernie Stautner	38		14	0							0	0	1	0	0			
82	George Tarasovic	33		8	0							0	0	1	0	0			
	Team Total	26.8		14			25	330	1	38	0	0	25	31	7	0			1
	Opp Total			14		30							31	12					

1964 PITTSBURGH STEELERS: 5-9-0, 6TH IN EAST, TIED FOR 12TH IN NFL
Head Coach: Buddy Parker

						Score		Offe					Defe				
Week	Day	Date	OT	Rec	Opp	Tm	Opp	1stD	TotYd	PassY	RushY	TO	1stD	TotYd	PassY	RushY	TO
1	Sun	September 13	L	0-1	Los Angeles Rams	14	26	11	167	48	119	8	9	175	27	148	1
2	Sun	September 20	W	1-1	New York Giants	27	24	14	214	77	137	2	24	356	209	147	2
3	Sun	September 27	W	2-1	Dallas Cowboys	23	17	16	291	160	131		19	320	170	150	2
4	Sun	October 4	L	2-2	Philadelphia Eagles	7	21	18	293	207	86	2	20	452	180	272	1
5	Sat	October 10	W	3-2	Cleveland Browns	23	7	28	477	123	354	1	14	217	121	96	
6	Sun	October 18	L	3-3	Minnesota Vikings	10	30	15	227	117	110	2	20	310	91	219	1
7	Sun	October 25	L	3-4	Philadelphia Eagles	10	34	11	305	118	187	2	21	391	237	154	2
8	Sun	November 1	L	3-5	Cleveland Browns	17	30	16	251	86	165	2	24	412	162	250	1
9	Sun	November 8	L	3-6	St. Louis Cardinals	30	34	21	355	239	116	3	24	351	227	124	1
10	Sun	November 15	L	3-7	Washington Redskins	0	30	16	267	156	111	5	13	286	184	102	3
11	Sun	November 22	W	4-7	New York Giants	44	17	26	429	191	238	2	22	305	226	79	4
12	Sun	November 29	L	4-8	St. Louis Cardinals	20	21	16	279	148	131	4	14	204	124	80	5
13	Sun	December 6	W	5-8	Washington Redskins	14	7	13	180	41	139	3	12	184	102	82	2
14	Sun	December 13	L	5-9	Dallas Cowboys	14	17	12	225	147	78	5	17	268	177	91	1

Passing

No.		Age	Pos	G	GS	QBrec	Cmp	Att	Cmp%	Yds	TD	TD%	Int	Int%	Lng	Y/A	AY/A	Y/C	Y/G	Rate	Sk	Yds
15	Ed Brown	36	QB/P	14	13	5-8-0	121	272	44.5	1990	12	4.4	19	7.0	54	7.3	5.1	16.4	142.1	55.2		
14	Bill Nelsen	23		5	1	0-1-0	16	42	38.1	276	2	4.8	3	7.1	44	6.6	4.3	17.3	55.2	47.3		
12	Terry Nofsinger	26		1	0		3	4	75.0	35	0	0.0	1	25.0	22	8.8	-2.5	11.7	35.0	61.5		
16	Tommy Wade	22		1	0		1	3	33.3	7	0	0.0	0	0.0	7	2.3	2.3	7.0	7.0	42.4		
85	Gary Ballman*	24	KR/FL	13	0		0	1	0.0	0	0	0.0	1	100.0	0	0.0	-45.0		0.0	0.0		
42	Dick Hoak	25	HB	14	0		0	1	0.0	0	0	0.0	0	0.0	0	0.0		0.0	0.0	39.6		
	Team Total	26.3		14		5-9-0	141	323	43.7	2308	14	4.3	24	7.4	54	7.1	4.7	16.4	164.9	51.7		
	Opp Total			14			185	378	48.9	2582	16	4.2	12	3.2		6.8	6.2	14.0	184.4	72.2	42	345

Rushing and Receiving

No.		Age	Pos	G	GS	Rush							Receiving							YScm
						Att	Yds	TD	Lng	Y/A	Y/G	A/G	Rec	Yds	Y/R	TD	Lng	R/G	Y/G	
35	John Henry Johnson*	35	FB	14	0	235	1048	7	45	4.5	74.9	16.8	17	69	4.1	1	21	1.2	4.9	1117
36	Clarence Peaks	29	fb	12	0	118	503	2	70	4.3	41.9	9.8	12	113	9.4	0	41	1.0	9.4	616
42	Dick Hoak	25	HB	14	0	84	258	2	17	3.1	18.4	6.0	12	137	11.4	3	22	0.9	9.8	395
46	Phil King	28		8	0	26	71	1	12	2.7	8.9	3.3	4	32	8.0	1	13	0.5	4.0	103
15	Ed Brown	36	QB/P	14	13	26	110	2	22	4.2	7.9	1.9								110
85	Gary Ballman*	24	KR/FL	13	0	11	43	0	11	3.9	3.3	0.8	47	935	19.9	7	47	3.6	71.9	978
20	Paul Martha	22	se	14	0	4	12	0	10	3.0	0.9	0.3	6	145	24.2	0	54	0.4	10.4	157
33	Theron Sapp	29		11	0	4	15	0	5	3.8	1.4	0.4	1	44	44.0	0	44	0.1	4.0	59
14	Bill Nelsen	23		5	1	3	17	0	13	5.7	3.4	0.6								17
28	Clendon Thomas	29	SE/ls	14	0	2	7	0	4	3.5	0.5	0.1	17	334	19.6	1	49	1.2	23.9	341
88	John Powers	24	TE	14	0	2	10	0	9	5.0	0.7	0.1	8	193	24.1	0	42	0.6	13.8	203
31	Ed Holler	24		13	0	1	8	0	8	8.0	0.6	0.1								8
89	Jim Kelly	22	te	6	0	0	0	0	0	0.0	0.0	0.0	10	186	18.6	1	27	1.7	31.0	186
86	John Burrell	24		14	0	0	0	0	0	0.0	0.0	0.0	6	113	18.8	0	43	0.4	8.1	113
82	Chuck Logan	21		14	0	0	0	0	0	0.0	0.0	0.0	1	7	7.0	0	7	0.1	0.5	7
	Team Total	26.3		14		516	2102	14	70	4.1	150.1	36.9	141	2308	16.4	14	54	10.1	164.9	4410
	Opp Total			14		454	1994	15		4.4	142.4	32.4	185	2237	12.1	16		13.2	159.8	4231

Defense

No.	Name	Age	Pos	G	GS	Sk	Def Int	Yds	TD	Lng	PD	Fumb FF	Fmb	FR	Yds	TD	Tack Tkl	Ast	Sfty
20	Paul Martha	22	se	14	0							0	5	2	0	0			
21	Jim Bradshaw	25	LS	14	0		1	39	0	39	0	0	1	3	80	2			
15	Ed Brown	36	QB/P	14	13							0	5	0	0	0			
35	John Henry Johnson*	35	FB	14	0							0	4	1	0	0			
26	Brady Keys	28	RCB/PR	14	0		2	11	0	11	0	0	2	1	0	0			
36	Clarence Peaks	29	fb	12	0							0	4	1	0	0			
85	Gary Ballman*	24	KR/FL	13	0							0	2	1	0	0			
27	Dick Haley	27	LCB	13	0		2	11	0	8	0	0	0	1	0	0			
30	Bob L. Harrison	27	RLB	11	0							0	0	3	0	0			
44	Willie Daniel	27	RS	14	0		2	4	0	4	0								
64	Chuck Hinton	25	RDT	14	0		1	8	1	8	0	0	0	1	0	0			
42	Dick Hoak	25	HB	14	0							0	2	0	0	0			
31	Ed Holler	24		13	0		1	2	0	2	0	0	1	0	0	0			
51	Buzz Nutter	33	C	14	0							0	0	2	0	0			
66	Myron Pottios*	25	MLB	7	0		1	8	0	8	0	0	0	1	0	0			
78	John Baker	29	RDE	14	0							0	0	1	0	0			
71	Charlie Bradshaw*	28	LT	14	0							0	0	1	0	0			
86	John Burrell	24		14	0							0	0	1	0	0			
89	Jim Kelly	22	te	6	0							0	1	0	0	0			
87	Dan LaRose	25		12	0							0	0	1	0	0			
72	Ray Lemek	30	RG	14	0							0	0	1	0	0			
54	Max Messner	26	LLB	7	0							0	0	1	0	0			
62	Mike Sandusky	29		6	0							0	0	1	0	0			
33	Theron Sapp	29		11	0							0	1	0	0	0			
50	Bill Saul	24	llb	13	0		1	13	0	13	0								
34	Robert Soleau	23		14	0							0	0	1	0	0			
28	Clendon Thomas	29	SE/ls	14	0		1	0	0	0	0								
	Team Total	26.3		14			12	96	1	39	0	0	28	25	80	2			
	Opp Total			14		51							24	10					

1965 PITTSBURGH STEELERS: 2-12-0, LAST IN EAST AND NFL
Head Coach: Mike Nixon

Week	Day	Date	OT	Rec	Opp	Score Tm	Opp	Offe 1stD	TotYd	PassY	RushY	TO	Defe 1stD	TotYd	PassY	RushY	TO
1	Sun	September 19	L	0-1	Green Bay Packers	9	41	15	193	101	92	4	21	354	220	134	
2	Sun	September 26	L	0-2	San Francisco 49ers	17	27	16	250	173	77	2	26	401	210	191	3
3	Sun	October 3	L	0-3	New York Giants	13	23	18	323	250	73	3	17	344	232	112	
4	Sat	October 9	L	0-4	Cleveland Browns	19	24	16	252	77	175	3	21	375	143	232	
5	Sun	October 17	L	0-5	St. Louis Cardinals	7	20	9	142	−16	158	4	12	344	275	69	3
6	Sun	October 24	W	1-5	Philadelphia Eagles	20	14	8	132	72	60	2	20	388	189	199	5
7	Sun	October 31	W	2-5	Dallas Cowboys	22	13	16	314	245	69	2	14	255	165	90	3
8	Sun	November 7	L	2-6	St. Louis Cardinals	17	21	18	339	201	138	1	16	276	171	105	
9	Sun	November 14	L	2-7	Dallas Cowboys	17	24	12	197	147	50	6	15	341	218	123	5
10	Sun	November 21	L	2-8	Washington Redskins	3	31	7	115	54	61	7	12	199	81	118	2
11	Sun	November 28	L	2-9	Cleveland Browns	21	42	13	358	221	137		20	360	119	241	
12	Sun	December 5	L	2-10	New York Giants	10	35	13	184	99	85	6	21	414	171	243	2
13	Sun	December 12	L	2-11	Philadelphia Eagles	13	47	19	324	266	58	12	17	302	111	191	2
14	Sun	December 19	L	2-12	Washington Redskins	14	35	14	231	86	145	5	11	177	145	32	2

Passing

No.	Name	Age	Pos	G	GS	QBrec	Cmp	Att	Cmp%	Yds	TD	TD%	Int	Int%	Lng	Y/A	AY/A	Y/C	Y/G	Rate	Sk	Yds
14	Bill Nelsen	24	QB	12	12	2-10-0	121	270	44.8	1917	8	3.0	17	6.3	87	7.1	4.9	15.8	159.8	52.7		
16	Tommy Wade	23		4	2	0-2-0	33	66	50.0	463	2	3.0	13	19.7	49	7.0	−1.2	14.0	115.8	43.5		
15	Ed Brown	37		13	0		7	18	38.9	123	0	0.0	5	27.8	39	6.8	−5.7	17.6	9.5	23.4		
	Team Total	26.3		14		2-12-0	161	354	45.5	2503	10	2.8	35	9.9	87	7.1	3.2	15.5	178.8	39.3		
	Opp Total			14			173	353	49.0	2703	25	7.1	12	3.4		7.7		7.5	15.6	193.1	84.3	33	253

Rushing and Receiving

No.		Age	Pos	G	GS	Rush Att	Yds	TD	Lng	Y/A	Y/G	A/G	Receiving Rec	Yds	Y/R	TD	Lng	R/G	Y/G	YScm
42	Dick Hoak	26	HB	14	0	131	426	5	42	3.3	30.4	9.4	19	228	12.0	1	48	1.4	16.3	654
38	Mike Lind	25	FB	14	0	111	375	1	20	3.4	26.8	7.9	25	236	9.4	1	39	1.8	16.9	611
36	Clarence Peaks	30		10	0	47	230	0	36	4.9	23.0	4.7	3	22	7.3	0	21	0.3	2.2	252
23	Cannonball Butler	22	KR	14	0	46	108	0	12	2.3	7.7	3.3	9	117	13.0	1	43	0.6	8.4	225
14	Bill Nelsen	24	QB	12	12	26	84	1	21	3.2	7.0	2.2	1	−5	−5.0	0	−5	0.1	−0.4	79
85	Gary Ballman*	25	FL	14	0	17	46	3	11	2.7	3.3	1.2	40	859	21.5	5	87	2.9	61.4	905
33	Theron Sapp	30		14	0	14	54	0	24	3.9	3.9	1.0	1	10	10.0	0	10	0.1	0.7	64
16	Tommy Wade	23		4	2	8	43	0	41	5.4	10.8	2.0								43
35	John Henry Johnson	36		1	0	3	11	0	7	3.7	11.0	3.0								11
20	Paul Martha	23		12	0	2	3	0	6	1.5	0.3	0.2	11	171	15.5	0	39	0.9	14.3	174
87	Roy Jefferson	22	PR	10	0	1	−1	0	−1	−1.0	−0.1	0.1	13	287	22.1	1	50	1.3	28.7	286
15	Ed Brown	37		13	0	1	−1	0	−1	−1.0	−0.1	0.1								−1
28	Clendon Thomas	30	SE	14	0	0	0	0	0		0.0	0.0	25	431	17.2	1	80	1.8	30.8	431
84	Lee Folkins	26		8	0	0	0	0	0		0.0	0.0	5	58	11.6	0	16	0.6	7.3	58
82	John Hilton	23	TE	14	0	0	0	0	0		0.0	0.0	4	32	8.0	0	12	0.3	2.3	32
27	Red Mack	28		2	0	0	0	0	0		0.0	0.0	3	41	13.7	0	17	1.5	20.5	41
25	Jerry Simmons	23		4	0	0	0	0	0		0.0	0.0	2	16	8.0	0	9	0.5	4.0	16
	Team Total	26.3		14		407	1378	10	42	3.4	98.4	29.1	161	2503	15.5	10	87	11.5	178.8	3881
	Opp Total			14		483	2080	19		4.3	148.6	34.5	173	2450	14.2	25		12.4	175.0	4530

Defense

No.		Age	Pos	G	GS	Sk	Def Int	Yds	TD	Lng	PD	FF	Fumb Fmb	FR	Yds	TD	Tack Tkl	Ast	Sfty
23	Cannonball Butler	22	KR	14	0							0	7	6	0	0			
42	Dick Hoak	26	HB	14	0							0	6	1	0	0			
16	Tommy Wade	23		4	2							0	6	1	0	0			
24	Jim Bradshaw	26	LS	12	0		5	117	1	82	0	0	0	1	0	0			
14	Bill Nelsen	24	QB	12	12							0	6	0	0	0			
38	Mike Lind	25	FB	14	0							0	3	2	0	0			
36	Clarence Peaks	30		10	0							0	3	2	7	0			
87	Roy Jefferson	22	PR	10	0							0	3	1	0	0			
63	Rod Breedlove	27		14	0							0	0	3	12	0			
15	Ed Brown	37		13	0							0	2	1	0	0			
28	Clendon Thomas	30	SE	14	0							0	2	1	0	0			
47	Marv Woodson	24	LCB	13	0		3	87	1	61	0								
85	Gary Ballman*	25	FL	14	0							0	2	0	0	0			
53	John Campbell	27	LLB	14	0							0	0	2	15	1			
44	Willie Daniel	28	RS	9	0		1	9	0	9	0	0	0	1	17	1			
26	Brady Keys	29	RCB	14	0		1	20	0	20	0	0	1	0	0	0			
75	Ken Kortas	23		14	0							0	0	2	0	0			
54	Max Messner	27		14	0		1	14	0	14	0	0	0	1	18	0			
78	John Baker	30	RDE	14	0							0	0	1	19	0			
84	Lee Folkins	26		8	0							0	0	1	18	1			
61	Riley Gunnels	28		14	0							0	0	1	0	0			
51	Ken Henson	22		4	0							0	0	1	0	0			
82	John Hilton	23	TE	14	0							0	0	1	0	0			
46	Frank Lambert	22	P	14	0							0	1	0	0	0			
68	Mike Magac	27	RG	8	0							0	0	1	0	0			
73	Ray Mansfield	24	LDT	14	0							0	0	1	0	0			
60	Ben McGee	26	LDE	13	0							0	0	1	0	0			
58	Ed Pine	25		8	0							0	0	1	0	0			
62	Mike Sandusky	30	LG	12	0							0	0	1	0	0			
49	Bob Sherman	23		11	0		1	35	0	35	0								
	Team Total	26.3		14			12	282	2	82	0	0	42	35	106	3			
	Opp Total			14		62							28	13					

1966 PITTSBURGH STEELERS: 5-8-1, 6TH IN EAST, 11TH IN NFL
Head Coach: Bill Austin

							Score		Offe					Defe				
Week	Day	Date		OT	Rec	Opp	Tm	Opp	1stD	TotYd	PassY	RushY	TO	1stD	TotYd	PassY	RushY	TO
1	Sun	September 11	T		0-0-1	New York Giants	34	34	25	404	266	138	3	8	279	247	32	5
2	Sun	September 18	W		1-0-1	Detroit Lions	17	3	15	256	143	113	1	9	158	89	69	4
3	Sun	September 25	L		1-1-1	Washington Redskins	27	33	15	278	206	72	6	17	320	228	92	2
4	Sun	October 2	L		1-2-1	Washington Redskins	10	24	16	249	180	69	4	11	333	249	84	
5	Sat	October 8	L		1-3-1	Cleveland Browns	10	41	12	204	182	22	6	31	467	226	241	2
6	Sun	October 16	L		1-4-1	Philadelphia Eagles	14	31	14	178	91	87	3	22	281	93	188	3
7	Sun	October 30	L		1-5-1	Dallas Cowboys	21	52	6	119	112	7	4	24	425	233	192	3
8	Sun	November 6	W		2-5-1	Cleveland Browns	16	6	12	267	132	135		19	307	176	131	6
9	Sun	November 13	W		3-5-1	St. Louis Cardinals	30	9	6	150	102	48	3	14	251	195	56	4
10	Sun	November 20	L		3-6-1	Dallas Cowboys	7	20	16	163	110	53	3	16	258	134	124	1
11	Sun	November 27	L		3-7-1	St. Louis Cardinals	3	6	8	78	46	32	2	15	228	29	199	1
12	Sun	December 4	L		3-8-1	Philadelphia Eagles	23	27	15	250	155	95	2	19	304	124	180	2
13	Sun	December 11	W		4-8-1	New York Giants	47	28	20	392	297	95	1	15	310	191	119	2
14	Sun	December 18	W		5-8-1	Atlanta Falcons	57	33	27	458	332	126	1	18	370	291	79	5

Passing

No.		Age	Pos	G	GS	QBrec	Cmp	Att	Cmp%	Yds	TD	TD%	Int	Int%	Lng	Y/A	AY/A	Y/C	Y/G	Rate	Sk	Yds
10	Ron C. Smith	24	QB	9	7	2-5-0	79	181	43.6	1249	8	4.4	12	6.6	84	6.9	4.8	15.8	138.8	54.3		
14	Bill Nelsen	25	qb	5	5	3-1-1	63	112	56.3	1122	7	6.3	1	0.9	68	10.0	10.9	17.8	224.4	107.8		
15	George Izo	29		4	2	0-2-0	35	81	43.2	360	2	2.5	8	9.9	37	4.4	0.5	10.3	90.0	25.3		
11	Ron Meyer	22		4	0		7	19	36.8	59	0	0.0	1	5.3	19	3.1	0.7	8.4	14.8	23.8		
42	Dick Hoak	27	HB	13	0		4	6	66.7	87	1	16.7	0	0.0	42	14.5	17.8	21.8	6.7	149.3		
30	Willie Asbury	23	FB	14	0		0	1	0.0	0	0	0.0	0	0.0	0	0.0	0.0		0.0	39.6		
49	Amos Bullocks	27		8	0		0	1	0.0	0	0	0.0	0	0.0	0	0.0	0.0		0.0	39.6		
	Team Total	25.6		14		5-8-1	188	401	46.9	2877	18	4.5	22	5.5	84	7.2	5.6	15.3	205.5	63.1		
	Opp Total			14			192	397	48.4	2849	27	6.8	24	6.0		7.2	5.8	14.8	203.5	69.8	38	344

Rushing and Receiving

						Rush							Receiving							
No.		Age	Pos	G	GS	Att	Yds	TD	Lng	Y/A	Y/G	A/G	Rec	Yds	Y/R	TD	Lng	R/G	Y/G	YScm
30	Willie Asbury	23	FB	14	0	169	544	7	45	3.2	38.9	12.1	19	228	12.0	2	37	1.4	16.3	772
42	Dick Hoak	27	HB	13	0	81	212	1	16	2.6	16.3	6.2	23	239	10.4	0	31	1.8	18.4	451
23	Cannonball Butler	23		14	0	46	114	2	19	2.5	8.1	3.3	4	93	23.3	1	66	0.3	6.6	207
49	Amos Bullocks	27		8	0	29	83	1	13	2.9	10.4	3.6	5	64	12.8	1	18	0.6	8.0	147
37	Bobby L. Smith	24		8	0	24	93	0	21	3.9	11.6	3.0	3	26	8.7	0	21	0.4	3.3	119
31	Dick Leftridge	22		4	0	8	17	2	5	2.1	4.3	2.0								17
14	Bill Nelsen	25	qb	5	5	6	18	0	9	3.0	3.6	1.2								18
10	Ron C. Smith	24	QB	9	7	4	−9	0	2	−2.3	−1.0	0.4								−9
38	Mike Lind	26		6	0	3	4	0	3	1.3	0.7	0.5								4
87	Roy Jefferson	23	SE/PR	14	0	2	36	0	24	18.0	2.6	0.1	32	772	24.1	4	84	2.3	55.1	808
15	George Izo	29		4	2	2	−18	0	−4	−9.0	−4.5	0.5								−18
11	Ron Meyer	22		4	0	1	−2	0	−2	−2.0	−0.5	0.3								−2
82	John Hilton	24	TE	14	0	0	0	0	0		0.0	0.0	46	603	13.1	4	32	3.3	43.1	603
85	Gary Ballman	26	KR/FL	13	0	0	0	0	0		0.0	0.0	41	663	16.2	5	79	3.2	51.0	663
86	J.R. Wilburn	23		14	0	0	0	0	0		0.0	0.0	7	103	14.7	0	42	0.5	7.4	103
25	Jerry Simmons	24		13	0	0	0	0	0		0.0	0.0	6	68	11.3	1	21	0.5	5.2	68
84	Tony Jeter	22		9	0	0	0	0	0		0.0	0.0	2	18	9.0	0	11	0.2	2.0	18
	Team Total	25.6		14		375	1092	13	45	2.9	78.0	26.8	188	2877	15.3	18	84	13.4	205.5	3969
	Opp Total			14		468	1786	11		3.8	127.6	33.4	192	2505	13.0	27		13.7	178.9	4291

Defense

No.		Age	Pos	G	GS	Sk	Int	Yds	TD	Lng	PD	FF	Fmb	FR	Yds	TD	Tkl	Ast	Sfty
30	Willie Asbury	23	FB	14	0							0	6	0	0	0			
26	Brady Keys*	30	RCB	14	0		4	0	0	0	0	0	2	0	0	0			
24	Jim Bradshaw	27		9	0		4	82	1	28	0	0	0	1	0	0			
87	Roy Jefferson	23	SE/PR	14	0							0	3	2	0	0			
23	Cannonball Butler	23		14	0							0	4	0	0	0			
53	John Campbell	28	LLB	13	0		2	6	0	6	0	0	0	2	8	0			
73	Ray Mansfield	25	C	14	0							0	1	3	−20	0			
20	Paul Martha	24	RS	12	0		3	44	0	35	0	0	0	1	0	0			
50	Bill Saul	26	MLB	14	0		2	21	0	13	0	0	0	2	0	0			
28	Clendon Thomas	31	LS	14	0		2	24	0	24	0	0	0	2	23	1			
47	Marv Woodson	25	LCB	14	0		4	91	1	56	0								
85	Gary Ballman	26	KR/FL	13	0							0	2	1	0	0			
71	Charlie Bradshaw	30	LT	14	0							0	0	3	0	0			
63	Rod Breedlove	28		11	0		2	10	0	9	0	0	0	1	0	0			
42	Dick Hoak	27	HB	13	0							0	3	0	0	0			
25	Jerry Simmons	24		13	0							0	1	2	0	0			
79	Larry Gagner	23	LG	14	14							0	0	2	0	0			
74	Riley Gunnels	29		14	0		1	2	0	2	0	0	0	1	0	0			
15	George Izo	29		4	2							0	2	0	0	0			
31	Dick Leftridge	22		4	0							0	1	1	0	0			
60	Ben McGee*	27	LDE	14	0							0	0	2	9	0			
14	Bill Nelsen	25	qb	5	5							0	1	1	0	0			
37	Bobby L. Smith	24		8	0							0	2	0	0	0			
10	Ron C. Smith	24	QB	9	7							0	2	0	0	0			
49	Amos Bullocks	27		8	0							0	1	0	0	0			
82	John Hilton	24	TE	14	0							0	1	0	0	0			
84	Tony Jeter	22		9	0							0	0	1	0	0			
75	Ken Kortas	24	LDT	14	0							0	0	1	0	0			
46	Frank Lambert	23	P	14	0							0	0	1	0	0			
68	Mike Magac	28	RG	14	0							0	0	1	0	0			
11	Ron Meyer	22		4	0							0	1	0	0	0			
58	Roger Pillath	25		6	0							0	0	1	0	0			
62	Ralph Wenzel	23		6	0							0	0	1	0	0			
86	J.R. Wilburn	23		14	0							0	1	0	0	0			
	Team Total	25.6		14			24	200	2	56	0	0	24	33	20	1			
	Opp Total			14		66							37	21						

1967 PITTSBURGH STEELERS: 4-9-1, LAST IN CENTURY, 13TH IN NFL
Head Coach: Bill Austin

Week	Day	Date	OT	Rec	Opp	Score Tm	Score Opp	Offe 1stD	TotYd	PassY	RushY	TO	Defe 1stD	TotYd	PassY	RushY	TO
1	Sun	September 17	W	1-0	Chicago Bears	41	13	23	393	198	195	2	6	95	79	16	6
2	Sun	September 24	L	1-1	St. Louis Cardinals	14	28	17	237	143	94	6	12	283	137	146	1
3	Sun	October 1	L	1-2	Philadelphia Eagles	24	34	19	318	165	153	3	17	319	271	48	1
4	Sat	October 7	L	1-3	Cleveland Browns	10	21	20	278	208	70	4	24	361	183	178	3
5	Sun	October 15	L	1-4	New York Giants	24	27	16	259	197	62	2	18	381	305	76	2
6	Sun	October 22	L	1-5	Dallas Cowboys	21	24	29	379	298	81	2	14	378	290	88	1
7	Sun	October 29	W	2-5	New Orleans Saints	14	10	19	267	88	179	4	19	308	225	83	1
8	Sun	November 5	L	2-6	Cleveland Browns	14	34	14	301	229	72	3	21	313	132	181	1
9	Sun	November 12	T	2-6-1	St. Louis Cardinals	14	14	21	274	192	82	1	19	258	145	113	3
10	Sun	November 19	L	2-7-1	New York Giants	20	28	18	281	210	71	3	18	238	171	67	4
11	Sun	November 26	L	2-8-1	Minnesota Vikings	27	41	7	117	52	65	6	16	212	102	110	5
12	Sun	December 3	W	3-8-1	Detroit Lions	24	14	19	330	233	97	1	18	254	167	87	3
13	Sun	December 10	L	3-9-1	Washington Redskins	10	15	20	280	226	54	5	11	246	155	91	3
14	Sun	December 17	W	4-9-1	Green Bay Packers	24	17	10	194	72	122	3	15	309	216	93	5

Passing

No.		Age	Pos	G	GS	QBrec	Cmp	Att	Cmp%	Yds	TD	TD%	Int	Int%	Lng	Y/A	AY/A	Y/C	Y/G	Rate	Sk	Yds
10	Kent Nix	23	QB	12	9	3-6-0	136	268	50.7	1587	8	3.0	19	7.1	66	5.9	3.3	11.7	132.3	49.5		
14	Bill Nelsen	26	qb	8	5	1-3-1	74	165	44.8	1125	10	6.1	9	5.5	58	6.8	5.6	15.2	140.6	65.3		
42	Dick Hoak*	28		14	0		4	8	50.0	69	1	12.5	1	12.5	21	8.6	5.5	17.3	4.9	79.7		
83	Mike Clark	27	K	14	0		0	1	0.0	0	0	0.0	0	0.0	0	0.0	0.0		0.0	39.6		
	Team Total	25.8		14		4-9-1	214	442	48.4	2781	19	4.3	29	6.6	66	6.3	4.2	13.0	198.6	55.6		
	Opp Total			14			201	397	50.6	2854	22	5.5	26	6.5		7.2	5.4	14.2	203.9	65.4	29	276

Rushing and Receiving

No.		Age	Pos	G	GS	Rush Att	Yds	TD	Lng	Y/A	Y/G	A/G	Rec	Receiving Yds	Y/R	TD	Lng	R/G	Y/G	YScm
25	Don Shy	22	KR/HB	14	0	99	341	4	33	3.4	24.4	7.1	12	152	12.7	1	55	0.9	10.9	493
23	Cannonball Butler	24	hb	11	0	90	293	0	24	3.3	26.6	8.2	4	23	5.8	0	13	0.4	2.1	316
30	Willie Asbury	24	FB	12	0	80	315	4	73	3.9	26.3	6.7	3	52	17.3	0	21	0.3	4.3	367
38	Earl Gros	27	fb	12	0	72	252	1	23	3.5	21.0	6.0	19	175	9.2	0	22	1.6	14.6	427
42	Dick Hoak*	28		14	0	52	142	1	11	2.7	10.1	3.7	17	111	6.5	1	20	1.2	7.9	253
10	Kent Nix	23	QB	12	9	15	45	2	15	3.0	3.8	1.3								45
14	Bill Nelsen	26	qb	8	5	9	−19	0	11	−2.1	−2.4	1.1								−19
36	Charlie Bivins	29		2	0	7	23	1	9	3.3	11.5	3.5	1	24	24.0	0	24	0.5	12.0	47
87	Roy Jefferson	24	se	13	0	5	−11	0	20	−2.2	−0.8	0.4	29	459	15.8	4	58	2.2	35.3	448
45	Dick Compton	27	SE	12	0	1	1	0	1	1.0	0.1	0.1	42	507	12.1	1	40	3.5	42.3	508
82	John Hilton	25	TE	13	0	1	15	0	15	15.0	1.2	0.1	26	343	13.2	5	43	2.0	26.4	358
86	J.R. Wilburn	24	FL	14	0	0	0	0	0		0.0	0.0	51	767	15.0	5	66	3.6	54.8	767
46	Chet Anderson	22		14	0	0	0	0	0		0.0	0.0	8	141	17.6	2	48	0.6	10.1	141
89	Marshall Cropper	23		7	0	0	0	0	0		0.0	0.0	1	11	11.0	0	11	0.1	1.6	11
85	Jerry Marion	23		7	0	0	0	0	0		0.0	0.0	1	16	16.0	0	16	0.1	2.3	16
	Team Total	25.8		14		431	1397	13	73	3.2	99.8	30.8	214	2781	13.0	19	66	15.3	198.6	4178
	Opp Total			14		418	1377	12		3.3	98.4	29.9	201	2578	12.8	22		14.4	184.1	3955

Defense

No.		Age	Pos	G	GS	Sk	Def Int	Yds	TD	Lng	PD	Fumb FF	Fmb	FR	Yds	TD	Tack Tkl	Ast	Sfty
14	Bill Nelsen	26	qb	8	5							0	7	3	0	0			
47	Marv Woodson*	26	LCB	14	0		7	49	0	24	0	0	0	2	0	0			
20	Paul Martha	25	RS	14	0		4	41	0	23	0	0	1	2	0	0			
25	Don Shy	22	KR/HB	14	0							0	5	2	0	0			
30	Willie Asbury	24	FB	12	0							0	4	0	0	0			
24	Jim Bradshaw	28	PR	13	0							0	2	2	0	0			
29	Bob Hohn	26	RCB	13	0		2	0	0	0	0	0	0	2	0	0			
26	Brady Keys	31		6	0		2	8	0	6	0	0	1	1	0	0			
10	Kent Nix	23	QB	12	9							0	2	2	−3	0			
78	John Baker	32		13	0		1	0	0	0	0	0	0	2	0	0			
42	Dick Hoak*	28		14	0							0	2	1	0	0			
73	Ray Mansfield	26	C	14	0							0	2	1	−21	0			
34	Andy Russell	26	RLB	14	0		3	50	0	42	0								
28	Clendon Thomas	32	LS	13	0		2	39	0	33	0	0	0	1	0	0			
53	John Campbell	29	LLB	14	0		2	52	0	30	0								
45	Dick Compton	27	SE	12	0							0	1	1	0	0			
87	Roy Jefferson	24	se	13	0							0	1	1	0	0			
50	Bill Saul	27	MLB	14	0		1	0	0	0	0	0	1	0	0	0			
66	Bruce Van Dyke	23	RG	14	14							0	0	2	0	0			
23	Cannonball Butler	24	hb	11	0							0	1	0	0	0			
83	Mike Clark	27	K	14	0							0	0	1	0	0			
6	Jim Elliott	23	P	14	0							0	1	0	0	0			
9	John Foruria	23		3	0							0	0	1	0	0			
38	Earl Gros	27	fb	12	0							0	1	0	0	0			
76	Mike Haggerty	22	LT	14	0							0	0	1	0	0			
64	Chuck Hinton	28	RDT	14	0							0	0	1	27	1			
75	Ken Kortas	25	LDT	14	0							0	0	1	5	1			
60	Ben McGee	28	LDE	10	0		1	21	1	21	0								
65	Lloyd Voss	25	RDE	13	0		1	4	0	4	0								
86	J.R. Wilburn	24	FL	14	0							0	1	0	0	0			
	Team Total	25.8		14			26	264	1	42	0	0	33	30	8	2			
	Opp Total			14		30							26	13					1

1968 PITTSBURGH STEELERS: 2-11-1, LAST IN CENTURY, 14TH IN NFL
Head Coach: Bill Austin

Week	Day	Date	OT	Rec	Opp	Tm	Opp	1stD	TotYd	PassY	RushY	TO	1stD	TotYd	PassY	RushY	TO
1	Sun	September 15	L	0-1	New York Giants	20	34	20	324	194	130	4	21	331	166	165	2
2	Sun	September 22	L	0-2	Los Angeles Rams	10	45	16	258	202	56	3	20	378	291	87	
3	Sun	September 29	L	0-3	Baltimore Colts	7	41	11	213	164	49	4	18	276	153	123	1
4	Sat	October 5	L	0-4	Cleveland Browns	24	31	19	272	156	116	2	24	374	190	184	3
5	Sun	October 13	L	0-5	Washington Redskins	13	16	17	287	104	183	3	19	294	178	116	2
6	Sun	October 20	L	0-6	New Orleans Saints	12	16	16	301	91	210	2	16	273	170	103	1
7	Sun	October 27	W	1-6	Philadelphia Eagles	6	3	13	249	126	123	1	15	287	171	116	2
8	Sun	November 3	W	2-6	Atlanta Falcons	41	21	25	402	288	114	1	16	343	257	86	5
9	Sun	November 10	T	2-6-1	St. Louis Cardinals	28	28	17	363	280	83		17	425	337	88	2
10	Sun	November 17	L	2-7-1	Cleveland Browns	24	45	21	353	188	165	7	18	399	352	47	3
11	Sun	November 24	L	2-8-1	San Francisco 49ers	28	45	22	351	280	71	5	18	399	269	130	1
12	Sun	December 1	L	2-9-1	St. Louis Cardinals	10	20	13	167	90	77	3	18	322	137	185	2
13	Sun	December 8	L	2-10-1	Dallas Cowboys	7	28	19	313	120	193	1	11	341	232	109	2
14	Sun	December 15	L	2-11-1	New Orleans Saints	14	24	16	350	199	151	4	13	343	258	85	

Passing

No.		Age	Pos	G	GS	QBrec	Cmp	Att	Cmp%	Yds	TD	TD%	Int	Int%	Lng	Y/A	AY/A	Y/C	Y/G	Rate	Sk	Yds
17	Dick Shiner	26	QB	13	11	2-8-1	148	304	48.7	1856	18	5.9	17	5.6	61	6.1	4.8	12.5	142.8	64.5		
10	Kent Nix	24		8	3	0-3-0	56	130	43.1	720	4	3.1	8	6.2	61	5.5	3.4	12.9	90.0	45.7		
42	Dick Hoak	29	HB	14	0		7	16	43.8	188	0	0.0	1	6.3	62	11.8	8.9	26.9	13.4	61.5		
39	Bobby Walden	30	P	14	0		0	1	0.0	0	0	0.0	0	0.0	0	0.0	0.0		0.0	39.6		
	Team Total	26.4		14		2-11-1	211	451	46.8	2764	22	4.9	26	5.8	62	6.1	4.5	13.1	197.4	58.8		
	Opp Total			14			220	413	53.3	3360	29	7.0	17	4.1		8.1	7.7	15.3	240.0	86.6	28	199

Rushing and Receiving

No.		Age	Pos	G	GS	Att	Yds	TD	Lng	Y/A	Y/G	A/G	Rec	Yds	Y/R	TD	Lng	R/G	Y/G	YScm
42	Dick Hoak	29	HB	14	0	175	858	3	77	4.9	61.3	12.5	28	253	9.0	1	30	2.0	18.1	1111
38	Earl Gros	28	FB	13	0	151	579	3	44	3.8	44.5	11.6	27	211	7.8	3	21	2.1	16.2	790
25	Don Shy	23		13	0	35	106	1	39	3.0	8.2	2.7	13	106	8.2	0	21	1.0	8.2	212
17	Dick Shiner	26	QB	13	11	14	53	0	12	3.8	4.1	1.1								53
87	Roy Jefferson*	25	SE/PR	14	0	6	57	0	22	9.5	4.1	0.4	58	1074	18.5	11	62	4.1	76.7	1131
26	Rocky Bleier	22		10	0	6	39	0	21	6.5	3.9	0.6	3	68	22.7	0	54	0.3	6.8	107
10	Kent Nix	24		8	3	6	15	0	12	2.5	1.9	0.8								15
30	Willie Asbury	25		7	0	4	9	0	4	2.3	1.3	0.6	3	27	9.0	0	16	0.4	3.9	36
39	Bobby Walden	30	P	14	0	2	5	0	5	2.5	0.4	0.1								5
86	J.R. Wilburn	25	FL	14	0	0	0	0	0		0.0	0.0	39	514	13.2	3	41	2.8	36.7	514
82	John Hilton	26	TE	14	0	0	0	0	0		0.0	0.0	20	285	14.3	1	37	1.4	20.4	285
88	Rich Kotite	26		12	0	0	0	0	0		0.0	0.0	6	65	10.8	2	20	0.5	5.4	65
45	Dick Compton	28		7	0	0	0	0	0		0.0	0.0	5	45	9.0	1	14	0.7	6.4	45
89	Marshall Cropper	24		5	0	0	0	0	0		0.0	0.0	4	54	13.5	0	17	0.8	10.8	54
24	Jon Henderson	24	KR	14	0	0	0	0	0		0.0	0.0	3	26	8.7	0	13	0.2	1.9	26
69	Jerry Hillebrand	28	LLB	14	0	0	0	0	0		0.0	0.0	1	27	27.0	0	27	0.1	1.9	27
84	Tony Jeter	24		2	0	0	0	0	0		0.0	0.0	1	9	9.0	0	9	0.5	4.5	9
	Team Total	26.4		14		399	1721	7	77	4.3	122.9	28.5	211	2764	13.1	22	62	15.1	197.4	4485
	Opp Total			14		441	1624	14		3.7	116.0	31.5	220	3161	14.4	29		15.7	225.8	4785

Defense

No.		Age	Pos	G	GS	Sk	Def					Fumb					Tack		Sfty
							Int	Yds	TD	Lng	PD	FF	Fmb	FR	Yds	TD	Tkl	Ast	
17	Dick Shiner	26	QB	13	11							0	7	2	0	0			
42	Dick Hoak	29	HB	14	0							0	5	0	0	0			
10	Kent Nix	24		8	3							0	4	1	0	0			
38	Earl Gros	28	FB	13	0							0	3	1	0	0			
24	Jon Henderson	24	KR	14	0							0	2	2	0	0			
87	Roy Jefferson*	25	SE/PR	14	0							0	3	1	0	0			
20	Paul Martha	26	RS	9	0		3	43	0	23	0	0	0	1	60	1			
28	Clendon Thomas	33	LS	14	0		3	0	0	0	0	0	0	1	2	0			
47	Marv Woodson	27	LCB	14	0		3	23	0	12	0	0	0	1	0	0			
59	Ray May	23	MLB	12	0		3	31	1	25	0								
34	Andy Russell*	27	RLB	14	0		2	2	0	2	0	0	0	1	0	0			
69	Jerry Hillebrand	28	LLB	14	0		2	32	0	32	0								
25	Don Shy	23		13	0							0	1	1	0	0			
39	Bobby Walden	30	P	14	0							0	1	1	-8	0			
26	Rocky Bleier	22		10	0							0	0	1	0	0			
53	John Campbell	30		8	0		1	20	0	20	0								
57	Sam Davis	24		14	0							0	0	1	0	0			
64	Chuck Hinton	29	RDT	14	0							0	0	1	0	0			
60	Ben McGee*	29	RDE	14	0							0	0	1	0	0			
78	Frank Parker	29	rdt	10	0							0	0	1	0	0			
77	Mike Taylor	23		14	0							0	0	1	9	0			
44	Bob Wade	24	RCB	14	0							0	0	1	0	0			
86	J.R. Wilburn	25	FL	14	0							0	0	1	15	0			
	Team Total	26.4		14			17	151	1	32	0	0	26	21	78	1			
	Opp Total			14		41							16	7					

1969 PITTSBURGH STEELERS: 1-13-0, LAST IN CENTURY, TIED FOR LAST IN NFL
Head Coach: Chuck Noll

Week	Day	Date	OT	Rec	Opp	Score		Offe					Defe				
						Tm	Opp	1stD	TotYd	PassY	RushY	TO	1stD	TotYd	PassY	RushY	TO
1	Sun	September 21	W	1-0	Detroit Lions	16	13	12	237	128	109	4	14	236	156	80	4
2	Sun	September 28	L	1-1	Philadelphia Eagles	27	41	19	355	254	101	2	19	460	318	142	2
3	Sun	October 5	L	1-2	St. Louis Cardinals	14	27	20	345	245	100	5	17	344	241	103	4
4	Sun	October 12	L	1-3	New York Giants	7	10	19	231	84	147	4	14	208	132	76	1
5	Sat	October 18	L	1-4	Cleveland Browns	31	42	20	320	183	137	8	16	283	139	144	4
6	Sun	October 26	L	1-5	Washington Redskins	7	14	17	301	130	171	2	14	214	117	97	3
7	Sun	November 2	L	1-6	Green Bay Packers	34	38	19	346	204	142	4	14	318	236	82	5
8	Sun	November 9	L	1-7	Chicago Bears	7	38	10	86	55	31	4	25	379	107	272	4
9	Sun	November 16	L	1-8	Cleveland Browns	3	24	15	278	107	171	4	23	390	263	127	2
10	Sun	November 23	L	1-9	Minnesota Vikings	14	52	10	145	97	48	5	25	329	215	114	4
11	Sun	November 30	L	1-10	St. Louis Cardinals	10	47	10	187	110	77	4	25	401	205	196	2
12	Sun	December 7	L	1-11	Dallas Cowboys	7	10	14	217	140	77	1	13	202	109	93	3
13	Sun	December 14	L	1-12	New York Giants	17	21	14	311	206	105	2	18	297	184	113	1
14	Sun	December 21	L	1-13	New Orleans Saints	24	27	11	267	141	126		23	340	247	93	2

Passing

No.		Age	Pos	G	GS	QBrec	Cmp	Att	Cmp%	Yds	TD	TD%	Int	Int%	Lng	Y/A	AY/A	Y/C	Y/G	Rate	Sk	Yds
17	Dick Shiner	27	QB	12	9	1-8-0	97	209	46.4	1422	7	3.3	10	4.8	63	6.8	5.3	14.7	118.5	60.3	24	157
5	Terry Hanratty	21	qb	8	5	0-5-0	52	126	41.3	716	8	6.3	13	10.3	41	5.7	2.3	13.8	89.5	41.7	20	168
10	Kent Nix	25		5	0		25	53	47.2	290	2	3.8	6	11.3	47	5.5	1.1	11.6	58.0	37.2	7	39
42	Dick Hoak	30	HB	14	0		2	3	66.7	30	0	0.0	0	0.0	16	10.0	10.0	15.0	2.1	99.3	1	10
	Team Total	25.9		14		1-13-0	176	391	45.0	2458	17	4.3	29	7.4	63	6.3	3.8	14.0	175.6	49.4	52	374
	Opp Total			14			227	410	55.4	2973	27	6.6	25		6.1		7.3	5.8	13.1	212.4	75.0	33	304

Rushing and Receiving

No.		Age	Pos	G	GS	Rush Att	Yds	TD	Lng	Y/A	Y/G	A/G	Receiving Rec	Yds	Y/R	TD	Lng	R/G	Y/G	YScm
42	Dick Hoak	30	HB	14	0	151	531	2	13	3.5	37.9	10.8	20	190	9.5	1	26	1.4	13.6	721
38	Earl Gros	29	FB	13	0	116	343	4	16	3.0	26.4	8.9	17	131	7.7	3	20	1.3	10.1	474
46	Warren Bankston	22		14	0	62	259	1	15	4.2	18.5	4.4	6	6	1.0	0	8	0.4	0.4	265
36	Don McCall	25		13	0	30	98	0	14	3.3	7.5	2.3	2	2	1.0	0	5	0.2	0.2	100
17	Dick Shiner	27	QB	12	9	14	55	1	18	3.9	4.6	1.2								55
5	Terry Hanratty	21	qb	8	5	10	106	0	31	10.6	13.3	1.3								106
10	Kent Nix	25		5	0	10	70	0	20	7.0	14.0	2.0								70
87	Roy Jefferson*+	26	SE	14	0	4	46	0	22	11.5	3.3	0.3	67	1079	16.1	9	63	4.8	77.1	1125
86	J.R. Wilburn	26	FL	10	0	2	29	0	35	14.5	2.9	0.2	20	373	18.7	0	53	2.0	37.3	402
23	Bob Campbell	22	PR/KR	14	0	1	5	0	5	5.0	0.4	0.1	1	32	32.0	0	32	0.1	2.3	37
24	Jon Henderson	25		9	0	0	0	0	0		0.0	0.0	12	188	15.7	3	45	1.3	20.9	188
82	John Hilton	27	TE	11	0	0	0	0	0		0.0	0.0	12	231	19.3	0	34	1.1	21.0	231
89	Marshall Cropper	25		4	0	0	0	0	0		0.0	0.0	9	116	12.9	0	19	2.3	29.0	116
85	Bob Adams	23		14	0	0	0	0	0		0.0	0.0	6	80	13.3	0	19	0.4	5.7	80
43	Erwin Williams	22		9	0	0	0	0	0		0.0	0.0	3	14	4.7	1	6	0.3	1.6	14
83	Don Alley	24		8	0	0	0	0	0		0.0	0.0	1	16	16.0	0	16	0.1	2.0	16
	Team Total	25.9		14		400	1542	8	35	3.9	110.1	28.6	176	2458	14.0	17	63	12.6	175.6	4000
	Opp Total			14		455	1732	17		3.8	123.7	32.5	227	2669	11.8	27		16.2	190.6	4401

Defense

No.		Age	Pos	G	GS	Sk	Def Int	Yds	TD	Lng	PD	Fumb FF	Fmb	FR	Yds	TD	Tack Tkl	Ast	Sfty
20	Paul Martha	27	RS	14	0		5	37	0	15	0	0	3	1	0	0			
23	Bob Campbell	22	PR/KR	14	0							0	5	3	0	0			
29	Bob Hohn	28	LCB	11	0		5	64	0	24	0	0	0	3	3	0			
46	Warren Bankston	22		14	0							0	6	0	0	0			
38	Earl Gros	29	FB	13	0							0	4	1	0	0			
64	Chuck Hinton	30	RDT	14	0		1	7	0	7	0	0	1	3	0	0			
21	Jim Shorter	30	RCB	14	0		3	47	0	23	0	0	0	2	50	0			
42	Dick Hoak	30	HB	14	0							0	4	0	0	0			
87	Roy Jefferson*+	26	SE	14	0							0	3	1	0	0			
17	Dick Shiner	27	QB	12	9							0	3	1	0	0			
5	Terry Hanratty	21	qb	8	5							0	3	0	0	0			
61	Brian Stenger	22		14	0		3	38	0	19	0								
66	Bruce Van Dyke	25	RG	14	0							0	0	3	0	0			
44	Lee Calland	28		8	0		2	0	0	0	0								
89	Marshall Cropper	25		4	0							0	0	2	0	0			
57	Sam Davis	25		12	2							0	2	0	0	0			
69	Jerry Hillebrand	29	LLB	10	0		1	14	0	14	0	0	0	1	0	0			
59	Ray May	24	MLB	14	0		2	4	0	4	0								
36	Don McCall	25		13	0							0	1	1	0	0			
34	Andy Russell	28	RLB	14	0		2	48	0	26	0								
77	Mike Taylor	24	LT	9	0							0	0	2	0	0			
65	Lloyd Voss	27	LDE	14	0							0	0	2	0	0			
47	Marv Woodson	28		8	0		1	0	0	0	0	0	0	1	0	0			
85	Bob Adams	23		14	0							0	0	1	0	0			
55	Jon Kolb	22		14	0							0	0	1	0	0			
56	Ray Mansfield	28	C	14	0							0	0	1	0	0			
10	Kent Nix	25		5	0							0	1	0	0	0			
27	Clancy Oliver	22		9	0							0	0	1	0	0			
67	Clarence Washington	23		13	0							0	0	1	0	0			
	Team Total	25.9		14			25	257	0	26	0	0	36	32	53	0			
	Opp Total			14		52							25	9					2

1970 PITTSBURGH STEELERS: 5-9-0, 4TH IN AFC CENTRAL DIVISION
Head Coach: Chuck Noll

Week	Day	Date	OT	Rec	Opp	Score		Offe					Defe				
						Tm	Opp	1stD	TotYd	PassY	RushY	TO	1stD	TotYd	PassY	RushY	TO
1	Sun	September 20	L	0-1	Houston Oilers	7	19	11	214	143	71	1	17	305	133	172	
2	Sun	September 27	L	0-2	Denver Broncos	13	16	14	245	227	18	3	12	226	144	82	4
3	Sat	October 3	L	0-3	Cleveland Browns	7	15	17	263	129	134	4	8	199	130	69	2
4	Sun	October 11	W	1-3	Buffalo Bills	23	10	12	209	38	171		16	285	200	85	5
5	Sun	October 18	W	2-3	Houston Oilers	7	3	11	241	186	55	4	17	259	124	135	4
6	Sun	October 25	L	2-4	Oakland Raiders	14	31	24	266	138	128	5	15	346	184	162	2
7	Mon	November 2	W	3-4	Cincinnati Bengals	21	10	13	281	195	86	1	18	282	143	139	3
8	Sun	November 8	W	4-4	New York Jets	21	17	14	277	123	154	2	20	246	142	104	3
9	Sun	November 15	L	4-5	Kansas City Chiefs	14	31	15	202	99	103	6	21	424	257	167	3
10	Sun	November 22	L	4-6	Cincinnati Bengals	7	34	23	321	183	138	6	17	332	146	186	1
11	Sun	November 29	W	5-6	Cleveland Browns	28	9	15	425	257	168	2	16	171	129	42	1
12	Sun	December 6	L	5-7	Green Bay Packers	12	20	13	274	143	131	6	14	317	235	82	4
13	Sun	December 13	L	5-8	Atlanta Falcons	16	27	14	193	94	99	6	11	221	74	147	2
14	Sun	December 20	L	5-9	Philadelphia Eagles	20	30	10	341	82	259	2	23	383	276	107	4

Passing

No.		Age	Pos	G	GS	QBrec	Cmp	Att	Cmp%	Yds	TD	TD%	Int	Int%	Lng	Y/A	AY/A	Y/C	Y/G	Rate	Sk	Yds
12	Terry Bradshaw	22	QB	13	8	3-5-0	83	218	38.1	1410	6	2.8	24	11.0	87	6.5	2.1	17.0	108.5	30.4	25	242
5	Terry Hanratty	22	qb	13	6	2-4-0	64	163	39.3	842	5	3.1	8	4.9	72	5.2	3.6	13.2	64.8	46.1	3	33
42	Dick Hoak	31		12	0		2	2	100.0	40	1	50.0	0	0.0	27	20.0	30.0	20.0	3.3	158.3	0	0
39	Bobby Walden	32	P	13	0		1	1	100.0	20	0	0.0	0	0.0	20	20.0	20.0	20.0	1.5	118.7	0	0
	Team Total	25.6		14		5-9-0	150	384	39.1	2312	12	3.1	32	8.3	87	6.0	2.9	15.4	165.1	35.4	28	275
	Opp Total			14			191	393	48.6	2555	21	5.3	23	5.9		6.5	4.9	13.4	182.5	63.1	26	238

Rushing and Receiving

No.		Age	Pos	G	GS	Rush							Receiving							YScm
						Att	Yds	TD	Lng	Y/A	Y/G	A/G	Rec	Yds	Y/R	TD	Lng	R/G	Y/G	
26	Preston Pearson	25	RB	14	0	173	503	2	30	2.9	35.9	12.4	6	71	11.8	0	18	0.4	5.1	574
33	John Fuqua	24	FB	14	0	138	691	7	85	5.0	49.4	9.9	23	289	12.6	2	57	1.6	20.6	980
42	Dick Hoak	31		12	0	40	115	1	13	2.9	9.6	3.3	4	25	6.3	0	18	0.3	2.1	140
12	Terry Bradshaw	22	QB	13	8	32	233	1	22	7.3	17.9	2.5								233
46	Warren Bankston	23		4	0	26	122	2	31	4.7	30.5	6.5	7	30	4.3	0	20	1.8	7.5	152
30	Terry Cole	25		10	0	9	8	0	6	0.9	0.8	0.9	3	31	10.3	0	20	0.3	3.1	39
86	J.R. Wilburn	27		6	0	5	25	0	10	5.0	4.2	0.8	6	77	12.8	0	15	1.0	12.8	102
5	Terry Hanratty	22	qb	13	6	4	−5	0	0	−1.3	−0.4	0.3								−5
32	Hubie Bryant	24	PR/wr	14	0	3	25	0	24	8.3	1.8	0.2	8	154	19.3	0	63	0.6	11.0	179
88	Dave L. Smith	23	WR	14	0	1	6	0	6	6.0	0.4	0.1	30	458	15.3	2	87	2.1	32.7	464
82	Dennis Hughes	22	TE	11	0	1	−8	0	−8	−8.0	−0.7	0.1	24	332	13.8	3	72	2.2	30.2	324
25	Ron Shanklin	22	WR	14	0	0	0	0	0		0.0	0.0	30	691	23.0	4	81	2.1	49.4	691
2	Jon Staggers	22		12	0	0	0	0	0		0.0	0.0	6	118	19.7	1	31	0.5	9.8	118
85	Bob Adams	24		14	0	0	0	0	0		0.0	0.0	3	36	12.0	0	17	0.2	2.6	36
	Team Total	25.6		14		432	1715	13	85	4.0	122.5	30.9	150	2312	15.4	12	87	10.7	165.1	4027
	Opp Total			14		487	1679	8		3.4	119.9	34.8	191	2317	12.1	21		13.6	165.5	3996

Defense

No.		Age	Pos	G	GS	Sk	Int	Yds	TD	Lng	PD	FF	Fmb	FR	Yds	TD	Tkl	Ast	Sfty
33	John Fuqua	24	FB	14	0							0	7	5	0	0			
44	Lee Calland	29	RCB	14	0		7	38	0	21	0	0	0	2	0	0			
26	Preston Pearson	25	RB	14	0							0	6	2	0	0			
58	Chuck Allen	31	MLB	14	0		4	48	0	30	0	0	0	2	6	0			
32	Hubie Bryant	24	PR/wr	14	0							0	3	2	0	0			
69	Jerry Hillebrand	30	LLB	12	0		2	14	0	14	0	0	1	1	0	0			
48	John Rowser	26	lcb	7	0		3	27	0	12	0	0	0	1	10	0			
34	Andy Russell*	29	RLB	14	0		3	64	0	37	0	0	0	1	0	0			
12	Terry Bradshaw	22	QB	13	8							0	3	0	0	0			
46	Warren Bankston	23		4	0							0	1	1	0	0			
29	Fred Barry	22		9	0							0	0	2	0	0			
37	Chuck Beatty	24	SS	12	0		2	49	1	30	0								
47	Mel Blount	22	LCB/KR	14	9		1	4	0	4	0	0	0	1	0	0			
5	Terry Hanratty	22	qb	13	6							0	1	1	0	0			
42	Dick Hoak	31		12	0							0	1	1	-2	0			
56	Ray Mansfield	29	C	14	0							0	0	2	4	0			
60	Ben McGee	31	RDE	14	0							0	0	2	0	0			
2	Jon Staggers	22		12	0							0	2	0	0	0			
28	Ocie Austin	23	FS	7	0		1	22	0	22	0								
30	Terry Cole	25		10	0							0	1	0	0	0			
64	Chuck Hinton	31	RDT	14	0							0	0	1	0	0			
82	Dennis Hughes	22	TE	11	0							0	1	0	0	0			
25	Ron Shanklin	22	WR	14	0							0	1	0	0	0			
88	Dave L. Smith	23	WR	14	0							0	1	0	0	0			
49	John Sodaski	22		3	0							0	0	1	0	0			
65	Lloyd Voss	28	LDE	14	0							0	0	1	0	0			
86	J.R. Wilburn	27		6	0							0	1	0	0	0			
	Team Total	25.6		14			23	266	1	37	0	0	30	29	18	0			
	Opp Total			14		28							29	14					3

1971 PITTSBURGH STEELERS: 6-8-0, 2ND IN AFC CENTRAL DIVISION
Head Coach: Chuck Noll

Week	Day	Date	OT	Rec	Opp	Tm	Opp	1stD	TotYd	PassY	RushY	TO	1stD	TotYd	PassY	RushY	TO
1	Sun	September 19	L	0-1	Chicago Bears	15	17	15	352	129	223	7	8	141	96	45	4
2	Sun	September 26	W	1-1	Cincinnati Bengals	21	10	15	288	208	80	3	15	253	225	28	1
3	Sun	October 3	W	2-1	San Diego Chargers	21	17	16	282	157	125	1	28	427	258	169	4
4	Sun	October 10	L	2-2	Cleveland Browns	17	27	11	222	112	110	1	20	350	219	131	3
5	Mon	October 18	L	2-3	Kansas City Chiefs	16	38	18	322	251	71	4	15	348	285	63	2
6	Sun	October 24	W	3-3	Houston Oilers	23	16	26	419	254	165	5	19	272	180	92	2
7	Sun	October 31	L	3-4	Baltimore Colts	21	34	14	181	155	26	2	19	383	312	71	2
8	Sun	November 7	W	4-4	Cleveland Browns	26	9	21	393	163	230	1	11	210	81	129	3
9	Sun	November 14	L	4-5	Miami Dolphins	21	24	17	288	219	69	4	11	309	189	120	4
10	Sun	November 21	W	5-5	New York Giants	17	13	11	175	60	115		22	419	273	146	3
11	Sun	November 28	L	5-6	Denver Broncos	10	22	12	225	67	158	3	14	276	150	126	2
12	Sun	December 5	L	5-7	Houston Oilers	3	29	10	132	59	73	3	15	275	128	147	
13	Sun	December 12	W	6-7	Cincinnati Bengals	21	13	16	272	146	126	3	14	348	222	126	5
14	Sun	December 19	L	6-8	Los Angeles Rams	14	23	24	331	144	187	5	14	237	140	89	

Passing

No.		Age	Pos	G	GS	QBrec	Cmp	Att	Cmp%	Yds	TD	TD%	Int	Int%	Lng	Y/A	AY/A	Y/C	Y/G	Rate	Sk	Yds
12	Terry Bradshaw	23	QB	14	13	5-8-0	203	373	54.4	2259	13	3.5	22	5.9	49	6.1	4.1	11.1	161.4	59.7	33	287
5	Terry Hanratty	23		6	1	1-0-0	7	29	24.1	159	2	6.9	3	10.3	40	5.5	2.2	22.7	26.5	33.3	3	32
16	Bob Leahy	24		1	0		3	11	27.3	18	0	0.0	1	9.1	9	1.6	−2.5	6.0	18.0	1.7	1	3
39	Bobby Walden	33	P	14	0		1	1	100.0	10	0	0.0	0	0.0	10	10.0	10.0	10.0	0.7	108.3	0	0
	Team Total	25.3		14		6-8-0	214	414	51.7	2446	15	3.6	26	6.3	49	5.9	3.8	11.4	174.7	55.7	37	322
	Opp Total			14			235	408	57.6	3060	16	3.9	17	4.2		7.5	6.4	13.0	218.6	77.0	33	294

Rushing and Receiving

No.		Age	Pos	G	GS	Rush Att	Yds	TD	Lng	Y/A	Y/G	A/G	Rec	Yds	Y/R	TD	Lng	R/G	Y/G	YScm
33	John Fuqua	25	FB	12	0	155	625	4	30	4.0	52.1	12.9	49	427	8.7	1	40	4.1	35.6	1052
26	Preston Pearson	26	RB	14	0	131	605	0	29	4.6	43.2	9.4	20	246	12.3	2	41	1.4	17.6	851
46	Warren Bankston	24		14	0	70	274	0	30	3.9	19.6	5.0	17	148	8.7	0	31	1.2	10.6	422
12	Terry Bradshaw	23	QB	14	13	53	247	5	39	4.7	17.6	3.8								247
25	Ron Shanklin	23	WR	14	0	2	1	0	2	0.5	0.1	0.1	49	652	13.3	6	42	3.5	46.6	653
88	Dave L. Smith	24	WR	14	0	1	−10	0	−10	−10.0	−0.7	0.1	47	663	14.1	5	49	3.4	47.4	653
2	Jon Staggers	23	PR	14	0	1	5	0	5	5.0	0.4	0.1	8	103	12.9	0	20	0.6	7.4	108
5	Terry Hanratty	23		6	1	1	3	1	3	3.0	0.5	0.2								3
16	Bob Leahy	24		1	0	1	−6	0	−6	−6.0	−6.0	1.0								−6
39	Bobby Walden	33	P	14	0	1	14	0	14	14.0	1.0	0.1								14
85	Bob Adams	25	TE	14	0	0	0	0	0		0.0	0.0	20	160	8.0	0	21	1.4	11.4	160
43	Frank Lewis	24		9	0	0	0	0	0		0.0	0.0	3	44	14.7	0	22	0.3	4.9	44
87	Larry Brown	22		13	0	0	0	0	0		0.0	0.0	1	3	3.0	1	3	0.1	0.2	3
	Team Total	25.3		14		416	1758	10	39	4.2	125.6	29.7	214	2446	11.4	15	49	15.3	174.7	4204
	Opp Total			14		440	1482	13		3.4	105.9	31.4	235	2766	11.8	16		16.8	197.6	4248

Defense

No.		Age	Pos	G	GS	Sk	Def Int	Yds	TD	Lng	PD	Fumb FF	Fmb	FR	Yds	TD	Tack Tkl	Ast	Sfty
12	Terry Bradshaw	23	QB	14	13							0	7	4	−2	0			
26	Preston Pearson	26	RB	14	0							0	7	3	0	1			
46	Warren Bankston	24		14	0							0	5	1	0	0			
85	Bob Adams	25	TE	14	0							0	1	4	15	0			
58	Chuck Allen	32	MLB	10	0		3	45	0	29	0	0	0	2	0	0			
68	L.C. Greenwood	25	LDE	14	14							0	0	5	0	0			
33	John Fuqua	25	FB	12	0							0	4	0	0	0			
48	John Rowser	27	LCB	12	0		4	94	1	70	0								
2	Jon Staggers	23	PR	14	0							0	3	1	0	0			
47	Mel Blount	23	RCB	14	9		2	16	0	16	0	0	1	0	0	0			
44	Lee Calland	30	rcb	13	0		2	0	0	0	0	0	0	1	6	0			
75	Joe Greene*	25	LDT	14	14							0	0	3	3	0			
59	Jack Ham	23	LLB	14	14		2	4	0	4	0	0	0	1	0	0			
16	Bob Leahy	24		1	0							0	2	1	0	0			
23	Mike Wagner	22	SS	12	0		2	53	0	27	0	0	1	0	0	0			
39	Bobby Walden	33	P	14	0							0	1	2	−7	0			
36	Jim Brumfield	24	KR	14	0							0	1	1	0	0			
43	Frank Lewis	24		9	0							0	1	1	0	0			
34	Andy Russell*	30	RLB	14	0							0	0	2	3	0			
61	Brian Stenger	24		14	0							0	0	2	8	0			
49	Ralph Anderson	22		7	0		1	14	0	14	0								
50	Jim Clack	24	c	14	0							0	1	0	−32	0			
27	Glen Edwards	24	FS	8	6		1	20	0	20	0								
25	Ron Shanklin	23	WR	14	0							0	1	0	0	0			
88	Dave L. Smith	24	WR	14	0							0	1	0	0	0			
65	Lloyd Voss	29	RDT	13	0							0	0	1	0	0			
78	Dwight White	22	RDE	14	0							0	0	1	4	0			
	Team Total	25.3		14			17	246	1	70	0	0	37	36	−2	1			
	Opp Total			14		37							27	9					2

1972 PITTSBURGH STEELERS: 11-3-0, 1ST IN AFC CENTRAL DIVISION
Head Coach: Chuck Noll

							Score		Offe					Defe				
Week	Day	Date	OT	Rec	Opp		Tm	Opp	1stD	TotYd	PassY	RushY	TO	1stD	TotYd	PassY	RushY	TO
1	Sun	September 17	W	1-0	Oakland Raiders		34	28	17	247	106	141	4	20	370	273	97	5
2	Sun	September 24	L	1-1	Cincinnati Bengals		10	15	14	205	131	74	3	13	269	148	121	4
3	Sun	October 1	W	2-1	St. Louis Cardinals		25	19	20	362	209	153	2	15	248	190	58	4
4	Sun	October 8	L	2-2	Dallas Cowboys		13	17	14	272	142	130	2	21	367	176	191	4
5	Sun	October 15	W	3-2	Houston Oilers		24	7	18	295	46	249		7	108		108	1
6	Sun	October 22	W	4-2	New England Patriots		33	3	19	426	183	243	1	17	276	149	127	4
7	Sun	October 29	W	5-2	Buffalo Bills		38	21	18	309	93	216	1	24	418	164	254	4
8	Sun	November 5	W	6-2	Cincinnati Bengals		40	17	20	415	185	230		21	366	221	145	3
9	Sun	November 12	W	7-2	Kansas City Chiefs		16	7	15	318	80	238	5	16	183	108	75	3
10	Sun	November 19	L	7-3	Cleveland Browns		24	26	15	314	103	211	2	24	389	172	217	2
11	Sun	November 26	W	8-3	Minnesota Vikings		23	10	12	292	86	206	3	16	320	225	95	3
12	Sun	December 3	W	9-3	Cleveland Browns		30	0	19	337	153	184	1	11	126	27	99	3
13	Sun	December 10	W	10-3	Houston Oilers		9	3	12	193	63	130	1	11	159	87	72	1
14	Sun	December 17	W	11-3	San Diego Chargers		24	2	15	246	131	115	1	12	172	116	56	7
		Playoffs																
Division	Sat	December 23	W	12-3	Oakland Raiders		13	7	13	252	144	108	1	13	216	78	138	4
Conf Champ	Sun	December 31	L	12-4	Miami Dolphins		17	21	13	250	122	128	2	19	314	121	193	1

Passing

No.		Age	Pos	G	GS	QBrec	Cmp	Att	Cmp%	Yds	TD	TD%	Int	Int%	Lng	Y/A	AY/A	Y/C	Y/G	Rate	Sk	Yds
12	Terry Bradshaw	24	QB	14	14	11-3-0	147	308	47.7	1887	12	3.9	12	3.9	78	6.1	5.2	12.8	134.8	64.1	29	237
17	Joe Gilliam	22		2	0		7	11	63.6	48	0	0.0	0	0.0	9	4.4	4.4	6.9	24.0	73.3	2	8
5	Terry Hanratty	24		7	0		2	4	50.0	23	0	0.0	0	0.0	14	5.8	5.8	11.5	3.3	67.7	1	2
39	Bobby Walden	34	P	14	0		0	1	0.0	0	0	0.0	0	0.0	0	0.0	0.0		0.0	39.6	0	0
	Team Total	25.3		14		11-3-0	156	324	48.1	1958	12	3.7	12	3.7	78	6.0	5.1	12.6	139.9	64.3	32	247
	Opp Total			14			206	411	50.1	2393	9	2.2	28	6.8		5.8		3.2	11.6	170.9	47.0	40	33

Rushing and Receiving

						Rush							Receiving							
No.		Age	Pos	G	GS	Att	Yds	TD	Lng	Y/A	Y/G	A/G	Rec	Yds	Y/R	TD	Lng	R/G	Y/G	YScm
32	Franco Harris*	22	RB	14	9	188	1055	10	75	5.6	75.4	13.4	21	180	8.6	1	29	1.5	12.9	1235
33	John Fuqua	26	FB	13	0	150	665	4	47	4.4	51.2	11.5	18	152	8.4	0	28	1.4	11.7	817
26	Preston Pearson	27	KR	11	0	67	264	0	21	3.9	24.0	6.1	11	79	7.2	0	15	1.0	7.2	343
12	Terry Bradshaw	24	QB	14	14	58	346	7	20	6.0	24.7	4.1								346
35	Steve Davis	24		11	0	20	85	1	28	4.3	7.7	1.8	1	5	5.0	0	5	0.1	0.5	90
46	Warren Bankston	25		7	0	7	20	0	11	2.9	2.9	1.0	1	5	5.0	0	5	0.1	0.7	25
43	Frank Lewis	25	WR	13	13	3	68	0	41	22.7	5.2	0.2	27	391	14.5	5	52	2.1	30.1	459
17	Joe Gilliam	22		2	0	2	0	0	0	0.0	0.0	1.0								0
89	John McMakin	22	TE	14	0	1	0	0	0	0.0	0.0	0.1	21	277	13.2	1	78	1.5	19.8	277
20	Rocky Bleier	26		14	0	1	17	0	17	17.0	1.2	0.1								17
25	Ron Shanklin	24	WR	14	0	0	0	0	0		0.0	0.0	38	669	17.6	3	57	2.7	47.8	669
88	Dave L. Smith	25	wr	6	0	0	0	0	0		0.0	0.0	10	98	9.8	0	25	1.7	16.3	98
31	Al Young	23		14	0	0	0	0	0		0.0	0.0	6	86	14.3	0	33	0.4	6.1	86
87	Larry Brown	23		9	0	0	0	0	0		0.0	0.0	1	13	13.0	1	13	0.1	1.4	13
72	Gerry Mullins	23	RT	14	0	0	0	0	0		0.0	0.0	1	3	3.0	1	3	0.1	0.2	3
	Team Total	25.3		14		497	2520	22	75	5.1	180.0	35.5	156	1958	12.6	12	78	11.1	139.9	4478
	Opp Total			14		445	1715	6		3.9	122.5	31.8	206	2056	10.0	9		14.7	146.9	3771

Defense

No.		Age	Pos	G	GS	Sk	Int	Yds	TD	Lng	PD	FF	Fmb	FR	Yds	TD	Tkl	Ast	Sfty
							Def					**Fumb**					**Tack**		
59	Jack Ham	24	LLB	14	14		7	83	1	32	0	0	1	4	0	0			
32	Franco Harris*	22	RB	14	9							0	7	1	−5	0			
49	Ralph Anderson	23	FS	14	0		3	68	0	41	0	0	0	3	0	0			1
12	Terry Bradshaw	24	QB	14	14							0	4	2	−9	0			
27	Glen Edwards	25	PR	12	0		1	14	0	14	0	0	4	1	0	0			
23	Mike Wagner	23	SS	14	0		6	77	0	35	0								
47	Mel Blount	24	RCB	14	14		3	75	0	34	0	0	0	2	35	1			
26	Preston Pearson	27	KR	11	0							0	4	1	0	0			
48	John Rowser	28	LCB	14	0		4	30	0	23	0								
34	Andy Russell*	31	RLB	14	0							0	0	4	0	0			
35	Steve Davis	24		11	0							0	3	0	0	0			
78	Dwight White*	23	RDE	14	0							0	0	3	9	0			
37	Chuck Beatty	26		8	0		2	16	0	16	0								
53	Henry Davis	30	MLB	14	0		2	32	0	28	0								
5	Terry Hanratty	24		7	0							0	1	1	0	0			
43	Frank Lewis	25	WR	13	13							0	1	1	0	0			
46	Warren Bankston	25		7	0							0	0	1	0	0			
20	Rocky Bleier	26		14	0							0	1	0	0	0			
87	Larry Brown	23		9	0							0	0	1	0	0			
57	Sam Davis	28	LG	11	11							0	0	1	0	0			
33	John Fuqua	26	FB	13	0							0	1	0	−2	0			
75	Joe Greene*+	26	LDT	14	14							0	0	1	0	0			
63	Ernie Holmes	24	rdt	14	0							0	0	1	0	0			
77	Mel Holmes	22		14	0							0	0	1	0	0			
60	Ben McGee	33	RDT	14	0							0	0	1	0	0			
72	Gerry Mullins	23	RT	14	0							0	0	1	0	0			
	Team Total	25.3		14			28	395	1	41	0	0	27	31	28	1			1
	Opp Total			14		32							37	17					1

1973 PITTSBURGH STEELERS: 10-4-0, 1ST IN AFC CENTRAL DIVISION
Coach: Chuck Noll

Week	Day	Date	OT	Rec	Opp	Tm	Opp	1stD	TotYd	PassY	RushY	TO	1stD	TotYd	PassY	RushY	TO
						Score		**Offe**					**Defe**				
1	Sun	September 16	W	1-0	Detroit Lions	24	10	29	395	154	241	2	17	301	193	108	3
2	Sun	September 23	W	2-0	Cleveland Browns	33	6	14	369	173	196	1	16	208	124	84	3
3	Sun	September 30	W	3-0	Houston Oilers	36	7	14	255	130	125	3	13	178	115	63	5
4	Sun	October 7	W	4-0	San Diego Chargers	38	21	15	286	132	154	5	20	348	181	167	6
5	Sun	October 14	L	4-1	Cincinnati Bengals	7	19	6	138	67	71	3	19	250	78	172	
6	Sun	October 21	W	5-1	New York Jets	26	14	19	360	146	214	2	9	118	46	72	3
7	Sun	October 28	W	6-1	Cincinnati Bengals	20	13	10	242	156	86	4	17	318	217	101	5
8	Mon	November 5	W	7-1	Washington Redskins	21	16	18	255	102	153	4	14	190	73	117	4
9	Sun	November 11	W	8-1	Oakland Raiders	17	9	8	194	82	112	1	26	395	223	172	5
10	Sun	November 18	L	8-2	Denver Broncos	13	23	12	300	217	83	3	20	257	73	184	
11	Sun	November 25	L	8-3	Cleveland Browns	16	21	16	380	210	170	2	10	250	146	104	4
12	Mon	December 3	L	8-4	Miami Dolphins	26	30	19	268	90	178	6	8	189	66	123	2
13	Sun	December 9	W	9-4	Houston Oilers	33	7	19	320	132	188	4	5	83	25	58	9
14	Sat	December 15	W	10-4	San Francisco 49ers	37	14	18	308	136	172		16	239	112	127	6
		Playoffs															
Division	Sat	December 22	L	10-5	Oakland Raiders	14	33	15	223	158	65	3	24	361	129	232	

Passing

No.		Age	Pos	G	GS	QBrec	Cmp	Att	Cmp%	Yds	TD	TD%	Int	Int%	Lng	Y/A	AY/A	Y/C	Y/G	Rate	Sk	Yds
12	Terry Bradshaw	25	QB	10	9	8-1-0	89	180	49.4	1183	10	5.6	15	8.3	67	6.6	3.9	13.3	118.3	54.5	24	186
5	Terry Hanratty	25			9	4	2-2-0	31	69	44.9	643	8	11.6	5	7.2	53	9.3	8.4	20.7	71.4	86.8	3	27
17	Joe Gilliam	23			5	1	0-1-0	20	60	33.3	331	2	3.3	6	10.0	46	5.5	1.7	16.6	66.2	24.4	3	17
	Team Total	26.0			14		10-4-0	140	309	45.3	2157	20	6.5	26	8.4	67	7.0	4.5	15.4	154.1	55.4	30	230
	Opp Total				14			164	359	45.7	1923	11	3.1	37	10.3		5.4	1.3	11.7	137.4	33.1	33	251

Rushing and Receiving

No.		Age	Pos	G	GS	Rush Att	Yds	TD	Lng	Y/A	Y/G	A/G	Receiving Rec	Yds	Y/R	TD	Lng	R/G	Y/G	YScm
32	Franco Harris*	23	RB	12	12	188	698	3	35	3.7	58.2	15.7	10	69	6.9	0	19	0.8	5.8	767
26	Preston Pearson	28	KR/FB	14	0	132	554	2	47	4.2	39.6	9.4	11	173	15.7	2	36	0.8	12.4	727
33	John Fuqua	27		11	0	117	457	2	25	3.9	41.5	10.6	17	150	8.8	0	22	1.5	13.6	607
35	Steve Davis	25		14	0	67	266	2	27	4.0	19.0	4.8	7	31	4.4	1	9	0.5	2.2	297
12	Terry Bradshaw	25	QB	10	9	34	145	3	21	4.3	14.5	3.4								145
17	Joe Gilliam	23		5	1	6	23	0	14	3.8	4.6	1.2								23
25	Ron Shanklin*	25	WR	13	0	3	1	0	10	0.3	0.1	0.2	30	711	23.7	10	67	2.3	54.7	712
20	Rocky Bleier	27		12	0	3	0	0	1	0.0	0.0	0.3								0
5	Terry Hanratty	25		9	4	3	0	0	0	0.0	0.0	0.3								0
43	Frank Lewis	26	WR	9	9	1	−1	0	−1	−1.0	−0.1	0.1	23	409	17.8	3	53	2.6	45.4	408
39	Bobby Walden	35	P	14	0	1	0	0	0	0.0	0.0	0.1								0
83	Barry Pearson	23		13	0	0	0	0	0		0.0	0.0	23	317	13.8	3	46	1.8	24.4	317
89	John McMakin	23	TE	14	0	0	0	0	0		0.0	0.0	13	195	15.0	1	44	0.9	13.9	195
87	Larry Brown	24		14	1	0	0	0	0		0.0	0.0	5	88	17.6	0	45	0.4	6.3	88
85	Dave Davis	25		2	0	0	0	0	0		0.0	0.0	1	14	14.0	0	14	0.5	7.0	14
	Team Total	26.0			14	555	2143	12	47	3.9	153.1	39.6	140	2157	15.4	20	67	10.0	154.1	4300
	Opp Total				14	488	1652	8		3.4	118.0	34.9	164	1672	10.2	11		11.7	119.4	3324

Defense

No.		Age	Pos	G	GS	Sk	Def Int	Yds	TD	Lng	PD	Fumb FF	Fmb	FR	Yds	TD	Tack Tkl	Ast	Sfty
23	Mike Wagner	24	SS	14	0		8	134	0	38	0	0	2	5	1	0			
27	Glen Edwards	26	PR/FS	14	14		6	186	1	86	0	0	2	2	0	0			
32	Franco Harris*	23	RB	12	12							0	8	2	0	0			
48	John Rowser	29	LCB	14	0		6	131	1	71	0	0	0	1	2	0			
47	Mel Blount	25	RCB	14	14		4	82	0	24	0	0	0	2	0	0			
5	Terry Hanratty	25		9	4							0	4	2	−2	0			
12	Terry Bradshaw	25	QB	10	9							0	3	1	−4	0			
35	Steve Davis	25		14	0							0	3	1	0	0			
17	Joe Gilliam	23		5	1							0	3	1	−12	0			
51	Loren Toews	22		14	0		2	13	0	8	0	0	0	2	0	0			
20	Rocky Bleier	27		12	0							0	2	1	0	0			
53	Henry Davis	31	MLB	14	0		2	23	0	15	0	0	0	1	0	0			
33	John Fuqua	27		11	0							0	3	0	0	0			
68	L.C. Greenwood*	27	LDE	14	14							0	0	3	0	0			
59	Jack Ham*	25	LLB	13	13		2	30	0	27	0	0	0	1	0	1			
41	Dennis Meyer	23		11	0							0	1	2	0	0			
34	Andy Russell*	32	RLB	14	0		3	54	1	45	0								
66	Bruce Van Dyke*	29	RG	14	0							0	0	3	0	0			
75	Joe Greene*+	27	LDT	14	13							0	0	2	0	0			
67	Craig Hanneman	24		14	0							0	0	2	0	0			
26	Preston Pearson	28	KR/FB	14	0							0	2	0	0	0			
39	Bobby Walden	35	P	14	0							0	1	1	−7	0			
78	Dwight White*	24	RDE	14	0		2	10	0	8	0								1
57	Sam Davis	29	LG	12	12							0	0	1	0	0			
79	John Dockery	29		10	0		1	0	0	0	0								
74	Tom Keating	31		12	0							0	0	1	0	0			
72	Gerry Mullins	24		13	0							0	0	1	0	0			
83	Barry Pearson	23		13	0							0	1	0	0	0			
25	Ron Shanklin*	25	WR	13	0							0	1	0	0	0			
24	J.T. Thomas	22		14	0		1	10	0	10	0								
	Team Total	26.0			14		37	673	3	86	0	0	36	38	−22	1			1
	Opp Total				14	30							41	23					

1974 PITTSBURGH STEELERS: 10-3-1, 1ST IN AFC CENTRAL DIVISION
Head Coach: Chuck Noll

1974 Super Bowl Champions

Week	Day	Date	OT	Rec	Opp	Tm	Opp	1stD	TotYd	PassY	RushY	TO	1stD	TotYd	PassY	RushY	TO
									Score				Offe				Defe
1	Sun	September 15	W	1-0	Baltimore Colts	30	0	18	392	289	103	2	11	166	48	118	4
2	Sun	September 22	T OT	1-0-1	Denver Broncos	35	35	33	484	324	160	4	20	332	176	156	3
3	Sun	September 29	L	1-1-1	Oakland Raiders	0	17	16	203	86	117	4	17	247	70	177	
4	Sun	October 6	W	2-1-1	Houston Oilers	13	7	18	386	202	184	3	10	240	121	119	3
5	Sun	October 13	W	3-1-1	Kansas City Chiefs	34	24	19	321	202	119	4	19	257	199	58	9
6	Sun	October 20	W	4-1-1	Cleveland Browns	20	16	15	231	66	165	1	16	262	127	135	3
7	Mon	October 28	W	5-1-1	Atlanta Falcons	24	17	21	355	120	235	4	13	167	59	108	3
8	Sun	November 3	W	6-1-1	Philadelphia Eagles	27	0	20	375	137	238		10	143	77	66	3
9	Sun	November 10	L	6-2-1	Cincinnati Bengals	10	17	20	289	128	161	1	22	329	193	136	3
10	Sun	November 17	W	7-2-1	Cleveland Browns	26	16	10	314	81	233	6	13	218	138	80	7
11	Mon	November 25	W	8-2-1	New Orleans Saints	28	7	18	334	62	272	4	15	178	69	109	4
12	Sun	December 1	L	8-3-1	Houston Oilers	10	13	6	84	9	75	3	11	158	61	97	
13	Sun	December 8	W	9-3-1	New England Patriots	21	17	16	253	69	184	2	12	184	105	79	3
14	Sat	December 14	W	10-3-1	Cincinnati Bengals	27	3	21	354	183	171	2	11	193	23	170	2
		Playoffs															
Division	Sun	December 22	W	11-3-1	Buffalo Bills	32	14	29	438	203	235	15	264	164	100	1	
Conf Champ	Sun	December 29	W	12-3-1	Oakland Raiders	24	13	20	319	95	224	3	15	278	249	29	3
Super Bowl	Sun	January 12	W	13-3-1	Minnesota Vikings	16	6	17	333	84	249	2	9	119	102	17	5

Passing

No.		Age	Pos	G	GS	QBrec	Cmp	Att	Cmp%	Yds	TD	TD%	Int	Int%	Lng	Y/A	AY/A	Y/C	Y/G	Rate	Sk	Yds
17	Joe Gilliam	24	qb	9	6	4-1-1	96	212	45.3	1274	4	1.9	8	3.8	61	6.0	4.7	13.3	141.6	55.4	7	79
12	Terry Bradshaw	26	QB	8	7	5-2-0	67	148	45.3	785	7	4.7	8	5.4	56	5.3	3.8	11.7	98.1	55.2	10	104
5	Terry Hanratty	26		3	1	1-0-0	3	26	11.5	95	1	3.8	5	19.2	35	3.7	-4.2	31.7	31.7	15.5	1	13
	Team Total	25.3		14		10-3-1	166	386	43.0	2154	12	3.1	21	5.4	61	5.6	3.8	13.0	153.9	48.9	18	196
	Opp Total			14			147	339	43.4	1872	14	4.1	25	7.4		5.5	3.0	12.7	133.7	44.3	52	406

Rushing and Receiving

No.		Age	Pos	G	GS	Att	Yds	TD	Lng	Y/A	Y/G	A/G	Rec	Yds	Y/R	TD	Lng	R/G	Y/G	YScm
						Rush							Receiving							
32	Franco Harris*	24	FB	12	12	208	1006	5	54	4.8	83.8	17.3	23	200	8.7	1	31	1.9	16.7	1206
20	Rocky Bleier	28	RB	12	0	88	373	2	18	4.2	31.1	7.3	7	87	12.4	0	24	0.6	7.3	460
35	Steve Davis	26	KR	14	0	71	246	2	22	3.5	17.6	5.1	11	152	13.8	1	61	0.8	10.9	398
26	Preston Pearson	29		9	0	70	317	4	53	4.5	35.2	7.8	11	118	10.7	0	31	1.2	13.1	435
33	John Fuqua	28		9	0	50	156	2	14	3.1	17.3	5.6	6	68	11.3	0	18	0.7	7.6	224
12	Terry Bradshaw	26	QB	8	7	34	224	2	34	6.6	28.0	4.3								224
17	Joe Gilliam	24	qb	9	6	14	41	1	13	2.9	4.6	1.6								41
46	Reggie Harrison	23		4	0	6	30	1	15	5.0	7.5	1.5	1	2	2.0	0	2	0.3	0.5	32
43	Frank Lewis	27	WR	12	12	2	25	0	22	12.5	2.1	0.2	30	365	12.2	4	31	2.5	30.4	390
82	John Stallworth	22		13	2	1	-9	0	-9	-9.0	-0.7	0.1	16	269	16.8	1	56	1.2	20.7	260
88	Lynn Swann	22	PR	11	2	1	14	0	14	14.0	1.3	0.1	11	208	18.9	2	54	1.0	18.9	222
5	Terry Hanratty	26		3	1	1	-6	0	-6	-6.0	-2.0	0.3								-6
25	Ron Shanklin	26	WR	12	0	0	0	0	0		0.0	0.0	19	324	17.1	1	35	1.6	27.0	324
87	Larry Brown	25	TE	14	12	0	0	0	0		0.0	0.0	17	190	11.2	1	35	1.2	13.6	190
84	Randy Grossman	22		14		0	0	0	0		0.0	0.0	13	164	12.6	0	32	0.9	11.7	164
72	Gerry Mullins	25	RG	12	0	0	0	0	0		0.0	0.0	1	7	7.0	1	7	0.1	0.6	7
	Team Total	25.3		14		546	2417	19	54	4.4	172.6	39.0	166	2154	13.0	12	61	11.9	153.9	4571
	Opp Total			14		472	1608	7		3.4	114.9	33.7	147	1466	10.0	14		10.5	104.7	3074

Defense

No.	Name	Age	Pos	G	GS	Sk	Int	Yds	TD	Lng	PD	FF	Fmb	FR	Yds	TD	Tkl	Ast	Sfty
							Def					**Fumb**					**Tack**		
32	Franco Harris*	24	FB	12	12							0	9	2	0	0			
27	Glen Edwards	27	FS	14	14		5	153	1	59	0	0	1	3	10	0			
17	Joe Gilliam	24	qb	9	6							0	5	2	−8	0			
88	Lynn Swann	22	PR	11	2							0	5	2	0	0			
75	Joe Greene*+	28	LDT	14	14		1	26	0	26	0	0	1	4	7	0			
59	Jack Ham*+	26	LLB	14	14		5	13	0	10	0	0	0	1	2	0			
24	J.T. Thomas	23	LCB	14	14		5	22	0	14	0	0	1	0	14	1			
23	Mike Wagner	25	SS	13	0		2	13	0	9	0	0	1	3	84	0			
47	Mel Blount	26	RCB	13	13		2	74	1	52	0	0	0	3	5	0			
58	Jack Lambert	22	MLB	14	14		2	19	0	13	0	0	1	1	11	0			
35	Steve Davis	26	KR	14	0							0	3	0	0	0			
68	L.C. Greenwood*+	28	LDE	14	14							0	0	3	9	0			1
51	Loren Toews	23		14	0							0	0	3	0	0			
20	Rocky Bleier	28	RB	12	0							0	2	0	0	0			
86	Reggie Garrett	23		14	0							0	0	2	0	0			
34	Andy Russell*	33	RLB	14	0		1	0	0	0	0	0	0	1	0	0			
31	Donnie Shell	22		14	0		1	0	0	0	0	0	0	1	0	0			
45	Jimmy Allen	22		14	1							0	1	0	0	0			
12	Terry Bradshaw	26	QB	8	7							0	1	0	0	0			
50	Jim Clack	27	lg	13	0							0	0	1	0	0			
71	Gordon Gravelle	25	RT	14	13							0	0	1	0	0			
5	Terry Hanratty	26		3	1							0	1	0	0	0			
54	Marv Kellum	22		14	0		1	0	0	0	0								
55	Jon Kolb	27	LT	14	14							0	0	1	0	0			
43	Frank Lewis	27	WR	12	12							0	1	0	0	0			
89	John McMakin	24		8	0							0	0	1	0	0			
	Team Total	25.3		14			25	320	2	59	0	0	33	35	134	1			1
	Opp Total			14	18								38	16					

1975 PITTSBURGH STEELERS: 12-2-0, 1ST IN AFC CENTRAL DIVISION
Head Coach: Chuck Noll

1975 Super Bowl Champions

Week	Day	Date	OT	Rec	Opp	Tm	Opp	1stD	TotYd	PassY	RushY	TO	1stD	TotYd	PassY	RushY	TO
						Score		**Offe**					**Defe**				
1	Sun	September 21	W	1-0	San Diego Chargers	37	0	24	443	238	205	2	9	146	58	88	4
2	Sun	September 28	L	1-1	Buffalo Bills	21	30	19	353	231	122	5	21	434	124	310	1
3	Sun	October 5	W	2-1	Cleveland Browns	42	6	23	501	367	134		19	221	99	122	2
4	Sun	October 12	W	3-1	Denver Broncos	20	9	14	327	190	137	2	17	277	153	124	4
5	Sun	October 19	W	4-1	Chicago Bears	34	3	25	303	146	157		16	242	46	196	1
6	Sun	October 26	W	5-1	Green Bay Packers	16	13	23	332	84	248	3	11	161	98	63	2
7	Sun	November 2	W	6-1	Cincinnati Bengals	30	24	20	369	130	239	4	17	367	298	69	3
8	Sun	November 9	W	7-1	Houston Oilers	24	17	22	352	169	183	2	18	298	206	92	3
9	Sun	November 16	W	8-1	Kansas City Chiefs	28	3	23	420	181	239	2	12	201	123	78	2
10	Mon	November 24	W	9-1	Houston Oilers	32	9	22	367	139	228	5	13	257	131	126	4
11	Sun	November 30	W	10-1	New York Jets	20	7	21	326	113	213		16	270	129	141	4
12	Sun	December 7	W	11-1	Cleveland Browns	31	17	17	258	98	160	2	15	237	115	122	4
13	Sat	December 13	W	12-1	Cincinnati Bengals	35	14	21	319	128	191	1	16	317	194	123	2
14	Sat	December 20	L	12-2	Los Angeles Rams	3	10	14	217	40	177	4	14	233	62	171	1
		Playoffs															
Division	Sat	December 27	W	13-2	Baltimore Colts	28	10	16	287	76	211	5	10	154	72	82	3
Conf Champ	Sun	January 4	W	14-2	Oakland Raiders	16	10	16	332	215	117	7	18	321	228	93	5
Super Bowl	Sun	January 18	W	15-2	Dallas Cowboys	21	17	13	339	190	149		14	270	162	108	3

Passing

No.		Age	Pos	G	GS	QBrec	Cmp	Att	Cmp%	Yds	TD	TD%	Int	Int%	Lng	Y/A	AY/A	Y/C	Y/G	Rate	Sk	Yds
12	Terry Bradshaw*	27	QB	14	14	12-2-0	165	286	57.7	2055	18	6.3	9	3.1	59	7.2	7.0	12.5	146.8	88.0	31	290
17	Joe Gilliam	25		4	0		24	48	50.0	450	3	6.3	3	6.3	53	9.4	7.8	18.8	112.5	77.6	0	0
39	Bobby Walden	37	P	14	0		2	3	66.7	39	0	0.0	0	0.0	20	13.0	13.0	19.5	2.8	109.7	0	0
	Team Total	26.3		14		12-2-0	191	337	56.7	2544	21	6.2	12	3.6	59	7.5	7.2	13.3	181.7	86.7	31	290
	Opp Total			14			183	396	46.2	2194	9	2.3	27	6.8		5.5	2.9	12.0	156.7	42.8	43	358

Rushing and Receiving

No.		Age	Pos	G	GS	Rush Att	Yds	TD	Lng	Y/A	Y/G	A/G	Rec	Receiving Yds	Y/R	TD	Lng	R/G	Y/G	YScm
32	Franco Harris*	25	FB	14	14	262	1246	10	36	4.8	89.0	18.7	28	214	7.6	1	44	2.0	15.3	1460
20	Rocky Bleier	29	RB	11	11	140	528	2	17	3.8	48.0	12.7	15	65	4.3	0	13	1.4	5.9	593
33	John Fuqua	29		14	3	74	285	1	18	3.9	20.4	5.3	18	146	8.1	0	21	1.3	10.4	431
46	Reggie Harrison	24		14	0	43	191	3	17	4.4	13.6	3.1	1	4	4.0	0	4	0.1	0.3	195
12	Terry Bradshaw*	27	QB	14	14	35	210	3	27	6.0	15.0	2.5								210
44	Mike Collier	22	KR	14	0	21	124	3	23	5.9	8.9	1.5	1	7	7.0	0	7	0.1	0.5	131
88	Lynn Swann*	23	WR	14	12	3	13	0	11	4.3	0.9	0.2	49	781	15.9	11	43	3.5	55.8	794
43	Frank Lewis	28	WR	10	10	2	36	0	24	18.0	3.6	0.2	17	308	18.1	2	40	1.7	30.8	344
5	Terry Hanratty	27		1	0	1	0	0	0	0.0	0.0	1.0								0
82	John Stallworth	23	wr	11	9	0	0	0	0		0.0	0.0	20	423	21.2	4	59	1.8	38.5	423
87	Larry Brown	26	TE	14	13	0	0	0	0		0.0	0.0	16	244	15.3	1	27	1.1	17.4	244
86	Reggie Garrett	24		14	3	0	0	0	0		0.0	0.0	13	178	13.7	1	45	0.9	12.7	178
84	Randy Grossman	23		14	1	0	0	0	0		0.0	0.0	11	135	12.3	1	21	0.8	9.6	135
31	Donnie Shell	23		14	2	0	0	0	0		0.0	0.0	2	39	19.5	0	20	0.1	2.8	39
	Team Total	26.3		14		581	2633	22	36	4.5	188.1	41.5	191	2544	13.3	21	59	13.6	181.7	5177
	Opp Total			14		431	1825	8		4.2	130.4	30.8	183	1836	10.0	9		13.1	131.1	3661

Defense

No.		Age	Pos	G	GS	Sk	Def Int	Yds	TD	Lng	PD	FF	Fumb Fmb	FR	Yds	TD	Tack Tkl	Ast	Sfty
47	Mel Blount*+	27	RCB	14	14		11	121	0	47	0	0	1	0	0	0			
32	Franco Harris*	25	FB	14	14							0	9	3	0	0			
20	Rocky Bleier	29	RB	11	11							0	7	2	0	0			
23	Mike Wagner*	26	SS	12	0		4	122	0	65	0	0	1	3	8	0			
12	Terry Bradshaw*	27	QB	14	14							0	6	0	0	0			
88	Lynn Swann*	23	WR	14	12							0	4	1	0	0			
27	Glen Edwards*	28	PR/FS	14	14		3	68	0	47	0	0	0	1	0	0			
44	Mike Collier	22	KR	14	0							0	2	1	0	0			
58	Jack Lambert*	23	MLB	14	14		2	35	0	24	0	0	0	1	21	0			
24	J.T. Thomas	24	LCB	14	14		3	44	0	33	0								
45	Jimmy Allen	23		14	0		2	0	0	0	0								
87	Larry Brown	26	TE	14	13		0	2	0	0	0								
59	Jack Ham*+	27	LLB	14	14		1	2	0	2	0	0	0	1	0	0			
72	Gerry Mullins	26	RG	14	14							0	0	2	2	1			
31	Donnie Shell	23		14	2		1	29	0	29	0	0	0	1	0	0			
76	John Banaszak	25		14	0							0	0	1	0	0			
36	Dave Brown	22		13	0							0	1	0	0	0			
33	John Fuqua	29		14	3							0	1	0	0	0			
71	Gordon Gravelle	26	RT	14	14							0	0	1	0	0			
63	Ernie Holmes	27	RDT	13	0							0	0	1	0	0			
54	Marv Kellum	23		14	0							0	0	1	0	0			
82	John Stallworth	23	wr	11	9							0	0	1	0	0			
	Team Total	26.3		14			27	421	0	65	0	0	34	21	52	2			1
	Opp Total			14		31							22	12					

1976 PITTSBURGH STEELERS: 10-4-0, 1ST IN AFC EAST DIVISION
Head Coach: Chuck Noll

Week	Day	Date	OT	Rec	Opp	Score		Offe					Defe				
						Tm	Opp	1stD	TotYd	PassY	RushY	TO	1stD	TotYd	PassY	RushY	TO
1	Sun	September 12	L	0-1	Oakland Raiders	28	31	24	438	242	196	3	28	440	324	116	4
2	Sun	September 19	W	1-1	Cleveland Browns	31	14	16	298	77	221	1	16	330	185	145	4
3	Sun	September 26	L	1-2	New England Patriots	27	30	24	416	247	169	6	18	399	257	142	4
4	Mon	October 4	L	1-3	Minnesota Vikings	6	17	12	225	52	173	6	11	178	26	152	4
5	Sun	October 10	L	1-4	Cleveland Browns	16	18	13	196	85	111	3	15	326	179	147	2
6	Sun	October 17	W	2-4	Cincinnati Bengals	23	6	16	253	52	201	2	11	171	96	75	3
7	Sun	October 24	W	3-4	New York Giants	27	0	18	331	101	230		10	151	63	88	2
8	Sun	October 31	W	4-4	San Diego Chargers	23	0	20	361	106	255	3	7	134	90	44	5
9	Sun	November 7	W	5-4	Kansas City Chiefs	45	0	26	451	121	330	1	14	257	223	34	6
10	Sun	November 14	W	6-4	Miami Dolphins	14	3	19	354	96	258		14	224	108	116	
11	Sun	November 21	W	7-4	Houston Oilers	32	16	17	248	105	143	2	12	225	124	101	4
12	Sun	November 28	W	8-4	Cincinnati Bengals	7	3	20	347	143	204	2	9	225	115	110	2
13	Sun	December 5	W	9-4	Tampa Bay Buccaneers	42	0	26	385	163	222	1	8	105	11	94	4
14	Sat	December 11	W	10-4	Houston Oilers	21	0	20	334	76	258	1	9	158	65	93	2
Playoffs																	
Division	Sun	December 19	W	11-4	Baltimore Colts	40	14	29	526	301	225	1	12	170	99	71	2
Conf Champ	Sun	December 26	L	11-5	Oakland Raiders	7	24	13	237	165	72	1	15	220	63	157	

Passing

No.		Age	Pos	G	GS	QBrec	Cmp	Att	Cmp%	Yds	TD	TD%	Int	Int%	Lng	Y/A	AY/A	Y/C	Y/G	Rate	Sk	Yds
12	Terry Bradshaw	28	QB	10	8	4-4-0	92	192	47.9	1177	10	5.2	9	4.7	50	6.1	5.1	12.8	117.7	65.4	16	164
15	Mike Kruczek	23	qb	10	6	6-0-0	51	85	60.0	758	0	0.0	3	3.5	64	8.9	7.3	14.9	75.8	74.5	11	105
	Team Total	26.8		14		10-4-0	143	277	51.6	1935	10	3.6	12	4.3	64	7.0	5.8	13.5	138.2	68.2	27	269
	Opp Total			14			158	373	42.4	2179	9	2.4	22	5.9		5.8	3.7	13.8	155.6	45.2	41	313

Rushing and Receiving

No.		Age	Pos	G	GS	Rush							Receiving							YScm
						Att	Yds	TD	Lng	Y/A	Y/G	A/G	Rec	Yds	Y/R	TD	Lng	R/G	Y/G	
32	Franco Harris*	26	FB	14	14	289	1128	14	30	3.9	80.6	20.6	23	151	6.6	0	39	1.6	10.8	1279
20	Rocky Bleier	30	RB	14	0	220	1036	5	28	4.7	74.0	15.7	24	294	12.3	0	32	1.7	21.0	1330
46	Reggie Harrison	25		12	0	54	235	4	27	4.4	19.6	4.5	2	19	9.5	0	10	0.2	1.6	254
12	Terry Bradshaw	28	QB	10	8	31	219	3	17	7.1	21.9	3.1								219
15	Mike Kruczek	23	qb	10	6	18	106	2	22	5.9	10.6	1.8								106
35	Jack Deloplaine	22		14	0	17	91	2	19	5.4	6.5	1.2	1	3	3.0	0	3	0.1	0.2	94
33	John Fuqua	30		14	0	15	63	1	12	4.2	4.5	1.1	1	4	4.0	0	4	0.1	0.3	67
39	Bobby Walden	38	P	14	0	3	7	0	7	2.3	0.5	0.2								7
43	Frank Lewis	29	WR	12	12	2	24	1	16	12.0	2.0	0.2	17	306	18.0	1	64	1.4	25.5	330
22	Ernest Pough	24	KR	14	0	2	8	0	6	4.0	0.6	0.1	8	161	20.1	1	50	0.6	11.5	169
88	Lynn Swann	24	WR	12	10	1	2	0	2	2.0	0.2	0.1	28	516	18.4	3	47	2.3	43.0	518
83	Theo Bell	23	PR	13	1	1	5	0	5	5.0	0.4	0.1	3	43	14.3	1	19	0.2	3.3	48
84	Randy Grossman	24	te	14	5	0	0	0	0		0.0	0.0	15	181	12.1	1	35	1.1	12.9	181
82	John Stallworth	24		8	3	0	47	1	47		5.9	0.0	9	111	12.3	2	25	1.1	13.9	158
87	Larry Brown	27	TE	13	8	0	0	0	0		0.0	0.0	7	97	13.9	0	35	0.5	7.5	97
89	Bennie Cunningham	22		12	0	0	0	0	0		0.0	0.0	5	49	9.8	1	20	0.4	4.1	49
	Team Total	26.8		14		653	2971	33	47	4.5	212.2	46.6	143	1935	13.5	10	64	10.2	138.2	4906
	Opp Total			14		452	1457	5		3.2	104.1	32.3	158	1866	11.8	9		11.3	133.3	3323

Defense

No.	Name	Age	Pos	G	GS	Sk	Def Int	Yds	TD	Lng	PD	Fumb FF	Fmb	FR	Yds	TD	Tack Tkl	Ast	Sfty
32	Franco Harris*	26	FB	14	14							0	8	2	0	0			
58	Jack Lambert*+	24	MLB	14	14		2	32	0	22	0	0	0	8	36	0			
83	Theo Bell	23	PR	13	1							0	5	4	0	0			
12	Terry Bradshaw	28	QB	10	8							0	7	2	–4	0			
47	Mel Blount*	28	RCB	14	14		6	75	0	28	0	0	1	1	0	0			
27	Glen Edwards*	29	FS	14	14		6	95	0	55	0								
20	Rocky Bleier	30	RB	14	0							0	4	0	0	0			
87	Larry Brown	27	TE	13	8							0	0	4	0	0			
64	Steve Furness	26		9	4							0	1	3	5	0			
59	Jack Ham*+	28	LLB	14	14		2	13	0	13	0	0	0	2	17	0			
15	Mike Kruczek	23	qb	10	6							0	2	2	0	0			
35	Jack Deloplaine	22		14	0							0	3	0	0	0			
24	J.T. Thomas*	25	LCB	14	14		2	43	0	38	0	0	1	0	27	0			
76	John Banaszak	26	rde	13	5							0	0	2	0	0			
33	John Fuqua	30		14	0							0	2	0	0	0			
46	Reggie Harrison	25		12	0							0	1	1	0	0			
63	Ernie Holmes	28	RDT	14	0							0	0	2	0	0			
22	Ernest Pough	24	KR	14	0							0	1	1	0	0			
31	Donnie Shell	24		14	0		1	4	0	4	0	0	0	1	0	0			
23	Mike Wagner*	27	SS	14	0		2	0	0	0	0								
39	Bobby Walden	38	P	14	0							0	1	1	–12	0			
52	Mike Webster	24	C	14	14							0	2	0	–15	0			
50	Jim Clack	29	RG	11	0							0	1	0	0	0			
89	Bennie Cunningham	22		12	0							0	0	1	0	0			
68	L.C. Greenwood*	30	LDE	13	12							0	0	1	0	0			
55	Jon Kolb	29	LT	14	14							0	0	1	0	0			
56	Ray Mansfield	35		14	0							0	0	1	0	0			
72	Gerry Mullins	27	RT	14	0							0	0	1	0	0			
34	Andy Russell	35	RLB	14	0		1	0	0	0	0								
78	Dwight White	27	RDE	9	0							0	0	1	0	0			
	Team Total	26.8		14			22	262	0	55	0	0	40	42	54	0			1
	Opp Total			14		27	22	262	0	55	0	0	42	18					

1977 PITTSBURGH STEELERS: 9-5-0, 1ST IN AFC CENTRAL DIVISION
Head Coach: Chuck Noll

Week	Day	Date	OT	Rec	Opp	Score Tm	Opp	Offe 1stD	TotYd	PassY	RushY	TO	Defe 1stD	TotYd	PassY	RushY	TO
1	Mon	September 19	W	1-0	San Francisco 49ers	27	0	19	308	133	175	1	8	101	19	82	3
2	Sun	September 25	L	1-1	Oakland Raiders	7	16	18	369	217	152	5	13	247	107	140	
3	Sun	October 2	W	2-1	Cleveland Browns	28	14	21	361	143	218	2	16	165	85	80	5
4	Sun	October 9	L	2-2	Houston Oilers	10	27	21	389	211	178	9	15	267	169	98	2
5	Mon	October 17	W	3-2	Cincinnati Bengals	20	14	18	253	87	166	3	20	311	208	103	5
6	Sun	October 23	W	4-2	Houston Oilers	27	10	19	352	227	125	6	10	119	–14	133	6
7	Sun	October 30	L	4-3	Baltimore Colts	21	31	18	383	219	164	6	22	318	158	160	
8	Sun	November 6	L	4-4	Denver Broncos	7	21	19	216	97	119	2	12	174	75	99	
9	Sun	November 13	W	5-4	Cleveland Browns	35	31	25	420	249	171	4	23	421	283	138	4
10	Sun	November 20	W	6-4	Dallas Cowboys	28	13	17	320	92	228	1	20	337	201	136	2
11	Sun	November 27	W	7-4	New York Jets	23	20	15	238	124	114	1	21	268	59	209	6
12	Sun	December 4	W	8-4	Seattle Seahawks	30	20	22	393	157	236	2	17	376	210	166	4
13	Sat	December 10	L	8-5	Cincinnati Bengals	10	17	21	362	239	123	5	17	413	302	111	3
14	Sun	December 18	W	9-5	San Diego Chargers	10	9	13	281	192	89	2	14	175	107	68	4
		Playoffs															
Division	Sat	December 24	L	9-6	Denver Broncos	21	34	18	304	177	127	4	15	258	155	103	1

Passing

No.		Age	Pos	G	GS	QBrec	Cmp	Att	Cmp%	Yds	TD	TD%	Int	Int%	Lng	Y/A	AY/A	Y/C	Y/G	Rate	Sk	Yds
12	Terry Bradshaw	29	QB	14	14	9-5-0	162	314	51.6	2523	17	5.4	19	6.1	65	8.0	6.4	15.6	180.2	71.4	26	235
16	Neil Graff	27		4	0		6	12	50.0	47	0	0.0	0	0.0	21	3.9	3.9	7.8	11.8	60.1	1	10
21	Tony Dungy	22		14	0		3	8	37.5	43	0	0.0	2	25.0	18	5.4	−5.9	14.3	3.1	16.1	0	0
15	Mike Kruczek	24		2	0		2	7	28.6	19	0	0.0	0	0.0	13	2.7	2.7	9.5	9.5	39.6	0	0
	Team Total	26.4		14		9-5-0	173	341	50.7	2632	17	5.0	21	6.2	65	7.7	5.9	15.2	188.0	67.5	27	245
	Opp Total	14					157	357	44.0	2254	16	4.5	31	8.7		6.3	3.3	14.4	161.0	43.8	32	285

Rushing and Receiving

No.		Age	Pos	G	GS	Rush Att	Yds	TD	Lng	Y/A	Y/G	A/G	Receiving Rec	Yds	Y/R	TD	Lng	R/G	Y/G	YScm
32	Franco Harris*+	27	FB	14	14	300	1162	11	61	3.9	83.0	21.4	11	62	5.6	0	15	0.8	4.4	1224
20	Rocky Bleier	31	RB	13	0	135	465	4	16	3.4	35.8	10.4	18	161	8.9	0	30	1.4	12.4	626
46	Reggie Harrison	26		14	1	36	175	0	33	4.9	12.5	2.6	3	11	3.7	0	7	0.2	0.8	186
12	Terry Bradshaw	29	QB	14	14	31	171	3	26	5.5	12.2	2.2								171
38	Sidney Thornton	23		13	0	27	103	2	18	3.8	7.9	2.1	1	5	5.0	0	5	0.1	0.4	108
28	Alvin Maxson	26		7	0	18	56	0	8	3.1	8.0	2.6	5	70	14.0	0	34	0.7	10.0	126
37	Laverne Smith	23		7	0	14	55	0	16	3.9	7.9	2.0								55
82	John Stallworth	25	WR	14	14	6	47	0	15	7.8	3.4	0.4	44	784	17.8	7	49	3.1	56.0	831
16	Neil Graff	27		4	0	5	3	0	4	0.6	0.8	1.3								3
21	Tony Dungy	22		14	0	3	8	0	6	2.7	0.6	0.2								8
88	Lynn Swann*	25	WR	14	14	2	6	0	14	3.0	0.4	0.1	50	789	15.8	7	46	3.6	56.4	795
35	Jack Deloplaine	23		8	0	2	7	0	5	3.5	0.9	0.3								7
15	Mike Kruczek	24		2	0	1	0	0	0	0.0	0.0	0.5								0
39	Bobby Walden	39	P	13	0	1	0	0	0	0.0	0.0	0.1								0
89	Bennie Cunningham	23	TE	12	10	0	0	0	0		0.0	0.0	20	347	17.4	2	43	1.7	28.9	347
43	Frank Lewis	30		10	0	0	0	0	0		0.0	0.0	11	263	23.9	1	65	1.1	26.3	263
84	Randy Grossman	25		13	4	0	0	0	0		0.0	0.0	5	57	11.4	0	20	0.4	4.4	57
86	Jim Smith	22	PR/KR	14	0	0	0	0	0		0.0	0.0	4	80	20.0	0	26	0.3	5.7	80
85	Ernest Pough	25		14	0	0	0	0	0		0.0	0.0	1	3	3.0	0	3	0.1	0.2	3
	Team Total	26.4		14		501	2250	20	61	3.9	161.3	41.5	173	2632	15.2	17	65	12.4	188.0	4890
	Opp Total			14		493	1723	9		3.5	123.1	35.2	157	1969	12.5	16		11.2	140.6	3692

Defense

No.		Age	Pos	G	GS	Sk	Def Int	Yds	TD	Lng	PD	Fumb FF	Fmb	FR	Yds	TD	Tack Tkl	Ast	Sfty
12	Terry Bradshaw	29	QB	14	14							0	10	4	−3	0			
32	Franco Harris*+	27	FB	14	14							0	10	0	0	0			
45	Jimmy Allen	25		12	0		5	76	0	48	0	0	2	2	0	0			
20	Rocky Bleier	31	RB	13	0							0	6	1	0	0			
47	Mel Blount	29	RCB	14	13		6	65	0	37	0	0	0	1	15	0			
59	Jack Ham*+	29	LLB	14	14		4	17	0	9	0	0	1	1	0	0			
21	Tony Dungy	22		14	0		3	37	0	29	0	0	1	0	−2	0			
27	Glen Edwards	30	FS	13	8		3	116	0	51	0	0	0	1	0	0			
31	Donnie Shell	25	SS	12	12		3	14	0	8	0	0	0	1	0	0			
86	Jim Smith	22	PR/KR	14	0							0	3	0	0	0			
51	Loren Toews	26	RLB	14	14							0	0	3	0	0			
39	Bobby Walden	39	P	13	0							0	2	1	−9	0			
56	Robin Cole	22		8	0							0	0	2	0	0			
24	J.T. Thomas	26	LCB	14	14		2	10	0	12	0								
78	Dwight White	28	RDE	14	14		2	27	0	19	0								
53	Dirt Winston	22		13	4		2	7	0	7	0								
79	Larry Brown	28	RT	14	14							0	0	1	0	0			
60	Brad Cousino	24		3	0							0	0	1	0	0			
64	Steve Furness	27	RDT/lde	14	14							0	0	1	0	0			
10	Roy Gerela	29	K	14	0							0	0	1	0	0			
75	Joe Greene+	31	LDT	13	13							0	0	1	0	0			

(Continued)

No.		Age	Pos	G	GS	Sk	Int	Yds	TD	Lng	PD	FF	Fmb	FR	Yds	TD	Tkl	Ast	Sfty
								Def					**Fumb**					**Tack**	
46	Reggie Harrison	26		14	1							0	0	1	0	0			
15	Mike Kruczek	24		2	0							0	1	0	−3	0			
54	Dave LaCrosse	22		14	0							0	0	1	0	0			
58	Jack Lambert*	25	MLB	11	10		1	5	0	5	0								
28	Alvin Maxson	26		7	0							0	1	0	0	0			
37	Laverne Smith	23		7	0							0	1	0	0	0			
82	John Stallworth	25	WR	14	14							0	1	0	0	0			
88	Lynn Swann*	25	WR	14	14							0	1	0	0	0			
38	Sidney Thornton	23		13	0							0	1	0	0	0			
	Team Total	26.4		14			31	374	0	51	0	0	41	24	−2	0			
	Opp Total			14		27							28	15					

1978 PITTSBURGH STEELERS: 14-2-0, 1ST IN AFC CENTRAL DIVISION
Head Coach: Chuck Noll

1978 Super Bowl Champions

Week	Day	Date	OT	Rec	Opp	Tm	Opp	1stD	TotYd	PassY	RushY	TO	1stD	TotYd	PassY	RushY	TO
						Score		**Offe**					**Defe**				
1	Sun	September 3	W	1-0	Buffalo Bills	28	17	21	359	217	142	1	16	264	164	100	1
2	Sun	September 10	W	2-0	Seattle Seahawks	21	10	26	336	185	151	1	18	247	154	93	3
3	Sun	September 17	W	3-0	Cincinnati Bengals	28	3	26	447	235	212	4	9	179	123	56	2
4	Sun	September 24	W OT	4-0	Cleveland Browns	15	9	18	339	200	139	3	19	199	102	97	2
5	Sun	October 1	W	5-0	New York Jets	28	17	20	327	189	138	2	18	297	142	155	1
6	Sun	October 8	W	6-0	Atlanta Falcons	31	7	28	387	206	181	3	20	257	144	113	4
7	Sun	October 15	W	7-0	Cleveland Browns	34	14	20	321	153	168		19	360	228	132	4
8	Mon	October 23	L	7-1	Houston Oilers	17	24	21	328	215	113	1	22	329	160	169	1
9	Sun	October 29	W	8-1	Kansas City Chiefs	27	24	17	215	80	135	3	20	322	141	181	3
10	Sun	November 5	W	9-1	New Orleans Saints	20	14	20	345	200	145	2	23	421	340	81	2
11	Sun	November 12	L	9-2	Los Angeles Rams	7	10	12	174	115	59	3	14	313	121	192	2
12	Sun	November 19	W	10-2	Cincinnati Bengals	7	6	14	154	84	70	5	15	246	149	97	5
13	Mon	November 27	W	11-2	San Francisco 49ers	24	7	22	380	168	212	4	12	141	74	67	5
14	Sun	December 3	W	12-2	Houston Oilers	13	3	17	251	74	177	2	9	164	83	81	6
15	Sat	December 9	W	13-2	Baltimore Colts	35	13	20	373	234	139	3	12	129	43	86	5
16	Sat	December 16	W	14-2	Denver Broncos	21	17	14	260	144	116	2	19	300	226	74	2
		Playoffs															
Division	Sat	December 30	W	15-2	Denver Broncos	33	10	24	425	272	153	2	15	218	131	87	2
Conf Champ	Sun	January 7	W	16-2	Houston Oilers	34	5	21	379	200	179	5	10	142	70	72	9
Super Bowl	Sun	January 21	W	17-2	Dallas Cowboys	35	31	19	357	291	66	3	20	330	176	154	3

Passing

No.		Age	Pos	G	GS	QBrec	Cmp	Att	Cmp%	Yds	TD	TD%	Int	Int%	Lng	Y/A	AY/A	Y/C	Y/G	Rate	Sk	Yds
12	Terry Bradshaw*+	30	QB	16	16	14-2-0	207	368	56.3	2915	28	7.6	20	5.4	70	7.9	7.0	14.1	182.2	84.7	21	222
15	Mike Kruczek	25		9	0		5	11	45.5	46	0	0.0	2	18.2	21	4.2	−4.0	9.2	5.1	17.8	4	40
32	Franco Harris*	28	FB	16	16		0	1	0.0	0	0	0.0	0	0.0	0	0.0	0.0		0.0	39.6	0	0
	Team Total	26.4		16		14-2-0	212	380	55.8	2961	28	7.4	22	5.8	70	7.8	6.7	14.0	185.1	81.5	25	262
	Opp Total			16			221	442	50.0	2755	10	2.3	27	6.1		6.2	3.9	12.5	172.2	51.8	44	361

Rushing and Receiving

No.		Age	Pos	G	GS	Rush							Receiving							YScm
						Att	Yds	TD	Lng	Y/A	Y/G	A/G	Rec	Yds	Y/R	TD	Lng	R/G	Y/G	
32	Franco Harris*	28	FB	16	16	310	1082	8	37	3.5	67.6	19.4	22	144	6.5	0	15	1.4	9.0	1226
20	Rocky Bleier	32	RB	16	0	165	633	5	24	3.8	39.6	10.3	17	168	9.9	1	32	1.1	10.5	801
38	Sidney Thornton	24		16	0	71	264	2	27	3.7	16.5	4.4	5	66	13.2	1	24	0.3	4.1	330
39	Rick Moser	22		15	0	42	153	0	15	3.6	10.2	2.8	1	−1	−1.0	0	−1	0.1	−0.1	152
12	Terry Bradshaw*+	30	QB	16	16	32	93	1	17	2.9	5.8	2.0								94
35	Jack Deloplaine	24		10	0	11	49	0	19	4.5	4.9	1.1								49
15	Mike Kruczek	25		9	0	5	7	0	8	1.4	0.8	0.6								7
28	Alvin Maxson	27		5	0	4	9	0	7	2.3	1.8	0.8								9
88	Lynn Swann*+	26	WR	16	16	1	7	0	7	7.0	0.4	0.1	61	880	14.4	11	62	3.8	55.0	887
82	John Stallworth	26	WR	16	16	0	0	0	0		0.0	0.0	41	798	19.5	9	70	2.6	49.9	798
84	Randy Grossman	26	TE	16	10	0	0	0	0		0.0	0.0	37	448	12.1	1	26	2.3	28.0	448
89	Bennie Cunningham	24	te	6	6	0	0	0	0		0.0	0.0	16	321	20.1	2	48	2.7	53.5	321
83	Theo Bell	25	PR	16	0	0	0	0	0		0.0	0.0	6	53	8.8	1	15	0.4	3.3	53
86	Jim Smith	23		9	0	0	0	0	0		0.0	0.0	6	83	13.8	2	29	0.7	9.2	83
	Team Total	26.4		16		641	2297	16	37	3.6	143.6	40.1	212	2961	14.0	28	70	13.3	185.1	5258
	Opp Total			16		513	1774	11		3.5	110.9	32.1	221	2394	10.8	10		13.8	149.6	4168

Defense

No.		Age	Pos	G	GS	Sk	Def					Fumb					Tack		Sfty
							Int	Yds	TD	Lng	PD	FF	Fmb	FR	Yds	TD	Tkl	Ast	
12	Terry Bradshaw*+	30	QB	16	16							0	8	1	−3	0			
21	Tony Dungy	23		16	2		6	95	0	65	0	0	0	2	8	0			
31	Donnie Shell*	26	SS	16	16		3	21	0	20	0	0	0	5	21	1			
20	Rocky Bleier	32	RB	16	0							0	6	1	0	0			
58	Jack Lambert*	26	MLB	16	16		4	41	0	24	0	0	0	2	0	0			
75	Joe Greene*	32	LDT	16	16							0	0	5	0	0			
59	Jack Ham*+	30	LLB	14	14		3	7	0	7	0	0	0	2	0	0			
32	Franco Harris*	28	FB	16	16							0	4	1	0	0			
29	Ron Johnson	22	LCB	16	16		4	24	0	21	0	0	0	1	0	0			
39	Rick Moser	22		15	0							0	3	2	0	0			
47	Mel Blount*	30	RCB	16	16		4	55	0	35	0	0	0	1	0	0			
38	Sidney Thornton	24		16	0							0	3	1	0	0			
82	John Stallworth	26	WR	16	16							0	2	1	0	0			
30	Larry Anderson	22	KR	16	1							0	2	0	0	0			
15	Mike Kruczek	25		9	0							0	1	1	0	0			
28	Alvin Maxson	27		5	0							0	2	0	0	0			
23	Mike Wagner	29	FS	14	0		2	34	0	20	0								
83	Theo Bell	25	PR	16	0							0	0	1	0	0			
77	Steve Courson	23		16	1							0	0	1	0	0			
89	Bennie Cunningham	24	te	6	6							0	1	0	0	0			
57	Sam Davis	34	LG	16	16							0	0	1	0	0			
67	Gary Dunn	25		16	0							0	0	1	0	0			
64	Steve Furness	28	rdt	10	6							0	0	1	12	0			
68	L.C. Greenwood*	32	LDE	14	14							0	0	1	0	0			
84	Randy Grossman	26	TE	16	10							0	1	0	0	0			
55	Jon Kolb	31	LT	16	16							0	0	1	0	0			
72	Gerry Mullins	29	RG	16	0							0	0	1	0	0			
74	Ray Pinney	24	RT	13	11							0	0	1	0	0			
86	Jim Smith	23		9	0							0	1	0	0	0			
51	Loren Toews	27	RLB	11	10		1	12	0	12	0								
52	Mike Webster*+	26	C	16	16							0	1	0	−2	0			
78	Dwight White	29	RDE	15	11							0	0	1	0	0			
53	Dirt Winston	23		16	0							0	0	1	0	0			
	Team Total	26.4		16			27	289	0	65	0	0	35	36	36	1			
	Opp Total			16		25							33	12					

1979 PITTSBURGH STEELERS: 12-4-0, 1ST IN AFC CENTRAL DIVISION
Head Coach: Chuck Noll

1979 Super Bowl Champions

							Score			Offe				Defe				
Week	Day	Date		OT	Rec	Opp	Tm	Opp	1stD	TotYd	PassY	RushY	TO	1stD	TotYd	PassY	RushY	TO
1	Mon	September 3	W	OT	1-0	New England Patriots	16	13	20	309	191	118	2	16	244	82	162	2
2	Sun	September 9	W		2-0	Houston Oilers	38	7	17	256	174	82	2	12	124	22	102	6
3	Sun	September 16	W		3-0	St. Louis Cardinals	24	21	25	398	234	164	4	12	212	106	106	1
4	Sun	September 23	W		4-0	Baltimore Colts	17	13	17	392	235	157	4	17	285	188	97	2
5	Sun	September 30	L		4-1	Philadelphia Eagles	14	17	19	308	169	139	4	18	283	148	135	2
6	Sun	October 7	W		5-1	Cleveland Browns	51	35	21	522	161	361	1	24	458	365	93	5
7	Sun	October 14	L		5-2	Cincinnati Bengals	10	34	16	327	263	64	9	19	284	114	170	4
8	Mon	October 22	W		6-2	Denver Broncos	42	7	27	530	294	236	3	16	329	276	53	3
9	Sun	October 28	W		7-2	Dallas Cowboys	14	3	16	288	115	173		16	278	199	79	1
10	Sun	November 4	W		8-2	Washington Redskins	38	7	26	545	372	173	3	17	237	149	88	4
11	Sun	November 11	W		9-2	Kansas City Chiefs	30	3	20	355	228	127	2	8	127	62	65	3
12	Sun	November 18	L		9-3	San Diego Chargers	7	35	14	191	125	66	8	14	218	120	98	4
13	Sun	November 25	W	OT	10-3	Cleveland Browns	33	30	36	606	351	255	3	22	345	283	62	1
14	Sun	December 2	W		11-3	Cincinnati Bengals	37	17	24	478	324	154	1	21	340	209	131	1
15	Mon	December 10	L		11-4	Houston Oilers	17	20	15	338	218	120	2	20	350	160	190	
16	Sun	December 16	W		12-4	Buffalo Bills	28	0	24	415	201	214	4	8	156	78	78	3
		Playoffs																
Division	Sun	December 30	W		13-4	Miami Dolphins	34	14	27	379	220	159	3	16	249	224	25	2
Conf Champ	Sun	January 6	W		14-4	Houston Oilers	27	13	22	358	197	161	2	11	227	203	24	3
Super Bowl	Sun	January 20	W		15-4	Los Angeles Rams	31	19	19	393	309	84	3	16	301	194	107	1

Passing

No.		Age	Pos	G	GS	QBrec	Cmp	Att	Cmp%	Yds	TD	TD%	Int	Int%	Lng	Y/A	AY/A	Y/C	Y/G	Rate	Sk	Yds
12	Terry Bradshaw*	31	QB	16	16	12-4-0	259	472	54.9	3724	26	5.5	25	5.3	65	7.9	6.6	14.4	232.8	77.0	24	196
15	Mike Kruczek	26		8	0		13	20	65.0	153	0	0.0	1	5.0	31	7.7	5.4	11.8	19.1	67.3	3	26
	Team Total	26.9		16		12-4-0	272	492	55.3	3877	26	5.3	26	5.3	65	7.9	6.6	14.3	242.3	76.6	27	222
	Opp Total			16			226	480	47.1	2912	19	4.0	27	5.6		6.1	4.3	12.9	182.0	56.4	49	351

Rushing and Receiving

						Rush							Receiving							
No.		Age	Pos	G	GS	Att	Yds	TD	Lng	Y/A	Y/G	A/G	Rec	Yds	Y/R	TD	Lng	R/G	Y/G	YScm
32	Franco Harris*	29	FB	15	15	267	1186	11	71	4.4	79.1	17.8	36	291	8.1	1	21	2.4	19.4	1477
38	Sidney Thornton	25	RB	13	10	118	585	6	75	5.0	45.0	9.1	16	231	14.4	4	32	1.2	17.8	816
20	Rocky Bleier	33	rb	16	0	92	434	4	70	4.7	27.1	5.8	31	277	8.9	0	28	1.9	17.3	711
27	Greg Hawthorne	23		15	0	28	123	1	19	4.4	8.2	1.9	8	47	5.9	0	17	0.5	3.1	170
12	Terry Bradshaw*	31	QB	16	16	21	83	0	28	4.0	5.2	1.3								83
33	Anthony Anderson	23		16	0	18	118	1	31	6.6	7.4	1.1								118
39	Rick Moser	23		16	0	11	33	1	8	3.0	2.1	0.7	1	6	6.0	0	6	0.1	0.4	39
15	Mike Kruczek	26		8	0	4	20	0	22	5.0	2.5	0.5								20
88	Lynn Swann	27	WR	13	11	1	9	1	9	9.0	0.7	0.1	41	808	19.7	5	65	3.2	62.2	817
86	Jim Smith	24		15	4	1	12	0	12	12.0	0.8	0.1	17	243	14.3	2	25	1.1	16.2	255
82	John Stallworth*+	27	WR	16	16	0	0	0	0		0.0	0.0	70	1183	16.9	8	65	4.4	73.9	1183
89	Bennie Cunningham	25	TE	15	8	0	0	0	0		0.0	0.0	36	512	14.2	4	28	2.4	34.1	512
84	Randy Grossman	27	te	16	8	0	0	0	0		0.0	0.0	12	217	18.1	1	54	0.8	13.6	217
83	Theo Bell	26	PR	13	1	0	0	0	0		0.0	0.0	3	61	20.3	0	31	0.2	4.7	61
79	Larry Brown	30	RT	15	14	0	0	0	0		0.0	0.0	1	1	1.0	1	1	0.1	0.1	1
	Team Total	26.9		16		561	2603	25	75	4.6	162.7	35.1	272	3877	14.3	26	65	17.0	242.3	6480
	Opp Total			16		506	1709	9		3.4	106.8	31.6	226	2561	11.3	19		14.1	160.1	4270

Defense

No.		Age	Pos	G	GS	Sk	Int	Yds	TD	Lng	PD	FF	Fmb	FR	Yds	TD	Tkl	Ast	Sfty
							Def					**Fumb**					**Tack**		
12	Terry Bradshaw*	31	QB	16	16							0	10	4	−10	0			
32	Franco Harris*	29	FB	15	15							0	11	0	0	0			
38	Sidney Thornton	25	RB	13	10							0	7	1	0	0			
31	Donnie Shell*+	27	SS	16	16		5	10	0	8	0	0	0	2	0	0			
82	John Stallworth*+	27	WR	16	16							0	4	3	0	0			
30	Larry Anderson	23	KR	16	0		1	19	0	19	0	0	4	1	0	0			
58	Jack Lambert*+	27	MLB	16	13		6	29	0	23	0								
53	Dirt Winston	24	RLB	16	11		3	48	1	41	0	0	0	3	0	0			
20	Rocky Bleier	33	rb	16	0							0	4	0	0	0			
47	Mel Blount*	31	RCB	16	16		3	1	0	1	0	0	0	1	15	0			
23	Mike Wagner	30		8	0		4	31	0	19	0								
83	Theo Bell	26	PR	13	1							0	1	2	22	0			
59	Jack Ham*+	31	LLB	15	15		2	8	0	8	0	0	0	1	0	0			
27	Greg Hawthorne	23		15	0							0	2	1	0	0			
33	Anthony Anderson	23		16	0							0	1	1	0	0			
76	John Banaszak	29	RDE	16	16		1	3	0	3	0	0	0	1	0	0			
67	Gary Dunn	26	RDT	16	15							0	0	2	0	0			
29	Ron Johnson	23	LCB	11	11		1	20	0	20	0	0	0	1	0	0			
86	Jim Smith	24		15	4							0	1	1	0	0			
52	Mike Webster*+	27	C	16	16							0	0	2	2	0			
79	Larry Brown	30	RT	15	14							0	0	1	0	0			
56	Robin Cole	24	rlb	13	8							0	0	1	0	0			
77	Steve Courson	24	RG	16	8							0	0	1	0	0			
89	Bennie Cunningham	25	TE	15	8							0	0	1	0	0			
63	Thom Dornbrook	23		16	1							0	1	0	0	0			
64	Steve Furness	29		12	2							0	0	1	0	0			
15	Mike Kruczek	26		8	0							0	1	0	0	0			
72	Gerry Mullins	30	rg	15	0							0	0	1	0	0			
78	Dwight White	30		11	0							0	0	1	0	0			
49	Dwayne Woodruff	22		16	1		1	31	0	31	0								
	Team Total	26.9		16			27	200	1	41	0	0	47	34	29	0			
	Opp Total			16		27							32	17					

1980 PITTSBURGH STEELERS: 9-7-0, 3RD IN AFC CENTRAL DIVISION
Head Coach: Chuck Noll

Week	Day	Date	OT	Rec	Opp	Tm	Opp	1stD	TotYd	PassY	RushY	TO	1stD	TotYd	PassY	RushY	TO
						Score		**Offe**					**Defe**				
1	Sun	September 7	W	1-0	Houston Oilers	31	17	20	356	237	119	4	16	292	232	60	5
2	Sun	September 14	W	2-0	Baltimore Colts	20	17	22	392	273	119	1	25	347	250	97	1
3	Sun	September 21	L	2-1	Cincinnati Bengals	28	30	18	393	265	128	6	17	309	173	136	
4	Sun	September 28	W	3-1	Chicago Bears	38	3	23	443	280	163	2	13	200	101	99	7
5	Sun	October 5	W	4-1	Minnesota Vikings	23	17	23	411	231	180	2	20	318	211	107	5
6	Sun	October 12	L	4-2	Cincinnati Bengals	16	17	15	331	208	123	2	17	304	184	120	1
7	Mon	October 20	L	4-3	Oakland Raiders	34	45	27	467	350	117	3	20	390	247	143	2
8	Sun	October 26	L	4-4	Cleveland Browns	26	27	21	393	306	87	1	26	439	348	91	4
9	Sun	November 2	W	5-4	Green Bay Packers	22	20	18	281	121	160	4	18	343	266	77	3
10	Sun	November 9	W	6-4	Tampa Bay Buccaneers	24	21	14	229	94	135	1	23	369	294	75	3
11	Sun	November 16	W	7-4	Cleveland Browns	16	13	21	319	240	79	4	14	266	171	95	1
12	Sun	November 23	L	7-5	Buffalo Bills	13	28	16	239	155	84	1	23	379	201	178	2
13	Sun	November 30	W	8-5	Miami Dolphins	23	10	20	435	267	168	3	14	224	143	81	4
14	Thu	December 4	L	8-6	Houston Oilers	0	6	18	278	118	160	5	13	268	177	91	1
15	Sun	December 14	W	9-6	Kansas City Chiefs	21	16	16	285	170	115	3	16	198	66	132	1
16	Mon	December 22	L	9-7	San Diego Chargers	17	26	16	302	253	49		27	488	308	180	

Passing

No.		Age	Pos	G	GS	QBrec	Cmp	Att	Cmp%	Yds	TD	TD%	Int	Int%	Lng	Y/A	AY/A	Y/C	Y/G	Rate	Sk	Yds
12	Terry Bradshaw	32	QB	15	15	9-6-0	218	424	51.4	3339	24	5.7	22	5.2	68	7.9	6.7	15.3	222.6	75.0	33	245
18	Cliff Stoudt	25		6	1	0-1-0	32	60	53.3	493	2	3.3	2	3.3	72	8.2	7.4	15.4	82.2	78.0	4	19
	Team Total	27.2		16		9-7-0	250	484	51.7	3832	26	5.4	24	5.0	72	7.9	6.8	15.3	239.5	75.4	37	264
	Opp Total			16			280	532	52.6	3517	25	4.7	26	4.		6.6	5.4	12.6	219.8	68.8	18	145

Rushing and Receiving

No.		Age	Pos	G	GS	Rush Att	Rush Yds	Rush TD	Rush Lng	Rush Y/A	Rush Y/G	Rush A/G	Rec	Rec Yds	Rec Y/R	Rec TD	Rec Lng	Rec R/G	Rec Y/G	YScm
32	Franco Harris*	30	FB	13	13	208	789	4	26	3.8	60.7	16.0	30	196	6.5	2	31	2.3	15.1	985
20	Rocky Bleier	34	RB	16	6	78	340	1	19	4.4	21.3	4.9	21	174	8.3	1	17	1.3	10.9	514
38	Sidney Thornton	26	rb	12	5	78	325	3	28	4.2	27.1	6.5	15	131	8.7	1	29	1.3	10.9	456
27	Greg Hawthorne	24	rb	15	6	63	226	4	15	3.6	15.1	4.2	12	158	13.2	0	33	0.8	10.5	384
12	Terry Bradshaw	32	QB	15	15	36	111	2	18	3.1	7.4	2.4								111
45	Russell Davis	24		14	2	33	132	1	12	4.0	9.4	2.4								132
18	Cliff Stoudt	25		6	1	9	35	0	13	3.9	5.8	1.5								35
44	Frank Pollard	23	KR	16	0	4	16	0	12	4.0	1.0	0.3								16
88	Lynn Swann	28	WR	13	11	1	−4	0	−4	−4.0	−0.3	0.1	44	710	16.1	7	68	3.4	54.6	706
86	Jim Smith	25	WR	12	10	1	−1	0	−1	−1.0	−0.1	0.1	37	711	19.2	9	45	3.1	59.3	710
5	Craig Colquitt	26	P	16	0	1	17	0	17	17.0	1.1	0.1								17
83	Theo Bell	27	PR/wr	14	9	0	0	0	0		0.0	0.0	29	748	25.8	2	72	2.1	53.4	748
84	Randy Grossman	28	TE	15	14	0	0	0	0		0.0	0.0	23	293	12.7	0	35	1.5	19.5	293
89	Bennie Cunningham	26		15	1	0	0	0	0		0.0	0.0	18	232	12.9	2	35	1.2	15.5	232
85	Calvin Sweeney	25		15	0	0	0	0	0		0.0	0.0	12	282	23.5	1	34	0.8	18.8	282
82	John Stallworth	28		3	2	0	0	0	0		0.0	0.0	9	197	21.9	1	50	3.0	65.7	197
	Team Total	27.2		16		512	1986	15	28	3.9	124.1	32.0	250	3832	15.3	26	72	15.6	239.5	5818
	Opp Total			16		486	1762	9		3.6	110.1	30.4	280	3372	12.0	25		17.5	210.8	5134

Defense

No.		Age	Pos	G	GS	Sk	Def Int	Def Yds	Def TD	Def Lng	Def PD	FF	Fmb	FR	Fumb Yds	Fumb TD	Tkl	Ast	Sfty
12	Terry Bradshaw	32	QB	15	15							0	13	3	−34	0			
32	Franco Harris*	30	FB	13	13							0	7	4	0	0			
27	Greg Hawthorne	24	rb	15	6							0	6	3	0	0			
31	Donnie Shell*+	28	SS	16	16		7	135	0	67	0	0	0	1	7	0			
23	Mike Wagner	31	FS	15	13		6	27	0	17	0	0	0	1	0	0			
38	Sidney Thornton	26	rb	12	5							0	5	1	0	0			
47	Mel Blount	32	RCB	16	16		4	28	0	17	0	0	0	1	32	0			
59	Jack Ham*	32	LLB	16	16		2	16	0	15	0	0	0	3	0	0			
53	Dirt Winston	25		14	3							0	0	4	0	0			
25	Marvin Cobb	27		6	0							0	1	1	0	0			
56	Robin Cole	25	RLB	14	12		1	34	0	34	0	0	0	1	14	0			
5	Craig Colquitt	26	P	16	0							0	1	1	0	0			
64	Steve Furness	30	RDT	16	16							0	0	2	0	0			
58	Jack Lambert*+	28	MLB	14	13		2	1	0	1	0								
86	Jim Smith	25	WR	12	10							0	1	1	0	0			
18	Cliff Stoudt	25		6	1							0	1	1	−2	0			
24	J.T. Thomas	29		16	3		2	0	0	0	0								
83	Theo Bell	27	PR/wr	14	9							0	1	0	0	0			
79	Larry Brown	31	RT	16	16							0	0	1	0	0			
68	L.C. Greenwood	34	LDE	15	15							0	0	1	0	0			
84	Randy Grossman	28	TE	15	14							0	0	1	0	0			
29	Ron Johnson	24	LCB	16	16		1	19	0	19	0								
66	Ted Petersen	25	LT	16	9							0	0	1	0	0			
44	Frank Pollard	23	KR	16	0							0	1	0	0	0			
88	Lynn Swann	28	WR	13	11							0	0	1	0	0			
85	Calvin Sweeney	25		15	0							0	1	0	0	0			
49	Dwayne Woodruff	23		16	0		1	0	0	0	0								
	Team Total	27.2		16			26	260	0	67	0	0	38	33	17	0			1
	Opp Total			16		37							23	9					

1981 PITTSBURGH STEELERS: 8-8-0, 2ND IN AFC CENTRAL DIVISION
Head Coach: Chuck Noll

							Score		Offe					Defe				
Week	Day	Date	OT	Rec	Opp		Tm	Opp	1stD	TotYd	PassY	RushY	TO	1stD	TotYd	PassY	RushY	TO
1	Sun	September 6	L		0-1	Kansas City Chiefs	33	37	29	408	319	89	7	17	353	214	139	2
2	Thu	September 10	L		0-2	Miami Dolphins	10	30	15	300	183	117	2	25	346	161	185	1
3	Sun	September 20	W		1-2	New York Jets	38	10	33	566	223	343	1	16	258	174	84	2
4	Sun	September 27	W	OT	2-2	New England Patriots	27	21	27	498	247	251		24	438	323	115	1
5	Sun	October 4	W		3-2	New Orleans Saints	20	6	19	406	269	137	3	16	180	102	78	5
6	Sun	October 11	W		4-2	Cleveland Browns	13	7	19	365	199	166	1	26	445	279	166	3
7	Sun	October 18	L		4-3	Cincinnati Bengals	7	34	10	205	140	65	1	25	494	330	164	
8	Mon	October 26	W		5-3	Houston Oilers	26	13	22	363	196	167	1	13	307	231	76	3
9	Sun	November 1	L		5-4	San Francisco 49ers	14	17	16	269	125	144	6	25	330	200	130	2
10	Sun	November 8	L		5-5	Seattle Seahawks	21	24	17	367	205	162	2	19	356	260	96	1
11	Sun	November 15	W		6-5	Atlanta Falcons	34	20	13	293	221	72	3	24	441	380	61	6
12	Sun	November 22	W		7-5	Cleveland Browns	32	10	25	362	223	139	5	22	365	219	146	7
13	Sun	November 29	W		8-5	Los Angeles Rams	24	0	18	381	170	211	3	12	174	103	71	4
14	Mon	December 7	L		8-6	Oakland Raiders	27	30	24	331	235	96	2	22	471	257	214	5
15	Sun	December 13	L		8-7	Cincinnati Bengals	10	17	14	207	120	87	2	19	318	215	103	2
16	Sun	December 20	L		8-8	Houston Oilers	20	21	17	277	151	126	2	18	376	335	41	2

Passing

No.		Age	Pos	G	GS	QBrec	Cmp	Att	Cmp%	Yds	TD	TD%	Int	Int%	Lng	Y/A	AY/A	Y/C	Y/G	Rate	Sk	Yds
12	Terry Bradshaw	33	QB	14	14	8-6-0	201	370	54.3	2887	22	5.9	14	3.8	90	7.8	7.3	14.4	206.2	83.9	17	155
16	Mark Malone	23		8	2	0-2-0	45	88	51.1	553	3	3.4	5	5.7	30	6.3	4.4	12.3	69.1	58.6	10	76
18	Cliff Stoudt	26		2	0		1	3	33.3	17	0	0.0	0	0.0	17	5.7	5.7	17.0	8.5	53.5	0	0
	Team Total	27.3		16		8-8-0	247	461	53.6	3457	25	5.4	19	4.1	90	7.5	6.7	14.0	216.1	78.9	27	231
	Opp Total			16			302	544	55.5	4108	22	4.0	30	5.5		7.6	5.9	13.6	256.8	70.3	40	325

Rushing and Receiving

No.		Age	Pos	G	GS	Rush							Receiving							YScm
						Att	Yds	TD	Lng	Y/A	Y/G	A/G	Rec	Yds	Y/R	TD	Lng	R/G	Y/G	
32	Franco Harris	31	FB	16	16	242	987	8	50	4.1	61.7	15.1	37	250	6.8	1	26	2.3	15.6	1237
44	Frank Pollard	24	RB	14	10	123	570	2	29	4.6	40.7	8.8	19	156	8.2	0	26	1.4	11.1	726
38	Sidney Thornton	27	rb	16	6	56	202	4	17	3.6	12.6	3.5	8	78	9.8	0	30	0.5	4.9	280
45	Russell Davis	25		16	0	47	270	1	28	5.7	16.9	2.9	4	34	8.5	0	19	0.3	2.1	304
12	Terry Bradshaw	33	QB	14	14	38	162	2	16	4.3	11.6	2.7								162
27	Greg Hawthorne	25		10	0	25	58	2	16	2.3	5.8	2.5	4	23	5.8	0	12	0.4	2.3	81
16	Mark Malone	23		8	2	16	68	2	19	4.3	8.5	2.0	1	90	90.0	1	90	0.1	11.3	158
18	Cliff Stoudt	26		2	0	3	11	0	10	3.7	5.5	1.5								11
82	John Stallworth	29	WR	16	16	1	17	0	17	17.0	1.1	0.1	63	1098	17.4	5	55	3.9	68.6	1115
86	Jim Smith	26	PR	15	3	1	15	0	15	15.0	1.0	0.1	29	571	19.7	7	46	1.9	38.1	586
39	Rick Moser	25		6	0	1	4	0	4	4.0	0.7	0.2	1	5	5.0	1	5	0.2	0.8	9
5	Craig Colquitt	27	P	16	0	1	8	0	8	8.0	0.5	0.1								8
89	Bennie Cunningham	27	TE	15	15	0	0	0	0		0.0	0.0	41	574	14.0	3	30	2.7	38.3	574
88	Lynn Swann	29	WR	13	12	0	0	0	0		0.0	0.0	34	505	14.9	5	44	2.6	38.8	505
84	Randy Grossman	29		16	1	0	0	0	0		0.0	0.0	3	19	6.3	1	14	0.2	1.2	19
85	Calvin Sweeney	26		14	0	0	0	0	0		0.0	0.0	2	53	26.5	0	32	0.1	3.8	53
74	Ray Pinney	27	LT	16	11	0	0	0	0		0.0	0.0	1	1	1.0	1	1	0.1	0.1	1
	Team Total	27.3		16		554	2372	21	50	4.3	148.3	34.6	247	3457	14.0	25	90	15.4	216.1	5829
	Opp Total			16		500	1869	10		3.7	116.8	31.3	302	3783	12.5	22		18.9	236.4	5652

Defense

No.		Age	Pos	G	GS	Sk	Int	Yds	TD	Lng	PD	FF	Fmb	FR	Yds	TD	Tkl	Ast	Sfty
								Def					**Fumb**					**Tack**	
12	Terry Bradshaw	33	QB	14	14							0	7	3	−23	0			
58	Jack Lambert*+	29	MLB	16	16		6	76	0	31	0	0	0	2	38	0			
31	Donnie Shell*	29	SS	14	14		5	52	0	25	0	0	0	2	0	0			
38	Sidney Thornton	27	rb	16	6							0	6	1	0	0			
47	Mel Blount*+	33	RCB	16	16		6	106	1	50	0								
32	Franco Harris	31	FB	16	16							0	6	0	0	0			
45	Russell Davis	25		16	0							0	3	2	0	0			
44	Frank Pollard	24	RB	14	10							0	5	0	−12	0			
24	J.T. Thomas	30	FS	16	16		4	18	0	16	0	0	0	1	0	0			
59	Jack Ham	33	LLB	12	11		1	23	0	23	0	0	0	3	0	0			
82	John Stallworth	29	WR	16	16							0	4	0	0	0			
42	Anthony Washington	23		16	1		3	46	0	35	0								
49	Dwayne Woodruff	24	LCB	16	14		1	17	0	17	0	0	1	1	0	0			
56	Robin Cole	26	RLB	14	13		1	29	0	29	0	0	0	1	0	0			
77	Steve Courson	26	RG	16	16							0	0	2	0	0			
29	Ron Johnson	25		12	3		2	8	0	8	0								
16	Mark Malone	23		8	2							0	2	0	0	0			
86	Jim Smith	26	PR	15	3							0	1	1	0	0			
88	Lynn Swann	29	WR	13	12							0	1	1	0	0			
54	Zack Valentine	24		16	0							0	0	2	0	0			
30	Larry Anderson	25	KR	16	0							0	1	0	0	0			
76	John Banaszak	31	RDE	12	12							0	0	1	0	0			
89	Bennie Cunningham	27	TE	15	15							0	0	1	0	0			
67	Gary Dunn	28	RDT	16	15							0	0	1	1	0			
27	Greg Hawthorne	25		10	0							0	1	0	0	0			
62	Tunch Ilkin	24		16	1							0	0	1	0	0			
90	Bob Kohrs	23	lde	16	6							0	0	1	0	0			
50	David Little	22		16	0							0	0	1	0	0			
85	Calvin Sweeney	26		14	0							0	1	0	0	0			
51	Loren Toews	30		16	4							0	0	1	0	0			
1	David Trout	24	K	16	0							0	0	1	0	0			
53	Dirt Winston	26		14	4		1	1	0	1	0								
	Team Total	27.3		16			30	376	1	50	0	0	39	30	4	0			
	Opp Total			16		27							31	15					

1982 PITTSBURGH STEELERS: 6-3-0, 2ND IN AFC CENTRAL DIVISION
Head Coach: Chuck Noll

Week	Day	Date	OT	Rec	Opp	Tm	Opp	1stD	TotYd	PassY	RushY	TO	1stD	TotYd	PassY	RushY	TO
						Score		**Offe**					**Defe**				
1	Mon	September 13	W	1-0	Dallas Cowboys	36	28	23	388	241	147	1	28	436	341	95	4
2	Sun	September 19	W OT	2-0	Cincinnati Bengals	26	20	20	295	269	26		24	379	310	69	3
3	Sun	November 21	W	3-0	Houston Oilers	24	10	20	362	199	163	3	16	292	199	93	4
4	Sun	November 28	L	3-1	Seattle Seahawks	0	16	12	218	135	83	5	21	290	166	124	1
5	Sun	December 5	W	4-1	Kansas City Chiefs	35	14	20	376	275	101	2	16	238	179	59	2
6	Sun	December 12	L	4-2	Buffalo Bills	0	13	6	94	−2	96	4	20	339	155	184	2
7	Sun	December 19	L	4-3	Cleveland Browns	9	10	15	222	124	98	5	15	224	186	38	2
8	Sun	December 26	W	5-3	New England Patriots	37	14	28	494	282	212	2	14	331	283	48	1
9	Sun	January 2	W	6-3	Cleveland Browns	37	21	27	521	260	261	3	20	345	293	52	6
		Playoffs															
Wild Card	Sun	January 9	L	6-4	San Diego Chargers	28	31	26	422	325	97	2	29	479	333	146	2

Passing

No.		Age	Pos	G	GS	QBrec	Cmp	Att	Cmp%	Yds	TD	TD%	Int	Int%	Lng	Y/A	AY/A	Y/C	Y/G	Rate	Sk	Yds
12	Terry Bradshaw	34	QB	9	9	6-3-0	127	240	52.9	1768	17	7.1	11	4.6	74	7.4	6.7	13.9	196.4	81.4	18	131
18	Cliff Stoudt	27		6	0		14	35	40.0	154	0	0.0	5	14.3	24	4.4	−2.0	11.0	25.7	14.2	1	8
	Team Total	26.1		9		6-3-0	141	275	51.3	1922	17	6.2	16	5.8	74	7.0	5.6	13.6	213.6	70.3	19	139
	Opp Total			9			176	329	53.5	2385	12	3.6	17	5.2		7.2	5.7	13.6	265.0	67.5	34	273

Rushing and Receiving

No.		Age	Pos	G	GS	Rush Att	Yds	TD	Lng	Y/A	Y/G	A/G	Receiving Rec	Yds	Y/R	TD	Lng	R/G	Y/G	YScm
32	Franco Harris	32	FB	9	9	140	604	2	21	4.3	67.1	15.6	31	249	8.0	0	20	3.4	27.7	853
44	Frank Pollard	25	RB	9	8	62	238	2	18	3.8	26.4	6.9	6	39	6.5	0	11	0.7	4.3	277
45	Russell Davis	26		7	0	24	72	0	9	3.0	10.3	3.4	1	11	11.0	0	11	0.1	1.6	83
34	Walter Abercrombie	23		6	0	21	100	2	34	4.8	16.7	3.5	1	14	14.0	0	14	0.2	2.3	114
27	Greg Hawthorne	26		9	1	15	68	0	11	4.5	7.6	1.7	12	182	15.2	3	46	1.3	20.2	250
18	Cliff Stoudt	27		6	0	11	28	0	8	2.5	4.7	1.8								28
12	Terry Bradshaw	34	QB	9	9	8	10	0	6	1.3	1.1	0.9								10
38	Sidney Thornton	28		4	0	6	33	1	13	5.5	8.3	1.5	1	4	4.0	0	4	0.3	1.0	37
82	John Stallworth*	30	WR	9	9	1	9	0	9	9.0	1.0	0.1	27	441	16.3	7	74	3.0	49.0	450
88	Lynn Swann	30	WR	9	8	1	25	0	25	25.0	2.8	0.1	18	265	14.7	0	60	2.0	29.4	290
89	Bennie Cunningham	28	TE	9	9	0	0	0	0		0.0	0.0	21	277	13.2	2	31	2.3	30.8	277
86	Jim Smith	27		8	0	0	0	0	0		0.0	0.0	17	387	22.8	4	51	2.1	48.4	387
85	Calvin Sweeney	27		7	1	0	0	0	0		0.0	0.0	5	50	10.0	0	17	0.7	7.1	50
74	Ray Pinney	28	LT	9	9	0	0	0	0		0.0	0.0	1	3	3.0	1	3	0.1	0.3	3
	Team Total	26.1		9		289	1187	7	34	4.1	131.9	32.1	141	1922	13.6	17	74	15.7	213.6	3109
	Opp Total			9		236	762	5		3.2	84.7	26.2	176	2112	12.0	12		19.6	234.7	2874

Defense

No.		Age	Pos	G	GS	Sk	Def Int	Yds	TD	Lng	PD	FF	Fumb Fmb	FR	Yds	TD	Tack Tkl	Ast	Sfty
65	Tom Beasley	28	RDE	7	7	6.0						0	0	1	0	0			
31	Donnie Shell*+	30	SS	9	9	1.0	5	27	0	18	0	0	0	1	0	0			
12	Terry Bradshaw	34	QB	9	9							0	5	1	−3	0			
67	Gary Dunn	29	NT	9	9	6.0													
58	Jack Lambert*+	30	RILB	8	8	4.0	1	6	0	6	0	0	0	1	1	0			
49	Dwayne Woodruff	25	LCB	9	9	1.0	5	53	0	30	0								
56	Robin Cole	27	ROLB	9	9	5.0													
59	Jack Ham	34	LOLB	8	8	3.0	1	2	0	2	0	0	0	1	0	0			
22	Rick Woods	23		5	0		1	12	0	12	0	0	2	2	0	0			
51	Loren Toews	31	LILB	9	9	2.5	1	20	0	20	0	0	0	1	0	0			
23	Fred Bohannon	24	KR	7	0							0	3	0	0	0			
90	Bob Kohrs	24		9	0	2.0						0	0	1	0	0			
44	Frank Pollard	25	RB	9	8							0	3	0	0	0			
34	Walter Abercrombie	23		6	0							0	0	2	0	0			
29	Ron Johnson	26	FS	9	9		2	5	0	5	0								
82	John Stallworth*	30	WR	9	9							0	2	0	0	0			
73	Craig Wolfley	24	LG	9	9							0	0	2	0	0			
95	John Goodman	24	LDE	9	9	1.5													
47	Mel Blount	34	RCB	9	9		1	2	0	2	0								
77	Steve Courson	27	RG	8	8							0	0	1	0	0			
32	Franco Harris	32	FB	9	9							0	1	0	−13	0			
53	Bryan Hinkle	23		9	1	1.0													
50	David Little	23		9	1							0	0	1	2	0			
64	Edmund Nelson	22		8	2							0	0	1	0	0			
86	Jim Smith	27		8	0							0	1	0	0	0			
18	Cliff Stoudt	27		6	0							0	1	0	0	0			
88	Lynn Swann	30	WR	9	8							0	0	1	0	0			
93	Keith Willis	23		9	0	1.0													
	Team Total	26.1		9		34.0	17	127	0	30	0	0	18	17	−13	0			
	Opp Total			9		19							17	9					

1983 PITTSBURGH STEELERS: 10-6-0, 1ST IN AFC CENTRAL DIVISION
Head Coach: Chuck Noll

Week	Day	Date	OT	Rec	Opp	Score Tm	Opp	1stD	TotYd	PassY	RushY	TO	1stD	TotYd	PassY	RushY	TO
1	Sun	September 4	L	0-1	Denver Broncos	10	14	21	314	191	123	7	14	139	1	138	3
2	Sun	September 11	W	1-1	Green Bay Packers	25	21	27	471	186	285		17	363	276	87	1
3	Sun	September 18	W	2-1	Houston Oilers	40	28	25	451	176	275	3	16	311	254	57	5
4	Sun	September 25	L	2-2	New England Patriots	23	28	30	448	238	210	3	12	296	208	88	1
5	Sun	October 2	W	3-2	Houston Oilers	17	10	14	225	88	137		19	270	147	123	3
6	Mon	October 10	W	4-2	Cincinnati Bengals	24	14	9	168	112	56	2	22	281	176	105	5
7	Sun	October 16	W	5-2	Cleveland Browns	44	17	19	332	186	146	2	27	449	290	159	7
8	Sun	October 23	W	6-2	Seattle Seahawks	27	21	26	340	158	182	2	14	254	197	57	4
9	Sun	October 30	W	7-2	Tampa Bay Buccaneers	17	12	21	338	209	129	7	13	236	105	131	
10	Sun	November 6	W	8-2	San Diego Chargers	26	3	19	288	132	156	2	11	218	159	59	4
11	Sun	November 13	W	9-2	Baltimore Colts	24	13	24	366	152	214	1	16	334	199	135	3
12	Sun	November 20	L	9-3	Minnesota Vikings	14	17	14	236	128	108	1	20	338	188	150	2
13	Thu	November 24	L	9-4	Detroit Lions	3	45	10	218	84	134	5	25	328	129	199	1
14	Sun	December 4	L	9-5	Cincinnati Bengals	10	23	9	154	70	84	5	21	354	159	195	
15	Sat	December 10	W	10-5	New York Jets	34	7	22	380	138	242	1	13	251	215	36	5
16	Sun	December 18	L	10-6	Cleveland Browns	17	30	22	285	156	129	2	18	310	196	114	1
Playoffs																	
Division	Sun	January 1	L	10-7	Los Angeles Raiders	10	38	17	331	169	162	2	24	413	225	188	

Passing

No.		Age	Pos	G	GS	QBrec	Cmp	Att	Cmp%	Yds	TD	TD%	Int	Int%	Lng	Y/A	AY/A	Y/C	Y/G	Rate	Sk	Yds
18	Cliff Stoudt	28	QB	16	15	9-6-0	197	381	51.7	2553	12	3.1	21	5.5	52	6.7	4.9	13.0	159.6	60.6	51	339
16	Mark Malone	25		2	0		9	20	45.0	124	1	5.0	2	10.0	38	6.2	2.7	13.8	62.0	42.5	1	11
12	Terry Bradshaw	35		1	1	1-0-0	5	8	62.5	77	2	25.0	0	0.0	24	9.6	14.6	15.4	77.0	133.9	0	0
	Team Total	26.2		16		10-6-0	211	409	51.6	2754	15	3.7	23	5.6	52	6.7	4.9	13.1	172.1	61.9	52	350
	Opp Total			16			238	447	53.2	3260	19	4.3	28	6.3		7.3	5.3	13.7	203.8	64.9	50	361

Rushing and Receiving

No.		Age	Pos	G	GS	Rush Att	Yds	TD	Lng	Y/A	Y/G	A/G	Rec	Yds	Y/R	TD	Lng	R/G	Y/G	YScm
32	Franco Harris	33	FB	16	16	279	1007	5	19	3.6	62.9	17.4	34	278	8.2	2	29	2.1	17.4	1285
30	Frank Pollard	26		16	3	135	608	4	32	4.5	38.0	8.4	16	127	7.9	0	17	1.0	7.9	735
34	Walter Abercrombie	24	RB	15	13	112	446	4	50	4.0	29.7	7.5	26	391	15.0	3	51	1.7	26.1	837
18	Cliff Stoudt	28	QB	16	15	77	479	4	23	6.2	29.9	4.8								479
27	Greg Hawthorne	27		10	4	5	47	0	20	9.4	4.7	0.5	19	300	15.8	0	52	1.9	30.0	347
43	Tim A. Harris	22		14	0	2	15	0	10	7.5	1.1	0.1								15
44	Henry Odom	24	KR	16	0	2	7	0	4	3.5	0.4	0.1								7
85	Calvin Sweeney	28	WR/wr	16	16	1	−2	0	−2	−2.0	−0.1	0.1	39	577	14.8	5	42	2.4	36.1	575
12	Terry Bradshaw	35		1	1	1	3	0	3	3.0	3.0	1.0								3
89	Bennie Cunningham	29	TE	16	16	0	0	0	0		0.0	0.0	35	442	12.6	3	29	2.2	27.6	442
86	Gregg Garrity	23		15	3	0	0	0	0		0.0	0.0	19	279	14.7	1	38	1.3	18.6	279
80	Wayne Capers	22		11	4	0	0	0	0		0.0	0.0	10	185	18.5	1	36	0.9	16.8	185
82	John Stallworth*	31	WR	4	4	0	0	0	0		0.0	0.0	8	100	12.5	0	20	2.0	25.0	100
81	Paul Skansi	23	PR	15	0	0	0	0	0		0.0	0.0	3	39	13.0	0	21	0.2	2.6	39
87	John Rodgers	23		15	1	0	0	0	0		0.0	0.0	2	36	18.0	0	25	0.1	2.4	36
	Team Total	26.2		16		614	2610	17	50	4.3	163.1	38.4	211	2754	13.1	15	52	13.2	172.1	5364
	Opp Total			16		509	1833	14		3.6	114.6	31.8	238	2899	12.2	19		14.9	181.2	4732

Defense

No.		Age	Pos	G	GS	Sk	Int	Yds	TD	Lng	PD	FF	Fmb	FR	Yds	TD	Tkl	Ast	Sfty
93	Keith Willis	24		14	4	14.0						0	0	1	0	0			
18	Cliff Stoudt	28	QB	16	15							0	10	2	0	0			
32	Franco Harris	33	FB	16	16							0	10	0	0	0			
92	Keith Gary	24		16	2	7.5						0	0	2	17	0			
58	Jack Lambert*+	31	RILB	15	15	4.0	2	−1	0	0	0	0	0	2	0	0			
56	Robin Cole	28	ROLB	16	16	5.0						0	0	2	20	0			
81	Paul Skansi	23	PR	15	0							0	5	2	0	0			
22	Rick Woods	24	FS	15	9		5	53	0	31	0	0	0	2	38	1			
67	Gary Dunn	30	NT	13	12	6.0													
30	Frank Pollard	26		16	3							0	5	1	0	0			
31	Donnie Shell	31	SS	16	16		5	18	0	18	0	0	0	1	0	0			
57	Mike Merriweather	23	LOLB	16	16	0.5	3	55	1	31	0	0	0	2	0	0			
47	Mel Blount	35	RCB	16	16		4	32	0	21	0	0	0	1	3	1			
89	Bennie Cunningham	29	TE	16	16							0	4	1	0	0			
65	Tom Beasley	29	RDE	16	14	2.5						0	0	2	0	0			
29	Ron Johnson	27	fs	12	7		3	84	1	34	0	0	0	1	5	0			
49	Dwayne Woodruff	26	LCB	15	15	1.0	3	85	0	47	0								
33	Harvey Clayton	22		14	0	2.0	1	70	1	70	0								
43	Tim A. Harris	22		14	0							0	2	1	0	0			
53	Bryan Hinkle	24		16	0		1	14	1	14	0	0	0	2	4	0			
64	Edmund Nelson	23	nt	16	5	3.0													
44	Henry Odom	24	KR	16	0							0	2	1	0	0			
90	Bob Kohrs	25		9	0	1.5						0	0	1	0	0			1
34	Walter Abercrombie	24	RB	15	13							0	2	0	0	0			
86	Gregg Garrity	23		15	3							0	1	1	0	0			
66	Ted Petersen	28	LT	13	13							0	0	2	0	0			
69	Gabe Rivera	22		6	0	2.0													
52	Mike Webster*+	31	C	16	16							0	0	2	0	0			
25	Greg Best	23		13	0							0	0	1	94	1			
71	Emil Boures	23		16	3							0	1	0	0	0			
95	John Goodman	25	LDE	14	11	1.0													
27	Greg Hawthorne	27		10	4							0	0	1	0	0			
62	Tunch Ilkin	26	RT	11	10							0	0	1	0	0			
16	Mark Malone	25		2	0							0	0	1	0	0			
41	Sam Washington	23		16	0		1	25	0	25	0								
73	Craig Wolfley	25	LG	14	14							0	0	1	0	0			
	Team Total	26.2		16		50.0	28	435	4	70	0	0	42	37	181	3			1
	Opp Total			16			52						34	17					

1984 PITTSBURGH STEELERS: 9-7-0, 1ST IN AFC CENTRAL DIVISION
Head Coach: Chuck Noll

Week	Day	Date	OT	Rec	Opp	Score Tm	Opp	Offe 1stD	TotYd	PassY	RushY	TO	Defe 1stD	TotYd	PassY	RushY	TO
1	Sun	September 2	L	0-1	Kansas City Chiefs	27	37	20	465	419	46	4	18	264	170	94	1
2	Thu	September 6	W	1-1	New York Jets	23	17	19	293	172	121	2	11	168	95	73	4
3	Sun	September 16	W	2-1	Los Angeles Rams	24	14	20	345	226	119	2	15	298	215	83	3
4	Sun	September 23	L	2-2	Cleveland Browns	10	20	12	219	148	71	3	17	413	285	128	1
5	Mon	October 1	W	3-2	Cincinnati Bengals	38	17	22	392	241	151	4	15	280	155	125	5
6	Sun	October 7	L	3-3	Miami Dolphins	7	31	17	287	208	79	3	20	342	226	116	1
7	Sun	October 14	W	4-3	San Francisco 49ers	20	17	23	324	149	175	1	22	358	241	117	1
8	Sun	October 21	L	4-4	Indianapolis Colts	16	17	18	405	278	127	1	21	301	174	127	1
9	Sun	October 28	W	5-4	Atlanta Falcons	35	10	17	314	141	173	3	15	296	193	103	3
10	Sun	November 4	W	6-4	Houston Oilers	35	7	17	322	131	191	3	17	273	176	97	4
11	Sun	November 11	L	6-5	Cincinnati Bengals	20	22	20	293	133	160	3	15	282	166	116	1
12	Mon	November 19	L	6-6	New Orleans Saints	24	27	18	332	217	115	4	16	265	176	89	3
13	Sun	November 25	W	7-6	San Diego Chargers	52	24	28	445	243	202		23	422	391	31	5
14	Sun	December 2	L OT	7-7	Houston Oilers	20	23	14	272	145	127	3	22	424	303	121	3
15	Sun	December 9	W	8-7	Cleveland Browns	23	20	16	347	222	125	2	21	342	202	140	4
16	Sun	December 16	W	9-7	Los Angeles Raiders	13	7	21	365	168	197	2	14	188	131	57	2
		Playoffs															
Division	Sun	December 30	W	10-7	Denver Broncos	24	17	25	381	212	169	2	15	250	199	51	2
Conf Champ	Sun	January 6	L	10-8	Miami Dolphins	28	45	22	455	312	143	4	28	569	435	134	2

Passing

No.		Age	Pos	G	GS	QBrec	Cmp	Att	Cmp%	Yds	TD	TD%	Int	Int%	Lng	Y/A	AY/A	Y/C	Y/G	Rate	Sk	Yds
16	Mark Malone	26	QB	13	9	6-3-0	147	272	54.0	2137	16	5.9	17	6.3	61	7.9	6.2	14.5	164.4	73.4	25	211
19	David Woodley	26	qb	7	7	3-4-0	85	156	54.5	1273	8	5.1	7	4.5	80	8.2	7.2	15.0	181.9	79.9	10	67
10	Scott Campbell	22		5	0		8	15	53.3	109	1	6.7	1	6.7	25	7.3	5.6	13.6	21.8	71.3	0	0
	Team Total	25.5		16		9-7-0	240	443	54.2	3519	25	5.6	25	5.6	80	7.9	6.5	14.7	219.9	75.6	35	278
	Opp Total			16			299	515	58.1	3689	19	3.7	31	6.0		7.2	5.2	12.3	230.6	67.5	47	390

Rushing and Receiving

No.		Age	Pos	G	GS	Rush Att	Yds	TD	Lng	Y/A	Y/G	A/G	Receiving Rec	Yds	Y/R	TD	Lng	R/G	Y/G	YScm
30	Frank Pollard	27	FB	15	15	213	851	6	52	4.0	56.7	14.2	21	186	8.9	0	18	1.4	12.4	1037
34	Walter Abercrombie	25	rb	14	7	145	610	1	31	4.2	43.6	10.4	16	135	8.4	0	59	1.1	9.6	745
24	Rich Erenberg	22	RB/KR	16	9	115	405	2	31	3.5	25.3	7.2	38	358	9.4	1	25	2.4	22.4	763
38	Elton Veals	23		15	1	31	87	0	9	2.8	5.8	2.1								87
16	Mark Malone	26	QB	13	9	25	42	3	13	1.7	3.2	1.9								42
40	Anthony Corley	24		14	0	18	89	0	23	4.9	6.4	1.3								89
19	David Woodley	26	qb	7	7	11	14	0	7	1.3	2.0	1.6								14
26	Scoop Gillespie	22		14	0	7	18	0	9	2.6	1.3	0.5	1	12	12.0	0	12	0.1	0.9	30
83	Louis Lipps*	22	WR/PR	14	8	3	71	1	36	23.7	5.1	0.2	45	860	19.1	9	80	3.2	61.4	931
10	Scott Campbell	22		5	0	3	−5	0	0	−1.7	−1.0	0.6								−5
80	Wayne Capers	23		16	0	1	−3	0	−3	−3.0	−0.2	0.1	7	81	11.6	0	19	0.4	5.1	78
5	Craig Colquitt	30	P	16	0	1	0	0	9	0.0	0.0	0.1								0
36	Todd Spencer	22		7	0	1	0	0	0	0.0	0.0	0.1								0
82	John Stallworth*	32	WR	16	16	0	0	0	0		0.0	0.0	80	1395	17.4	11	51	5.0	87.2	1395
87	Weegie Thompson	23	wr	16	7	0	0	0	0		0.0	0.0	17	291	17.1	3	59	1.1	18.2	291
84	Chris Kolodziejski	23		7	3	0	0	0	0		0.0	0.0	5	59	11.8	0	22	0.7	8.4	59
89	Bennie Cunningham	30		7	4	0	0	0	0		0.0	0.0	4	64	16.0	1	29	0.6	9.1	64
86	Gregg Garrity	24		6	0	0	0	0	0		0.0	0.0	2	22	11.0	0	12	0.3	3.7	22
81	Darrell Nelson	23	TE	11	9	0	0	0	0		0.0	0.0	2	31	15.5	0	19	0.2	2.8	31
85	Calvin Sweeney	29		9	1	0	0	0	0		0.0	0.0	2	25	12.5	0	16	0.2	2.8	25
	Team Total	25.5		16		574	2179	13	52	3.8	136.2	35.9	240	3519	14.7	25	80	15.0	219.9	5698
	Opp Total			16		454	1617	12		3.6	101.1	28.4	299	3299	11.0	19		18.7	206.2	4916

Defense

No.		Age	Pos	G	GS	Sk	Int	Yds	TD	Lng	PD	FF	Fmb	FR	Yds	TD	Tkl	Ast	Sfty
57	Mike Merriweather*	24	LOLB	16	16	15.0	2	9	0	8	0	0	0	1	0	0			
30	Frank Pollard	27	FB	15	15							0	9	2	0	0			
53	Bryan Hinkle	25	ROLB	15	15	5.5	3	77	0	43	0	0	0	2	21	1			
83	Louis Lipps*	22	WR/PR	14	8							0	8	2	0	0			
64	Edmund Nelson	24	rde	16	5	7.0													
31	Donnie Shell	32	SS	16	16		7	61	1	52	0								
36	Todd Spencer	22		7	0							0	5	2	0	0			
19	David Woodley	26	qb	7	7							0	5	2	-4	0			
24	Rich Erenberg	22	RB/KR	16	9							0	3	3	0	0			
16	Mark Malone	26	QB	13	9							0	4	2	0	0			
41	Sam Washington	24	RCB	14	14		6	138	2	69	0								
21	Eric T. Williams	24	FS	16	12	2.0	3	49	0	44	0	0	0	1	6	0			
93	Keith Willis	25		12	2	5.0						0	0	1	0	0			
49	Dwayne Woodruff	27	LCB	16	14		5	56	1	42	0	0	0	1	65	1			
92	Keith Gary	25	RDE	16	11	4.0						0	0	1	6	0			
56	Robin Cole*	29	RILB	16	16	2.0	1	12	0	12	0	0	0	1	8	0			
80	Wayne Capers	23		16	0							0	1	2	2	0			
33	Harvey Clayton	23		14	0	1.0	1	0	0	0	0	0	0	1	0	0			
26	Scoop Gillespie	22		14	0							0	1	2	0	0			
95	John Goodman	26	LDE	14	14	2.5													
23	Chris D. Brown	22		16	4		1	31	0	31	0	0	0	1	0	0			
10	Scott Campbell	22		5	0							0	1	1	0	0			
40	Anthony Corley	24		14	0							0	0	2	0	0			
22	Rick Woods	25		15	4		2	0	0	0	0								
54	Craig Bingham	25		11	1							0	0	1	0	0			
67	Gary Dunn	31	NT	16	16	1.0													
50	David Little	25	LILB	16	13	1.0													
74	Terry Long	25	rg	12	7							0	1	0	0	0			
72	Ray Snell	26	lt	13	6							0	0	1	0	0			
82	John Stallworth*	32	WR	16	16							0	1	0	0	0			
87	Weegie Thompson	23	wr	16	7							0	1	0	0	0			
38	Elton Veals	23		15	1							0	0	1	0	0			
	Team Total	25.5		16		46.0	31	433	4	69	0	0	40	33	104	2			
	Opp Total			16			35						30	19					

1985 PITTSBURGH STEELERS: 7-9-0, 2ND IN AFC CENTRAL DIVISION
Head Coach: Chuck Noll

Week	Day	Date	OT	Rec	Opp	Score Tm	Opp	1stD	Offe TotYd	PassY	RushY	TO	Defe 1stD	TotYd	PassY	RushY	TO
1	Sun	September 8	W	1-0	Indianapolis Colts	45	3	30	445	282	163	1	9	159	112	47	2
2	Mon	September 16	I	1-1	Cleveland Browns	7	17	15	216	162	54	2	21	293	148	145	1
3	Sun	September 22	W	2-1	Houston Oilers	20	0	22	335	102	233		8	134	84	50	2
4	Mon	September 30	L	2-2	Cincinnati Bengals	24	37	27	453	340	113	3	23	366	144	222	2
5	Sun	October 6	L	2-3	Miami Dolphins	20	24	15	282	145	137	1	24	399	277	122	4
6	Sun	October 13	L	2-4	Dallas Cowboys	13	27	14	315	231	84	3	18	374	241	133	2
7	Sun	October 20	W	3-4	St. Louis Cardinals	23	10	15	326	184	142	1	22	286	160	126	3
8	Sun	October 27	L	3-5	Cincinnati Bengals	21	26	14	256	169	87	6	20	306	221	85	2
9	Sun	November 3	W	4-5	Cleveland Browns	10	9	17	238	83	155		9	153	87	66	
10	Sun	November 10	W	5-5	Kansas City Chiefs	36	28	17	396	251	145	1	13	295	259	36	2
11	Sun	November 17	W	6-5	Houston Oilers	30	7	24	378	130	248	2	10	162	56	106	2
12	Sun	November 24	L	6-6	Washington Redskins	23	30	20	308	206	102	3	16	259	176	83	1
13	Sun	December 1	L	6-7	Denver Broncos	23	31	22	327	250	77	4	20	331	238	93	1
14	Sun	December 8	L	6-8	San Diego Chargers	44	54	28	427	275	152	4	23	448	364	84	3
15	Sun	December 15	W	7-8	Buffalo Bills	30	24	25	434	264	170	3	14	323	134	189	5
16	Sat	December 21	L	7-9	New York Giants	10	28	10	214	99	115	2	23	371	82	289	2

Passing

No.		Age	Pos	G	GS	QBrec	Cmp	Att	Cmp%	Yds	TD	TD%	Int	Int%	Lng	Y/A	AY/A	Y/C	Y/G	Rate	Sk	Yds
16	Mark Malone	27	QB	10	8	3-5-0	117	233	50.2	1428	13	5.6	7	3.0	45	6.1	5.9	12.2	142.8	75.5	10	80
19	David Woodley	27	qb	9	6	4-2-0	94	183	51.4	1357	6	3.3	14	7.7	69	7.4	4.6	14.4	150.8	54.8	13	84
10	Scott Campbell	23		16	2	0-2-0	43	96	44.8	612	4	4.2	6	6.3	51	6.4	4.4	14.2	38.3	53.8	10	60
	Team Total	25.9		16		7-9-0	254	512	49.6	3397	23	4.5	27	5.3	69	6.6	5.2	13.4	212.3	64.1	33	224
	Opp Total			16			287	484	59.3	3088	18	3.7	20	4.1		6.4	5.3	10.8	193.0	73.3	36	305

Rushing and Receiving

No.		Age	Pos	G	GS	Rush Att	Yds	TD	Lng	Y/A	Y/G	A/G	Rec	Yds	Y/R	TD	Lng	R/G	Y/G	YScm
30	Frank Pollard	28	FB	16	16	233	991	3	56	4.3	61.9	14.6	24	250	10.4	0	20	1.5	15.6	1241
34	Walter Abercrombie	26	RB	16	16	227	851	7	32	3.7	53.2	14.2	24	209	8.7	2	27	1.5	13.1	1060
24	Rich Erenberg	23		14	0	17	67	0	12	3.9	4.8	1.2	33	326	9.9	3	35	2.4	23.3	393
19	David Woodley	27	qb	9	6	17	71	2	13	4.2	7.9	1.9								71
16	Mark Malone	27	QB	10	8	15	80	1	25	5.3	8.0	1.5								80
36	Todd Spencer	23	KR	16	0	13	56	0	11	4.3	3.5	0.8	3	25	8.3	0	13	0.2	1.6	81
10	Scott Campbell	23		16	2	9	28	0	14	3.1	1.8	0.6								28
47	Steve Morse	22		16	0	8	17	0	9	2.1	1.1	0.5								17
83	Louis Lipps*	23	WR/PR	16	16	2	16	1	15	8.0	1.0	0.1	59	1134	19.2	12	51	3.7	70.9	1150
82	John Stallworth	33	WR	16	16	0	0	0	0		0.0	0.0	75	937	12.5	5	41	4.7	58.6	937
85	Calvin Sweeney	30		16	0	0	0	0	0		0.0	0.0	16	234	14.6	0	69	1.0	14.6	234
87	Weegie Thompson	24		16	0	0	0	0	0		0.0	0.0	8	138	17.3	1	42	0.5	8.6	138
89	Bennie Cunningham	31	TE	11	11	0	0	0	0		0.0	0.0	6	61	10.2	0	17	0.5	5.5	61
86	Preston Gothard	23		16	0	0	0	0	0		0.0	0.0	6	83	13.8	0	24	0.4	5.2	83
	Team Total	25.9		16		541	2177	14	56	4.0	136.1	33.8	254	3397	13.4	23	69	15.9	212.3	5574
	Opp Total			16		470	1876	19		4.0	117.3	29.4	287	2783	9.7	18		17.9	173.9	4659

Defense

No.		Age	Pos	G	GS	Sk	Def Int	Yds	TD	Lng	PD	FF	Fumb Fmb	FR	Yds	TD	Tack Tkl	Ast	Sfty
19	David Woodley	27	qb	9	6							0	8	2	0	0			
83	Louis Lipps*	23	WR/PR	16	16							0	5	4	3	0			
56	Robin Cole	30	RILB	16	16	3.0	1	4	0	4	0	0	0	3	0	0			
57	Mike Merriweather*	25	LOLB	16	16	4.0	2	36	1	35	0	0	1	0	0	0			
34	Walter Abercrombie	26	RB	16	16							0	5	1	0	0			
10	Scott Campbell	23		16	2							0	3	3	0	0			
16	Mark Malone	27	QB	10	8							0	3	3	–5	0			
31	Donnie Shell	33	SS	16	16		4	40	0	26	0	0	0	2	0	0			
67	Gary Dunn	32	NT	10	7	2.5						0	0	3	0	0			
93	Keith Willis	26	LDE	16	16	5.5													
53	Bryan Hinkle	26	ROLB	14	14	5.0													
50	David Little	26	LILB	16	16	1.0	2	0	0	3	0	0	0	2	11	0			
49	Dwayne Woodruff	28	LCB	12	10		5	80	0	33	0								
78	Mark Catano	23	nt	15	6	3.0						0	0	1	17	0			
92	Keith Gary	26	RDE	12	7	3.0						0	0	1	0	0			
36	Todd Spencer	23	KR	16	0							0	3	1	0	0			
21	Eric T. Williams	25	FS	14	14		4	47	0	29	0								
91	Gregg Carr	23		16	2	1.0						0	0	2	0	0			
30	Frank Pollard	28	FB	16	16							0	2	1	0	0			
95	John Goodman	27	rde	12	6	2.0													
99	Darryl Sims	24		16	0	2.0													
26	John Swain	26		9	1		2	4	0	4	0								
24	Rich Erenberg	23		14	0							0	1	0	–12	0			
86	Preston Gothard	23		16	0							0	0	1	0	0			
62	Tunch Ilkin	28	RT	16	16							0	0	1	0	0			
47	Steve Morse	22		16	0							0	0	1	0	0			
64	Edmund Nelson	25	rde	6	6	1.0													
85	Calvin Sweeney	30		16	0							0	0	1	0	0			
41	Sam Washington	25		7	0							0	0	1	0	0			
52	Mike Webster*	33	C	16	16							0	0	1	0	0			
73	Craig Wolfley	27	LG	13	13							0	0	1	0	0			
22	Rick Woods	26	lcb	16	9	1.0													
	Team Total	25.9		16		34.0	20	211	1	35	0	0	31	36	14	0			
	Opp Total			16		33							34	20					

1986 PITTSBURGH STEELERS: 6-10-0, 3RD IN AFC CENTRAL DIVISION
Head Coach: Chuck Noll

Week	Day	Date	OT	Rec	Opp	Score		Offe					Defe				
						Tm	Opp	1stD	TotYd	PassY	RushY	TO	1stD	TotYd	PassY	RushY	TO
1	Sun	September 7	L	0-1	Seattle Seahawks	0	30	9	146	61	85	5	20	374	172	202	2
2	Mon	September 15	L	0-2	Denver Broncos	10	21	17	236	206	30	3	20	326	235	91	1
3	Sun	September 21	L	0-3	Minnesota Vikings	7	31	13	235	154	81	3	22	412	250	162	1
4	Sun	September 28	W OT	1-3	Houston Oilers	22	16	22	375	161	214	2	19	281	200	81	3
5	Sun	October 5	L	1-4	Cleveland Browns	24	27	19	308	132	176	4	16	270	162	108	3
6	Mon	October 13	L	1-5	Cincinnati Bengals	22	24	15	288	180	108	1	16	359	211	148	1
7	Sun	October 19	L	1-6	New England Patriots	0	34	11	168	54	114	4	16	317	243	74	1
8	Sun	October 26	W	2-6	Cincinnati Bengals	30	9	22	332	94	238		23	371	249	122	2
9	Sun	November 2	W	3-6	Green Bay Packers	27	3	19	321	195	126	2	11	240	179	61	4
10	Sun	November 9	L	3-7	Buffalo Bills	12	16	11	185	132	53	1	18	248	76	172	1
11	Sun	November 16	W	4-7	Houston Oilers	21	10	20	287	116	171	1	19	291	220	71	2
12	Sun	November 23	L OT	4-8	Cleveland Browns	31	37	20	339	197	142	1	35	536	414	122	1
13	Sun	November 30	L OT	4-9	Chicago Bears	10	13	18	291	159	132	3	25	406	235	171	3
14	Sun	December 7	W	5-9	Detroit Lions	27	17	23	421	218	203	3	13	281	178	103	3
15	Sat	December 13	W	6-9	New York Jets	45	24	25	364	189	175	1	22	369	223	146	4
16	Sun	December 21	L	6-10	Kansas City Chiefs	19	24	28	515	340	175	2	8	171	133	38	1

Passing

No.		Age	Pos	G	GS	OBrec	Cmp	Att	Cmp%	Yds	TD	TD%	Int	Int%	Lng	Y/A	AY/A	Y/C	Y/G	Rate	Sk	Yds
16	Mark Malone	28	QB	14	14	6-8-0	216	425	50.8	2444	15	3.5	18	4.2	48	5.8	4.6	11.3	174.6	62.5	13	97
6	Bubby Brister	24		2	2	0-2-0	21	60	35.0	291	0	0.0	2	3.3	58	4.9	3.4	13.9	145.5	37.6	6	57
10	Scott Campbell	24		3	0		0	4	0.0	0	0	0.0	0	0.0	0	0.0	0.0		0.0	39.6	1	5
18	Harry Newsome	23	P	16	0		1	2	50.0	12	1	50.0	0	0.0	12	6.0	16.0	12.0	0.8	108.3	0	0
	Team Total	26.4		16		6-10-0	238	491	48.5	2747	16	3.3	20	4.1	58	5.6	4.4	11.5	171.7	59.7	20	159
	Opp Total			16			311	536	58.0	3669	22	4.1	20	3.7		6.8	6.0	11.8	229.3	77.1	43	289

Rushing and Receiving

No.		Age	Pos	G	GS	Rush							Receiving							YScm
						Att	Yds	TD	Lng	Y/A	Y/G	A/G	Rec	Yds	Y/R	TD	Lng	R/G	Y/G	
43	Earnest Jackson*	27	FB	13	12	216	910	5	31	4.2	70.0	16.6	17	169	9.9	0	28	1.3	13.0	1079
34	Walter Abercrombie	27	RB	16	14	214	877	6	38	4.1	54.8	13.4	47	395	8.4	2	27	2.9	24.7	1272
24	Rich Erenberg	24		16	1	42	170	1	17	4.0	10.6	2.6	27	217	8.0	3	19	1.7	13.6	387
16	Mark Malone	28	QB	14	14	31	107	5	45	3.5	7.6	2.2								107
30	Frank Pollard	29		3	3	24	86	0	12	3.6	28.7	8.0	2	15	7.5	0	10	0.7	5.0	101
36	David Hughes	27		5	0	14	32	0	8	2.3	6.4	2.8	10	98	9.8	0	22	2.0	19.6	130
40	Dan Reeder	25		11	0	6	20	0	6	3.3	1.8	0.5	2	4	2.0	0	3	0.2	0.4	24
6	Bubby Brister	24		2	2	6	10	1	9	1.7	5.0	3.0								10
83	Louis Lipps	24	WR	13	12	4	−3	0	8	−0.8	−0.2	0.3	38	590	15.5	3	48	2.9	45.4	587
45	Chuck Sanders	22		14	2	4	12	0	13	3.0	0.9	0.3	2	19	9.5	0	10	0.1	1.4	31
80	Warren Seitz	24		16	0	3	2	0	2	0.7	0.1	0.2								2
82	John Stallworth	34	WR	11	9	0	0	0	0		0.0	0.0	34	466	13.7	1	40	3.1	42.4	466
86	Preston Gothard	24	TE	16	16	0	0	0	0		0.0	0.0	21	246	11.7	1	34	1.3	15.4	246
85	Calvin Sweeney	31	wr	16	7	0	0	0	0		0.0	0.0	21	337	16.0	1	58	1.3	21.1	337
87	Weegie Thompson	25		16	4	0	0	0	0		0.0	0.0	17	191	11.2	5	20	1.1	11.9	191
	Team Total	26.4		16		564	2223	18	45	3.9	138.9	35.3	238	2747	11.5	16	58	14.9	171.7	4970
	Opp Total			16		471	1872	10		4.0	117.0	29.4	311	3380	10.9	22		19.4	211.3	5252

Defense

No.		Age	Pos	G	GS	Sk	Def					Fumb					Tack		Sfty
							Int	Yds	TD	Lng	PD	FF	Fmb	FR	Yds	TD	Tkl	Ast	
98	Gerald Williams	23		16	0	3.5											14	0	
93	Keith Willis	27	LDE	16	16	12.0													
57	Mike Merriweather*	26	LOLB	16	16	6.0	2	14	0	11	0	0	0	2	18	0			
53	Bryan Hinkle	27	ROLB	16	16	4.5	3	7	0	6	0	0	0	1	0	0			
16	Mark Malone	28	QB	14	14							0	7	1	-8	0			
64	Edmund Nelson	26	RDE	16	16	5.0						0	0	2	0	0			
92	Keith Gary	27		16	0	6.5													
28	Lupe Sanchez	25	KR	11	4		3	71	1	67	0	0	2	1	0	0			
22	Rick Woods	27	PR	15	0		3	26	0	23	0	0	2	0	0	0			
34	Walter Abercrombie	27	RB	16	14							0	4	0	0	0			
36	David Hughes	27		5	0							0	3	1	0	0			
43	Earnest Jackson*	27	FB	13	12							0	3	1	0	0			
21	Eric T. Williams	26	FS	16	16		3	44	0	25	0	0	0	1	0	0			
67	Gary Dunn	33	NT	16	16	2.5						0	0	1	0	0			
33	Harvey Clayton	25	RCB	15	12		3	18	0	14	0								
83	Louis Lipps	24	WR	13	12							0	2	1	0	0			
31	Donnie Shell	34	SS	15	15		3	29	0	17	0								
56	Robin Cole	31	RILB	16	16	0.5						0	0	2	0	0			
37	Donnie Elder	24		9	0							0	1	1	0	0			
24	Rich Erenberg	24		16	1							0	1	1	0	0			
99	Darryl Sims	25		16	0	1.0						0	0	1	2	0			
6	Bubby Brister	24		2	2							0	1	0	0	0			
96	Anthony Henton	23		16	0							0	0	1	0	0			
74	Terry Long	27	RG	16	16							0	0	1	0	0			
30	Frank Pollard	29		3	3							0	1	0	0	0			
80	Warren Seitz	24		16	0							0	0	1	0	0			
55	Dirt Winston	31		16	0							0	0	1	0	0			
73	Craig Wolfley	28	LG	9	9							0	0	1	0	0			
50	David Little	27	LILB	16	16	0.5													
	Team Total	26.4		16		42.0	20	218	1	67	0	0	27	22	12	0	14	0	1
	Opp Total			16		20.0							31	18					

1987 PITTSBURGH STEELERS: 8-7-0, 3RD IN AFC CENTRAL DIVISION
Head Coach: Chuck Noll

Week	Day	Date	OT	Rec	Opp	Score		Offe					Defe				
						Tm	Opp	1stD	TotYd	PassY	RushY	TO	1stD	TotYd	PassY	RushY	TO
1	Sun	September 13	W	1-0	San Francisco 49ers	30	17	21	266	83	183		24	356	309	47	4
2	Sun	September 20	L	1-1	Cleveland Browns	10	34	17	185	127	58	6	18	304	180	124	2
3	Sun	October 4	W	2-1	Atlanta Falcons	28	12	19	361	219	142	3	13	215	148	67	4
4	Sun	October 11	L	2-2	Los Angeles Rams	21	31	16	319	170	149	1	15	313	141	172	2
5	Sun	October 18	W	3-2	Indianapolis Colts	21	7	23	378	126	252	1	15	270	195	75	5
6	Sun	October 25	W	4-2	Cincinnati Bengals	23	20	17	282	204	78		17	433	292	141	2
7	Sun	November 1	L	4-3	Miami Dolphins	24	35	22	315	199	116	1	26	478	332	146	3
8	Sun	November 8	W	5-3	Kansas City Chiefs	17	16	25	391	141	250	4	15	224	123	101	5
9	Sun	November 15	L	5-4	Houston Oilers	3	23	8	170	84	86	3	21	373	221	152	1
10	Sun	November 22	W	6-4	Cincinnati Bengals	30	16	14	328	194	134	2	28	448	373	75	5
11	Sun	November 29	L	6-5	New Orleans Saints	16	20	17	284	172	112	6	15	258	144	114	2
12	Sun	December 6	W	7-5	Seattle Seahawks	13	9	18	308	99	209		16	215	80	135	2
13	Sun	December 13	W	8-5	San Diego Chargers	20	16	14	254	150	104	1	27	435	321	114	5
14	Sun	December 20	L	8-6	Houston Oilers	16	24	22	348	172	176	3	17	283	221	62	1
15	Sat	December 26	L	8-7	Cleveland Browns	13	19	10	221	126	95	2	22	315	230	85	1

Passing

No.		Age	Pos	G	GS	QBrec	Cmp	Att	Cmp%	Yds	TD	TD%	Int	Int%	Lng	Y/A	AY/A	Y/C	Y/G	Rate	Sk	Yds
16	Mark Malone	29	QB	12	12	6-6-0	156	336	46.4	1896	6	1.8	19	5.7	63	5.6	3.5	12.2	158.0	46.7	18	151
15	Steve Bono	25		3	3	2-1-0	34	74	45.9	438	5	6.8	2	2.7	57	5.9	6.1	12.9	146.0	76.3	6	30
6	Bubby Brister	25		2	0		4	12	33.3	20	0	0.0	3	25.0	10	1.7	−9.6	5.0	10.0	2.8	2	14
7	Reggie Collier	26		2	0		4	7	57.1	110	2	28.6	1	14.3	49	15.7	15.0	27.5	55.0	101.8	1	3
	Team Total	25.7		15		8-7-0	198	429	46.2	2464	13	3.0	25	5.8	63	5.7	3.7	12.4	164.3	50.3	27	198
	Opp Total			15			290	481	60.3	3506	22	4.6	27	5.6		7.3	5.7	12.1	233.7	74.6	26	196

Rushing and Receiving

No.		Age	Pos	G	GS	Rush Att	Yds	TD	Lng	Y/A	Y/G	A/G	Rec	Yds	Y/R	TD	Lng	R/G	Y/G	YScm
43	Earnest Jackson	28	FB	12	9	180	696	1	39	3.9	58.0	15.0	7	52	7.4	0	23	0.6	4.3	748
30	Frank Pollard	30	fb	12	7	128	536	3	33	4.2	44.7	10.7	14	77	5.5	0	17	1.2	6.4	613
34	Walter Abercrombie	28	RB	12	12	123	459	2	28	3.7	38.3	10.3	24	209	8.7	0	24	2.0	17.4	668
16	Mark Malone	29	QB	12	12	34	162	3	42	4.8	13.5	2.8								162
20	Dwight Stone	23	KR	14	0	17	135	0	51	7.9	9.6	1.2	1	22	22.0	0	22	0.1	1.6	157
45	Chuck Sanders	23		5	0	11	65	1	14	5.9	13.0	2.2	1	11	11.0	0	11	0.2	2.2	76
15	Steve Bono	25		3	3	8	27	1	23	3.4	9.0	2.7	1	2	2.0	0	2	0.3	0.7	29
44	Rodney Carter	23		11	2	5	12	0	4	2.4	1.1	0.5	16	180	11.3	3	26	1.5	16.4	192
7	Reggie Collier	26		2	0	4	20	0	12	5.0	10.0	2.0								20
33	Merril Hoge	22		13	0	3	8	0	5	2.7	0.6	0.2	7	97	13.9	1	27	0.5	7.5	105
18	Harry Newsome	24	P	12	0	2	16	0	16	8.0	1.3	0.2								16
40	Dan Reeder	26		2	0	2	8	0	4	4.0	4.0	1.0								8
82	John Stallworth	35	WR	12	11	0	0	0	0		0.0	0.0	41	521	12.7	2	45	3.4	43.4	521
87	Weegie Thompson	26		12	3	0	0	0	0		0.0	0.0	17	313	18.4	1	63	1.4	26.1	313
85	Calvin Sweeney	32	WR	9	6	0	0	0	0		0.0	0.0	16	217	13.6	0	34	1.8	24.1	217
88	Joey Clinkscales	23		7	3	0	0	0	0		0.0	0.0	13	240	18.5	1	57	1.9	34.3	240
84	Danzell Lee	24	TE	13	13	0	0	0	0		0.0	0.0	12	124	10.3	0	24	0.9	9.5	124
83	Louis Lipps	25		4	2	0	0	0	0		0.0	0.0	11	164	14.9	0	27	2.8	41.0	164
89	Charles Lockett	22		11	1	0	0	0	0		0.0	0.0	7	116	16.6	1	25	0.6	10.5	116
81	Lyneal Alston	23		3	1	0	0	0	0		0.0	0.0	3	84	28.0	2	42	1.0	28.0	84
86	Preston Gothard	25		2	2	0	0	0	0		0.0	0.0	2	9	4.5	1	7	1.0	4.5	9
83	Russell Hairston	23		3	2	0	0	0	0		0.0	0.0	2	16	8.0	1	11	0.7	5.3	16
80	Theo Young	22		12	1	0	0	0	0		0.0	0.0	2	10	5.0	0	6	0.2	0.8	10
65	Jim Boyle	25		3	3	0	0	0	0		0.0	0.0	1	0	0.0	0	0	0.3	0.0	0
	Team Total	25.7		15		517	2144	11	51	4.1	142.9	34.5	198	2464	12.4	13	63	13.2	164.3	4608
	Opp Total			15		455	1610	8		3.5	107.3	30.3	290	3310	11.4	22		19.3	220.7	4920

Defense

No.		Age	Pos	G	GS	Sk	Def					Fumb					Tack		Sfty
							Int	Yds	TD	Lng	PD	FF	Fmb	FR	Yds	TD	Tkl	Ast	
27	Thomas Everett	23	FS	12	9		3	22	0	21	0	1	1	2	7	0	72	0	
26	Rod Woodson	22	PR	8	0		1	45	1	45	0	0	3	2	0	0	20	0	
98	Gerald Williams	24		9	1	1.0						0	0	1	0	0	17	0	
54	Hardy Nickerson	22		12	0							0	0	1	0	0	17	0	
16	Mark Malone	29	QB	12	12							0	10	5	–3	0			
57	Mike Merriweather	27	LOLB	12	12	5.5	2	26	0	15	0	0	0	4	4	0			
78	Tim Johnson	22		12	0												5	0	
15	Steve Bono	25		3	3							0	5	3	0	0			
34	Walter Abercrombie	28	RB	12	12							0	4	3	2	0			
53	Bryan Hinkle	28	ROLB	12	12	2.0	3	15	0	8	0	0	1	1	0	0			
35	Delton Hall	22	RCB	12	12		3	29	1	25	0	0	1	2	50	1			
43	Earnest Jackson	28	FB	12	9							0	2	3	0	0			
49	Dwayne Woodruff	30	LCB	12	12		5	91	1	33	0								
92	Keith Gary	28	rde	11	6	4.0													
29	Cornell Gowdy	24		13	3		2	50	1	45	0	0	0	2	1	0			
30	Frank Pollard	30	fb	12	7							0	3	1	1	0			
91	Gregg Carr	25		12	0	3.0													1
56	Robin Cole	32	RILB	12	12	1.0	1	0	0	0	0	0	0	1	0	0			
93	Keith Willis	28	LDE	11	10	3.0													
50	David Little	28	LILB	12	12	1.5						0	0	1	0	0			
86	Ralph Britt	22		3	0							0	1	1	0	0			
33	Larry Griffin	24		7	3		2	2	0	2	0								
89	Charles Lockett	22		11	1							0	1	1	0	0			
18	Harry Newsome	24	P	12	0							0	1	1	–17	0			
99	Avon Riley	29		3	0		1	4	0	4	0	0	1	0	0	0			
31	Donnie Shell	35	SS	13	13		1	50	1	50	0	0	0	1	19	1			
95	Xavier Warren	23		2	0	1.0						0	0	1	11	0			
72	Buddy Aydelette	31	lt	12	5							0	0	1	5	0			
91	Tommy Dawkins	22		2	2	1.0													
67	Gary Dunn	34	NT	13	13							0	0	1	0	0			
42	Dave Edwards	25		3	3		1	0	0	0	0								
85	Russell Hairston	23		3	2							0	1	0	0	0			
84	Danzell Lee	24	TE	13	13							0	0	1	0	0			
64	Edmund Nelson	27	RDE	10	8							0	0	1	0	0			
28	Lupe Sanchez	26		12	3							0	1	0	0	0			
41	Chris Sheffield	24		5	0		1	2	0	2	0								
82	John Stallworth	35	WR	12	11							0	1	0	0	0			
20	Dwight Stone	23	KR	14	0							0	0	1	0	0			
87	Weegie Thompson	26		12	3							0	0	1	0	0			
94	Bert Williams	23		3	3							0	0	1	0	0			
97	Joe Williams	22		3	0	1.0													
35	Ray Williams	22		1	0		1	0	0	0	0								
73	Craig Wolfley	29	LG	12	12							0	0	1	0	0			
	Team Total	25.7		15		24.0	27	336	5	50	0	1	37	45	80	2	131	0	1
	Opp Total			15		27							41	24					2

1988 PITTSBURGH STEELERS: 5-11-0, LAST IN AFC CENTRAL DIVISION
Head Coach: Chuck Noll

Week	Day	Date	OT	Rec	Opp	Score Tm	Opp	Offe 1stD	TotYd	PassY	RushY	TO	Defe 1stD	TotYd	PassY	RushY	TO
1	Sun	September 4	W	1-0	Dallas Cowboys	24	21	17	356	214	142		25	414	280	134	3
2	Sun	September 11	L	1-1	Washington Redskins	29	30	14	341	258	83	1	25	515	422	93	3
3	Sun	September 18	L	1-2	Cincinnati Bengals	12	17	19	319	195	124	6	20	306	190	116	1
4	Sun	September 25	L	1-3	Buffalo Bills	28	36	25	408	314	94	5	22	398	282	116	3
5	Sun	October 2	L	1-4	Cleveland Browns	9	23	13	183	94	89	5	15	299	131	168	1
6	Sun	October 9	L	1-5	Phoenix Cardinals	14	31	10	203	125	78	2	21	388	285	103	3
7	Sun	October 16	L	1-6	Houston Oilers	14	34	23	344	251	93	4	18	309	185	124	
8	Sun	October 23	W	2-6	Denver Broncos	39	21	18	386	130	256	2	15	323	278	45	4
9	Sun	October 30	L	2-7	New York Jets	20	24	15	352	209	143	4	15	196	112	84	1
10	Sun	November 6	L	2-8	Cincinnati Bengals	7	42	15	198	97	101		28	559	338	221	2
11	Sun	November 13	L	2-9	Philadelphia Eagles	26	27	19	361	197	164	1	27	358	252	106	3
12	Sun	November 20	L	2 10	Cleveland Browns	7	27	18	285	167	118	4	11	262	192	70	
13	Sun	November 27	W	3-10	Kansas City Chiefs	16	10	19	336	122	214	1	19	366	278	88	2
14	Sun	December 4	W	4-10	Houston Oilers	37	34	23	426	332	94		23	403	269	134	4
15	Sun	December 11	L	4-11	San Diego Chargers	14	20	20	302	172	130	3	17	324	144	180	
16	Sun	December 18	W	5-11	Miami Dolphins	40	24	24	404	99	305	1	18	385	303	82	3

Passing

No.		Age	Pos	G	GS	QBrec	Cmp	Att	Cmp%	Yds	TD	TD%	Int	Int%	Lng	Y/A	AY/A	Y/C	Y/G	Rate	Sk	Yds
6	Bubby Brister	26	QB	13	13	4-9-0	175	370	47.3	2634	11	3.0	14	3.8	89	7.1	6.0	15.1	202.6	65.3	36	292
14	Todd Blackledge	27		3	3	1-2-0	38	79	48.1	494	2	2.5	3	3.8	34	6.3	5.1	13.0	164.7	60.8	4	25
13	Steve Bono	26		2	0		10	35	28.6	110	1	2.9	2	5.7	15	3.1	1.1	11.0	55.0	25.9	1	8
24	Rodney Carter	24		14	1		2	3	66.7	56	0	0.0	0	0.0	40	18.7	18.7	28.0	4.0	109.7	0	0
83	Louis Lipps	26	WR	16	16		1	2	50.0	13	1	50.0	1	50.0	13	6.5	−6.0	13.0	0.8	70.8	1	6
	Team Total	25.6		16		5-11-0	226	489	46.2	3307	15	3.1	20	4.1	89	6.8	5.5	14.6	206.7	62.0	42	331
	Opp Total			16			309	532	58.1	4086	25	4.7	20	3.8		7.7	6.9	13.2	255.4	82.5	19	145

Rushing and Receiving

No.		Age	Pos	G	GS	Rush Att	Yds	TD	Lng	Y/A	Y/G	A/G	Receiving Rec	Yds	Y/R	TD	Lng	R/G	Y/G	YScm
33	Merril Hoge	23	FB	16	8	170	705	3	20	4.1	44.1	10.6	50	487	9.7	3	40	3.1	30.4	1192
42	Warren Williams	23	RB	15	8	87	409	0	33	4.7	27.3	5.8	11	66	6.0	1	21	0.7	4.4	475
43	Farnest Jackson	29	fb	12	6	74	315	3	29	4.3	26.3	6.2	9	84	9.3	0	24	0.8	7.0	399
6	Bubby Brister	26	QB	13	13	45	209	6	20	4.6	16.1	3.5								209
20	Dwight Stone	24	rb	16	6	40	127	0	11	3.2	7.9	2.5	11	196	17.8	1	72	0.7	12.3	323
24	Rodney Carter	24		14	1	36	216	3	64	6.0	15.4	2.6	32	363	11.3	2	33	2.3	25.9	579
30	Frank Pollard	31		10	3	31	93	0	7	3.0	9.3	3.1	2	22	11.0	0	19	0.2	2.2	115
14	Todd Blackledge	27		3	3	8	25	1	10	3.1	8.3	2.7								25
83	Louis Lipps	26	WR	16	16	6	129	1	39	21.5	8.1	0.4	50	973	19.5	5	89	3.1	60.8	1102
18	Harry Newsome	25	P	16	0	2	0	0	0	0.0	0.0	0.1								0
89	Charles Lockett	23	wr	16	5	0	0	0	0		0.0	0.0	22	365	16.6	1	44	1.4	22.8	365
87	Weegie Thompson	27	WR	16	11	0	0	0	0		0.0	0.0	16	370	23.1	1	50	1.0	23.1	370
86	Preston Gothard	26	TE	16	15	0	0	0	0		0.0	0.0	12	121	10.1	1	26	0.8	7.6	121
85	Troy Johnson	26		14	0	0	0	0	0		0.0	0.0	10	237	23.7	0	60	0.7	16.9	237
81	Mike Hinnant	22		16	1	0	0	0	0		0.0	0.0	1	23	23.0	0	23	0.1	1.4	23
	Team Total	25.6		16		499	2228	17	64	4.5	139.3	31.2	226	3307	14.6	15	89	14.1	206.7	5535
	Opp Total			16		516	1864	20		3.6	116.5	32.3	309	3941	12.8	25		19.3	246.3	5805

Defense

No.		Age	Pos	G	GS	Sk	Def					Fumb					Tack		Sfty
							Int	Yds	TD	Lng	PD	FF	Fmb	FR	Yds	TD	Tkl	Ast	
54	Hardy Nickerson	23	RILB	15	10	3.5	1	0	0	0	0	1	0	1	0	0	99	0	
26	Rod Woodson	23	RCB/PR/KR	16	16	0.5	4	98	0	29	0	1	3	3	2	0	88	0	
27	Thomas Everett	24	FS	14	12		3	31	0	29	0	0	0	2	38	0	60	0	
98	Gerald Williams	25	NT	16	16	3.5						0	0	1	1	0	41	0	
78	Tim Johnson	23	LDE/rde	15	12	4.0											34	0	
95	Greg Lloyd	23		9	4	0.5						2	0	1	0	0	33	0	
97	Aaron Jones	22	ROLB/lde	15	12	1.5											20	0	
33	Merril Hoge	23	FB	16	8							0	8	6	0	0			
6	Bubby Brister	26	QB	13	13							0	8	2	0	0			
14	Todd Blackledge	27		3	3							0	4	2	−2	0			
55	Darin Jordan	24		15	2		1	28	1	28	0	0	0	4	0	0			
20	Dwight Stone	24	rb	16	6							0	5	0	0	0			
91	Gregg Carr	26	rolb	13	5	3.5	1	27	0	27	0								
22	Larry Griffin	25		15	3		2	63	0	33	0	0	1	1	0	0			
49	Dwayne Woodruff	31	LCB	14	13		4	109	1	78	0								
43	Earnest Jackson	29	fb	12	6							0	3	0	0	0			
50	David Little	29	LILB	16	14		1	0	0	0	0	0	0	2	2	0			
42	Warren Williams	23	RB	15	8							0	3	0	0	0			
53	Bryan Hinkle	29	LOLB	13	13	0.5	1	1	0	1	0	0	0	1	5	0			
83	Louis Lipps	26	WR	16	16							0	2	0	0	0			
28	Lupe Sanchez	27		16	2		1	0	0	0	0	0	0	1	0	0			
52	Mike Webster	36	C	16	16							0	2	0	−58	0			
60	Brian Blankenship	25	LG	13	12							0	0	1	0	0			
86	Preston Gothard	26	TE	16	15							0	0	1	0	0			
29	Cornell Gowdy	25	SS	16	14		1	24	0	24	0								
74	Terry Long	29	RG	12	11							0	0	1	0	0			
18	Harry Newsome	25	P	16	0							0	0	1	0	0			
30	Frank Pollard	31		10	3							0	1	0	0	0			
64	Jerry Reese	24		15	0	1.0													
79	John Rienstra	25		5	4							0	0	1	0	0			
69	Ben Thomas	27	lde	8	5	0.5													
	Team Total	25.6		16		19.0	20	381	2	78	0	4	40	32	−12	0	375	0	
	Opp Total			16		42							35	22					1

1989 PITTSBURGH STEELERS: 9-7-0, 2ND IN AFC CENTRAL DIVISION
Head Coach: Chuck Noll

Week	Day	Date	OT	Rec	Opp	Score		Offe					Defe				
						Tm	Opp	1stD	TotYd	PassY	RushY	TO	1stD	TotYd	PassY	RushY	TO
1	Sun	September 10	L	0-1	Cleveland Browns	0	51	5	53	17	36	8	19	357	205	152	
2	Sun	September 17	L	0-2	Cincinnati Bengals	10	41	18	274	188	86		31	520	328	192	1
3	Sun	September 24	W	1-2	Minnesota Vikings	27	14	23	278	119	159	1	17	258	146	112	2
4	Sun	October 1	W	2-2	Detroit Lions	23	3	20	315	213	102		13	240	222	18	4
5	Sun	October 8	L	2-3	Cincinnati Bengals	16	26	25	340	168	172	1	21	382	192	190	1
6	Sun	October 15	W	3-3	Cleveland Browns	17	7	16	231	138	93	2	17	260	153	107	7
7	Sun	October 22	L	3-4	Houston Oilers	0	27	10	132	100	32	4	22	361	229	132	1
8	Sun	October 29	W	4-4	Kansas City Chiefs	23	17	19	312	232	80	1	23	438	318	120	2
9	Sun	November 5	L	4-5	Denver Broncos	7	34	7	170	77	93	1	22	414	261	153	2
10	Sun	November 12	L	4-6	Chicago Bears	0	20	10	216	162	54	6	20	337	134	203	4
11	Sun	November 19	W	5-6	San Diego Chargers	20	17	14	191	103	88	1	20	359	225	134	3
12	Sun	November 26	W	6-6	Miami Dolphins	34	14	13	292	161	131		15	302	222	80	5
13	Sun	December 3	L	6-7	Houston Oilers	16	23	15	212	43	169	1	19	284	144	140	3
14	Sun	December 10	W	7-7	New York Jets	13	0	17	317	160	157	1	19	313	243	70	3
15	Sun	December 17	W	8-7	New England Patriots	28	10	18	347	128	219	1	26	403	282	121	3
16	Sun	December 24	W	9-7	Tampa Bay Buccaneers	31	22	14	316	169	147	3	19	321	237	84	1
		Playoffs															
Wild Card	Sun	December 31	W OT	10-7	Houston Oilers	26	23	17	289	112	177	1	22	380	315	65	2
Division	Sun	January 7	L	10-8	Denver Broncos	23	24	19	404	229	175	2	19	364	226	138	1

Passing

No.		Age	Pos	G	GS	QBrec	Cmp	Att	Cmp%	Yds	TD	TD%	Int	Int%	Lng	Y/A	AY/A	Y/C	Y/G	Rate	Sk	Yds
6	Bubby Brister	27	QB	14	14	8-6-0	187	342	54.7	2365	9	2.6	10	2.9	79	6.9	6.1	12.6	168.9	73.1	45	452
14	Todd Blackledge	28		3	2	1-1-0	22	60	36.7	282	1	1.7	3	5.0	30	4.7	2.8	12.8	94.0	36.9	4	25
24	Rodney Carter	25		15	0		1	1	100.0	15	0	0.0	0	0.0	15	15.0	15.0	15.0	1.0	118.7	2	7
11	Rick Strom	24		3	0		0	1	0.0	0	0	0.0	0	0.0	0	0.0	0.0		0.0	39.6	0	0
	Team Total	25.4		16		9-7-0	210	404	52.0	2662	10	2.5	13	3.2	79	6.6	5.6	12.7	166.4	67.7	51	484
	Opp Total			16			290	548	52.9	3721	17	3.1	21	3.8		6.8	5.7	12.8	232.6	68.8	31	180

Rushing and Receiving

No.		Age	Pos	G	GS	Rush Att	Rush Yds	Rush TD	Rush Lng	Rush Y/A	Rush Y/G	Rush A/G	Rec	Rec Yds	Rec Y/R	Rec TD	Rec Lng	Rec R/G	Rec Y/G	YScm
38	Tim Worley	23	RB	15	14	195	770	5	38	3.9	51.3	13.0	15	113	7.5	0	19	1.0	7.5	883
33	Merril Hoge	24	FB	16	16	186	621	8	31	3.3	38.8	11.6	34	271	8.0	0	22	2.1	16.9	892
42	Warren Williams	24		5	2	37	131	1	13	3.5	26.2	7.4	6	48	8.0	0	16	1.2	9.6	179
6	Bubby Brister	27	QB	14	14	27	25	0	15	0.9	1.8	1.9	1	−10	−10.0	0	−10	0.1	−0.7	15
83	Louis Lipps	27	WR	16	16	13	180	1	58	13.8	11.3	0.8	50	944	18.9	5	79	3.1	59.0	1124
24	Rodney Carter	25		15	0	11	16	1	7	1.5	1.1	0.7	38	267	7.0	3	22	2.5	17.8	283
20	Dwight Stone	25	wr	16	8	10	53	0	32	5.3	3.3	0.6	7	92	13.1	0	16	0.4	5.8	145
14	Todd Blackledge	28		3	2	9	20	0	11	2.2	6.7	3.0								20
43	Ray Wallace	26		9	0	5	10	1	5	2.0	1.1	0.6								10
11	Rick Strom	24		3	0	4	−3	0	0	−0.8	−1.0	1.3								−3
18	Harry Newsome	26	P	16	0	2	−8	0	0	−4.0	−0.5	0.1								−8
23	Tim Tyrrell	28		7	0	1	3	0	3	3.0	0.4	0.1								3
82	Derek Hill	22	WR	16	8	0	0	0	0		0.0	0.0	28	455	16.3	1	53	1.8	28.4	455
84	Mike Mularkey	28	TE	14	14	0	0	0	0		0.0	0.0	22	326	14.8	1	34	1.6	23.3	326
80	Mark Stock	23		8	0	0	0	0	0		0.0	0.0	4	74	18.5	0	27	0.5	9.3	74
87	Weegie Thompson	28		16	0	0	0	0	0		0.0	0.0	4	74	18.5	0	28	0.3	4.6	74
85	Terry O'Shea	23		16	2	0	0	0	0		0.0	0.0	1	8	8.0	0	8	0.1	0.5	8
	Team Total	25.4		16		500	1818	17	58	3.6	113.6	31.3	210	2662	12.7	10	79	13.1	166.4	4480
	Opp Total			16		498	2008	16		4.0	125.5	31.1	290	3541	12.2	17		18.1	221.3	5549

Defense

No.		Age	Pos	G	GS	Sk	Def Int	Def Yds	Def TD	Def Lng	Def PD	Fumb FF	Fumb Fmb	Fumb FR	Fumb Yds	Fumb TD	Tack Tkl	Tack Ast	Sfty
95	Greg Lloyd	24	ROLB	16	16	7.0	3	49	0	31	0	1	1	3	0	0	92	0	
26	Rod Woodson*+	24	RCB/PR/KR	15	14		3	39	0	39	0	4	3	4	1	0	80	0	
27	Thomas Everett	25	FS	16	16		3	68	0	32	0	0	1	1	21	0	81	0	
37	Carnell Lake	22	SS	15	15	1.0	1	0	0	0	0	2	0	6	2	0	70	0	
98	Gerald Williams	26	NT	16	16	3.0						1	0	1	0	0	54	0	
92	Jerry Olsavsky	22	rilb	16	8	1.0											41	0	
78	Tim Johnson	24	RDE	14	14	4.5						1	0	0	0	0	35	0	
54	Hardy Nickerson	24	RILB	10	8	1.0											35	0	
91	Jerrol Williams	22		16	3	3.0											23	0	
97	Aaron Jones	23		16	2	2.0											21	0	
44	D.J. Johnson	23		16	0		1	0	0	0	0						12	0	
38	Tim Worley	23	RB	15	14							0	9	1	0	0			
50	David Little	30	LILB	16	16	2.0	3	23	0	13	0	0	0	2	0	0			
93	Keith Willis	30	LDE	16	16	6.5													
6	Bubby Brister	27	QB	14	14							0	4	1	0	0			
49	Dwayne Woodruff	32	LCB	16	16		4	57	0	35	0	0	0	1	21	1			
33	Merril Hoge	24	FB	16	16							0	2	2	0	0			
14	Todd Blackledge	28		3	2							0	3	0	0	0			
83	Louis Lipps	27	WR	16	16							0	2	1	0	0			
20	Dwight Stone	25	wr	16	8							0	2	1	0	0			
22	Larry Griffin	26		16	1		1	15	0	15	0	0	0	1	0	0			
35	Delton Hall	24		16	2		1	6	0	6	0	0	0	1	0	0			
82	Derek Hill	22	WR	16	8							0	2	0	0	0			
53	Bryan Hinkle	30	LOLB	13	13		1	4	0	4	0	0	0	1	0	0			
88	Jason Johnson	24		14	0							0	1	1	0	0			

(Continued)

No.		Age	Pos	G	GS	Sk	Def					Fumb					Tack		Sfty
							Int	Yds	TD	Lng	PD	FF	Fmb	FR	Yds	TD	Tkl	Ast	
18	Harry Newsome	26	P	16	0							0	1	1	−13	0			
90	Tyronne Stowe	24		16	0							0	0	2	3	0			
79	John Rienstra	26	LG	15	14							0	0	1	0	0			
11	Rick Strom	24		3	0							0	1	0	−18	0			
23	Tim Tyrrell	28		7	0							0	0	1	0	0			
42	Warren Williams	24		5	2							0	0	1	0	0			
	Team Total	25.4		16		31.0	21	261	0	39	0	9	32	34	17	1	544	0	
	Opp Total			16		51							40	19					2

1990 PITTSBURGH STEELERS: 9-7-0, TIED FOR 1ST IN AFC CENTRAL DIVISION
Head Coach: Chuck Noll

Week	Day	Date	OT	Rec	Opp	Score		Offe					Defe				
						Tm	Opp	1stD	TotYd	PassY	RushY	TO	1stD	TotYd	PassY	RushY	TO
1	Sun	September 9	L	0-1	Cleveland Browns	3	13	14	210	161	49	3	11	158	78	80	1
2	Sun	September 16	W	1-1	Houston Oilers	20	9	10	123	55	68		20	309	258	51	4
3	Sun	September 23	L	1-2	Los Angeles Raiders	3	20	18	208	118	90	3	16	273	148	125	1
4	Sun	September 30	L	1-3	Miami Dolphins	6	28	8	160	119	41	3	20	324	202	122	1
5	Sun	October 7	W	2-3	San Diego Chargers	36	14	25	374	191	183	1	14	188	96	92	3
6	Sun	October 14	W	3-3	Denver Broncos	34	17	25	451	343	108	2	16	244	178	66	1
7	Sun	October 21	L	3-4	San Francisco 49ers	7	27	14	200	103	97	2	22	304	154	150	3
8	Mon	October 29	W	4-4	Los Angeles Rams	41	10	18	345	156	189	1	13	217	173	44	3
9	Sun	November 4	W	5-4	Atlanta Falcons	21	9	10	333	214	119	3	21	332	239	93	5
10					Bye Week												
11	Sun	November 18	L	5-5	Cincinnati Bengals	3	27	11	206	112	94	1	20	312	134	178	1
12	Sun	November 25	W	6-5	New York Jets	24	7	22	333	175	158	3	8	173	100	73	2
13	Sun	December 2	L	6-6	Cincinnati Bengals	12	16	16	305	226	79	2	17	319	154	165	3
14	Sun	December 9	W	7-6	New England Patriots	24	3	21	417	166	251	3	9	182	126	56	3
15	Sun	December 16	W	8-6	New Orleans Saints	9	6	14	232	154	78	1	12	195	95	100	1
16	Sun	December 23	W	9-6	Cleveland Browns	35	0	20	329	132	197	2	10	158	133	25	9
17	Sun	December 30	L	9-7	Houston Oilers	14	34	17	299	220	79	2	28	427	232	195	1

Passing

No.		Age	Pos	G	GS	QBrec	Cmp	Att	Cmp%	Yds	TD	TD%	Int	Int%	Lng	Y/A	AY/A	Y/C	Y/G	Rate	Sk	Yds
6	Bubby Brister	28	QB	16	16	9-7-0	223	387	57.6	2725	20	5.2	14	3.6	90	7.0	6.4	12.2	170.3	81.6	28	213
11	Rick Strom	25		6	0		14	21	66.7	162	0	0.0	1	4.8	22	7.7	5.6	11.6	27.0	69.9	5	29
	Team Total	25.6		16		9-7-0	237	408	58.1	2887	20	4.9	15	3.7	90	7.1	6.4	12.2	180.4	81.0	33	242
	Opp Total			16			236	460	51.3	2728	9	2.0	24	5.2		5.9	4.0	11.6	170.5	54.3	34	228

Rushing and Receiving

No.		Age	Pos	G	GS	Rush							Receiving							YScm
						Att	Yds	TD	Lng	Y/A	Y/G	A/G	Rec	Yds	Y/R	TD	Lng	R/G	Y/G	
33	Merril Hoge	25	FB	16	15	203	772	7	41	3.8	48.3	12.7	40	342	8.6	3	27	2.5	21.4	1114
38	Tim Worley	24	RB	11	8	109	418	0	38	3.8	38.0	9.9	8	70	8.8	0	27	0.7	6.4	488
42	Warren Williams	25		14	4	68	389	3	70	5.7	27.8	4.9	5	42	8.4	1	13	0.4	3.0	431
29	Barry Foster	22		16	1	36	203	1	38	5.6	12.7	2.3	1	2	2.0	0	2	0.1	0.1	205
6	Bubby Brister	28	QB	16	16	25	64	0	11	2.6	4.0	1.6								64
21	Richard Bell	23		8	1	5	18	0	12	3.6	2.3	0.6	12	137	11.4	1	43	1.5	17.1	155
11	Rick Strom	25		6	0	4	10	0	10	2.5	1.7	0.7								10

No.		Age	Pos	G	GS	Rush							Receiving							YScm
						Att	Yds	TD	Lng	Y/A	Y/G	A/G	Rec	Yds	Y/R	TD	Lng	R/G	Y/G	
4	Dan Stryzinski	25	P	16	0	3	17	0	9	5.7	1.1	0.2								17
20	Dwight Stone	26		16	2	2	−6	0	10	−3.0	−0.4	0.1	19	332	17.5	1	90	1.2	20.8	326
83	Louis Lipps	28	WR	14	14	1	−5	0	−5	−5.0	−0.4	0.1	50	682	13.6	3	37	3.6	48.7	677
86	Eric Green	23	te	13	7	0	0	0	0		0.0	0.0	34	387	11.4	7	46	2.6	29.8	387
84	Mike Mularkey	29	TE	16	15	0	0	0	0		0.0	0.0	32	365	11.4	3	28	2.0	22.8	365
82	Derek Hill	23	WR	16	11	0	0	0	0		0.0	0.0	25	391	15.6	0	66	1.6	24.4	391
88	Chris Calloway	22		16	2	0	0	0	0		0.0	0.0	10	124	12.4	1	20	0.6	7.8	124
85	Terry OShea	24		16	0	0	0	0	0		0.0	0.0	1	13	13.0	0	13	0.1	0.8	13
	Team Total	25.6		16		456	1880	11	70	4.1	117.5	28.5	237	2887	12.2	20	90	14.8	180.4	4767
	Opp Total			16		446	1615	13		3.6	100.9	27.9	236	2500	10.6	9		14.8	156.3	4115

Defense

No.		Age	Pos	G	GS	Sk	Def					Fumb					Tack		Sfty
							Int	Yds	TD	Lng	PD	FF	Fmb	FR	Yds	TD	Tkl	Ast	
26	Rod Woodson*+	25	RCB/PR/KR	16	16		5	67	0	34	0	1	3	3	0	0	66	0	
44	D.J. Johnson	24	LCB	16	15		2	60	1	34	0	0	0	1	9	0	69	0	
37	Carnell Lake	23	SS	16	16	1.0	1	0	0	0	0	2	0	1	0	0	67	0	
54	Hardy Nickerson	25	LILB	16	14	2.0						2	0	0	0	0	67	0	
95	Greg Lloyd	25	ROLB	15	14	4.5	1	9	0	9	0	1	0	0	0	0	62	0	
98	Gerald Williams	27	NT	16	15	6.0						1	0	0	0	0	49	0	
27	Thomas Everett	26	FS	15	14		3	2	0	2	0	2	0	0	0	0	35	0	
66	Donald Evans	26	RDE	16	16	3.0						0	0	3	59	0	26	0	
64	Kenny Davidson	23		14	0	3.5											22	0	
57	Jerrol Williams	23		16	1	1.0						2	1	2	1	0	15	0	
97	Aaron Jones	24		7	1	2.0	1	3	0	3	0	0	0	1	0	0	10	0	
91	Craig Veasey	24		10	0							0	0	1	0	0	9	0	
25	Gary Jones	23		16	1												9	0	
6	Bubby Brister	28	QB	16	16							0	9	4	−28	0			
55	Jerry Olsavsky	23		15	0							2	0	0	0	0	6	0	
33	Merril Hoge	23	FB	16	15							0	6	2	0	0			
93	Keith Willis	31	LDE	16	16	5.0	1	5	0	5	0	0	0	1	0	0			
22	Larry Griffin	27		16	3		4	75	0	36	0	0	1	1	1	0			
30	Tim Worley	24	RB	11	8							0	6	0	0	0			
53	Bryan Hinkle	31	LOLB	16	16	2.0	1	19	0	19	0	0	0	2	0	0			
42	Warren Williams	25		14	4							0	5	0	0	0			
49	Dwayne Woodruff	33		15	1		3	110	0	59	0	0	0	1	13	0			
29	Barry Foster	22		16	1							0	2	1	0	0			
68	Lorenzo Freeman	26		11	1	2.0						0	0	1	0	0			
50	David Little*	31	RILB	16	14		1	35	0	35	0	0	0	2	6	0			
20	Dwight Stone	26		16	2							0	1	2	0	0			
86	Eric Green	23	te	13	7							0	1	1	0	0			
82	Derek Hill	23	WR	16	11							0	1	1	0	0			
99	A.J. Jenkins	24		5	0	2.0													
11	Rick Strom	25		6	0							0	1	1	−3	0			
60	Brian Blankenship	27	LG	16	13							0	1	0	0	0			
35	Delton Hall	25		12	1		1	0	0	0	0								
62	Tunch Ilkin	33	RT	13	13							0	0	1	0	0			
83	Louis Lipps	28	WR	14	14							0	1	0	0	0			
84	Mike Mularkey	29	TE	16	15							0	1	0	0	0			
90	Tyronne Stowe	25		16	0							0	0	1	0	0			1
4	Dan Stryzinski	25	P	16	0							0	0	1	0	0			
	Team Total	25.6		16		34.0	24	385	1	59	0	13	40	35	58	0	512	0	1
	Opp Total			16		33							33	15						2

1991 PITTSBURGH STEELERS: 7-9-0, 2ND IN AFC CENTRAL DIVISION
Head Coach: Chuck Noll

						Score		Offe					Defe				
Week	Day	Date	OT	Rec	Opp	Tm	Opp	1stD	TotYd	PassY	RushY	TO	1stD	TotYd	PassY	RushY	TO
1	Sun	September 1	W	1-0	San Diego Chargers	26	20	16	390	266	124	2	20	281	186	95	2
2	Sun	September 8	L	1-1	Buffalo Bills	34	52	14	265	113	152	1	31	537	343	194	3
3	Sun	September 15	W	2-1	New England Patriots	20	6	16	290	247	43	2	12	174	92	82	2
4	Sun	September 22	L	2-2	Philadelphia Eagles	14	23	11	226	160	66	1	20	374	279	95	1
5					Bye Week												
6	Sun	October 6	W	3-2	Indianapolis Colts	21	3	17	292	172	120	3	15	189	147	42	2
7	Mon	October 14	L	3-3	New York Giants	20	23	20	377	229	148	1	17	311	114	197	
8	Sun	October 20	L	3-4	Seattle Seahawks	7	27	12	240	162	78	3	18	324	259	65	
9	Sun	October 27	L	3-5	Cleveland Browns	14	17	18	282	207	75	2	19	262	179	83	
10	Sun	November 3	L	3-6	Denver Broncos	13	20	19	309	163	146	1	17	274	130	144	2
11	Sun	November 10	W OT	4-6	Cincinnati Bengals	33	27	18	352	294	58		25	406	336	70	3
12	Sun	November 17	L	4-7	Washington Redskins	14	41	16	282	241	41	2	23	462	365	97	
13	Sun	November 24	W	5-7	Houston Oilers	26	14	16	294	155	139	2	21	331	307	24	6
14	Thu	November 28	L	5-8	Dallas Cowboys	10	20	17	199	134	65	1	20	297	181	116	
15	Sun	December 8	L	5-9	Houston Oilers	6	31	14	232	147	85	4	23	350	233	117	2
16	Sun	December 15	W	6-9	Cincinnati Bengals	17	10	18	326	177	149	5	13	195	120	75	2
17	Sun	December 22	W	7-9	Cleveland Browns	17	10	12	225	87	138		26	401	315	86	5

Passing

No.		Age	Pos	G	GS	QBrec	Cmp	Att	Cmp%	Yds	TD	TD%	Int	Int%	Lng	Y/A	AY/A	Y/C	Y/G	Rate	Sk	Yds
14	Neil ODonnell	25	QB	12	8	2-6-0	156	286	54.5	1963	11	3.8	7	2.4	89	6.9	6.5	12.6	163.6	78.8	30	214
6	Bubby Brister	29	qb	8	8	5-3-0	103	190	54.2	1350	9	4.7	9	4.7	65	7.1	5.9	13.1	168.8	72.9	15	145
	Team Total	25.8		16		7-9-0	259	476	54.4	3313	20	4.2	16	3.4	89	7.0	6.3	12.8	207.1	76.4	45	359
	Opp Total			16			334	535	62.4	3843	21	3.9	19	3.6		7.2	6.4	11.5	240.2	82.3	38	257

Rushing and Receiving

						Rush							Receiving							
No.		Age	Pos	G	GS	Att	Yds	TD	Lng	Y/A	Y/G	A/G	Rec	Yds	Y/R	TD	Lng	R/G	Y/G	YScm
33	Merril Hoge	26	FB	16	16	165	610	2	24	3.7	38.1	10.3	49	379	7.7	1	25	3.1	23.7	989
29	Barry Foster	23	RB	10	9	96	488	1	56	5.1	48.8	9.6	9	117	13.0	1	31	0.9	11.7	605
42	Warren Williams	26		16	3	57	262	4	21	4.6	16.4	3.6	15	139	9.3	0	29	0.9	8.7	401
38	Tim Worley	25		2	0	22	117	0	16	5.3	58.5	11.0								117
34	Leroy Thompson	22		13	0	20	60	0	14	3.0	4.6	1.5	14	118	8.4	0	32	1.1	9.1	178
14	Neil ODonnell	25	QB	12	8	18	82	1	22	4.6	6.8	1.5								82
6	Bubby Brister	29	qb	8	8	11	17	0	8	1.5	2.1	1.4								17
4	Dan Stryzinski	26	P	16	0	4	−11	0	0	−2.8	−0.7	0.3								−11
20	Dwight Stone	27	WR	16	8	1	2	0	2	2.0	0.1	0.1	32	649	20.3	5	89	2.0	40.6	651
83	Louis Lipps	29	WR	15	14	0	0	0	0		0.0	0.0	55	671	12.2	2	35	3.7	44.7	671
86	Eric Green	24	TE	11	11	0	0	0	0		0.0	0.0	41	582	14.2	6	49	3.7	52.9	582
88	Chris Calloway	23		12	0	0	0	0	0		0.0	0.0	15	254	16.9	1	33	1.3	21.2	254
87	Adrian Cooper	23	te	16	8	0	0	0	0		0.0	0.0	11	147	13.4	2	47	0.7	9.2	147
85	Keith Cash	22		5	0	0	0	0	0		0.0	0.0	7	90	12.9	1	20	1.4	18.0	90
84	Mike Mularkey	30	te	9	6	0	0	0	0		0.0	0.0	6	67	11.2	0	21	0.7	7.4	67
89	Ernie Mills	23		16	2	0	0	0	0		0.0	0.0	3	79	26.3	1	35	0.2	4.9	79
81	Jeff Graham	22		13	1	0	0	0	0		0.0	0.0	2	21	10.5	0	15	0.2	1.6	21
	Team Total	25.8		16		394	1627	8	56	4.1	101.7	24.6	259	3313	12.8	20	89	16.2	207.1	4940
	Opp Total			16		466	1582	14		3.4	98.9	29.1	334	3586	10.7	21		20.9	224.1	5168

Defense

No.		Age	Pos	G	GS	Sk	Def					Fumb					Tack		Sfty
							Int	Yds	TD	Lng	PD	FF	Fmb	FR	Yds	TD	Tkl	Ast	
54	Hardy Nickerson	26	LILB	16	14	1.0						2	0	0	0	0	94	0	
37	Carnell Lake	24	SS	16	16	1.0											83	0	
95	Greg Lloyd*	26	ROLB	16	16	8.0	1	0	0	0	0	6	1	2	0	0	76	0	
26	Rod Woodson*	26	RCB/PR/KR	15	15	1.0	3	72	0	41	0	1	3	3	15	0	71	0	
44	D.J. Johnson	25	LCB	16	16	1.0	1	0	0	0	0						74	0	
27	Thomas Everett	27	FS	16	16		4	53	0	27	0	1	0	2	18	0	67	0	
57	Jerrol Williams	24		16	4	9.0						1	0	1	38	1	47	0	
98	Gerald Williams	28	NT	16	15	2.0											50	0	
66	Donald Evans	27	RDE	16	14	2.0						0	0	1	0	0	35	0	
55	Jerry Olsavsky	24		16	4												32	0	
97	Aaron Jones	25	LDE	16	7	2.0											30	0	
91	Craig Veasey	25		13	2	2.0											22	0	
25	Gary Jones	24		9	1		1	0	0	0	0						16	0	
64	Kenny Davidson	24		13	1												13	0	
94	Jeff Brady	23		16	0												11	0	
14	Neil ODonnell	25	QB	12	8							0	11	2	-3	0			
93	Keith Willis	32	lde	16	7	7.0						0	0	1	0	0			
6	Bubby Brister	29	qb	8	8							0	4	2	0	0			
29	Barry Foster	23	RB	10	9							0	5	1	1	0			
53	Bryan Hinkle	32	LOLB	14	14	2.0	2	68	1	57	0	0	0	1	0	0			
24	Richard Shelton	25		14	2		3	57	1	57	0	0	0	2	0	0			
33	Merril Hoge	26	FB	16	16							0	3	1	0	0			
63	Dermontti Dawson	26	C	16	16							0	2	1	2	0			
4	Dan Stryzinski	26	P	16	0							0	1	2	0	0			
42	Warren Williams	26		16	3							0	2	1	0	0			
86	Eric Green	24	TE	11	11							0	2	0	0	0			
34	Leroy Thompson	22		13	0							0	1	1	0	0			
43	Shawn Vincent	23		10	1		2	52	0	27	0								
88	Chris Calloway	23		12	0							0	0	1	0	0			
22	Larry Griffin	28		6	0		1	22	0	22	0								
77	Carlton Haselrig	25	RG	16	16							0	0	1	2	0			
65	John Jackson	26	LT	16	16							0	0	1	0	0			
83	Louis Lipps	29	WR	15	14							0	1	0	0	0			
50	David Little	32	RILB	14	10		1	5	0	5	0								
74	Terry Long	32		8	3							0	0	1	0	0			
89	Ernie Mills	23		16	2							0	0	1	0	0			
38	Tim Worley	25		2	0							0	1	0	0	0			
	Team Total	25.8		16		38.0	19	329	2	57	0	11	37	29	73	1	721	0	
	Opp Total			16		45							27	16					

1992 PITTSBURGH STEELERS: 11-5-0, 1ST IN AFC CENTRAL DIVISION
Head Coach: Bill Cowher

Week	Day	Date	OT	Rec	Opp	Score		Offe					Defe				
						Tm	Opp	1stD	TotYd	PassY	RushY	TO	1stD	TotYd	PassY	RushY	TO
1	Sun	September 6	W	1-0	Houston Oilers	29	24	19	381	245	136	2	24	434	330	104	5
2	Sun	September 13	W	2-0	New York Jets	27	10	17	370	155	215	5	12	239	129	110	7
3	Sun	September 20	W	3-0	San Diego Chargers	23	6	15	272	205	67	3	15	330	221	109	3
4	Sun	September 27	L	3-1	Green Bay Packers	3	17	16	353	208	145	1	16	294	195	99	
5					Bye Week												
6	Sun	October 11	L	3-2	Cleveland Browns	9	17	20	348	228	120	1	12	253	168	85	1
7	Mon	October 19	W	4-2	Cincinnati Bengals	20	0	26	424	251	173	1	6	118	70	48	2
8	Sun	October 25	W	5-2	Kansas City Chiefs	27	3	16	263	109	154		13	179	58	121	3
9	Sun	November 1	W	6-2	Houston Oilers	21	20	20	302	183	119	3	21	283	228	55	2
10	Sun	November 8	L	6-3	Buffalo Bills	20	28	17	233	146	87		31	458	284	174	2
11	Sun	November 15	W	7-3	Detroit Lions	17	14	18	316	164	152	2	20	376	286	90	6
12	Sun	November 22	W	8-3	Indianapolis Colts	30	14	20	362	109	253	2	16	329	258	71	3
13	Sun	November 29	W	9-3	Cincinnati Bengals	21	9	17	240	141	99	2	15	228	68	160	1
14	Sun	December 6	W	10-3	Seattle Seahawks	20	14	16	306	168	138	5	10	220	153	67	2
15	Sun	December 13	L	10-4	Chicago Bears	6	30	10	140	105	35	4	20	283	71	212	
16	Sun	December 20	L	10-5	Minnesota Vikings	3	6	17	288	130	158	1	18	341	125	216	3
17	Sun	December 27	W	11-5	Cleveland Browns	23	13	20	308	203	105		17	293	173	120	3
		Playoffs															
Division	Sat	January 9	L	11-6	Buffalo Bills	3	24	18	240	111	129	3	19	325	156	169	

Passing

No.		Age	Pos	G	GS	QBrec	Cmp	Att	Cmp%	Yds	TD	TD%	Int	Int%	Lng	Y/A	AY/A	Y/C	Y/G	Rate	Sk	Yds
14	Neil O'Donnell*	26	QB	12	12	9-3-0	185	313	59.1	2283	13	4.2	9	2.9	51	7.3	6.8	12.3	190.3	83.6	27	208
6	Bubby Brister	30		6	4	2-2-0	63	116	54.3	719	2	1.7	5	4.3	42	6.2	4.6	11.4	119.8	61.0	13	88
29	Barry Foster*+	24	RB	16	15		0	1	0.0	0	0	0.0	0	0.0	0	0.0	0.0		0.0	39.6	0	0
3	Mark Royals	27	P	16	0		1	1	100.0	44	0	0.0	0	0.0	44	44.0	44.0	44.0	2.8	118.7	0	0
	Team Total	26.0		16		11-5-0	249	431	57.8	3046	15	3.5	14	3.2	51	7.1	6.3	12.2	190.4	77.7	40	296
	Opp Total			16			252	478	52.7	3065	15	3.1	22	4.6		6.4	5.0	12.2	191.6	64.0	36	248

Rushing and Receiving

No.		Age	Pos	G	GS	Rush Att	Yds	TD	Lng	Y/A	Y/G	A/G	Rec	Yds	Y/R	TD	Lng	R/G	Y/G	YScm
29	Barry Foster*+	24	RB	16	15	390	1690	11	69	4.3	105.6	24.4	36	344	9.6	0	42	2.3	21.5	2034
33	Merril Hoge	27	FB	16	11	41	150	0	15	3.7	9.4	2.6	28	231	8.3	1	20	1.8	14.4	381
34	Leroy Thompson	23		15	2	35	157	1	25	4.5	10.5	2.3	22	278	12.6	0	29	1.5	18.5	435
14	Neil ODonnell*	26	QB	12	12	27	5	1	9	0.2	0.4	2.3								5
20	Dwight Stone	28	WR	15	12	12	118	0	30	9.8	7.9	0.8	34	501	14.7	3	49	2.3	33.4	619
6	Bubby Brister	30		6	4	10	16	0	8	1.6	2.7	1.7								16
42	Warren Williams	27		16	0	2	0	0	2	0.0	0.0	0.1	1	44	44.0	0	44	0.1	2.8	44
89	Ernie Mills	24		16	4	1	20	0	20	20.0	1.3	0.1	30	383	12.8	3	22	1.9	23.9	403
81	Jeff Graham	23	WR	14	10	0	0	0	0		0.0	0.0	49	711	14.5	1	51	3.5	50.8	711
87	Adrian Cooper	24	TE	16	15	0	0	0	0		0.0	0.0	16	197	12.3	3	27	1.0	12.3	197
86	Eric Green	25	te	7	5	0	0	0	0		0.0	0.0	14	152	10.9	2	24	2.0	21.7	152
80	Charles Davenport	24		15	1	0	0	0	0		0.0	0.0	9	136	15.1	0	31	0.6	9.1	136
84	Tim Jorden	26		15	4	0	0	0	0		0.0	0.0	6	28	4.7	2	8	0.4	1.9	28
88	Mark Didio	23		2	0	0	0	0	0		0.0	0.0	3	39	13.0	0	18	1.5	19.5	39
82	Yancey Thigpen	23		12	0	0	0	0	0		0.0	0.0	1	2	2.0	0	2	0.1	0.2	2
	Team Total	26.0		16		518	2156	13	69	4.2	134.8	32.4	249	3046	12.2	15	51	15.6	190.4	5202
	Opp Total			16		435	1841	6		4.2	115.1	27.2	252	2817	11.2	15		15.8	176.1	4658

Defense

No.		Age	Pos	G	GS	Sk	Def Int	Yds	TD	Lng	PD	FF	Fmb	FR	Yds	TD	Tkl	Ast	Sfty
54	Hardy Nickerson	27	LILB	15	15	2.0						0	0	2	44	0	114	0	
26	Rod Woodson*+	27	PR/LCB/KR	16	16	6.0	4	90	0	57	0	4	2	1	9	0	100	0	
95	Greg Lloyd*	27	ROLB	16	16	6.5	1	35	0	35	0	5	1	4	0	0	96	0	
57	Jerrol Williams	25	LOLB	16	16	4.5	1	4	0	4	0	2	0	2	18	0	96	0	
66	Donald Evans	28	RDE	16	16	3.0						0	0	2	0	0	88	0	
37	Carnell Lake	25	SS	16	16	2.0						2	0	1	12	0	85	0	
39	Darren Perry	24	FS	16	16		6	69	0	34	0	0	0	1	0	0	61	0	
44	D.J. Johnson	26	RCB	15	15		5	67	0	35	0	0	0	2	0	0	56	0	
98	Gerald Williams	29	NT	10	10	3.0						1	0	0	0	0	43	0	
97	Aaron Jones	26		13	0	2.0						0	0	1	0	0	33	0	
64	Kenny Davidson	25	LDE	16	13	2.0											33	0	
78	Garry Howe	24		11	2	2.0											24	0	
93	Joel Steed	23		11	4												8	0	
29	Barry Foster*+	24	RB	16	15							0	9	2	−20	0			
99	Levon Kirkland	23		16	0												5	0	
14	Neil ODonnell*	26	QB	12	12							0	6	4	−20	0			
94	Darryl Ford	26		8	0												4	0	
55	Jerry Olsavsky	25		7	0							1	0	0	0	0	3	0	
50	David Little	33	RILB	16	12	3.0	2	6	0	6	0								
6	Bubby Brister	30		6	4							0	2	2	−2	0			
22	Larry Griffin	29		14	2		3	98	1	65	0								
33	Merril Hoge	27	FB	16	11							0	3	0	0	0			
89	Ernie Mills	24		16	4							0	2	0	0	0			
24	Richard Shelton	26		16	3							0	0	2	0	0			
34	Leroy Thompson	23		15	2							0	2	0	0	0			
87	Adrian Cooper	24	TE	16	15							0	1	0	0	0			
80	Charles Davenport	24		15	1							0	0	1	34	1			

No.		Age	Pos	G	GS	Sk	Int	Yds	TD	Lng	PD	FF	Fmb	FR	Yds	TD	Tkl	Ast	Sfty
								Def					Fumb					Tack	
77	Carlton Haselrig*	26	RG	16	16							0	0	1	4	0			
84	Tim Jorden	26		15	4							0	0	1	0	0			
67	Duval Love	29	LG	16	16							0	0	1	7	0			
23	Sammy Walker	23		16	4							0	0	1	0	0			
	Team Total	26.0		16		36.0	22	384	1	65	0	15	28	31	86	1	849	0	
	Opp Total			16		40							34	13					

1993 PITTSBURGH STEELERS: 9-7-0, 2ND IN AFC CENTRAL DIVISION
Head Coach: Bill Cowher

Week	Day	Date		OT	Rec	Opp	Tm	Opp	1stD	TotYd	PassY	RushY	TO	1stD	TotYd	PassY	RushY	TO
							Score		Offe					Defe				
1	Sun	September 5	L		0-1	San Francisco 49ers	13	24	12	211	109	102	3	21	326	240	86	3
2	Sun	September 12	L		0-2	Los Angeles Rams	0	27	11	175	120	55	3	20	314	215	99	2
3	Sun	September 19	W		1-2	Cincinnati Bengals	34	7	23	404	181	223	1	11	170	126	44	1
4	Mon	September 27	W		2-2	Atlanta Falcons	45	17	22	368	259	109	1	16	220	176	44	6
5						Bye Week												
6	Sun	October 10	W		3-2	San Diego Chargers	16	3	15	304	156	148		12	138	119	19	3
7	Sun	October 17	W		4-2	New Orleans Saints	37	14	22	393	192	201	3	11	264	215	49	5
8	Sun	October 24	L		4-3	Cleveland Browns	23	28	26	440	348	92	2	12	245	147	98	1
9						Bye Week												
10	Sun	November 7	W		5-3	Cincinnati Bengals	24	16	21	390	244	146	2	14	199	96	103	1
11	Mon	November 15	W		6-3	Buffalo Bills	23	0	26	400	173	227		9	157	110	47	1
12	Sun	November 21	L		6-4	Denver Broncos	13	37	19	349	248	101	3	23	364	257	107	
13	Sun	November 28	L		6-5	Houston Oilers	3	23	18	234	169	65	4	20	391	266	125	1
14	Sun	December 5	W		7-5	New England Patriots	17	14	14	217	92	125		20	349	296	53	6
15	Mon	December 13	W		8-5	Miami Dolphins	21	20	19	265	145	120		21	348	299	49	3
16	Sun	December 19	L		8-6	Houston Oilers	17	26	21	385	347	38	3	20	383	266	117	2
17	Sun	December 26	L		8-7	Seattle Seahawks	6	16	18	380	264	116	2	25	368	101	267	1
18	Sun	January 2	W		9-7	Cleveland Browns	16	9	20	320	185	135		12	295	234	61	2
		Playoffs																
Wild Card	Sat	January 8	L	OT	9-8	Kansas City Chiefs	24	27	21	369	272	97		28	401	276	125	

Passing

No.		Age	Pos	G	GS	QBrec	Cmp	Att	Cmp%	Yds	TD	TD%	Int	Int%	Lng	Y/A	AY/A	Y/C	Y/G	Rate	Sk	Yds
14	Neil ODonnell	27	QB	16	15	9-6-0	270	486	55.6	3208	14	2.9	7	1.4	71	6.6	6.5	11.9	200.5	79.5	41	331
18	Mike Tomczak	31		7	1	0-1-0	29	54	53.7	398	2	3.7	5	9.3	39	7.4	3.9	13.7	56.9	51.3	7	43
	Team Total	26.1		16		9-7-0	299	540	55.4	3606	16	3.0	12	2.2	71	6.7	6.3	12.1	225.4	76.7	48	374
	Opp Total			16			277	521	53.2	3440	16	3.1	24	4.6		6.6	5.1	12.4	215.0	64.9	42	277

Rushing and Receiving

No.		Age	Pos	G	GS	Att	Yds	TD	Lng	Y/A	Y/G	A/G	Rec	Yds	Y/R	TD	Lng	R/G	Y/G	YScm
						Rush							Receiving							
34	Leroy Thompson	24	rb	15	6	205	763	3	36	3.7	50.9	13.7	38	259	6.8	0	28	2.5	17.3	1022
29	Barry Foster*	25	RB	9	9	177	711	8	38	4.0	79.0	19.7	27	217	8.0	1	21	3.0	24.1	928
33	Merril Hoge	28	FB	16	13	51	249	1	30	4.9	15.6	3.2	33	247	7.5	4	18	2.1	15.4	496
14	Neil ODonnell	27	QB	16	15	26	111	0	27	4.3	6.9	1.6								111
20	Dwight Stone	29	WR	16	15	12	121	1	38	10.1	7.6	0.8	41	587	14.3	2	44	2.6	36.7	708
38	Tim Worley	27		5	0	10	33	0	8	3.3	6.6	2.0	3	13	4.3	0	9	0.6	2.6	46
18	Mike Tomczak	3		7	1	5	−4	0	2	−0.8	−0.6	0.7								−4
89	Ernie Mills	25	wr	14	5	3	12	0	19	4.0	0.9	0.2	29	386	13.3	1	30	2.1	27.6	398
42	Randy Cuthbert	23		10	0	1	7	0	7	7.0	0.7	0.1	1	3	3.0	0	3	0.1	0.3	10
26	Rod Woodson*+	28	PR/LCB/KR	16	16	1	0	0	0	0.0	0.0	0.1								0
86	Eric Green*	26	TE	16	16	0	0	0	0		0.0	0.0	63	942	15.0	5	71	3.9	58.9	942
81	Jeff Graham	24	WR	15	12	0	0	0	0		0.0	0.0	38	579	15.2	0	51	2.5	38.6	579
87	Adrian Cooper	25		14	3	0	0	0	0		0.0	0.0	9	112	12.4	0	38	0.6	8.0	112
82	Yancey Thigpen	24		12	0	0	0	0	0		0.0	0.0	9	154	17.1	3	39	0.8	12.8	154
80	Charles Davenport	25		16	0	0	0	0	0		0.0	0.0	4	51	12.8	0	19	0.3	3.2	51
88	Andre Hastings	22		6	0	0	0	0	0		0.0	0.0	3	44	14.7	0	18	0.5	7.3	44
84	Tim Jorden	27		16	1	0	0	0	0		0.0	0.0	1	12	12.0	0	12	0.1	0.8	12
	Team Total	26.1		16		491	2003	13	38	4.1	125.2	30.7	299	3606	12.1	16	71	18.7	225.4	5609
	Opp Total			16		399	1368	6		3.4	85.5	24.9	277	3163	11.4	16		17.3	197.7	4531

Defense

No.		Age	Pos	G	GS	Sk	Def Int	Yds	TD	Lng	PD	Fumb FF	Fmb	FR	Yds	TD	Tack Tkl	Ast	Sfty
95	Greg Lloyd*+	28	ROLB	15	15	6.0						5	0	1	0	0	111	0	
99	Levon Kirkland	24	LILB	16	13	1.0						4	0	2	24	1	103	0	
26	Rod Woodson*+	28	PR/LCB/KR	16	16	2.0	8	138	1	63	0	2	2	1	0	0	95	0	
37	Carnell Lake	26	SS	14	14	5.0	4	31	0	26	0	1	0	2	0	0	91	0	
39	Darren Perry	25	FS	16	16		4	61	0	30	0						94	0	
66	Donald Evans	29	RDE	16	16	6.5											84	0	
91	Kevin Greene	31	LOLB	16	16	12.5						3	0	3	5	0	67	0	
94	Chad Brown	23	RILB	16	9	3.0						2	0	0	0	0	69	0	
44	D.J. Johnson	27	RCB	16	15		3	51	0	26	0	1	0	0	0	0	62	0	
64	Kenny Davidson	26	LDE	16	9	2.5	1	6	0	6	0	0	0	1	18	1	51	0	
93	Joel Steed	24	NT	14	12	1.5						1	0	1	0	0	41	0	
21	Deon Figures	23		15	4		1	78	0	78	0	1	2	2	6	0	38	0	
55	Jerry Olsavsky	26	rilb	7	7												39	0	
25	Gary Jones	26		13	2		2	11	0	11	0	0	0	1	0	0	34	0	
98	Gerald Williams	30	lde	10	8	1.0											27	0	
90	Jeff Zgonina	23		5	0							0	0	1	0	0	16	0	
50	Reggie Barnes	24		16	0												12	0	
27	Willie J. Williams	23		16	0							1	0	0	0	0	9	0	
76	Kevin Henry	25		12	1	1.0	1	10	0	10	0						7	0	
34	Leroy Thompson	24	rb	15	6							0	7	1	0	0			
14	Neil ODonnell	27	QB	16	15							0	5	0	−2	0			
29	Barry Foster*	25	RB	9	9							0	3	0	0	0			
86	Eric Green*	26	TE	16	16							0	3	0	0	0			
20	Dwight Stone	29	WR	16	15							0	2	1	0	0			
18	Mike Tomczak	31		7	1							0	2	1	0	0			
87	Adrian Cooper	25		14	3							0	1	0	0	0			
63	Dermontti Dawson*+	28	C	16	16							0	1	0	0	0			
33	Merril Hoge	28	FB	16	13							0	0	1	4	0			
65	John Jackson	28	LT	16	13							0	0	1	0	0			
84	Tim Jorden	27		16	1							0	0	1	2	0			
72	Leon Searcy	24	RT	16	16							0	0	1	0	0			
73	Justin Strzelczyk	25	RG	16	12							0	0	1	0	0			
	Team Total	26.1		16		42.0	24	386	1	78	0	21	28	23	57	2	1050	0	
	Opp Total			16		48							37	23						

1994 PITTSBURGH STEELERS: 12-4-0, 1ST IN AFC CENTRAL DIVISION
Head Coach: Bill Cowher

Week	Day	Date	OT	Rec	Opp	Score Tm	Opp	Offe 1stD	TotYd	PassY	RushY	TO	Defe 1stD	TotYd	PassY	RushY	TO
1	Sun	September 4	L	0-1	Dallas Cowboys	9	26	14	126	71	55		26	442	245	197	1
2	Sun	September 11	W	1-1	Cleveland Browns	17	10	17	315	199	116		18	278	197	81	5
3	Sun	September 18	W	2-1	Indianapolis Colts	31	21	32	500	239	261	2	10	175	102	73	1
4	Sun	September 25	L	2-2	Seattle Seahawks	13	30	29	452	321	131	4	20	297	152	145	1
5	Mon	October 3	W	3-2	Houston Oilers	30	14	21	379	164	215		14	290	221	69	2
6					Bye Week												
7	Sun	October 16	W	4-2	Cincinnati Bengals	14	10	16	243	129	114	1	11	241	135	106	2
8	Sun	October 23	W	5-2	New York Giants	10	6	16	296	121	175	4	8	215	162	53	3
9	Sun	October 30	L OT	5-3	Arizona Cardinals	17	20	12	317	232	85	3	16	335	236	99	1
10	Sun	November 6	W OT	6-3	Houston Oilers	12	9	17	266	155	111		17	244	160	84	1
11	Mon	November 14	W	7-3	Buffalo Bills	23	10	10	226	140	86	1	24	326	198	128	3
12	Sun	November 20	W OT	8-3	Miami Dolphins	16	13	21	423	335	88		20	323	283	40	2
13	Sun	November 27	W	9-3	Los Angeles Raiders	21	3	19	306	131	175		14	179	122	57	2
14	Sun	December 4	W	10-3	Cincinnati Bengals	38	15	23	308	123	185		13	195	119	76	3
15	Sun	December 11	W	11-3	Philadelphia Eagles	14	3	20	269	145	124	2	9	105	34	71	1
16	Sun	December 18	W	12-3	Cleveland Browns	17	7	18	276	153	123		21	331	245	86	3
17	Sat	December 24	L	12-4	San Diego Chargers	34	37	22	442	306	136		21	350	263	87	
		Playoffs															
Division	Sat	January 7	W	13-4	Cleveland Browns	29	9	23	424	186	238	1	10	186	131	55	2
Conf Champ	Sun	January 15	L	13-5	San Diego Chargers	13	17	22	415	349	66	1	13	226	160	66	1

Passing

No.		Age	Pos	G	GS	QBrec	Cmp	Att	Cmp%	Yds	TD	TD%	Int	Int%	Lng	Y/A	AY/A	Y/C	Y/G	Rate	Sk	Yds
14	Neil ODonnell	28	QB	14	14	10-4-0	212	370	57.3	2443	13	3.5	9	2.4	60	6.6	6.2	11.5	174.5	78.9	35	250
18	Mike Tomczak	32		6	2	2-0-0	54	93	58.1	804	4	4.3	0	0.0	84	8.6	9.5	14.9	134.0	100.8	4	33
	Team Total	26.5		16		12-4-0	266	463	57.5	3247	17	3.7	9	1.9	84	7.0	6.9	12.2	202.9	83.3	39	283
	Opp Total			16			280	532	52.6	3256	12	2.3	17	3.2		6.1	5.1	11.6	203.5	65.6	55	382

Rushing and Receiving

No.		Age	Pos	G	GS	Rush Att	Yds	TD	Lng	Y/A	Y/G	A/G	Rec	Yds	Y/R	TD	Lng	R/G	Y/G	YScm
29	Barry Foster	26	RB	11	10	216	851	5	29	3.9	77.4	19.6	20	124	6.2	0	27	1.8	11.3	975
33	Bam Morris	22	rb	15	6	198	836	7	20	4.2	55.7	13.2	22	204	9.3	0	49	1.5	13.6	1040
22	John L. Williams	30	FB	15	12	68	317	1	23	4.7	21.1	4.5	51	378	7.4	2	23	3.4	25.2	695
14	Neil O'Donnell	28	QB	14	14	31	80	1	18	2.6	5.7	2.2								80
35	Fred McAfee	26		6	0	16	56	1	13	3.5	9.3	2.7								56
81	Charles Johnson	22	WR/KR	16	9	4	−1	0	7	−0.3	−0.1	0.3	38	577	15.2	3	84	2.4	36.1	576
18	Mike Tomczak	32		6	2	4	22	0	13	5.5	3.7	0.7								22
89	Ernie Mills	26	wr	15	6	3	18	0	17	6.0	1.2	0.2	19	384	20.2	1	43	1.3	25.6	402
20	Dwight Stone	30		15	1	2	7	0	4	3.5	0.5	0.1	7	81	11.6	0	25	0.5	5.4	88
43	Steve Avery	28		14	1	2	4	0	5	2.0	0.3	0.1	1	2	2.0	0	2	0.1	0.1	6
1	Gary Anderson	35	K	16	0	1	3	0	3	3.0	0.2	0.1								3
3	Mark Royals	29	P	16	0	1	−13	0	−13	−13.0	−0.8	0.1								−13
86	Eric Green*	27	TE	15	14	0	0	0	0		0.0	0.0	46	618	13.4	4	46	3.1	41.2	618
82	Yancey Thigpen	25	wr	15	6	0	0	0	0		0.0	0.0	36	546	15.2	4	60	2.4	36.4	546
88	Andre Hastings	23	WR	16	8	0	0	0	0		0.0	0.0	20	281	14.1	2	46	1.3	17.6	281
85	Jonathan Hayes	32	te	16	6	0	0	0	0		0.0	0.0	5	50	10.0	1	17	0.3	3.1	50
87	Craig Keith	23		16	1	0	0	0	0		0.0	0.0	1	2	2.0	0	2	0.1	0.1	2
	Team Total	26.5		16		546	2180	15	29	4.0	136.3	34.1	266	3247	12.2	17	84	16.6	202.9	5427
	Opp Total			16		421	1452	7		3.4	90.8	26.3	280	2874	10.3	12		17.5	179.6	4326

Defense

No.		Age	Pos	G	GS	Sk	Def Int	Yds	TD	Lng	PD	FF	Fmb	FR	Yds	TD	Tkl	Ast	Sfty
94	Chad Brown	24	RILB	16	16	8.5	1	9	0	9	0	2	0	0	0	0	90	29	
99	Levon Kirkland	25	LILB	16	15	3.0	2	0	0	0	0						70	30	
95	Greg Lloyd*+	29	ROLB	15	15	10.0	1	8	0	8	0	5	0	1	0	0	69	18	
26	Rod Woodson*+	29	PR/LCB	15	15	3.0	4	109	2	37	0	3	2	1	0	0	67	16	
37	Carnell Lake*	27	SS	16	16	1.0	1	2	0	2	0	3	0	1	0	0	68	14	
91	Kevin Greene*+	32	LOLB	16	16	14.0						1	0	3	0	0	53	16	
21	Deon Figures	24	RCB	16	15	1.0						1	0	1	0	0	56	14	
39	Darren Perry	26	FS	16	16		7	112	0	42	0	0	0	2	0	0	49	16	
93	Joel Steed	25	NT	16	16	2.0						2	0	0	0	0	40	12	
97	Ray Seals	29	RDE	13	11	7.0						0	0	2	0	0	28	8	
98	Gerald Williams	31	LDE	11	11	1.5						0	0	1	0	1	26	13	
24	Tim McKyer	31		16	2							0	0	1	0	0	26	3	
96	Brentson Buckner	23	rde	13	5	2.0						0	0	1	0	0	13	5	
25	Gary Jones	27		14	0		1	0	0	0	0	0	0	1	0	0	13	6	
76	Kevin Henry	26	rde	16	5							0	0	1	0	0	12	5	
90	Jeff Zgonina	24		16	0							0	1	1	0	0	6	5	
51	Ed Robinson	24		16	0							0	0	1	0	0	8	1	
92	Jason Gildon	22		16	1	2.0											4	0	
40	Myron Bell	23		15	0												4	0	
27	Willie J. Williams	24		16	1												3	0	
14	Neil O'Donnell	28	QB	14	14							0	4	1	0	0			
78	Taase Faumui	23		5	0												2	0	
33	Bam Morris	22	rb	15	6							0	3	1	0	0			
86	Eric Green*	27	TE	15	14							0	2	0	0	0			
65	John Jackson	29	LT	16	16							0	0	2	0	0			
81	Charles Johnson	22	WR/KR	16	9							0	2	0	0	0			
18	Mike Tomczak	32		6	2							0	2	0	−1	0			
53	Reggie Clark	27		5	0							0	0	1	0	0			
85	Jonathan Hayes	32	te	16	6							0	1	0	0	0			
89	Ernie Mills	26	wr	15	6							0	1	0	0	0			
	Team Total	26.5		16		55.0	17	240	2	42	0	17	18	22	−1	1	707	211	
	Opp Total			16		39							31	17						

1995 PITTSBURGH STEELERS: 11-5-0, 1ST IN AFC CENTRAL DIVISION, AFC CHAMPIONS

Head Coach: Bill Cowher

Week	Day	Date	OT	Rec	Opp	Score Tm	Opp	Offe 1stD	TotYd	PassY	RushY	TO	Defe 1stD	TotYd	PassY	RushY	TO
1	Sun	September 3	W		1-0	Detroit Lions	23	20	26	354	204	150	4	16	302	180	122	1
2	Sun	September 10	W		2-0	Houston Oilers	34	17	19	250	123	127	1	19	216	178	38	3
3	Mon	September 18	L		2-1	Miami Dolphins	10	23	21	366	273	93	5	16	256	210	46	
4	Sun	September 24	L		2-2	Minnesota Vikings	24	44	22	405	335	70	7	20	378	244	134	4
5	Sun	October 1	W		3-2	San Diego Chargers	31	16	21	261	141	120	1	20	327	232	95	4
6	Sun	October 8	L		3-3	Jacksonville Jaguars	16	20	16	350	282	68	1	17	267	171	96	
7						Bye Week												
8	Thu	October 19	L		3-4	Cincinnati Bengals	9	27	24	468	347	121	1	18	368	275	93	
9	Sun	October 29	W		4-4	Jacksonville Jaguars	24	7	20	316	178	138	1	14	229	145	84	1
10	Sun	November 5	W	OT	5-4	Chicago Bears	37	34	27	383	298	85	4	20	343	223	120	5
11	Mon	November 13	W		6-4	Cleveland Browns	20	3	22	310	157	153		7	120	43	77	1
12	Sun	November 19	W		7-4	Cincinnati Bengals	49	31	28	556	365	191	2	19	265	208	57	2
13	Sun	November 26	W		8-4	Cleveland Browns	20	17	19	318	258	60		19	253	178	75	3
14	Sun	December 3	W		9-4	Houston Oilers	21	7	17	358	205	153	4	11	249	174	75	2
15	Sun	December 10	W		10-4	Oakland Raiders	29	10	21	355	211	144	2	9	190	162	28	4
16	Sat	December 16	W		11-4	New England Patriots	41	27	14	321	226	95	1	28	439	322	117	3
17	Sun	December 24	L		11-5	Green Bay Packers	19	24	27	398	314	84		19	359	295	64	1
Playoffs																		
Division	Sat	January 6	W		12-5	Buffalo Bills	40	21	23	409	262	147	2	18	250	156	94	4
Conf Champ	Sun	January 14	W		13-5	Indianapolis Colts	20	16	21	285	205	80	1	16	328	245	83	
Super Bowl	Sun	January 28	L		13-6	Dallas Cowboys	17	27	25	310	207	103	3	15	254	198	56	

Passing

No.		Age	Pos	G	GS	QBrec	Cmp	Att	Cmp%	Yds	TD	TD%	Int	Int%	Lng	Y/A	AY/A	Y/C	Y/G	Rate	Sk	Yds
14	Neil O'Donnell	29	QB	12	12	9-3-0	246	416	59.1	2970	17	4.1	7	1.7	71	7.1	7.2	12.1	247.5	87.7	15	126
18	Mike Tomczak	33		7	4	2-2-0	65	113	57.5	666	1	0.9	9	8.0	29	5.9	2.5	10.2	95.1	44.3	6	42
16	Jim Miller	24		3	0		32	56	57.1	397	2	3.6	5	8.9	42	7.1	3.8	12.4	132.3	53.9	2	8
10	Kordell Stewart	23		10	2		5	7	71.4	60	1	14.3	0	0.0	32	8.6	11.4	12.0	6.0	136.9	1	0
	Team Total	26.8		16		11-5-0	348	592	58.8	4093	21	3.5	21	3.5	71	6.9	6.0	11.8	255.8	76.9	24	176
	Opp Total			16			314	531	59.1	3512	24	4.5	22	4.1		6.6	5.7	11.2	219.5	76.7	42	272

Rushing and Receiving

No.		Age	Pos	G	GS	Rush Att	Yds	TD	Lng	Y/A	Y/G	A/G	Receiving Rec	Yds	Y/R	TD	Lng	R/G	Y/G	YScm
20	Erric Pegram	26	RB	15	11	213	813	5	38	3.8	54.2	14.2	26	206	7.9	1	22	1.7	13.7	1019
33	Bam Morris	23		13	4	148	559	9	30	3.8	43.0	11.4	8	36	4.5	0	13	0.6	2.8	595
25	Fred McAfee	27		16	1	39	156	1	22	4.0	9.8	2.4	15	88	5.9	0	18	0.9	5.5	244
22	John L. Williams	31	FB	11	9	29	110	0	31	3.8	10.0	2.6	24	127	5.3	1	20	2.2	11.5	237
14	Neil O'Donnell	29	QB	12	12	24	45	0	14	1.9	3.8	2.0								45
10	Kordell Stewart	23		10	2	15	86	1	22	5.7	8.6	1.5	14	235	16.8	1	71	1.4	23.5	321
18	Mike Tomczak	33		7	4	11	25	0	11	2.3	3.6	1.6								25
89	Ernie Mills	27	KR	16	4	5	39	0	20	7.8	2.4	0.3	39	679	17.4	8	62	2.4	42.4	718
34	Tim Lester	27		6	1	5	9	1	3	1.8	1.5	0.8								9
82	Yancey Thigpen*	26	WR	16	15	1	1	0	1	1.0	0.1	0.1	85	1307	15.4	5	43	5.3	81.7	1308
88	Andre Hastings	24	PR	16	0	1	14	0	14	14.0	0.9	0.1	48	502	10.5	1	36	3.0	31.4	516
81	Charles Johnson	23	WR	15	10	1	−10	0	−10	−10.0	−0.7	0.1	38	432	11.4	0	33	2.5	28.8	422
43	Steve Avery	29		11	2	1	3	0	3	3.0	0.3	0.1	11	82	7.5	1	18	1.0	7.5	85
16	Jim Miller	24		3	0	1	2	0	2	2.0	0.7	0.3								2
87	Mark Bruener	23	TE	16	13	0	0	0	0		0.0	0.0	26	238	9.2	3	29	1.6	14.9	238
85	Jonathan Hayes	33	te	16	6	0	0	0	0		0.0	0.0	11	113	10.3	0	32	0.7	7.1	113
80	Johnnie Barnes	27		3	0	0	0	0	0		0.0	0.0	3	48	16.0	0	25	1.0	16.0	48
	Team Total	26.8		16		494	1852	17	38	3.7	115.8	30.9	348	4093	11.8	21	71	21.8	255.8	5945
	Opp Total			16		370	1321	9		3.6	82.6	23.1	314	3240	10.3	24		19.6	202.5	4561

Defense

No.		Age	Pos	G	GS	Sk	Int	Yds	TD	Lng	PD	FF	Fmb	FR	Yds	TD	Tkl	Ast	Sfty
							Def					**Fumb**					**Tack**		
95	Greg Lloyd*+	30	ROLB	16	16	6.5	3	85	0	52	0	6	0	0	0	0	88	28	
27	Willie J. Williams	25	LCB	16	15		7	122	1	63	0	1	0	1	0	0	69	8	
99	Levon Kirkland	26	LILB	16	16	1.0						0	0	2	0	0	58	30	
37	Carnell Lake*	28	RCB/ss	16	16	1.5	1	32	1	32	0	1	0	1	0	0	63	10	
39	Darren Perry	27	FS	16	16		4	71	0	26	0	0	1	2	0	0	61	9	
91	Kevin Greene*	33	LOLB	16	16	9.0	1	0	0	0	0	2	0	0	0	0	34	14	
97	Ray Seals	30	RDE	16	16	8.5	1	0	0	0	0	2	0	1	4	0	33	14	
96	Brentson Buckner	24	LDE/nt	16	16	3.0						1	0	1	46	1	29	19	
28	Alvoid Mays	29	rcb	13	6		2	35	1	32	0	1	0	0	0	0	34	3	
40	Myron Bell	24	SS	16	9		2	4	0	4	0	2	0	1	0	0	25	11	
55	Jerry Olsavsky	28	rilb	15	5	1.0											24	10	
94	Chad Brown	25	RILB	10	10	5.5											20	10	
93	Joel Steed	26	NT	12	11	1.0											23	7	
76	Kevin Henry	27	lde	13	5	2.0											12	3	
24	Chris Oldham	27		15	0		1	12	0	12	0	0	0	1	23	1	10	5	
92	Jason Gildon	23		16	0	3.0						2	0	1	1	0	8	4	
90	Bill E. Johnson	27		9	0							0	0	1	0	0	9	2	
21	Deon Figures	25		14	1												10	0	
29	Randy Fuller	25		13	0												7	1	
57	Eric Ravotti	24		6	1												7	0	
20	Erric Pegram	26	RB	15	11							0	9	1	0	0			
54	Donta Jones	23		16	0												2	0	
98	Oliver Gibson	23		12	0												1	1	
89	Ernie Mills	27	KR	16	4							0	2	1	0	0			
33	Bam Morris	23		13	4							0	3	0	0	0			
14	Neil O'Donnell	29	QB	12	12							0	2	1	0	0			
18	Mike Tomczak	33		7	4							0	2	1	0	0			
22	John L. Williams	31	FB	11	9							0	2	1	0	0			
88	Andre Hastings	24	PR	16	0							0	1	0	0	0			
81	Charles Johnson	23	WR	15	10							0	0	1	0	0			
25	Fred McAfee	27		16	1							0	0	1	0	0			
16	Jim Miller	24		3	0							0	1	0	0	0			
66	Tom Newberry	33	LG	16	15							0	0	1	0	0			
72	Leon Searcy	26	RT	16	16							0	0	1	0	0			
82	Yancey Thigpen*	26	WR	16	15							0	1	0	0	0			
26	Rod Woodson	30		1	1												0	1	
	Team Total	26.8		16		42.0	22	361	3	63	0	18	24	21	74	2	627	190	
	Opp Total			16		24							30	18					

1996 PITTSBURGH STEELERS: 10-6-0, 1ST IN AFC CENTRAL DIVISION
Head Coach: Bill Cowher

Week	Day	Date	OT	Rec	Opp	Tm	Opp	1stD	TotYd	PassY	RushY	TO	1stD	TotYd	PassY	RushY	TO
						Score			**Offe**					**Defe**			
1	Sun	September 1	L	0-1	Jacksonville Jaguars	9	24	13	187	86	101	2	22	313	194	119	2
2	Sun	September 8	W	1-1	Baltimore Ravens	31	17	26	397	191	206	2	17	251	154	97	3
3	Mon	September 16	W	2-1	Buffalo Bills	24	6	22	382	160	222	1	11	185	99	86	4
4					Bye Week												
5	Sun	September 29	W	3-1	Houston Oilers	30	16	15	309	197	112	2	16	273	193	80	5
6	Mon	October 7	W	4-1	Kansas City Chiefs	17	7	21	436	338	98	3	17	300	170	130	3
7	Sun	October 13	W	5-1	Cincinnati Bengals	20	10	17	306	182	124	2	20	252	158	94	2
8	Sun	October 20	L	5-2	Houston Oilers	13	23	12	275	192	83	2	23	328	237	91	2
9	Sun	October 27	W	6-2	Atlanta Falcons	20	17	20	311	184	127		19	301	234	67	1
10	Sun	November 3	W	7-2	St. Louis Rams	42	6	20	348	100	248	1	18	201	137	64	3
11	Sun	November 10	L	7-3	Cincinnati Bengals	24	34	18	317	180	137	4	25	372	260	112	3
12	Sun	November 17	W	8-3	Jacksonville Jaguars	28	3	15	198	90	108	1	20	239	161	78	4
13	Mon	November 25	W	9-3	Miami Dolphins	24	17	23	381	239	142	3	15	312	237	75	1
14	Sun	December 1	L	9-4	Baltimore Ravens	17	31	18	333	214	119	1	19	372	250	122	1
15	Sun	December 8	W	10-4	San Diego Chargers	16	3	21	327	160	167	4	8	148	83	65	4
16	Sun	December 15	L	10-5	San Francisco 49ers	15	25	23	368	248	120	3	21	288	232	56	2
17	Sun	December 22	L	10-6	Carolina Panthers	14	18	12	265	80	185	2	15	227	148	79	2
Playoffs																	
Wild Card	Sun	December 29	W	11-6	Indianapolis Colts	42	14	24	407	176	231	3	8	146	105	41	2
Division	Sun	January 5	L	11-7	New England Patriots	3	28	12	213	90	123	2	17	346	152	194	2

Passing

No.		Age	Pos	G	GS	QBrec	Cmp	Att	Cmp%	Yds	TD	TD%	Int	Int%	Lng	Y/A	AY/A	Y/C	Y/G	Rate	Sk	Yds
18	Mike Tomczak	34	QB	16	15	10-5-0	222	401	55.4	2767	15	3.7	17	4.2	70	6.9	5.7	12.5	172.9	71.8	16	105
10	Kordell Stewart	24		16	2		11	30	36.7	100	0	0.0	2	6.7	15	3.3	0.3	9.1	6.3	18.8	3	37
16	Jim Miller	25		2	1	0-1-0	13	25	52.0	123	0	0.0	0	0.0	17	4.9	4.9	9.5	61.5	65.9	2	7
	Team Total	26.7		16		10-6-0	246	456	53.9	2990	15	3.3	19	4.2	70	6.6	5.3	12.2	186.9	68.0	21	149
	Opp Total			16			322	547	58.9	3316	17	3.1	23	4.2		6.1	4.8	10.3	207.3	69.2	51	369

Rushing and Receiving

No.		Age	Pos	G	GS	Rush Att	Yds	TD	Lng	Y/A	Y/G	A/G	Rec	Yds	Y/R	TD	Lng	R/G	Y/G	YScm
36	Jerome Bettis*+	24	RB	16	12	320	1431	11	50	4.5	89.4	20.0	22	122	5.5	0	16	1.4	7.6	1553
20	Erric Pegram	27		12	4	97	509	1	27	5.2	42.4	8.1	17	112	6.6	0	14	1.4	9.3	621
10	Kordell Stewart	24		16	2	39	171	5	80	4.4	10.7	2.4	17	293	17.2	3	48	1.1	18.3	464
18	Mike Tomczak	34	QB	16	15	22	−7	0	6	−0.3	−0.4	1.4								−7
38	Jon Witman	24		16	4	17	69	0	15	4.1	4.3	1.1	2	15	7.5	0	11	0.1	0.9	84
34	Tim Lester	28	FB	16	13	8	20	1	5	2.5	1.3	0.5	7	70	10.0	0	19	0.4	4.4	90
25	Fred McAfee	28		14	0	7	17	0	5	2.4	1.2	0.5	5	21	4.2	0	9	0.4	1.5	38
44	Terry Richardson	25		1	0	5	17	0	8	3.4	17.0	5.0								17
88	Andre Hastings	25	WR/PR	16	10	4	71	0	37	17.8	4.4	0.3	72	739	10.3	6	38	4.5	46.2	810
89	Ernie Mills	28		9	3	2	24	0	15	12.0	2.7	0.2	7	92	13.1	1	22	0.8	10.2	116
16	Jim Miller	25		2	1	2	−4	0	0	−2.0	−2.0	1.0								−4
80	Jahine Arnold	23	KR	9	0	1	−3	0	−3	−3.0	−0.3	0.1	6	76	12.7	0	26	0.7	8.4	73
14	Shayne Edge	25		4	0	1	−16	0	−16	−16.0	−4.0	0.3								−16
81	Charles Johnson	24	WR	16	12	0	0	0	0		0.0	0.0	60	1008	16.8	3	70	3.8	63.0	1008
87	Mark Bruener	24	TE	12	12	0	0	0	0		0.0	0.0	12	141	11.8	0	36	1.0	11.8	141
82	Yancey Thigpen	27		6	2	0	0	0	0		0.0	0.0	12	244	20.3	2	39	2.0	40.7	244
84	Kirk Botkin	25		16	0	0	0	0	0		0.0	0.0	4	36	9.0	0	17	0.3	2.3	36
85	Jonathan Hayes	34	te	16	6	0	0	0	0		0.0	0.0	2	14	7.0	0	7	0.1	0.9	14
83	Corey Holliday	25		12	0	0	0	0	0		0.0	0.0	1	7	7.0	0	7	0.1	0.6	7
	Team Total	26.7		16		525	2299	18	80	4.4	143.7	32.8	246	2990	12.2	15	70	15.4	186.9	5289
	Opp Total			16		411	1415	7		3.4	88.4	25.7	322	2947	9.2	17		20.1	184.2	4362

Defense

No.		Age	Pos	G	GS	Sk	Def Int	Yds	TD	Lng	PD	Fumb FF	Fmb	FR	Yds	TD	Tack Tkl	Ast	Sfty
99	Levon Kirkland*	27	LILB	16	16	4.0	4	12	0	6	0	2	0	0	0	0	75	38	
94	Chad Brown*+	26	ROLB	14	14	13.0	2	20	0	16	0	3	1	2	0	0	50	31	
39	Darren Perry	28	FS	16	16	1.0	5	115	1	28	0	2	1	2	0	0	61	18	
27	Willie J. Williams	26	RCB	15	14	1.0	1	1	0	1	0	2	0	1	0	0	66	10	
26	Rod Woodson*	31	LCB	16	16	1.0	6	121	1	43	0	0	1	3	42	1	57	10	
21	Deon Figures	26		16	3		2	13	0	13	0	0	0	1	0	0	54	5	
92	Jason Gildon	24	LOLB	14	13	7.0						2	0	0	0	0	47	12	
55	Jerry Olsavsky	29	RILB	15	13	0.5	1	5	0	5	0	0	0	1	6	0	46	17	
37	Carnell Lake*	29	SS	13	13	2.0	1	47	1	47	0	2	0	2	85	1	44	10	
93	Joel Steed	27	NT	16	14							0	0	1	0	0	32	13	
40	Myron Bell	25		16	4	2.0						3	0	2	0	0	28	8	
96	Brentson Buckner	25	LDE	15	14	3.0						0	1	1	13	0	24	12	
90	Bill E. Johnson	28	lde	15	8	1.0						0	0	1	0	0	18	11	
76	Kevin Henry	28	RDE	12	10	1.5						1	0	1	4	0	13	10	
98	Oliver Gibson	24		16	0	2.5											7	8	
54	Donta Jones	24		15	2	1.0											9	3	
50	Earl Holmes	23		3	1	1.0											9	1	
29	Randy Fuller	26		14	1		1	0	0	0	0						7	2	
24	Chris Oldham	28		16	0	2.0											7	0	
57	Eric Ravotti	25		15	2	2.0						0	0	1	9	0	5	3	

No.		Age	Pos	G	GS	Sk	Int	Yds	TD	Lng	PD	FF	Fmb	FR	Yds	TD	Tkl	Ast	Sfty
								Def					Fumb				Tack		
51	Carlos Emmons	23		15	0	2.5						1	0	1	0	0	5	2	
36	Jerome Bettis*+	24	RB	16	12							0	7	2	0	0			
18	Mike Tomczak	34	QB	16	15							0	7	2	0	0			
41	Lee Flowers	23		16	0												3	0	
95	Greg Lloyd	31		1	1	1.0											2	0	
71	Orpheus Roye	23		13	1							0	0	1	0	0	1	2	
88	Andre Hastings	25	WR/PR	16	10							0	3	1	0	0			
91	Israel Raybon	23		3	0	1.0											1	0	
20	Erric Pegram	27		12	4							0	1	1	0	0			
80	Jahine Arnold	23	KR	9	0							0	1	0	0	0			
65	John Jackson	31	LT	16	16							0	0	1	0	0			
81	Charles Johnson	24	WR	16	12							0	1	0	0	0			
34	Tim Lester	28	FB	16	13							0	1	0	0	0			
16	Jim Miller	25		2	1							0	1	0	-4	0			
89	Ernie Mills	28		9	3							0	0	1	5	0			
10	Kordell Stewart	24		16	2							0	1	0	0	0			
	Team Total	26.7		16		50.0	23	334	3	47	0	18	27	29	160	2	671	226	
	Opp Total			16		21							28	11						3

1997 PITTSBURGH STEELERS: 11-5-0, 1ST IN AFC CENTRAL DIVISION
Head Coach: Bill Cowher

Week	Day	Date	OT	Rec	Opp	Tm	Opp	1stD	TotYd	PassY	RushY	TO	1stD	TotYd	PassY	RushY	TO
						Score		Offe					Defe				
1	Sun	August 31	L	0-1	Dallas Cowboys	7	37	15	174	89	85	2	21	380	295	85	
2	Sun	September 7	W	1-1	Washington Redskins	14	13	23	295	73	222	1	19	354	285	69	3
3					Bye Week												
4	Mon	September 22	L	1-2	Jacksonville Jaguars	21	30	19	306	153	153	2	23	343	303	40	
5	Sun	September 28	W	2-2	Tennessee Oilers	37	24	19	399	262	137	1	20	284	226	58	3
6	Sun	October 5	W	3-2	Baltimore Ravens	42	34	22	431	217	214	3	20	332	280	52	5
7	Sun	October 12	W	4-2	Indianapolis Colts	24	22	17	327	142	185	6	18	270	101	70	2
8	Sun	October 19	W	5-2	Cincinnati Bengals	26	10	24	412	246	166	2	13	236	165	71	4
9	Sun	October 26	W	OT	6-2	Jacksonville Jaguars	23	17	26	439	298	141	3	16	267	194	73	1
10	Mon	November 3	L	6-3	Kansas City Chiefs	10	13	12	235	93	142	1	24	392	209	183	2
11	Sun	November 9	W	7-3	Baltimore Ravens	37	0	19	341	198	143		11	172	112	60	7
12	Sun	November 16	W	8-3	Cincinnati Bengals	20	3	20	309	123	186		16	244	128	116	3
13	Sun	November 23	L	8-4	Philadelphia Eagles	20	23	22	383	272	111	5	19	326	229	97	
14	Sun	November 30	W	OT	9-4	Arizona Cardinals	26	20	25	342	165	177		18	291	243	48	
15	Sun	December 7	W	10-4	Denver Broncos	35	24	22	476	290	186	2	18	320	231	89	1
16	Sat	December 13	W	OT	11-4	New England Patriots	24	21	22	404	266	138	2	15	253	211	42	2
17	Sun	December 21	L	11-5	Tennessee Oilers	6	16	19	269	176	93	3	14	241	85	156	1
		Playoffs															
Division	Sat	January 3	W	12-5	New England Patriots	7	6	16	279	134	145	1	15	280	244	36	4
Conf Champ	Sun	January 11	L	12-6	Denver Broncos	21	24	23	354	193	161	4	23	345	195	150	2

Passing

No.		Age	Pos	G	GS	QBrec	Cmp	Att	Cmp%	Yds	TD	TD%	Int	Int%	Lng	Y/A	AY/A	Y/C	Y/G	Rate	Sk	Yds
10	Kordell Stewart	25	QB	16	16	11-5-0	236	440	53.6	3020	21	4.8	17	3.9	69	6.9	6.1	12.8	188.8	75.2	20	152
18	Mike Tomczak	35		16	0		16	24	66.7	185	1	4.2	2	8.3	28	7.7	4.8	11.6	11.6	68.9	0	0
11	Mike Quinn	23		1	0		1	2	50.0	10	0	0.0	0	0.0	10	5.0	5.0	10.0	10.0	64.6	0	0
	Team Total	27.2		16		11-5-0	253	466	54.3	3215	22	4.7	19	4.1	69	6.9	6.0	12.7	200.9	74.8	20	152
	Opp Total			16			295	554	53.2	3681	24	4.3	20	3.6		6.6	5.9	12.5	230.1	73.5	48	294

Rushing and Receiving

No.		Age	Pos	G	GS	Rush Att	Yds	TD	Lng	Y/A	Y/G	A/G	Rec	Yds	Y/R	TD	Lng	R/G	Y/G	YScm
36	Jerome Bettis*	25	RB	15	15	375	1665	7	34	4.4	111.0	25.0	15	110	7.3	2	19	1.0	7.3	1775
10	Kordell Stewart	25	QB	16	16	88	476	11	74	5.4	29.8	5.5								476
43	George Jones	24		16	1	72	235	1	32	3.3	14.7	4.5	16	96	6.0	1	25	1.0	6.0	331
25	Fred McAfee	29		14	0	13	41	0	9	3.2	2.9	0.9	2	44	22.0	0	30	0.1	3.1	85
18	Mike Tomczak	35		16	0	7	13	0	17	1.9	0.8	0.4								13
88	Courtney Hawkins	28		15	3	5	17	0	11	3.4	1.1	0.3	45	555	12.3	3	44	3.0	37.0	572
38	Jon Witman	25		16	2	5	11	0	4	2.2	0.7	0.3	1	3	3.0	0	3	0.1	0.2	14
89	Will Blackwell	22	PR/KR	14	0	2	14	0	11	7.0	1.0	0.1	12	168	14.0	1	46	0.9	12.0	182
34	Tim Lester	29	FB	16	13	2	9	0	6	4.5	0.6	0.1	10	51	5.1	0	14	0.6	3.2	60
82	Yancey Thigpen*	28	WR	16	15	1	3	0	3	3.0	0.2	0.1	79	1398	17.7	7	69	4.9	87.4	1401
17	Curtis Marsh	27		5	0	1	2	0	2	2.0	0.4	0.2	2	14	7.0	0	8	0.4	2.8	16
4	Josh Miller	27	P	16	0	1	−7	0	−7	−7.0	−0.4	0.1								−7
81	Charles Johnson	25	WR	13	11	0	0	0	0		0.0	0.0	46	568	12.3	2	49	3.5	43.7	568
87	Mark Bruener	25	TE	16	16	0	0	0	0		0.0	0.0	18	117	6.5	6	18	1.1	7.3	117
85	Mitch Lyons	27		10	3	0	0	0	0		0.0	0.0	4	29	7.3	0	13	0.4	2.9	29
86	Mike Adams	23		6	0	0	0	0	0		0.0	0.0	1	39	39.0	0	39	0.2	6.5	39
84	Kirk Botkin	26		13	1	0	0	0	0		0.0	0.0	1	11	11.0	0	11	0.1	0.8	11
46	Troy Sadowski	32		6	0	0	0	0	0		0.0	0.0	1	12	12.0	0	12	0.2	2.0	12
	Team Total	27.2		16		572	2479	19	74	4.3	154.9	35.8	253	3215	12.7	22	69	15.8	200.9	5694
	Opp Total			16		403	1318	5		3.3	82.4	25.2	295	3387	11.5	24		18.4	211.7	4705

Defense

No.		Age	Pos	G	GS	Sk	Def Int	Yds	TD	Lng	PD	Fumb FF	Fmb	FR	Yds	TD	Tack Tkl	Ast	Sfty
99	Levon Kirkland*+	28	LILB	16	16	5.0	2	14	0	11	0	1	0	1	0	0	95	31	
50	Earl Holmes	24	RILB	16	16	4.0						0	0	1	0	0	67	29	
39	Darren Perry	29	FS	16	16	1.0	4	77	0	42	0	1	0	0	0	0	68	10	
37	Carnell Lake*+	30	RCB/ss	16	16	6.0	3	16	0	11	0	2	0	1	38	1	43	17	
40	Myron Bell	26	SS	16	8	1.5	1	10	0	7	0	0	0	1	0	0	40	18	
92	Jason Gildon	25	LOLB	16	16	5.0						0	0	2	32	1	41	12	
21	Donnell Woolford	31	LCB	15	12		4	91	0	34	0						46	5	
30	Chad Scott	23	rcb	13	9		2	−4	0	0	0						45	2	
76	Kevin Henry	29	RDE	16	16	4.5	1	36	0	36	0	0	0	2	0	0	35	16	
95	Greg Lloyd	32	ROLB	12	12	3.5						3	1	3	61	0	30	22	
93	Joel Steed*	28	NT	16	16	1.0						0	0	1	0	0	27	21	
29	Randy Fuller	27		12	3	1.0						1	0	0	0	0	28	2	
74	Nolan Harrison	28	LDE	16	16	4.0						2	0	0	0	0	22	9	
24	Chris Oldham	29		16	0	4.0	2	16	0	8	0	3	0	0	0	0	21	2	
96	Mike Vrabel	22		15	0	1.5						2	0	1	0	0	14	3	
98	Oliver Gibson	25		16	0	1.0						0	0	1	0	0	9	1	
54	Donta Jones	25		16	0	4						0	0	1	6	0	6	6	
53	Steve Conley	25		16	0	4.0	1	−3	0	−3	0						5	1	
27	J. B. Brown	30		13	0												5	0	
71	Orpheus Roye	24		16	0	1.0						1	0	0	0	0	3	1	
36	Jerome Bettis*	25	RB	15	15							0	6	1	0	0			
55	Jerry Olsavsky	30		16	0												3	1	
10	Kordell Stewart	25	QB	16	16							0	6	1	−1	0			
89	Will Blackwell	22	PR/KR	14	0							0	3	2	0	0			
43	George Jones	24		16	1							0	3	1	0	0			
41	Lee Flowers	24		10	0							0	0	1	0	0	1	0	
51	Carlos Emmons	24		5	0												1	0	
82	Yancey Thigpen*	28	WR	16	15							0	1	1	0	0			
86	Mike Adams	23		6	0							0	1	0	0	0			
87	Mark Bruener	25	TE	16	16							0	1	0	0	0			
19	Andre Coleman	25		8	0							0	1	0	0	0			
88	Courtney Hawkins	28		15	3							0	1	0	0	0			
25	Fred McAfee	29		14	0							0	1	0	0	0			
	Team Total	27.2		16		48.0	20	253	0	42	0	16	25	22	136	2	655	209	
	Opp Total			16		20							26	12					1

1998 PITTSBURGH STEELERS: 7-9-0, 3RD IN AFC CENTRAL DIVISION
Head Coach: Bill Cowher

Week	Day	Date	OT	Rec	Opp	Score		Offe					Defe				
						Tm	Opp	1stD	TotYd	PassY	RushY	TO	1stD	TotYd	PassY	RushY	TO
1	Sun	September 6	W	1-0	Baltimore Ravens	20	13	14	271	157	114	3	17	376	264	112	
2	Sun	September 13	W	2-0	Chicago Bears	17	12	17	251	109	142	1	19	320	190	130	2
3	Sun	September 20	L	2-1	Miami Dolphins	0	21	13	200	78	122	3	11	219	109	110	1
4	Sun	September 27	W	3-1	Seattle Seahawks	13	10	16	285	100	185		14	230	169	61	4
5					Bye Week												
6	Sun	October 11	L	3-2	Cincinnati Bengals	20	25	20	386	129	257	1	17	389	281	108	
7	Sun	October 18	W	4-2	Baltimore Ravens	16	6	13	241	162	79	2	16	230	134	96	5
8	Mon	October 26	W	5-2	Kansas City Chiefs	20	13	20	272	90	182	1	16	290	218	72	3
9	Sun	November 1	L	5-3	Tennessee Oilers	31	41	26	401	347	54	3	19	321	152	169	
10	Mon	November 9	W	6-3	Green Bay Packers	27	20	19	360	218	142	1	17	256	217	39	1
11	Sun	November 15	L	6-4	Tennessee Oilers	14	23	16	310	231	79	2	18	338	230	108	1
12	Sun	November 22	W	7-4	Jacksonville Jaguars	30	15	18	329	208	121		17	301	204	97	4
13	Thu	November 26	L	OT	7-5	Detroit Lions	16	19	22	293	208	85	2	13	283	213	70	2
14	Sun	December 6	L		7-6	New England Patriots	9	23	13	249	195	54	3	19	377	304	73	3
15	Sun	December 13	L		7-7	Tampa Bay Buccaneers	3	16	10	166	78	88	5	14	253	109	144	1
16	Sun	December 20	L		7-8	Cincinnati Bengals	24	25	11	211	86	125	2	23	483	359	124	2
17	Mon	December 28	L		7-9	Jacksonville Jaguars	3	21	20	361	156	205	3	16	297	168	129	

Passing

No.		Age	Pos	G	GS	QBrec	Cmp	Att	Cmp%	Yds	TD	TD%	Int	Int%	Lng	Y/A	AY/A	Y/C	Y/G	Rate	Sk	Yds
10	Kordell Stewart	26	QB	16	16	7-9-0	252	458	55.0	2560	11	2.4	18	3.9	55	5.6	4.3	10.2	160.0	62.9	33	211
18	Mike Tomczak	36		16	0		21	30	70.0	204	2	6.7	2	6.7	42	6.8	5.1	9.7	12.8	83.2	2	18
86	Hines Ward	22		16	0		1	1	100.0	17	0	0.0	0	0.0	17	17.0	17.0	17.0	1.1	118.7	0	0
	Team Total	27.2		16		7-9-0	274	489	56.0	2781	13	2.7	20	4.1	55	5.7	4.4	10.1	173.8	64.3	35	229
	Opp Total			16			268	482	55.6	3559	17	3.5	16	3.3		7.4	6.6	13.3	222.4	77.1	41	238

Rushing and Receiving

No.		Age	Pos	G	GS	Rush							Receiving							
						Att	Yds	TD	Lng	Y/A	Y/G	A/G	Rec	Yds	Y/R	TD	Lng	R/G	Y/G	YScm
36	Jerome Bettis	26	RB	15	15	316	1185	3	42	3.8	79.0	21.1	16	90	5.6	0	26	1.1	6.0	1275
10	Kordell Stewart	26	QB	16	16	81	406	2	56	5.0	25.4	5.1	1	17	17.0	0	17	0.1	1.1	423
33	Richard Huntley	26		16	1	55	242	1	48	4.4	15.1	3.4	3	18	6.0	0	7	0.2	1.1	260
25	Fred McAfee	30		14	0	18	111	0	14	6.2	7.9	1.3	9	27	3.0	0	11	0.6	1.9	138
88	Courtney Hawkins	29	WR/PR	15	14	10	41	0	14	4.1	2.7	0.7	66	751	11.4	1	53	4.4	50.1	792
45	Chris Fuamatu-Maafala	21		12	0	7	30	2	10	4.3	2.5	0.6	9	84	9.3	1	26	0.8	7.0	114
81	Charles Johnson	26	WR	16	16	1	4	0	4	4.0	0.3	0.1	65	815	12.5	7	55	4.1	50.9	819
86	Hines Ward	22		16	0	1	13	0	13	13.0	0.8	0.1	15	246	16.4	0	45	0.9	15.4	259
38	Jon Witman	26	FB	16	8	1	2	0	2	2.0	0.1	0.1	13	74	5.7	0	15	0.8	4.6	76
89	Will Blackwell	23		16	2	0	0	0	0		0.0	0.0	32	297	9.3	1	24	2.0	18.6	297
87	Mark Bruener	26	TE	16	16	0	0	0	0		0.0	0.0	19	157	8.3	2	20	1.2	9.8	157
83	David Dunn	26	KR	10	0	0	0	0	0		0.0	0.0	9	87	9.7	0	24	0.9	8.7	87
34	Tim Lester	30	fb	9	7	0	0	0	0		0.0	0.0	9	46	5.1	0	9	1.0	5.1	46
83	Andre Coleman	26		4	0	0	0	0	0		0.0	0.0	4	49	12.3	1	13	1.0	12.3	49
85	Mitch Lyons	28		15	0	0	0	0	0		0.0	0.0	3	19	6.3	0	11	0.2	1.3	19
84	Harold Bishop	28		7	1	0	0	0	0		0.0	0.0	1	4	4.0	0	4	0.1	0.6	4
	Team Total	27.2		16		490	2034	8	56	4.2	127.1	30.6	274	2781	10.1	13	55	17.1	173.8	4815
	Opp Total			16		479	1642	8		3.4	102.6	29.9	268	3321	12.4	17		16.8	207.6	4963

Defense

No.		Age	Pos	G	GS	Sk	Int	Yds	TD	Lng	PD	FF	Fmb	FR	Yds	TD	Tkl	Ast	Sfty
								Def					**Fumb**				**Tack**		
99	Levon Kirkland	29	LILB	16	16	2.5	1	1	0	1	0	3	0	0	0	0	79	38	
41	Lee Flowers	25	SS	16	16	1.0	1	2	0	2	0	3	0	2	0	0	78	23	
20	Dewayne Washington	26	RCB	16	16		5	178	2	78	0	0	0	2	0	0	79	14	
37	Carnell Lake	31	LCB	16	16	1.0	4	33	1	27	0	0	0	1	-2	0	63	6	
50	Earl Holmes	25	RILB	14	14	1.5	1	36	0	36	0						55	25	
39	Darren Perry	30	FS	14	14	0.5	2	69	0	40	0	1	1	1	0	0	54	14	
51	Carlos Emmons	25	ROLB	15	14	3.5	1	2	0	2	0	2	0	1	0	0	46	17	
92	Jason Gildon	26	LOLB	16	16	11.0						2	0	1	0	0	42	12	
93	Joel Steed	29	NT	16	16	1.0						1	0	0	0	0	37	12	
71	Orpheus Roye	25	LDE	16	9	3.5											29	13	
76	Kevin Henry	30	RDE	16	16	4.0											27	13	
24	Chris Oldham	30		16	1	0.5	1	14	0	14	0	0	0	5	79	1	17	8	
54	Donta Jones	26		16	4	3.0											17	11	
74	Nolan Harrison	29	lde	9	7	3.5											11	8	
98	Oliver Gibson	26		16	0	2.0											10	5	
26	Deshea Townsend	23		12	0												9	2	
56	Mike Vrabel	23		11	0	2.5											6	3	
23	Jason Simmons	22		6	0							1	0	0	0	0	7	1	
33	Richard Huntley	26		16	1							0	5	0	0	0			
21	Bo Orlando	32		11	1												2	1	
10	Kordell Stewart	26	QB	16	16							0	3	2	0	0			
53	Steve Conley	26		2	0												1	1	
36	Jerome Bettis	26	RB	15	15							0	2	0	0	0			
29	Lance Brown	26		16	0							0	0	2	1	0			
57	John Fiala	25		16	0												0	2	
88	Courtney Hawkins	29	WR/PR	15	14							0	1	1	0	0			
97	Rod Manuel	24		2	0												1	0	
18	Mike Tomczak	36		16	0							0	2	0	0	0			
89	Will Blackwell	23		16	2							0	1	0	0	0			
83	Andre Coleman	26		4	0							0	1	0	0	0			
63	Dermontti Dawson*+	33	C	16	16							0	1	0	-25	0			
83	David Dunn	26	KR	10	0							0	1	0	0	0			
77	Will Wolford	34	LT	13	13							0	0	1	0	0			
	Team Total	27.2		16		41.0	16	335	3	78	0	13	18	19	53	1	670	229	
	Opp Total			16		35							28	15					

1999 PITTSBURGH STEELERS: 6-10-0, 4TH IN AFC CENTRAL DIVISION
Head Coach: Bill Cowher

Week	Day	Date	OT	Rec	Opp	Tm	Opp	1stD	TotYd	PassY	RushY	TO	1stD	TotYd	PassY	RushY	TO
						Score		**Offe**					**Defe**				
1	Sun	September 12	W	1-0	Cleveland Browns	43	0	33	464	247	217		2	40	31	9	4
2	Sun	September 19	W	2-0	Baltimore Ravens	23	20	19	270	121	149		16	292	167	125	3
3	Sun	September 26	L	2-1	Seattle Seahawks	10	29	15	272	207	65	5	16	341	251	90	2
4	Sun	October 3	L	2-2	Jacksonville Jaguars	3	17	14	216	99	117	2	13	204	80	124	1
5	Sun	October 10	L	2-3	Buffalo Bills	21	24	17	255	207	48	1	24	365	254	111	1
6	Sun	October 17	W	3-3	Cincinnati Bengals	17	3	18	255	125	130		14	261	177	84	3
7	Mon	October 25	W	4-3	Atlanta Falcons	13	9	14	226	115	111	1	20	236	187	49	1
8					Bye Week												
9	Sun	November 7	W	5-3	San Francisco 49ers	27	6	14	271	130	141		16	313	90	223	2
10	Sun	November 14	L	5-4	Cleveland Browns	15	16	17	298	130	168	2	14	235	161	74	2
11	Sun	November 21	L	5-5	Tennessee Titans	10	16	14	267	161	106	1	17	261	149	112	1
12	Sun	November 28	L	5-6	Cincinnati Bengals	20	27	20	391	280	111	3	18	415	235	180	1
13	Thu	December 2	L	5-7	Jacksonville Jaguars	6	20	15	235	172	63		24	466	298	168	1
14	Sun	December 12	L	5-8	Baltimore Ravens	24	31	21	352	243	109	1	12	374	242	132	
15	Sat	December 18	L	5-9	Kansas City Chiefs	19	35	21	376	269	107	4	16	363	145	218	
16	Sun	December 26	W	6-9	Carolina Panthers	30	20	21	293	82	211	1	17	375	256	119	3
17	Sun	January 2	L	6-10	Tennessee Titans	36	47	22	433	295	138	4	21	343	203	140	3

Passing

No.		Age	Pos	G	GS	QBrec	Cmp	Att	Cmp%	Yds	TD	TD%	Int	Int%	Lng	Y/A	AY/A	Y/C	Y/G	Rate	Sk	Yds
10	Kordell Stewart	27	QB	16	12	5-6-0	160	275	58.2	1464	6	2.2	10	3.6	42	5.3	4.1	9.2	91.5	64.9	22	131
18	Mike Tomczak	37	qb	16	5	1-4-0	139	258	53.9	1625	12	4.7	8	3.1	49	6.3	5.8	11.7	101.6	75.8	15	104
36	Jerome Bettis	27	RB	16	16		1	1	100.0	21	1	100.0	0	0.0	21	21.0	41.0	21.0	1.3	158.3	0	0
7	Pete Gonzalez	25		1	0		1	1	100.0	8	0	0.0	0	0.0	8	8.0	8.0	8.0	8.0	100.0	0	0
	Team Total	26.4		16		6-10-0	301	535	56.3	3118	19	3.6	18	3.4	49	5.8	5.0	10.4	194.9	71.1	37	235
	Opp Total			16			245	463	52.9	3167	20	4.3	14	3.0		6.8	6.3	12.9	197.9	76.5	39	241

Rushing and Receiving

No.		Age	Pos	G	GS	Rush Att	Yds	TD	Lng	Y/A	Y/G	A/G	Rec	Yds	Y/R	TD	Lng	R/G	Y/G	YScm
36	Jerome Bettis	27	RB	16	16	299	1091	7	35	3.6	68.2	18.7	21	110	5.2	0	17	1.3	6.9	1201
33	Richard Huntley	27	KR	16	2	93	567	5	52	6.1	35.4	5.8	27	253	9.4	3	25	1.7	15.8	820
10	Kordell Stewart	27	QB	16	12	56	258	2	21	4.6	16.1	3.5	9	113	12.6	1	28	0.6	7.1	371
21	Amos Zereoue	23		8	0	18	48	0	8	2.7	6.0	2.3	2	17	8.5	0	14	0.3	2.1	65
18	Mike Tomczak	37	qb	16	5	16	19	0	17	1.2	1.2	1.0								19
38	Jon Witman	27	FB	16	11	6	18	0	7	3.0	1.1	0.4	12	106	8.8	0	38	0.8	6.6	124
86	Hines Ward	23	WR	16	14	2	−2	0	3	−1.0	−0.1	0.1	61	638	10.5	7	42	3.8	39.9	636
7	Pete Gonzalez	25		1	0	2	−3	0	−1	−1.5	−3.0	2.0								−3
4	Josh Miller	29	P	16	0	2	−9	0	0	−4.5	−0.6	0.1								−9
45	Chris Fuamatu-Maafala	22		10	0	1	4	0	4	4.0	0.4	0.1								4
81	Troy Edwards	22	PR/wr	16	6	0	0	0	0		0.0	0.0	61	714	11.7	5	41	3.8	44.6	714
88	Courtney Hawkins	30	WR	11	11	0	0	0	0		0.0	0.0	30	285	9.5	0	23	2.7	25.9	285
82	Bobby Shaw	24		15	1	0	0	0	0		0.0	0.0	28	387	13.8	3	49	1.9	25.8	387
89	Will Blackwell	24		11	1	0	0	0	0		0.0	0.0	20	186	9.3	0	26	1.8	16.9	186
87	Mark Bruener	27	TE	14	14	0	0	0	0		0.0	0.0	18	176	9.8	0	29	1.3	12.6	176
85	Mitch Lyons	29		14	2	0	0	0	0		0.0	0.0	8	81	10.1	0	25	0.6	5.8	81
80	Matt Cushing	24		7	1	0	0	0	0		0.0	0.0	2	29	14.5	0	22	0.3	4.1	29
83	Malcolm Johnson	22		6	0	0	0	0	0		0.0	0.0	2	23	11.5	0	18	0.3	3.8	23
	Team Total	26.4		16		495	1991	14	52	4.0	124.4	30.9	301	3118	10.4	19	49	18.8	194.9	5109
	Opp Total			16		451	1958	10		4.3	122.4	28.2	245	2926	11.9	20		15.3	182.9	4884

Defense

No.		Age	Pos	G	GS	Def Sk	Int	Yds	TD	Lng	PD	Fumb FF	Fmb	FR	Yds	TD	Tack Tkl	Ast	Sfty
50	Earl Holmes	26	RILB	16	16							0	0	1	0	0	89	26	
99	Levon Kirkland	30	LILB	16	16	2.0	1	23	0	23	0	4	0	2	0	0	89	22	
41	Lee Flowers	26	SS	15	15	5.0						1	0	0	0	0	64	15	
51	Carlos Emmons	26	ROLB	16	16	6.0	1	22	0	22	0	1	0	3	2	0	51	16	
92	Jason Gildon	27	LOLB	16	16	8.5						1	0	0	0	0	42	15	
20	Dewayne Washington	27	RCB	16	16		4	1	0	1	0						50	2	
71	Orpheus Roye	26	LDE	16	16	4.5	1	2	0	2	0	1	0	1	0	0	41	17	
27	Travis Davis	26	FS	16	16		1	1	0	1	0	1	0	1	102	1	43	15	
30	Chad Scott	25	LCB	13	12		1	16	0	16	0						49	1	
26	Deshea Townsend	24		16	4												27	4	
76	Kevin Henry	31	RDE	16	13	1.0											22	8	
93	Joel Steed	30	NT	14	14	3.0						0	0	1	4	0	16	14	
47	Scott Shields	23		16	1	1.0	4	75	0	25	0	1	0	0	0	0	14	4	
24	Chris Oldham	31		15	0	3.0	1	9	0	9	0	1	0	1	0	0	12	1	
55	Joey Porter	22		16	0	2.0						1	0	2	50	1	10	0	
94	Jeremy Staat	23		16	2												8	3	
56	Mike Vrabel	24		10	0	2.0						1	0	1	0	0	4	1	
74	Nolan Harrison	30		5	3							0	0	1	0	0	4	2	
23	Jason Simmons	23		16	0							0	0	1	0	0	3	1	
81	Troy Edwards	22	PR/wr	16	6							0	4	3	0	0			

(Continued)

							Def					Fumb					Tack		
No.		Age	Pos	G	GS	Sk	Int	Yds	TD	Lng	PD	FF	Fmb	FR	Yds	TD	Tkl	Ast	Sfty
36	Jerome Bettis	27	RB	16	16							0	2	3	1	0			
10	Kordell Stewart	27	QB	16	12							0	4	1	0	0			
33	Richard Huntley	27	KR	16	2							0	3	0	0	0			
91	Aaron Smith	23		6	0												1	1	
18	Mike Tomczak	37	qb	16	5							0	3	0	−6	0			
87	Mark Bruener	27	TE	14	14							0	0	2	4	0			
89	Will Blackwell	24		11	1							0	1	0	0	0			
29	Lance Brown	27		16	0	1.0													
97	Chad Kelsay	22		6	0												0	1	
4	Josh Miller	29	P	16	0							0	1	0	−11	0			
86	Hines Ward	23	WR	16	14							0	1	0	0	0			
	Team Total	26.4		16		39.0	14	149	0	25	0	13	19	24	146	2	639	169	
	Opp Total			16		37							29	15					5

2000 PITTSBURGH STEELERS: 9-7-0, 3RD IN AFC CENTRAL DIVISON

Head Coach: Bill Cowher

							Score		Offe					Defe				
Week	Day	Date		OT	Rec	Opp	Tm	Opp	1stD	TotYd	PassY	RushY	TO	1stD	TotYd	PassY	RushY	TO
1	Sun	September 3	L		0-1	Baltimore Ravens	0	16	12	223	193	30	1	18	336	196	140	
2							**Bye Week**											
3	Sun	September 17	L		0-2	Cleveland Browns	20	23	19	336	166	170	1	14	377	316	61	1
4	Sun	September 24	L		0-3	Tennessee Titans	20	23	20	364	249	115	1	15	372	287	85	3
5	Sun	October 1	W		1-3	Jacksonville Jaguars	24	13	22	332	123	209	3	17	206	180	26	2
6	Sun	October 8	W		2-3	New York Jets	20	3	21	330	137	193		12	206	94	112	4
7	Sun	October 15	W		3-3	Cincinnati Bengals	15	0	13	274	171	103		12	232	112	120	3
8	Sun	October 22	W		4-3	Cleveland Browns	22	0	17	248	105	143		5	104	55	49	3
9	Sun	October 29	W		5-3	Baltimore Ravens	9	6	14	231	111	120	1	14	274	139	135	3
10	Sun	November 5	L		5-4	Tennessee Titans	7	9	10	167	93	74	3	21	364	216	148	1
11	Sun	November 12	L	OT	5-5	Philadelphia Eagles	23	26	21	322	140	182	1	21	290	202	88	1
12	Sun	November 19	L		5-6	Jacksonville Jaguars	24	34	15	302	155	147	5	20	417	177	240	2
13	Sun	November 26	W		6-6	Cincinnati Bengals	48	28	21	372	187	185		23	309	100	209	3
14	Sun	December 3	W		7-6	Oakland Raiders	21	20	19	311	112	199	1	20	390	273	117	2
15	Sun	December 10	L		7-7	New York Giants	10	30	17	264	217	47	1	20	394	326	68	
16	Sat	December 16	W		8-7	Washington Redskins	24	3	21	374	174	200	1	14	271	207	64	5
17	Sun	December 24	W		9-7	San Diego Chargers	34	21	21	316	185	131	2	6	171	140	31	2

Passing

No.		Age	Pos	G	GS	QBrec	Cmp	Att	Cmp%	Yds	TD	TD%	Int	Int%	Lng	Y/A	AY/A	Y/C	Y/G	Rate	Sk	Yds
10	Kordell Stewart	28	QB	16	11	7-4-0	151	289	52.2	1860	11	3.8	8	2.8	45	6.4	6.0	12.3	116.3	73.6	30	150
11	Kent Graham	32	qb	14	5	2-3-0	66	148	44.6	878	1	0.7	1	0.7	77	5.9	5.8	13.3	62.7	63.4	13	70
36	Jerome Bettis	28	RB	16	16		0	2	0.0	0	0	0.0	1	50.0	0	0.0	−22.5		0.0	0.0	0	0
	Team Total	26.3		16		9-7-0	217	439	49.4	2738	12	2.7	10	2.3	77	6.2	5.8	12.6	171.1	68.9	43	220
	Opp Total			16			280	521	53.7	3249	13	2.5	17	3.3		6.2	5.3	11.6	203.1	67.6	39	229

Rushing and Receiving

No.		Age	Pos	G	GS	Att	Yds	TD	Lng	Y/A	Y/G	A/G	Rec	Yds	Y/R	TD	Lng	R/G	Y/G	YScm
36	Jerome Bettis	28	RB	16	16	355	1341	8	30	3.8	83.8	22.2	13	97	7.5	0	25	0.8	6.1	1438
10	Kordell Stewart	28	QB	16	11	78	436	7	45	5.6	27.3	4.9								436
33	Richard Huntley	28		13	0	46	215	3	30	4.7	16.5	3.5	10	91	9.1	0	19	0.8	7.0	306
45	Chris Fuamatu-Maafala	23		7	1	21	149	1	23	7.1	21.3	3.0	11	107	9.7	0	25	1.6	15.3	256
11	Kent Graham	32	qb	14	5	8	7	0	7	0.9	0.5	0.6								7
21	Amos Zereoue	24		12	0	6	14	0	11	2.3	1.2	0.5								14
86	Hines Ward	24	WR	16	15	4	53	0	23	13.3	3.3	0.3	48	672	14.0	4	77	3.0	42.0	725
81	Troy Edwards	23		14	1	3	4	0	15	1.3	0.3	0.2	18	215	11.9	0	27	1.3	15.4	219
38	Jon Witman	28	fb	6	5	3	5	0	2	1.7	0.8	0.5	5	33	6.6	0	11	0.8	5.5	38
35	Dan Kreider	23	FB	10	7	2	24	0	22	12.0	2.4	0.2	5	42	8.4	0	14	0.5	4.2	66
4	Josh Miller	30	P	16	0	1	0	0	0	0.0	0.0	0.1								0
82	Bobby Shaw	25		16	0	0	0	0	0		0.0	0.0	40	672	16.8	4	45	2.5	42.0	672
80	Plaxico Burress	23	WR	12	8	0	0	0	0		0.0	0.0	22	273	12.4	0	39	1.8	22.8	273
88	Courtney Hawkins	31	wr	13	5	0	0	0	0		0.0	0.0	19	238	12.5	1	33	1.5	18.3	238
87	Mark Bruener	28	TE	16	16	0	0	0	0		0.0	0.0	17	192	11.3	3	30	1.1	12.0	192
48	Matt Cushing	25		7	1	0	0	0	0		0.0	0.0	4	17	4.3	0	5	0.6	2.4	17
85	Cory Geason	25		9	3	0	0	0	0		0.0	0.0	3	66	22.0	0	36	0.3	7.3	66
89	Will Blackwell	25		5	0	0	0	0	0		0.0	0.0	2	23	11.5	0	14	0.4	4.6	23
	Team Total	26.3		16		527	2248	19	45	4.3	140.5	32.9	217	2738	12.6	12	77	13.6	171.1	4986
	Opp Total			16		425	1693	9		4.0	105.8	26.6	280	3020	10.8	13		17.5	188.8	4713

Defense

No.		Age	Pos	G	GS	Sk	Int	Yds	TD	Lng	PD	FF	Fmb	FR	Yds	TD	Tkl	Ast	Sfty
50	Earl Holmes	27	RILB	16	16	1.0						1	0	1	4	0	87	41	
99	Levon Kirkland	31	LILB	16	16		1	1	0	1	0	0	0	1	0	0	65	21	
92	Jason Gildon*	28	LOLB	16	16	13.5						4	0	4	22	1	58	19	
20	Dewayne Washington	28	RCB	16	16		5	59	0	31	0						69	9	
41	Lee Flowers	27	SS	14	14	1.0	1	0	0	0	0	4	0	3	0	0	61	24	
27	Brent Alexander	29	FS	16	16	1.5	3	31	0	15	0	1	0	1	0	0	61	15	
30	Chad Scott	26	LCB	16	16		5	49	0	33	0	0	0	2	6	0	64	6	
55	Joey Porter	23	ROLB	16	16	10.5	1	0	0	0	0	2	0	1	32	1	43	17	1
91	Aaron Smith	24	LDE	16	15	4.0											28	14	
76	Kevin Henry	32	RDE	15	15							0	0	1	0	0	20	18	
67	Kimo von Oelhoffen	29	NT	16	16	1.0						1	0	0	0	0	26	13	
26	Deshea Townsend	25		16	0	3.5											22	7	
28	Ainsley Battles	22		16	2	1.0						0	1	2	-1	0	13	4	
23	Jason Simmons	24		15	0							2	0	0	0	0	15	1	
74	Chris Sullivan	27		15	2							0	0	2	0	0	8	9	
47	Scott Shields	24		10	1							0	1	2	-5	0	10	2	
96	Kendrick Clancy	22		9	0												5	3	
94	Jeremy Staat	24		7	0												4	5	
10	Kordell Stewart	28	QB	16	11							0	8	3	-1	0			
57	John Fiala	27		16	0												4	2	
56	Mike Vrabel	25		15	0	1.0						0	0	1	0	0	3	2	
22	Hank Poteat	23	PR/KR	15	0							0	3	0	0	0	2	0	
73	Chris Combs	24		6	0												3	0	
86	Hines Ward	24	WR	16	15							0	2	1	0	0			
36	Jerome Bettis	28	RB	16	16							0	1	1	1	0			
4	Josh Miller	30	P	16	0							0	1	1	-18	0			
82	Bobby Shaw	25		16	0							0	2	0	0	0			
80	Plaxico Burress	23	WR	12	8							0	1	0	0	0			
24	Nakia Codie	24		6	0		1	14	0	14	0								
62	Roger Duffy	33	c	13	7							0	1	0	-10	0			
81	Troy Edwards	23		14	1							0	1	0	0	0			
66	Alan Faneca	24	LG	16	16							0	0	1	0	0			
72	Wayne Gandy	29	LT	16	16							0	0	1	0	0			
11	Kent Graham	32	qb	14	5							0	1	0	0	0			
33	Richard Huntley	28		13	0							0	1	0	0	0			
61	Tom Myslinski	32		6	0							0	0	1	0	0			
	Team Total	26.3		16		38.0	17	154	0	33	0	15	24	30	30	2	677	232	1
	Opp Total			16		43							25	7						

2001 PITTSBURGH STEELERS: 13-3-0, 1ST IN AFC CENTRAL DIVISION
Head Coach: Bill Cowher

Week	Day	Date	OT	Rec	Opp	Score Tm	Opp	Offe 1stD	TotYd	PassY	RushY	TO	Defe 1stD	TotYd	PassY	RushY	TO
1	Sun	September 9	L	0-1	Jacksonville Jaguars	3	21	15	281	161	120	4	16	299	198	101	
2	Sun	September 30	W	1-1	Buffalo Bills	20	3	16	270	100	170		14	172	120	52	2
3	Sun	October 7	W	2-1	Cincinnati Bengals	16	7	19	413	138	275	2	15	214	149	65	1
4	Sun	October 14	W	3-1	Kansas City Chiefs	20	17	16	316	113	203		19	271	106	165	1
5	Sun	October 21	W	4-1	Tampa Bay Buccaneers	17	10	17	344	124	220	3	19	278	214	64	1
6	Mon	October 29	W	5-1	Tennessee Titans	34	7	24	405	272	133		15	214	157	57	4
7	Sun	November 4	L	5-2	Baltimore Ravens	10	13	21	348	225	123	1	10	183	142	41	1
8	Sun	November 11	W	OT	6-2	Cleveland Browns	15	12	20	428	181	247	1	15	187	113	74	
9	Sun	November 18	W	7-2	Jacksonville Jaguars	20	7	20	402	257	145		14	234	186	48	3
10	Sun	November 25	W	8-2	Tennessee Titans	34	24	20	377	247	130		21	405	324	81	2
11	Sun	December 2	W	9-2	Minnesota Vikings	21	16	21	364	157	207	2	12	385	340	45	3
12	Sun	December 9	W	10-2	New York Jets	18	7	23	345	211	134		14	220	159	61	
13	Sun	December 16	W	11-2	Baltimore Ravens	26	21	22	476	318	158		15	207	149	58	1
14	Sun	December 23	W	12-2	Detroit Lions	47	14	25	429	214	215		11	151	77	74	3
15	Sun	December 30	L	OT	12-3	Cincinnati Bengals	23	26	16	313	240	73	5	32	544	403	141	3
16	Sun	January 6	W	13-3	Cleveland Browns	28	7	19	376	155	221	3	12	173	105	68	3
17																	
		Playoffs															
Division	Sun	January 20	W	14-3	Baltimore Ravens	27	10	21	297	143	154	1	7	150	128	22	4
Conf Champ	Sun	January 27	L	14-4	New England Patriots	17	24	23	306	248	58	4	15	259	192	67	

Passing

No.		Age	Pos	G	GS	QBrec	Cmp	Att	Cmp%	Yds	TD	TD%	Int	Int%	Lng	Y/A	AY/A	Y/C	Y/G	Rate	Sk	Yds
10	Kordell Stewart*	29	QB	16	16	13-3-0	266	442	60.2	3109	14	3.2	11	2.5	90	7.0	6.5	11.7	194.3	81.7	29	175
8	Tommy Maddox	30		3	0		7	9	77.8	154	1	11.1	1	11.1	57	17.1	14.3	22.0	51.3	116.2	1	4
36	Jerome Bettis*	29	RB	11	11		1	2	50.0	32	1	50.0	0	0.0	32	16.0	26.0	32.0	2.9	135.4	0	0
86	Hines Ward*q	25	WR	16	16		0	1	0.0	0	0	0.0	0	0.0	0	0.0	0.0		0.0	39.6	1	3
	Team Total	26.3		16		13-3-0	274	454	60.4	3295	16	3.5	12	2.6	90	7.3	6.8	12.0	205.9	83.4	31	182
	Opp Total			16			295	525	56.2	3309	19	3.6	16	3.0		6.3	5.7	11.2	206.8	74.5	55	367

Rushing and Receiving

No.		Age	Pos	G	GS	Rush Att	Yds	TD	Lng	Y/A	Y/G	A/G	Receiving Rec	Yds	Y/R	TD	Lng	R/G	Y/G	YScm
36	Jerome Bettis*	29	RB	11	11	225	1072	4	48	4.8	97.5	20.5	8	48	6.0	0	16	0.7	4.4	1120
45	Chris Fuamatu-Maafala	24	rb	16	5	120	453	3	46	3.8	28.3	7.5	16	127	7.9	1	54	1.0	7.9	580
10	Kordell Stewart*	29	QB	16	16	96	537	5	48	5.6	33.6	6.0								537
21	Amos Zereoue	25		14	0	85	441	1	32	5.2	31.5	6.1	13	154	11.8	1	62	0.9	11.0	595
33	R.J. Bowers	27		3	0	18	84	1	21	4.7	28.0	6.0	1	0	0.0	0	0	0.3	0.0	84
86	Hines Ward*	25	WR	16	16	10	83	0	36	8.3	5.2	0.6	94	1003	10.7	4	34	5.9	62.7	1086
35	Dan Kreider	24		13	1	7	29	1	12	4.1	2.2	0.5	2	5	2.5	0	5	0.2	0.4	34
8	Tommy Maddox	30		3	0	6	9	1	8	1.5	3.0	2.0								9
81	Troy Edwards	24	KR	16	0	5	28	1	12	5.6	1.8	0.3	19	283	14.9	0	57	1.2	17.7	311
38	Jon Witman	29	FB	15	12	5	24	0	14	4.8	1.6	0.3	6	32	5.3	0	12	0.4	2.1	56
3	Kris Brown	25	K	16	0	1	6	0	6	6.0	0.4	0.1								6
17	Tee Martin	23		1	0	1	8	0	8	8.0	8.0	1.0								8
4	Josh Miller	31	P	16	0	1	0	0	0	0.0	0.0	0.1								0
80	Plaxico Burress	24	WR	16	16	0	0	0	0	0.0	0.0		66	1008	15.3	6	43	4.1	63.0	1008
82	Bobby Shaw	26		16	0	0	0	0	0	0.0	0.0		24	409	17.0	2	90	1.5	25.6	409
87	Mark Bruener	29	TE	9	9	0	0	0	0	0.0	0.0		12	98	8.2	0	21	1.3	10.9	98
84	Jerame Tuman	25	te	16	7	0	0	0	0	0.0	0.0		7	96	13.7	1	32	0.4	6.0	96
48	Matt Cushing	26		13	3	0	0	0	0	0.0	0.0		5	24	4.8	1	9	0.4	1.8	24
89	Will Blackwell	26		1	0	0	0	0	0	0.0	0.0		1	8	8.0	0	8	1.0	8.0	8
	Team Total	26.3		16		580	2774	17	48	4.8	173.4	36.3	274	3295	12.0	16	90	17.1	205.9	6069
	Opp Total			16		339	1195	5		3.5	74.7	21.2	295	2942	10.0	19		18.4	183.9	4137

Defense

No.		Age	Pos	G	GS	Sk	Def Int	Yds	TD	Lng	PD	Fumb FF	Fmb	FR	Yds	TD	Tack Tkl	Ast	Sfty
50	Earl Holmes	28	LILB	16	16	2.0	0	0	0	0	2	2	0	1	0	0	85	33	
97	Kendrell Bell*	23	RILB	16	16	9.0	0	0	0	0	1	1	0	0	0	0	69	13	
30	Chad Scott	27	LCB	15	15		5	204	2	62	19						71	9	
20	Dewayne Washington	29	RCB	16	16	1.0	1	15	0	15	18	0	0	1	63	1	66	11	
27	Brent Alexander	30	FS	16	16	2.0	4	39	0	22	10	1	0	0	0	0	52	17	
55	Joey Porter	24	ROLB	15	15	9.0	0	0	0	0	4	4	0	1	0	0	47	14	
92	Jason Gildon*+	29	LOLB	16	16	12.0	1	0	0	0	8	3	0	2	27	1	43	13	
41	Lee Flowers	28	SS	15	15	1.0	0	0	0	0	4						48	13	
91	Aaron Smith	25	LDE	16	16	8.0	0	0	0	0	1	1	0	0	0	0	22	7	
67	Kimo von Oelhoffen	30	RDE	15	15	4.0						0	0	2	0	0	20	8	
31	Mike Logan	27		16	1	2.0	2	2	0	2	8	1	0	2	14	0	20	3	
26	Deshea Townsend	26		16	1	2.0	2	7	0	7	8						20	4	
98	Casey Hampton	24	NT	16	11	1.0						0	0	1	0	0	10	13	
40	Myron Bell	30		16	1		0	0	0	0	1	0	0	1	0	0	13	0	
51	Mike Jones	32		15	0							1	0	0	0	0	10	3	
94	Rodney Bailey	22		16	1	2.0	0	0	0	0	1						8	4	
96	Kendrick Clancy	23		16	4		1	3	0	3	1						6	4	
10	Kordell Stewart*	29	QB	16	16							0	11	5	−11	0			
23	Jason Simmons	25		12	0		0	0	0	0	1						4	1	
53	Clark Haggans	24		16	1							1	0	0	0	0	3	2	
22	Hank Poteat	24	PR	13	0							0	4	2	0	0	1	0	
36	Jerome Bettis*	29	RB	11	11							0	3	2	0	0			
57	John Fiala	28		16	0		0	0	0	0	1	0	0	1	0	0	1	2	
21	Amos Zereoue	25		14	0							0	3	1	0	0			
90	Justin Kurpeikis	24		3	0												1	1	
3	Kris Brown	25	K	16	0							0	1	1	0	0			
73	Chris Combs	25		2	0												1	0	
81	Troy Edwards	24	KR	16	0							0	1	1	32	1			
79	Oliver Ross	27	rg	16	7							0	0	2	0	0			
87	Mark Bruener	29	TE	9	9							0	0	1	0	0			
80	Plaxico Burress	24	WR	16	16							0	1	0	0	0			
8	Tommy Maddox	30		3	0							0	1	0	0	0			
4	Josh Miller	31	P	16	0							0	1	0	−9	0			
02	Bobby Shaw	26		16	0							0	1	0	0	0			
86	Hines Ward*	25	WR	16	16							0	1	0	0	0			
	Team Total	26.3		16		55.0	16	270	2	62	88	15	28	27	116	3	621	175	
	Opp Total			16		31							27	15					2

2002 PITTSBURGH STEELERS: 10-5-1, 1ST IN AFC NORTH DIVISION
Head Coach: Bill Cowher

								Score		Offe					Defe				
Week	Day	Date		OT	Rec		Opp	Tm	Opp	1stD	TotYd	PassY	RushY	TO	1stD	TotYd	PassY	RushY	TO
1	Mon	September 9	L		0-1		New England Patriots	14	30	20	283	209	74	5	20	343	280	63	1
2	Sun	September 15	L		0-2		Oakland Raiders	17	30	14	273	201	72	5	27	464	369	95	2
3						Bye Week													
4	Sun	September 29	W	OT	1-2		Cleveland Browns	16	13	21	358	265	93	2	13	245	122	123	2
5	Sun	October 6	L		1-3		New Orleans Saints	29	32	23	364	244	120	2	17	315	194	121	
6	Sun	October 13	W		2-3		Cincinnati Bengals	34	7	21	408	197	211	2	18	268	190	78	4
7	Mon	October 21	W		3-3		Indianapolis Colts	28	10	22	364	182	182	1	23	367	295	72	3
8	Sun	October 27	W		4-3		Baltimore Ravens	31	18	16	283	179	104	1	26	360	293	67	5
9	Sun	November 3	W		5-3		Cleveland Browns	23	20	25	391	255	136	1	9	193	157	36	3
10	Sun	November 10	T	OT	5-3-1		Atlanta Falcons	34	34	30	645	463	182	3	21	447	279	168	2
11	Sun	November 17	L		5-4-1		Tennessee Titans	23	31	20	357	312	45	3	22	378	257	121	1
12	Sun	November 24	W		6-4-1		Cincinnati Bengals	29	21	21	391	235	156		17	352	298	54	1
13	Sun	December 1	W		7-4-1		Jacksonville Jaguars	25	23	23	403	184	219	1	13	226	124	102	
14	Sun	December 8	L		7-5-1		Houston Texans	6	24	24	422	294	128	5	3	47	10	37	1
15	Sun	December 15	W		8-5-1		Carolina Panthers	30	14	19	332	203	129	2	11	131	81	50	4
16	Mon	December 23	W		9-5-1		Tampa Bay Buccaneers	17	7	19	327	233	94	1	18	277	203	74	3
17	Sun	December 29	W		10-5-1		Baltimore Ravens	34	31	25	351	176	175	2	21	422	308	114	4
		Playoffs																	
Wild Card	Sun	January 5	W		11-5-1		Cleveland Browns	36	33	30	432	343	89	3	21	447	409	38	1
Division	Sat	January 11	L	OT	11-6-1		Tennessee Titans	31	34	21	324	257	67	1	29	430	331	99	4

Passing

No.		Age	Pos	G	GS	QBrec	Cmp	Att	Cmp%	Yds	TD	TD%	Int	Int%	Lng	Y/A	AY/A	Y/C	Y/G	Rate	Sk	Yds
8	Tommy Maddox	31	QB	15	11	7-3-1	234	377	62.1	2836	20	5.3	16	4.2	72	7.5	6.7	12.1	189.1	85.2	26	148
10	Kordell Stewart	30	qb	8	5	3-2-0	109	166	65.7	1155	6	3.6	6	3.6	64	7.0	6.1	10.6	144.4	82.8	7	46
82	Antwaan Randle El	23	PR/KR	16	0		7	8	87.5	45	0	0.0	0	0.0	25	5.6	5.6	6.4	2.8	90.1	1	10
	Team Total	26.8		16		10-5-1	350	551	63.5	4036	26	4.7	22	4.0	72	7.3	6.5	11.5	252.3	84.6	34	204
	Opp Total			16			336	573	58.6	3773	19	3.3	19	3.3		6.6	5.8	11.2	235.8	75.6	50	313

Rushing and Receiving

						Rush							Receiving						
No.		Age	Pos	G	GS	Att	Yds	TD	Lng	Y/A	Y/G	A/G	Rec	Yds	Y/R	TD	Lng	R/G	Y/G	YScm
21	Amos Zereoue	26	rb	16	5	193	762	4	42	3.9	47.6	12.1	42	341	8.1	0	54	2.6	21.3	1103
36	Jerome Bettis	30	RB	13	11	187	666	9	41	3.6	51.2	14.4	7	57	8.1	0	15	0.5	4.4	723
10	Kordell Stewart	30	qb	8	5	43	191	2	25	4.4	23.9	5.4								191
45	Chris Fuamatu-Maafala	25		8	0	23	115	0	17	5.0	14.4	2.9	2	12	6.0	0	6	0.3	1.5	127
82	Antwaan Randle El	23	PR/KR	16	0	19	134	0	24	7.1	8.4	1.2	47	489	10.4	2	36	2.9	30.6	623
8	Tommy Maddox	31	QB	15	11	19	43	0	21	2.3	2.9	1.3								43
86	Hines Ward*	26	WR	16	16	12	142	0	39	11.8	8.9	0.8	112	1329	11.9	12	72	7.0	83.1	1471
34	Verron Haynes	23		14	0	10	51	0	20	5.1	3.6	0.7	3	10	3.3	0	7	0.2	0.7	61
35	Dan Kreider	25	FB	16	13	6	16	0	5	2.7	1.0	0.4	18	122	6.8	1	15	1.1	7.6	138
80	Plaxico Burress	25	WR	16	15	0	0	0	0		0.0	0.0	78	1325	17.0	7	62	4.9	82.8	1325
88	Terance Mathis	35		16	0	0	0	0	0		0.0	0.0	23	218	9.5	2	22	1.4	13.6	218
87	Mark Bruener	30	TE	12	12	0	0	0	0		0.0	0.0	13	66	5.1	1	10	1.1	5.5	66
84	Jerame Tuman	26	te	13	7	0	0	0	0		0.0	0.0	4	63	15.8	1	27	0.3	4.8	63
48	Matt Cushing	27		6	0	0	0	0	0		0.0	0.0	1	4	4.0	0	4	0.2	0.7	4
	Team Total	26.8		16		512	2120	15	42	4.1	132.5	32.0	350	4036	11.5	26	72	21.9	252.3	6156
	Opp Total			16		359	1375	16		3.8	85.9	22.4	336	3460	10.3	19		21.0	216.3	4835

Defense

No.	Name	Age	Pos	G	GS	Sk	Int	Yds	TD	Lng	PD	FF	Fmb	FR	Yds	TD	Tkl	Ast	Sfty
55	Joey Porter*+	25	ROLB	16	16	9.0	4	153	0	84	10	2	0	2	6	0	61	28	
30	Chad Scott	28	LCB	15	15		2	30	1	30	16						66	17	
51	James Farrior	27	RILB	14	14		0	0	0	0	1	0	0	1	4	0	60	22	
91	Aaron Smith	26	LDE	16	16	5.5	0	0	0	0	2	0	0	3	0	0	55	17	
41	Lee Flowers	29	SS	16	15	4.0	2	31	0	25	0	0	0	1	3	0	52	21	
27	Brent Alexander	31	FS	16	16	1.0	4	37	0	25	0						50	25	
92	Jason Gildon*	30	LOLB	16	16	9.0											45	21	
20	Dewayne Washington	30	RCB	16	16		3	51	0	28	0	0	0	1	0	0	45	9	
97	Kendrell Bell	24	LILB	12	12	4.0	0	0	0	0	2	0	0	1	0	0	37	13	
26	Deshea Townsend	27		16	3		3	3	0	2	10						40	7	
31	Mike Logan	28		14	0	0.5	1	46	0	46	9	2	0	0	0	0	33	9	
53	Clark Haggans	25		16	1	6.5	0	0	0	0	8	2	0	0	0	0	24	15	
98	Casey Hampton	25	NT	16	15	2.0						2	0	1	36	0	24	17	
94	Rodney Bailey	23		16	0	5.5	0	0	0	0	2	0	0	1	0	0	18	7	
28	Chris Hope	22		14	0								0	0	1	0	0	19	4	
67	Kimo von Oelhoffen	31	RDE	16	16	3.0	0	0	0	0	2	0	0	1	0	0	12	10	
22	Hank Poteat	25		13	0		0	0	0	0	1	0	1	1	0	0	16	3	
50	Larry Foote	22		14	3								0	0	1	0	0	13	7	
29	Chidi Iwuoma	24		13	0													11	3	
8	Tommy Maddox	31	QB	15	11								0	8	5	−3	0			
57	John Fiala	29		11	1								0	0	1	0	0	4	1	
99	Brett Keisel	24		1	0								0	0	1	0	0	3	1	
10	Kordell Stewart	30	qb	8	5								0	4	2	−10	0			
82	Antwaan Randle El	23	PR/KR	16	0								0	4	1	0	0			
80	Plaxico Burress	25	WR	16	15								0	2	1	0	0			
96	Kendrick Clancy	24		7	0													1	0	
66	Alan Faneca*+	26	LG	16	16								0	0	2	0	0			
21	Amos Zereoue	26	rb	16	5								0	2	0	0	0			
36	Jerome Bettis	30	RB	13	11								0	1	0	0	0			
95	Mike Jones	33		6	1								0	0	1	0	0			
35	Dan Kreider	25	FB	16	13								0	1	0	0	0			
56	Chukky Okobi	24	c	13	5								0	1	0	−13	0			
2	Todd Peterson	32	K	10	0								0	1	0	0	0			
86	Hines Ward*	26	WR	16	16								0	1	0	0	0			
	Team Total	26.8		16		50.0	19	351	1	84	63	8	26	29	23	0	689	257	
	Opp Total			16		34							22	5						

2003 PITTSBURGH STEELERS: 6-10-0, 3RD IN AFC NORTH DIVISION
Head Coach: Bill Cowher

Week	Day	Date	OT	Rec	Opp	Score Tm	Opp	Offe 1stD	TotYd	PassY	RushY	TO	Defe 1stD	TotYd	PassY	RushY	TO
1	Sun	September 7	W	1-0	Baltimore Ravens	34	15	21	339	251	88	1	17	231	143	88	2
2	Sun	September 14	L	1-1	Kansas City Chiefs	20	41	16	380	320	60	4	19	282	123	159	2
3	Sun	September 21	W	2-1	Cincinnati Bengals	17	10	22	376	238	138	1	11	182	125	57	1
4	Sun	September 28	L	2-2	Tennessee Titans	13	30	25	376	307	69	2	9	198	158	40	
5	Sun	October 5	L	2-3	Cleveland Browns	13	33	11	209	149	60	3	22	324	200	124	2
6	Sun	October 12	L	2-4	Denver Broncos	14	17	17	215	130	85	1	15	242	165	77	3
7					Bye Week												
8	Sun	October 26	L	2-5	St. Louis Rams	21	33	11	245	151	94	4	26	448	359	89	
9	Sun	November 2	L	2-6	Seattle Seahawks	16	23	19	320	215	105		19	289	191	98	
10	Sun	November 9	W	3-6	Arizona Cardinals	20	15	11	246	159	87	1	19	379	283	96	1
11	Mon	November 17	L	3-7	San Francisco 49ers	14	30	21	349	305	44	2	17	423	254	169	
12	Sun	November 23	W	4-7	Cleveland Browns	13	6	11	168	59	109		19	303	213	90	5
13	Sun	November 30	L	4-8	Cincinnati Bengals	20	24	23	384	299	85	2	18	379	266	113	
14	Sun	December 7	W	5-8	Oakland Raiders	27	7	21	399	266	133	2	9	161	39	122	3
15	Sun	December 14	L	5-9	New York Jets	0	6	16	231	137	94		15	319	144	175	1
16	Sun	December 21	W	6-9	San Diego Chargers	40	24	21	341	160	181		21	344	228	116	3
17	Sun	December 28	L	OT	6-10	Baltimore Ravens	10	13	9	214	158	56	5	14	279	151	128	2

Passing

No.		Age	Pos	G	GS	QBrec	Cmp	Att	Cmp%	Yds	TD	TD%	Int	Int%	Lng	Y/A	AY/A	Y/C	Y/G	Rate	Sk	Yds
8	Tommy Maddox	32	QB	16	16	6-10-0	298	519	57.4	3414	18	3.5	17	3.3	53	6.6	5.8	11.5	213.4	75.3	41	242
16	Charlie Batch	29		4	0		4	8	50.0	47	0	0.0	0	0.0	22	5.9	5.9	11.8	11.8	68.2	1	2
82	Antwaan Randle El	24	PR	16	1		3	4	75.0	6	0	0.0	0	0.0	9	1.5	1.5	2.0	0.4	77.1	0	0
4	Josh Miller	33	P	16	0		1	1	100.0	81	1	100.0	0	0.0	81	81.0	101.0	81.0	5.1	158.3	0	0
	Team Total	26.9		16		6-10-0	306	532	57.5	3548	19	3.6	17	3.2	81	6.7	5.9	11.6	221.8	76.4	42	244
	Opp Total			16			294	484	60.7	3245	20	4.1	14	2.9		6.7	6.2	11.0	202.8	82.4	35	203

Rushing and Receiving

No.		Age	Pos	G	GS	Rush Att	Rush Yds	Rush TD	Rush Lng	Rush Y/A	Rush Y/G	Rush A/G	Rec	Rec Yds	Rec Y/R	Rec TD	Rec Lng	Rec R/G	Rec Y/G	YScm
36	Jerome Bettis	31	RB	16	10	246	811	7	21	3.3	50.7	15.4	13	86	6.6	0	16	0.8	5.4	897
21	Amos Zereoue	27	rb	16	6	132	433	2	22	3.3	27.1	8.3	40	310	7.8	0	29	2.5	19.4	743
34	Verron Haynes	24		12	0	20	63	0	15	3.2	5.3	1.7	7	57	8.1	0	13	0.6	4.8	120
82	Antwaan Randle El	24	PR	16	1	15	75	0	32	5.0	4.7	0.9	37	364	9.8	1	32	2.3	22.8	439
8	Tommy Maddox	32	QB	16	16	13	12	0	6	0.9	0.8	0.8								12
86	Hines Ward*	27	WR	16	16	11	61	0	25	5.5	3.8	0.7	95	1163	12.2	10	50	5.9	72.7	1224
35	Dan Kreider	26	FB	16	12	7	29	1	9	4.1	1.8	0.4	9	107	11.9	0	26	0.6	6.7	136
80	Plaxico Burress	26	WR	16	16	1	-7	0	-7	-7.0	-0.4	0.1	60	860	14.3	4	47	3.8	53.8	853
16	Charlie Batch	29		4	0	1	11	0	11	11.0	2.8	0.3								11
83	Chris Doering	30		16	0	0	0	0	0		0.0	0.0	18	240	13.3	1	53	1.1	15.0	240
84	Jerame Tuman	27	TE	16	12	0	0	0	0		0.0	0.0	12	113	9.4	0	23	0.8	7.1	113
85	Jay Riemersma	30	te	11	7	0	0	0	0		0.0	0.0	10	138	13.8	1	24	0.9	12.5	138
87	Mark Bruener	31		14	0	0	0	0	0		0.0	0.0	2	12	6.0	1	11	0.1	0.9	12
89	Lee Mays	25		16	0	0	0	0	0		0.0	0.0	2	17	8.5	0	9	0.1	1.1	17
28	Chris Hope	23		16	0	0	0	0	0		0.0	0.0	1	81	81.0	1	81	0.1	5.1	81
	Team Total	26.9		16		446	1488	10	32	3.3	93.0	27.9	306	3548	11.6	19	81	19.1	221.8	5036
	Opp Total			16		449	1741	14		3.9	108.8	28.1	294	3042	10.3	20		18.4	190.1	4783

Defense

No.		Age	Pos	G	GS	Sk	Def Int	Def Yds	Def TD	Def Lng	Def PD	Fumb FF	Fumb Fmb	Fumb FR	Fumb Yds	Fumb TD	Tack Tkl	Tack Ast	Sfty
51	James Farrior	28	LILB	16	16		1	9	0	9	4	0	1	1	0	0	96	45	
97	Kendrell Bell	25	RILB	16	16	5.0	1	61	0	42	3	1	0	1	0	0	81	19	
31	Mike Logan	29	SS	16	15	1.0	0	0	0	0	5	1	0	3	14	0	71	23	
27	Brent Alexander	32	FS	16	16	1.0	4	63	0	34	6	0	0	2	2	0	60	21	
55	Joey Porter	26	ROLB	14	14	5.0	0	0	0	0	4	1	0	1	0	0	50	16	
92	Jason Gildon	31	LOLB	16	16	6.0	1	1	0	1	6	1	1	1	0	0	42	19	
20	Dewayne Washington	31	RCB	16	12		1	7	0	7	8	0	1	0	0	0	50	5	
30	Chad Scott	29	LCB	12	12		3	50	1	26	9	1	0	0	0	0	44	12	
26	Deshea Townsend	28	lcb	16	8	1.0	3	24	1	25	14	1	0	1	0	0	39	7	
91	Aaron Smith	27	LDE	16	16	2.0	0	0	0	0	7	1	0	0	0	0	36	9	
67	Kimo von Oelhoffen	32	RDE	16	16	8.0						1	0	1	0	0	27	8	
43	Troy Polamalu	22		16	0	2.0	0	0	0	0	4	1	0	0	0	0	29	9	
98	Casey Hampton*	26	NT	16	16	1.0	0	0	0	0	2						27	12	
24	Ike Taylor	23	KR	16	1		0	0	0	0	2	0	1	0	0	0	26	6	
28	Chris Hope	23		16	0		0	0	0	0	1						22	5	
53	Clark Haggans	26		16	2	1.0	0	0	0	0	1	1	0	0	0	0	18	9	
57	Clint Kriewaldt	27		15	0							1	0	1	0	0	17	3	
29	Chidi Iwuoma	25		15	0							0	0	1	0	0	11	3	
94	Rodney Bailey	24		16	0	2.0											7	2	
50	Larry Foote	23		16	0							0	0	1	0	0	5	1	
96	Kendrick Clancy	25		12	0							0	0	1	0	0	3	0	
82	Antwaan Randle El	24	PR	16	1							0	5	2	-7	0			
36	Jerome Bettis	31	RB	16	10							0	5	1	0	0			
8	Tommy Maddox	32	QB	16	16							0	5	1	-6	0			
34	Verron Haynes	24		12	0							0	2	1	0	0			
4	Josh Miller	33	P	16	0							0	1	1	0	0			
16	Charlie Batch	29		4	0							0	1	0	0	0			
80	Plaxico Burress	26	WR	16	16							0	1	0	0	0			
73	Kendall Simmons	24	RG	16	16							0	0	1	0	0			
86	Hines Ward*	27	WR	16	16							0	0	1	0	0			
	Team Total	26.9		16		35.0	14	215	2	42	76	11	24	23	3	0	761	234	
	Opp Total			16		42							24	13					1

2004 PITTSBURGH STEELERS: 15-1-0, 1ST IN AFC NORTH DIVISION
Head Coach: Bill Cowher

							Score		Offe					Defe				
Week	Day	Date		OT	Rec	Opp	Tm	Opp	1stD	TotYd	PassY	RushY	TO	1stD	TotYd	PassY	RushY	TO
1	Sun	September 12	W		1-0	Oakland Raiders	24	21	17	237	130	107	1	18	358	297	61	4
2	Sun	September 19	L		1-1	Baltimore Ravens	13	30	16	310	217	93	3	15	259	87	172	
3	Sun	September 26	W		2-1	Miami Dolphins	13	3	15	314	161	153	1	13	169	117	52	4
4	Sun	October 3	W		3-1	Cincinnati Bengals	28	17	23	333	168	165	2	22	293	156	137	3
5	Sun	October 10	W		4-1	Cleveland Browns	34	23	21	401	231	170	1	17	305	207	98	1
6	Sun	October 17	W		5-1	Dallas Cowboys	24	20	21	297	172	125		20	348	248	100	1
7						Bye Week												
8	Sun	October 31	W		6-1	New England Patriots	34	20	25	417	196	221		19	248	243	5	4
9	Sun	November 7	W		7-1	Philadelphia Eagles	27	3	25	420	168	252	2	7	113	90	23	1
10	Sun	November 14	W		8-1	Cleveland Browns	24	10	18	300	120	180	1	12	228	160	68	4
11	Sun	November 21	W		9-1	Cincinnati Bengals	19	14	21	235	84	151	1	10	209	147	62	1
12	Sun	November 28	W		10-1	Washington Redskins	16	7	15	207	100	107		10	156	105	51	1
13	Sun	December 5	W		11-1	Jacksonville Jaguars	17	16	15	316	196	120		20	359	259	100	
14	Sun	December 12	W		12-1	New York Jets	17	6	15	262	142	120	2	15	296	189	107	3
15	Sat	December 18	W		13-1	New York Giants	33	30	27	469	309	160	2	18	278	182	96	1
16	Sun	December 26	W		14-1	Baltimore Ravens	20	7	20	404	221	183	2	16	248	177	71	1
17	Sun	January 2	W		15-1	Buffalo Bills	29	24	15	262	105	157	3	16	267	171	96	3
		Playoffs																
Division	Sat	January 15	W	OT	16-1	New York Jets	20	17	23	364	171	193	3	17	275	165	110	1
Conf Champ	Sun	January 23	L		16-2	New England Patriots	27	41	19	388	225	163	4	18	322	196	126	

Passing

No.		Age	Pos	G	GS	QBrec	Cmp	Att	Cmp%	Yds	TD	TD%	Int	Int%	Lng	Y/A	AY/A	Y/C	Y/G	Rate	Sk	Yds
7	Ben Roethlisberger	22	QB	14	13	13-0-0	196	295	66.4	2621	17	5.8	11	3.7	58	8.9	8.4	13.4	187.2	98.1	30	213
8	Tommy Maddox	33		4	3	2-1-0	30	60	50.0	329	1	1.7	2	3.3	39	5.5	4.3	11.0	82.3	58.3	6	37
36	Jerome Bettis*	32	RB	15	6		1	1	100.0	10	1	100.0	0	0.0	10	10.0	30.0	10.0	0.7	147.9	0	0
82	Antwaan Randle El	25	PR/wr	16	7		1	1	100.0	10	1	100.0	0	0.0	10	10.0	30.0	10.0	0.6	147.9	0	0
2	Brian St. Pierre	25		1	0		0	1	0.0	0	0	0.0	0	0.0	0	0.0	0.0		0.0	39.6	0	0
	Team Total	27.4		16		15-1-0	228	358	63.7	2970	20	5.6	13	3.6	58	8.3	7.8	13.0	185.6	93.2	36	250
	Opp Total			16			269	484	55.6	3060	14	2.9	19	3.9		6.3	5.1	11.4	191.3	68.0	41	225

Rushing and Receiving

No.		Age	Pos	G	GS	Rush							Receiving							YScm
						Att	Yds	TD	Lng	Y/A	Y/G	A/G	Rec	Yds	Y/R	TD	Lng	R/G	Y/G	
36	Jerome Bettis*	32	RB	15	6	250	941	13	29	3.8	62.7	16.7	6	46	7.7	0	20	0.4	3.1	987
22	Duce Staley	29	rb	10	10	192	830	1	38	4.3	83.0	19.2	6	55	9.2	0	21	0.6	5.5	885
7	Ben Roethlisberger	22	QB	14	13	56	144	1	20	2.6	10.3	4.0								144
34	Verron Haynes	25		13	0	55	272	0	18	4.9	20.9	4.2	18	142	7.9	2	26	1.4	10.9	414
39	Willie Parker	24		8	0	32	186	0	58	5.8	23.3	4.0	3	16	5.3	0	12	0.4	2.0	202
8	Tommy Maddox	33		4	3	9	15	0	10	1.7	3.8	2.3								15
82	Antwaan Randle El	25	PR/wr	16	7	8	34	0	12	4.3	2.1	0.5	43	601	14.0	3	39	2.7	37.6	635
86	Hines Ward*	28	WR	16	16	7	25	1	16	3.6	1.6	0.4	80	1004	12.6	4	58	5.0	62.8	1029
35	Dan Kreider	27	FB	16	9	4	18	0	6	4.5	1.1	0.3	10	75	7.5	1	13	0.6	4.7	93
2	Brian St. Pierre	25		1	0	4	-3	0	2	-0.8	-3.0	4.0								-3
46	Dante Brown	24		1	0	1	2	0	2	2.0	2.0	1.0								2
80	Plaxico Burress	27	WR	11	11	0	0	0	0		0.0	0.0	35	698	19.9	5	48	3.2	63.5	698
89	Lee Mays	26		16	1	0	0	0	0		0.0	0.0	9	137	15.2	0	46	0.6	8.6	137
84	Jerame Tuman	28	TE	16	16	0	0	0	0		0.0	0.0	9	89	9.9	3	26	0.6	5.6	89
85	Jay Riemersma	31		11	2	0	0	0	0		0.0	0.0	7	82	11.7	2	26	0.6	7.5	82
48	Matt Cushing	29		16	0	0	0	0	0		0.0	0.0	1	17	17.0	0	17	0.1	1.1	17
81	Sean Morey	28		16	0	0	0	0	0		0.0	0.0	1	8	8.0	0	8	0.1	0.5	8
	Team Total	27.4		16		618	2464	16	58	4.0	154.0	38.6	228	2970	13.0	20	58	14.3	185.6	5434
	Opp Total			16		357	1299	8		3.6	81.2	22.3	269	2835	10.5	14		16.8	177.2	4134

Defense

No.	Name	Age	Pos	G	GS	Sk	Def					Fumb					Tack		Sfty
							Int	Yds	TD	Lng	PD	FF	Fmb	FR	Yds	TD	Tkl	Ast	
51	James Farrior*+	29	LILB	16	16	3.0	4	113	1	41	12	3	0	3	0	0	67	28	
43	Troy Polamalu*	23	SS	16	16	1.0	5	58	1	26	14	1	0	0	0	0	68	29	
28	Chris Hope	24	FS	16	16		1	41	0	41	5	1	0	0	0	0	59	31	
50	Larry Foote	24	RILB	16	16	3.0	1	1	0	1	2	1	0	1	0	0	53	17	
26	Deshea Townsend	29	RCB	15	15	4.0	4	54	1	39	10	1	0	1	0	0	47	9	
55	Joey Porter*	27	ROLB	15	15	7.0	1	3	0	3	12	3	0	0	0	0	37	17	
91	Aaron Smith*	28	LDE	16	15	8.0	0	0	0	0	1	3	0	2	54	0	31	13	
92	James Harrison	26		16	4	1.0	0	0	0	0	3	0	0	1	18	1	36	9	
53	Clark Haggans	27	LOLB	13	13	6.0	0	0	0	0	1	2	0	1	0	0	30	8	
30	Chad Scott	30	lcb	7	7		1	23	0	23	7						27	2	
21	Ricardo Colclough	22	KR	16	0	1.5	0	0	0	0	3	2	3	0	0	0	21	6	
67	Kimo von Oelhoffen	33	RDE	16	15	1.0	0	0	0	0	1	0	0	2	21	0	16	8	
76	Chris Hoke	28	NT	14	10	1.0											13	11	
29	Chidi Iwuoma	26		14	0							1	0	0	0	0	16	2	
33	Russell Stuvaints	24		15	0		0	0	0	0	4	0	0	1	24	1	14	3	
24	Ike Taylor	24		13	1		1	0	0	0	5	0	1	0	0	0	10	6	
57	Clint Kriewaldt	28		15	0	0.5						1	0	0	0	0	10	6	
98	Casey Hampton	27	nt	6	6												8	7	
90	Travis Kirschke	30		16	1	1.0											6	6	
23	Tyrone Carter	28		9	0												8	0	
96	Kendrick Clancy	26		8	0												7	1	
97	Kendrell Bell	26		3	0												6	2	
99	Brett Keisel	26		13	0												5	4	
31	Mike Logan	30		3	0							1	0	0	0	0	5	3	
82	Antwaan Randle El	25	PR/wr	16	7							0	5	2	0	0			
95	Alonzo Jackson	24		7	0												2	1	
22	Duce Staley	29	rb	10	10							0	3	1	0	0			
8	Tommy Maddox	33		4	3							0	3	0	0	0			
37	Ainsley Battles	26		1	0												1	0	
36	Jerome Bettis*	32	RB	15	6							0	1	1	0	0			
80	Plaxico Burress	27	WR	11	11							0	1	1	0	0			
35	Dan Kreider	27	FB	16	9							0	0	2	0	0			
7	Ben Roethlisberger	22	QB	14	13							0	2	0	-6	0			
27	Willie J. Williams	34	LCB	16	10	1.0	1	0	0	0	0								
34	Verron Haynes	25		13	0							0	0	1	2	0			
89	Lee Mays	26		16	1							0	0	1	0	0			
86	Hines Ward*	28	WR	16	16							0	1	0	0	0			
	Team Total	27.4		16		39.0	19	293	3	41	80	20	20	21	113	2	603	229	
	Opp Total			16		36							28	15					

2005 PITTSBURGH STEELERS: 11-5-0, 1ST IN AFC NORTH DIVISION
Head Coach: Bill Cowher

2005 Super Bowl Champions

Week	Day	Date	OT	Rec	Opp	Score Tm	Score Opp	Offe 1stD	Offe TotYd	Offe PassY	Offe RushY	Offe TO	Defe 1stD	Defe TotYd	Defe PassY	Defe RushY	Defe TO
1	Sun	September 11	W	1-0	Tennessee Titans	34	7	18	424	218	206		16	303	206	97	4
2	Sun	September 18	W	2-0	Houston Texans	27	7	18	388	253	135		16	221	108	113	1
3	Sun	September 25	L	2-1	New England Patriots	20	23	14	269	190	79	1	24	426	346	80	3
4					Bye Week												
5	Mon	October 10	W	3-1	San Diego Chargers	24	22	25	311	207	104	1	20	279	213	66	2
6	Sun	October 16	L OT	3-2	Jacksonville Jaguars	17	23	16	218	145	73	4	17	246	153	93	1
7	Sun	October 23	W	4-2	Cincinnati Bengals	27	13	20	304	83	221	2	20	302	211	91	2
8	Mon	October 31	W	5-2	Baltimore Ravens	20	19	19	261	160	101	2	20	318	246	72	3
9	Sun	November 6	W	6-2	Green Bay Packers	20	10	13	213	59	154	1	16	268	203	65	3
10	Sun	November 13	W	7-2	Cleveland Browns	34	21	25	382	223	159		16	303	242	61	2
11	Sun	November 20	L OT	7-3	Baltimore Ravens	13	16	17	282	212	70	2	18	241	137	104	2
12	Mon	November 28	L	7-4	Indianapolis Colts	7	26	10	197	111	86	2	17	366	239	127	1
13	Sun	December 4	L	7-5	Cincinnati Bengals	31	38	28	474	379	95	4	21	324	222	102	
14	Sun	December 11	W	8-5	Chicago Bears	21	9	20	363	173	190		15	268	185	83	
15	Sun	December 18	W	9-5	Minnesota Vikings	18	3	14	275	133	142	1	11	185	131	54	3
16	Sat	December 24	W	10-5	Cleveland Browns	41	0	20	457	248	209	1	12	186	123	63	1
17	Sun	January 1	W	11-5	Detroit Lions	35	21	20	331	132	199	2	16	308	203	105	2
		Playoffs															
Wild Card	Sun	January 8	W	12-5	Cincinnati Bengals	31	17	19	346	202	144		19	327	243	84	2
Division	Sun	January 15	W	13-5	Indianapolis Colts	21	18	21	295	183	112	2	15	305	247	58	
Conf Champ	Sun	January 22	W	14-5	Denver Broncos	34	17	20	358	268	90		16	308	211	97	4
Super Bowl	Sun	February 5	W	15-5	Seattle Seahawks	21	10	14	339	158	181	2	20	396	259	137	1

Passing

No.		Age	Pos	G	GS	QBrec	Cmp	Att	Cmp%	Yds	TD	TD%	Int	Int%	Lng	Y/A	AY/A	Y/C	Y/G	Rate	Sk	Yds
7	Ben Roethlisberger	23	QB	12	12	9-3-0	168	268	62.7	2385	17	6.3	9	3.4	85	8.9	8.7	14.2	198.8	98.6	23	129
8	Tommy Maddox	34		5	2	0-2-0	34	71	47.9	406	2	2.8	4	5.6	32	5.7	3.7	11.9	81.2	51.7	8	43
16	Charlie Batch	31		4	2	2-0-0	23	36	63.9	246	1	2.8	1	2.8	43	6.8	6.1	10.7	61.5	81.5	1	6
82	Antwaan Randle El	26	WR/PR	16	15		3	3	100.0	67	1	33.3	0	0.0	51	22.3	29.0	22.3	4.2	158.3	0	0
17	Chris Gardocki	35	P	16	0		0	1	0.0	0	0	0.0	0	0.0	0	0.0	0.0		0.0	39.6	0	0
	Team Total	27.5		16		11-5-0	228	379	60.2	3104	21	5.5	14	3.7	85	8.2	7.6	13.6	194.0	89.4	32	178
	Opp Total			16			315	549	57.4	3480	15	2.7	15	2.7		6.3	5.7	11.0	217.5	74.0	47	312

Rushing and Receiving

No.		Age	Pos	G	GS	Rush Att	Rush Yds	Rush TD	Rush Lng	Rush Y/A	Rush Y/G	Rush A/G	Rec	Rec Yds	Rec Y/R	Rec TD	Rec Lng	Rec R/G	Rec Y/G	YScm
39	Willie Parker	25	RB	15	15	255	1202	4	80	4.7	80.1	17.0	18	218	12.1	1	48	1.2	14.5	1420
36	Jerome Bettis	33		12	0	110	368	9	39	3.3	30.7	9.2	4	40	10.0	0	16	0.3	3.3	408
34	Verron Haynes	26		14	0	74	274	3	20	3.7	19.6	5.3	11	113	10.3	0	18	0.8	8.1	387
22	Duce Staley	30		5	1	38	148	1	17	3.9	29.6	7.6	6	34	5.7	0	9	1.2	6.8	182
7	Ben Roethlisberger	23	QB	12	12	31	69	3	13	2.2	5.8	2.6								69
82	Antwaan Randle El	26	WR/PR	16	15	12	73	0	43	6.1	4.6	0.8	35	558	15.9	1	63	2.2	34.9	631
16	Charlie Batch	31		4	2	11	30	1	15	2.7	7.5	2.8								30
8	Tommy Maddox	34		5	2	8	26	0	16	3.3	5.2	1.6								26
86	Hines Ward	29	WR	15	15	3	10	0	7	3.3	0.7	0.2	69	975	14.1	11	85	4.6	65.0	985
35	Dan Kreider	28	FB	16	9	3	21	0	12	7.0	1.3	0.2	7	43	6.1	0	9	0.4	2.7	64
38	Noah Herron	23		2	0	3	2	0	1	0.7	1.0	1.5								2
80	Cedrick Wilson	27		16	1	1	0	0	0	0.0	0.0	0.1	26	451	17.3	0	46	1.6	28.2	451
83	Heath Miller	23	TE	16	14	0	0	0	0		0.0	0.0	39	459	11.8	6	50	2.4	28.7	459
11	Quincy Morgan	28	KR	16	0	0	0	0	0		0.0	0.0	9	150	16.7	2	31	0.6	9.4	150
84	Jerame Tuman	29	te	15	9	0	0	0	0		0.0	0.0	3	57	19.0	0	27	0.2	3.8	57
88	Matt Kranchick	26		4	1	0	0	0	0		0.0	0.0	1	6	6.0	0	6	0.3	1.5	6
	Team Total	27.5		16		549	2223	21	80	4.0	138.9	34.3	228	3104	13.6	21	85	14.3	194.0	5327
	Opp Total			16		402	1376	10		3.4	86.0	25.1	315	3168	10.1	15		19.7	198.0	4544

Defense

No.		Age	Pos	G	GS	Sk	Def					Fumb					Tack		Sfty
							Int	Yds	TD	Lng	PD	FF	Fmb	FR	Yds	TD	Tkl	Ast	
51	James Farrior	30	LILB	14	14	2.0	0	0	0	0	4	2	0	1	0	0	76	45	
50	Larry Foote	25	RILB	16	16	3.0	0	0	0	0	2	0	0	1	27	0	76	26	1
43	Troy Polamalu*+	24	SS	16	16	3.0	2	42	0	36	8	1	0	2	78	1	74	18	
28	Chris Hope	25	FS	16	16		3	60	0	55	5	1	0	1	6	0	70	27	
24	Ike Taylor	25	LCB	16	15		1	0	0	0	20	0	0	2	8	0	75	16	
53	Clark Haggans	28	LOLB	13	13	9.0	0	0	0	0	2	4	0	0	0	0	42	19	
55	Joey Porter*	28	ROLB	16	16	10.5	2	9	0	9	4	4	0	1	0	0	40	17	
26	Deshea Townsend	30	RCB	16	15	3.0	2	26	0	26	12	1	0	1	2	0	41	14	
92	James Harrison	27		16	3	3.0	1	25	0	25	3	0	0	1	0	0	36	9	
91	Aaron Smith	29	LDE	16	16	2.0	1	0	0	0	3	1	0	1	0	0	30	10	
98	Casey Hampton*	28	NT	16	15												25	17	
67	Kimo von Oelhoffen	34	RDE	16	16	3.5	0	0	0	0	4	1	0	0	0	0	23	12	
99	Brett Keisel	27		16	0	3.0	0	0	0	0	2	1	0	1	0	0	23	10	
21	Ricardo Colclough	23		14	0	1.0	1	14	0	14	2	0	1	0	0	0	24	6	
57	Clint Kriewaldt	29		16	2		0	0	0	0	1						25	6	
23	Tyrone Carter	29		16	0	1.0	1	3	0	3	3	2	0	2	0	0	20	6	
31	Mike Logan	31		12	1		0	0	0	0	1						16	8	
20	Bryant McFadden	24		12	1	1.0	1	0	0	0	7	1	0	1	9	0	17	1	
29	Chidi Iwuoma	27		16	0							1	0	0	0	0	10	3	
90	Travis Kirschke	31		16	0	1.0						0	0	1	0	0	7	6	
94	Andre Frazier	23		11	0	1.0						1	0	0	0	0	8	0	
76	Chris Hoke	29		15	0												3	3	
39	Willie Parker	25	RB	15	15							0	4	2	0	0			
82	Antwaan Randle El	26	WR/PR	16	15							0	4	0	0	0			
33	Russell Stuvaints	25		4	0												2	0	
16	Charlie Batch	31		4	2							0	1	2	0	0			
34	Verron Haynes	26		14	0							0	2	1	0	0			
7	Ben Roethlisberger	23	QB	12	12							0	2	1	−1	0			
66	Alan Faneca*+	29	LG	16	16							0	0	2	0	0			
8	Tommy Maddox	34		5	2							0	2	0	−9	0			
22	Duce Staley	30		5	1							0	1	1	0	0			
54	Rian Wallace	23		4	0												1	0	
80	Cedrick Wilson	27		16	1							0	1	1	0	0			
64	Jeff Hartings*	33	C	16	16							0	1	0	−9	0			
83	Heath Miller	23	TE	16	14							0	0	1	0	0			
81	Sean Morey	29		15	0							0	0	1	0	0			
11	Quincy Morgan	28	KR	16	0							0	1	0	0	0			
86	Hines Ward	29	WR	15	15							0	1	0	0	0			
60	Greg Warren	24		16	0							0	1	0	0	0			
	Team Total	27.5		16		47.0	15	179	0	55	83	21	22	28	111	1	764	279	1
	Opp Total			16		32							30	15					

2006 PITTSBURGH STEELERS: 8-8-0, TIED FOR 2ND IN AFC NORTH DIVISION
Head Coach: Bill Cowher

Week	Day	Date	OT	Rec	Opp	Tm	Opp	1stD	TotYd	PassY	RushY	TO	1stD	TotYd	PassY	RushY	TO
						Score		**Offe**					**Defe**				
1	Thu	September 7	W	1-0	Miami Dolphins	28	17	20	342	196	146	1	15	278	240	38	2
2	Mon	September 18	L	1-1	Jacksonville Jaguars	0	9	9	153	127	26	2	17	362	252	110	1
3	Sun	September 24	L	1-2	Cincinnati Bengals	20	28	27	365	195	170	5	15	246	159	87	3
4					Bye Week												
5	Sun	October 8	L	1-3	San Diego Chargers	13	23	16	265	197	68	2	22	341	222	119	1
6	Sun	October 15	W	2-3	Kansas City Chiefs	45	7	23	457	238	219	1	14	213	175	38	3
7	Sun	October 22	L OT	2-4	Atlanta Falcons	38	41	27	473	418	55	3	24	399	226	173	2
8	Sun	October 29	L	2-5	Oakland Raiders	13	20	15	360	271	89	4	9	98	17	81	1
9	Sun	November 5	L	2-6	Denver Broncos	20	31	27	499	403	96	6	13	336	221	115	
10	Sun	November 12	W	3-6	New Orleans Saints	38	31	19	467	250	217		29	513	393	120	3
11	Sun	November 19	W	4-6	Cleveland Browns	24	20	23	338	261	77	3	15	302	203	99	2
12	Sun	November 26	L	4-7	Baltimore Ravens	0	27	17	172	151	21	3	19	275	161	114	
13	Sun	December 3	W	5-7	Tampa Bay Buccaneers	20	3	13	267	191	76	1	16	254	144	110	4
14	Thu	December 7	W	6-7	Cleveland Browns	27	7	26	528	225	303	1	11	294	276	18	2
15	Sun	December 17	W	7-7	Carolina Panthers	37	3	20	306	147	159		12	240	197	43	2
16	Sun	December 24	L	7-8	Baltimore Ravens	7	31	16	251	188	63	3	23	359	256	103	3
17	Sun	December 31	W OT	8-8	Cincinnati Bengals	23	17	29	482	275	207	2	15	295	251	44	

Passing

No.		Age	Pos	G	GS	QBrec	Cmp	Att	Cmp%	Yds	TD	TD%	Int	Int%	Lng	Y/A	AY/A	Y/C	Y/G	Rate	Sk	Yds
7	Ben Roethlisberger	24	QB	15	15	7-8-0	280	469	59.7	3513	18	3.8	23	4.9	67	7.5	6.1	12.5	234.2	75.4	46	280
16	Charlie Batch	32		8	1	1-0-0	31	53	58.5	492	5	9.4	0	0.0	87	9.3	11.2	15.9	61.5	121.0	3	13
80	Cedrick Wilson	28	WR	15	12		1	1	100.0	21	0	0.0	0	0.0	21	21.0	21.0	21.0	1.4	118.7	0	0
	Team Total	27.3		16		8-8-0	312	523	59.7	4026	23	4.4	23	4.4	87	7.7	6.6	12.9	251.6	80.2	49	293
	Opp Total			16			319	529	60.3	3619	21	4.0	20	3.8		6.8	5.9	11.3	226.2	78.3	39	226

Rushing and Receiving

No.		Age	Pos	G	GS	Att	Yds	TD	Lng	Y/A	Y/G	A/G	Rec	Yds	Y/R	TD	Lng	R/G	Y/G	YScm
						Rush							**Receiving**							
39	Willie Parker*	26	RB	16	16	337	1494	13	76	4.4	93.4	21.1	31	222	7.2	3	25	1.9	13.9	1716
44	Najeh Davenport	27	KR	13	0	60	221	1	48	3.7	17.0	4.6	15	193	12.9	1	32	1.2	14.8	414
7	Ben Roethlisberger	24	QB	15	15	32	98	2	20	3.1	6.5	2.1								98
34	Verron Haynes	27		7	0	15	78	0	13	5.2	11.1	2.1	18	95	5.3	0	16	2.6	13.6	173
16	Charlie Batch	32		8	1	13	15	0	12	1.2	1.9	1.6								15
85	Nate Washington	23		16	2	3	8	0	8	2.7	0.5	0.2	35	624	17.8	4	49	2.2	39.0	632
86	Hines Ward	30	WR	14	14	2	30	0	21	15.0	2.1	0.1	74	975	13.2	6	70	5.3	69.6	1005
80	Cedrick Wilson	28	WR	15	12	2	14	0	14	7.0	0.9	0.1	37	504	13.6	1	38	2.5	33.6	518
42	John Kuhn	24		9	0	2	18	0	16	9.0	2.0	0.2	1	15	15.0	0	15	0.1	1.7	33
10	Santonio Holmes	22	WR/PR	16	4	1	13	0	13	13.0	0.8	0.1	49	824	16.8	2	67	3.1	51.5	837
35	Dan Kreider	29	FB	16	12	1	5	0	5	5.0	0.3	0.1	8	62	7.8	0	15	0.5	3.9	67
20	Bryant McFadden	25	rcb	16	9	1	-2	0	-2	-2.0	-0.1	0.1								-2
83	Heath Miller	24	TE	16	16	0	0	0	0		0.0	0.0	34	393	11.6	5	87	2.1	24.6	393
84	Jerame Tuman	30		15	4	0	0	0	0		0.0	0.0	7	73	10.4	1	21	0.5	4.9	73
81	Sean Morey	30		16	0	0	0	0	0		0.0	0.0	2	29	14.5	0	15	0.1	1.8	29
18	Walter Young	27		2	0	0	0	0	0		0.0	0.0	1	17	17.0	0	17	0.5	8.5	17
	Team Total	27.3		16		469	1992	16	76	4.2	124.5	29.3	312	4026	12.9	23	87	19.5	251.6	6018
	Opp Total			16		408	1412	9		3.5	88.3	25.5	319	3393	10.6	21		19.9	212.1	4805

Defense

No.		Age	Pos	G	GS	Sk	Def					Fumb					Tack		Sfty
							Int	Yds	TD	Lng	PD	FF	Fmb	FR	Yds	TD	Tkl	Ast	
51	James Farrior	31	LILB	16	16	4.0	1	1	0	1	6	2	0	1	0	0	85	43	
50	Larry Foote	26	RILB	16	16	4.0	1	11	0	11	3	2	0	1	0	0	62	29	
53	Clark Haggans	29	LOLB	15	15	6.0	1	0	0	0	4	2	0	1	0	0	53	24	
43	Troy Polamalu*	25	SS	13	13	1.0	3	51	0	49	9	1	0	0	0	0	57	20	
24	Ike Taylor	26	LCB	16	11		2	34	0	34	12	0	0	1	0	0	60	9	
25	Ryan Clark	27	FS	13	12		1	−1	0	−1	4	0	0	3	5	0	48	24	
91	Aaron Smith	30	LDE	16	16	4.5	0	0	0	0	2	1	0	1	0	0	46	17	
20	Bryant McFadden	25	rcb	16	9		3	39	0	39	12	0	0	3	0	0	47	7	
55	Joey Porter	29	ROLB	14	14	7.0	2	49	1	42	5						39	16	
99	Brett Keisel	28	RDE	16	16	5.5	0	0	0	0	4	0	0	1	1	0	38	18	
26	Deshea Townsend	31	RCB	16	12	2.0	2	6	0	6	11	2	0	0	0	0	37	4	
23	Tyrone Carter	30		16	3	2.0	0	0	0	0	2	1	0	1	0	0	31	12	
98	Casey Hampton*	29	NT	15	15		0	0	0	0	1	1	0	0	0	0	26	15	
27	Anthony Smith	23		16	4		2	40	0	20	5						21	5	
92	James Harrison	28		11	1												14	6	
57	Clint Kriewaldt	30		14	0		1	12	0	12	1						12	5	
31	Mike Logan	32		12	0												11	2	
37	Anthony Madison	25		13	0												10	2	
76	Chris Hoke	30		16	1												9	3	
54	Rian Wallace	24		12	0		1	30	1	30	1						5	3	
94	Chad Brown	36		9	0	1.0											3	4	
90	Travis Kirschke	32		16	0	2.0											2	5	
93	Rodney Bailey	27		12	0		0	0	0	0	1						2	4	
39	Willie Parker*	26	RB	16	16							0	7	0	0	0			
21	Ricardo Colclough	24		3	0							0	1	0	0	0	2	1	
10	Santonio Holmes	22	PR	16	4							0	5	1	0	0			
29	Chidi Iwuoma	28		2	0												2	1	
7	Ben Roethlisberger	24	QB	15	15							0	5	0	−1	0			
44	Najeh Davenport	27	KR	13	0							0	2	1	0	0			
28	Jovon Johnson	23		2	0												1	1	
80	Cedrick Wilson	28	WR	15	12							0	2	1	−7	0			
66	Alan Faneca*+	30	LG	16	16							0	0	2	0	0			
95	Richard Seigler	26		2	0												1	0	
86	Hines Ward	30	WR	14	14							0	2	0	0	0			
16	Charlie Batch	32		8	1							0	1	0	0	0			
64	Jeff Hartings	34	C	14	14							0	0	1	0	0			
34	Verron Haynes	27		7	0							0	1	0	0	0			
68	Chris Kemoeatu	23		3	2							0	0	1	0	0			
83	Heath Miller	24	TE	16	16							0	0	1	0	0			
81	Sean Morey	30		16	0							0	1	0	0	0			
77	Marvel Smith	28	LT	16	16							0	0	1	0	0			
	Team Total	27.3		16		39.0	20	272	2	49	83	12	27	22	−2	0	724	280	
	Opp Total			16		49							16	7					

2007 PITTSBURGH STEELERS: 10-6-0, TIED FOR 1ST IN AFC NORTH DIVISION
Head Coach: Mike Tomlin

Week	Day	Date	OT	Rec	Opp	Score		Offe					Defe				
						Tm	Opp	1stD	TotYd	PassY	RushY	TO	1stD	TotYd	PassY	RushY	TO
1	Sun	September 9	W	1-0	Cleveland Browns	34	7	17	365	159	206	1	13	221	175	46	5
2	Sun	September 16	W	2-0	Buffalo Bills	26	3	24	420	236	184	1	10	223	121	102	
3	Sun	September 23	W	3-0	San Francisco 49ers	37	16	19	350	145	205	1	17	289	198	91	1
4	Sun	September 30	L	3-1	Arizona Cardinals	14	21	17	282	205	77	2	19	301	215	86	2
5	Sun	October 7	W	4-1	Seattle Seahawks	21	0	19	342	179	163		8	144	106	38	1
4					Bye Week												
7	Sun	October 21	L	4-2	Denver Broncos	28	31	24	379	260	119	3	21	324	234	90	2
8	Sun	October 28	W	5-2	Cincinnati Bengals	24	13	23	390	230	160	1	15	296	205	91	1
9	Mon	November 5	W	6-2	Baltimore Ravens	38	7	14	291	201	90	1	5	104	40	64	4
10	Sun	November 11	W	7-2	Cleveland Browns	31	28	22	401	242	159	1	13	163	123	40	1
11	Sun	November 18	L	OT	7-3	New York Jets	16	19	16	263	151	112	2	20	297	146	151	1
12	Mon	November 26	W	8-3	Miami Dolphins	3	0	13	216	132	84	1	9	159	110	49	2
13	Sun	December 2	W	9-3	Cincinnati Bengals	24	10	20	285	184	101	4	15	249	175	74	1
14	Sun	December 9	L	9-4	New England Patriots	13	34	19	349	168	181	1	21	421	399	22	
15	Sun	December 16	L	9-5	Jacksonville Jaguars	22	29	13	217	102	115		25	421	197	224	1
16	Thu	December 20	W	10-5	St. Louis Rams	41	24	24	425	259	166		17	316	226	90	2
17	Sun	December 30	L	10-6	Baltimore Ravens	21	27	14	264	218	46	3	21	334	154	180	1
		Playoffs															
Wild Card	Sat	January 5	L	10-7	Jacksonville Jaguars	29	31	24	340	297	43	4	14	239	104	135	2

Passing

No.		Age	Pos	G	GS	QBrec	Cmp	Att	Cmp%	Yds	TD	TD%	Int	Int%	Lng	Y/A	AY/A	Y/C	Y/G	Rate	Sk	Yds
7	Ben Roethlisberger*	25	QB	15	15	10-5-0	264	404	65.3	3154	32	7.9	11	2.7	83	7.8	8.2	11.9	210.3	104.1	47	347
16	Charlie Batch	33		7	1	0-1-0	17	36	47.2	232	2	5.6	3	8.3	59	6.4	3.8	13.6	33.1	52.1	0	0
39	Willie Parker*	27	RB	15	15		0	1	0.0	0	0	0.0	0	0.0	0	0.0	0.0		0.0	39.6	0	0
9	Daniel Sepulveda	23	P	16	0		1	1	100.0	32	0	0.0	0	0.0	32	32.0	32.0	32.0	2.0	118.7	0	0
	Team Total	27.0		16		10-6-0	282	442	63.8	3418	34	7.7	14	3.2	83	7.7	7.8	12.1	213.6	99.9	47	347
	Opp Total			16			292	536	54.5	3067	22	4.1	11	2.1		5.7	5.6	10.5	191.7	76.5	36	243

Rushing and Receiving

No.		Age	Pos	G	GS	Rush							Receiving							YScm
						Att	Yds	TD	Lng	Y/A	Y/G	A/G	Rec	Yds	Y/R	TD	Lng	R/G	Y/G	
39	Willie Parker*	27	RB	15	15	321	1316	2	32	4.1	87.7	21.4	23	164	7.1	0	22	1.5	10.9	1480
44	Najeh Davenport	28		15	1	107	499	5	45	4.7	33.3	7.1	18	184	10.2	2	32	1.2	12.3	683
7	Ben Roethlisberger*	25	QB	15	15	35	204	2	30	5.8	13.6	2.3								204
38	Carey Davis	26	FB	16	7	17	68	0	12	4.0	4.3	1.1	12	49	4.1	0	10	0.8	3.1	117
16	Charlie Batch	33		7	1	12	-7	0	0	-0.6	-1.0	1.7								-7
33	Gary Russell	21		3	0	7	21	0	8	3.0	7.0	2.3								21
10	Santonio Holmes	23	WR	13	13	5	17	0	11	3.4	1.3	0.4	52	942	18.1	8	83	4.0	72.5	959
86	Hines Ward	31	WR	13	13	3	11	0	7	3.7	0.8	0.2	71	732	10.3	7	25	5.5	56.3	743
80	Cedrick Wilson	29		16	1	2	37	0	37	18.5	2.3	0.1	18	207	11.5	1	18	1.1	12.9	244
85	Nate Washington	24		16	4	1	0	0	0	0.0	0.0	0.1	29	450	15.5	5	40	1.8	28.1	450
35	Dan Kreider	30		10	4	1	2	0	2	2.0	0.2	0.1	1	15	15.0	0	15	0.1	1.5	17
83	Heath Miller	25	TE	16	16	0	0	0	0		0.0	0.0	47	566	12.0	7	29	2.9	35.4	566
89	Matt Spaeth	24	te	14	5	0	0	0	0		0.0	0.0	5	34	6.8	3	13	0.4	2.4	34
15	Willie Reid	25		6	0	0	0	0	0		0.0	0.0	4	54	13.5	0	25	0.7	9.0	54
34	Verron Haynes	28		1	0	0	0	0	0		0.0	0.0	1	12	12.0	0	12	1.0	12.0	12
84	Jerame Tuman	31		6	1	0	0	0	0		0.0	0.0	1	9	9.0	1	9	0.2	1.5	9
	Team Total	27.0		16		511	2168	9	45	4.2	135.5	31.9	282	3418	12.1	34	83	17.6	213.6	5586
	Opp Total			16		361	1438	6		4.0	89.9	22.6	292	2824	9.7	22		18.3	176.5	4262

Defense

No.		Age	Pos	G	GS	Sk	Def					Fumb					Tack		Sfty
							Int	Yds	TD	Lng	PD	FF	Fmb	FR	Yds	TD	Tkl	Ast	
92	James Harrison*	29	ROLB	16	16	8.5	1	20	0	20	3	7	0	3	0	0	77	21	
51	James Farrior	32	LILB	16	16	6.5	1	0	0	0	7	2	0	0	0	0	64	30	
24	Ike Taylor	27	LCB	16	16	1.0	3	56	1	51	16	1	0	1	0	0	69	11	
50	Larry Foote	27	RILB	16	16	3.0	1	14	0	14	5	3	0	0	0	0	45	36	
27	Anthony Smith	24	FS	16	10		2	50	0	50	2	1	0	1	0	0	52	16	
43	Troy Polamalu*	26	SS	11	11		0	0	0	0	9	3	0	1	13	0	45	13	
26	Deshea Townsend	32	RCB	16	16		2	44	0	23	16						45	7	
23	Tyrone Carter	31	ss	16	5	0.5	0	0	0	0	2	3	0	0	0	0	41	16	
53	Clark Haggans	30	LOLB	16	16	4.0	0	0	0	0	1	0	0	1	0	0	36	21	
99	Brett Keisel	29	RDE	16	16	2.0	0	0	0	0	7						24	16	
91	Aaron Smith	31	LDE	11	11	2.5						0	0	2	0	0	23	8	
98	Casey Hampton*	30	NT	15	15	0.5											17	16	
90	Travis Kirschke	33		16	4	2.0											17	9	
20	Bryant McFadden	26		13	0		1	50	1	50	3	0	0	1	0	0	20	2	
25	Ryan Clark	28	fs	6	6	1.0	0	0	0	0	3	1	0	0	0	0	17	5	
22	William Gay	22		16	0		0	0	0	0	2	0	1	1	0	0	13	6	
56	LaMarr Woodley	23		13	0	4.0						1	0	0	0	0	14	0	
94	Lawrence Timmons	21		16	0							0	0	2	5	0	11	2	
93	Nick Eason	27		16	1												10	4	
37	Anthony Madison	26		9	0							0	0	1	0	0	10	1	
54	Andre Frazier	25		8	0							0	0	1	0	0	8	2	
57	Clint Kriewaldt	31		14	0												3	7	
7	Ben Roethlisberger*	25	QB	15	15							0	9	4	−16	0			
30	Allen Rossum	32	PR/KR	15	0							0	3	0	0	0	3	2	
76	Chris Hoke	31		16	1	0.5											4	1	
39	Willie Parker*	27	RB	15	15							0	4	1	0	0			
21	Ricardo Colclough	25		3	0												1	0	
44	Najeh Davenport	28		15	1							0	1	1	0	0			
10	Santonio Holmes	23	WR	13	13							0	2	0	0	0			
38	Carey Davis	26	FB	16	7							0	0	1	0	0			
66	Alan Faneca*+	31	LG	16	16							0	0	1	0	0			
83	Heath Miller	25	TE	16	16							0	0	1	0	0			
15	Willie Reid	25		6	0							0	1	0	0	0			
73	Kendall Simmons	28	RG	16	16							0	0	1	0	0			
	Team Total	27.0		16		36.0	11	234	2	51	76	22	21	25	2	0	669	252	
	Opp Total			16		47							30	16					

2008 PITTSBURGH STEELERS: 12-4-0, 1ST IN AFC NORTH DIVISION
Head Coach: Mike Tomlin

2008 Super Bowl Champions

Week	Day	Date		OT	Rec	Opp	Score Tm	Opp	Offe 1stD	TotYd	PassY	RushY	TO	Defe 1stD	TotYd	PassY	RushY	TO
1	Sun	September 7	W		1-0	Houston Texans	38	17	21	305	122	183	1	20	234	159	75	3
2	Sun	September 14	W		2-0	Cleveland Browns	10	6	14	281	164	117		17	208	155	53	2
3	Sun	September 21	L		2-1	Philadelphia Eagles	6	15	14	181	147	34	3	16	260	195	65	3
4	Mon	September 29	W	OT	3-1	Baltimore Ravens	23	20	11	237	168	69	1	16	243	140	103	1
5	Sun	October 5	W		4-1	Jacksonville Jaguars	26	21	28	415	286	129	1	14	213	175	38	
4						Bye Week												
7	Sun	October 19	W		5-1	Cincinnati Bengals	38	10	20	375	250	125		16	212	128	84	1
8	Sun	October 26	L		5-2	New York Giants	14	21	12	249	154	95	4	14	282	199	83	
9	Mon	November 3	W		6-2	Washington Redskins	23	6	15	229	165	64	1	13	221	161	60	2
10	Sun	November 9	L		6-3	Indianapolis Colts	20	24	18	326	271	55	3	17	290	228	62	
11	Sun	November 16	W		7-3	San Diego Chargers	11	10	24	410	286	124		16	218	152	66	2
12	Thu	November 20	W		8-3	Cincinnati Bengals	27	10	20	364	243	121	1	11	208	165	43	1
13	Sun	November 30	W		9-3	New England Patriots	33	10	19	333	172	161	1	19	267	145	122	5
14	Sun	December 7	W		10-3	Dallas Cowboys	20	13	13	238	168	70	2	15	289	194	95	5
15	Sun	December 14	W		11-3	Baltimore Ravens	13	9	18	311	220	91	2	12	202	90	112	2
16	Sun	December 21	L		11-4	Tennessee Titans	14	31	23	374	301	73	4	16	322	205	117	
17	Sun	December 28	W		12-4	Cleveland Browns	31	0	20	369	193	176	1	8	126	20	106	2
		Playoffs																
Division	Sun	January 11	W		13-4	San Diego Chargers	35	24	22	342	177	165		15	290	275	15	2
Conf Champ	Sun	January 18	W		14-4	Baltimore Ravens	23	14	11	275	223	52	1	13	198	125	73	4
Super Bowl	Sun	February 1	W		15-4	Arizona Cardinals	27	23	20	292	234	58	1	23	407	374	33	2

Passing

No.		Age	Pos	G	GS	QBrec	Cmp	Att	Cmp%	Yds	TD	TD%	Int	Int%	Lng	Y/A	AY/A	Y/C	Y/G	Rate	Sk	Yds
7	Ben Roethlisberger	26	QB	16	16	12-4-0	281	469	59.9	3301	17	3.6	15	3.2	65	7.0	6.3	11.7	206.3	80.1	46	284
4	Byron Leftwich	28		5	0		21	36	58.3	303	2	5.6	0	0.0	50	8.4	9.5	14.4	80.8	104.3	3	22
2	Dennis Dixon	23		1	0		1	1	100.0	3	0	0.0	0	0.0	3	3.0	3.0	3.0	3.0	79.2	0	0
	Team Total	27.2		16		12-4-0	303	506	59.9	3607	19	3.8	15	3.0	65	7.1	6.5	11.9	225.4	81.9	49	306
	Opp Total			16			301	533	56.5	2861	12	2.3	20	3.8		5.4	4.1	9.5	178.8	63.4	51	350

Rushing and Receiving

No.		Age	Pos	G	GS	Rush Att	Yds	TD	Lng	Y/A	Y/G	A/G	Receiving Rec	Yds	Y/R	TD	Lng	R/G	Y/G	YScm
39	Willie Parker	28	RB	11	11	210	791	5	34	3.8	71.9	19.1	3	13	4.3	0	5	0.3	1.2	804
21	Mewelde Moore	26		16	4	140	588	5	32	4.2	36.8	8.8	40	320	8.0	1	25	2.5	20.0	908
7	Ben Roethlisberger	26	QB	16	16	34	101	2	17	3.0	6.3	2.1	1	−7	−7.0	0	−7	0.1	−0.4	94
33	Gary Russell	22	KR	12	0	28	77	3	15	2.8	6.4	2.3	1	−2	−2.0	0	−2	0.1	−0.2	75
34	Rashard Mendenhall	21		4	1	19	58	0	12	3.1	14.5	4.8	2	17	8.5	0	11	0.5	4.3	75
38	Carey Davis	27		14	3	12	35	0	11	2.9	2.5	0.9	5	27	5.4	0	14	0.4	1.9	62
85	Nate Washington	25		16	1	5	18	0	8	3.6	1.1	0.3	40	631	15.8	3	65	2.5	39.4	649
4	Byron Leftwich	28		5	0	4	7	1	8	1.8	1.4	0.8								7
10	Santonio Holmes	24	WR/PR	15	15	2	9	0	10	4.5	0.6	0.1	55	821	14.9	5	48	3.7	54.7	830
44	Najeh Davenport	29		4	0	2	5	0	3	2.5	1.3	0.5								5
2	Dennis Dixon	23		1	0	2	−3	0	−1	−1.5	−3.0	2.0								−3
86	Hines Ward	32	WR	16	15	1	4	0	4	4.0	0.3	0.1	81	1043	12.9	7	49	5.1	65.2	1047
17	Mitch Berger	36	P	13	0	1	0	0	0	0.0	0.0	0.1								0
83	Heath Miller	26	TE	14	14	0	0	0	0		0.0	0.0	48	514	10.7	3	22	3.4	36.7	514
89	Matt Spaeth	25	TE	16	13	0	0	0	0		0.0	0.0	17	136	8.0	0	13	1.1	8.5	136
14	Limas Sweed	24		11	0	0	0	0	0		0.0	0.0	6	64	10.7	0	17	0.5	5.8	64
49	Sean McHugh	26		15	3	0	0	0	0		0.0	0.0	3	24	8.0	0	15	0.2	1.6	24
81	Dallas Baker	26		8	0	0	0	0	0		0.0	0.0	1	6	6.0	0	6	0.1	0.8	6
	Team Total	27.2		16		460	1690	16	34	3.7	105.6	28.8	303	3607	11.9	19	65	18.9	225.4	5297
	Opp Total			16		390	1284	7		3.3	80.3	24.4	301	2511	8.3	12		18.8	156.9	3795

Defense

No.		Age	Pos	G	GS	Sk	Def					Fumb					Tack		Sfty
							Int	Yds	TD	Lng	PD	FF	Fmb	FR	Yds	TD	Tkl	Ast	
51	James Farrior*	33	LILB	16	16	3.5	0	0	0	0	5	1	0	1	0	0	89	44	
92	James Harrison*+	30	ROLB	15	15	16.0	1	33	0	33	3	7	1	0	−18	0	59	34	1
25	Ryan Clark	29	FS	14	14		1	0	0	0	6						50	35	
43	Troy Polamalu*+	27	SS	16	16		7	59	0	23	17						54	19	
56	LaMarr Woodley	24	LOLB	15	15	11.5	1	6	0	6	2	2	0	4	9	1	41	19	
24	Ike Taylor	28	LCB	16	16		1	0	0	0	14						47	15	
91	Aaron Smith	32	LDE	16	16	5.5	0	0	0	0	4						44	16	
94	Lawrence Timmons	22		16	2	5.0	1	89	0	89	3	1	0	1	0	0	35	22	
50	Larry Foote	28	RILB	16	16	1.5	0	0	0	0	3	1	0	0	0	0	34	29	
20	Bryant McFadden	27	RCB	10	8	1.0	2	0	0	0	8	0	0	1	0	0	36	4	
90	Travis Kirschke	34	rde	16	6	2.0						0	0	1	0	0	30	16	
99	Brett Keisel	30	RDE	10	10	1.0	0	0	0	0	2						22	19	
22	William Gay	23		16	4		1	12	0	12	7						26	8	
26	Deshea Townsend	33		12	4		2	27	1	25	8	0	1	1	0	0	16	4	
98	Casey Hampton	31	NT	13	13	1.0	0	0	0	0	1						13	9	
23	Tyrone Carter	32		16	2		3	64	1	32	5						11	4	
93	Nick Eason	28		15	0	1.5	0	0	0	0	1						10	7	
76	Chris Hoke	32		16	3	0.5											12	4	
7	Ben Roethlisberger	26	QB	16	16							0	14	3	−5	0	2	0	
54	Andre Frazier	26		15	0	1.0											4	3	
83	Heath Miller	26	TE	14	14							0	1	0	0	0	5	0	
57	Keyaron Fox	26		13	0							0	0	2	18	0	1	6	
96	Orpheus Roye	35		6	0		0	0	0	0	1						3	3	
31	Fernando Bryant	31		2	0												3	0	
10	Santonio Holmes	24	WR/PR	15	15							0	4	2	0	0			
46	Patrick Bailey	23		12	0												0	5	
33	Gary Russell	22	KR	12	0												1	3	
27	Anthony Smith	25		14	0												2	1	
14	Limas Sweed	24		11	0							0	2	1	0	0	1	0	
38	Carey Davis	27		14	3							0	2	1	0	0	0	1	
62	Justin Hartwig	30	C	16	16												2	0	
68	Chris Kemoeatu	25	LG	16	16							0	0	2	0	0	1	0	
37	Anthony Madison	27		16	0												1	2	
21	Mewelde Moore	26		16	4							0	2	0	0	0	1	0	
39	Willie Parker	28	RB	11	11												2	0	
86	Hines Ward	32	WR	16	15							0	1	0	0	0	1	0	
85	Nate Washington	25		16	1												1	1	
74	Willie Colon	25	RT	16	16							0	0	2	0	0			
49	Sean McHugh	26		15	3												1	0	
89	Matt Spaeth	25	TE	16	13												1	0	
78	Max Starks	26	LT	16	11												1	0	
95	Donovan Woods	23		5	0												0	2	
44	Najeh Davenport	29		4	0												0	1	
61	Jared Retkofsky	25		9	0												0	1	
73	Kendall Simmons	29		4	4												0	1	
60	Greg Warren	27		7	0												0	1	
Team Total		27.2		16		51.0	20	290	2	89	90	12	28	22	4	1	663	339	1
Opp Total				16		49							22	13					2

2009 PITTSBURGH STEELERS: 9-7-0, TIED FOR 2ND IN AFC NORTH DIVISION
Head Coach: Mike Tomlin

						Score		Offe					Defe				
Week	Day	Date	OT	Rec	Opp	Tm	Opp	1stD	TotYd	PassY	RushY	TO	1stD	TotYd	PassY	RushY	TO
1	Thu	September 10	W OT	1-0	Tennessee Titans	13	10	19	357	321	36	3	18	320	234	86	2
2	Sun	September 20	L	1-1	Chicago Bears	14	17	21	308	203	105	2	17	275	231	44	
3	Sun	September 27	L	1-2	Cincinnati Bengals	20	23	17	373	271	102	1	19	273	173	100	
4	Sun	October 4	W	2-2	San Diego Chargers	38	28	32	497	320	177	1	17	251	235	16	1
5	Sun	October 11	W	3-2	Detroit Lions	28	20	18	344	262	82	1	21	335	225	110	1
6	Sun	October 18	W	4-2	Cleveland Browns	27	14	28	543	403	140	4	12	197	106	91	4
7	Sun	October 25	W	5-2	Minnesota Vikings	27	17	14	259	152	107	1	21	386	297	89	2
8					Bye Week												
9	Mon	November 9	W	6-2	Denver Broncos	28	10	21	375	202	173	2	12	242	215	27	3
10	Sun	November 15	L	6-3	Cincinnati Bengals	12	18	16	226	146	80	1	14	218	157	61	
11	Sun	November 22	L OT	6-4	Kansas City Chiefs	24	27	27	516	402	114	3	13	282	214	68	1
12	Sun	November 29	L OT	6-5	Baltimore Ravens	17	20	16	298	145	153	1	21	393	261	132	2
13	Sun	December 6	L	6-6	Oakland Raiders	24	27	19	401	269	132	1	19	396	287	109	
14	Thu	December 10	L	6-7	Cleveland Browns	6	13	16	218	141	77		12	255	84	171	
15	Sun	December 20	W	7-7	Green Bay Packers	37	36	28	537	472	65		18	436	376	60	
16	Sun	December 27	W	8-7	Baltimore Ravens	23	20	17	286	238	48	2	20	323	148	175	3
17	Sun	January 3	W	9-7	Miami Dolphins	30	24	22	403	201	202	2	20	303	204	99	3

Passing

No.		Age	Pos	G	GS	QBrec	Cmp	Att	Cmp%	Yds	TD	TD%	Int	Int%	Lng	Y/A	AY/A	Y/C	Y/G	Rate	Sk	Yds
7	Ben Roethlisberger	27	QB	15	15	9-6-0	337	506	66.6	4328	26	5.1	12	2.4	60	8.6	8.5	12.8	288.5	100.5	50	348
2	Dennis Dixon	24		1	1	0-1-0	12	26	46.2	145	1	3.8	1	3.8	33	5.6	4.6	12.1	145.0	60.6	0	0
16	Charlie Batch	35		1	0		1	2	50.0	17	0	0.0	0	0.0	17	8.5	8.5	17.0	17.0	79.2	0	0
10	Santonio Holmes	25	WR	16	16		0	1	0.0	0	0	0.0	0	0.0	0	0.0	0.0		0.0	39.6	0	0
21	Mewelde Moore	27		16	0		1	1	100.0	6	1	100.0	0	0.0	6	6.0	26.0	6.0	0.4	131.2	0	0
	Team Total	27.4		16		9-7-0	351	536	65.5	4496	28	5.2	13	2.4	60	8.4	8.3	12.8	281.0	98.9	50	348
	Opp Total			16			319	548	58.2	3761	22	4.0	12	2.2		6.9	6.7	11.8	235.1	83.4	47	314

Rushing and Receiving

No.		Age	Pos	G	GS	Rush							Receiving							YScm
						Att	Yds	TD	Lng	Y/A	Y/G	A/G	Rec	Yds	Y/R	TD	Lng	R/G	Y/G	
34	Rashard Mendenhall	22	RB	16	12	242	1108	7	60	4.6	69.3	15.1	25	261	10.4	1	26	1.6	16.3	1369
39	Willie Parker	29		14	3	98	389	0	34	4.0	27.8	7.0	6	64	10.7	1	27	0.4	4.6	453
7	Ben Roethlisberger	27	QB	15	15	40	82	2	15	2.1	5.5	2.7								82
21	Mewelde Moore	27		16	0	35	118	0	15	3.4	7.4	2.2	21	153	7.3	2	19	1.3	9.6	271
17	Mike Wallace	23		16	4	5	48	0	21	9.6	3.0	0.3	39	756	19.4	6	60	2.4	47.3	804
10	Santonio Holmes	25	WR	16	16	3	6	0	7	2.0	0.4	0.2	79	1248	15.8	5	57	4.9	78.0	1254
2	Dennis Dixon	24		1	1	3	27	1	24	9.0	27.0	3.0								27
38	Carey Davis	28		6	0	2	15	0	14	7.5	2.5	0.3								15
86	Hines Ward	33	WR	16	16	0	0	0	0		0.0	0.0	95	1167	12.3	6	54	5.9	72.9	1167
83	Heath Miller*	27	TE	16	16	0	0	0	0		0.0	0.0	76	789	10.4	6	41	4.8	49.3	789
89	Matt Spaeth	26	TE	16	8	0	0	0	0		0.0	0.0	5	25	5.0	1	9	0.3	1.6	25
85	David Johnson	22		15	3	0	0	0	0		0.0	0.0	2	9	4.5	0	5	0.1	0.6	9
19	Tyler Grisham	22		4	0	0	0	0	0		0.0	0.0	1	14	14.0	0	14	0.3	3.5	14
11	Stefan Logan	28	PR/KR	16	1	0	0	0	0		0.0	0.0	1	5	5.0	0	5	0.1	0.3	5
14	Limas Sweed	25		9	0	0	0	0	0		0.0	0.0	1	5	5.0	0	5	0.1	0.6	5
	Team Total	27.4		16		428	1793	10	60	4.2	112.1	26.8	351	4496	12.8	28	60	21.9	281.0	6289
	Opp Total			16		372	1438	7		3.9	89.9	23.3	319	3447	10.8	22		19.9	215.4	4885

Defense

No.	Name	Age	Pos	G	GS	Sk	Def Int	Yds	TD	Lng	PD	Fumb FF	Fmb	FR	Yds	TD	Tack Tkl	Ast	Sfty
51	James Farrior	34	LILB	16	16	3.0	1	18	0	18	5	1	0	1	0	0	68	34	
25	Ryan Clark	30	FS	15	15		3	0	0	0	8						68	20	
92	James Harrison*	31	ROLB	16	16	10.0	0	0	0	0	3	5	0	2	0	0	60	19	
22	William Gay	24	RCB	16	14	1.0	0	0	0	0	10	1	0	0	0	0	67	8	
94	Lawrence Timmons	23	RILB	14	13	7.0	0	0	0	0	4	4	0	0	0	0	55	22	
56	LaMarr Woodley*	25	LOLB	16	16	13.5	0	0	0	0	6	1	0	1	77	1	51	11	
24	Ike Taylor	29	LCB	16	16	1.0	1	20	0	20	13	0	0	1	1	0	52	9	
23	Tyrone Carter	33	SS	16	12	1.0	2	53	1	48	4	1	0	1	6	0	49	12	
99	Brett Keisel	31	RDE	15	15	3.0	0	0	0	0	2	1	0	2	0	0	36	18	
98	Casey Hampton*	32	NT	16	16	2.5											23	20	
26	Deshea Townsend	34		16	2		1	−1	0	−1	3						24	3	
57	Keyaron Fox	27		16	3		1	82	1	82	1	0	0	1	5	0	18	13	
90	Travis Kirschke	35	LDE	12	7	1.0											16	10	
43	Troy Polamalu	28	ss	5	5		3	17	0	16	7						18	2	
93	Nick Eason	29	lde	8	5												15	1	
29	Ryan Mundy	24		16	0		0	0	0	0	1	0	0	1	0	0	5	8	
91	Aaron Smith	33	lde	5	5	2.0											6	3	
96	Ziggy Hood	22		16	0	1.0	0	0	0	0	2	0	0	1	−1	0	5	3	
83	Heath Miller*	27	TE	16	16							0	2	0	0	0	4	2	
27	Joe Burnett	23		15	0												3	5	
7	Ben Roethlisberger	27	QB	15	15							0	7	2	−6	0			
11	Stefan Logan	28	PR/KR	16	1							0	3	0	0	0	0	5	
34	Rashard Mendenhall	22	RB	16	12							0	3	1	0	0	2	0	
31	Keiwan Ratliff	28		8	0												4	0	
17	Mike Wallace	23		16	4							0	1	0	0	0	3	0	
54	Andre Frazier	27		14	0												0	6	
97	Arnold Harrison	27		8	0												0	5	
76	Chris Hoke	33		16	0												1	3	
78	Max Starks	27	LT	16	16												2	1	
50	Rocky Boiman	29		6	0												0	4	
37	Anthony Madison	28		5	0												0	3	
39	Willie Parker	29		14	3							0	2	1	0	0			
62	Justin Hartwig	31	C	16	16												1	0	
10	Santonio Holmes	25	WR	16	16												1	0	
35	Corey Ivy	32		1	0		0	0	0	0	1						1	0	
64	Doug Legursky	23		8	0												1	0	
21	Mewelde Moore	27		16	0												1	0	
89	Matt Spaeth	26	TE	16	8							0	1	1	0	0			
14	Limas Sweed	25		9	0												1	0	
86	Hines Ward	33	WR	16	16							0	2	0	0	0			
38	Carey Davis	28		6	0							0	0	1	0	0			
95	Donovan Woods	24		1	0												0	1	
	Team Total	27.4		16		46.0	12	189	2	82	70	14	21	17	82	1	661	251	
	Opp Total			16		50							21	11					

2010 PITTSBURGH STEELERS: 12-4-0, 1ST IN AFC NORTH DIVISION, 2010 AFC CHAMPIONS

Head Coach: Mike Tomlin

Week	Day	Date	OT	Rec	Opp	Score Tm	Score Opp	1stD	TotYd	PassY	RushY	TO	1stD	TotYd	PassY	RushY	TO
1	Sun	September 12	W OT	1-0	Atlanta Falcons	15	9	14	354	211	143	1	18	295	237	58	1
2	Sun	September 19	W	2-0	Tennessee Titans	19	11	7	127	21	106	1	14	238	192	46	7
3	Sun	September 26	W	3-0	Tampa Bay Buccaneers	38	13	17	387	186	201	2	18	303	228	75	2
4	Sun	October 3	L	3-1	Baltimore Ravens	14	17	14	210	126	84	1	22	320	250	70	2
5					Bye Week												
6	Sun	October 17	W	4-1	Cleveland Browns	28	10	22	378	257	121	1	17	327	258	69	3
7	Sun	October 24	W	5-1	Miami Dolphins	23	22	15	348	290	58	2	15	313	249	64	2
8	Sun	October 31	L	5-2	New Orleans Saints	10	20	13	279	171	108	2	19	318	288	30	2
9	Mon	November 8	W	6-2	Cincinnati Bengals	27	21	14	314	193	121	2	18	272	218	54	2
10	Sun	November 14	L	6-3	New England Patriots	26	39	27	425	349	76	1	26	453	350	103	
11	Sun	November 21	W	7-3	Oakland Raiders	35	3	18	431	269	162	1	17	182	121	61	3
12	Sun	November 28	W OT	8-3	Buffalo Bills	19	16	28	426	220	206	1	19	329	255	74	2
13	Sun	December 5	W	9-3	Baltimore Ravens	13	10	17	288	234	54	1	14	269	226	43	1
14	Sun	December 12	W	10-3	Cincinnati Bengals	23	7	18	354	231	123		14	190	156	34	3
15	Sun	December 19	L	10-4	New York Jets	17	22	25	377	231	146		17	276	170	106	
16	Thu	December 23	W	11-4	Carolina Panthers	27	3	22	408	293	115	2	7	119	45	74	2
17	Sun	January 2	W	12-4	Cleveland Browns	41	9	24	418	318	100		17	225	182	43	3
Playoffs																	
Division	Sat	January 15	W	13-4	Baltimore Ravens	31	24	21	263	192	71	2	12	126	91	35	3
Conf Champ	Sun	January 23	W	14-4	New York Jets	24	19	23	287	121	166	2	17	289	219	70	1
Super Bowl	Sun	February 6	L	14-5	Green Bay Packers	25	31	19	387	261	126	3	15	338	288	50	

Passing

No.		Age	Pos	G	GS	QBrec	Cmp	Att	Cmp%	Yds	TD	TD%	Int	Int%	Lng	Y/A	AY/A	Y/C	Y/G	Rate	Sk	Yds
7	Ben Roethlisberger	28	QB	12	12	9-3-0	240	389	61.7	3200	17	4.4	5	1.3	56	8.2	8.5	13.3	266.7	97.0	32	220
16	Charlie Batch	36		3	2	1-1-0	29	49	59.2	352	3	6.1	3	6.1	46	7.2	5.7	12.1	117.3	76.2	4	21
10	Dennis Dixon	25		2	2	2-0-0	22	32	68.8	254	0	0.0	1	3.1	52	7.9	6.5	11.5	127.0	79.4	5	41
4	Byron Leftwich	30		1	0		5	7	71.4	42	0	0.0	0	0.0	14	6.0	6.0	8.4	42.0	86.6	2	7
82	Antwaan Randle El	31		16	0		2	2	100.0	42	2	100.0	0	0.0	39	21.0	41.0	21.0	2.6	158.3	0	0
	Team Total	27.5		16		12-4-0	298	479	62.2	3890	22	4.6	9	1.9	56	8.1	8.2	13.1	243.1	95.2	43	289
	Opp Total			16			363	593	61.2	3744	15	2.5	21	3.5		6.3	5.2	10.3	234.0	73.1	48	319

Rushing and Receiving

No.		Age	Pos	G	GS	Rush Att	Rush Yds	Rush TD	Rush Lng	Rush Y/A	Rush Y/G	Rush A/G	Rec	Rec Yds	Rec Y/R	Rec TD	Rec Lng	Rec R/G	Rec Y/G	YScm
34	Rashard Mendenhall	23	RB	16	16	324	1273	13	50	3.9	79.6	20.3	23	167	7.3	0	24	1.4	10.4	1440
33	Isaac Redman	26		16	0	53	247	0	23	4.7	15.4	3.3	9	72	8.0	2	16	0.6	4.5	319
21	Mewelde Moore	28		15	0	33	99	0	18	3.0	6.6	2.2	26	205	7.9	0	29	1.7	13.7	304
7	Ben Roethlisberger	28	QB	12	12	33	176	2	31	5.3	14.7	2.8								176
27	Jonathan Dwyer	21		1	0	9	28	0	7	3.1	28.0	9.0								28
16	Charlie Batch	36		3	2	7	30	0	24	4.3	10.0	2.3								30
17	Mike Wallace	24	WR	16	16	5	39	0	19	7.8	2.4	0.3	60	1257	21.0	10	56	3.8	78.6	1296
10	Dennis Dixon	25		2	2	5	32	0	21	6.4	16.0	2.5								32
86	Hines Ward	34	WR	16	15	1	-2	0	-2	-2.0	-0.1	0.1	59	755	12.8	5	43	3.7	47.2	753
82	Antwaan Randle El	31		16	0	1	2	0	2	2.0	0.1	0.1	22	253	11.5	0	34	1.4	15.8	255
83	Heath Miller	28	TE	14	14	0	0	0	0		0.0	0.0	42	512	12.2	2	36	3.0	36.6	512
88	Emmanuel Sanders	27	WR/KR	13	1	0	0	0	0		0.0	0.0	28	376	13.4	2	35	2.2	28.9	376
84	Antonio Brown	24	WR/PR	9	0	0	0	0	0		0.0	0.0	16	167	10.4	0	26	1.8	18.6	167
89	Matt Spaeth	27	TE	14	13	0	0	0	0		0.0	0.0	9	80	8.9	1	13	0.6	5.7	80
85	David Johnson	23	te	16	5	0	0	0	0		0.0	0.0	4	46	11.5	0	25	0.3	2.9	46
	Team Total	27.5		16		471	1924	15	50	4.1	120.3	29.4	298	3890	13.1	22	56	18.6	243.1	5814
	Opp Total			16		333	1004	5		3.0	62.8	20.8	363	3425	9.4	15		22.7	214.1	4429

Defense

No.	Name	Age	Pos	G	GS	Sk	Def					Fumb					Tack		Sfty
							Int	Yds	TD	Lng	PD	FF	Fmb	FR	Yds	TD	Tkl	Ast	
94	Lawrence Timmons	24	RILB	16	15	3.0	2	5	0	5	10	2	0	2	0	0	95	39	
51	James Farrior	35	LILB	16	16	6.0	0	0	0	0	5	1	0	1	8	0	80	29	
92	James Harrison*+	32	ROLB	16	16	10.5	2	2	0	2	4	6	0	1	0	0	70	30	
20	Bryant McFadden	29	LCB	16	16	2.0	2	−3	0	0	10	2	0	0	0	0	74	8	
25	Ryan Clark	31	FS	16	15		2	34	0	23	7	0	0	1	5	0	57	33	
43	Troy Polamalu*+	29	SS	14	14	1.0	7	101	1	45	11	1	0	1	0	0	49	15	
24	Ike Taylor	30	RCB	16	15	1.0	2	9	0	9	10	1	0	0	0	0	46	15	
56	LaMarr Woodley	26	LOLB	16	16	10.0	2	22	1	14	5	3	0	2	19	0	35	15	
22	William Gay	25		16	4	2.0	0	0	0	0	11	1	0	0	0	0	34	7	
99	Brett Keisel*	32	RDE	11	11	3.0	1	79	1	79	7	2	0	0	0	0	17	16	
50	Larry Foote	30		16	0	1.0	0	0	0	0	1						16	5	
96	Ziggy Hood	23	LDE	16	9	3.0	0	0	0	0	1						15	5	
29	Ryan Mundy	25		16	2		0	0	0	0	4						14	6	
98	Casey Hampton	33	NT	15	14	1.0						1	0	0	0	0	10	10	
93	Nick Eason	30	rde	16	5	1.5	0	0	0	0	1						7	9	
91	Aaron Smith	34	lde	6	6												7	8	
76	Chris Hoke	34		15	1							0	0	1	0	0	7	4	
57	Keyaron Fox	28		16	0		0	0	0	0	2	1	0	2	0	0	5	6	
37	Anthony Madison	29		16	1	1.0	1	−1	0	−1	1	0	0	1	0	0	3	9	
97	Jason Worilds	22		14	0	2.0	0	0	0	0	1	0	0	1	0	0	2	5	
86	Hines Ward	34	WR	16	15							0	1	0	0	0	4	0	
26	Will Allen	28		14	0							0	0	1	0	0	3	1	
23	Keenan Lewis	24		9	0							1	0	0	0	0	2	3	
83	Heath Miller	28	TE	14	14							0	1	0	0	0	3	0	
7	Ben Roethlisberger	28	QB	12	12							0	6	1	−6	0			
55	Stevenson Sylvester	22		16	0							1	0	0	0	0	3	1	
34	Rashard Mendenhall	23	RB	16	16							0	2	0	0	0	2	0	
33	Isaac Redman	26		16	0							0	2	1	−6	0	1	1	
88	Emmanuel Sanders	27	KR	13	1							1	2	0	0	0	0	4	
69	Steve McLendon	24		7	0							0	0	1	0	0	2	0	
53	Maurkice Pouncey*	21	C	16	16							0	0	2	0	0	1	0	
82	Antwaan Randle El	31		16	0							0	2	2	0	0			
71	Flozell Adams	35	RT	16	16							0	0	1	0	0	1	0	
16	Charlie Batch	36		3	2							0	2	1	−3	0			
84	Antonio Brown	24	PR	9	0							0	1	0	0	0	1	0	
21	Mewelde Moore	28		15	0							0	0	1	0	0	1	0	
81	Arnaz Battle	30		15	0												0	2	
10	Dennis Dixon	25		2	2							0	2	0	−4	0			
68	Chris Kemoeatu	27	LG	15	15												1	0	
17	Mike Wallace	24	WR	16	16							0	1	1	0	0			
60	Greg Warren	29		16	0												0	2	
6	Shaun Suisham	29		7	0												0	1	
	Team Total	27.5		16		48.0	21	248	3	79	91	24	22	25	13	0	668	289	
	Opp Total			16		43							28	14					

2011 PITTSBURGH STEELERS: 12-4-0, 1ST IN AFC NORTH DIVISION
Head Coach: Mike Tomlin

Week	Day	Date	OT	Rec	Opp	Score Tm	Score Opp	Offe 1stD	Offe TotYd	Offe PassY	Offe RushY	Offe TO	Defe 1stD	Defe TotYd	Defe PassY	Defe RushY	Defe TO
1	Sun	September 11	L	0-1	Baltimore Ravens	7	35	20	312	246	66	7	17	385	215	170	
2	Sun	September 18	W	1-1	Seattle Seahawks	24	0	23	421	297	124		8	164	133	31	
3	Sun	September 25	W	2-1	Indianapolis Colts	23	20	19	408	341	67	3	14	241	144	97	1
4	Sun	October 2	L	2-2	Houston Texans	10	17	20	296	178	118	1	17	318	138	180	
5	Sun	October 9	W	3-2	Tennessee Titans	38	17	26	431	257	174	1	20	306	240	66	1
6	Sun	October 16	W	4-2	Jacksonville Jaguars	17	13	15	370	185	185		16	209	76	133	
7	Sun	October 23	W	5-2	Arizona Cardinals	32	20	26	445	354	91		23	330	257	73	1
8	Sun	October 30	W	6-2	New England Patriots	25	17	29	427	329	98	1	19	213	170	43	
9	Sun	November 6	L	6-3	Baltimore Ravens	20	23	20	392	322	70	2	23	356	289	67	1
10	Sun	November 13	W	7-3	Cincinnati Bengals	24	17	24	328	223	105	1	14	279	170	109	2
11					Bye Week												
12	Sun	November 27	W	8-3	Kansas City Chiefs	13	9	18	290	182	108	2	15	252	162	90	4
13	Sun	December 4	W	9-3	Cincinnati Bengals	35	7	22	295	159	136		13	232	128	104	2
14	Thu	December 8	W	10-3	Cleveland Browns	14	3	20	416	269	147	3	19	304	206	98	2
15	Mon	December 19	L	10-4	San Francisco 49ers	3	20	20	389	305	84	4	17	287	187	100	
16	Sat	December 24	W	11-4	St. Louis Rams	27	0	17	377	208	169	1	15	232	68	164	
17	Sun	January 1	W	12-4	Cleveland Browns	13	9	22	360	199	161	2	14	240	168	72	1
		Playoffs															
Wild Card	Sun	January 8	L OT	12-5	Denver Broncos	23	29	21	400	244	156	1	18	447	316	131	1

Passing

No.		Age	Pos	G	GS	QBrec	Cmp	Att	Cmp%	Yds	TD	TD%	Int	Int%	Lng	Y/A	AY/A	Y/C	Y/G	Rate	Sk	Yds
7	Ben Roethlisberger*	29	QB	15	15	11-4-0	324	513	63.2	4077	21	4.1	14	2.7	95	7.9	7.5	12.6	271.8	90.1	40	269
16	Charlie Batch	37	qb	4	1	1-0-0	15	24	62.5	208	0	0.0	1	4.2	46	8.7	6.8	13.9	52.0	72.9	2	10
88	Emmanuel Sanders	28	wr	11	1		1	1	100.0	15	0	0.0	0	0.0	15	15.0	15.0	15.0	1.4	118.7	0	0
9	Daniel Sepulveda	27	p	8	0		1	1	100.0	33	0	0.0	0	0.0	33	33.0	33.0	33.0	4.1	118.7	0	0
	Team Total	27.0		16		12-4-0	341	539	63.3	4333	21	3.9	15	2.8	95	8.0	7.6	12.7	270.8	89.7	42	279
	Opp Total			16			289	530	54.5	2981	15	2.8	11	2.1		5.6	5.3	10.3	186.3	71.7	35	230

Rushing and Receiving

No.		Age	Pos	G	GS	Rush Att	Rush Yds	Rush TD	Rush Lng	Rush Y/A	Rush Y/G	Rush A/G	Rec Rec	Rec Yds	Rec Y/R	Rec TD	Rec Lng	Rec R/G	Rec Y/G	YScm
34	Rashard Mendenhall	24	RB	15	15	228	928	9	68	4.1	61.9	15.2	18	154	8.6	0	35	1.2	10.3	1082
33	Isaac Redman	27	rb	16	1	110	479	3	27	4.4	29.9	6.9	18	78	4.3	0	12	1.1	4.9	557
7	Ben Roethlisberger*	29	QB	15	15	31	70	0	11	2.3	4.7	2.1								70
21	Mewelde Moore	29		12	0	22	157	0	21	7.1	13.1	1.8	11	104	9.5	1	24	0.9	8.7	261
27	Jonathan Dwyer	22		7	0	16	123	0	76	7.7	17.6	2.3	1	6	6.0	0	6	0.1	0.9	129
38	John Clay	23		2	0	10	41	1	10	4.1	20.5	5.0								41
84	Antonio Brown*	25	wr	16	3	7	41	0	10	5.9	2.6	0.4	69	1108	16.1	2	79	4.3	69.3	1149
17	Mike Wallace*	25	WR	16	14	5	57	0	21	11.4	3.6	0.3	72	1193	16.6	8	95	4.5	74.6	1250
16	Charlie Batch	37	qb	4	1	3	-2	0	0	-0.7	-0.5	0.8								-2
83	Heath Miller	29	TE	16	16	1	6	0	6	6.0	0.4	0.1	51	631	12.4	2	39	3.2	39.4	637
82	Jerricho Cotchery	29		13	0	1	3	0	3	3.0	0.2	0.1	16	237	14.8	2	36	1.2	18.2	240
86	Hines Ward	35	WR	15	9	0	0	0	0		0.0	0.0	46	381	8.3	2	31	3.1	25.4	381
88	Emmanuel Sanders	28	wr	11	1	0	0	0	0		0.0	0.0	22	288	13.1	2	32	2.0	26.2	288
85	David Johnson	24	fb/TE	16	16	0	0	0	0		0.0	0.0	12	91	7.6	1	25	0.8	5.7	91
44	Weslye Saunders	22	te	16	5	0	0	0	0		0.0	0.0	4	29	7.3	1	14	0.3	1.8	29
29	Ryan Mundy	26		16	0	0	0	0	0		0.0	0.0	1	33	33.0	0	33	0.1	2.1	33
	Team Total	27.0		16		434	1903	13	76	4.4	118.9	27.1	341	4333	12.7	21	95	21.3	270.8	6236
	Opp Total			16		399	1597	7		4.0	99.8	24.9	289	2751	9.5	15		18.1	171.9	4348

Defense

No.	Name	Age	Pos	G	GS	Sk	Int	Yds	TD	Lng	PD	FF	Fmb	FR	Yds	TD	Tkl	Ast	Sfty
25	Ryan Clark	32	FS	16	16	1.0	1	10	0	10	5						71	29	
43	Troy Polamalu*+	30	SS	16	16	1.0	2	33	0	33	14	0	0	1	16	1	66	29	
94	Lawrence Timmons	25	RILB	16	16	2.0	1	0	0	0	5	1	0	0	0	0	68	26	
51	James Farrior	36	LILB	14	14	2.0	0	0	0	0	3						57	24	
22	William Gay	26	CB	16	14		2	12	0	12	14	0	0	1	2	0	53	12	
92	James Harrison	33	ROLB	11	11	9.0	0	0	0	0	1	2	0	0	0	0	50	12	
24	Ike Taylor	31	RCB	16	16		2	29	0	29	14						39	11	
99	Brett Keisel	33	DE	14	14	3.0	0	0	0	0	6	2	0	1	0	0	33	15	
56	LaMarr Woodley	27	LOLB	10	10	9.0	1	1	0	1	2	0	0	1	0	0	28	13	
50	Larry Foote	31	lb	15	5	1.5	0	0	0	0	1						29	17	
23	Keenan Lewis	25	cb	16	1		1	9	0	9	6						28	7	
93	Jason Worilds	23	lb	12	7	3.0						1	0	0	0	0	25	11	
96	Ziggy Hood	24	de	16	7	1.5	0	0	0	0	1						23	12	
29	Ryan Mundy	26		16	0		1	5	0	5	1	2	0	0	0	0	20	17	
98	Casey Hampton	34	NT	13	12												17	14	
95	Cameron Heyward	22		16	0	1.0	0	0	0	0	1	1	0	0	0	0	13	2	
69	Steve McLendon	25	dt	14	1	1.0											11	5	
7	Ben Roethlisberger*	29	QB	15	15							0	9	3	−10	0	2	0	
83	Heath Miller	29	TE	16	16							0	1	1	0	0	6	0	
28	Cortez Allen	23		15	0												5	3	
91	Aaron Smith	35	de	4	4												3	5	
20	Bryant McFadden	30	cb/lcb	13	2		0	0	0	0	1	1	0	0	0	0	3	3	
84	Antonio Brown*	25	wr	16	3												3	0	
65	Marcus Gilbert	23	RT/t	14	13												3	0	
76	Chris Hoke	35	nt	6	2												3	0	
17	Mike Wallace*	25	WR	16	14							0	1	0	0	0	2	0	
21	Mewelde Moore	29		12	0							0	2	0	0	0	1	0	
88	Emmanuel Sanders	28	wr	11	1							0	0	1	0	0	1	1	
26	Will Allen	29		16	0												0	3	
81	Arnaz Battle	31		10	0												0	3	
31	Curtis Brown	23		12	0							1	0	0	0	0	0	3	
54	Chris Carter	22		8	0												1	1	
64	Doug Legursky	25	c/lg/rg	11	10							0	1	0	−23	0	1	0	
34	Rashard Mendenhall	24	RB	15	15							0	1	0	0	0	1	0	
6	Shaun Suisham	30	k	16	0												0	3	
55	Stevenson Sylvester	23	lilb	15	1							1	0	0	0	0	0	3	
86	Hines Ward	35	WR	15	9							0	1	0	0	0	1	0	
82	Jerricho Cotchery	29		13	0												1	0	
73	Ramon Foster	25	lg/RG/t	15	14												1	0	
53	Maurkice Pouncey*+	22	C	14	14												1	0	
33	Isaac Redman	27	rb	16	1							0	2	0	0	0			
44	Weslye Saunders	22	te	16	5												1	0	
72	Jonathan Scott	28	lt/rt/t	13	6												1	0	
78	Max Starks	29	LT/t	12	11												1	0	
27	Jonathan Dwyer	22		7	0												0	1	
79	Trai Essex	29	lg/lt	16	3							0	0	1	0	0			
60	Greg Warren	30		16	0												0	1	
	Team Total	27.0		16		35.0	11	99	0	33	75	12	18	10	−15	1	673	286	2
	Opp Total			16		42						0	13	4	0	0			

A/G: attempts (either passing or rushing) per game; Ast: assists on tackles; Att: attempts; BB (position): blocking back (in the single wing); Cmp%: completion percentage: completions/(passing attempts); Fmb: fumbles; FR: fumble recoveries; G: games played; GS: games started; Int: in a passing table, this means interceptions thrown—in a defensive table, it means interceptions caught; LH (position): left halfback; Lng: long gain; LS (position): left safety; MG (position): middle guard (in a 5–2 defense); NY/A: net yards per passing attempt; PD: passes defended; Pos: position; R/G: receptions per game; Rate: passer rating; Rec: record; RH (position): right halfback; RS (position): right safety; SE (position): split end; Sk: sacks; TB (position): tailback (in the single wing); TD: touchdowns; TD%: passing TD percentage; Tkl: tackles; WB (position): wingback (in the single wing); Y/A: yards per attempt; Y/C: yards per completion; Y/G: yards per game; Y/R: yards per reception; Yds: yards; Yscm: yards from scrimmage.

* Pro Bowl player

+ Voted All-Pro

CHUCK FINDER was a sportswriter and columnist at the *Pittsburgh Post-Gazette* for 25 years, covering the Steelers in Super Bowls XXX, XL, and XLIII. He also served as a correspondent to CBSSports.com and the *New York Times*. A contributor to several books about Pittsburgh and Pennsylvania sports, he has also worked for the *Birmingham News* and the *Atlanta Journal-Constitution*.

CORE COLLECTION 2012